PMENT

2004

erty

ld

D P

Published
for the United Nations
Development Programme
(UNDP)

ISBN 0-19-522146-X

9 8 7 6 5 4 3 2 1
Printed by Hoechstetter Printing Co. on chlorine-free paper with vegetable inks and
produced by means of environmentally compatible technology.

Cover and design: Gerald Quinn, Quinn Information Design, Cabin John, Maryland
Information design: Grundy & Northedge, London
Editing, desktop composition and production management: Communications Development Incorporated,
Washington, DC

For a listing of any errors or omissions in HDR2004 found subsequent to printing, please visit our website at
http://hdr.undp.org

TEAM FOR THE PREPARATION OF
Human Development Report 2004

Director and Lead Author
Sakiko Fukuda-Parr

Core team

Carla De Gregorio, Haishan Fu (Chief of Statistics), Ricardo Fuentes, Arunabha Ghosh, Claes Johansson, Christopher Kuonqui, Santosh Mehrotra, Tanni Mukhopadhyay, Stefano Pettinato, David Stewart and Emily White

Statistical adviser: Tom Griffin

Editors: Cait Murphy and Bruce Ross-Larson

Cover and layout design: Gerald Quinn
Information design: Grundy & Northedge

Principal consultants

Amartya Sen (Chapter 1), Lourdes Arizpe, Robert Bach, Rajeev Bhargava, Elie Cohen, Emmanuel de Kadt, Nicholas Dirks, K.S. Jomo, Will Kymlicka, Valentine Moghadam, Joy Moncrieffe, Sam Moyo, Brendan O'Leary, Kwesi Kwaa Prah, Barnett R. Rubin, Daniel Sabbagh, D.L. Sheth, Rodolfo Stavenhagen, Alfred Stepan, Deborah Yashar and Aristide Zolberg

HDRO colleagues

The team expresses its sincere gratitude for the invaluable support and contributions from their colleagues in the Human Development Report Office (HDRO). Administrative support for the Report's preparation was provided by Oscar Bernal, Renuka Corea-Lloyd and Mamaye Gebretsadik. Outreach and promotional work for the Report were provided by Nena Terrell with Maria Kristina Dominguez and Anne-Louise Winsløv. HDRO operations were managed by Yves Sassenrath with Marie Suzanne Ndaw. And the team collaborated with members of the National Human Development Report (NHDR) Unit including: Sarah Burd-Sharps (Deputy Director HDRO and Chief NHDR Unit), Marcia de Castro, Sharmila Kurukulasuriya, Juan Pablo Mejia and Mary Ann Mwangi.

Foreword

At a time when the notion of a global "clash of cultures" is resonating so powerfully—and worryingly—around the world, finding answers to the old questions of how best to manage and mitigate conflict over language, religion, culture and ethnicity has taken on renewed importance. For development practitioners this is not an abstract question. If the world is to reach the Millennium Development Goals and ultimately eradicate poverty, it must first successfully confront the challenge of how to build inclusive, culturally diverse societies. Not just because doing so successfully is a precondition for countries to focus properly on other priorities of economic growth, health and education for all citizens. But because allowing people full cultural expression is an important development end in itself.

Human development is first and foremost about allowing people to lead the kind of life they choose—and providing them with the tools and opportunities to make those choices. In recent years *Human Development Report* has argued strongly that this is as much a question of politics as economics—from protecting human rights to deepening democracy. Unless people who are poor and marginalized—who more often than not are members of religious or ethnic minorities or migrants—can influence political action at local and national levels, they are unlikely to get equitable access to jobs, schools, hospitals, justice, security and other basic services.

This year's Report builds on that analysis, by carefully examining—and rejecting—claims that cultural differences necessarily lead to social, economic and political conflict or that inherent cultural rights should supersede political and economic ones. Instead, it provides a powerful argument for finding ways to "delight in our differences", as Archbishop Desmond Tutu has put it. It also offers some concrete ideas on what it means in practice to build and manage the politics of identity and culture in a manner consistent with the bedrock principles of human development.

Sometimes, that is relatively easy—for example, a girl's right to an education will always trump her father's claim to a cultural right to forbid her schooling for religious or other reasons. But the question can get much more complicated. Take education in the mother tongue. There is persuasive evidence that young children are more successful learning in their own language. However, what is an advantage at one point in life—and indeed may remain an indispensable bedrock of identity throughout life—can turn into a disadvantage in other ways when lack of proficiency in more widely used national or international languages can severely handicap employment opportunities. As this Report makes clear, from affirmative action to the role of the media, there are no easy—or one size fits all—rules for how best to build working multicultural societies.

Even so, one overarching lesson is clear: succeeding is not simply a question of legislative and policy changes, necessary though they be. Constitutions and legislation that provide protections and guarantees for minorities, indigenous people and other groups are a critical foundation for broader freedoms. But unless the political culture also changes—unless citizens come to think, feel and act in ways that genuinely accommodate the needs and aspirations of others—real change will not happen.

When the political culture does not change, the consequences are disturbingly clear. From disaffected indigenous groups across Latin America, to unhappy minorities in Africa and Asia, to new immigrants across the developed world, failing to address the grievances of marginalized groups does not just create injustice. It builds real problems for the future: unemployed, disaffected youth, angry with the status quo and demanding change, often violently.

That is the challenge. But there are also real opportunities. The overarching message of this Report is to highlight the vast potential of building a more peaceful, prosperous world by bringing issues of culture to the mainstream of development thinking and practice. Not to substitute for more traditional priorities that will remain our bread and butter—but to complement and strengthen them. The flip side of the development divide is that developing countries are often able to draw on richer, more diverse cultural traditions—whether captured in language, art, music or other forms—than their wealthier counterparts in the North. The globalization of mass culture—from books to films to television—clearly poses some significant threats to these traditional cultures. But it also opens up opportunities, from the narrow sense of disadvantaged groups like Australian Aborigines or Arctic Inuit tapping global art markets, to the broader one of creating more vibrant, creative, exciting societies.

Like all *Human Development Reports*, this is an independent study intended to stimulate debate and discussion around an important issue, not a statement of United Nations or UNDP policy. However, by taking up an issue often neglected by development economists and putting it firmly within the spectrum of priorities in building better, more fulfilled lives, it presents important arguments for UNDP and its partners to consider and act on in their broader work. This year, I would also like to pay particular tribute to Sakiko Fukuda-Parr, who is stepping down after 10 successful years leading our Human Development Report Office. I would also like to extend special thanks to Amartya Sen, one of the godfathers of human development, who has not only contributed the first chapter but been an enormous influence in shaping our thinking on this important issue.

Mark Malloch Brown
Administrator, UNDP

Acknowledgements

This Report could not have been prepared without the generous contributions of many individuals and organizations.

The team expresses its sincere gratitude to Professor Amartya Sen, who provided the conceptual framework for the Report.

CONTRIBUTORS

The team is particularly grateful for its collaboration with the Director-General of UNESCO, Koïchiro Matsuura, and his staff, especially Ann-Belinda Preis, Katarina Stenou and Rene Zapata.

Many background studies, papers and notes were prepared on thematic issues related to identity, cultural diversity and cultural liberty. These were contributed by Lourdes Arizpe, Robert Bach, Rajeev Bhargava, Elie Cohen, Emanuel De Kadt, Carolyn Deere, Nicholas Dirks, K.S. Jomo, Will Kymlicka, Valentine Moghadam, Joy Moncrieffe, Sam Moyo, Brendan O'Leary, Kwesi Kwaa Prah, Barnett R. Rubin, Daniel Sabbagh, Amartya Sen, D.L. Sheth, Rodolfo Stavenhagen, Alfred Stepan, Deborah Yashar and Aristide Zolberg. Chapter 2 benefited from the country maps and associated information on conflict provided by the Bureau for Crisis Prevention and Recovery, especially from the work of Meegan Murray, Praveen Pardeshi and Pablo Ruiz.

Several organizations generously shared their data and other research materials: Carbon Dioxide Information and Analysis Center; Caribbean Community Secretariat; Center for International Comparisons at the University of Pennsylvania; Economic and Social Commission for Asia and the Pacific; Food and Agriculture Organization; International Institute for Strategic Studies; International Labour Organization; International Monetary Fund; International Organizations for Migration; International Telecommunication Union; Inter-Parliamentary Union; Joint United Nations Programme on HIV/AIDS; Luxembourg Income Study; Organisation for Economic Co-operation and Development; Stockholm International Peace Research Institute; United Nations Children's Fund; United Nations Conference on Trade and Development; United Nations Economic Commission for Latin America and the Caribbean; United Nations Educational, Scientific and Cultural Organization Institute for Statistics; United Nations High Commissioner for Refugees; United Nations Office on Drugs and Crime; United Nations Office of Legal Affairs; United Nations Population Division; United Nations Statistics Division; World Bank; World Health Organization and World Intellectual Property Organization.

The team also expresses its appreciation for the support received from the Rockefeller Foundation, especially Ram Manikkalingam, Janet Maughan, Joan Shigekawa, Lynn Szwaja, Tomas Ybarro-Frausto as well as Gianna Celli and Nadia Giladroni at the Bellagio Rockefeller Foundation Conference and Study Center.

ADVISORY PANEL

The Report benefited greatly from intellectual advice and guidance provided by an external advisory panel of eminent experts. The panel included Arjun Appadurai, Robert Bach, Seyla Benhabib, Nancy Birdsall, Jody Narandran Kollapen, Mahmood Mamdani, Sonia Picado, Surin Pitsuwan, Jorge F. Quiroga,

Paul Streeten, Victoria Tauli-Corpus, Ngaire Woods, Rene Zapata and Antonina Zhelyazkova. An advisory panel on statistics included Sudhir Anand, Paul Cheung, Willem DeVries, Lamine Diop, Carmen Feijo, Andrew Flatt, Paolo Garonna, Robert Johnston, Irena Krizman, Nora Lustig, Ian Macredie, Marion McEwin, Wolf Scott, Tim Smeeding and Michael Ward.

CONSULTATIONS

Many individuals consulted during the preparation of the Report provided invaluable advice, information and material. The Report team thanks Carla Abouzahr, Yasmin Ahmad, Patricia Alexander, Serge Allegrezza, Anna Alvazzi del Frate, Shaida Badiee, Yusuf Bangura, Nefise Bazoglu, Grace Bediako, Matt Benjamin, Yonas Biru, Ties Boerma, Eduard Bos, Thomas Buettner, Tony Burton, Rosario Garcia Calderon, Joe Chamie, Shaohua Chen, Paul Cheung, Martin Chungong, David Cieslikowski, Lee Cokorinos, Patrick R. Cornu, Kim Cragin, Trevor Croft, Gaurav Datt, Ian Dennis, Yuri Dikhanov, Dennis Drescher, Asghar Ali Engineer, Hubert Escaith, Kareen Fabre, Yousef Falah, Richard Fix, Karl Franklin, Nancy Fraser, Rodolfo Roque Fuentes, Enrique Ganuza, Peter Ghys, Erlinda Go, Rui Gomes, Ray Gordon, Marilyn Gregerson, Ted Robert Gurr, Brian Hammond, Philomen Harrison, Sabinne Henning, Alan Heston, Misako Hiraga, Frederick W.H. Ho, Joop van Holsteyn, Béla Hovy, Piero Ignazi, Chandika Indikadahena, Jens Johansen, Lawrence Jeff Johnson, Robert Johnston, Vasantha Kandiah, Alison Kennedy, Sio Suat Kheng, Elizabeth Kielman, Taro Komatsu, Karoly Kovacs, Olivier Labe, Frank Laczko, Henrik Larsen, Georges Lemaitre, Denise Lievesley, Rolf Luyendijk, Nyein Nyein Lwin, Doug Lynd, Esperanza C. Magpantay, Mary Mahy, Heikki S. Mattila, Clare Menozzi, Jorge Mernies, Michael Minges, Anjali Mody, Catherine Monagle, Bruno Moro, Ron Morren, Philip Mukungu, Angela Ferriol Muruaga, Jack Nagel, Keiko Osaki, Jude Padyachy, Sonia Palmieri, Rosario Pardo, Amy Pate, Sulekha Patel, François Pelletier, Bob Pember, Indira Persaud, Francesca Perucci, Rudolphe Petras, Spyridon Pilos, Lionel Pintopontes, William Prince, Lakshmi Puri, Agnès Puymoyen, Hantamalala Rafalimanana, Markandey Rai, Vijayendra Rao, Luca Renda, Clinton Robinson, David Roodman, Ricardo Sibrián, Shaguni Singh, Armin Sirco, Carl Skau, Petter Stalenheim, Elsa Stamatopoulou, Mark Stoker, Diane Stukel, Ilpo Survo, Eric Swanson, Tony Taubman, Benedicte Terryn, Michel Thieren, Anne Thomas, Barbara Trudell, Elisa Tsakiri, Rafael Tuts, Erica Usher, Said Voffal, Rick Wacek, Neff Walker, Steve Walter, Tessa Wardlaw, Jayashree Watal, Glenys Waters, Catherine Watt, Wendy Wendland, Patrick Werquin, Siemon Wezeman, Anders Widfeldt, Boris Wijkström, Jonathan Wilkenfeld, Diane Wroge, A. Sylvester Young, Elizabeth Zaniewski and Hania Zlotnik.

An informal consultation with UN agencies provided the team with helpful comments and suggestions. The team thanks Food and Agriculture Organization; International Fund for Agricultural Development; International Labour Organization; International Monetary Fund; Joint United Nations Programme on HIV/AIDS; United Nations Children's Fund; United Nations Conference on Trade and Development; United Nations Department of Economic and Social Affairs; United Nations Educational, Scientific and Cultural Organization; United Nations Environment Programme; United Nations High Commissioner for Human Rights; United Nations High Commissioner for Refugees; United Nations Human Settlements Programme; United Nations Institute for Training and Research; United Nations Population Fund; World Health Organization; World Intellectual Property Organization and World Bank.

The team would like to thank members of the UNDP human development reports network (HDR-Net) and civil society network who provided many insightful comments and suggestions during the network discussions.

UNDP READERS

A Readers Group, made up of colleagues in UNDP, provided extremely useful comments, suggestions and inputs during the writing of the

Report. The Report team is especially grateful to Randa Aboul-Hosn, Fernando Calderon, Moez Doraid, Gilbert Fossoun Houngbo, Andrey Ivanov, Selim Jahan, Bruce Jenks, Freddy Justiniano, Inge Kaul, Douglas Keh, Thierry Lemaresquier, Lamin Manneh, Saraswathi Menon, Kalman Mizsei, Balasubramaniam Murali, Shoji Nishimoto, Omar Noman, William Orme, Eugenio Ortega, Hilda Paqui, Ravi Rajan, Ramaswamy Sudarshan, Mark Suzman, Julia V. Taft, Gulden Turkoz-Cosslett, Louisa Vinton, Mourad Wahba and Gita Welch.

EDITING, PRODUCTION AND TRANSLATION

As in previous years, the Report benefited from the editors at Communications Development Incorporated: Meta de Coquereaumont, Elizabeth McCrocklin, Thomas Roncoli, Bruce Ross-Larson and Christopher Trott. The Report (including cover) was designed by Gerald Quinn and laid out by Elaine Wilson. Statistical information appearing in the Report was designed by Grundy & Northedge.

The production, translation, distribution and promotion of the Report benefited from the help and support of the Communications Office of the Administrator: Djibril Diallo, Maureen Lynch, Trygve Olfarnes, Bill Orme, Hilda Paqui as well as Elizabeth Scott Andrews. Translations were reviewed by Helene Castel, Cielo Morales, Vladimir Scherbov, Andrey Ivanov, and Ali Al-Kasimi.

The Report also benefited from the dedicated work of interns: Valentina Azzarello, Alexandra Lopoukhine, Rachel Sorrentino and Rati Tripathi. Emmanuel Boudard and Jessica Lopatka made valuable contributions to the statistical team.

Liliana Izquierdo and Gerardo Nunez of the UN Office of Project Services provided critical administrative support and management services.

*   *   *

The team expresses sincere appreciation to the Report's peer reviewer, Will Kymlicka, who carefully reviewed drafts and shared his expertise and insights. The team is also grateful to Ian Macredie, Lene Mikkelsen and David Pearce, the statistical peer reviewers who scrutinized the data in the Report and lent their statistical expertise.

Finally, the authors are especially grateful to Mark Malloch Brown, UNDP's Administrator, for his leadership and vision. And although thankful for all the support they have received, the authors assume full responsibility for the opinions expressed in the Report.

S. Fukud-Parr

Sakiko Fukuda-Parr
Director
Human Development Report 2004

Contents

SPECIAL CONTRIBUTIONS

BOXES

TABLES

FIGURES

MAPS

FEATURES

HUMAN DEVELOPMENT INDICATORS

MONITORING HUMAN DEVELOPMENT: ENLARGING PEOPLE'S CHOICES. . .

. . . TO LEAD A LONG AND HEALTHY LIFE. . .

. . . TO ACQUIRE KNOWLEDGE . . .

. . . TO HAVE ACCESS TO THE RESOURCES NEEDED FOR A DECENT STANDARD OF LIVING. . .

. . . WHILE PRESERVING IT FOR FUTURE GENERATIONS . . .

Cultural liberty in today's diverse world

How will the new constitution of Iraq satisfy demands for fair representation for Shiites and Kurds? Which—and how many—of the languages spoken in Afghanistan should the new constitution recognize as the official language of the state? How will the Nigerian federal court deal with a Sharia law ruling to punish adultery by death? Will the French legislature approve the proposal to ban headscarves and other religious symbols in public schools? Do Hispanics in the United States resist assimilation into the mainstream American culture? Will there be a peace accord to end fighting in Côte d'Ivoire? Will the President of Bolivia resign after mounting protests by indigenous people? Will the peace talks to end the Tamil-Sinhala conflict in Sri Lanka ever conclude? These are just some headlines from the past few months. Managing cultural diversity is one of the central challenges of our time.

Long thought to be divisive threats to social harmony, choices like these—about recognizing and accommodating diverse ethnicities, religions, languages and values—are an inescapable feature of the landscape of politics in the 21st century. Political leaders and political theorists of all persuasions have argued against explicit recognition of cultural identities—ethnic, religious, linguistic, racial. The result, more often than not, has been that cultural identities have been suppressed, sometimes brutally, as state policy—through religious persecutions and ethnic cleansings, but also through everyday exclusion and economic, social and political discrimination.

New today is the rise of identity politics. In vastly different contexts and in different ways—from indigenous people in Latin America to religious minorities in South Asia to ethnic minorities in the Balkans and Africa to immigrants in Western Europe—people are mobilizing anew around old grievances along ethnic,

religious, racial and cultural lines, demanding that their identities be acknowledged, appreciated and accommodated by wider society. Suffering discrimination and marginalization from social, economic and political opportunities, they are also demanding social justice. Also new today is the rise of coercive movements that threaten cultural liberty. And, in this era of globalization, a new class of political claims and demands has emerged from individuals, communities and countries feeling that their local cultures are being swept away. They want to keep their diversity in a globalized world.

Why these movements today? They are not isolated. They are part of a historic process of social change, of struggles for cultural freedom, of new frontiers in the advance of human freedoms and democracy. They are propelled and shaped by the spread of democracy, which is giving movements more political space for protest, and the advance of globalization, which is creating new networks of alliances and presenting new challenges.

Cultural liberty is a vital part of human development because being able to choose one's identity—who one is—without losing the respect of others or being excluded from other choices is important in leading a full life. People want the freedom to practice their religion openly, to speak their language, to celebrate their ethnic or religious heritage without fear of ridicule or punishment or diminished opportunity. People want the freedom to participate in society without having to slip off their chosen cultural moorings. It is a simple idea, but profoundly unsettling.

States face an urgent challenge in responding to these demands. If handled well, greater recognition of identities will bring greater cultural diversity in society, enriching people's lives. But there is also a great risk.

These struggles over cultural identity, if left unmanaged or managed poorly, can quickly

Cultural liberty is a vital part of human development

become one of the greatest sources of instability within states and between them—and in so doing trigger conflict that takes development backwards. Identity politics that polarize people and groups are creating fault lines between "us" and "them". Growing distrust and hatred threaten peace, development and human freedoms. Just in the last year ethnic violence destroyed hundreds of homes and mosques in Kosovo and Serbia. Terrorist train bombings in Spain killed nearly 200. Sectarian violence killed thousands of Muslims and drove thousands more from their homes in Gujarat and elsewhere in India, a champion of cultural accommodation. A spate of hate crimes against immigrants shattered Norwegians' belief in their unshakable commitment to tolerance.

Struggles over identity can also lead to regressive and xenophobic policies that retard human development. They can encourage a retreat to conservatism and a rejection of change, closing off the infusion of ideas and of people who bring cosmopolitan values and the knowledge and skills that advance development.

Managing diversity and respecting cultural identities are not just challenges for a few "multiethnic states". Almost no country is entirely homogeneous. The world's nearly 200 countries contain some 5,000 ethnic groups. Two-thirds have at least one substantial minority—an ethnic or religious group that makes up at least 10% of the population.

At the same time the pace of international migration has quickened, with startling effects on some countries and cities. Nearly half the population of Toronto was born outside of Canada. And many more foreign-born people maintain close ties with their countries of origin than did immigrants of the last century. One way or another every country is a multicultural society today, containing ethnic, religious or linguistic groups that have common bonds to their own heritage, culture, values and way of life.

Cultural diversity is here to stay—and to grow. States need to find ways of forging national unity amid this diversity. The world, ever more interdependent economically, cannot function unless people respect diversity and build unity through common bonds of humanity. In this age of globalization the demands for cultural recognition can no longer be ignored by any state or by the international community. And confrontations over culture and identity are likely to grow—the ease of communications and travel have shrunk the world and changed the landscape of cultural diversity, and the spread of democracy, human rights and new global networks have given people greater means to mobilize around a cause, insist on a response and get it.

Five myths debunked. Policies recognizing cultural identities and encouraging diversity to flourish do not result in fragmentation, conflict, weak development or authoritarian rule. Such policies are both viable, and necessary, for it is often the suppression of culturally identified groups that leads to tensions.

This Report makes a case for respecting diversity and building more inclusive societies by adopting policies that explicitly recognize cultural differences—multicultural policies. But why have many cultural identities been suppressed or ignored for so long? One reason is that many people believe that allowing diversity to flourish may be desirable in the abstract but in practice can weaken the state, lead to conflict and retard development. The best approach to diversity, in this view, is assimilation around a single national standard, which can lead to the suppression of cultural identities. However, this Report argues that these are not premises—they are myths. Indeed, it argues that a multicultural policy approach is not just desirable but also viable and necessary. Without such an approach the imagined problems of diversity can become self-fulfilling prophecies.

Myth 1. People's ethnic identities compete with their attachment to the state, so there is a trade-off between recognizing diversity and unifying the state.

Not so. Individuals can and do have multiple identities that are complementary—ethnicity, language, religion and race as well as citizenship. Nor is identity a zero sum game. There is no inevitable need to choose between state unity and recognition of cultural differences.

This Report makes a case for respecting diversity and building more inclusive societies by adopting policies that explicitly recognize cultural differences— multicultural policies

A sense of identity and belonging to a group with shared values and other bonds of culture is important for individuals. But each individual can identify with many different groups. Individuals have identity of citizenship (for example, being French), gender (being a woman), race (being of West African origin), language (being fluent in Thai, Chinese and English), politics (having left-wing views) and religion (being Buddhist).

Identity also has an element of choice: within these memberships individuals can choose what priority to give to one membership over another in different contexts. Mexican Americans may cheer for the Mexican soccer team but serve in the US Army. Many white South Africans chose to fight apartheid as South Africans. Sociologists tell us that people have boundaries of identity that separate "us" from "them", but these boundaries shift and blur to incorporate broader groups of people.

"Nation building" has been a dominant objective of the 20th century, and most states have aimed to build culturally homogeneous states with singular identities. Sometimes they succeeded but at the cost of repression and persecution. If the history of the 20th century showed anything, it is that the attempt either to exterminate cultural groups or to wish them away elicits a stubborn resilience. By contrast, recognizing cultural identities has resolved never-ending tensions. For both practical and moral reasons, then, it is far better to accommodate cultural groups than to try to eliminate them or to pretend that they do not exist.

Countries do not have to choose between national unity and cultural diversity. Surveys show that the two can and often do coexist. In Belgium citizens overwhelmingly replied when asked that they felt both Belgian and Flemish or Walloon and in Spain, that they felt Spanish as well as Catalan or Basque.

These countries and others have worked hard to accommodate diverse cultures. They have also worked hard to build unity by fostering respect for identities and trust in state institutions. The states have held together. Immigrants need not deny their commitment to their families in their countries of origin when they develop loyalties to their new countries. Fears that if immigrants do not "assimilate", they will fragment the country are unfounded. Assimilation without choice is no longer a viable—or a necessary—model of integration.

There is no trade-off between diversity and state unity. Multicultural policies are a way to build diverse and unified states.

Myth 2. Ethnic groups are prone to violent conflict with each other in clashes of values, so there is a trade-off between respecting diversity and sustaining peace.

No. There is little empirical evidence that cultural differences and clashes over values are in themselves a cause of violent conflict.

It is true, particularly since the end of the cold war, that violent conflicts have arisen not so much between states but within them between ethnic groups. But on their causes, there is wide agreement in recent research by scholars that cultural differences by themselves are not the relevant factor. Some even argue that cultural diversity reduces the risk of conflict by making group mobilization more difficult.

Studies offer several explanations for these wars: economic inequalities between the groups as well as struggles over political power, land and other economic assets. In Fiji indigenous Fijians initiated a coup against the Indian-dominated government because they feared that land might be confiscated. In Sri Lanka the Sinhalese majority gained political power, but the Tamil minority had access to more economic resources, triggering decades of civil conflict. In Burundi and Rwanda, at different points in time, Tutsis and Hutus were each excluded from economic opportunities and political participation.

Cultural identity does have a role in these conflicts—not as a cause but as a driver for political mobilization. Leaders invoke a single identity, its symbols and its history of grievances, to "rally the troops". And a lack of cultural recognition can trigger violent mobilization. Underlying inequalities in South Africa were at the root of the Soweto riots in 1976, but they were triggered by attempts to impose Afrikaans on black schools.

While the coexistence of culturally distinct groups is not, in itself, a cause of violent conflict,

A sense of identity and belonging to a group with shared values and other bonds of culture is important for all individuals. But each individual can identify with many different groups

it is dangerous to allow economic and political inequality to deepen between these groups or to suppress cultural differences, because cultural groups are easily mobilized to contest these disparities as injustice.

There is no trade-off between peace and respect for diversity, but identity politics need to be managed so that they do not turn violent.

Myth 3. Cultural liberty requires defending traditional practices, so there could be a trade-off between recognizing cultural diversity and other human development priorities such as progress in development, democracy and human rights.

No. Cultural liberty is about expanding individual choices, not about preserving values and practices as an end in itself with blind allegiance to tradition.

Culture is not a frozen set of values and practices. It is constantly recreated as people question, adapt and redefine their values and practices to changing realities and exchanges of ideas.

Some argue that multiculturalism is a policy of conserving cultures, even practices that violate human rights, and that movements for cultural recognition are not governed democratically. But neither cultural freedom nor respect for diversity should be confused with the defence of tradition. Cultural liberty is the capability of people to live and be what they choose, with adequate opportunity to consider other options.

"Culture", "tradition" and "authenticity" are not the same as "cultural liberty". They are not acceptable reasons for allowing practices that deny individuals equality of opportunity and violate their human rights—such as denying women equal rights to education.

Interest groups led by self-appointed leaders may not reflect the views of the membership at large. It is not rare for groups to be dominated by people who have an interest in maintaining the status quo under the justification of "tradition" and who act as gatekeepers of traditionalism to freeze their cultures. Those making demands for cultural accommodation should also abide by democratic principles and the objectives of human freedom and human rights. One good model is the Sami people in Finland,

who enjoy autonomy in a parliament that has democratic structures and follows democratic procedures but is part of the Finnish state.

There does not need to be any trade-off between respect for cultural difference and human rights and development. But the process of development involves active participation of people in fighting for human rights and shifts in values.

Myth 4. Ethnically diverse countries are less able to develop, so there is a trade-off between respecting diversity and promoting development.

No. There is no evidence of a clear relationship, good or bad, between cultural diversity and development.

Some argue, however, that diversity has been an obstacle to development. But while it is undeniably true that many diverse societies have low levels of income and human development, there is no evidence that this is related to cultural diversity. One study argues that diversity has been a source of poor economic performance in Africa—but this is related to political decision-making that follows ethnic rather than national interests, not to diversity itself. Just as there are multi-ethnic countries that have stagnated, there are others that were spectacularly successful. Malaysia, with 62% of its people Malays and other indigenous groups, 30% Chinese and 8% Indian, was the world's 10th fastest growing economy during 1970–90, years when it also implemented affirmative action policies. Mauritius ranks 64 in the human development index, the highest in Sub-Saharan Africa. It has a diverse population of African, Indian, Chinese and European origin—with 50% Hindu, 30% Christian and 17% Muslim.

Myth 5. Some cultures are more likely to make developmental progress than others, and some cultures have inherent democratic values while others do not, so there is a trade-off between accommodating certain cultures and promoting development and democracy.

Again, no. There is no evidence from statistical analysis or historical studies of a causal

Cultural liberty is the capability of people to live and be what they choose

relationship between culture and economic progress or democracy.

Cultural determinism—the idea that a group's culture explains economic performance and the advance of democracy—as an obstacle or a facilitator, has enormous intuitive appeal. But these theories are not supported by econometric analysis or history.

Many theories of cultural determinism have been advanced, starting with Max Weber's explanation of the Protestant ethic as a key factor behind successful growth in capitalist economies. Persuasive in explaining the past, these theories have been repeatedly proven wrong in predicting the future. When Weber's theory of the Protestant ethic was being touted, Catholic countries (France and Italy) were growing faster than Protestant Britain and Germany, so the theory was expanded to mean Christian or Western. When Japan, the Republic of Korea, Thailand and other East Asian countries achieved record growth rates, the notion that Confucian values retard growth had to be jettisoned.

Understanding cultural traditions can offer insights to human behaviour and social dynamics that influence development outcomes. But these insights do not offer a grand theory of culture and development. In explaining economic growth rates, for example, economic policy, geography and the burden of disease are found to be highly relevant factors. But culture, such as whether a society is Hindu or Muslim, is found to be insignificant.

The same is true with reference to democracy. A new wave of cultural determinism is starting to hold sway in some policy debates, attributing the failures of democratization in the non-Western world to inherent cultural traits of intolerance and "authoritarian values". At the global level some theorists have argued that the 21st century will see a "clash of civilizations", that the future of democratic and tolerant Western states is threatened by non-Western states with more authoritarian values. There are reasons to be sceptical. For one thing, the theory exaggerates the differences between "civilization" groups and ignores the similarities among them.

Moreover, the West has no monopoly on democracy or tolerance, and there is no unique line of historical division between a tolerant and democratic West and a despotic East. Plato and Augustine were no less authoritarian in their thinking than were Confucius and Kautilya. There were champions of democracy not just in Europe but elsewhere as well. Take Akbar, who preached religious tolerance in 16th century India, or Prince Shotoku who in 7th century Japan introduced the constitution (*kempo*) that insisted that "decisions on important matters should not be made by one person alone. They should be discussed by many". Notions of participatory decision-making on important public issues have been a central part of many traditions in Africa and elsewhere. And more recent findings of the World Values survey show that people in Muslim countries have as much support for democratic values as do people in non-Muslim countries.

A basic problem with these theories is the underlying assumption that culture is largely fixed and unchanging, allowing the world to be neatly divided into "civilizations" or "cultures". This ignores the fact that while there can be great continuity in values and traditions in societies, cultures also change and are rarely homogeneous. Nearly all societies have undergone shifts in values—for example, shifts in values about the role of women and gender equality over the last century. And radical changes in social practices have occurred everywhere, from Catholics in Chile to Muslims in Bangladesh to Buddhists in Thailand. Such changes and tensions within societies drive politics and historical change, so that the way power relationships affect those dynamics now dominates research in anthropology. Paradoxically, just as anthropologists have discarded the concept of culture as a bounded and fixed social phenomenon, mainstream political interest in finding core values and traits of "a people and their culture" is growing.

Theories of cultural determinism deserve critical assessment since they have dangerous policy implications. They can fuel support for nationalistic policies that denigrate or oppress "inferior" cultures argued to stand in the way of national unity, democracy and development. Such attacks on cultural values would then fuel violent reactions that could feed tensions both within and between nations.

A new wave of cultural determinism is starting to hold sway

Human development requires more than health, education, a decent standard of living and political freedom. People's cultural identities must be recognized and accommodated by the state, and people must be free to express these identities without being discriminated against in other aspects of their lives. In short: cultural liberty is a human right and an important aspect of human development—and thus worthy of state action and attention.

Human development is the process of widening choices for people to do and be what they value in life. Previous *Human Development Reports* have focused on expanding social, political and economic opportunities to expand these choices. They have explored ways that policies of equitable growth, expansion of social opportunities and deepening of democracy can enhance those choices for all people.

A further dimension of human development, difficult to measure and even to define, is vitally important: cultural liberty is central to the capability of people to live as they would like. The advance of cultural liberty must be a central aspect of human development, and this requires going beyond social, political and economic opportunities since they do not guarantee cultural liberty.

Cultural liberty is about allowing people the freedom to choose their identities—and to lead the lives they value—without being excluded from other choices important to them (such as those for education, health or job opportunities). In practice there are two forms of cultural exclusion. First is living mode exclusion, which denies recognition and accommodation of a lifestyle that a group would choose to have and that insists that individuals must live exactly like all others in society. Examples include religious oppression or the insistence that immigrants drop their cultural practices and language. Second is participation exclusion, when people are discriminated against or suffer disadvantage in social, political and economic opportunities because of their cultural identity.

Both types of exclusion exist on an extensive scale, across every continent, at every level of development, in democracies and authoritarian states. The *Minorities at Risk* data set, a research project including issues relating to cultural exclusion that has reviewed the situation of minority groups worldwide, estimates that about 900 million people belong to groups that are subject to some form of either living mode or participation exclusion not faced by other groups in the state—around one in every seven people around the world.

Of course, suppressions of cultural liberty fill the spectrum. At one extreme is ethnic cleansing. Then there are formal restrictions on the practice of religion, language and citizenship. But more frequently cultural exclusion comes from a simple lack of recognition or respect for the culture and heritage of people—or from some cultures being considered inferior, primitive or uncivilized. This can be reflected in state policies, as in national calendars that do not observe a minority's religious holiday, schoolbooks that leave out or belittle the achievements of minority leaders and support to literature and other arts that celebrate the achievements of the dominant culture.

Living mode exclusion often overlaps with social, economic and political exclusion through discrimination and disadvantage in employment, housing, schooling and political representation. The occupational castes in Nepal have under-five mortality rates of more than 17%, compared with around 7% for the Newar and Brahmin. In Serbia and Montenegro 30% of Roma children have never attended primary school. Latin Americans of European descent often express pride that they are colour blind and insist that their states are too. But across the continent indigenous groups are poorer and less represented politically than the non-indigenous. In Mexico, for example, 81% of indigenous people are reckoned to have incomes below the poverty line, compared with 18% for the general population.

Living mode and participation exclusion, however, do not always overlap. People of Chinese ancestry in South-East Asia, for example, are economically dominant yet have been culturally excluded, for example, with Chinese language schools restricted, publishing in Chinese prohibited and people of Chinese descent socially pressured to adopt local names. But more often

Cultural liberty is a human right and an important aspect of human development—and thus worthy of state action and attention

living mode exclusion reinforces exclusion from other opportunities. This is particularly so for language. Many groups, especially large minorities such as the Kurds in Turkey and the indigenous people of Guatemala, are excluded from political participation and economic opportunities because the state does not recognize their language in schools, law courts and other official arenas. This is why groups fight so hard for their languages to be recognized and used in instruction and in political and legal processes.

None of this is utopian. Incorporating multicultural policies is not always easy. Democracy, equitable development and state cohesion are essential, and many countries are successfully developing multicultural policies to address cultural exclusion.

Cultural liberty will not just happen, any more than health, education and gender equity just happen. Fostering it should be a core concern of governments, even where there are no explicit policies of persecution or discrimination.

Some argue that guaranteeing individuals civil and political rights—such as freedom of worship, speech and association—is enough to give them the ability to practice their religion, speak their language and be free of discrimination in employment, schooling and many other types of exclusion. They argue that cultural exclusion is a by-product of economic and political exclusions and that once these are resolved, the cultural exclusion will disappear of its own accord.

This has not happened. Many rich and democratic countries, for example, profess to treat all citizens equally, but are nonetheless home to minorities who lack proper representation in politics, and for whom harassment and difficulty in accessing public services are their daily fare.

To expand cultural freedoms requires explicit policies to address denials of cultural liberty—multicultural policies. To do this, states need to recognize cultural differences in their constitutions, their laws and their institutions. They also need to formulate policies to ensure that the interests of particular groups—whether minorities or historically marginalized majorities—are not

ignored or overridden by the majority or by dominant groups. And they need to do so in ways that do not contradict other goals and strategies of human development, such as consolidating democracy, building a capable state and ensuring equal opportunities to all citizens. This is not easy, but there are many examples of countries around the world adopting innovative approaches for managing cultural diversity. This Report focuses particularly on five central policy areas: political participation, religion, access to justice, language and access to socioeconomic opportunities.

Policies for ensuring political participation

Many historically marginalized groups are still excluded from real political power, and so they often feel alienated from the state. In some cases the exclusion is due to a lack of democracy or the denial of political rights. If so, democratization would be an essential first step. However, something more is required, because even when members of minorities have equal political rights in a democracy, they may be consistently underrepresented or outvoted, and so view the central government as alien and oppressive. Not surprisingly, many minorities resist alien or oppressive rule and seek more political power. That is why a "multicultural" conception of democracy is often required.

Several emerging models of multicultural democracy provide effective mechanisms for power sharing between culturally diverse groups. These kinds of power-sharing arrangements are crucial for securing the rights of diverse cultural groups and minorities and for preventing violations—either by majoritarian imposition or by the dominance of the ruling political elite.

Electoral reforms addressed the chronic underrepresentation of Maoris in New Zealand. With the introduction of proportional representation in place of the winner-takes-all formula, Maori representation rose from 3% in 1993 to 16% in the 2002 elections, in line with their share of the population. Reserved seats and quotas have been critical to ensuring that the scheduled tribes and castes had a voice in India and that ethnic minorities were represented in Croatia.

Several emerging models of multicultural democracy provide effective mechanisms for power sharing between culturally diverse groups

Federal arrangements are an important approach to power sharing. Almost every one of the dozen ethnically diverse countries that are longstanding democracies has asymmetrical federal arrangements in which subunits of the federal state do not all have the same powers. This arrangement responds more flexibly to the needs of different groups. For example, Sabah and Sarawak have a special status in Malaysia, as do the Basques and 14 other *comunidades autonomas* in Spain, with autonomy in areas such as education, language and culture.

Some indigenous people, such as the Inuits in Canada, have also negotiated self-governing territories. The lesson is that such power sharing arrangements have broadly proven to be critical in resolving tensions in countries historically confronted with secessionist movements, as in Spain. Introduced early enough, when tensions are mounting, they can forestall violent conflict.

Policies for ensuring religious freedom

Many religious minorities suffer various forms of exclusion, sometimes due to explicit suppression of religious freedom or discrimination against that group—a problem particularly common in non-secular countries where the state upholds an established religion.

But in other cases the exclusion may be less direct and often unintended, as when the public calendar does not recognize a minority's religious holidays. India officially celebrates 5 Hindu holidays but also 4 Muslim, 2 Christian, 1 Buddhist, 1 Jain and 1 Sikh in recognition of a diverse population. France celebrates 11 national holidays, 5 are non-denominational and of the 6 religious holidays all celebrate events in the Christian calendar, though 7% of the population is Muslim and 1% Jewish. Similarly, the dress codes in public institutions may conflict with a minority's religious dress. Or state rules about marriage and inheritance may differ from those of religious codes. Or zoning regulations may be at odds with a minority's burial practices.

These sorts of conflicts can arise even in secular states with strong democratic institutions that protect civil and political rights. Given the profound importance of religion to people's identities, it is not surprising that religious minorities often mobilize to contest these exclusions. Some religious practices are not difficult to accommodate, but often they present difficult choices and trade-offs. France is grappling with whether headscarves in state schools violate state principles of secularism and democratic values of gender equality that state education aims to impart. Nigeria is struggling with whether to uphold the ruling of a Sharia court in a case of adultery.

What is important from the human development perspective is to expand human freedoms and human rights—and to recognize equality. Secular and democratic states are most likely to achieve these goals where the state provides reasonable accommodation of religious practices, where all religions have the same relation to the state and where the state protects human rights.

Policies for legal pluralism

In many multicultural societies indigenous people and people from other cultural groups have pressed for recognition of their traditional legal systems to gain access to justice. For example, the Maya in Guatemala suffered centuries of oppression, and the state legal system became part of their oppression. The communities lost faith in the state system of rule of law, because it did not secure justice and because it was not embedded in the society and its values.

Several countries such as Guatemala, India and South Africa are developing approaches to legal pluralism, recognizing the role of the judicial norms and institutions of the communities in different ways. Demands for legal pluralism meet opposition from those who fear that it undermines the principle of a unified legal system or that it would promote traditional practices contrary to democracy and human rights. For sure, conflicts do arise—South Africa, for example, is grappling with the conflict between the rights of women to inheritance under state constitution and the rights denied under customary law. There are real trade-offs societies must face, but legal pluralism does not require wholesale adoption of all traditional practices. Culture does evolve, and cultural liberty is not a knee-jerk defence of tradition.

Power sharing arrangements have broadly proven to be critical in resolving tensions

Language policies

Language is often the most contested issue in multicultural states. Some countries have tried to suppress people's languages, labelling their use subversive. But the more frequent source of widespread exclusion in even well-established democracies is monolingual policy. The choice of official language—the language of instruction in schools, the language of legislative debates and civic participation, the language of commerce—shapes the barriers and advantages individuals face in life—political, social, economic and cultural. In Malawi the Constitution requires all parliamentarians to speak and read English. English and Afrikaans are still the de facto languages used in the courts of South Africa, even though nine other languages are now officially recognized. Recognizing a language means more than just the use of that language. It symbolizes respect for the people who speak it, their culture and their full inclusion in society.

The state can be blind to religion, but it cannot be mute to language. Citizens need to communicate to feel a sense of belonging, and the choice of official language symbolizes the national identity. That is why many states resist recognizing multiple languages even when they champion civil and political freedoms.

Many countries are finding ways to accommodate the twin objectives of unity and diversity by adopting two or three languages, recognizing a unifying national language as well as local languages. In many colonized countries this has meant recognizing the language of administration (such as English or French), the most widely used local language and a mother tongue at local levels. Tanzania has promoted the use of Kiswahili along with English in schools and government. India has practised a three-language formula for decades; children are taught in the official language of their state (Bengali in West Bengal, for example) and are also taught the two official languages of the country, Hindi and English.

Socio-economic policies

Socio-economic injustices and inequalities in income, education and health outcomes have been the defining feature of many multi-ethnic societies with marginal groups—blacks in South Africa and indigenous people in Guatemala and Canada. These exclusions reflect long historical roots of conquest and colonization—as well as entrenched structures of hierarchy, such as caste systems.

Economic and social policies that promote equity are critical in addressing these inequalities. Redressing biases in public spending as well as targeting basic services to people with lower health and education outcomes would help—but would not be enough. Multicultural policies that recognize differences between groups are needed to address the injustices that are historically rooted and socially entrenched. For example, simply spending more on education for children of indigenous groups would not be enough, for they are disadvantaged if school instruction is in the official language only. Bilingual education would help. Claims over land—such as the claims of indigenous people over land with mineral resources or the land settled by white colonizers in Southern Africa—cannot be resolved with policies that expand socio-economic opportunities.

Experience in India, Malaysia, South Africa and the United States shows that affirmative action can reduce inequalities between groups. In Malaysia the ratio of average income between Chinese and Malay populations declined from 2.3 in 1970 to 1.7 in 1990. In the United States the proportion of black lawyers rose from 1.2% to 5.1% of the total and the proportion of black physicians from 2% to 5.6%. In India the allocation of government jobs, admission to higher education and legislative seats to scheduled castes and tribes has helped members of these groups climb out of poverty and join the middle class.

None of these policies is without its complexities, but the experience of many countries shows that solutions are possible. Bilingual education may be contested as ineffective, but that is because it receives too little support to ensure quality. Affirmative action programmes may be contested as creating permanent sources of inequality or becoming a source of patronage—but they can be better managed. These are ways of responding to demands for cultural inclusion. But we must also recognize that in the world today there are also more movements for cultural domination that seek to suppress diversity.

Multicultural policies that recognize differences between groups are needed to address injustices historically rooted and socially entrenched

Movements for cultural domination threaten cultural liberty. Fighting them with illegal and undemocratic measures violates human rights and does not make the problem go away. Democratic accommodation is more effective in exposing the intolerant agendas of such movements and undermining their appeal.

People leading movements for cultural domination believe in their own cultural superiority and try to impose their ideologies on others, both within and outside their community. Not all such movements are violent. Some coerce others using political campaigns, threats and harassment. In the extreme they use violent means as well—hate attacks, expulsions, ethnic cleansing and genocide. As a political force intolerance is threatening to overwhelm political processes in countries around the world. Movements for cultural domination take different forms: political parties, militias, violent groups, international networks and even the state. It is naïve to assume that democratic societies are immune to intolerance and hatred.

The underlying causes for the rise of movements for cultural domination often include manipulative leadership, poverty and inequality, weak or ineffectual states, outside political interventions and linkages with the diaspora. These factors can also inspire nationalist movements— say, for autonomy or secession. But movements for national autonomy are not the same as movements for cultural domination. For one thing, movements for cultural domination can often arise within the majority group that already dominates the state—such as extreme right parties in many European countries. Conversely, many movements for national autonomy can be quite liberal, recognizing the importance of accommodating diversity within an autonomous territory and seeking only the same respect and recognition as other nations. What distinguishes movements for cultural domination is their assertion of cultural superiority and their intolerance. Their targets are freedom and diversity.

The question is how to deal with them? States have often tried to confront these movements with repressive and undemocratic methods— bans on parties, extrajudicial detentions and trials, legislation that violates fundamental rights and even indiscriminate force and torture. These measures often suppress legitimate political demands and processes, resulting in much more extreme reactions. When the Islamist Salvation Front (FIS) won the first round of elections in 1991 in Algeria, the military intervened and banned the party. The result: a civil war that cost more than 100,000 lives and spurred the growth of intolerant and violent groups.

Instead, democratic accommodation works. Allowing extreme right parties to contest in elections can force them to moderate their positions as well, for example, with the Freedom Party (FPÖ) in Austria or the Justice and Development Party in Morocco. Electoral competition exposes the fringe appeal of other groups (the Progress Party in Denmark). Democratic accommodation also gives states the legitimacy to prosecute hate crimes, reform the curriculum of religious schools (in Indonesia and Malaysia) and experiment with community initiatives to improve relations (Mozambique and Rwanda).

The maintenance of a liberal society depends on respecting the rule of law, listening to political claims and protecting fundamental human rights—even those of vile people. Intolerance is a real challenge for cultural liberty—that is why the means to deal with it must be legitimate.

Globalization can threaten national and local identities. The solution is not to retreat to conservatism and isolationist nationalism—it is to design multicultural policies to promote diversity and pluralism.

So far the focus has been on how states should manage diversity within their borders. But in an era of globalization states also face challenges from outside their borders, in the form of international movements of ideas, capital, goods and people.

Expanding cultural freedom in this age of globalization presents new challenges and dilemmas. Contacts between people, their values, ideas and ways of life have been growing and deepening in unprecedented ways. For many, this new diversity is exciting, even empowering. For others, it is disquieting and disempowering. Many fear that globalization means a loss of

The maintenance of a liberal society depends on respecting the rule of law, listening to political claims and protecting fundamental human rights—even those of vile people

their values and ways of life—a threat to local and national identity. An extreme reaction is to shut out foreign influences, an approach that is not only xenophobic and conservative but also regressive, shrinking rather than expanding freedoms and choice.

This Report advocates an alternative approach that respects and promotes diversity while keeping countries open to global flows of capital, goods and people. That requires policies reflecting the goal of cultural liberty. Policies need to explicitly recognize and respect cultural difference. They also need to address imbalances in economic and political power that lead to loss of cultures and identities.

Such alternatives are being developed and debated in three hotly contested areas:

- Indigenous people are protesting investments in extractive sectors and misappropriations of traditional knowledge that threaten their livelihoods.
- Countries are demanding that cultural goods (mainly cinema and audiovisual products) not be treated as any other goods in international trade since imports of cultural goods can weaken national cultural industries.
- Migrants are demanding accommodation of their way of life and respect for the multiple identities they have in both the local community and their country of origin. But local communities are demanding that immigrants assimilate, or be turned away, for they fear that their societies are becoming divided and that national values and identity are being eroded.

How can these demands be accommodated? How should diversity be respected, and the asymmetries addressed?

Indigenous people, extractive industries and traditional knowledge

Investments that disregard indigenous people's rights to land and its cultural significance as well as its value as an economic resource will inevitably invite opposition. So will patenting traditional knowledge under the same conditions. Three principles are critical: recognizing indigenous people's rights over knowledge and land, ensuring that indigenous groups have voice (seeking their prior informed consent)

and developing strategies for sharing benefits.

Some initiatives, though still limited, are being taken by corporations and national governments to work with indigenous communities in developing new investments. In Peru government and corporations have learned the lessons of previous confrontations and have been involving indigenous communities in decision-making in the Antamina zinc and copper mine since 2001. In Papua New Guinea investments in community development projects accompany extraction activities. Collaborative ventures between mining companies and indigenous people in North America and Australia have brought monetary benefits while preserving traditional lifestyles.

Many national governments are taking steps to recognize traditional knowledge. Bangladesh recognizes community-based rights to biological resources and associated traditional knowledge. Lao PDR documents knowledge in its Traditional Medicines Resource Centre. South Africa has promised to share with the San Bushmen the proceeds from drugs developed based on their knowledge. Countries have already found ways of using existing intellectual property rights systems to protect traditional knowledge. Industrial designs are used to protect carpets and headdresses in Kazakhstan. Geographical indications protect liquors and teas in Venezuela and Viet Nam. Copyrights and trademarks are used for traditional art in Australia and Canada.

Recognizing diversity means that different notions of property rights and the cultural significance of knowledge and art forms be accommodated within global regimes. This requires international action. If current intellectual property standards cannot accommodate commonly known traditional knowledge or its attributes of group ownership, the rules will need to be revised. Loans to countries and companies for projects that wrongly acquire property or do not compensate communities should be withdrawn.

Cultural goods

Should cultural goods be protected in international trade to help protect cultural diversity in the world? Are films and audiovisual products cultural goods? Two principles are critical: recognize the role of cultural goods in nurturing

This Report advocates an approach that respects and promotes diversity while keeping countries open to global flows of capital, goods and people

creativity and diversity, and recognize the disadvantage of small film and audiovisual industries in global markets.

Diversity in cultural goods has its own value because it increases consumer choice and enriches people's cultural experience. But cultural goods also enjoy economies of scale. So the products of large producers tend to crowd out the products of smaller producers, particularly in poorer countries.

How can diversity be promoted? Mounting barriers to trade is not the answer, since that reduces choice. Support to cultural industries rather than tariffs would do more for diversity. Argentina, Brazil and France have successfully experimented with production subsidies and tax breaks for cultural industries, without stopping the flows of cultural products from overseas to local markets. Hungary diverts 6% of television receipts to promote domestic films. Egypt uses public-private partnerships to finance the infrastructure for film making.

Immigration

Should immigrants have to assimilate or should their cultures be recognized? Three principles are critical: respect diversity, recognize multiple identities and build common bonds of belonging to the local community. No country has advanced by closing its borders. International migration brings skills, labour and ideas, enriching people's lives. Just as traditionalism and religious practices that violate human rights cannot be defended, forced assimilation cannot be a viable solution.

Identities are not a zero sum game. Consider this, from a Malaysian in Norway: "I am often asked how long I have lived here; '20 years', I say. The next remark often is 'Oh, you are almost Norwegian!' The assumption here is that I have become less Malaysian because it is common to think about identity as a zero sum game; if you have more of one identity, you have less of another. Identity is somehow imagined like a square box with a fixed size."

Two approaches to immigration dominate most countries' policies: differentialism (migrants keeping their identities but not integrating into the rest of society) and assimilation

Individuals have to shed rigid identities if they are to become part of diverse societies and uphold cosmopolitan values of tolerance and respect for universal human rights

(without the choice of keeping the old identity). But new approaches of multiculturalism are being introduced that recognize multiple identities. This involves promoting tolerance and cultural understanding, but also specifically accommodating religious practice, dress and other aspects of everyday life. It also involves acknowledging that immigrants are voiceless and insecure in the face of exploitation and providing support for integration such as language training and job search services.

Countries are expanding the rights of civic participation to non-citizenship—"denizenship" (Belgium, Sweden). And more than 30 countries now accept dual citizenship. To reduce misconceptions and prejudices the Commissioner's Office of the Berlin Senate for Integration and Migration funds immigrant organizations, uses public information campaigns and offers legal consultations in 12 languages to help with jobs and tackle discrimination.

But these policies are contested. Bilingual education in the United States and the wearing of headscarf in France are divisive issues. Some fear that they challenge some of the most fundamental values of society—such as commitment to adopt the American culture, or the French principles of secularism and gender equality.

*   *   *

Expanding cultural freedoms is an important goal in human development—one that needs urgent attention in the 21st century. All people want to be free to be who they are. All people want to be free to express their identity as members of a group with shared commitments and values—whether it is nationality, ethnicity, language or religion, whether it is family, profession or avocation.

Globalization is driving ever-increasing interactions among the world's people. This world needs both greater respect for diversity and stronger commitment to unity. Individuals have to shed rigid identities if they are to become part of diverse societies and uphold cosmopolitan values of tolerance and respect for universal human rights. This Report provides a basis for discussing how countries can make that happen. If the short history of the 21st century has taught us nothing else, it is that ducking these questions is not an option.

CHAPTER 1

Cultural liberty and human development

Human deprivation can occur in many ways, some more remediable than others. The human development approach has been extensively used in the development literature (including earlier *Human Development Reports*) to analyze several prominent sources of affliction, ranging from illiteracy and a lack of health care to unemployment and indigence. In this year's Report there is a substantial expansion of coverage and reach focusing in particular on the importance of cultural liberty and on the personal and social loss that can result from its dearth.

This refocusing does not abandon the basic commitments of the human development approach. The underlying motivation continues to be to search for ways of enhancing people's lives and the freedoms they can enjoy. Denial of cultural liberty can generate significant deprivations, impoverishing human lives and excluding people from the cultural connections they have reason to seek. So the human development perspective can be extended to accommodate the importance of cultural liberty.

The cultural dimensions of human development require careful attention for three reasons. First, cultural liberty is an important aspect of human freedom, central to the capability of people to live as they would like and to have the opportunity to choose from the options they have—or can have. The advance of cultural liberty must be a central aspect of human development, and it requires us to go beyond social, political and economic opportunities, since by themselves they do not guarantee cultural liberty.

Second, even though there has been much discussion in recent years about culture and civilization, the focus has been less on cultural liberty and more on recognizing—even celebrating—cultural conservatism. The human development approach has something to offer in clarifying the importance of human freedom in cultural spheres. Rather than glorify unreasoned endorsement of inherited traditions, or warn the world about the alleged inevitability of clashes of civilizations, the human development perspective demands that attention go to the importance of freedom in cultural spheres (as in others), and to the ways of defending and expanding the cultural freedoms that people can enjoy. The critical issue is not just the significance of traditional culture—it is the far-reaching importance of cultural choices and freedoms.

Third, cultural liberty is important not only in the cultural sphere, but in the successes and failures in social, political and economic spheres. The different dimensions of human life have strong interrelations. Even poverty, a central economic idea, cannot be adequately understood without bringing in cultural considerations. Indeed, the close link between cultural deprivation and economic poverty was noted by no less an economist than Adam Smith, whose works have, as it happens, illuminated the relevance of human development.

Smith argued not only that poverty takes the gross shape of hunger and physical deprivation, but that it can also arise in the difficulties that some groups experience in taking part in the social and cultural life of the community. In particular, the analysis of poverty and the diagnosis of what commodities count as "necessaries" cannot be independent (Smith argued) of the demands of local culture. As he wrote: "By necessaries I understand not only the commodities which are indispensably necessary for the support of life, but whatever the custom of the country renders it indecent for creditable people, even the lowest order, to be without….Custom has rendered leather shoes a necessary of life in England. The poorest creditable person of either sex would be ashamed to appear in public without them."[1]

Indeed, culture establishes an important relation between relative incomes and absolute human capabilities. Relative deprivation in

The underlying motivation continues to be to search for ways of enhancing people's lives and the freedoms they can enjoy

incomes in the local community can lead to absolute social deprivation. For example, being relatively poor in income in a rich society can generate absolute poverty because of one's inability to afford the commodities that the established lifestyle in that society requires—even though the person may have a higher income than most people in poorer countries elsewhere. So, the very notion of economic poverty demands cultural investigation. In giving adequate recognition to cultural freedom and cultural influences in human development, we have to take note of the leverage of established cultures on our lives, and the significance of the interconnections between the cultural aspects of human life and the other aspects.

PARTICIPATION AND RECOGNITION

Deprivation of freedom, including cultural freedom, takes many forms. So does discrimination that can lead to a loss of freedom. As discussed in this Report, parts of the population can be subjected to discrimination in different spheres: political, socio-economic and cultural. The many dimensions of deprivation—and of discrimination—demand understanding the distinctions between different, if interrelated, processes through which people's freedoms are curtailed.

Deprivation often works through processes of exclusion. Cultural exclusion has recently received much attention. But two forms of cultural exclusion must be clearly distinguished.

PARTICIPATION EXCLUSION

First, the cultural exclusion of a person or group may sometimes take the form of not allowing this person or group to participate in society in the way that others are allowed and encouraged to do. This can be called "participation exclusion". Excluding people from participation can be linked to various characteristics of the persons involved, such as gender, ethnicity or religion.

The primary basis of discrimination in many cases of participation exclusion is the cultural affiliation of the people involved, resulting in their exclusion from participation in education or employment or political decision-making.

Even though cultural correlates are very often bogus, they clear the road to discrimination and exclusion

Arguments used to justify such exclusion tend to invoke alleged cultural correlates of the groups involved. Particular ethnic groups are said to be lazy or rowdy or irresponsible, members of minority religions are suspected of having conflicting loyalties to religious authorities and to the state and so on. Even though these cultural correlates are very often bogus, they clear the road to discrimination and exclusion. In some cases the identifying characteristics used in discriminatory policy directly invoke cultural attributes. This is particularly so with discrimination against religious communities, but it can also apply to groups defined by language, social origin or other identifying characteristic.

LIVING MODE EXCLUSION

A second kind of cultural exclusion denies recognition of a lifestyle that a group would choose to have. And this intolerance can go with the insistence that members of the group must live exactly like others in the society. This "living mode exclusion" figures prominently in religious intolerance—an important challenge addressed by John Stuart Mill in his famous essay, "On Liberty" (1859).

Living mode exclusions continue to be strong in many contexts today, with various manifestations. Religious intolerance, obviously, is still an important kind of exclusion. Intolerance of some behaviour patterns in purely personal lives is another example: discriminatory treatment of gays and lesbians is a common form of living mode exclusion. These exclusions involve direct violation of cultural liberty, and here the violation of liberty goes with a denial of diversity as well.

This type of exclusion can also be a momentous issue in multicultural societies with ethnic diversity, particularly with recently arrived immigrant populations. The insistence that immigrants give up their traditional lifestyles and adopt the dominant lifestyle in the society to which they have immigrated illustrates a common type of lifestyle intolerance in the contemporary world.

The demand can extend even to minute behavioural issues about the conduct of immigrants, made famous in Great Britain by Lord Tebbit's far-reaching "cricket test" (a legitimate immigrant must cheer for England in test matches against the country of the person's origin). Tebbit's test has the merit of definiteness, which can otherwise be a problem in a multicultural society in identifying what the dominant lifestyle actually happens to be. For example, now that curry has been described as "authentic British fare" by the British Tourist Board (in line with the prevailing consumption patterns of the natives of that island), a South Asian immigrant to Britain may have some difficulty, without Tebbit's algorithmic help, in determining what is the behaviour pattern to which he or she is being asked to conform!

Living mode exclusion can be a serious area of injustice.[2] This has been the subject of much recent work, including what is called the "politics of recognition", which includes "claims for the recognition of the distinctive perspectives of ethnic, 'racial,' and sexual minorities, as well as of gender difference".[3] These considerations are indeed important for an adequately broad view of justice, but in the context of human development they are most immediately seen as relevant to the exercise of cultural liberty, which—like other freedoms—must figure in the assessment of human development and in the appraisal of its lapses.

FREEDOMS, HUMAN RIGHTS AND THE ROLE OF DIVERSITY

The importance of human freedoms can be the basis of linking them with the idea of human rights. The recognition of human rights need not await their legalization in the form of justiciable entitlements. Often enough, they provide the motivation behind such legislation. Indeed, even the naming of some laws as "human rights laws" indicates this connection. As Herbert Hart, the distinguished legal theorist, put it in a justly famous essay, people "speak of their moral rights mainly when advocating their incorporation in a legal system".[4]

Indeed, going further, the ethical acknowledgement of human rights, sustained by public discussions and reasoning, can—and does—go beyond serving only as the basis for possible legislation.[5] Through the activism of individuals and groups (including dedicated human rights organizations), the freedoms reflected in the acknowledgement of human rights can provide the grounds for public demands, even widespread collective action and agitation (for example, for the right of minorities to have the freedom to choose their own lifestyles). The United Nations itself has been strongly engaged (particularly through the UN High Commissioners for Human Rights and for Refugees) in the pursuit of human rights even where national legislation has lagged behind ethical norms.

As pronouncements in social ethics, sustained by open public reasoning, human rights call for diverse forms of implementation. The underlying freedoms can be advanced through a variety of public actions, including recognition, monitoring and agitation, in addition to legislation and the moral commitments of concerned people. Affirmation of human rights, founded on the importance of human freedom in diverse forms, goes with the need to appreciate the reasons for acknowledging corresponding duties. Sometimes the duties are exactly specifiable, and sometimes they are only broadly characterized (they include both "perfect obligations" and "imperfect obligations", to make use of an old Kantian distinction). The nature and demands of human rights were extensively explored in *Human Development Report 2000*.

To be emphasized here is the basic recognition that the idea of human rights links directly to the safeguarding and advance of human freedoms. This gives reason enough, depending on circumstances, to defend and promote particular institutions and social arrangements. But such programmes have only derivative and contingent value, which has to be assessed in terms of what they actually do to human freedoms. The ethical force of human rights ultimately depends on the importance of human freedoms and cannot be detached from that connection. This elementary recognition has an extensive reach.[6]

One of the subjects that has received considerable attention in the contemporary cultural literature is cultural diversity. Sometimes it is even seen as a human right that groups of people, taken together, have. Group rights have many ambiguities, but it is not hard to argue that if they are to be taken seriously, their role in enhancing the freedoms of human beings must be

Intolerance can go with the insistence that members of the group must live exactly like others in the society

demonstrated. Even without entering deeply into the complex debates surrounding the idea of groups rights, the basic need to link rights to freedoms can be readily recognized.

This immediately raises questions about the value of cultural diversity, since it is not itself a characteristic of human freedoms. It is, however, easy to show that diversity can be important in the cultural sphere. If diversity is not allowed, many choices become unviable. Nevertheless, if our focus is on freedom (including cultural liberty), the significance of cultural diversity must vary along with its causal connections to human freedom.

Quite often these connections are positive and strong. Indeed, diversity may be both a consequence of the exercise of human freedom (particularly cultural liberty) and a source of societal enrichment (particularly cultural enrichment). Cultural diversity may well result if individuals are allowed and encouraged to live as they would value living. This would tend to follow from the earlier discussion on living mode inclusion. For example, the persistence of ethnically diverse lifestyles and the recognition of, and respect for, sexual minorities can make a society more culturally diverse precisely as a result of the exercise of cultural liberty. In these cases the importance of cultural diversity will follow directly from the value of cultural liberty, since the first is a consequence of the second.

Cultural diversity can also play a positive role of its own. For example, a culturally diverse society can bring benefits to others through the variety of experiences that they are, as a consequence, in a position to enjoy. To illustrate, it can be plausibly argued that the rich tradition of African American music—with its African lineage and American evolution—has not only helped to enhance the cultural freedom and self-respect of African Americans, but has also expanded the cultural options of all people (African American or not) and enriched the cultural landscape of America, and indeed the world.

However, the relation between cultural liberty and cultural diversity requires further examination. The simplest way of having cultural diversity may well be a conservative continuation of the variety of cultures that happen to be present at this time. A similar point can be made for

cultural diversity within an individual country, if it happens to have a variety of cultures within its borders. Does the championing of cultural diversity then demand support for cultural conservatism, asking that people stick to their own cultural background and not try to move to other lifestyles? That would immediately deliver us to an anti-freedom position, which would look for ways of blocking the choice of a changed living mode that many people may wish to have. Indeed, we could then also be in the territory of a different kind of exclusion: participation exclusion as opposed to living mode exclusion, since people from minority cultures would be excluded from participating in the mainstream.

The insistence on cultural conservatism can discourage—or prevent—people from adopting a different lifestyle, indeed even from joining the lifestyle that others, from a different cultural background, standardly follow in the society in question. Diversity will then be achieved at the cost of cultural liberty. If what is ultimately important is cultural liberty, then the valuing of cultural diversity must take a contingent and conditional form. Much will depend on how that diversity is brought about and sustained.

Indeed, to argue for cultural diversity on the ground that this is what the different groups of people have inherited is clearly not reasoning based on cultural liberty (even though the argument is sometimes presented as if it were pro-freedom reasoning). Nothing can be justified in the name of freedom without actually giving an opportunity for the exercise of that freedom, or at least without assessing how an opportunity of choice would be exercised if it were available. Diversity may well be sought for reasons other than cultural liberty. But to justify the maintenance of pre-existing diversities on the supposed ground of cultural liberty must, in the absence of some further argument, be a straightforward non sequitur.

IDENTITY, COMMUNITY AND FREEDOM

The reasons for being sceptical of giving automatic priority to inherited culture can be seen in terms of who makes what choices. Being born in a particular cultural milieu is not an exercise of freedom—quite the contrary. It becomes aligned to cultural liberty only if the person chooses to continue to live within the terms of that culture, and does so having had the opportunity of considering other alternatives. The central issue in cultural liberty is the capability of people to live as they would choose, with adequate opportunity to consider other options. The normative weight of freedom can hardly be invoked when no choice—real or potential—is actually considered.

As it happens, some communitarian theories have glorified the absence of choice involved in the "discovery" of one's real identity. Michael Sandel has helpfully explained this claim, which is part of the "constitutive conception" of community: "community describes not just what they *have* as fellow citizens but also what they *are,* not a relationship they choose (as in a voluntary association) but an attachment they discover, not merely an attribute but a constituent of their identity."[7] "The self came by its ends", as Sandel further explains, "not by choice but by reflection, as knowing (or inquiring) subject to object of (self-) understanding."[8] In this perspective, social organization can be seen (as another communitarian author, Crowley, puts it) as attempts to "create opportunities for men to give voice to what they have discovered about themselves and the world and to persuade others of its worth".[9]

The claim that identity is not a matter of choice but ultimately one of discovery needs further examination, and that larger issue will be taken up below. For the present argument it is relevant to note that the special importance and exceptional gravity that are connected, in this communitarian perspective, to inherited affiliations and attachments relate to its discovery-based foundation, in contradistinction to things that are "merely chosen". Whatever may be the persuasive power of that claim (it certainly needs some justification), it is in real tension with attaching importance to choice and the freedom to choose.

The communitarians are right, however, in emphasizing the importance of a sense of identity in leading one's life. Less clear is how identity can be a matter of just discovering something about oneself, rather than, explicitly or by implication, exercising a choice. These choices are constantly being made—quite often implicitly

but sometimes explicitly, with clear awareness. For example, when Mohandas Gandhi decided, after considerable reflection, to give priority to his identification with Indians seeking independence from British rule over his identity as a trained barrister pursuing English legal justice, there can be no question that he was consciously and firmly making a choice. In other cases the choice may be implicit or obscure, and also far less grandly defended than Gandhi's decision, but the choice may be no less authentic for that reason.

Typically, each individual can identify with many different groups. A person may have an identity of citizenship (for example, being French), gender (being a woman), race (being of Chinese origin), regional ancestry (having come from Thailand), language (being fluent in Thai, Chinese and English, in addition to French), politics (having left-wing views), religion (being a Buddhist), profession (being a lawyer), location (being a resident of Paris), sports affiliation (being a badminton player and a golf fanatic), musical taste (loving jazz and hip-hop), literary preference (enjoying detective stories), food habit (being a vegetarian) and so on.

The choices are not unlimited (you cannot choose the identity, for example, of an Inuit or a Sumo wrestler, if you are not one). But within the range of the memberships that you actually have, you can choose what priority to give to one membership or another, in a particular context. The fact that you have all these—and many other—memberships may be a matter of "discovery", but you still have to think and decide on what relative priorities to give to your various affiliations. The fact that discoveries occur does not exempt you from the need to choose, even if the choice is made implicitly.[10]

The possibility of choice is important in preventing what Anthony Appiah has called "new tyrannies" in the form of newly asserted identities, which can tyrannize by eliminating the claims of other identities that we may also have reason to accept and respect. Appiah illustrates this with the identity of being an African American. That identity has certainly helped in the past—and continues to do so today—in seeking racial justice in America. But it can also be oppressive if it is taken to be the only identity

Within the range of the memberships that you actually have, you can choose what priority to give to one membership or another, in a particular context

a black person has, with no other claims being given a hearing. Appiah puts the issue thus:

> In policing this imperialism of identity—an imperialism as visible in racial identities as anywhere else—it is crucial to remember always that we are not simply black or white or yellow or brown, gay or straight or bisexual, Jewish, Christian, Moslem, Buddhist or Confucian, but we are also brothers and sisters; parents and children; liberals, conservatives and leftists; teachers and lawyers and auto-makers and gardeners; fans of the Padres and the Bruins; amateurs of grunge rock and lovers of Wagner; movie buffs; MTV-holics, mystery-readers; surfers and singers; poets and pet-lovers; students and teachers; friends and lovers. Racial identity can be the basis of resistance to racism—and though we have made great progress, we have further still to go—let us not let our racial identities subject us to new tyrannies.[11]

Consider a different—and more ominous—example. When Hutu instigators a decade ago tried (and to some extent succeeded) in persuading other members of the Hutu community in Rwanda that they could plainly see that they were indubitably Hutus (not to be confused with "those awful Tutsis"), the unreasoned killings that followed could have been resisted by invoking broader identities of Hutus, for example, as Rwandans, or as Africans, or more broadly still as human beings. To see identity merely as a matter of discovery can not only be a conceptual confusion. It can also lead to a dereliction of duty by thinking human beings—a moral duty to consider how they would like to see themselves and with whom they would like to identify (whether only with the community of Hutus or also with the nation of Rwandans, the category of Africans or the collectivity of human beings). Freedom to choose is important not only for the individuals who would make the choice, but it can also be important for others, when the responsibility that goes with choice is adequately seized.

BIGOTRY AND ALIENATION

Complicated theory can sometimes bolster uncomplicated bigotry and make the world a more combustible place than it would otherwise be.[12] Rapid-fire cultural generalizations can displace a deeper understanding of culture and serve as a tool of sectarian prejudice, social discrimination and even political tyranny. Simple cultural generalizations, with great power in shaping ways of thinking, abound in popular beliefs and informal communication. A subject of many ethnic jokes and slurs, these underexamined beliefs can also surface as pernicious grand theories. An accidental correlation between cultural prejudice and social observation (no matter how casual) leads to the birth of a theory that may live on even after the chance correlation vanishes.

For example, jokes about the Irish (such as "How many Irishmen do you need to change a light bulb?") have had some currency in England for a long time. They appeared to fit well with the depressing predicament of the Irish economy, when it was in a long-term slump. But when the economy started growing with astonishing speed, the cultural stereotyping and its allegedly profound economic and social relevance were not discarded. Theories have lives of their own, often in defiance of the world that can actually be observed.

The connections between cultural bigotry and political tyranny can also be very close. The asymmetry of power between ruler and ruled, when combined with cultural prejudices, can result in injurious failures of governance, as was devastatingly observed in the Irish famines of the 1840s. As Richard Lebow has argued, poverty in Ireland was widely viewed in England as caused by laziness, indifference and ineptitude, so that "Britain's mission" was not seen to be to "alleviate Irish distress but to civilize her people and lead them to feel and act like human beings".[13] Similar uses of cultural prejudice for political purposes can be seen in the history of European empires in Africa and Asia. Winston Churchill's famous remark that the Bengal famines of 1943 were caused by the tendency of people there to "breed like rabbits" belongs to this general tradition of blaming the colonial victim. And it had a profound effect on relief efforts during that disastrous famine. Cultural critiques of the victims can be used by the rulers to justify hugely inefficient—as well as deeply iniquitous—tyrannies.

Cultural critiques of the victims can be used by the rulers to justify hugely inefficient—as well as deeply iniquitous—tyrannies

While the marriage of cultural prejudice and political asymmetry can be lethal, the need to be cautious about jumping to cultural conclusions is more pervasive.[14] Unexamined cultural assumptions can even influence the way experts view economic development. Theories are often derived from scanty evidence. Half-truths or quarter-truths can grossly mislead—sometimes even more than straightforward falsity, which is easier to expose.

Consider this argument from the influential book jointly edited by Lawrence Harrison and Samuel Huntington, *Culture Matters*. In the introductory essay, "Cultures count," Huntington writes:

> In the early 1990s, I happened to come across economic data on Ghana and South Korea in the early 1960s, and I was astonished to see how similar their economies were then. ....Thirty years later, South Korea had become an industrial giant with the fourteenth largest economy in the world, multinational corporations, major exports of automobiles, electronic equipment, and other sophisticated manufactures, and per capita income approximately that of Greece. Moreover it was on its way to the consolidation of democratic institutions. No such changes had occurred in Ghana, whose per capita income was now about one-fifteenth that of South Korea's. How could this extraordinary difference in development be explained? Undoubtedly, many factors played a role, but it seemed to me that culture had to be a large part of the explanation. South Koreans valued thrift, investment, hard work, education, organization, and discipline. Ghanians had different values. In short, cultures count.[15]

There may well be something of interest in this engaging comparison (perhaps even a quarter-truth torn out of context), and the contrast does call for probing examination. But the causal story is extremely deceptive. There were many important differences—other than cultural predispositions—between Ghana and the Republic of Korea in the 1960s, when the countries appeared to Huntington to be much the same, except for culture. The class structures in the two countries were quite different, with a much larger role of business classes in Korea. The politics were very different too, with the government in Korea eager to play a prime-moving role in initiating business-centred economic development in a way that did not apply to Ghana. The close relationship between the Korean economy and the Japanese and US economies also made a big difference, at least in the early stages of Korean development. Perhaps most important, by the 1960s Korea had a much higher literacy rate and a more extensive school system than Ghana had. The Korean changes had been brought about largely through resolute public policy since the Second World War, and were not simply a reflection of age-old Korean culture.

There have, of course, been earlier attempts to use cultural determinism to explain economic development. A century ago Max Weber (1930) presented a major thesis on the decisive role of the Protestant ethic (in particular, Calvinism) in the successful development of a capitalist industrial economy. Weber's analysis of the role of culture in the emergence of capitalism drew on the world as he observed it in the late 19th century. His analysis is of particular interest in the contemporary world, especially in the light of the recent success of market economies in non-Protestant societies.

There may be much to learn from these theories, and the empirical connections they expose may be insightful. And yet it is also remarkable how often specific aspects of cultural explanations, based on observing the past, have been undermined by later experiences. Indeed, theories of cultural determinism have often been one step behind the real world.

GLOBALIZATION, ASYMMETRY AND DEMOCRACY

There is more to be said on the choice of identity, in particular about problems of equity—and of distributive justice—that have to be faced in examining the implications of cultural inclusion as well as cultural diversity. But before doing that, it is useful to examine two special phenomena—or alleged phenomena—of the contemporary world that have exerted

Theories of cultural determinism have often been one step behind the real world

considerable influence on recent discussions of cultural identity. They can be jointly called—for want of a better expression—the future of cultural diversity in the globalized world. They deal with the impact of globalization and the asymmetric power that goes with it and with the thesis that there is a persistent tendency for civilizations to clash, which can make the world a very violent and disruptive place.

GLOBALIZATION'S ASYMMETRIC POWER?

One of the worries that many people have in contemplating the safeguarding of cultural liberty today concerns the overwhelming influence of Western culture, especially its "consumerism", in the globalized world in which we live. The point is often made, plausibly, that being free to choose one's lifestyle is not, in the present world, just a matter of being allowed to choose freely. It is also an issue of whether people in more marginalized civilizations are able to resist the Western influence. This concern certainly deserves attention, given the evident precariousness of local cultures in a world so dominated by thunderous exposure to Western influences.

At least two issues are of particular interest here. First, there is the power and force of market culture in general, which is part and parcel of the form that economic globalization has increasingly taken. Those who find the values and priorities of market-related cultures to be vulgar and impoverishing (even many in the West have this view) tend to find economic globalization itself to be quite objectionable. And yet often enough, they also see market-based globalization as hard to resist, given the reach and strength of the market economy and the sheer volume of resources it can bring to bear on reshaping the world.

The second problem concerns the asymmetry of power between the West and other countries and the likelihood that this asymmetry will translate into destruction of local cultures (poetry, drama, music, dancing, food habits and so on). Such a loss, it is plausibly argued, would culturally impoverish non-Western societies. Given the constant cultural bombardment that tends to come from the Western metropolis (from fast food to blast music), there are genuine fears that native traditions may be overwhelmed by the fusillade.

These threats are undoubtedly real, and to a considerable extent they may also be difficult to escape. The solution can hardly lie in stopping the globalization of trade and exchange, both because international commerce can bring economic benefits that many countries value greatly and because the forces of economic exchange and division of labour are hard to resist in an interacting world.

A plausible line of response to the problem of asymmetry can, however, take the form of strengthening the constructive opportunities that local cultures have—and can be helped to have—to protect their own and to resist being outgunned by the forces of cultural invasion. If foreign imports dominate because of greater control over the radio waves, television channels and so on, surely a counteracting policy must involve expanding the facilities available to local culture to present its own creations, both locally and beyond. The costs involved in following that constructive route may not be as forbidding as people might think, since communication has become so much cheaper in the contemporary world. This would also be a positive response, unlike the temptation, which rears its head with some frequency, to ban foreign influence through legislation or executive decree.

The constructive possibility of providing much more support for local cultural activities would not only help to strengthen them—it would also allow them to face a more equal competition. In the pro-freedom perspective there is much merit in taking that route, rather than making local cultures prevail simply through proscribing the competition. It is important to make sure that the baby of cultural liberty is not thrown away with the bath water of unequal competition.

The deciding issue, ultimately, has to be one of democracy. An overarching value must be the need for participatory decision-making on the kind of society people want to live in, based on open discussion, with adequate opportunity for the expression of minority positions. The issue of political inclusion (giving people the freedom to participate in political

An overarching value must be the need for participatory decision-making on the kind of society people want to live in

choices, rather than being ignored by authoritarian potentates) is particularly relevant here in the safeguarding of cultural liberty (in the freedom of people to choose their own lifestyles). We cannot both want democracy and yet rule out certain choices, on traditionalist grounds, because of their "foreignness" (irrespective of what people would choose, in an informed and reflective way). The value of democracy has to resist the banishing of citizens' freedom of choice through the fiat of political authorities (or orders of religious establishments or pronouncements of grand guardians of "national taste"), no matter how unbecoming those authorities (or establishments or guardians) find the new predilections to be. This is one field, among others, in which cultural liberty and political freedom can be fruitfully viewed together.[16]

CIVILIZATIONS AND GLOBAL HISTORY

If fear of globalization is one general concern that many people express in dealing with cultural liberty, the dread of a "clash of civilizations" (as Huntington calls it) is another that has received considerable articulation in recent years. The thesis has many components, but a general concern seems to be that pluralist and tolerant Western civilization is now under constant threat from less lenient and more authoritarian cultures.

Indeed, if we were to assume that people in non-Western civilizations are constantly tempted by authoritarian values (and perhaps even by the lure of violence), then the dread that the world's cultural diversity must have grave consequences would not be hard to understand. But how sound is the cultural analysis that underlies that fear? And how reliable is the reading of history that sustains that cultural analysis? There are reasons to be sceptical of both. Civilizational categories are far from clear-cut, and the simulated history that goes with the thesis of clashing civilizations exaggerates these contrasts, partly by neglecting the heterogeneities within each culture, but also by ignoring historical interactions between the different cultures.

The specific claim that tolerance is a special—and very nearly unique—feature of Western civilization, extending way back into history, is particularly hard to sustain. This is not to deny

that tolerance and liberty are among the important achievements of modern Europe (despite some aberrations, such as brutal imperialist rules over two centuries and the Nazi atrocities six decades ago). The world indeed has much to learn from the recent history of Europe and the Western world, particularly since the period of European Enlightenment. But to see a unique line of historical division there—going back through history—is remarkably fanciful. The history of the world does not suggest anything like a division between a long-run history of Western toleration and that of non-Western despotism.

Political liberty and tolerance in their full contemporary form are not an old historical feature in any country or civilization. Plato and Augustine were no less authoritarian in thinking than were Confucius and Kautilya. There were, of course, champions of tolerance in classical European thought, but there are plenty of similar examples in other cultures as well. For example, Emperor Ashoka's dedicated championing of religious and other kinds of tolerance in India in the third century BCE (arguing that "the sects of other people all deserve reverence for one reason or another") is certainly among the earliest political defences of tolerance anywhere. Similarly, when a later Indian emperor, Akbar, the Great Moghal, was making comparable pronouncements on religious tolerance at the end of the 16th century (such as: "no one should be interfered with on account of religion, and anyone is to be allowed to go over to a religion that pleases him"), the Inquisition was in full swing in Europe. To take another illustration, when the Jewish philosopher Maimonides was forced to emigrate from an intolerant Europe in the 12th century, he found a tolerant refuge in the Arab world and was given an honoured and influential position in the court of Emperor Saladin in Cairo. His tolerant host was the same Saladin who fought hard for Islam in the Crusades.

Indeed, the very idea of democracy, in the form of participatory public reasoning, has appeared in different civilizations at different periods in world history.[17] In early seventh century Japan, the Buddhist Prince Shotoku, regent to his mother Empress Suiko, introduced a relatively liberal constitution or *kempo* (known as

The specific claim that tolerance is a special feature of Western civilization, extending way back into history, is particularly hard to sustain

"the constitution of 17 articles") in 604 CE. In the spirit of the Magna Carta (signed six centuries later, in 1215 CE), the *kempo* insisted: "Decisions on important matters should not be made by one person alone. They should be discussed with many." On the subject of tolerance, it says: "Nor let us be resentful when others differ from us. For all men have hearts, and each heart has its own leanings. Their right is our wrong, and our right is their wrong."[18]

Examples of championing public discussion and seeking different—and conflicting—points of view have figured in the history of other countries in the world, both in the West and outside it. They continue to be of contemporary relevance in thinking about the feasibility of a tolerant democracy in today's world. When India became independent in 1947, the committee that drafted its constitution, led by B.R. Ambedkar, had to consider India's own traditions (including those of political tolerance and local democracy), in addition to learning from the gradual emergence of Western democracies over the previous two centuries.

Similarly, Nelson Mandela, in his autobiography, *Long Walk to Freedom,* describes how influenced he was, as a young boy, by the democratic nature of the local meetings that were held in the regent's house in Mqhekezweni:

> Everyone who wanted to speak did so. It was democracy in its purest form. There may have been a hierarchy of importance among the speakers, but everyone was heard, chief and subject, warrior and medicine man, shopkeeper and farmer, landowner and laborer.... The foundation of self-government was that all men were free to voice their opinions and equal in their value as citizens.[19]

The hard lines that have recently been drawn to give shape to the fear of a clash of civilizations are especially blind to world history. The classifications are often based in an extraordinarily crude and extreme historical innocence. The diversity of traditions within distinct civilizations is effectively ignored, and major global interventions in science, technology, mathematics and literature over millennia are made to disappear so as to give credence to a parochial view of the uniqueness of Western civilization.

There is a fundamental methodological problem in assuming that a partitioning civilization is the uniquely relevant distinction and must swamp other ways of identifying people. Other divisions (say, between rich and poor, between members of different classes and occupations, between people of different politics, between distinct nationalities and places of residence, between language groups and so on) are all submerged by this allegedly preeminent way of seeing the differences between people. It is not enough that those who would foment global confrontation or local sectarian violence try to impose a pre-chosen unitary and divisive identity on the people who are recruited as the foot-soldiers of political brutality. They are indirectly aided in that task by the implicit support that the warriors get from theories of singular categorization of the people of the world.

There is a remarkable neglect of the role of choice and reasoning in decisions about what importance to attach to membership in any particular group or any particular identity. By adopting a unique and allegedly predominant way of categorizing people, partitioning civilization can materially contribute to conflict in the world. To deny choice when it does exist is not only a misunderstanding of what the world is like. It is also ethical delinquency and a political dereliction of responsibility.

CONCLUSIONS

The building of humane and just societies demands adequate recognition of the importance of freedoms in general, which include cultural liberty. This calls for securing and constructively expanding the opportunities that people have to choose how they would live and to consider alternative lifestyles. Cultural considerations can figure prominently in these choices.

Emphasizing cultural liberty is not exactly the same as going all out for cultural diversity. It is certainly true that allowing diversity in cultural practices can be extremely important, since the exercise of cultural liberty depends on it. This, however, is not the same as championing cultural diversity for its own sake. Much would depend on how cultural diversity comes about and the extent to which the people involved can exercise

The building of humane and just societies demands adequate recognition of the importance of freedoms in general, which include cultural liberty

Human rights embody the fundamental values of human civilizations

People are different, and so are their cultures.

People live in different ways, and civilizations also differ.

People speak in a variety of languages.

People are guided by different religions.

People are born different colours, and many traditions influence their lives with varying colours and shades.

People dress differently and adapt to their environment in different ways.

People express themselves differently. Music, literature and art reflect different styles as well.

But despite these differences, all people have one single common attribute: they are all human beings—nothing more, nothing less.

And however different they may be, all cultures embrace certain common principles:

No culture tolerates the exploitation of human beings.

No religion allows the killing of the innocent.

No civilization accepts violence or terror.

Torture is abhorrent to the human conscience.

Brutality and cruelty are appalling in every tradition.

In short, these common principles, which are shared by all civilizations, reflect our fundamental human rights. These rights are treasured and cherished by everyone, everywhere.

So cultural relativity should never be used as a pretext to violate human rights, since these rights embody the most fundamental values of human civilizations. The Universal Declaration of Human Rights is needed universally, applicable to both East and West. It is compatible with every faith and religion. Failing to respect our human rights only undermines our humanity.

Let us not destroy this fundamental truth; if we do, the weak will have nowhere to turn.

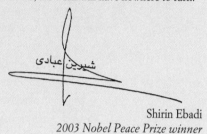

Shirin Ebadi
2003 Nobel Peace Prize winner

their freedom. It would be a serious mistake to regard cultural diversity as valuable no matter how it is brought about. Indeed, cultural diversity, particularly in the perspective of human development, cannot be evaluated without taking note of the processes involved and the role of human freedom in the way things get decided.

The analysis in this chapter leads to some clear conclusions, pursued in the chapters that follow. First, a greater extent of cultural diversity can be a consequence of the exercise of cultural liberty by all (including ethnic or sexual or social minorities). When that is the case, there is a strong argument for celebrating cultural diversity and for doing what can be done to safeguard it. The applause for diversity, in this reasoning, comes from the value of cultural liberty—a value that fits fully with the importance of freedoms in general.

Second, cultural diversity in a society can also give all the people in that society—irrespective of their background—the opportunity to enjoy a wider range of cultural choice. This, too, links ultimately with cultural liberty, in this case as a facilitator, rather than (as in the last case) as a consequence of the exercise of cultural liberty. Here too cultural diversity should get cheers, in expanding the cultural range of social life and thereby enhancing the options that people actually enjoy to choose their ways of living. This is also a part of a freedom-based defence of cultural diversity.

Third, the exercise of cultural liberty may sometimes lead to a reduction of—rather than an increase in—cultural diversity, when people adapt to the lifestyles of others and choose, in a reasoned way, to go in that direction (unhindered by living mode exclusion). When that occurs, to oppose cultural liberty on the ground that it reduces cultural diversity would be a blunder, since liberty has constitutive—and intrinsic—importance of its own in a way that diversity does not.

Related to that issue is the prizing of cultural conservatism, often championed on the ground that retaining one's "own" culture is a move in favour of freedom. But to assume that a compulsion to retain one's ancestral and inherited culture must somehow be an exercise of freedom is a conceptual confusion. That subject relates also to the role of choice in the determination of identity. Since all individuals belong to many groups, have many different ways of identifying themselves and have to decide how to deal with the correspondingly different—possibly conflicting—priorities, there is no way of avoiding choice (even if it is done implicitly and perhaps imperceptibly). This does not deny that "discoveries" are frequently made about whether one belongs to one group or another (and these could be important discoveries), but that does not eliminate the need for choice.

To deny choice when a choice exists is not only a factual mistake, it can also have grave moral consequences in a world where identity-based conflicts—and brutalities—are common. The inclusiveness of a society will depend greatly on bringing clarity to the role of choice in identity and to the need to "reason before identity". Indeed, understanding the responsibility of choice can help greatly in making sure that the relevant moral issues related to one's social existence are adequately addressed.

The importance of freedom links well with the need for equity in the pursuit of freedom. The freedoms of different people are involved, and focusing on freedom requires that attention be paid to the freedoms of all—and this connects with considerations of equity. It is important to keep the issue of equity constantly in view, because of its extensive reach. There is no basic tension—as is sometimes alleged—between freedom and equity. Indeed, equity can be seen in terms of equitable advancement of the freedoms of all people (rather than merely in terms of the distribution of income, or in terms of the even more limited perspective of "redistribution" from an ultimately arbitrary starting point). Seen in this way, it is possible to make consistent use of both the basic concepts of liberty and equity in assessing the demands of social inclusion and the contingent merits of cultural diversity.

A difficult—or allegedly difficult—case may be considered briefly to illustrate the arguments that may be invoked. The question has been asked, with considerable perspicacity: "Is multiculturalism bad for women?"[20] That issue relates to the well discussed fact that continuation of many of the practices in a traditional male-dominated society may go against the interests and opportunities of women. To argue for retaining them on the ground of the importance of multiculturalism does not well serve the interests of women. Extreme cases of this kind of conflict can involve particular practices (such as bodily mutilations) that are sanctioned by the rules of some prevailing cultures but that may be especially harmful to women's ability to lead their own lives and to exercise their own freedoms.

In pursuing this question, it is important to see cultural liberty in a broad enough perspective. In defence of ongoing practices it is sometimes pointed out that women themselves typically accept these cultural rules without protest. But many iniquities in the world continue to survive and prosper by making allies of the victims, by denying them the opportunity to consider alternatives and obstructing knowledge of other feasible arrangements in other communities. So it is particularly important not to fall into the confusion of taking unexamined traditionalism to be part of the exercise of cultural liberty. It is necessary to ask whether the underdogs in society—in this case the women whose lives may be badly affected by these practices—have had the opportunity to consider alternatives and have the freedom to know how people in the rest of the world live. The need for reasoning and for freedom is central to the perspective that is being used here.

Putative defences of conservative traditionalism could be—and have been—proposed on other grounds. Can such practices be defended on the ground of the value of multiculturalism? Can they be championed in the cause of cultural diversity? The second question is fairly easy to answer. Cultural diversity is not, as has already been discussed, a value in itself, at least not in the human development approach (with its focus on human freedoms and their equitable advancement). The value of cultural diversity rests on its positive connection—as is often the case—with cultural liberty. Invoking the contingent value of cultural diversity in defence of practices that deny women their basic freedom to choose would be manifestly perverse, since the freedom of the women involved is violated, not promoted, through these arrangements. Nor can equity, in the sense of equity of freedoms, be promoted in this way.

If, however, the expansion of cultural diversity, or any increase of "multiculturalism", is taken to be an object of value in itself—no matter what it does to the lives of the people involved—then we are in a territory whose limitations have already been much discussed in the human development literature. Even economic opulence—important as it is—could not be taken to be valuable in itself and had to be seen as important only to the extent that it conforms to what people would value having. In the human development perspective multiculturalism must be assessed for what it does to the lives and freedoms of the people involved.

Indeed, seeing the expansion of multiculturalism as an end in itself can easily yield a situation in which the freedoms of individual members of a community—in this case female members—are severely violated. This goes deeply against the importance of human freedom, which applies to women as well as men, and to the underdogs of a traditional society as well as to its leading figures and thunderous spokesmen. The need for equity points to the fundamental difficulties involved in taking the enlargement of multiculturalism as an end in itself.

As this chapter shows, deprivation of human freedom can arise from many causes and reflect diverse forms of discrimination, involving cultural as well as political and socio-economic influences on human lives. In the chapters that follow the different forms of exclusion, and their implications for human deprivation, are extensively investigated and assessed. Attention is paid to institutional features as well as values that profoundly influence human lives.

The practical importance of multiculturalism and cultural diversity figures in these analyses. Their merit, which can of course be very great, depends on their connections with the freedoms of the people involved, including equity and evenhandedness in the distribution of their freedoms. That basic principle is a central feature of the human development approach.

CHAPTER 2

 Challenges for cultural liberty

Some of the most socially divisive debates today are on cultural identity and diversity—in vastly different contexts, in many different ways. The debates can be about the choice of official language (Afghanistan's new Constitution), political representation of ethnic or religious groups (Sunnis and Shiites in Iraq), relations between the state and religion (Muslims in France), claims of indigenous people against mining by multinational corporations (Amazon region of Brazil), immigration policies (United Kingdom) or naturalization procedures (Germany). Such tensions can also be at the heart of violent conflicts (Rwanda, Yugoslavia). Globalization adds yet another dimension, as ethnic groups, indigenous people and nation-states challenge international agreements on trade and investment on the grounds that they diminish cultural diversity.

Around the world people are more assertive in demanding respect for their cultural identities. Often, their demands are for social justice, for greater political voice. But that is not all. Their demands are also for recognition and respect (box 2.1). People care about jobs and schools. But they also care about whether their history is acknowledged, their heroes are respected and their religious celebrations are recognized as official holidays. And they care about whether they and their children will live in a society that is diverse or one in which everyone is expected to conform to a single dominant culture.

Many states face an urgent challenge in responding to these demands. But responding can threaten ruling elites who impose their language, religion and ways of life to consolidate power and control of the state. And many states fear that recognizing diverse identities gets in the way of other important objectives: state unity, economic growth, development, democracy, peace and stability.

People have been persecuted for their identities for millennia. But suppressing identities is

becoming more difficult in today's world. Political movements for cultural recognition are difficult to suppress without resorting to extreme repression or violence, strategies that are less feasible in today's world of instant communication and strong international human rights networks.

All countries, and the world as a whole, face the challenges of promoting diversity and expanding the cultural choices of all people. These are not just challenges for a few "multiethnic states", for almost no country is homogeneous. The world's nearly 200 countries include some 5,000 ethnic groups.[1] Two-thirds of countries have more than one ethnic or religious group making up at least 10% of the population.[2] Many countries have large indigenous populations that were marginalized by colonization and settlers.

Around the world people are more assertive in demanding respect for their cultural identities

---

BOX 2.1

Two aspects of cultural exclusion

Cultural liberty is the freedom people have to choose their identity—to be who they are and who they want to be—and to live without being excluded from other choices that are important to them. Cultural liberty is violated by the failure to respect or recognize the values, institutions and ways of life of cultural groups and by discrimination and disadvantage based on cultural identity.

Living mode exclusion

Living mode exclusion occurs when the state or social custom denigrates or suppresses a group's culture, including its language, religion or traditional customs or lifestyles. Needed are policies that give some form of public recognition, accommodation and support to a group's culture. Through such policies of cultural inclusion members of the group see their cultures in the symbols and institutions of the state and in the respect of society.

Source: Chapter 1 and Kymlicka 2004.

Participation exclusion

Participation exclusion—social, economic and political exclusion along ethnic, linguistic or religious lines—refers to discrimination or disadvantage based on cultural identity. Such exclusions operate through discriminatory policies from the state (such as the denial of citizenship or of the right to vote or run for office), past discrimination that has not been remedied (lower performance in education) or social practice (such as less access in the media to a cultural group's point of view, or discrimination in job interviews). Needed are approaches that integrate multicultural policies with human development strategies.

Specific remedies required

There is much reinforcement between living mode exclusion and social, economic and political exclusion, and some of their causes (viewing some cultures as "backward"). Each type of exclusion requires its own analysis and remedies.

Figure
2.1

Most countries are culturally diverse

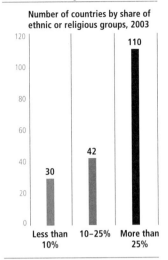

Number of countries by share of ethnic or religious groups, 2003

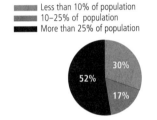

Share of world population, 2003

- Less than 10% of population
- 10–25% of population
- More than 25% of population

30%
52%
17%

Note: Percentages refer to all ethnic or religious groups except the largest.
Source: CIA 2003.

The pace of international migration has quickened, with startling effects on some cities. In Toronto 44% of the population was born outside of Canada.[3] One way or another every country is a multicultural society—containing ethnic, religious, linguistic and racial groups that have common bonds to a heritage, culture, values and way of life.

In the agenda for human development in the 21st century, expanding cultural liberty is an important, and often neglected, challenge (box 2.2). This chapter explores the nature of that challenge.

CULTURAL LIBERTY—AN UNCHARTED DIMENSION OF HUMAN DEVELOPMENT

Human development is about people. It is about enlarging the choices people have to do and be what they value in life. Much work on human development—including the human development index and previous *Human Development Reports*—has focused on greater access to health and education, on pro-poor economic growth and on democratization as the main challenges. But as chapter 1 explains, people must also be free to be who they are and to choose their cultural identity accordingly—as a Thai, a Quaker, a Wolof speaker, a South African of Indian descent—and to enjoy the respect of others and live in dignity. They must also be free to make cultural choices without penalty, without being excluded from other choices—for jobs, schooling, housing, healthcare, political voice and many other opportunities critical to human well-being. They must be allowed to choose multiple identities—as Thai and Muslim, for example, or as Wolof and Senegalese.

The core argument of this Report is that societies should embrace, not suppress, such multiple and complementary identities. The challenge for policy-makers in the 21st century is to broaden choices—so that people need not renounce their identities to have access to the full range of social and economic opportunities.

DIVERSE FORMS AND ORIGINS OF CLAIMS FOR CULTURAL LIBERTY

Throughout history, in all regions of the world, cultural identities have been suppressed. Conquerors, colonizers, despots and democratically elected governments alike have tried to impose

---

BOX 2.2

Defining cultural rights lags behind defining civil, political, economic and social rights—why?

Of the five categories of human rights—civil, cultural, economic, social and political—cultural rights have received the least attention. The first-ever resolution on cultural rights adopted by the Commission on Human Rights was in 2002, on "Promotion of the enjoyment of the cultural rights of everyone and respect for different cultural identities".

This neglect has its roots in the heated debates that arose during the drafting of the Universal Declaration of Human Rights. At issue was whether cultural rights should explicitly recognize minority rights. Canada, most Latin American countries and the United States argued against minority rights, while the Eastern bloc countries and India argued for them. In the end, minority rights were not recognized in the final wording. It was not until 1966 that the International Covenant on Civil and Political Rights recognized that people belonging to ethnic, linguistic or religious minorities "shall not be denied the right, in community with other members of their group, to enjoy their culture, to profess and practice their religion, or to use their own language".

These reservations reflect the unease that surrounds the notion of cultural rights:

- Cultural rights can provoke arguments about cultural relativism, arguments that use culture to defend violations of human rights.
- Cultural rights are difficult to operationalize because they are tied up with the concept of culture, which is a moving target.
- Cultural rights, according to some, are a "luxury", to be addressed once the other rights have been achieved.
- Cultural rights cannot be addressed without confronting the cultural "wrongs" that exist in societies. These are traditions and practices that violate human rights. States are cautious about recognizing such wrongs.
- Cultural rights evoke the scary spectrum of group identities and group rights that some people fear threaten the nation-state.

Some human rights and political philosophy theorists argue that ensuring the civil and political rights of individuals—such as freedom of worship, speech and association—is sufficient to allow individuals to freely pursue their cultural beliefs and practices.

Though slow to start, the work of human rights bodies has made important strides in clarifying the elements of human rights to participate in cultural life, including equality and non-discrimination, freedom from interference in the enjoyment of cultural life and the freedom to create and contribute to it, freedom to choose in which culture and which cultural life to participate, freedom to disseminate, freedom to cooperate internationally and freedom to participate in the definition and implementation of policies on culture. Overriding all these elements is the fundamental principle that cultural rights are an indivisible part of human rights, although not every custom or practice is a right.

Sources: Stamatopoulou 2002; Kymlicka 2004; and Arizpe 2004.

a particular language, religion or way of life on the people under their rule. In some places non-favoured cultures have been labelled "inferior" or "backward". In others, such as apartheid South Africa, rulers sought to keep people separated, in part by denying some groups the same rights of citizenship and participation as others enjoyed. Worst of all are the places that have tried to obliterate groups through genocide, such as in Nazi Germany and Rwanda.

The result is a legacy of widespread cultural exclusion, both living mode exclusion and exclusion in political, social and economic participation along ethnic, linguistic or religious lines (participation exclusion). This Report explores such exclusions in three categories: minorities in multi-ethnic states, indigenous people and migrants.

Minorities in multi-ethnic states. More than 150 countries have significant minority ethnic or religious groups, and only 30 countries do not have a religious or ethnic minority that constitutes at least 10% of the population (figure 2.1). An example is the ethnic groups in former colonial states, especially in Africa, where boundaries did not coincide with ethnic identities, creating highly diverse states. In most of these groups members share a common history or at least perceive a shared experience.

Not all these groups are discriminated against or disadvantaged, and the situations they face vary widely. African Americans have twice the unemployment rate of their white counterparts and nearly three times the infant mortality rate (see figure 3.4 in chapter 3). They are also underrepresented politically in upper and lower houses of legislatures. But civil rights struggles have led to greater respect for African American culture and affirmation of the African American identity as a source of pride. Other minorities may be economically privileged but culturally or politically sidelined. In Indonesia the ethnic Chinese constitute 3% of the population but control about 70% of the private economy.[4] Despite their economic power they face restrictions on Chinese-language education and publishing. In many countries in South-East Asia residents of Chinese descent are considered "foreigners" even when they have lived there for generations.

For some groups discrimination is widerspread. The Roma of Eastern Europe have unemployment rates averaging 45% and rising above 60% in some areas. They also suffer from substandard health and living conditions.[5] Only one in three Roma children in Serbia and Montenegro has ever attended primary school, and no more than 0.4% of Serbian Roma have a university education.[6] Often perceived as lazy, unclean, uneducated and petty thieves, Roma disproportionately suffer violent attacks in countries such as Bulgaria, the Czech Republic and Slovakia.[7]

Indigenous people. Around 300 million people belong to the world's indigenous groups,[8] representing some 4,000 languages in more than 70 countries.[9] Latin America's 50 million indigenous people make up 11% of the region's population. Indigenous people are not always in the minority.[10] In Bolivia and Guatemala indigenous people make up more than half the population.[11]

These groups are heirs to unique cultures and unique ways of relating to other people and the environment. They maintain political, cultural and economic characteristics distinct from mainstream society. In Australasia, the Americas and elsewhere the sound of foreign feet on indigenous soil was too often a death knell. Military conquest, ecological destruction, forced labour and lethal diseases reduced indigenous populations in the Americas and Australia by as much as 95%.[12] In Australia alone some 500 languages have been lost since the arrival of Europeans.[13]

For those who remain, the struggle continues. The world's indigenous people share many challenges, such as poverty and poor health (figure 2.2) and education. While many culturally identifiable groups face inequalities in these areas, indigenous people share some distinct problems. Often the lands they use for productive purposes and to maintain historical and spiritual links are not secure and so are being taken over for logging, mining, tourism and infrastructure. From occupying most of the earth's ecosystems two centuries ago indigenous people today have the legal right to use about 6% of the earth's territory. And in many cases the rights are partial or qualified.[14] In most South-East Asian countries, for example, there are no laws granting indigenous people the right to

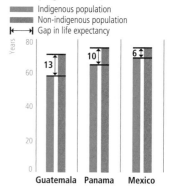

Figure 2.2 **Indigenous people can expect a shorter life**

Gap in life expectancy in selected developing countries, 1997–2000

Source: During 1993 (share of indigenous peoples); WHO 2001 (Guatemala); UNDP 2002b (Panama); Mexico, Ministry of Health 2004 (Mexico).

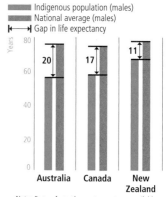

Gap in life expectancy in selected industrial countries, 1997–2000

Note: Data refer to the most recent year available during the period specified.
Source: Australian Bureau of Statistics 2004 (Australia); Justiniano and Litchfield 2003 (Canada); WHO 2001 (New Zealand).

Figure
2.3 **Europe's non-European migrant population has increased significantly...**

Foreign-born population from outside Europe

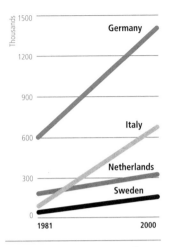

... and migrants are coming from more places

Migrant groups in Sweden with populations greater than 1,000

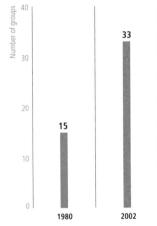

Source: Wanner 2002; Statistics Sweden 2004.

their land. And not only their land is being coveted and taken—so is their knowledge. Multinational corporations have discovered its commercial potential, and the race is on to patent, privatize and appropriate.

Migrants. The number of international migrants—defined as people living outside their country of birth—more than doubled since the mid-1970s—to about 175 million.[15] The numbers have increased most dramatically in the richest countries. The number of migrants to the European Union from outside Europe is up 75% since 1980.[16] Migrants are coming from a wider range of countries, too, so that more people of different cultures are living together. In London children in state schools speak some 300 different languages.[17] And in Sweden migrants come from twice as many countries as they did in 1980 (see figure 2.3 and feature 5.1 in chapter 5).[18]

While the inflow is fastest in the richest countries, migration is an issue in all regions. People have moved from poorer to more prosperous developing countries (such as the migration into the oil-rich countries in the 1970s and 1980s) and from countries experiencing political upheaval or persecution to neighbouring countries (see figure 5.2 in chapter 5). As a result developing countries make up 10 of the 15 countries with the highest proportion of foreign-born residents, including the top three (United Arab Emirates, Kuwait and Jordan).[19] Saudi Arabia has the fifth largest foreign-born population, at more than 5 million.[20]

In both richer and poorer countries one of the greatest challenges for migrants is their legal status in the receiving country. For immigrants there is a sea of gray between full citizenship and illegal status. This uncertainty affects their civic participation, such as receiving health and education services, being able to drive legally and being able to enter the workforce without being subjected to discrimination. Often immigrants' uncertain legal status culminates in their having no political voice and being vulnerable to human rights abuses. Their uncertain status also puts recognition of their cultural identity in jeopardy. Immigrants, particularly those deemed illegitimate, can face severe restrictions on building houses of worship, celebrating holidays and wearing their traditional or religious clothing or

symbols. In the United Kingdom, for example, 69% of Muslims surveyed felt that the rest of society did not regard them as an integral part of it.[21]

CULTURAL EXCLUSION IS WIDESPREAD

In many areas of human development much work has been done to document performance and the nature and the size of the problems to be overcome. Measurement techniques, developed through decades of research and established traditions in data collection, provide numerical evidence: 1.2 billion people survive on less than $1 a day,[22] 828 million go to bed hungry,[23] 114 million children of primary school age are not in school,[24] 11 million children die each year of preventable causes,[25] and 1.8 billion people live in countries lacking the key elements of formal democracy.[26]

Capturing living mode exclusion is intrinsically more difficult than capturing social, economic and political exclusion. Living mode exclusion happens when the culture of a group—whether ethnic, linguistic or religious—is denied recognition and respect. It is often reflected in a culture being considered "inferior" or in its practices not being recognized. The most extreme forms of exclusion result from state policies to suppress or prohibit the use of languages or religious or other important practices such as dress that are visible markers of identity—for example, turbans worn by Sikhs or the headscarf worn by some Muslim women.

State policies of living mode exclusion include official language laws—where a national language must be used in the bureaucracy, courts, public services and education—and restrictions on religious freedoms. Policies of exclusion also include elevating state symbols celebrating the history and culture of dominant groups through national holidays and the naming of streets and buildings while ignoring the history and culture of other groups.[27]

Charting living mode exclusion is difficult (box 2.3). Few national or international statistical agencies track such exclusion. As with data on gender and the environment—also once novel to statistical offices—this must change. But the challenges are enormous, and not just the technical aspects. Language, religion, history, clothing, customs, ceremonies and cuisine are just some of the areas that define cultural identity. Just as there are myriad ways to understand "culture", there are myriad ways to curtail cultural liberty and to fail to recognize cultural identities. A comprehensive understanding of culture and cultural liberty will always be out of statistical reach.

But attempts can be made to gain a rough idea of the scope of the problem based on some key cultural markers such as religion, language and ceremonial practices. The *Minorities at Risk* data set attempts to capture the exclusion of people and groups on the basis of cultural identity (see feature 2.1). It estimates that almost 900 million people—around one of seven—belong to groups that are discriminated against or disadvantaged as a result of their identity, facing cultural, economic or political exclusion.

Of course, these categories often overlap, and many people in these groups face some combination of these exclusions. About 518 million of them belong to groups that are estimated to face living mode exclusion, including restrictions on religion, language, ceremonies and appearance (see figure 1 in feature 2.1).

Recognition of religion. History is full of examples of religious persecution. In the 14th century BCE Egyptian Pharaoh Akhenaten proclaimed that there was no god but Ra and ordered references to all other gods to be expunged, forbidding even the use of the plural form of the word *god*.[28] The infamous Spanish Inquisition of the 15th century sought to discover and punish Jews and Moors who had publicly converted to Christianity under duress but continued practicing their true beliefs. In mid-19th

---

BOX 2.3

Measuring cultural liberty

To date, cultural statistics have dealt mainly with the production and consumption of "cultural goods"—film, books and theatre. But can cultural liberty—and its opposites, living mode exclusion and social, economic and political exclusion along ethnic, linguistic or religious lines—be measured?

Measuring living mode exclusion
Language, religion, history, clothing, customs, ceremonies, cuisine and values, among others, interact to define cultural identity. All of these ways to understand culture provide ways to exclude cultural identities such as language policies, treatment of different religions, school curricula and attitudes within society. Information can be collected on these issues, but rarely is. Beyond the simple data availability problems are the analytical challenges of converting information into statistically useful numbers. One possible approach is qualitative assessments—expert assessments of the severity of the situation—on issues that are important to many cultural identities, such as language and religion. This Report, for example, includes information from the *Minorities at Risk* data set of the University of Maryland (see feature 2.1), which does not capture the whole detail or scope of cultural exclusions but can provide useful evidence for understanding the problem.

Measuring participation exclusion
Measurement of social, economic and to a lesser extent political exclusions along ethnic, linguistic

and religious lines is more advanced. Often lacking, however, is a breakdown by culturally identified groups. Some data collection does include questions on religious, ethnic and linguistic identity and some post-censal surveys focus specifically on these cultural groups, but they could be much more comprehensive and comparable. An important issue is allowing people to register multiple identities. Political exclusion is more difficult to capture. There are some hard data, such as representation in parliament and voter participation (although they could be more disaggregated), but other issues, such as freedom of expression, movement and organization, are more difficult to capture and require qualitative approaches.

Next steps
More work can be done at the country level, where understanding of the issues may be greater. This could involve improved data monitoring and collection—such as including questions on identities in survey questionnaires and post-censal surveys targeted at specific cultural groups—as well as qualitative assessments.

At the international level leadership by an international statistical body could bring sharper focus to what is a formidable and urgent task. For example, the UNESCO Institute of Statistics has already done much work in measuring culture. The coordinating institution could advocate for the collection of information, such as the inclusion in national surveys of questions on cultural identity, and could be the lead depository for

these data. In more qualitative areas of cultural and political exclusions enormous benefits could accrue from having an international institution take the lead on comprehensive approaches to these complex issues at the country level.

No index of cultural liberty
There are demands not only to produce statistics on issues of culture but to go farther and produce a cultural liberty index. A lesson of the human development index and other composite indicators is that such measures need to be grounded in a conceptual framework and must be policy relevant as well as measurable and comparable.

As this Report acknowledges, data on issues of cultural liberty are extremely limited. And the conceptual and methodological challenges are enormous for capturing such issues as discriminatory policy and social practice and the extent of historical neglect that cultural groups face.

And the problem is more than empirical. Unlike some other aspects of human development, such as health and education, where many countries face common challenges, the challenges in dealing with cultural exclusion are more diverse. It will never be fully possible to compare homogeneous Japan with diverse India, or how Europe is dealing with issues posed by immigration with how Latin America is meeting the demands of indigenous people for land and self-rule.

Sources: Goldstone 1998; Fukuda-Parr 2001; Kymlicka 2004; and Valdés 2002.

The *Minorities at Risk* data set, created by researchers at the University of Maryland's Center for International Development and Conflict Management, collects data on groups that suffer discrimination and disadvantage and that organize politically on the basis of their group identity. Discrimination and disadvantage include exclusion through public policy and through social practice, both current and the lingering effects of historical patterns of discrimination.

These data track a group's status relative to that of the majority. If the minority groups are not worse off than others in the country, their situation is not reflected in the data. While this may miss many people living in countries where cultural freedom is restricted for all, focusing on discrimination is at the heart of this Report—capturing the different treatment of cultural groups in society and the suppression of cultural identities.

What is a minority at risk?

The project deals with "communal groups" whose members share a "distinctive and enduring collective identity" based on shared history, religion, language, ethnicity or other factors. Group identity is not seen as rigid, unchanging or inextricably linked to a particular feature of the group, but as a perception shared by the group or society.

While the project tracks many variables for each group, of particular interest for this Report are the variables on cultural (living mode), political and socio-economic discrimination and disadvantage. Data used for this report are current through 2000 and are derived from the project's most recent global survey, completed in 2002.

- *Cultural (living mode) discrimination and disadvantage* were assessed according to discriminatory policy and practice in several fields: restrictions on religion (affecting groups with some 359 million members); on the use of language, including for instruction (334 million); on ceremonies (305 million), appearance and family life (144 million); and on cultural organizations. For each category the project assessed restrictions giving a value from zero (no restrictions) to three (activities sharply restricted). The scores were summed to give a broad overview of cultural restrictions. The project found that 129 groups with around 518 million people face at least some of these restrictions (figure 1).
- *Political discrimination and disadvantage* were graded on a five-point scale. Zero means no discrimination, and one signifies a situation in which public policies are actively trying to remedy historical patterns of discrimination. Two refers to situations where there are historical patterns of discrimination, but no

remedial public policy. Three refers to exclusion based on prevailing social practice without remedial public policy. And four refers to cases in which public policy actively discriminates against a group. There were also detailed assessments of discrimination in key political rights: freedom of expression, freedom of movement, rights in judicial proceedings, freedom to organize, right to vote and access to the police and military, civil service and higher office. For the last case, the absence of minorities in these fields is not enough to signal discrimination. There needs to be evidence of discriminatory policy or governmental practice. According to the project 191 groups, with around 832 million people, were considered to be discriminated against politically (figure 2).
- *Economic discrimination and disadvantage* were also graded on a four-point scale. For the 189 groups with about 750 million people that faced economic discrimination, zero refers to the case where public policy aims to reduce

disadvantages, for example, through affirmative action. Four refers to the case where both policies and prevailing social practice actively discriminate against the group.

The data from the *Minorities at Risk* data set can be used to reveal a good deal about the living mode and participation exclusions faced by members of culturally identified groups, showing not only how extensive these exclusions are but also how frequently they overlap (see figure 1). The data set can also reveal some specific aspects of the living mode exclusion that some minorities face, as well as the varying causes—from discrimination by the state to historic neglect of cultural groups that has not been remedied (see figure 2).

Caveats

The data set is a pioneering effort to measure the conditions that minority groups experience and the policies affecting them. Subjective data capture aspects of the traits and challenges of groups not available through other means. The Minorities at Risk Project consults multiple sources—including journalistic accounts, international organization reports, human rights reports, government accounts and expert opinion—when scoring groups on their various characteristics. Every effort is made to ensure consistent coding across cases and to minimize the dangers of ideological bias. Additional information on the project is available online at www.cidcm.umd.edu/inscr/mar. Data updated through 2003 will be available by the end of 2004.

This Report uses the data carefully, to give a broad overview of the immense challenges of cultural discrimination, not as an attempt to rank or evaluate specific countries for their policies. Used in that way, the data set is a useful tool and a great step forward in measurement.

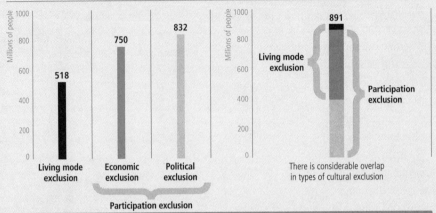

Figure 1 Discrimination and disadvantage of culturally identified groups can be cultural, political and economic—with considerable overlap

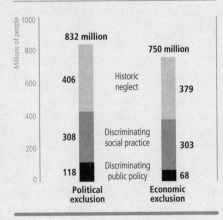

Figure 2 Political and economic exclusion have different causes

Sources: Gurr 1993, 2000; MAR 2003; Kymlicka 2004.

century Korea several hundred Christians were killed for their beliefs. And non-Catholic Christian denominations were not recognized in Italy until 1984 and in Spain until 1992.[29]

In some countries religious restrictions can affect everyone; in others they focus on people with certain beliefs. The *Minorities at Risk* data set found that some 359 million people (of the 518 million who belong to groups that face some form of cultural exclusion) are disadvantaged or discriminated against relative to others in the state in following their beliefs (see feature 2.1).

In many cases the religious activities of groups discriminated against are closely controlled. For example, religious activities and organizations of the 80% Muslim population of Uzbekistan are banned unless the group is registered, allowing the state to exert close control over religion. In other instances discrimination against religion is more active.[30] Since 1997 Turkmenistan has officially allowed religious activities for only two religious denominations—Sunni Islam and Orthodox Christianity. All other religions have been severely persecuted, including Jehovah's Witnesses, Pentecostals, Baptists, Adventists and Hare Krishnas, and the Shiite community has been denied registration. However, registration requirements were formally lifted by the president in early 2004.[31] In Iran the Baha'i community—the largest religious minority, with 300,000 members—is not recognized in the Constitution, which essentially considers them "non-persons".[32]

These are just three examples. Not only is the issue widespread and a direct concern to cultural liberty and human development. It is contentious and emotive. Of the many unmet claims of current political movements, the claim for religious freedom is often central.

Language recognition. Language is often a key element of an individual's cultural identity. Limitations on people's ability to use their mother tongue—and limited facility in speaking the dominant or official national language—can exclude people from education, political life and access to justice. There is no more powerful means of "encouraging" individuals to assimilate to a dominant culture than having the economic, social and political returns stacked against their mother tongue. Such assimilation is not freely chosen if the choice is between

one's mother tongue and one's future. In 19th century Belgium, for example, the Flemish who strived for upward mobility had little choice but to learn French—the sole official language—and in time many abandoned their ancestral language altogether.[33] These pressures have not gone away in other countries: the indigenous people of Guatemala are much more likely to prosper speaking Spanish.

An indication of the resulting assimilation is the death of the world's languages. Of the estimated 10,000 languages that have existed over time, only about 6,000 are spoken today.[34] And the number is projected to drop by 50–90% over the next 100 years.[35]

The challenges are greatest where linguistic diversity is greatest. Sub-Saharan Africa has more than 2,500 languages (although, as chapter 3 shows, many of these languages share commonalities), but the ability of many people to use their language in education and in dealings with the state is particularly limited. In more than 30 countries in the region—with 518 million people, 80% of the region's total—the official language is different from the one most commonly used.[36] Only 13% of the children who receive primary education do so in their mother tongue (figure 2.4).

Does a lack of education in one's mother tongue stall development? Research suggests that the answer might be yes. In the United States children educated in their mother tongue for the first six years of school perform much better than those immediately immersed in English. And there is every reason to believe that the process of learning would follow a similar pattern in developing countries (chapter 3).[37]

While the ability to use one's mother tongue in public as well as private life is important, this does not make the use of multiple languages in government, the courts and education easy or practical. Chapter 3 looks in detail at the costs and benefits states face in their language policy.

Other aspects of living mode exclusion. Language and religion are often important parts of an individual's cultural identity, but there are many ways different cultures can be respected and recognized. According to the *Minorities at Risk* data set, 60% of people who face cultural discrimination are restricted in

There is no more powerful means of "encouraging" individuals to assimilate to a dominant culture than having the economic, social and political returns stacked against their mother tongue

Figure
2.4 **Many lack access to primary education in their mother tongue**

Region or group	Number of spoken languages	Population with access to education in mother tongue in 2000	Total population (millions)
Sub-Saharan Africa	2,632	13%	641
East Asia and the Pacific	2,815	62%	1,918
South Asia	811	66%	1,480
Central and Eastern Europe and the CIS	625	74%	409
High-income OECD	1,299	87%	912
Latin America and the Caribbean	1,086	91%	530

Source: SIL International 2004b.

performing ceremonies. A further 25% face restrictions in the clothes they wear and how they can appear in public, including many indigenous people in Latin America and the Roma in parts of Eastern Europe.[38]

Also important is the way the state recognizes and respects the history of different cultural groups within its borders. This is not an easy matter on which to collect data, particularly by region or city. One way of assessing how diverse groups are recognized and accepted is by the way national holidays celebrate key moments in the history or religion of cultural groups in a country or the way streets are named.

In the United States most national holidays are non-denominational. In India central government employees have 17 holidays, 14 of which celebrate the diversity of its religions (figure 2.5). But in France 6 of 11 national holidays are of religious origin, all Christian, and 5 are non-denominational although almost 1 in 13 French citizens is Muslim.

POLITICAL, ECONOMIC AND SOCIAL
EXCLUSION BASED ON CULTURAL IDENTITY

Facing restrictions in expressing one's identity (living mode exclusion) is only part of the challenge for cultural liberty. Many groups, because of their cultural identities, face discrimination or disadvantage in other aspects of human development. More than 750 million people are estimated to belong to groups that are disadvantaged or discriminated against in economic or political life (see feature 2.1).

Political participation. The limits of political participation are obvious in dictatorships or one-party states. But inequalities in political participation can be widespread even in established democracies. Political processes can be rigged or restricted in many ways to create obstacles to members of certain ethnic, linguistic and religious groups. The *Minorities at Risk* data set estimates that more than 300 million people belong to groups that face restrictions on access to higher office relative to others in the state as a result of their identity. Just under 300 million belong to groups that have restricted access to the civil service. Some 250 million belong to groups that do not have equal rights to organize. About 280 million belong to groups that do not enjoy equal freedom of expression. And 83 million belong to groups that do not have equal voting rights.[39]

Denial of citizenship is one of the most direct ways of excluding groups of people from the political process. More than 300,000 people of the "hill tribe" minority in Thailand have been denied nationality and the rights and privileges afforded to full citizens, and Myanmar has denied citizenship to more than 250,000 Rohingya Muslims who had previously fled the country because of persecution. Despite a growing parliamentary lobby Kuwait continues to deny citizenship to more than 100,000 Bidun, many of whom have lived in the country for generations.[40]

Ensuring equality at all stages of the political process is vital for preventing discrimination against culturally identified groups, but it is difficult to assess. Looking at outcomes, which are easier to define and measure, can be more revealing. Of high-income OECD countries with data, only in the Netherlands is the proportion of ethnic minorities in parliament similar to their share in the population. The United States comes in second and Belgium third (table 2.1).

The problem is more widespread, of course. In Brazil only 2 of the 33 cabinet members are Afro-Brazilian, even though they make up almost half the population.[41] In Kenya the number of Kikuyu cabinet members dropped from 31% in 1979 to 3% in 1998, even though their share of the population remained steady at around 20%.[42] The situation changed again in the 2003 elections. In Fiji ethnic Fijians occupied 19 of 21

Figure
2.5

National holidays are important ways to recognize—or ignore—cultural identities

Religions reflected in national holidays, 2003

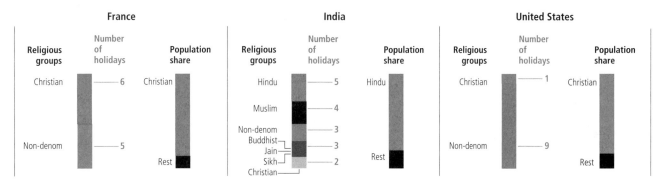

Source: National holidays: France 2004; India, Ministry of Personnel 2004; Office of Personnel Management 2003; religious populations: India, Office of the Registrar General 2004; France and United States, CIA 2003.

cabinet seats in 2001 although they make up just half the population.[43] In Trinidad and Tobago citizens of Indian descent (especially Hindus) were essentially excluded from cabinet positions from 1961 to 1986 (the situation has improved since then).[44]

The *Minorities at Risk* data set estimates that more than 800 million people are part of more than 200 culturally identified groups that face political disadvantage or discrimination based on ethnic, linguistic or religious identities,[45] with around 130 million of them facing directly discriminatory public policy. The rest are discriminated against because of social customs in the country or the lingering effects of historic discrimination (see feature 2.1).

Remedying this is vital. Politics is power. Too often inequalities in political participation are at the heart of the unresolved claims of cultural groups, which are discussed in the rest of this Report.

Health, education and income. Rarely are levels of human development—or its progress—spread evenly in a country. Certain religious, ethnic and linguistic groups are too often left behind (box 2.4). These pockets of poverty matter in their own right. But inequalities along cultural lines can be a key source of tension in society.

Few states collect information on life expectancy, infant mortality, literacy and school enrolment by ethnic, linguistic and religious group, even though population censuses can be an effective means for collecting such information.

Available data show consistent patterns of inequality. According to the *Minorities at Risk*

TABLE 2.1

Political representation of ethnic minorities in selected OECD parliaments

Country (year of last election with data)	Ethnic minorities in parliaments[a]			
	Number in lower house/ total	Share in lower house (%)	Share in population (%)	Ratio in house to ratio in population
Netherlands (2003)	13/150	8.7	9.0	1.0
United States (2002)	69/440	15.7	28.1	0.6
Belgium (1999)	6/150	4.0	10.0	0.4
Canada (2000)	12/301	4.3	13.4	0.3
United Kingdom (2001)	12/659	1.8	8.7	0.2
New Zealand (1999)	2/120	1.7	10.9	0.2
Denmark (2001)	2/179	1.1	5.8	0.2
Australia (2001)	1/150	0.7	6.0	0.1
Germany (2002)	5/603	0.8	8.5	0.1
France (2002)	0/577	0.0	8.0	0.0
Switzerland (1999)	0/200	0.0	6.0	0.0

a. Refers to visible ethnic minorities based on census or academic reports. Non-visible immigrants (of European descent) are not included. The share of ethnic minorities is likely to be lower than the reported figure because reports include citizens and non-citizens and ethnic minority groups tend to be disproportionately young compared to the majority population. Does not include aboriginals or members of dominant linguistic or national minority groups.

Source: Bird 2003.

data set, around 750 million people in the world belong to groups that face socio-economic discrimination or disadvantage because of their cultural identities. Many groups face both kinds of discrimination (see feature 2.1). For some 68 million of them this is a result of direct government policies of discrimination. But the more common causes are discriminatory social practices or unremedied neglect.

Around the globe people with different cultural identities live side by side, but often in different worlds. Black South Africans still earn about a fifth of the incomes of whites.[46] Romas in the Czech Republic, Hungary and Slovakia believe that their ethnicity is the main reason they cannot find a job.[47] Black men and women in São Paolo, Brazil, have half the salaries of whites.[48] In Guatemala there are clear overlaps between indigenous groups and social exclusion (map 2.1).

The same patterns are found in health and education. Life expectancies are consistently lower for indigenous people than for non-indigenous people (see figure 2.2). The Dalit population of Nepal has a life expectancy almost 20 years less than the national average.[49] Of Roma children in Serbia and Montenegro 30% have never attended primary school, and one in five of those who do attend will drop out.[50] In South Africa almost a quarter of the black population has had no schooling.[51]

PROMOTING CULTURAL LIBERTY REQUIRES RECOGNIZING DIFFERENCES IN IDENTITY

Living mode exclusion and participation exclusion require different policy solutions. Traditional policy approaches alone cannot address participation exclusion in social, economic and political life, and removing barriers to social, economic and political participation will not eliminate issues of living mode exclusion. New approaches are needed that integrate multicultural policies into human development strategies (table 2.2).

CULTURAL EXCLUSIONS REQUIRE THEIR OWN POLICY APPROACHES

There is no evidence that eliminating economic and political inequalities would erase living mode inequalities. Some groups are economically privileged but culturally (and politically) marginalized, such as the Chinese in South-East Asia.[52] Nationalist minorities like the Catalans in Spain or the Québécois in Canada enjoy the same standard of living as the majority, and in some cases a higher than average income, and their right to participate in the political process is well protected. Yet they have suffered living mode exclusion as their language and traditions were marginalized by the central government.[53]

So while it is common for living mode exclusion and political or economic exclusion to go together, they are distinct (see chapter 1). Living mode exclusion requires its own analysis and remedies. Too often cultural policy-making has been more concerned with the promotion of arts and the protection of cultural heritage than with the promotion of cultural liberty. Even today, key debates on cultural policies focus largely on protecting cultural heritage. But while these issues are important, the fundamental question of promoting cultural liberty has largely been forgotten (box 2.5).[54] To promote cultural

---

BOX 2.4

The human development index: capturing inequalities across groups

Large disparities exist between cultural groups within countries 2000

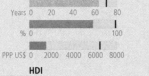

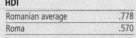

The human development index has become an invaluable tool for capturing human development and a country's development performance—roughly—in one number.

One of the index's most effective uses is in comparing the performance of neighbouring or similar countries, creating a healthy sense of competition. While creating a similar index for cultural liberty (see box 2.3) or including cultural liberty in the human development index is not possible, disaggregating the human development index by ethnic, linguistic or religious groups can shed some light on exclusion in health, education and income. This is rarely done, however.

In the rare cases when the human development index is calculated by cultural group, a revealing picture often emerges. The Roma in Romania, for example, have a human development index well below the Romanian average (see figure). Romania is ranked 72 in the human development index, but its Roma population would rank 128.

Namibia is the only country to have calculated a human development index by linguistic group. Again, the differences are staggering. The German-speaking population would finish comfortably ahead of Norway at the top of the rankings, with the English and Afrikaans speakers not far behind. San speakers would come 174 places below, with speakers of Tswana, Otjiherero, Oshiwambo, Rukavango, Caprivi-Lozi and Nama-Damara falling in between.

These examples show the huge challenges. Spotlighting these challenges is the first step in solving them. Governments are often reluctant to collect and disseminate this sort of information. Where data are available, they should be considered an important first step, not a damning revelation.

Source: Sen 2004b; UNDP 2000b.

liberty, policies of cultural inclusion need to give public recognition, accommodation and support to suppressed cultural identities. When this happens, disadvantaged cultural groups can see their identities reflected in the symbols and institutions of the state, removing many of the sources of their discontent.

INCORPORATING MULTICULTURALISM INTO HUMAN DEVELOPMENT STRATEGIES

Many traditional approaches to social, economic and political equality have been based on assimilation. Groups are expected to take on the language of the dominant culture at the expense of their own and must sometimes deny their religious and other traditions to succeed. There is nothing wrong with identifying with a dominant culture, but people should not be forced to make a stark choice between their identities and economic or political progress. Cultural liberty and human development require that individuals be as free to maintain their identities as they are to change them. For that, multicultural policies

need to be integrated into human development strategies (see table 2.2).

For example, while democracy is the only form of government consistent with all freedoms (including cultural freedoms), majoritarian rule does not always protect claims for cultural recognition and respect. As chapter 3 argues, asymmetric federalism (different rights—such as language rights—for different regions based on cultural need) and power sharing through proportionality and representative electoral arrangements are options to consider when majoritarian democracy falls short. Nor can socio-economic exclusion be addressed simply through policies of pro-poor growth and redistribution. Special programmes may be appropriate, even essential, to overcome discrimination and redress past wrongs. Bilingual education can give non-dominant language groups equal opportunities. In essence, multicultural policies require looking at equity in a new way. Where groups have specific cultural needs or are disadvantaged as a result of past wrongs, identical policy approaches will not produce equal opportunities—differentiated policy approaches are required (see table 2.2).

Map 2.1

Guatemala exhibits substantial overlap between linguistic communities and social exclusion

1998

▨ Indigenous linguistic communities

▨ Non-indigenous linguistic communities

▥ High social exclusion

Source: UNDP 2004.

TABLE 2.2

Integrating multicultural policies into human development strategies

Three pillars of the human development strategy	Necessary for cultural liberty	But not sufficient for cultural liberty	Additional multicultural policies	Potential contradictions between aims of multiculturalism and three pillars
Democracy	Democracy is the only form of government consistent with all human freedoms and human rights, including cultural freedoms and rights.	Democracy does little to accommodate minority interests. Well developed democracies have neglected claims for cultural recognition from ethnic, linguistic and religious groups, including indigenous groups and immigrants. Democracy also permits the rise of violent extremist groups.	Incorporate accommodation of minority identities and adopt policies of multiculturalism. Consider asymmetric federalism and executive power sharing. Recognize multiple identities and multiple citizenship.	Claims for cultural recognition often made by non-democratic groups. Demands can be antithetical to building democracy, freezing traditional practices that are oppressive in the name of "authenticity", and may not be supported by many members of the relevant group.
Pro-poor growth	Pro-poor growth is necessary to redress socio-economic exclusion (participation exclusion) of cultural groups.	Pro-poor growth is not enough to overcome discrimination and redress past wrongs.	Develop special support programmes for jobs, training and credit. Institute affirmative action programmes.	Affirmative action is contrary to principles of equality. Are special programmes an alternative to affirmative action?
Equitable expansion of social opportunities	Equitable expansion of social opportunities is necessary to redress socio-economic exclusion of cultural groups.	Equitable expansion of social opportunities is not enough to overcome discrimination and redress past wrongs. Also, does not address demand for different opportunities, such as different kinds of education.	Develop special support programmes for excluded groups. Institute affirmative action programmes. Offer separate publicly funded provisions, such as schools.	Affirmative action is contrary to principles of equality. Are special programmes an alternative to affirmative action? May involve "unfair inclusion" and exclusion from many choices and opportunities open to all other citizens.

Source: Human Development Report Office.

BOX 2.5
Cultural policies—protecting cultural heritage and promoting cultural liberty

In 1969 the United Nations Educational, Scientific and Cultural Organization (UNESCO) introduced the notion of "cultural policies", calling on governments to explicitly recognize cultural actions as an important end of public policy. The world community has step by step heeded this call: the 1982 World Conference on Cultural Policies in Mexico, the UN declaration of 1988 through 1997 as the Decade for Culture and Development, the 1998 Stockholm Intergovernmental Conference on Cultural Policies for Development and the increasing number of states establishing cultural ministries are all evidence of the realization that culture is development and vice versa.

In the beginning, the notion of cultural policy-making was concerned with the promotion of arts and the protection of cultural heritage. It is now increasingly related to cultural liberty, as the World Commission on Culture and Development proposed in its 1995 report, *Our Creative Diversity*. Cultural liberty is inseparable from respect and recognition of cultural diversity and the safeguarding of cultural heritage, both physical and intangible.

The cycle of cultural policy must end where it began a quarter of a century ago, with people, and their cultural freedom and fulfilment, the central end of cultural policy-making.

Source: Arizpe 2004.

THREE MYTHS SURROUNDING CULTURAL LIBERTY AND DEVELOPMENT

Few countries have attempted formal multicultural polices. Most countries have resisted them. Political scientists and philosophers have debated whether multiculturalism is consistent with democracy and human rights. Part of the reason lies in the realities of majority politics. The vulnerable are easy to ignore. Policy-makers have serious concerns about the effect of such policies on the country as a whole. Perceptions persist that ensuring cultural liberty is a luxury: it would be nice, but the costs are just too high.

Many of these perceptions are based on misconceptions about the role that cultural liberty, cultural diversity and even cultures themselves play in a society's development. Here, three such myths are examined in detail:

- Some cultures are more likely to make development progress than others.
- Cultural diversity inevitably leads to clashes over values.
- Cultural diversity is an obstacle to development.

MYTH 1: SOME CULTURES ARE MORE LIKELY TO MAKE DEVELOPMENT PROGRESS THAN OTHERS

There is no clear relationship between culture and development.[55] The idea that a group's culture matters for its development has enormous intuitive appeal, allowing cultural stereotypes to be turned into explanations for the state of the world. This idea is not new. It goes back at least as far as de Tocqueville's view of American democracy in the early 19th century and Weber's idealization of the Protestant work ethic. But a new wave of cultural determinism is emerging—attributing the failures of growth and democratization to inherent flaws in cultural traits.

These are dangerous ideas—that can lead to extreme policy conclusions. If some cultures in a society are believed not to be attuned to economic growth or democracy, it is not a long step to argue that they must be suppressed or assimilated. To overgeneralize, if Africa's failure to progress can be blamed on culture, why bother with political and economic policies or with foreign aid?

Proponents of cultural determinism often label large parts of the world as simply "African" or "Islamic".[56] But culture is not a homogeneous attribute. There are huge variations in language, religion, literature, art and living styles within the same cultural "group".[57] Moreover, culture is not uniquely pivotal in determining our lives and identities. Class, gender, profession and politics also matter hugely. Without being able to identify these clear and common cultural traits, a meaningful theory of cultural determinism struggles to get off the ground.[58]

There can be great continuity in a culture, but even in cultures with very long traditions rapid changes can occur over one or two generations.[59] For example, it is difficult to ascribe Japan's development to "Japanese culture" when interaction with the industrializing West in the mid-19th century led to the Meiji restoration and the determination to change the face of Japanese education. Even aspects of culture than seem entrenched can be altered. Bangladesh, for example, has taken great strides in reducing practices of gender inequality. Because cultures evolve, a society's culture today may determine very little of its future development. And these changes happen not as a result of targeted policies of cultural change, as cultural determinists might propose. They happen through economic and political interactions with other cultures and through better education—a policy conclusion that differs little from those in other areas of development theory.[60]

Even what is perceived as valuable for development in a culture is apt to change, and Western economies can no longer be assumed to be the model for the world.[61] Consider Japan again, which drew from a different class of cultural values than did the West for economic operations, emphasizing company loyalty, responsibility, interpersonal trust and implicit contracts to drive tremendous economic progress in the 20th century—values now espoused in every management training course in the West. But it was not always this way. So, predicting the value—and future—of cultural traits is far from straightforward.

It is not that culture offers no insights into the development process—cultural influences can make a difference. Some analysis has found, for example, that work ethic, thrift, honesty and openness to strangers can play a role in economic growth.[62] And when those influences are understood to be varied and changeable and one source of influence among many, culture can offer constructive insights into human behaviour and development. But there is no grand cultural theory of development here. The econometric evidence underlines this. In explaining growth rates, for example, economic policy, geography and the burden of disease were all found to be highly relevant. Cultural factors—such as whether a society is Hindu or Muslim—were found to be insignificant.[63]

So, while statistical analysis can help in assessing the validity of a theory, history is perhaps its greatest judge: and so far the history of cultural determinism exposes a theory one step behind the real world. By the time Weber's glowing assessment of the Protestant ethic was being recognized, many Catholic countries (France, Italy) were growing faster than Protestant Britain or Germany. The theory was then expanded to be more generally Christian and Western. But then Japan had to be included. And soon, East Asia was growing fastest, and old views that Confucian values do not promote conditions for growth had to be quickly jettisoned. Then Thailand, essentially a Buddhist country, became the fastest growing, so the theory had to be altered again.[64] So far, then, cultural determinism has not been able to catch up. Are today's views better founded and better able to predict a culture's influence on development—say, in Africa—or the compatibility of some religions with democracy—say, Islam?

Growth and development in Africa. Some propose that culture is determining development in Sub-Saharan Africa. A problematic "African culture" the argument goes, is unsuited to economic, political and social development.[65]

It is a convenient tautology for the cultural determinist to combine the idea of an "African culture" with the fact that Africa is failing. But African countries have much more in common than their cultures, and many of these factors may be more relevant in their struggles to develop.

Human Development Report 2003 identified 38 "priority" countries in Sub-Saharan Africa that have both low levels of development and weak progress towards the Millennium Development Goals (see Statistical feature 1, *The state of human development*). Of these, 21 are landlocked or have a large proportion of their populations living far from the coast. And most are small—only 4 have more than 40 million people. These countries are also highly dependent on primary commodities, which make up more than two-thirds of exports for 16 of the 23 countries with data. The disease burden in these countries is also extreme: in 22 of them more than 5% of the population has HIV/AIDS, and malaria remains prevalent.

In the examples showcased to argue the decisive role of culture in development, realities such as these often lie just below the surface. An often cited example, discussed in detail in chapter 1, is that of the Republic of Korea and Ghana in the 1960s, whose rapid divergence in the following decades has frequently been attributed to cultural differences. But analysis, as chapter 1 points out, has shown more important differences, such as levels of investment in education.[66] The example demonstrates that economic and social policy can have an enormous influence. Focusing internal and external resources on health and education is the first step out of the poverty trap. Even handicaps of geography—such as small internal markets and limited access to world trading routes—can be addressed through regional integration and cooperation.

African success stories are emerging. In Cape Verde, Mauritius, Mozambique and Uganda

By the time Weber's glowing assessment of the Protestant ethic was being recognized, many Catholic countries (France, Italy) were growing faster than Protestant Britain or Germany

GDP per capita grew at more than 3% in the 1990s.[67] Benin, Mali and Senegal increased primary enrolment rates by more than 15 percentage points.[68] Despite the growing HIV/AIDS epidemic in Africa, Guinea and Niger reduced child mortality rates by more than 5 percentage points.[69]

The world has the knowledge and the resources to overcome such policy challenges, offering the possibility that Africa can take its place as a full partner in the global economy. It would not be the first time the cultural determinist thesis had to adjust—this time bringing "African culture" into the fold.

Islam and democracy. All religions contain some ideas that can be helpful to development and some that can be harmful.[70] Islam is sometimes alleged to be incompatible with democracy, another way that culture is said to determine development (see also chapter 1). Yet there are basic Islamic principles that lay a foundation for democracy including the *shura* (consultation), *ijithad* (independent reasoning), *ijma* (consensus) and the Qur'anic injunction that there be no compulsion in matters of religion.[71]

The idea that Islam is incompatible with democracy is counter not only to the word of Islam, but also to the practice of states with Muslim majorities. Driving this misunderstanding, perhaps, is the coincidence that many Arab countries are both Islamic and have non-democratic regimes. But the difference between Arab countries with Muslim majorities and non-Arab countries with Muslim majorities is stark. None of the Arab countries that is predominantly Muslim has had five consecutive years of moderate or strong political and electoral rights in the past quarter of a century. In the non-Arab Islamic world 8 of 29 countries have enjoyed such rights.

With one set of Islamic countries performing poorly on democracy and another performing strongly, their common trait, Islam, cannot be the lone reason for a failure of democracy. The evidence shows that Islamic countries can perform as strongly as non-Islamic countries on measures of democracy. Among the world's poorest countries (to control for income because richer countries are more likely to be democratic) non-Arab Islamic countries are as likely to be democracies as non-Islamic countries.[72]

The *Arab Human Development Report 2003* identified a freedom deficit in the Arab region relative to other world regions. The reason for this deficit does not appear to lie with the people of the Arab states or with an anti-democratic culture: surveys have shown that as many if not more people in the Arab countries believe that democracy is the best form of government as in any other part of the world including the United States and Europe.[73] Perhaps the answer lies in the history of power politics. And in a lack of openness to ideas and culture from outside the region—only 330 books were translated into Arabic in the whole Arab world in 1995. Greek, a language with one-twelfth the number of speakers, had five times the number of books translated.[74]

MYTH 2: CULTURAL DIVERSITY INEVITABLY LEADS TO CLASHES OVER VALUES

There is little evidence to justify this claim. Since the 1950s, 70 territorially concentrated ethnic groups have engaged in violent conflict.[75] These types of conflict rose sharply with the end of the cold war, doubling between the 1970s and 1980s and reaching a peak of 48 in 1991. At the start of 2003, 22 such conflicts continued, and another 76 groups sought greater autonomy but used tactics short of full-fledged war (such as protests or isolated acts of violence).[76]

A popular explanation of such violence points to cultural or ethnic differences as fundamentally responsible—arguing for some innate propensity among people from different cultures to fight one another for domination and autonomy over differences in values that are incompatible. This view is captured by Samuel Huntington's well known prediction of a "clash of civilizations".[77] These ideas have also been used to explain interethnic conflicts within nations, as in Liberia and the former Yugoslavia.

It certainly is true that many conflicts have a cultural dimension. The opposing groups each see themselves as belonging to a common culture (ethnicity or religion) and fighting (at least partly) for cultural autonomy. For this reason conflicts have been attributed to primordial ethnic passions, making conflict appear unavoidable and intractable.[78]

Chapter 1 points out the serious flaws in this approach, based as it is on an incorrect view of the formation, role and malleability of identities. This argument also diverts attention from important economic and political factors. Extensive evidence on how identities form and change and why their salience varies over time indicates that while a culture is inherited, it is also constructed and chosen. Many people have multiple identities.[79] Cultural differences are not the primary cause of conflict. And in some cases diversity might even reduce the risk of conflict by making group mobilization more difficult.[80] So, what causes these tensions?

Ethnic conflicts—or greed and inequality? Many conflicts do fall along cultural lines, because people engaged on each side of these wars see themselves as belonging to a common culture. But the root causes are rarely the cultures themselves or an incompatibility of values. Recent research offers two other explanations: greed and horizontal inequalities. The struggle to control valuable natural resources, such as oil or diamonds, may be at the heart of ethnic warfare, as in Liberia, Sierra Leone and Sudan. What often appears to be ethnic conflict may simply be a resource grab by elite groups that have manipulated ethnic loyalties.

Declining economic performance and high poverty levels are other important incitements to war, as in Sierra Leone and Somalia. Behind many other conflicts are inequalities among ethnic, religious or linguistic groups (horizontal inequalities). When the cultural, political or socio-economic claims of different groups remain unmet, tension builds and can boil over into violence.

Recent research shows that many conflicts have erupted when groups have had unequal access to economic assets, income or employment opportunities, social services or political opportunities (box 2.6). Work by the UNDP Bureau of Conflict Prevention and Recovery shows that the likelihood of conflict increases with rising

---

BOX 2.6

Inequalities between groups can fuel conflict and tension

The root causes of violent conflict are rarely simple. But as the examples below show, a common theme is emerging from recent research into conflict: the role that socio-economic and political inequalities between groups can play in causing tensions and violence. Less research has been done on the role that cultural exclusions of groups may play (such as lack of recognition of languages or religious practices), but as this Report argues, these are also issues that can lead to mobilization and protests and so may also be important root causes or triggers of conflict.

- Severe rioting against the Chinese in **Malaysia** in the late 1960s has been attributed largely to the animosity felt by the politically dominant but economically sidelined Bumiputera majority towards the economically dominant Chinese minority.
- Civil war in **Sri Lanka** since the early 1980s has been linked to tensions resulting from inequalities between the Tamil minority and Sinhalese majority. Colonial administrators had favoured the Tamil minority economically, but this advantage was sharply reversed once the Sinhalese gained power and increasingly sidelined the Tamil minority in such areas as educational

opportunities, civil service recruitment and language policy.
- In **Uganda** the Bantu-speaking people (largely in the centre and south) have been economically dominant but politically sidelined compared with the non-Bantu-speaking people (largely in the north). These economic and political inequities have played a role in major conflicts, including the violence initiated by Idi Amin (1970s) and by the second Obote regime (1983–85).
- Indigenous people in the state of Chiapas, **Mexico,** have long suffered political and socio-economic deprivations. They have demanded greater political autonomy, improved socio-economic conditions and protection of their cultural heritage, culminating in uprisings against the Mexican state in four municipalities.
- In **South Africa** before 1994 the black majority was severely disadvantaged politically and socio-economically. That led to many uprisings between 1976 and the transfer of power in 1993.
- Catholics in **Northern Ireland** have suffered economic and political deprivations since the 16th century. The establishment of Northern Ireland as part of the United

Kingdom in the 1920s ensured that Protestants would enjoy permanent political and economic dominance—fuelling demands by northern Catholics to become part of the predominantly Catholic Republic of Ireland. Violent conflict started in the late 1960s and began to ease in the 1990s following systematic efforts to reduce these inequalities.
- Constitutional crises and coups have occurred in **Fiji,** notably in 1987 and 1999, as economically sidelined indigenous Fijians have feared losing political control to the economically dominant Indian-origin Fijians.
- Increasing tensions between Muslims and Christians in Poso, Central Sulawesi, **Indonesia,** began surfacing in the mid-1990s as the Muslim community increasingly gained more than indigenous Christians from new economic policies.
- Since colonial times the indigenous people of **Guatemala** have suffered political and economic discrimination, contributing to the country's ongoing conflicts.
- The Maoist insurgency launched in **Nepal** in 1996 may be attributed to deep grievances stemming from the systematic marginalization and exclusion of certain ethnic groups, castes and women.

Source: Stewart 2002; UNDP 2004; Fraenkel 2003.

group inequality, as in Indonesia and Nepal. The root of conflict in the Solomon Islands was the struggle for scarce and poorly managed resources (box 2.7). In Bolivia the government of Gonzalo Sanchez de Lozada was forced to resign in October 2003 in large part because of the activism and uprisings of the indigenous majority and their supporters, aroused by their poverty and political marginalization. In Ecuador, too, indigenous groups mobilized around issues of poverty and inequality and joined other groups in protest against the government of Jamil Mahuad, who was forced to resign in January 2000.[81] In some cases groups have been both economically and politically deprived (as in Mexico and South Africa), while in others a group may be politically dominant yet economically deprived (as in Malaysia, Sri Lanka and Uganda).

The industrialized world is not immune to this sort of violence. Race riots in US cities have been linked to severe racial disparities in income and public spending.[82] In Northern Ireland the Catholic minority suffered both economic and political discrimination. Statistical evidence supports this in-depth research. A study of 233 groups in 93 countries strongly supports the hypothesis that such inequalities between groups are liable to lead to violence.[83]

Most research on these conflicts has focused on economic and political inequalities, but a lack of cultural recognition can also be important. The introduction of the "Sinhala only" language policy was a strong impetus to the dramatic escalation of conflict in Sri Lanka. Language policy also played a role in the civil war in Moldova. And the Soweto riots in South Africa were triggered not by new economic or political deprivations but by attempts to impose Afrikaans on black schools. The peace agreement that ended more than 30 years of fighting in Guatemala included the Agreement on the Identity and Rights of Indigenous People (as part of the general peace accords), which gave official recognition to the country's multi-ethnicity.

The state's typical response to cultural differences is suppression and assimilation—to build a homogeneous nation. But suppression of cultural liberty is an attack on human development. And attempts to suppress and assimilate can heighten the tensions in society—so much so that they spill over into violent conflict.

Multiple identities can reduce conflict. Identities based on common cultural characteristics, such as religion, language or ethnicity, appear to promote stronger loyalty among group members than identities based on other characteristics. From that, leaders have learned that uniting groups based on a single cultural bond may be the best way to "rally the troops". The idea that individuals have a single rigid identity is divisive and confrontational. There is no question that this has been important in many conflicts.

Creating an environment in which multiple identities flourish is no easy task. It begins with encouraging cultural liberty and equality between groups in cultural, political and socio-economic opportunities. People must be free to choose how to define themselves and must be afforded the same rights and opportunities that their neighbours enjoy. This Report asserts that a main hope for harmony lies in promoting our multiple identities.

MYTH 3: CULTURAL DIVERSITY IS AN OBSTACLE TO DEVELOPMENT

There is no clear relationship, good or bad, between diversity and development. An argument

Creating an environment in which multiple identities flourish begins with encouraging cultural liberty and equality between groups in cultural, political and socio-economic opportunities

---

BOX 2.7

Solomon Islands' ethnic difference not the cause of conflict

In the conflict in the Solomon Islands, ethnicity issues diverted attention from the core issues of land tenure, economic development and more accountable governance that underpinned the protests. The peace agreement, for example, refers to the victims of "ethnic unrest" and the need to restore "ethnic harmony" in the Solomon Islands. But it is naïve and potentially dangerous for would-be peacemakers to view the conflict solely through the lens of interethnic hostility. Situated in a culturally diverse region with more than 1,000 languages, the Solomon Islands (where at least 70 distinct languages are spoken) is a weak and impoverished modern state, incapable of collecting taxes or delivering basic services. With hundreds of tribal groups and small clans known as *wantoks,* the concept of larger ethnic loyalties is almost as foreign and artificial as the notion of the state.

Although an ethnic feud on the surface, the recent intense social unrest in the Solomon Islands stems more from the struggle for scarce and poorly managed resources, whose ownership was previously vested in the clan, tribe or line. With the arrival of increasing numbers of migrant workers in the 1990s on the resource-rich island of Guadalcanal, resentment grew among the island's native settlers. Starting in 1998 armed groups of Guadalcanal youth (known as the Isatabu Freedom Movement, or IFM) engaged in belligerent actions that resulted in the internal displacement of more than 35,000 Solomon Islanders. Clashes ensued, predominantly with inhabitants from the neighbouring island of Malaita, and continued until late 2000 and the signing of an Australian-brokered peace agreement.

Source: Ponzio 2004 citing Reilly 2002; Schoorl and Friesen 2000.

Diversity—from divisive to inclusive

On 27 April 1994 the people of South Africa founded a nation on the pledge that we would undo the legacy of our divided past in order to build a better life for all.

It was not a pledge that we made lightly.

For generations, millions had been deliberately reduced to poverty. And to perpetuate itself, the apartheid system that claimed to be ordained from on high was sustained only by brute force, robbing us all of our humanity—oppressed and oppressor alike.

For decades we had fought for a non-racial, non-sexist society, and even before we came into power in the historic elections of 1994, our vision of democracy was defined by the principle, among others, that no person or groups of persons shall be subjected to oppression, domination or discrimination by virtue of race, gender, ethnic origin, colour or creed.

Once we won power, we chose to regard the diversity of colours and languages that had once been used to divide us as a source of strength.

We ensured that the basic law of our land, our Constitution and Bill of Rights, promoted unity and gave unique attention to social and economic rights. Our path of inclusiveness was not new, nor had it been chosen in haste. For decades the African National Congress had promoted national unity, and even at the height of oppression, when racial interaction led to prison and death, we never gave up on our aim to build a society grounded on friendship and common humanity.

Now, although laws no longer enforce the old divisions, they are still visible in social and economic life, in our residential areas, in our workplaces and in the growing inequality between rich and poor.

When we took on the project to transform our society, one of our rallying cries was "freedom from want". Our goal was to banish hunger, illiteracy and homelessness and ensure that everyone had access to food, education and housing. We saw freedom as inseparable from human dignity and equality. Now the foundation for a better life has been laid, and construction has begun. We are fully aware that our freedom and our rights will only gain their full meaning as we succeed together in overcoming the divisions and inequalities of our past and in improving the lives of all, especially the poor. Today, we are starting to reap some of the harvest we sowed at the end of a South African famine.

Many in the international community, observing from a distance how our society defied the prophets of doom and their predictions of endless conflict, have spoken of a miracle. Yet those who have been closely involved in the transition will know that it has been the product of human decision.

Mandela

Nelson Mandela
1993 Nobel Peace Prize Winner

---

for suppressing cultural groups and encouraging assimilation is that cultural diversity hampers development. Historically, one of the ideological backbones of the nation-state is that it functions much more effectively if it has a single cultural identity.

Much fuel for that argument today comes from Sub-Saharan Africa. A region rich in diversity but struggling with economic growth and development leads to speculation that diversity itself might be the cause of the problem. But the literature reveals an important distinction: problems arise not simply when diverse groups live together but also when tensions between these groups lead to inefficient political decision-making and disproportionate access for one or more groups to material resources and patronage.[84]

In Kenya, for example, President Daniel arap Moi took over from Jomo Kenyatta in 1978. By 1988 the share of road building in the "home regions" of the Kenyatta coalition was a third of what it had been at the end of the Kenyatta years, while road building in the Moi home regions almost doubled. The picture was similar for health spending in 1988, which was 18% in the regions of the Kenyatta coalition and 49% in the regions of the Moi coalition.[85]

The way to overall economic growth, and to high levels of health and education, is to formulate policies for the country, not for interest groups. Interest group politics are a problem in all countries, not just the culturally diverse. Indeed, the purpose of democracies is to manage conflicting interests through a transparent political system and open dialogue. Many established and prosperous democracies are constantly balancing the interests of powerful groups and those of the country.

In culturally diverse countries that are performing poorly, how much can diversity be blamed? Many of the poorest countries face enormous hurdles: high levels of HIV/AIDS and malaria, low levels of education, a location far from world markets. Resolving the tensions between groups is clearly not going to solve these problems. Consider Botswana, a homogeneous country with a stable political situation—and the highest HIV/AIDS prevalence in the world.

Again, the idea that diversity is bad for development is demolished by the many success stories of societies that recognize diversity.

Malaysia, with 62% of its people Malays and other indigenous groups, 30% ethnic Chinese and 8% Indian, was the world's 10th fastest growing economy during 1970–90, years when it implemented a broad range of affirmative action policies.[86] India has managed its diverse cultures with pluralist policies and 15 official languages—and made remarkable progress in economic growth and in health and education.

These success stories of culturally diverse countries point to the importance of pluralist policies. To the extent that cultural diversity can lead to tensions between groups and to inefficient political decision-making, the solution lies in reducing these tensions. As this Report argues from beginning to end, attempts to suppress and assimilate diverse cultural groups are not only morally wrong—they are often ineffective, heightening tensions. Needed instead are accommodating pluralist policies for incorporating individuals with diverse cultural identities into society.

Economic benefits of migration. A special case in the relationship between diversity and development is migration to the more developed countries. Unlike managing existing diversity, accepting economic migrants—or turning a blind eye to illegal immigrants looking for work—is a clear policy decision to increase diversity for economic gain.

The positive impact of migration on the ageing demographic profile of the West lies behind softer approaches to economic migration. Large inflows of migrants are needed for countries to maintain the ratio of working to non-working citizens—the European Union needs about 3 million immigrants a year, roughly twice the current number.[87] Immigrants also bring entrepreneurial skills—30% of the new companies in Silicon Valley in California in 1995–98 were started by Chinese and Indian immigrants (these ideas are further developed in chapter 5).[88]

And while debate continues on the brain drain from developing countries, the economic benefits of migration are not just one way. Remittances have soared, adding up to $80 billion in 2002, outstripping foreign aid and providing one of the biggest sources of revenue for some poor countries.[89]

But there are losers as well as winners. People already residing in the country feel threatened by the new immigrants and unfairly treated, through perceptions about a depressing impact on wages and employment. Key issues arise for the immigrants too. Needed for their labour and not their culture, their cultural freedoms are often not protected. Chapter 5 looks at the delicate policy balances of ensuring the benefits of migration while avoiding growing tensions between groups within a country and the negative consequences that can follow.

Diversity and dynamism through an exchange of ideas. Diverse societies can reap real benefits through the dynamism and creativity arising from the interactions of different cultural groups. Such effects are not easy to capture. They are most visible at the international level, where benefits can accrue from interactions between countries through trade and a sharing of experiences. A key element in Japan's emergence as one of the world's richest economies was a reversal of isolationist policies, with a firm commitment to "seek knowledge throughout the world".[90, 91] And *Arab Human Development Report 2003* identifies the lack of openness to ideas as a major factor holding back progress in that region.[92]

Effects within countries can be similar. The United States is the leading example of a country founded on diversity and tolerance where enormous economic success has followed. Benefits can come directly from interactions between groups. And businesses and entrepreneurs can be drawn to cities and societies where cultural freedom and diversity flourish. A study by the Brookings Institution finds that 11 of the metropolitan areas in the United States with the highest overall diversity are among the top 15 high-technology areas.[93] The implication is that diverse and tolerant environments foster the creation and innovation necessary for high-technology industries.

TODAY'S CHALLENGES FOR CULTURAL LIBERTY

This Report argues that multicultural approaches to managing diversity (see table 2.2) need not end in conflict, fragmentation and weak development. Indeed, such approaches may help avoid problems by easing tensions before they become acute. In the big picture the arguments for these policies are clear. But for policy-makers the contradictions, trade-offs and clashes with other aspects of human development can monopolize their attention.

For example, should London provide instruction in the 300 different languages that students in its state schools speak when there is so much demand for resources elsewhere? Does affirmative action violate principles of equity? How can a secular state balance the varying needs of religious groups? These are difficult questions. Ignoring the problem will not make it go away.

In some areas policies for cultural recognition will not interfere with human development. In others innovative policy solutions are needed to manage trade-offs. As the following chapters show, the tensions and policy trade-offs can be managed, despite what current discourse might suggest, especially where the costs have been exaggerated and the benefits ignored.

In a world where about 900 million people belong to groups that experience cultural exclusion in some form, promoting cultural liberty is an enormous challenge. Almost twice as many people are discriminated against or disadvantaged socially, economically or politically. The rest of this Report focuses on the policy issues for addressing the challenges to cultural liberty.

CHAPTER 3

 # Building multicultural democracies

Chapter 2 chronicles the widespread suppression of cultural liberty and the discrimination based on cultural identity—ethnic, religious and linguistic. How can states be more inclusive? Democracy, equitable development and state cohesion are essential. But also needed are multicultural policies that explicitly recognize cultural differences. But such policies are resisted because ruling elites want to keep their power, and so they play on the flawed assumptions of the "myths" detailed in chapter 2. And these policies are challenged for being undemocratic and inequitable. This chapter argues that multicultural policies are not only desirable but also feasible and necessary. That individuals can have multiple and complementary identities. That cultures, far from fixed, are constantly evolving. And that equitable outcomes can be achieved by recognizing cultural differences.

This chapter also argues that states can formulate policies of cultural recognition in ways that do not contradict other goals and strategies of human development, such as consolidating democracy, building a capable state and fostering more equal socio-economic opportunities. To do this, states need to recognize cultural differences in their constitutions, their laws and their institutions.[1] They also need to formulate policies to ensure that the interests of particular groups—whether minorities or historically marginalized majorities—are not ignored or overriden by the majority or by other dominant groups.[2]

RESOLVING STATE DILEMMAS IN RECOGNIZING CULTURAL DIFFERENCE

Pursuing multicultural policies is not easy—given the complexities and controversial trade-offs—and opponents of such policies criticize multicultural interventions on several grounds. Some believe that such policies undermine the building of a cohesive nation state with a homogeneous cultural identity, the dominant political project of the 20th century. Most states influenced by this thinking were deeply committed to fostering a single, homogeneous national identity with a shared sense of history, values and beliefs. Recognition of ethno-cultural diversity, especially of organized, politically active and culturally differentiated groups and minorities, was viewed as a serious threat to state unity, destabilizing to the political and social unity achieved after historic struggles[3] (feature 3.1). Other critics, often classical liberals, argue that group distinctions—such as reserved seats in parliaments for ethnic groups, special advantages in access to jobs, or the wearing of religious symbols—contradict principles of individual equality.

The issues at stake are further complicated by demands for cultural recognition by groups that are not internally democratic or representative of all their members, or by demands that restrict rather than expand freedoms. Demands to continue traditional practices—such as the hierarchies of caste in Hindu society—may reflect the interests of the dominant group in communities intent on preserving traditional sources of power and authority, rather than the interests of all members of the group.[4] Legitimizing such claims could risk solidifying undemocratic practices in the name of "tradition" and "authenticity".[5] It is an ongoing challenge to respond to these kinds of political claims.

Everywhere around the world these demands for cultural recognition and the critical responses to them also reflect historical injustices and inequities. In much of the developing world contemporary complications of cultural identity are intertwined with long histories of colonial rule and its societal consequences. Colonial views of cultural groups as fixed categories, formalized through colonial policies of divide and rule (racial and ethnic categories in the Caribbean[6] or religious categories in

How can states be more inclusive? Democracy, equitable development and state cohesion are essential. But also needed are multicultural policies that explicitly recognize cultural differences

Feature 3.1 State unity or ethnocultural identity? Not an inevitable choice

Historically, states have tried to establish and enhance their political legitimacy through nation-building strategies. They sought to secure their territories and borders, expand the administrative reach of their institutions and acquire the loyalty and obedience of their citizens through policies of assimilation or integration. Attaining these objectives was not easy, especially in a context of cultural diversity where citizens, in addition to their identification with their country, might also feel a strong sense of identity with their community—ethnic, religious, linguistic and so on.

Most states feared that the recognition of such difference would lead to social fragmentation and prevent the creation of a harmonious society. In short, such identity politics was considered a threat to state unity. In addition, accommodating these differences is politically challenging, so many states have resorted to either suppressing these diverse identities or ignoring them in the political domain.

Policies of assimilation—often involving outright suppression of the identities of ethnic, religious or linguistic groups—try to erode the cultural differences between groups. Policies of integration seek to assert a single national identity by attempting to eliminate ethno-national and cultural differences from the public and political arena, while allowing them in the private domain.[1] Both sets of policies assume a singular national identity.

Nation building strategies privileging singular identities

Assimilationist and integrationist strategies try to establish singular national identities through various interventions:[2]

- Centralization of political power, eliminating forms of local sovereignty or autonomy historically enjoyed by minority groups, so that all important decisions are made in forums where the dominant group constitutes a majority.
- Construction of a unified legal and judicial system, operating in the dominant group's language and using its legal traditions, and the abolition of any pre-existing legal systems used by minority groups.
- Adoption of official-language laws, which define the dominant group's language as the only official national language to be used in the bureaucracy, courts, public services, the army, higher education and other official institutions.
- Construction of a nationalized system of compulsory education promoting standardized curricula and teaching the dominant group's language, literature and history and

defining them as the "national" language, literature and history.

- Diffusion of the dominant group's language and culture through national cultural institutions, including state-run media and public museums.
- Adoption of state symbols celebrating the dominant group's history, heroes and culture, reflected in such things as the choice of national holidays or the naming of streets, buildings and geographic characteristics.
- Seizure of lands, forests and fisheries from minority groups and indigenous people and declaring them "national" resources.
- Adoption of settlement policies encouraging members of the dominant national group to settle in areas where minority groups historically resided.
- Adoption of immigration policies that give preference to immigrants who share the same language, religion or ethnicity as the dominant group.

These strategies of assimilation and integration sometimes worked to ensure political stability, but at risk of terrific human cost and denial of human choice. At worst, coercive assimilation involved genocidal assaults and explusions of some groups. In less extreme cases

these strategies involved many forms of cultural exclusion, as documented in chapter 2, that made it difficult for people to maintain their ways of life, language and religion or to hand down their values to their children. People feel strongly about such matters, and so resentment often festered. In today's world of increasing democratization and global networks policies that deny cultural freedoms are less and less acceptable. People are increasingly assertive about protesting assimilation without choice.

Assimilation policies were easier to pursue with illiterate peasant populations, as with Turkey's language reform in 1928 propagating a single language and script. But with the rapid spread of a culture of universal human rights these conditions are fast disappearing. Efforts to impose such a strategy would be greatly challenged today. In any case the historical evidence suggests that there need be no contradiction between a commitment to one national identity and recognition of diverse ethnic, religious and linguistic identities.[3]

Bolstering multiple and complementary identities

If a country's constitution insists on the notion of a single people, as in Israel and Slovakia, it

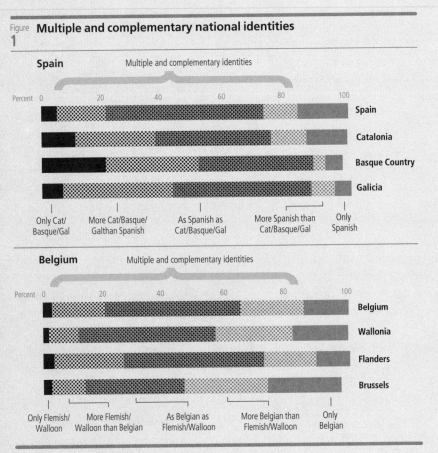

Figure 1 **Multiple and complementary national identities**

Spain — Multiple and complementary identities

Spain
Catalonia
Basque Country
Galicia

Only Cat/Basque/Gal | More Cat/Basque/Galthan Spanish | As Spanish as Cat/Basque/Gal | More Spanish than Cat/Basque/Gal | Only Spanish

Belgium — Multiple and complementary identities

Belgium
Wallonia
Flanders
Brussels

Only Flemish/Walloon | More Flemish/Walloon than Belgian | As Belgian as Flemish/Walloon | More Belgian than Flemish/Walloon | Only Belgian

becomes difficult to find the political space to articulate the demands of other ethnic, religious or linguistic minorities and indigenous people. Constitutions that recognize multiple and complementary identities, as in South Africa,[4] enable political, cultural and socio-economic recognition of distinct groups.

A cursory look around the globe shows that national identity need not imply a single homogeneous cultural identity. Efforts to impose one can lead to social tensions and conflicts. A state can be multi-ethnic, multilingual and multireligious.[5] It can be explicitly binational (Belgium) or multi-ethnic (India). Citizens can have a solid commitment both to their state identity and to their own cultural (or distinct national) identity.[6]

Belgium and Spain show how appropriate policies can foster multiple and complementary identities (figure 1). Appropriate policies—undertaken by Belgium since the 1830s and in Spain since its 1978 Constitution—can diminish polarization between groups within society, with the majority of citizens now asserting multiple and complementary identities.

Obviously, if people felt loyalty and affection only for their own group, the larger state could fall apart—consider the former Yugoslavia.

Countries such as Iceland, the Republic of Korea and Portugal are close to the ideal of a culturally homogeneous nation-state. But over time even states known for their homogeneity can be challenged by waves of immigration, as has happened in the Netherlands and Sweden.

Fostering trust, support and identification among all groups to build a democratic "state nation"

The solution could be to create institutions and polices that allow for both self-rule that creates a sense of belonging and a pride in one's ethnic group and for shared rule that creates attachment to a set of common institutions and symbols. An alternative to the nation state, then, is the "state nation", where various "nations"—be they ethnic, religious, linguistic or indigenous identities—can coexist peacefully and cooperatively in a single state polity.[7]

Case studies and analyses demonstrate that enduring democracies can be established in polities that are multicultural. Explicit efforts are required to end the cultural exclusion of diverse groups (as highlighted in the Spanish and Belgian cases) and to build multiple and complementary identities. Such responsive policies provide incentives to build a feeling of unity in diversity—

a "we" feeling. Citizens can find the institutional and political space to identify with both their country and their other cultural identities, to build their trust in common institutions and to participate in and support democratic politics. All of these are key factors in consolidating and deepening democracies and building enduring "state-nations".

India's constitution incorporates this notion. Although India is culturally diverse, comparative surveys of long-standing democracies including India show that it has been very cohesive, despite its diversity. But modern India is facing a grave challenge to its constitutional commitment to multiple and complementary identities with the rise of groups that seek to impose a singular Hindu identity on the country. These threats undermine the sense of inclusion and violate the rights of minorities in India today.[8] Recent communal violence raises serious concerns for the prospects for social harmony and threatens to undermine the country's earlier achievements.

And these achievements have been considerable. Historically, India's constitutional design recognized and responded to distinct group claims and enabled the polity to hold together despite enormous regional, linguistic and cultural diversity.[9] As evident from India's performance on indicators of identification, trust and support (figure 2), its citizens are deeply committed to the country and to democracy, despite the country's diverse and highly stratified society. This performance is particularly impressive when compared with that of other long-standing—and wealthier—democracies. The challenge is in reinvigorating India's commitment to practices of pluralism, institutional accommodation and conflict resolution through democratic means.

Critical for building a multicultural democracy is a recognition of the shortcomings of historical nation-building exercises and of the benefits of multiple and complementary identities. Also important are efforts to build the loyalties of all groups in society through identification, trust and support.

National cohesion does not require the imposition of a single identity and the denunciation of diversity. Successful strategies to build "state-nations" can and do accommodate diversity constructively by crafting responsive policies of cultural recognition. They are effective solutions for ensuring the longer terms objectives of political stability and social harmony.

Figure 2

Trust, support and identification: poor and diverse countries can do well with multicultural policies

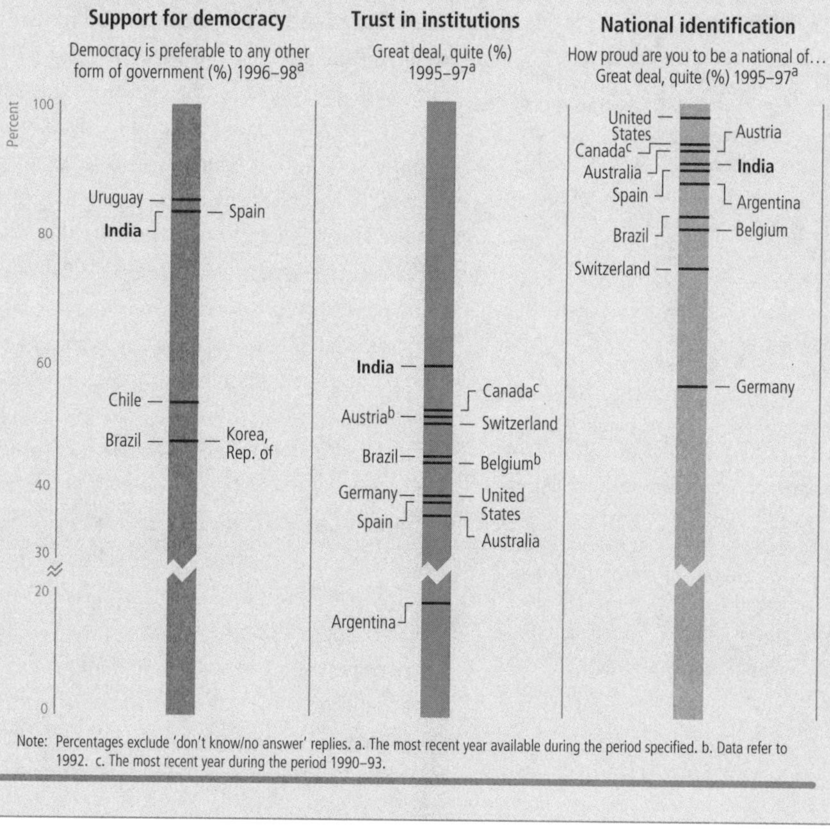

Note: Percentages exclude 'don't know/no answer' replies. a. The most recent year available during the period specified. b. Data refer to 1992. c. The most recent year during the period 1990–93.

Source: Bhargava 2004; Kymlicka 2004; Stepan, Linz and Yadav 2004.

South Asia, for example), continue to have profound consequences.[7] Contemporary states thus cannot hope to address these problems without some appreciation of the historical legacies of racism, slavery and colonial conquest.

But while multicultural policies thus must confront complexity and challenges in balancing cultural recognition and state unity, successful resolution is possible (see feature 3.1). Many states have accommodated diverse groups and extended their cultural freedoms without compromising their unity or territorial integrity. Policy interventions to minimize exclusive and conflictual political identities have often prevented or helped to end violent conflict. Policies of multicultural accommodation have also enhanced state capacity and promoted social harmony by bolstering multiple and complementary identities.

Redressing the cultural exclusion of minorities and other marginalized groups requires more than providing for their civil and political freedoms through instruments of majoritarian democracy and equitable socio-economic policies.[8] It requires explicit multicultural policies to ensure cultural recognition.[9] This chapter explores how states are integrating cultural recognition into their human development strategies in five areas:

- Policies for ensuring the political participation of diverse cultural groups.
- Policies on religion and religious practice
- Policies on customary law and legal pluralism.
- Policies on the use of multiple languages.
- Policies for redressing socio-economic exclusion.

POLICIES FOR ENSURING THE POLITICAL PARTICIPATION OF DIVERSE CULTURAL GROUPS

Many minorities and other historically marginalized groups are excluded from real political power and so feel alienated from the state (chapter 2). In some cases the exclusion is due to a lack of democracy or a denial of political rights. If so, moving to democracy will help. But something more is required, because even when members of such groups have equal political rights in a democracy, they may be consistently underrepresented or outvoted, and so view the central government as alien and oppressive. Not surprisingly, many minorities resist alien or oppressive rule and seek more political power. That is why a multicultural conception of democracy is often required. Several models of multicultural democracies have developed in recent years that provide effective mechanisms of power sharing between culturally diverse groups. Such arrangements are crucial for securing the rights of diverse cultural groups and for preventing violations of these rights by majoritarian imposition or by the political dominance of the ruling elite.

Considered here are two broad categories of democratic arrangements in which culturally diverse groups and minorities can share power within political processes and state institutions. The first involves sharing power territorially through federalism and its various forms. Federal arrangements involve establishing territorial subunits within a state for minorities to exercise considerable autonomy (box 3.1). This form of power-sharing arrangement is relevant where minorities are territorially concentrated and where they have a tradition of self-government that they are unwilling to surrender.

Redressing the cultural exclusion of minorities and other marginalized groups requires explicit multicultural policies to ensure cultural recognition

---

BOX 3.1

A rough guide to federalism

Federalism is a system of political organization based on a constitutionally guaranteed balance between shared rule and self-rule. It involves at least two levels of government—a central authority and its constituent regional units. The constituent units enjoy autonomy and power over constitutionally defined subjects—they can also play a role in shaping the policies of the central government. The degree and scope of autonomy varies widely. Some countries, such as Brazil, grant considerable powers to their regions. Others, such as Argentina, retain overriding control at the centre.

Some other important distinctions:

Coming together or holding together. In "coming together" federal arrangements, as in Australia or Switzerland, the regions chose to form a single federal polity. In "holding together" arrangements, such as in Belgium, Canada and Spain, the central government devolved political authority to the regions to maintain a single unified state.

One identity or many. "Mono-national" or "national" federations assert a single national identity, as in Australia, Austria and Germany. "Multi-national" federations, such as Malaysia and Switzerland, constitutionally recognize multiple identities. Other states combine the two. India and Spain assert a single national identity but recognize plural aspects of their heterogeneous polity—say, by accommodating diverse linguistic groups.

Symmetric or asymmetric. In symmetric federalism the constituent units have identical—that is symmetric—powers, relations and obligations relative to the central authority and each other, as in Australia. In asymmetric federalism some provinces enjoy different powers. In Canada, for example, asymmetric federal powers provided a way of reconciling Quebec to the federal system by awarding it specific powers connected to the protection and promotion of French-Canadian language and culture.

Source: Stepan 2001.

The second category of arrangements involves power sharing through consociations, using a series of instruments to ensure the participation of culturally diverse groups dispersed throughout the country. These arrangements address claims made by groups that are not territorially concentrated or do not demand autonomy or self-rule. Consociations are based on the principle of proportionality: the ethnic or cultural composition of society is proportionally mirrored in the institutions of the state. Achieving proportionality requires specific mechanisms and policies. Electoral arrangements such as proportional representation can better reflect group composition, as can the use of reserved seats and quotas in the executive and legislature.

Both federal and consociational types of power-sharing arrangements are common around the world. Neither is a panacea, but there are many successful examples of both. This chapter looks at a particular kind of federal arrangement and some specific mechanisms of consociation that are particularly suited to enabling the political participation of diverse cultural groups.

POWER SHARING THROUGH FEDERAL ARRANGEMENTS: ASYMMETRIC FEDERALISM

Federalism provides practical ways of managing conflict in multicultural societies[10] through democratic and representative institutions—and of enabling people to live together even as they maintain their diversity.[11] Sometimes the political demands of culturally diverse groups can be accommodated by explicitly recognizing group diversity and treating particular regions differently from others on specific issues. In such "asymmetric" federal systems the powers granted to subunits are not identical. Some regions have different areas of autonomy from others. Federal states can thus accommodate some subunits by recognizing specific distinctions in their political, administrative and economic structures, as Malaysia did when the Borneo states of Sabah and Sarawak joined the federation in 1963. This allows greater flexibility to respond to distinct demands and to accommodate diversity. These special measures enable territorially concentrated group distinctions to politically coexist with the central authority, thereby reducing violent clashes and demands for secession.

There are several flourishing examples of such entities. Almost every peaceful, long-standing democracy that is ethnically diverse is not only federal but asymmetrically so. For instance, Belgium is divided into three regions (the Walloon, Flemish, and Brussels-Capital regions), two established according to linguistic criteria (the Walloon region for French- and German-speaking people and the Flemish region for Dutch-speaking people). The Swiss federation also encompasses different linguistic and cultural identities.

In Spain the status of "comunidades autónomas" has been accorded to the Basque country, Catalonia, Galicia and 14 other entities. These communities have been granted a broad, and widely varying, range of autonomous powers in such areas as culture, education, language and economy. The three historic regions were given distinct areas of autonomy and self-rule. The Basque communities and Navarra have been granted explicit tax and expenditure powers beyond those of other autonomous communities. Spain's willingness to accommodate the distinct demands of its regions has helped to mitigate conflicts and separatist movements. Such proactive interventions have helped to foster acceptance of multiple identities and to marginalize the exclusive ones—identities solely as Basque, Galician, Catalan or Spanish (see feature 3.1).

Many federations have failed, however.[12] Federal arrangements that attempted to create ethnically "pure" mono-national subterritories have broken down in many parts of the world. Yugoslavia is a prominent example. The federal arrangements were not democratic. The units in the federation had been "put together" and were ruled with highly unequal shares of political and economic power among the key groups, an arrangement that fostered ethnic conflict that eventually became territorial conflict, and the federation fell apart. This collapse is sometimes attributed to a flawed federal design that failed to establish free and democratic processes and institutions through which ethnic groups could articulate multiple identities and build complementarity. Instead it reinforced demands for separation, thus ending in political disintegration.

Several models of multicultural democracies provide effective mechanisms of power sharing between culturally diverse groups

The success of federal arrangements depends on careful design and the political will to enhance the system's democratic functioning. What matters is whether the arrangements accommodate important differences, yet buttress national loyalties. For example, federal structures that merely respond to demands for the designation of "exclusive" or "mono-national" home-republics for ethnic groups may go against the idea of multiple and complementary identities. Such political deals, and communal concessions that do not foster loyalty to common institutions, can introduce divisive tendencies in the polity, which present ongoing challenges, as in the case of Nigeria (box 3.2).

In addition, history shows that asymmetric federalism, introduced early enough, can help reduce the likelihood of violent secessionist movements. The avoidance of violent conflict through various federal arrangements introduced in the early stages of emerging secessionist movements

The success of federal arrangements depends on careful design and the political will to enhance the system's democratic functioning

is often worth much more than the administrative costs that such arrangements incur.[13]

Many states fear that self-rule or "home rule" could undermine their unity and integrity. Yet many states have granted territorial autonomy without negative consequences. These efforts to enhance group representation and participation have sometimes staved off political violence and secessionist movements. For example, after decades-long struggle, the First Nations people of northern Canada negotiated a political agreement[14] with the federal government to create the self-governing territory of Nunavut in 1999.[15] In Panama several indigenous people—the Bri Bri, Bugle, Embera, Kuna, Naso, Ngobe and Wounaan—have constituted semiautonomous regions governed by local councils.

Article 1 of the International Covenant on Civil and Political Rights expresses the world's agreement that "All peoples have the right of self-determination. By virtue of that right they

---

BOX 3.2

The challenge of federalism: Nigeria's troubled political trajectory and prospects

Nigeria is home to more than 350 ethnic groups, but more than half the country's 121 million people belong to three main groups: the Hausa-Fulani, Muslims in the north; the Yoruba, followers of both Christian and Islamic faiths, in the South-West; and the Igbo, most of whom are Christians, in the South-East. Smaller groups have tended to cluster around these three groups, creating unstable and ethnically divisive politics.

Africa's largest country has had a troubled political history marked by military coups and failed civilian governments. The country has had military governments for 28 of its 44 years of independence. Nigeria is attempting to ensure that its return to civilian rule after 16 years of dictatorship under the Abacha regime will be a genuine process of democratic consolidation.

The 1999 Constitution addresses the two concerns of an excessively powerful centre and parochial concerns at the state levels, as well as the unhealthy dynamic of patronage, rent-seeking and competition between these levels. It has instituted several reforms, including:

- Gradually dissolving the three federal regimes inherited from the colonial era and replacing them with a decentralized system of 36 states and 775 local governments. The three regions were transformed into four in 1963. The 4 regions became 12 states in 1967, 19 in

1976, 21 in 1987, 30 in 1991 and 36 in 1999. The hope was that this would encourage more flexible ethnic loyalties and alliances. More immediately, this expanding federal structure has helped contain local ethnic disputes, diffusing the power of the three major ethnic groups and preventing the absolute domination of the more than 350 smaller minority groups.

- Devising electoral rules to produce governments that would enjoy broadly national and majority support. In the elections for the Second Republic of 1979–83, a presidential candidate with a plurality of the votes could be declared winner only after obtaining at least 25% of the votes in two-thirds of the states. The 1999 Constitution updated the threshold rule: to compete for the elections a party must secure at least 5% of the votes cast in at least 25 of the 36 states in local government elections. While the threshold rule relating to party formation was rescinded in 2003, the threshold rule for declaring a party the winner, and thus for forming a government, still holds, encouraging the formation of multi-ethnic parties. Many other issues of federal relations introduced by the 1999 Constitution continue to be hotly contested, including those on revenues, property rights, legal codes and states' prerogatives.

- Instituting affirmative action policies in education and the civil service. This has come to include rotation of the presidency among six geopolitical zones: north-west, north-east, north-central, south-west, south-east and south-central and appointment of at least one federal minister from each of the 36 states according to the zoning principle. These measures provide a functional framework for economic distribution that tries to avoid unitary and centralizing excesses and domination by the centre.

The return of democracy has reanimated regional, ethnic, religious and local identities and intensified communal mobilization. This has led to the social violence that has engulfed the country since the return to civilian rule, whereas previously such conflicts were coercively suppressed by the military regimes. Political stability in Nigeria is still threatened by massive structural socio-economic inequalities between the North and South, the high level of state dependence on federally collected oil revenues and the intense competition and corruption of public life linked to its distribution—and the unresolved question of rotating the presidency between the six ethno-political zones, which has incited violence and ethnic cleavages. The challenges are tremendous—and ongoing.

Source: Bangura 2004; Lewis 2003; Rotimi 2001.

---

freely determine their political status and freely pursue their economic, social and cultural development". The application of this principle to people within independent states and to indigenous people remains controversial. The constitutions of such countries as Mexico and the Philippines have taken some steps to recognize the rights of indigenous people to self-determination, but others avoid it.

One of the legal instruments indigenous people have used to mobilize around these issues is the International Labour Organization's Convention (169) Concerning Indigeonous and Tribal Peoples in Independent Countries, passed in 1989 and open for ratification since 1990.[16] As of 2003 it had only 17 signatories—Argentina, Bolivia, Brazil, Colombia, Costa Rica, Denmark, Dominica, Ecuador, Fiji, Guatemala, Honduras, Mexico, the Netherlands, Norway, Paraguay, Peru and Venezuela.[17] Chile's Congress has voted against several initiatives in this direction. The Organization of Africa Unity approved the African Charter on Human and People's Rights, but nowhere is the term "people" defined.

Another sign that these struggles for cultural recognition have entered the global debate is the recent meetings of the Permanent Forum on Indigenous Issues at the United Nations. Political developments seem to be concentrated in regions of the world that have explicitly recognized claims of indigenous people, who have mobilized to contest their exclusion. Some see such mobilizations as politically disruptive—as their violent and reactionary versions can be—but these movements also reflect greater awareness of cultural liberty. States can no longer afford to ignore or suppress these claims.

There have been some imaginative initiatives to grant autonomy and self-rule, especially when groups extend across national boundaries. An example is the Council for Cooperation on Sami issues set up jointly by Finland, Norway and Sweden.

POWER SHARING THROUGH CONSOLIATION: PROPORTIONALITY AND REPRESENTATIVE ELECTORAL ARRANGEMENTS

Consolidation applies the principle of proportionality in four key areas: through executive power sharing, proportional representation in electoral systems, provisions for cultural autonomy, and safeguards in the form of mutual vetoes. These instruments can help to prevent one segment of society from imposing its views on another. In their most effective form they can help to reflect the diverse cultural composition of a society in its state institutions. Consolidation arrangements are sometimes criticized as undemocratic because they are seen as an instrument of elite dominance, through the co-option of opposition or vulnerable groups.[18] But they need not involve a "grand coalition" of parties: they require only cross-community representation in the executive and legislature. The challenge is to ensure that neither self-rule (for minorities) nor shared rule (of the state as a whole) outweighs the other. These arrangements also have to be addressed through prudent and responsible politics.

This section focuses on two mechanisms of consolidations—executive power sharing and proportional representation—that prevent the dominance of a majority community.[19] From a constitutional point of view measures that privilege minorities in election procedures raise questions of equal treatment. But small and scattered minorities do not stand a chance of being represented in majoritarian democracies without assistance. Executive power sharing can protect their interests. Proportionality in such political and executive arrangements mirrors the diverse composition of society in its state institutions.

Belize, Guyana, Suriname, and Trinidad and Tobago have long used power-sharing mechanisms to address racial and ethnic divisions, with varying success.[20] The mechanisms involve elements of autonomy (self-government for each community) and integration (joint government of all the communities). Political power is shared in executives, in legislatures and (in principle) in judiciaries.[21]

Care has to be taken to ensure that a minority's potential for winning the appropriate number of seats is not sabotaged—as in Northern Ireland. During the era of "home rule" from 1920 to 1972 constituencies were repeatedly gerrymandered to the disadvantage of the Catholic nationalist parties and others and in favour of the

Another sign that these struggles for cultural recognition have entered the global debate is the recent meetings of the Permanent Forum on Indigenous Issues at the United Nations

Exclusion may be less direct and perhaps even unintended, as when the public calendar does not recognize a minority's religious holidays

dominant Ulster Unionist Party, which governed uninterrupted, often without taking the interests of the nationalist minority into account. This eventually provoked a long-lasting reaction of conflict and violence. The Good Friday Agreement of 1998 sought to avoid repeating this history. The agreement calls for key decisions at the Assembly of Northern Ireland to be decided on a "cross-community basis". This requires either parallel consent of both blocs independently or in a weighted majority of 60% of votes, with 40% of voting members of each bloc.[22] The idea is that no important decision can be taken without some support from both sides, providing a framework for negotiation.

In Belgium the Assembly and Senate are divided into language groups—one Dutch- and one French-speaking group, with the German-speaking group defined as a part of the French group. Certain key questions have to be decided by a majority in each group and by an overall majority of two-thirds of votes. In majoritarian democracy the majority rules; in consociational democracies power-sharing majorities from all groups rule.

Proportional representation, another instrument of consociation, allows each significant community to be represented politically in rough accord with its share of the population, particularly when parties are ethnically based. Even when they are not, proportional representation provides greater incentives for political parties to seek votes from dispersed groups who do not form majorities in any particular geographical constituency—and this also boosts minority representation. Proportional representation does not guarantee successful accommodation, and a winner-takes-all system can sometimes be compatible with multinational and multilingual federations, as Canada and India have demonstrated. But both countries also use other measures to ensure political representation for various groups, and winner-takes-all systems can also lead to tyrannies of the majority.

None of the many electoral rules of proportional representation provide perfect proportionality. But they can address the problem of winner-takes-all systems and enable greater representation of minorities and other groups, as shown in the impact of recent reforms in New Zealand (box 3.3).[23] Proportional representation is most effective in stable democracies and can remedy some of the major deficiencies of majoritarian electoral systems by strengthening the electoral voice of minorities. Proportional representation is not the sole solution in all circumstances. Innovations in winner-takes-all systems can also bolster the voice of minorities, though such arrangements are considerably more difficult to engineer.

Other approaches to ensuring representation of cultural minorities include reserving seats for certain groups, as New Zealand does for the Maoris,[24] India for scheduled tribes and castes and Croatia for Hungarians, Italians, Germans and others. Reserved seats and quotas are sometimes criticized because they "fix" peoples' identities and preferences in the electoral mechanism. And negotiating quotas and reservations can lead to conflict and grievances. In Lebanon Muslim grievances over a quota of 6:5 seats in the parliament between Christians and Muslims, fixed on the basis of the 1932 census, became an important source of tension and led to civil war when the demographic weight of the two communities changed.[25] These approaches can be more problematic than proportional electoral systems, which leave people free to choose their identifications.

POLICIES ON RELIGION AND RELIGIOUS PRACTICE

As chapter 2 shows, many religious minorities around the world suffer various forms of exclusion. In some cases this is due to explicit discrimination against a religious minority—a problem particularly common in non-secular countries where the state has the task of upholding and promoting an established religion. But in other cases the exclusion may be less direct and perhaps even unintended, as when the public calendar does not recognize a minority's religious holidays, or the dress codes in public institutions conflict with a minority's religious dress, or state rules on marriage and inheritance differ from those of a minority religion, or zoning regulations conflict with a minority's burial practices. These sorts of conflicts can arise even in secular states. Given the profound importance of religion to people's identities, it is not surprising that

BOX 3.3

Proportional representation or winner takes all? New Zealand makes a switch

Majoritarian democracies have a dismal record on political participation by minorities, under-representing them and marginalizing their electoral voice. How can multicultural societies be more inclusive and ensure adequate participation of minorities and other marginalized cultural groups? One way is through proportional representation rather than winner-takes-all systems. In winner-takes-all (also called first-past-the-post) systems, the political party with the most votes gets a majority of the legislative seats. In the United Kingdom, for example, a party can (and often does) win less than 50% of the vote but gets a much bigger share of seats in the House of Commons. In the 2001 election the Labour party won 41% of the vote and walked away with 61% of the seats. In the same election Liberal Democrats received 19.4% of the vote but only 7.5% of the seats. In proportional representation systems legislatures are elected from multiseat districts in proportion to the number of votes received: 20% of the popular vote wins 20% of the seats.

Because winner-takes-all systems exclude those who do not support the views of the party in power, they do not lend themselves to culturally inclusive environments. But in proportional representation systems parties that get a significant number of votes are likely to get a share of power. As a rule, then, proportional representation voting systems provide a more accurate reflection of public opinion and are likely to foster the inclusion of minorities (as long as minorities organize themselves in political form).

Several multicultural states rely on proportional representation systems, including Angola, Bosnia and Herzegovina, Guyana and Latvia. In Western Europe 21 of 28 countries use some form of proportional representation.

Critics of proportional representation argue that the incorporation of fragmented groups could lead to unstable, inefficient governments, with shifting coalitions; Italy is often cited. But such problems are neither endemic nor insurmountable. Indeed, several mechanisms can prevent stalemates and deadlocks. For example, instituting minimum vote requirements, as in Germany, or changing the number of districts to reflect the geographic dispersion of public opinion can alleviate these problems while maintaining inclusive legislative systems. And stalemate and deadlock may be preferable to a minority imposing its will on the majority—as often happens with governments elected under winner-takes-all systems.

Others resist these policies on grounds that such changes would entail tremendous upheavals and political instability—as feared by the political elite in many Latin American countries where indigenous populations are increasingly demanding greater political voice and representation. However, this argument cannot be used to defend policies that result in the continued exclusion of certain groups and sections. Transitions to prudent politics that encourage greater participation and enable more effective representation are possible, as the experiences of other democratic countries show.

Largely to address the underrepresentation of the indigenous Maori population, New Zealand in 1993 voted to undertake a major electoral reform, from winner takes all to proportional representation. Colonial legislation dating to 1867 assigned 4 of the 99 seats in government to the Maori, far short of their 15% share in the population. Voters chose a mixed-member proportional system, a hybrid in which half the legislative seats come from single-seat, winner-takes-all districts and half are allocated according to the percentage of votes won by each party.

New Zealand also incorporated a "dual constituency" system in which individuals of Maori descent were given the option of voting either for an individual from the Maori roll or for an individual on the general electoral roll. Maori seats are allocated based on the Maori census and by the proportion of Maori individuals who choose to register on the Maori roll.

New Zealand's first election under proportional representation (in 1996) was difficult. A majority coalition did not form for nine months, and public opinion swayed back in favour of the winner-takes-all system. But the 1999 and 2002 elections ran smoothly, restoring public support for proportional representation. Maori political representation increased from around 3% in 1993 to almost 16% in 2002. Despite problems along the way it is clear that electoral transition went a long way towards improving the representation of the Maori population in New Zealand.

Source: O'Leary 2004; Boothroyd 2004; Nagel 2004.

---

religious minorities often mobilize to contest these exclusions. If not managed properly, these mobilizations can become violent. So it is vital for states to learn how to manage these claims.

The state is responsible for ensuring policies and mechanisms that protect individual choice. This is best achieved when public institutions do not discriminate between believers and non-believers, not just among followers of different religions. Secular principles have been proven to work best towards these goals, but no one single model of secularism is demonstrably better than others in all circumstances. Various links between state and religious authorities have evolved over time. Similarly, states that profess to be secular do so differently both in principle and in practice. And these differences have implications

for the state's ability to protect individual choice and religious freedoms (box 3.4).

Sometimes problems arise because of too many formal links between regions and the state or too much influence by religious authorities in matters of state. This can happen when, say, a small clerical elite controls the institutions of the state in accord with what it considers divinely commissioned laws, as in Afghanistan under the Taliban. These politically dominant religious elites are unlikely to tolerate internal differences, let alone dissent, and unlikely to extend freedoms even to their own members outside the small ruling elite, much less to members of other religious groups. Such states do not accommodate other religious groups or dissenters or treat them equally.

The many forms of secular and non-secular states and their effects on religious freedom

States have treated religion in different ways.

Non-secular states

A non-secular state extends official recognition to specific religions and can assume different forms depending on its formal and substantive links with religious authority.

- A state governed by divine law—that is, a theocracy, such as the Islamic Republic of Iran run by ayatollahs or Afghanistan under the Taliban.
- A state where one religion benefits from a formal alliance with the government—that is, having an "established" religion. Examples include Islam in Bangladesh, Libya and Malaysia; Hinduism in Nepal; Catholicism in Argentina, Bolivia and Costa Rica; and Buddhism in Bhutan, Burma and Thailand.
- A state that has an established church or religion, but that nonetheless respects more than one religion, that recognizes and perhaps attempts to nurture all religions without any preference of one over the other. Such states may levy a religious tax on all citizens and yet grant them the freedom to remit the tax money to religious organizations of their choice. They may financially assist schools run by religious institutions but in a non-discriminatory way. Examples of such states include Sweden and the United Kingdom. Both are virtually secular and have established religions only in name. Other examples of this pattern of non-secular states are Denmark, Iceland and Norway.

Anti-religious, secular states

The state excludes religion from its own affairs without excluding itself from the affairs of religion. In such a state the right to religious freedom is very limited, and often the state intervenes to restrict religious freedoms and practice. Communist regimes in China and former communist regimes in the Soviet Union and Eastern Europe are examples.

Neutral or disengaged states

There are two ways of expressing this kind of neutrality. The state may profess a policy of "mutual exclusion", or the "strict separation of religion and state". This means that not only does the state prevent religious authorities from intervening in the affairs of state, but the state also avoids interfering in the internal affairs of religious groups. One consequence of this mutual exclusion is that the state may be unable or unwilling to interfere in practices designated as "religious" even when they threaten individual rights and democratic values. Or the state may have a policy of neutrality towards all religions. The clearest examples are the state of Virginia (after the disestablishment of the Anglican Church in 1786), the United States (particularly after the First Amendment to its Constitution in 1791) and France, especially after the Separation Law of 1905.

Secular states asserting equal respect and principled distance

The state is secular, in the sense that it does not have an established church and does not promote one religion over others, but rather accords equal respect to all religions (and to non-believers).

However, it is willing to defend universal principles of human rights and equal citizenship and is able to intervene in the internal affairs of religious groups in what can be called "principled distance". This engagement may take the form of even-handed support for religions (such as public funding of religious schools or state recognition of religious personal law) or even of intervention to monitor and reform religious practices that contradict human rights (such as regulating religious schools or reforming personal laws to ensure gender equality). With principled distance, whether the state intervenes or refrains from interfering depends on what measures really strengthen religious liberty and equality of citizenship. The state may not relate to every religion in exactly the same way or intervene to the same degree or in the same manner. But it ensures that the relations between religious and political institutions are guided by consistent, non-sectarian principles of liberty and human rights.

An example is the secular design in the Indian Constitution. While the growth of communal violence makes observers skeptical of the secular credentials of Indian politicians these days, the Constitution established India as a secular state. It was this policy of secularism with principled distance that enabled the Indian state in the early years after independence to recognize the customary laws, codes and practices of minority religious communities and enable their cultural integration. It enabled positive interventions upholding principles of equality and liberty by reforming a range of customary practices, such as prohibiting erstwhile "untouchables" from entering temples.

Source: Bhargava 2004.

In other instances the state may profess neutrality and purportedly exclude itself from matters of religion and exclude religion from matters of state—a policy of "mutual exclusion". But in reality this stance may become distorted through policies that are blind to actual violations of religious freedoms or through ad hoc interventions motivated by political expedience.

Whatever the historical links with religion, states have a responsibility to protect rights and secure freedoms for all their members and not discriminate (for or against) on grounds of religion. It is difficult to propose an optimal design for the relations between state institutions and religious authority. But non-discriminatory states should protect three dimensions of religious freedom and individual choice:

- Every individual or sect within a religious group should have the right to criticize, revise or challenge the dominance of a particular interpretation of core beliefs. All religions have numerous interpretations and practices—they are multivocal—and no single interpretation should be sponsored by the state. Clergy or other religious hierarchies should have the same status as other citizens and should not claim greater political or societal privilege.
- States must give space to all religions for interfaith discussion and, within limits, for

critiques. People of one religion must be allowed to be responsibly critical of the practices and beliefs of other religions.

- Individuals must be free not only to criticize the religion into which they are born, but to reject it for another or to remain without one.

Some challenges to secularism arise from a country's historical links with religion or from the legacy of colonialism. The British divide-and-rule policies in South Asia, which attempted to categorize religious and cultural identities, fixing their relative positions in the polity and in society, have been a source of continuing political conflict even after the territorial partitions in the region.[26] These historically entrenched divisions remain as serious barriers to secular policies in a region that has witnessed so much communal trauma. The Spanish colonial rulers, with their historical links with the Catholic Church, left a legacy of similar links between state and church in their former colonies, especially in Latin America, with implications for concerns of gender equality, among others.

Sometimes this historical baggage appears in contemporary dilemmas—of whether to recognize different religious laws in a democratic environment where all citizens have equality before the law. As the ongoing discussions on the uniform civil code in India demonstrates, the arguments for women's rights and principles of equality get entangled with concerns for minority rights and cultural recognition (box 3.5). Building consensus on these issues to advance universal principles of human rights, gender equality and human development has to be the guiding principle for resolving them.[27]

POLICIES ON CUSTOMARY LAW AND LEGAL PLURALISM

Certain religious and ethnic minorities and indigenous groups feel alienated from the larger legal system, for a number of reasons. In some countries judges and other court officials have historically been prejudiced against them, or ignorant of their conditions, resulting in the unfair and biased application of the law. In

The arguments for women's rights and principles of equality get entangled with concerns for minority rights and cultural recognition

---

BOX 3.5

Hindu and Muslim personal law: the ongoing debate over a uniform civil code

Legal pluralism and legal universalism are hotly debated in India today. Should a single legal system apply to members of all communities? The differences highlight the apparent contradiction of the constitutional recognition of Hindu and Muslim personal laws and the parallel constitutional commitment to a uniform civil code. The debate is thus embedded in larger concerns about India as a multicultural secular state.

Personal laws, specific to different religious communities, govern marriage, divorce, guardianship, adoption, inheritance and succession. They vary widely between and even within the same community. Court cases involving personal law also raise their own more particular issues, sometimes pitting minority religious groups' rights against women's rights.

The debate over personal laws often comes down to the following:

- *Gender equality*—how patriarchal customs and laws, be they Hindu or Muslim, treat men and women differently in terms of their legal entitlements.
- *Cultural freedoms and minority rights*— whether the state should reserve the right to

intervene in matters of religious practice to assert liberty and equality while protecting the right of groups to practice their religion.

It is important to understand the debate in historical context. India's leadership at independence was committed to a secular India, not just a state for its Hindu majority. This was politically imperative given the fears of the Muslim minority immediately after the brutal partition of the subcontinent. The Indian Constitution recognized and accommodated its colonially inherited system of legal pluralism as its multicultural reality. The ultimate goal of a unified civil code was included in the Constitution, and the Special Marriages Act of 1954 offered couples a non-religious alternative to personal laws.

A brief scan of legal developments over the 1980s and 1990s highlights how the argument for uniformity has overlooked concerns for equality—and how the secular agenda has been depicted as being antithetical to the principle of special recognition of the cultural rights of minorities. The ongoing debate is important because of the contemporary political context. Supporters of the code assert principles of

equality before the law, but fail to appreciate the difficult position of minorities. This is particularly relevant in the light of growing communal tensions. The Muslim minority often views the code as an underhand abrogation of their cultural freedom.

Personal laws of all communities have been criticized for disadvantaging women, and there are strong arguments for reforming almost all traditional (and usually patriarchal) laws and customs in the country, bringing Hindu and Muslim personal or customary laws in line with gender equality and universal human rights. But implementing equality—an objective that is central to concerns of human development—is not the same as implementing uniformity.

What is needed is internal reform of all customary laws, upholding gender equality rather than imposing identical gender-biased, prejudicial laws across all communities. Crucial in this is a genuine effort to establish consensus on the code. Legislation imposing uniformity will only widen the majority-minority divide—detrimental both for communal harmony and for gender equality.

Source: Engineer 2003; Mody 2003; Rudolph 2001.

many countries indigenous people are almost entirely unrepresented in the judiciary. This reality of bias and exclusion is exacerbated by the inaccessibility of the legal system to these groups for additional reasons, including geographical distance, financial cost and language or other cultural barriers.

Plural legal systems can counter this exclusion. But some critics argue that plural legal systems can legitimize traditional practices that are inconsistent with expansion of freedoms. Many traditional practices reject the equality of women, for example, in property rights, inheritance, family law and other realms.[28] But legal pluralism does not require the wholesale adoption of all practices claimed to be "traditional". The accommodation of customary law cannot be seen as an entitlement to maintain practices that violate human rights, no matter how "traditional" or "authentic" they may claim to be.[29]

From a human development perspective all legal systems—whether unitary or plural—must conform to international standards of human rights, including gender equality. Other critics therefore argue that if the legal system of the larger society respects human rights norms, and if indigenous people accept these norms, there is no need to maintain legal pluralism. But even where there is a consensus on human rights norms, there may still be a valuable role for legal pluralism.

Plural legal systems exist in almost all societies, evolving as local traditions were historically accommodated along with other formal systems of jurisprudence.[30] Customary practices, which acquired the force of law over time, coexisted alongside introduced systems of jurisprudence. Such legal pluralism often had roots in the colonial logic of protection of minority rights, which allowed certain customary systems to continue while imposing the colonizer's own laws.

COLONIAL CONSTRUCTIONS, YET CONTEMPORARY REALITIES

The colonial imprint can be marked. Indeed, it often is difficult to determine which legal processes are genuinely traditional and which can be seen as a hybrid by-product of colonial manipulation and control. An added complication in separating authentic from imposed practices is that colonial rule and its "civilizing mission" unilaterally claimed responsibility for introducing modern values, beliefs and institutions to the colonies.[31]

In Africa European colonialists introduced their own metropolitan law and system of courts. But they retained much customary law and many elements of the African judicial process that they deemed consistent with their sense of justice and morality. Western-type courts were presided over by expatriate magistrates and judges whose jurisdiction extended over all persons, African and non-African, in criminal and civil matters. Often referred to as "general courts", they applied European law and local statutes based on European practices. A second group of "native-authority courts" or "African courts" or "people's courts" comprised either traditional chiefs or local elders. These courts had jurisdiction over only Africans and for the most part applied the prevailing customary law. Throughout Malawi's colonial history, for example, jurisdiction over Africans was left to the traditional courts for cases involving customary law and for simple criminal cases.[32]

Towards the end of the colonial period, officials began to integrate the dual courts system, with the general courts supervising the workings of the customary courts. The Anglophone colonies retained much of the dual legal structure created during colonial rule while attempting to reform and adapt customary law to notions of English law. Francophone and Lusophone colonies tried to absorb customary law into the general law. Ethiopia and Tunisia abolished some aspects of customary law. But in no African country, either during or after the colonial era, has customary law been totally disregarded or proscribed.

CUSTOMARY LAW CAN PROMOTE ACCESS TO JUSTICE SYSTEMS

Accommodating customary law can help protect the rights of indigenous people and ensure a fairer application of the rule of law. Efforts to accord public recognition to customary law can help create a sense of inclusion

All legal systems must conform to international standards of human rights, including gender equality

in the wider society. Often the most pragmatic case for customary law, especially in parts of failed states, is that the choice is between customary law and no law. Recognizing the ability of indigenous people to adopt and administer their own laws is also a repudiation of historic prejudice—and can be an important part of self-government for indigenous people.[33]

Countries from Australia to Canada to Guatemala to South Africa have recognized legal pluralism. In Australia there has been a renewed focus on recognizing Aboriginal and Torres Strait Islander customary law, which has opened the way to indigenous community mechanisms of justice, aboriginal courts, greater regional autonomy and indigenous governance. In Canada most local criminal matters are dealt with by the indigenous community so that the accused can be judged by jurors of peers who share cultural norms. In Guataemala the 1996 peace accords acknowledged the need to recognize Mayan law as an important part of genuine reform (box 3.6).

In post-apartheid South Africa a groundswell of innovation is instilling new authority, resources and dignity into customary law. The aim is to rebuild trust in the criminal justice system and respect for the rule of law and to recognize customary laws. The challenge lies in integrating common and customary law in line with the new constitution, enshrining such principles as gender equality. This harmonization process marks a major step in South Africa's enormous task of legal reform. The first step was repealing apartheid laws. Next was reconstituting the Law Commission, dominated by conservative judges of the old regime. Now South Africa must shape new laws to govern a new social order.

Customary law is often the only form of justice known to many South Africans. About half the population lives in the countryside, where traditional courts administer customary law in more than 80% of villages.[34] These courts, also found in some urban townships, deal with petty theft, property disagreements and domestic affairs—from marriage to divorce to inheritance. Justice is swift and cheap as the courts are run with minimal formalities in venues close to the disputants' homes and charge less than

a dollar for a hearing. The judges use everyday language, and the rules of evidence allow the community to interject and question testimony.

The system has its critics—particularly women, who are barred from serving as judges and are often discriminated against as litigants. Even so, women's groups, under the umbrella of the Rural Women's Movement, are on the vanguard of efforts to recognize customary law and adapt it to post-apartheid society. They are leading discussions about how to elevate customary law and make it fairer to women.

Still a concern, therefore, is how customary law compromises or ensures human rights standards.[35] Any legal system—conventional or customary—is open to criticism over its formulation. A legal tradition is a set of deeply rooted, historically conditioned attitudes about the nature of law, about the role of law in society, about the proper organization and operation of a legal system and about the way law should be made, applied, studied, perfected and taught.

Accommodating customary law can help protect the rights of indigenous people and ensure a fairer application of the rule of law

BOX 3.6

Access to justice and cultural recognition in Guatemala

For the more than 500 years since the arrival of the Spanish conquistadors Guatemala's indigenous people have suffered violent subordination and exclusion. The armed internal conflict that lasted from 1960 until the signing of the peace accords in 1996 was particularly devastating. Indigenous people, constituting more than half the population, endured massacres and gross violations of human rights. The military dictatorship of 1970–85 undermined the independence of local community authorities.

Little surprise, then, that rural communities lost faith in the judicial system and the rule of law. Public lynchings became the alternative to the formal justice system, notorious for its inability to sentence the perpetrators of crimes and its tendency to release criminals through a corrupt bail tradition. The political establishment cynically misrepresents the lynchings as the traditional practices of indigenous people.

The 1996 accords acknowledged the need for genuine reform with commitments to acknowledge traditional Mayan law and authority. The Accord on Indigenous Identity and Rights, for example, states that "the lack of knowledge by the national legislative

body of the customary norms that regulate indigenous community life as well as the lack of access that the indigenous population has to the resources of the national justice system, have caused negation of rights, discrimination and marginalization".

The government and the opposition have agreed to:

- Recognize the management of internal issues of the indigenous communities according to their own judicial norms.
- Include cultural considerations in the practice of law.
- Develop a permanent programme for judges and members of the Public Ministry on the culture and identity of indigenous people.
- Ensure free judicial advisory services for people with limited resources.
- Offer free services for interpretation of judicial proceedings into indigenous languages.

These developments are first steps in acknowledging the distinct cultures of indigenous people in Guatemala. The challenge now is to develop the customary systems in a way consistent with human rights and gender equality.

Source: Buvollen 2002.

POLICIES ON THE USE OF MULTIPLE LANGUAGES

By choosing one or a few languages over others, a state often signals the dominance of those for whom the official language is their mother tongue. This choice can limit the freedom of many non-dominant groups—feeding intergroup tensions (see chapter 2). It becomes a way of excluding people from politics, education, access to justice and many other aspects of civic life. It can entrench socio-economic inequalities between groups. It can become a divisive political issue, as in Sri Lanka where, in place of English, Sinhala (spoken by the majority) was made the only official language in 1956 despite the opposition of the Tamil minority, who wanted both Sinhala and Tamil recognized.

While it is possible and even desirable for a state to remain "neutral" on ethnicity and religion, this is impractical for language. The citizenry needs a common language to promote mutual understanding and effective communication. And no state can afford to provide services and official documents in every language spoken on its territory. The difficulty, however, is that most states, especially in the developing world and Eastern Europe, are multilingual—and they are the focus of much of the discussion here. Once again, multicultural policies are needed.

In multilingual societies plural language policies provide recognition to distinct linguistic groups. Plural language policies safeguard the parallel use of two or more languages by saying, in essence, "Let us each retain our own language in certain spheres, such as schools and universities, but let us also have a common language for joint activities, especially in civic life." Language conflicts can be managed by providing some spheres in which minority languages are used freely and by giving incentives to learn other languages, especially a national or official language. This can be promoted by an appropriate social reward structure, such as by making facility in a national language a criterion for professional qualification and promotion.

There is no universal "right to language".[36] But there are human rights with an implicit linguistic content that multilingual states must acknowledge in order to comply with their international obligations under such instruments as the International Covenant on Civil and Political Rights. Especially important are the rights to freedom of expression and equality. Freedom of expression and the use of a language are inseparable. This is the most obvious example of the importance of language in matters of law. For example, until 1994 members of the Kurd minority in Turkey were prohibited by law from using their language in public. Reform of this law was an important element in the government's response to the demands of the Kurdish minority. In 2002 the Turkish Parliament passed legislation allowing private institutions to teach the language of the sizeable Kurdish minority, and the first Kurdish language teaching centre opened in March 2004 in Batman, in the southeast.

Experience around the world shows that plural language policies can expand opportunities for people in many ways, if there is a deliberate effort to teach all citizens some of the country's major languages (box 3.7). Very often what multilingual countries need is a three-language formula (as UNESCO recommends) that gives public recognition to the use of three languages:

- One international language—in former colonial countries this is often the official language of administration. In this era of globalization all countries need to be proficient in an international language to participate in the global economy and networks.
- One lingua franca—a local link language facilitates communication between different linguistic groups such as Swahili in East African countries, where many other languages are also spoken.
- Mother tongue—people want and need to be able to use their mother tongue when it is neither the lingua franca nor the international language.

Countries need to recognize all three as official languages or at least recognize their use and relevance in different circumstances, such as in courts or schools. There are many versions of such three-language formulas, depending on the country.

The main questions that states face on language policy relate to the language of instruction in schools and the language used in government institutions.

Multilingual education in Papua New Guinea

Nestled between the South Pacific Ocean and the Coral Sea, Papua New Guinea is the most linguistically and culturally diverse nation in the world, accounting for approximately a sixth of the world's 6,000 languages. A century of colonial occupation created a lingua franca, a neo-Melanesian pidgin, *tok pisin,* derived from English, German, Spanish, Malay and Papua New Guinea's own languages and spoken by half of the population of 5 million.

To meet the needs of indigenous people for relevant basic education, the Department of Education implemented a major education reform in 1993, introducing mother tongue instruction in the first three years of schooling. After that, the medium of instruction is English. By 2001, 369 indigenous languages had been introduced in 3,600 elementary schools. A third of children now start elementary school in their mother tongue.

No statistical study has been done, but there is abundant anecdotal evidence that children become literate and learn English faster and more easily when they start their schooling in their mother tongue. Access is improving, and the dropout rate, particularly of girls, has come down. More than 70% of grade 6 students go on to grade 7, compared with less than 40% in 1992. Lower-secondary enrolments have doubled since 1992, and upper-secondary numbers have quadrupled. Teachers report that children appear more self-confident and inquisitive.

The education reform came after 20 years of widespread public consultation, and implementation was gradual. Non-governmental organizations got grants to develop a writing system for some languages that had never been written before. Communities wanting to convert

their schools to the local language had to agree to build new facilities, assist in the life of the school or share their culture with the children. The learning material is deliberately simple: copies of a prototype textbook are printed with blank lines to be filled in with the local language. Costs were kept in check by using black and white text and soft covers. Communities choose local people with at least a grade 10 education as teachers. They are paid less than nationally recruited certified teachers, but many are pleased to be doing worthwhile work for a steady income.

Papua New Guinea sought and received large donor support from Australia to introduce the reform, but it is expected that the system will be cost-efficient and sustainable over the longer term. Studies are under way to assess its results.

Source: Klaus 2003; SIL International 2004a; CRIP 2004.

LANGUAGE POLICY IN SCHOOLS

Low educational attainment continues to be a major source of exclusion for immigrants, ethnic groups and indigenous people. In such cases offering bilingual education not only recognizes their cultural traditions but it can also enhance learning and reduce educational disparities—widening people's choices (see box 3.7).

Children learn best when they are taught in their mother tongue, particularly in the earliest years. Experience in many countries shows that bilingual education, which combines instruction in the mother tongue with teaching in the dominant national language, can open educational and other opportunities. In the Philippines students proficient in the two languages of the bilingual education policy (Tagalog and English) outperformed students who did not speak Tagalog at home. In Canada students from the English-speaking majority in bilingual immersion programmes outperform peers in traditional programmes of learning in the second language (French). In the United States Navajo students instructed throughout their primary school years in their first language (Navajo) as well as their second language (English) outperformed their Navajo-speaking peers educated only in English.[37]

In Latin America bilingualism is an established strategy for reducing the educational exclusion of indigenous children, who have the worst education indicators. Studies in Bolivia, Brazil, Guatemala, Mexico, Paraguay and Peru show that providing instruction to minority groups in their own language and using teachers from the same group is highly effective. Bilingual education leads to much less repetition, lower drop-out rates and higher educational attainment among indigenous children. In Guatemala the Q'eqchi' communities, which had fewer bilingual education opportunities than three other indigenous groups surveyed, had much higher drop-out and repetition rates.[38]

Studies in Africa find the same results, with bilingual schools more effective than conventional monolingual schools, as in Burkina Faso (table 3.1). Studies of bilingual education in Mali, Niger, Nigeria and Zambia find that it ensures continuity among families, communities and schools, strengthening interactions among them. It stimulates the production of school and cultural materials in the second language, broadening the body of knowledge and facilitating learners' integration into social and cultural life. And it encourages a blending of cultures, since it enhances the standing of both languages and the cultures they convey. Monolingual schools,

TABLE 3.1
Indicators of internal output and costs of conventional and bilingual schools in Burkina Faso

Indicator	Bilingual school	Conventional monolingual school
Chance of success in obtaining a primary education certificate	72%	14%
Average duration to gain a diploma	6 pupil years	37 pupil years
Internal output rate (allowing for repetition and drop-out)	68%	16%
Annual recurrent costs (teachers, supplies, maintenance) per student (total recurrent costs divided by number of students)	77,447 CFA francs	104,962 CFA francs

Source: Ndoye 2003.

whether in a Western or an African language, perform much less well.[39]

India, too, has extensive experience with multilingual education. For four decades it has had a three-language formula in which each child is taught in the official language of the state (Bengali in West Bengal, for example), with the two official national languages (English and Hindi) as second and third languages. Indian state boundaries have been drawn along linguistic lines since 1956, so each state has one dominant state language, each with its own script, rich vocabulary and literature going back hundreds, if not thousands, of years.

Often, bilingual education is stigmatized as being lower in quality, especially in the country's economic and political activities. Bilingual education can then be thought to restrict opportunities. Surveys among Hispanics in the American Southeast show that most prefer English-only classes and view their children's "restricted" early access to English as a deprivation. Bilingualism should be introduced only where there is demand for it. However, evidence suggests that there is no trade-off between the two goals of bilingual education and high quality education, especially in teaching the dominant language.

Nor is cost a real issue. An examination of the costs and benefits of bilingual education for indigenous people in Guatemala estimated that there would be a $5 million cost savings thanks to reduced repetitions, savings equal to the cost of providing primary education to about 100,000 students a year.[40]

It is true that the unit costs of producing local language materials are often higher than those of producing majority language materials because of the smaller quantities. But sharing by countries with the same local language can help hold unit costs down. Costs include those for modernizing and standardizing the orthography of the local language and for developing materials, training teachers in their use and distributing them. These financial costs have to be weighed against the social and political costs of inequality and unfairness. And since local language materials are produced in small quantities, they have little effect on the average unit cost of producing materials in all languages. In Senegal the production of materials in Wolof and other local languages barely pushes up the average unit cost of production of materials in all languages since the number of French books produced is much higher than the number of Wolof or Pulaar language books.

Bilingual education is a long-term investment, but nowhere do the costs appear prohibitive. In Guatemala bilingual education accounted for 0.13% of the primary education recurrent budget, increasing the unit cost of primary education by 9% annually (over the traditional Spanish-only instruction system).[41] In India producing materials in local languages adds 5–10% to total recurrent cost.[42] But as noted earlier, the gains can be massive, because of fewer dropouts and repetitions.

Most countries in Sub-Saharan Africa have local language education in schools in the first three grades, but after that almost all countries use French, English or Portuguese. These countries may find introducing local language education particularly difficult because of the many languages spoken. But most languages are related, and there are only 15 core language groups for the 45 Sub-Saharan countries (box 3.8). Developing local language education would require greater investment and regional cooperation to standardize and develop these languages. Standardization would require translating texts into these languages and introducing the texts to education at higher grades. These costs could be met through some additional donor support.

Standardization of texts and translation into the 15 core languages shared by communities spread across several national boundaries would help to keep costs down through economies of scale. Cooperation among countries in the region would be required to make this work. In the medium run such standardization would help to bolster the role of these 15 core languages as lingua franca and as the languages of the education and state administrative (legislative and judicial) systems.

Bilingual schooling can run up against unfavourable perceptions, problems of transition from the first language to the second and poor follow-up, evaluation and support systems. But most of these problems are linked to poor planning and a failure to make adjustments in curricula, teaching, training and promotion of the use of the language in official and public spheres.[43] Once these conditions are met, bilingual strategies improve learning, contribute to a multicultural identity and have a transforming effect on society.

Since knowledge of Western languages is often a means of upward mobility, the goal is not to remove Western languages, which would narrow choices and access to international knowledge. The goal is to give local languages equal or superior status. This reduces the heavy burden of repetitions and drop-outs and thus builds human skills.

LANGUAGE POLICY IN GOVERNMENT INSTITUTIONS

In multilingual societies a multiple language policy is the only way to ensure full democratic participation. Otherwise, much of a country's population can be excluded by an inability to speak the official language of the state. The Malawi Parliament uses English exclusively, and the Constitution (1994) requires all candidates standing for Parliament "to speak and to read the English language well enough to take an active part in the proceedings of Parliament" (see chapter 5).[44] The record of parliamentary proceedings is also published in English. The only way that people who do not know English are informed about parliamentary proceedings is through the national radio, which provides highly abridged versions in Chichewa.

The exclusive use of English creates a barrier between the political elite and the masses and reduces the pool of possible legislators. It can particularly disadvantage women, who are less likely to be literate or fluent in English. Tanzania has extended political participation in the legislature to the majority through the deliberate use of its national lingua franca, Kiswahili.

Language policies for the judiciary should not deny justice. The use of English as the primary language of legal discourse is common in Anglophone Africa, where judicial systems are based on the British legal system. This often alienates the people from the law since most of them have little or no facility in English.

South Africa has attempted to widen choices for non-English and non-Afrikaans speakers by calling for 11 constitutionally recognized official languages (since 1994)—9 indigenous, plus English and Afrikaans. Despite an ambitious court interpreter programme that puts most other countries to shame, there is still a bias towards English. One study of the courts in Qwaqwa in the Free State, a mainly Sesotho-speaking area, found that even when the magistrate, the prosecutor and the defendant were all Africans who spoke Southern Sotho as their mother tongue, the cases were conducted "in mediocre English with the assistance of a court interpreter from and into Sesotho for the benefit of the defendant".[45]

In multilingual societies a multiple language policy is the only way to ensure full democratic participation

---

BOX 3.8

How many languages are there in Africa?
85% of Africans speak 15 core languages

The profusion of languages in Africa gives the impression of unending fragmentation. Closer examination reveals convergences and structural similarities for superficially distinct cultures, clans and languages. Colonial administrators and missionaries, sometimes for administrative expediency and sometimes for proselytizing reasons (biblical translations, in particular), elevated small dialects to the status of languages and narrow local groups to the status of tribes. Just as colonial-era ethnologists would eagerly "discover" tribes that were often more appropriately parts of much larger groups, so languages in Africa have much greater affinity to each other than is commonly believed.

Most of what are counted as distinct languages in Africa are actually dialects of core languages. As first, second or third language speakers (most Africans are multilingual), more than 75% of Africans speak 12 core languages: Nguni, Soth-Tswana, Swahili, Amharic, Fulful, Mandenkan, Igbo, Hausa, Yoruba, Luo, Eastern Inter-lacustrine and Western Interlacustrine (Kitara). Some 85% of the African population of the continent speak 15 core languages (the three additional languages are Somali-Samburu-Rendille, Oromo-Borana and Gur). Though lexically different, these languages are similar morphologically, syntactically and phonologically.

If linguists across national boundaries in Sub-Saharan Africa were to work together to standardize vocabularies, it would be possible to use these languages to teach not just in the first three grades of primary school, but eventually in higher grades.

Source: Prah 2004.

Recognition of linguistic diversity in Afghanistan's Constitution

On 4 January 2004 Afghanistan's new Constitution was adopted by a Loya Jirga (or grand assembly) of 502 representatives from all parts of Afghanistan. While the adoption itself is a significant milestone achieved over the past two years, certain aspects of the new Constitution are particularly noteworthy. For example, in recognizing the linguistic diversity in Afghanistan, the Constitution takes a step that is unprecedented in the history not only of Afghanistan, but of the region as a whole.

Afghanistan has two major official languages, Pashto and Dari, which we have proudly spoken for centuries. The Constitution provides for the equal application of these two languages as the official medium of communication in all state organizations. Many state institutions will need to work to implement this, but some, including my own Office, do this already. It is gratifying to me as an Afghan, and as President, to be able to switch between Dari and Pashto when speaking publicly, as the occasion requires.

In addition to the two major official languages the delegates to the Loya Jirga agreed to give official status to all minority languages in the areas where these languages are spoken.

This is an important step that has precedence, I think, only in societies that are strong and solid. It is a powerful indication that, even though we are a society that has just emerged from war and disorder, we have the courage and broadmindedness to be inclusive and to recognize diversity. It makes us proud that today our Baluch, Nuristani, Pamiri, Pashai, Turkmen and Uzbek fellow Afghans are enjoying the right to use their own languages and to have them recognized as official. I am confident that this step will make Afghanistan a stronger nation, prouder than before, and an exemplary nation in the region.

Having taken the first step, Afghanistan now needs to work to make the words of the Constitution a reality. While we are confident about the feasibility of making regional languages official in their respective regions, it is indeed not a small task to put the infrastructure in place for this purpose. To teach people to read and write in their mother tongue requires incorporating the language into the school curriculum. This will require changes in our mainstream education system. We will need to train more teachers and to print more books.

But above all, we need to proceed carefully to ensure that making regional languages official contributes to national integration, rather than reinforcing the isolation of communities. In the 21st century, people around the world are increasingly searching for commonalities, including commonality in language. Learning a local language should not become a countercurrent. And it should not reduce the quality of education for our children.

The Loya Jirga representatives ensured that our new Constitution represents not only the deep aspirations of the nation but also the diverse preferences of the people of Afghanistan. Turning their vision into reality may indeed be a challenge, but it is a challenge we are confident that we can meet. Recognizing our diversity, while affirming our nationhood, will further solidify the foundations of a democratic Afghanistan.

Hamid Karzai
President
Transitional Islamic State of Afghanistan

In Tanzania, by contrast, Kiswahili is the judicial language in the primary courts. Bills come to Parliament in English but are debated in Kiswahili, before being written into law in English. In the lower courts both English and Kiswahili are used, but sentences are written in English. In 1980 Kiswahili was used 80% of the time in lower courts; only English is used in the high court.[46]

In 1987 New Zealand, with a 14% indigenous Maori population, declared Maori an official language, giving any person (not just a defendant) the right to speak Maori in any legal proceeding, regardless of the person's proficiency in English.[47] It is the judge's responsibility to ensure that a competent interpreter is available. Since most Maori speak English as their first language, this provision views language as a right, not as a problem as most other countries view it.

When a new language policy is being explored or implemented, a special state language board should be created, as was done in Quebec, Catalonia and the Baltic States. The board should include experts to analyze the socio-lingual situation, draft policy proposals and organize language learning programmes, especially needed if a new language policy includes language requirements for civil service jobs, licensing or naturalization. If the state openly acknowledges that facility in a language is required for access to public services, it has a duty to assist and monitor the acquisition of that language—otherwise conflict is inevitable between the deprived and the dominant. A state language board with expert commissions and a permanent staff naturally requires substantial resources, as do language learning programmes.

With new states there may be unprecedented opportunities to resolve ethnic conflicts by negotiating an agreement that involves trade-offs for various groups. For instance, it may be possible to negotiate more language autonomy in return for less territorial self-rule. Under the recent Ohrid agreement the Albanians in Macedonia gave up claims to territorial autonomy in return for official-language status throughout the country. In newly independent Malaysia in 1956 the Chinese accepted the public dominance of the Malay language in return for a liberal naturalization policy. The Chinese diaspora safeguards the survival of its languages by importing books, supporting cultural associations and sending students to Chinese universities abroad. In addition, there are still Chinese language schools where the Chinese community can study in Chinese as the medium of instruction. Students in these schools are merely required to sit an examination in the national language, Bahasa Malaysia.

In Soviet Latvia Russian was the dominant language, and Latvian was rarely used in official affairs. Since independence in 1991 Latvian has become the language of state and other public affairs. A massive state-sponsored language programme was begun so that Russian residents could learn Latvian, in order to end a situation in which mostly bilingual Latvians had to accommodate monolingual Russians. Russians have been able to continue schooling in Russian-language public schools.

Not that tensions have completely dissipated. There are restrictions on the use of Russian on signs and public election posters, and there are time quotas for Russian on radio and television.[48]

In addition to issues of language use in national institutions, there is also a risk that national information media could be monopolized by speakers of one (or two) dominant languages. Even though most countries that gained their independence after the collapse of the Soviet Union have large Russian majorities, nationalists attempt to protect the informational space under their control from "foreign" influence—that is, from the impact of Russian media—by limiting newspapers and broadcasts in non-state languages (Russian). That narrows people's choices, though satellite dishes can broaden them by providing access to television programming in Russian.

POLICIES FOR REDRESSING SOCIO-ECONOMIC EXCLUSION

Ethnic minorities and indigenous people are often the poorest groups in most parts of the world. As chapter 2 documents, they have shorter life expectancies and lower education attainments and other social indicators. They also are most likely to suffer socio-economic exclusion. Redressing that exclusion requires a combination of policies, including:

- Addressing unequal social investments to achieve equality of opportunity.
- Recognizing legitimate collective claims to land and livelihoods.
- Taking affirmative action in favour of disadvantaged groups.

But minorities are not always disadvantaged in access to social and economic opportunities. In fact, perhaps the most politically dangerous exclusion occurs when an ethnic minority holds a large part of the wealth (agricultural land, key industries and services). For example, the Chinese in Burma, Indonesia, Malaysia, the Philippines and Thailand own a large part of the industry in these countries.[49] Their economic dominance has been a factor in civil conflict, for example when the Suharto regime was replaced in Indonesia. Similarly, white settlers in southern Africa have dominant control over agricultural land. The response to such domination, whether induced by the market or the colonial state, is likely to take the form of affirmative action for the disadvantaged majority.

ADDRESSING UNEQUAL SOCIAL INVESTMENTS TO ACHIEVE EQUALITY OF OPPORTUNITY

Policies that promote growth with equity are necessary to achieve socio-economic inclusion for all groups. For most developing countries this would include investing in the agricultural and other labour-intensive sectors and broadening access to assets, especially agricultural land. But too often development policies become a source of intergroup tension. In other words, development itself can create, sustain and often intensify inequalities between groups and between individuals.

In many African countries state-based control and distribution of mineral resources became a key source of ethno-regional wealth differentials. Thus, in Sudan the discovery and exploitation of oil became the major source of post-independence conflict, with the government annexing oil-bearing lands in the South.

In addition to issues of language use in national institutions, there is also a risk that national information media could be monopolized by speakers of one (or two) dominant languages

And in Nigeria the oil resources in the South-East and the use of oil revenues have heightened ethnic tensions, sparking the civil war in Biafra. Botswana, by contrast, used its mineral wealth to invest in social infrastructure and human development—perhaps precisely because it is almost entirely made up of a single ethnic group, the Batswana.[50]

As noted earlier, colonial governance entrenched ethnic identities in Africa. It also promoted ethnic dominance through structures of state power that gave predominance to some ethnic identities and not to others.[51] External factors remain critical today. External forces are usually subregional or interventions by neighbouring states, as in the Democratic Republic of Congo, Liberia, Mozambique and Nigeria. But developed country (often the former metropolitan country) interventions, by governments or by multinationals, are more generalized in Africa, albeit more prominent in the mineral resource–rich African states (Angola, Democratic Republic of Congo, Liberia, Sierra Leone).

Since international firms are usually involved in the extractive industries in most developing countries, corporations should sign on to the "Publish what you pay" campaign—revealing publicly what they pay to developing country governments in the form of taxes, royalties and other fees. Such information would make it much more difficult for developing country governments to use the revenues and rents from mineral resources to benefit particular ethnic groups or individuals. When such information is publicly available, affected communities can track the flow and use of resources. They can question whether the resources benefit only local or national elites. And they can demand that resources also be made available for investments in their area.

Indigenous people are more likely to be poor than non-indigenous people (figure 3.1). A World Bank study in Bolivia, Guatemala, Mexico and Peru suggests that if human capital characteristics (health and education services and their use) were equalized, much of the earnings differential between indigenous and non-indigenous workers would disappear.[52] Distance cannot excuse a failure to provide services: if logging and mining infrastructure can

be provided in the remotest corners of the Amazon basin, so can social infrastructure.[53]

In many countries public spending in basic social services systematically discriminates against minorities and indigenous people. The low provision of services can be a result of lower financial allocations or of distance and isolation. Indigenous people often receive fewer health care inputs and have worse health outcomes than the average population. The Brazilian government spent $7 per capita on health care for the indigenous population, compared with $33 on average for the country.[54] Indigenous people may also be underserved because health infrastructure and medical personnel are concentrated in urban areas. In South Africa race has been associated with major differences in infant mortality rates and with enormous inequities in the resources allocated per health intervention (figure 3.2). In Mexico there are 79 hospital beds and 96 doctors per 100,000 people on a national level, but the number of hospital beds falls to 8 and doctors to 14 per 100,000 in areas where indigenous people constitute more than two-fifths of the population.[55]

In Bolivia and Peru surveys show that indigenous people are more likely to have been sick in the previous month than are non-indigenous people but are much less likely to consult a physician.[56] Poorer uptake of health services by indigenous people may sometimes reflect their view that the services are culturally inappropriate because they fail to consider the spiritual dimensions of good health or fail to incorporate their traditional medicine, based on herbs and other plants. These issues need to be addressed if the health of indigenous people is to improve, and this can be done without additional financial resources.

The right to education is often also compromised for indigenous people. Bilingual education, though it can be very effective, often remains underresourced and so of poor quality. Indigenous children's schooling also suffers from a lack of school facilities in areas where they live and a shortage of qualified teachers, partly because indigenous education is given a lower priority. The problem is often the low relevance of teaching content, especially if teachers are not drawn from indigenous communities.

In many countries public spending in basic social services systematically discriminates against minorities and indigenous people

It is not easy to universalize access to basic services where there is ethnic fragmentation and identities have been politicized. A study in Kenya finds lower primary school funding in more ethnically diverse districts.[57] Using a sample of US cities, one study finds that the level and variety of public goods provided worsens as ethnic diversity increases.[58] Another US study shows that individuals' support for public welfare spending increases if a larger fraction of welfare recipients in their area belong to their racial group.[59] So, even though comparatively disadvantaged minorities or groups may need favourable public policies to enable them to escape deprivation, such policies may not be forthcoming because of the absence of a national consensus and the required tax base to finance such policies.

RECOGNIZING LEGITIMATE CLAIMS TO LAND AND LIVELIHOODS

Rights to traditional lands. An important political trend over the last decade has been the rise of powerful indigenous movements around the world—from Bolivia to Cambodia to Canada to Ecuador. At the core of these movements is the demand to protect indigenous people's rights to historic lands and mineral wealth. These claims have to be recognized for what they are: claims for who owns the land and the right to use its soil and resources (water, minerals, plants, forests). Only then can policy instruments appropriately address the claims. Indigenous people often have a special relationship with the land—for many it is still their source of livelihood and sustenance and the basis of their existence as communities. The right to own, occupy and use land collectively is inherent in the self-conception of indigenous people, and this right is generally vested not in the individual but in the local community, the tribe or the indigenous nation.

Convention 169 of the International Labour Organization, adopted in 1989, calls on states to respect indigenous lands and territories and proclaims the right of indigenous people to control their natural resources. But only 17 countries have ratified it (mostly in Latin America). Many of the current conflicts over land and territory relate to the possession, control, exploitation and use of natural resources. In many

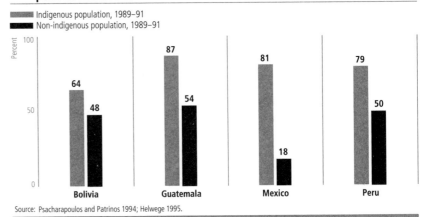

Figure 3.1 **Indigenous people are more likely than non-indigenous people to be poor in Latin America**

Indigenous population, 1989–91
Non-indigenous population, 1989–91

Source: Psacharapoulos and Patrinos 1994; Helwege 1995.

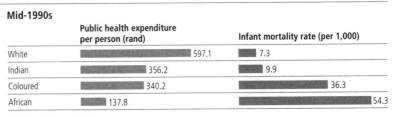

Figure 3.2 **Non-whites benefit less than whites from public health spending in South Africa**

Mid-1990s

	Public health expenditure per person (rand)	Infant mortality rate (per 1,000)
White	597.1	7.3
Indian	356.2	9.9
Coloured	340.2	36.3
African	137.8	54.3

Source: Mehrotra and Delamonica forthcoming.

countries the state claims the right to control such resources. And in many instances multinational corporations assert their own economic interests, unleashing conflicts. In Chile one law recognizes the rights of indigenous people over their lands, but other laws allow any private party to claim possession of subsoil and water resources on those lands, making it hard for indigenous communities to defend their ancestral claims.

Some countries protect such claims through legislation, but in many places indigenous people lack private ownership title. Powerful economic interests often turn communal possession into private property. From southern Chile to the Amazon basin to Canada's northern forests to the tropical jungles of South-East Asia to the bush of southern Africa, there is no territory not coveted by some international corporation. It is coveted for its mineral wealth, its oil deposits, its pastures, its forests, its medicinal plants, its suitability for commercial plantations, its water resources or its tourist potential. When the national government signs agreements with international companies for resources (logging, mines) on lands inhabited by indigenous people without their participation in decision-making, indigenous people become victims of globalized development (see chapter 5 for a more detailed discussion of this issue).

The claims of indigenous people over land and natural resources are collective and therefore complex. The idea of collective rights is troubling in a democracy because it seems to contradict individual rights. But the lack of legal recognition of collective rights violates individual rights. Countries such as Bolivia, Colombia, Ecuador and Mexico have begun to find ways to recognize diversity in their constitutions. Countries such as Bolivia, Ecuador and Mexico have also recognized degrees of territorial autonomy. Countries such as Bolivia, Brazil and Guatemala have established institutions to address the morass of incomplete or contradictory land titling and the challenge of land reform. And countries such as the Philippines have recognized the land rights of indigenous people (box 3.9).

In Africa the problem is similar, but with different roots. Despite movements towards democracy over the last decade, in many cases authoritarian regimes have broadly retained control over security forces, economic resources and funding from industrialized countries and multilateral institutions. Economic austerity programmes have often been used to advantage

Liberation struggles against colonialism were also struggles over access to land

by the ruling elites. And the dismantling of significant parts of the public sector, which market-oriented reforms usually require, without first creating a true market, has recentralized power in many cases. In that sense the structural adjustments of the 1980s and 1990s might be said to have had similar outcomes to the nationalizations of the 1960s and 1970s.

Unequal ownership of land. Independence and reconciliation policies in Namibia and Zimbabwe, and the end of apartheid in South Africa, led many to believe that racial conflicts would be mitigated. Liberation struggles against colonialism were also struggles over access to land, expropriated illegally during colonial times. But the post-colonial failure of national governments and their international partners to mobilize finance to acquire land on the market has fuelled perceptions that white landowners are being protected. The legacy of racially unequal land control afflicts the main agricultural settler areas of Namibia, South Africa and Zimbabwe, as well as of Botswana, Malawi and Swaziland. And the shift to the market has brought new migrations of white farmers to Mozambique and Zambia.

Most settler agriculture is on large farms, claimed to be more efficient than the small subsistence farms of black farmers. The fact that large farms provide most of the agricultural

---

BOX 3.9

Land rights in the Philippines

After decades of struggle the Philippine government passed the Indigenous People's Rights Act in 1997. This is the first time that a state in the region explicitly recognized the rights of indigenous people to their ancestral domain, to self-determination and to the free exercise of their culture. The act affirms that native title is the main basis of the ancestral domain rights of indigenous people. It offers an option to apply for a Certificate of Ancestral Domain Title, which formally acknowledges such rights.

As of July 2003 the National Commission on Indigenous People announced that 11 Certificates of Ancestral Domain Titles had been awarded covering 367,000 hectares. Around 76,000 indigenous people are direct beneficiaries of these certificates, a tiny proportion of the total indigenous population of 8 million.

The act defines ancestral domain as all areas belonging to indigenous cultural communities and indigenous people. This includes lands, inland waters and coastal areas occupied or possessed by indigenous people since time immemorial. The interruption of this possession because of war, force majeure, deceit or government projects does not invalidate the right. Ancestral domain also includes forests, pastures, burial grounds, worship areas, mineral and other resources that indigenous people may no longer exclusively occupy and use but to which they had access for their subsistence and traditional activities.

This provision is important because it clearly acknowledges the integral link of indigenous cultures and traditions with the land. This is consistent with Article 27 of the International

Covenant on Civil and Political Rights, which protects linguistic, cultural and religious rights and for indigenous people includes land, resource, subsistence and participation rights.

For those who were dispossessed of their lands, the law recognizes their cultural rights. It also recognizes their inherent right to self-governance and self-determination and respects the integrity of their values, practices and institutions. The state thus guarantees their right to freely pursue their economic, social and cultural development.

However, implementation of the act has also proved difficult, primarily because of bureaucratic inadequacies and discriminatory behaviour of politicians and civil servants. Indigenous people and their advocates must be vigilant in converting words to actions. The international community can help in this.

Source: National Commission on Indigenous Peoples 2004a, 2004b; UN 1994.

surplus for export and urban consumption ignores the well established research in agricultural economics: that small farms are more efficient than large ones. Land reform thus has to become a much greater state priority in the region.

Yet colonial land expropriations continue to be reinforced by new land concessions to foreign investors. Some of the biggest landowners in southern Africa are multinational companies with cattle ranches and mining concessions. These companies now control wildlife and safari parks—in the name of eco-tourism—which are growing in Mozambique, Namibia, South Africa and Zimbabwe. Few of the benefits of such activities go to the local inhabitants. In response, some of these countries have begun to take steps to alter the situation, such as setting up smaller game parks that are not controlled by large companies.

To date land reform in southern Africa has been slow, and accelerating the process will require donor support. Land reform should preferably be carried out in a transparent manner that allows poor, indigenous groups fair and productive use of land, which in addition to being a critical economic asset is a potent political symbol.

Land issues have remained relevant to race relations in Latin America as well. In the mid-20th century, as part of a corporatist state model, laws recognized indigenous people as candidates for citizenship rather than as objects of local control. When the corporatist state granted indigenous communities land titles and provided social services, it gave them the means for securing a basic standard of living. And peasant federations provided Indians with institutional avenues for accessing and interacting with the state.

However, in the 1980s and 1990s there has been a steady erosion of the citizenship regimes of corporatist states and a simultaneous politicization of ethnic cleavages in the Andean and Mesomerican countries of Bolivia, Ecuador, Guatemala, Mexico and Peru. The dismantling of rural programmes (including land reforms and credit programmes) has increased uncertainty about property regimes among Indian peasants. Liberalizing states have made it clear that they will not maintain (in Bolivia, Ecuador and Mexico) or re-establish (in Guatemala and Peru) special forms of property rights, credit and subsidies for Indian peasants. Thus the contemporary period challenges access to the state and its resources for poor indigenous people. Rural organizing and protests respond to this material uncertainty, as peasants fear indebtedness, declining incomes and loss of land. Unless these issues are addressed, indigenous people cannot realize the promise of democracy in the region. The potential loss of land also affects the viability and autonomy of local indigenous political institutions.[60]

TAKING AFFIRMATIVE ACTION IN FAVOUR OF DISADVANTAGED GROUPS

Affirmative action policies allocate jobs, promotions, public contracts, business loans, admissions to higher education and legislative seats on the basis of membership in a disadvantaged group. Such policies are needed when the disadvantage is cultural exclusion. Relying only on general policies of economic growth with equity for removing such group inequalities would take an insupportably long time, leading to resentment or even civil conflict.

Some affirmative action policies allocate numerical quotas; others set more flexibly defined goals. Affirmative action can be voluntary or legislatively mandated. In some countries, such as Malaysia, affirmative action has been used as a policy to address participation exclusion—to remove group distinctions so that racial, ethnic or linguistic identification is not identical to low socio-economic status. In other countries, such as South Africa, it is part of a policy of redressing past wrongs and reducing inequalities between groups (box 3.10).

Affirmative action has reduced intergroup inequalities in places where it has been effectively implemented. But studies of countries with extensive recorded data and a long history of affirmative action—India, Malaysia and the United States and, over a shorter period, South Africa—show that inequalities between individuals (vertical inequalities) as opposed to inequalities between groups (horizontal inequalities) have either increased or remained stable. The Chinese to Bumiputera disparity ratio in mean monthly

Relying only on general policies of economic growth with equity for removing such group inequalities would take an insupportably long time, leading to resentment or even civil conflict

BOX 3.10

Experiences with affirmative action in Malaysia and South Africa

Affirmative action, defined as public policy to reduce group inequalities, takes different forms. In South Africa over the past decade and Malaysia over the past three decades, affirmative action has increased the designated groups' representation in the elite and middle classes, but progress has not prevented increasing inequality between rich and poor, both within the formerly disadvantaged groups, as well as generally throughout society.

Malaysia

At independence in the late 1950s Malays and other indigenous groups (Bumiputera), though a numerical majority, were economically far behind the Chinese minority. Malays owned only 10% of registered businesses and 1.5% of invested capital. The Constitution granted Chinese and Indian residents citizenship and at the same time conferred special rights on Malays to land ownership, government jobs, education and business permits.

Following interethnic rioting in May 1969, the government adopted the New Economic Policy to eradicate poverty among all Malaysians and to restructure Malaysian society so that identification of race with economic function and geographical location is reduced and eventually eliminated through rapid economic expansion. The government legislated Malay quotas for trading and business licences and equity ownership and provided special assistance through credit, training and business sites. It also acquired shares in private corporations on behalf of the Bumiputera, with a view to achieving 30% corporate ownership.

While incomes have risen for all groups since 1969, group income disparities have fallen, an impressive achievement. But income inequality

within groups has risen since the late 1980s, especially among the Bumiputera, where the gap between rich and poor has widened substantially.

The growing abuse of ethnic privileges, especially by the politically well connected, has probably contributed to the cultural alienation of recent decades, with dissent being expressed among the Malays. With privatization opportunities from the mid-1980s largely decided by the government on a discretionary basis, there have been accusations of rent-seeking. Thus while the specific socio-economic targets of the New Economic Program have been largely achieved, national unity has remained somewhat elusive. Identifying improved interethnic relations almost exclusively with reduced disparities in participation in business communities and the middle class has generated greater ethnic resentment and suspicion on both sides.

South Africa

At the end of the apartheid era in 1995 whites accounted for 13% of the population and earned 59% of personal income; Africans, 76% of the population, earned 29%.[1] In a 2000 survey of 161 large firms employing 560,000 workers, whites still held 80% of management positions. The racial wage differential was also substantial although much smaller than before: at the end of the 1990s white workers earned an average of five times as much as Africans (although half of that discrepancy was explained by a difference in education and location).

In the post-apartheid era the democratic government introduced a range of programs designed to narrow these gaps. The 1998 Employment Equity Act requires employers to submit data on compensation and benefits for each occupational category by race and gender

and to take appropriate measures if disproportionate income differentials exist. Firms above a certain size are obliged to provide the government with annual reports outlining how they plan to make their workforce more demographically representative at all levels. The law also states that a protected group member's lack of necessary "experience" is not sufficient reason for hiring someone else as long as the applicant has the "capacity to acquire, within a reasonable time, the ability to do the job".[2] In addition, "black empowerment charters" for every industry set targets for the proportion of shares that must be transferred to blacks (indigenous Africans, coloureds and Asians). Charters have already been published for the oil, mining and banking sectors. The general thrust is that about a quarter of South African shares should be in black hands within a decade or so.

How have these efforts worked? About half of South Africa's middle managers and a quarter of top managers are black, up from hardly any a decade ago. Blacks have been promoted especially fast in the public sector—the government does not face competitors. However, since many underqualified people had been promoted, the government had to hire a large number of consultants to assist them, but that situation is changing. Efficiency is an issue. Under procurement rules black-owned firms can charge more and still win government contracts, leaving less money for public goods such as roads, bridges and houses. As for the empowerment charters, it is still unclear how this transfer of shares will be funded. The current practice of black empowerment "has created no new products or independent new companies that are not propped up by large white corporations", according to Moeletsi Mbeki, a well known commentator.

1. "Coloureds" and "Asians" made up 11% of the population.
2. The employer "may not unfairly discriminate against a person solely on the grounds of that person's lack of relevant experience", South Africa Employment Equity Act, no 55 of 1998, section 20 (5).
Source: Sabbagh 2004; Jomo 2004; *The Economist* 2004a; van der Westhuizen. 2002; Schultz and Mwabo 1998.

household income declined from 2.3 in 1970 to 1.8 in 2000 and that for Indians and Bumiputera fell from 1.73 to 1.3 (figure 3.3). And after decades of affirmative action policies in the United States the percentage of African Americans in the professions—lawyers, judges, physicians, engineers, college and university professors—has increased (figure 3.4). Thus the size of the African American elite has grown, and the dilemma now may be whether the second generation of this elite should continue to receive the benefits. In fact, in university admissions

the shift from affirmative action to colour blind policies, as enforced in Texas and California since 1996, has led to significant drops in minority enrolment in elite institutions.

India has one of the longest histories of any country in implementing affirmative action policies. Affirmative action rules (also known as "reservations") apply to three groups: the scheduled castes (Hindu untouchables and the deprived segments of religious minorities), scheduled tribes and "other backward classes" (caste groups that lie between the untouchables and the twice-born Dvija). Colonial regimes excluded these three groups from the structure of power. The result was that for centuries poverty was systematically concentrated in certain social groups. Reservations, which cover about 65% of the population, are designed to bring power to these peoples.

There are quotas for the scheduled castes (15% of the population) and scheduled tribes (8%) in legislative bodies at all government levels (local, provincial and national), in government jobs and in educational institutions.[61] Since 1991 the other backward classes, the largest and most heterogeneous group, have had quotas in government jobs and higher education institutions (27% at the national and state levels, a little over half of their proportion in the population), but not in legislative bodies since they constitute a majority in many states in India and their representation in legislatures has increased greatly through normal processes of competitive politics.

Reservations have changed the nature and composition of the Indian middle class. A sizeable portion of the middle class now consists of the second and third generation beneficiaries of reservations. At Independence the scheduled castes, scheduled tribes and other backward classes could aspire only to a limited degree of upward mobility. Reservations have broadened their opportunities. Education has become a social and cultural value, helping to create an upper crust whose members serve both as role models and as "spearheads" for their people to enter the economic and political mainstream.[62] One result is that middle-class identity is no longer perceived in ritual status terms.

Educational and occupational reservations have also made a lasting impact on India's political system. The entire structure of political power has changed since Independence, beginning with the south Indian states. A new political leadership has emerged from among the scheduled castes, scheduled tribes and other backward classes. In almost all states the beneficiaries of reservations occupy important positions in government and positions in lower levels of the bureaucracy. This new political class has ended the monopoly on power of the Congress Party.

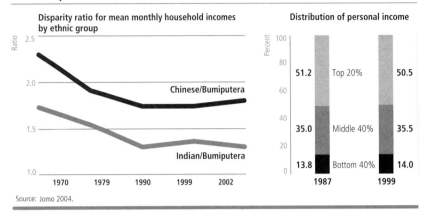

Figure 3.3 Group inequalities have declined in Malaysia, but personal inequalities have not

Source: Jomo 2004.

Figure 3.4 The record of affirmative action in the United States is mixed

Report card on equality

| | Circa 1980 | | Circa 2000 | |
	White	Black	White	Black
Life expectancy (years)	74.4	68.1	77.7	72.2
Maternal deaths (per thousand births)	6.7	21.5	5.1	17.1
Infant mortality rate (per thousand births)	10.9	22.2	5.2	14
People below the poverty line (percent)	10.2	32.5	9.5	22.5
Unemployment rate (16 and older)	6.3	14.3	3.5	7.6
Unemployment rate (16- to 19-year-olds)	15.5	38.5	11.4	24.5

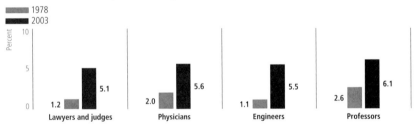

Blacks as share of professionals (percent)

Source: U.S. Census Bureau 2004b; U.S. Department of Labor 2004.

While affirmative action policies have had many successes, income inequalities between individuals have continued to increase even in societies that have tried to reduce group inequalities through affirmative action (India, Malaysia, South Africa and the United States). True, these inequalities might have been worse without the affirmative action policies. But to reduce individual inequalities and build truly inclusive and equitable societies, other policies are needed—of the kind discussed in previous *Human Development Reports*—such as policies that promote equitable economic development.

The original rationale of affirmative action was to redress past racial wrongs. US blacks were victimized first by slavery and then by a century of legal, and frequently violent, discrimination. Affirmative action was intended as a temporary measure. Instead, it has become a feature of US life. Now its rationale, supported not only by top universities but also by most large companies and even the military, is the pursuit of "diversity". The United States is slowly moving towards a model of formally colour blind policies, whose most distinctive feature is a principled negation of race as a legal category. For example, one suggested policy measure is to transform preferences based on race to preferences based on economic class. For university admissions, however, given that high-scoring poor white students outnumber high-scoring poor Hispanics and blacks on tests six to one, class-based preference will not foster racial equality.[63]

In India the intention was to end reservations once affected groups caught up. That has not happened. Instead, the preferences have become self-perpetuating. Reserved legislative districts, which were supposed to end 10 years after the Constitution of 1950, have been extended at 10-year intervals. Following a strategy of "we are more backward than you are", people try to get classified as members of preferred castes to be eligible for preferences. Reservations in some form now cover 65% of the population.

Such widespread gaming of the system has increased the rancour, bordering on animosity, of the "forward" castes and classes towards the "backward" ones. Several confrontations have resulted in the destruction of property and

the loss of life, raising the question of whether the polarization is worth the preference. The reasons:

- The scope of reservations in public employment has been widened from recruitment to promotions.
- The broadening of reservations constricts opportunities for the forward castes.
- Governments have used reservations as a populist policy to get votes.
- The reservations have led to the relaxation of standards for admitting members of the designated classes into professional schools.

Despite these concerns affirmative action policies have been quite successful in achieving their goals, and political considerations will probably prevent their retirement. And without them, group inequalities and socio-economic exclusions would likely be worse than they are today. Hence, there is no question that affirmative action has been necessary in the countries examined here.

One worrying aspect remains. Most countries that have adopted such policies have also experienced an increase in overall inequalities in personal income (accompanied by growing inequality within the underprivileged group). This suggests strongly that many other forces require action on a broader front: unequal land and resource ownership, inequalities in the provision of basic social services, and patterns of development that exploit or exclude indigenous people—just the factors underlying culturally driven socio-economic exclusion.

CHAPTER 4

Confronting movements for cultural domination

This Report argues that people should be free to be who they are, to choose their identities and to live accordingly. It further argues that the recognition of multiple and complementary identities—with individuals identifying themselves as citizens of a state as well as members of ethnic, religious and other cultural groups—is the cornerstone of cultural liberty. But movements hostile to these principles seek to eliminate diversity in the name of cultural superiority. Such movements, and their underlying sources of support, must be confronted. The question is: How?

This chapter is about coercive movements for cultural domination—those that are motivated by an ideology of cultural supremacy and domination and that use coercion to suppress the cultural identities of others. These movements are a familiar part of the political landscape in many countries and may even be growing in strength.

It is important to clarify what is distinctive about this sort of movement. Many types of movements use coercive strategies of violence or intimidation, but not all such movements are movements for cultural domination. Many historically disadvantaged or subordinated groups feel compelled to use coercive strategies, particularly if they are excluded from or marginalized within the normal political process. Their tactics may involve coercion, but their goal is the pursuit of equal rights, power sharing, autonomy and a more inclusive society (for example, the Zapatistas in Mexico). Insofar as the recommendations discussed in chapters 3 and 5 are adopted, the use of coercive strategies by such groups would no longer be necessary or justified.

This chapter, by contrast, focuses on movements that typically seek to create ethnically or religiously "pure" states by expelling, coercively assimilating or even killing anyone viewed as "other". For such movements the sorts of multiculturalist policies defended in this Report are anathema. It is the intolerance or hatred of other ways—and organizing to spread that intolerance while denying people choice over their identities—that makes a movement coercive (figure 4.1). The target: freedom and diversity.

Such movements are often misleadingly described as religious "fundamentalist" movements. But it is important to emphasize that the focus in this chapter is both broader and narrower than the phenomenon of religious fundamentalism. On the one hand, many forms of religious fundamentalism do not believe in the use of violence to achieve their aims. Nor do they necessarily seek to coercively impose their ideology on others. They may work solely within the democratic system. Tibetan or Trappist monks have strong religious beliefs but do not impinge on the religious freedom of others. On the other hand, there are cases of coercive movements for cultural domination that are not based primarily on religion, but rather on appeals to racial or ethnic purity. Thus, religious fundamentalism is neither a necessary nor a sufficient condition to qualify as a coercive movement for cultural domination.

This chapter focuses on movements that typically seek to create ethnically or religiously "pure" states by expelling, coercively assimilating or even killing anyone viewed as "other"

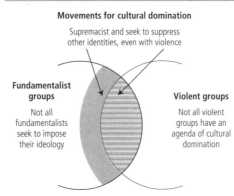

Figure
4.1

Movements for cultural domination—not the same as all fundamentalist or all violent movements

Movements for cultural domination

Supremacist and seek to suppress other identities, even with violence

Fundamentalist groups

Not all fundamentalists seek to impose their ideology

Violent groups

Not all violent groups have an agenda of cultural domination

Source: Human Development Report Office.

How can states respond to such movements without compromising their democratic principles? States have two options: to repress such movements or to undermine their bases of support by democratically accommodating their underlying concerns and grievances. States have a legitimate right, and responsibility, to prosecute criminal acts. At times, the use of force is necessary. But states have to ensure that measures to restrict movements for cultural domination do not repress fundamental rights and freedoms. This chapter argues that repression seldom works. The absence of democracy often creates conditions for the rise of such movements, while political accommodation can often moderate the sources of conflict and strengthen liberal democracy.

The absence of democracy often creates conditions for the rise of such movements, while political accommodation can often moderate the sources of conflict and strengthen liberal democracy

Movements for cultural domination— today's challenges

Coercive and intolerant movements are not new, but they have been on the rise. In many countries movements for cultural domination are becoming a prominent force in national politics. Among the disturbing indications:

- In Europe extreme right parties have had election successes in several countries, obtaining as much as 26.9% of the vote in Austria in 1999 (figure 4.2).
- In North America and Europe hate crimes and xenophobic violence—motivated by

racist, ethnic or religious bias—remain widespread. In 2002 there were 12,933 such crimes in Germany and 2,391 in Sweden, 3,597 prosecutions in the United Kingdom and 7,314 offences in the United States.[1] These countries are not unique in experiencing extreme intolerance; they are among the few, however, that collect such data.

- In 2003, 13 of 65 (one in five) groups engaging in terrorism could be identified as seeking religious domination or ethnic cleansing.[2]
- In Africa the Lord's Resistance Army, which aims to establish a government based on the Ten Commandments, has inflicted brutal violence in northern Uganda since 1988, including kidnapping, torture and rape. The Interahamwe Hutu rebels, perpetrators of the 1994 genocide, continue to pose a threat in Rwanda.
- In South Asia organized violent attacks on Christian churches and missions have increased. India, despite its long secular tradition, has experienced considerable communal violence, with rising intensity: 36.2% of casualties due to communal violence since 1954 occurred in 1990–2002.[3] In Pakistan certain organizations (the Sipah-e-Sahaba, Lashkar-e-Jhangvi and Tehreek-i-Jafariya) have stoked brutal sectarian violence between Sunnis and Shiites since 1989 (table 4.1).[4]
- In South-East Asia the militant Jemaah Islamiyah, with networks in Indonsia, Malaysia, the Philippines and Singapore, seeks to establish an Asian Islamic state. Some of its members were convicted for the Bali bombing in October 2002.
- Such movements are often found on the fringes, but they can also be segments of a political party or even a state. In seeking to impose a particular notion of national identity and ideology, while suppressing other cultural identities, coercive states have committed some of the worst brutalities of recent history—the genocide of non-communists by the Khmer Rouge and the ethnic cleansing of Muslims by Serbian forces in Kosovo.

Political activism for cultural domination exists in all major religions. In the United States Christian extremists bomb abortion clinics. In

Figure **4.2** **Some European extreme right parties have won steadily increasing vote shares**

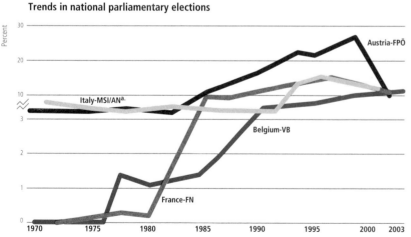

Trends in national parliamentary elections

a. The AN party in Italy was in the electoral alliance Casa Delle Liberta, which included Forza Italia, Lega Nord and the New Italian Socialist Party (the alliance recieved 45.4% of the vote.) The vote percentage shown refers to the proportional part of the election, in which 155 of the 630 deputies are elected.
Source: Electionworld.org 2004; Ignazi 2003; Jackman and Volpert 1996; Widfeldt 2004.

TABLE 4.1
Casualties resulting from sectarian violence in Pakistan, 1989–2003

Year	Number killed	Number injured
1989	18	102
1990	32	328
1991	47	263
1992	58	261
1993	39	247
1994	73	326
1995	59	189
1996	86	168
1997	193	219
1998	157	231
1999	86	189
2000	149	..
2001	261	495
2002	121	257
2003	102	103

.. Not available.

Note: Data for 2000 are for terrorist attacks using explosives only. Data on casualties and incidents of other terrorist activity are not available. Source: SATP 2004.

India Hindu extremists have fomented anti-Muslim violence in Gujarat even as Muslim extremists have targeted Hindus. The Jewish Gush Emunim, a militant settler group, aims to recreate Biblical Israel and has used violence to expel Palestinians. The Armed Islamic Group in Algeria threatens to kill those who do not pray or women who choose not to wear a headscarf. In Japan the Aum Shinrikyo cult, which claimed to be associated with Buddhism, poisoned commuters on the Tokyo subway system in 1995.

Nor is religion the only wellspring of extremism. Brutalities on the basis of ethnicity or race include the attempted extermination of Jews by the Nazis in Germany and the massacre of Tutsis by Hutus in Rwanda.

IDENTIFYING MOVEMENTS FOR CULTURAL DOMINATION

Movements for cultural domination share some key elements. They distinguish themselves by their cultural identity—whether ethnic, racial or religious—and they attempt to impose their ideology by coercion, even extermination. They:

- Believe in the superiority of their culture and reject all others.
- Act on this belief to impose their ideology on others and create a "pure" society.
- Often, though not always, resort to violence to achieve their aims.

Movements for cultural domination are supremacist and often predatory. They espouse an ideology that demonizes other identities to justify the creation of a "pure", sacred and homogeneous homeland. They view anyone who does not belong to the core community as inferior, unwanted and unworthy of respect. The Jemaah Islamiyah blames Indonesia's problems on "Kaffir Chinese and Christians"[5]— this is its justification for seeking to create an Islamic state at the cost of Indonesian secularism. The National Alliance—the largest neo-Nazi organization in the United States—wants to create a new government "answerable to white people only".[6]

Movements for cultural domination are exclusionary and seek to impose their ideology on others. They build support by engendering a sense of fear that their own values and identity are under threat (chapter 1). A study of extreme right parties in Europe revealed common characteristics: they foment xenophobia, leading to demands to create mono-cultural societies, to exclude "outsiders" from welfare policies and to mould a strong state that can protect the nation from "evil forces".[7] Movements of cultural domination also target members of their own community by denigrating and suppressing dissenting opinions and questioning integrity and loyalty (purity of faith or patriotism).

Other motives may be at work. Many ethnic conflicts are also about political or economic power (chapter 2), and ethnic identity is a way to mobilize allies. The Rwandan genocide, for example, was a manifestation of the struggle for political and economic power between the Tutsi, excluded under the Hutu-dominated government, and the Hutu, excluded under colonial rule. What distinguishes these movements is that they pursue cultural domination in the name of identity. Inciting an ideology of hatred against the Tutsis, the Hutu militants redefined Hutu identity in racial terms, claiming that Hutus were the original inhabitants and deriding Tutsis as "foreigners" from Ethiopia.

Not all movements for cultural domination are overtly violent. Threats, harassment and electoral politics are also common tactics. Moreover, the same organization might use a range of strategies—propaganda, electoral politics, soliciting of external support, forcible demands

Movements for cultural domination are exclusionary and seek to impose their ideology on others

for local support, and guerrilla or terrorist campaigns. Electoral politics is not always an alternative to coercion—many parties instil fear and insecurity to gain votes and to threaten members of other communities. While violence is not a universal characteristic of coercive movements, it is a common one. Coercive ideologies spread intolerance, which can inspire acts of random violence. The Christian Identity movement in the United States inspired racist shootings and murders by members of the Aryan Nations in 1998.

WHY DO THESE MOVEMENTS EXIST—AND WHY IS THEIR INFLUENCE GROWING?

Ideology. Discrimination. Poverty and inequality. Manipulative leadership. A weak or ineffectual state. Outside political interventions. Linkages with alienated diaspora. All are among the reasons for the rise and staying power of coercive movements for cultural domination. Failures of development and governance can leave a vacuum that coercive movements are only too eager to fill. A consistent characteristic of such movements is that they offer a simple (often distorted) explanation for the world's failings—and a simple agenda to correct them (expelling immigrants, killing members of other communities).

Identity politics often has underlying economic explanations of grievance or greed. In Western Europe extreme right parties have gained votes when there has been a significant loss of trust in mainstream parties over issues ranging from corruption to globalization.[8] Religious movements offer doctrinal salvation to people who see modernization as alien and repressive in contexts where neither democratization nor economic development has succeeded. So, even a threatened middle class and professionally frustrated intelligentsia might join the ranks of the economically and socially marginalized in coercive movements. This was evident in the role of the "oppositional lay intelligentsia" in the rise of many coercive Islamist movements until the 1970s. In recent years clerics have played the dominant role.[9]

When the state fails, coercive movements may step in to offer education, insurance or law and order. The Taliban initially helped secure

trading routes. The Gush Emunim briefly provided security to its members' settlements in the West Bank and Gaza. The Adolat brigades in Uzbekistan gained popularity when they took the law into their own hands to reduce crime and lower food prices.

The lack of resources to send children to secular (government or private) schools is one reason individuals rely on religious schools that provide free education. In principle, this is unobjectionable. Islamic schools, for example, can provide cultural and economic benefits to students who might otherwise not get an education. But in some communities such schools have also promoted coercive cultural ideologies and encouraged students to engage in coercive activities. While 2–3% of Pakistan's Islamic schools are said to be recruiting children into coercive movements, only about half the estimated 15,000–20,000 religious schools are officially registered.[10] It becomes difficult for the state to oversee and regulate such unregistered schools. In Thailand 300 of the 550 Islamic schools offer no secular education (the state is investigating their involvement in recruiting and training militants).[11]

But even state schools can preach intolerance. Nazism was propagated in state schools. Ideologies of white supremacy were part of the curriculum in South Africa under the apartheid regime. Control over education resources permits states to revise textbooks to distort history, target particular communities and encourage racist stereotypes.

Leaders define the ideology of a movement. One of their main functions is to interpret religious doctrine to persuade members of the "divine" rightness of their acts. Because militias have a high risk of defection, leaders might demand that members prove their loyalty by studying religious texts for years or by committing acts of destruction. They also change the organization's ideology or target, depending on the circumstances. And leaders convert wanton acts of coercion into a corporate effort. They recruit, indoctrinate and train their cadres (sometimes children). They plan terrorist acts and prepare publicity materials. And they secure funds to compensate family members of cadres who die in action and are then glorified as heroes (box 4.1).

When the state fails, coercive movements may step in to offer education, insurance or law and order

Long-term immigrant communities abroad can contribute to the rise of coercive movements in their countries of origin. As members of the diaspora they struggle between retaining their original identity and cultural traditions and adapting to their new environment. When they feel insecure or unappreciated, they may separate themselves from mainstream society. There is evidence of such dissatisfaction among Muslim populations in Germany and the Netherlands.[12] Coercive movements can exploit such sentiments to tap the diaspora for financial and political support. In the early 1990s "weekend fighters" came from Germany to fight for their ethnic groups in Bosnia.[13]

Many of these underlying factors in the rise of movements of cultural domination also inspire nationalist movements. Many of these factors are the reasons why discriminated-against groups struggle for political rights. But many movements for autonomy can be liberal and recognize the importance of accommodating diversity within an autonomous region. By contrast, movements for cultural domination can arise even within the majority and politically dominant group. Racists do not seek territorial autonomy; instead, they target all who are viewed as "other" or inferior. Movements for cultural domination are adept at using people's genuine grievances to gain supporters. What distinguishes them is their agenda of cultural superiority and elimination of diversity and tolerance.

DILEMMAS FOR DEMOCRACIES—RESTRICTIVE OR ACCOMMODATIVE MEASURES?

Coercive movements can be a powerfully destabilizing force. A challenge for all states, they present a particular dilemma for democratic ones. If movements for cultural domination use violent means, threaten law and order or deny the human rights of their members, governments have every right to take forceful action against them. But the problem is much broader than crime and punishment. In states that respect the right of free speech, movements for cultural domination use the freedoms of democratic societies to try to undermine them. It is possible—indeed, common— to advocate exclusion, discrimination and the denial of civil and political liberties without ever breaking the law.

The dilemma is that democratic states, which hold their values of freedom dear, do not want to stand accused of improperly restricting free speech and rights of assembly. Nor do they want to ignore threats to communal peace or intimidation of minority groups. If the rights of some groups are restricted, while the rest of society enjoys them, there is a danger of provoking extreme, even violent reactions. The challenge is to protect freedom while discouraging coercive movements.

Coercive movements tend to be more powerful, and threatening, in non-democratic states. They make themselves heard through violence and extremism because the public sphere is otherwise closed to them. By definition, non-democratic states embody little or no allegiance to such values as free speech or the right to organize politically. For non-democratic regimes the trade-off between liberty and repression is less acute because there is less liberty to start with.

For non-democratic governments, moving towards more liberal politics can be an effective

Coercive movements can be a powerfully destabilizing force

BOX 4.1
Leadership, ideological manipulation and recruiting supporters

Leaders of movements for cultural domination build group identities and mobilize their followers to adopt coercive methods against others. Leaders use their organizational skills to gain supporters, modify ideologies to suit their needs, arrange finances at home and abroad and give weapons and training to militant cadres. Such leaders pursue two core aims: creating an ideology of intolerance and altering the balance of political power.

The easiest way to breed intolerance is to use self-serving interpretations of history to describe and vilify other groups. By doing so, leaders emphasize the quest for justice and focus on the losses their group allegedly suffered. The focus is not on solving real grievances but on using ostensible grievances as rallying cries. The Web site of the Bajrang Dal, a Hindu extremist group, accuses the Indian state of appeasing "anti-national elements (muslims)" and demands that Indian Muslims "prove that

they are not the heirs and followers" of past invaders who destroyed Hindu temples. In the United States after the 1993 Waco tragedy involving Federal Bureau of Investigation (FBI) agents and the Branch Davidian cult, leaders of religious cults and white supremacist organizations tried to rally support by attacking the federal government for perpetrating what they claimed was an injustice.

Leaders also seek to change the structure of governance, such as substituting theological law for secular rules, repudiating electoral processes or restricting the constitutional rights of others. All these measures serve to impose one group's authority and superiority over others. Notwithstanding the violent activities of the Tamil Tigers (LTTE) in Sri Lanka, in the past Buddhist monks have regularly opposed any moves towards granting autonomy to Tamils in the northeast.

Source: ADL 2003; *The Economist* 2000; Grove and Carter 1999; HinduUnity.org 2004; IRR 2003; Stern 2003.

strategy (box 4.2). Democratic societies, better suited to dealing with movements of cultural domination, have more options.

RESTRICTIVE MEASURES

Restricting the activities of coercive movements is the first step. When these movements threaten, intimidate and violently target other groups, states need to restrain them, even if that requires the use of force. Common measures to restrict (and eventually eliminate) the activities of coercive movements include:

- Erecting institutional barriers against coercive political parties.
- Enacting legislation and using judicial intervention.
- Applying force.

Erecting barriers against coercive political parties. Institutional barriers that exclude certain types of organizations from participating freely in electoral politics or civil society are a common way for democratic societies to keep cultural extremism from infecting the larger society. Barriers include requiring a minimum share of votes to enter the legislature, controlling campaign funds, restricting access to broadcast services and

Restricting the activities of coercive movements is only the first step

banning certain types of political parties through constitutional provisions. Non-democratic governments use similar measures to suppress opposition, compromising their ability to deal with coercive movements when a specific threat arises because there are no lines of communication.

In Germany a political party must get 5% of the national vote to take a seat in the legislature. This threshold has helped to exclude from power all major extreme right parties since the end of the Second World War—the National Democratic Party (NPD), Republican Party (REP) and the German People's Union (DVU). Israel's threshold of 1.5%, by contrast, was not high enough to keep Rabbi Kahane of the racist Kach Party from winning a seat in the Knesset in 1984. In response, parliament adopted section 7A of the Basic Law, which blocks a slate of candidates from participating in elections if its purposes include, among others, "denial of the democratic character of the state" or "incitement to racism". The government banned Kach in 1988 for inciting racism and declared it a terrorist organization in 1994. In both Germany and Israel coercive groups, even if permitted to contest elections, found their freedoms constrained when authorities identified them as hostile to the constitution.

BOX 4.2

Central Asia—the danger in restricting political and cultural liberties

By the end of Soviet rule in Central Asia Islam was polarized and new Islamist movements had emerged. There was official Islam, as regulated (and suppressed) by the Soviet state; traditional Islam, as organized around unofficial clergy; and reformist Islam, as espoused by the ahl al-Quran—"people of the Book"—who wanted to establish "pure Islam" and believed in strict adherence to Sharia law. With the repression of movements expressing popular aspirations, each successive religious movement became more ideologically extreme and coercive.

Repression seldom works ...

In the early 1990s the pan-Central Asian Islamic Revival Party (IRP) sought to purify Islam but lacked a coherent structure. Despite being generally moderate, the IRP was banned in Uzbekistan in 1991. Around the same time the Adolat (justice) movement became a force, demanding that Uzbekistan become an Islamic state. It gained popularity as bands of volunteers

patrolled the Ferghana Valley to reduce crime and demand lower food prices. Fearing alleged links with the IRP, authorities prosecuted Adolat leaders. This only boosted their popular appeal and forced the movement underground. In 1999–2000 the Islamic Movement of Uzbekistan (IMU), headed by former Adolat leaders, sought to depose the Uzbek government and establish an Islamic state.

Another Islamist group, the Hizb-ut Tahrir (HT), has gained supporters throughout the Ferghana Valley region of Kyrgyzstan, Tajikistan and Uzbekistan. It wants to establish an Islamic caliphate in Central Asia. But it strongly criticizes the violence of the IMU, relying instead on grass-roots campaigns, distribution of leaflets and similar tactics. However, the HT also espouses radical ideas, rejecting democracy, imposing Sharia and threatening the possible use of force in future. The HT has been banned in all three states, but its popularity has not waned.

... but democratic accommodation can

Tajikistan's civil war (1992–97) was largely a power struggle between different ethnic groups. After the United Tajik Opposition had been expelled from its strongholds, religious activists took over its leadership and renamed the group the Movement for the Islamic Revival of Tajikistan (MIRT), trying to reshape it as a religious force. In areas under its control the MIRT threatened to punish people who did not pray and demanded that women wear veils. Many moderate opposition leaders left the MIRT. After a peace agreement in 1997 former opposition members (including those from the relegalized Islamic Revival Party of Tajikistan) received government positions. More moderate leaders joined the party. The IRPT has kept its commitment—surrendering weapons, upholding the constitution, supporting a secular democratic state. The IRPT continues to advocate inclusion of religious values in the legal system, though it has limited political influence.

Source: Cornell and Spector 2002; *The Economist* 2003b; Rotar' 2002; Rubin 2004; Zelkina 1999.

Such bans on political participation may be legitimate if a party has been implicated in criminal behaviour. But restrictions on political parties only because they adhere to a particular ideology might not work for two reasons. First, a movement that expresses a genuine public concern seldom withers away. Second, opposition against the regime can increase, and take more extreme forms, if the public considers such bans illegitimate. Morocco's experience shows that wider political participation can increase moderation. After constitutional changes expanded the electoral playing field, the Islamist Justice and Development Party became the main opposition party in 2002. Within a year its leaders were arguing less about imposing Islamic law and more about advancing development.

Enacting legislation and using judicial intervention. Laws restricting coercive groups differ in scope and implementation. Despite strong anti-racism laws in Sweden the Parliament rejected a ban on extreme right groups. But at times stringent laws against terrorism become necessary. In the United Kingdom the Anti-Terrorism, Crime and Security Act of 2001 extended its scope to include both racially and religiously aggravated crimes. This law and India's Prevention of Terrorism Act of 2002 extend the period of detention of suspects without trial. Malaysia and Singapore have used similar provisions for decades.

But there are lively debates about anti-terror legislation almost everywhere—Germany, Indonesia, Malaysia, New Zealand, Russia, the United Kingdom and the United States—because there is also a danger that anti-terror laws, enacted to deal with a crisis, will be abused or will remain in use in perpetuity. It is important to regularly review these laws for their need and effectiveness to justify their continuing application. The Indian government allowed its earlier anti-terror law to lapse in 1995 after accusations of human rights abuses. The UK anti-terror law was introduced as a temporary measure in 1974 (in the wake of Northern Ireland-related terrorism) and amended in 1976, 1984, 1989 and 1996. When made permanent, such laws compromise guarantees of civil liberties in democratic societies. The UK legislation has no expiry date.

The effectiveness of laws that seek to cut the ground out from under movements for cultural domination depends not on how much they restrict civil liberties but on how much they protect them. The role of a functioning civilian justice system is critical for prosecuting coercive movements and individuals but also to serve as a check on government actions.

Courts have come to different conclusions about the proper balance between protecting liberty and permitting the spread of hatred. In 1996 the Swedish Supreme Court interpreted a 1948 law that prohibited agitation against other ethnic groups (*hets mot folkgrupp*) to allow the banning of any display of emblems, symbols or clothing connected with racial hatred. The Dutch are also working through such complexities. In early 2001 the mayor of the municipality of Kerkrade invoked the Law on Public Events to forbid a march by the Netherlands People's Union, an extreme right party with a racist ideology. A court in Maastricht overturned the order, and the march took place. The legitimacy of actions rests on acceptance of internationally recognized laws and norms. Coercive movements often develop international networks. If due process of law is not followed in one country, then a movement might gain sympathy and support in other countries as well.

Applying force. All states, democratic or not, have a right to use force when faced with violent movements. What matters is how they use it. The use of force loses much or all of its legitimacy when the state restricts political rights, avoids civilian jurisdiction or uses torture.

There is a practical argument against the use of force as the first option: it often does not work. Repression of the generally moderate Islamic Revival Party in Uzbekistan in the early 1990s led to the growth of extremist groups like the Adolat movement, and by 1999 the Islamic Movement of Uzbekistan was attempting to overthrow the government and engaging in terrorism (see box 4.2).

Ensuring that force is used legitimately is not always easy. Force should be used only against groups that are coercive, not against groups demanding rights for political participation. It is sometimes difficult to make that distinction, however. Members of the same movement might

There is a practical argument against the use of force as the first option: it often does not work

espouse different ideologies and objectives, some coercive, others not. States become wary that giving freedom to a coercive movement could encourage more intolerance. Egypt shows just how difficult it has been to identify coercive movements—and yet how important it is to choose the right policy response (box 4.3).

But certain strategies should be avoided. States have resorted to torture, arguing that it is justified under certain circumstances. No matter how infrequent or moderate the use, there is always the danger of abuse when the law condones such actions. In 1987 an Israeli judicial commission recommended allowing "moderate physical pressure" in interrogations.[14] But the abuse of Palestinian prisoners by Shin Bet, the security service, became widespread. Recognizing this reality, the Israeli Supreme Court declared all such methods illegal in 1999. As of March 2004, 58 of 191 United Nations member states had not ratified the Convention against Torture and Other Cruel, Inhuman or Degrading Treatment or Punishment (indicator table 30).

Most democratic states, and even some non-democratic ones, apply five basic principles in their judicial processes: no arbitrary detention, no torture, habeas corpus, access to trial by civilian magistrate and access to a defence lawyer. Confronting coercive movements does not mean that these principles have to be compromised. Doing so makes restrictive measures repressive—and even ineffective.

States should go beyond restrictive measures to contain intolerant ideologies and coercive movements

DEMOCRATIC ACCOMMODATION

States should avoid using only restrictive measures to contain intolerant ideologies and coercive movements. Why? Because the measures can undermine democratic principles—and are frequently ineffective. There is no evidence, for example, that banning political parties and movements with a racist agenda ends racism. Movements for cultural domination exploit real grievances; if banned, they simply go underground. Restriction, especially repression, provokes resistance not only from the movements—it can also turn popular opinion against the state.

Coercive movements are sustainable at least in part because they give expression to people's concerns and sentiments. Such concerns can be addressed only if they can be expressed and understood.

BOX 4.3

Egypt—distinguishing between moderates and extremists

Islamist groups are not all alike. Treating them so is not only poor politics, it is also ineffective in addressing the concerns that animate them. At the same time, distinguishing between groups and their ideologies is not always easy. This can be seen clearly in Egypt.

For the better part of a century Egypt has contended with Islamist movements. The Muslim Brotherhood (founded in 1928), al-Jama'a al-Islamiyya and al-Jihad are the most prominent. From the 1940s to the 1960s the Muslim Brotherhood had a violent element involving high-profile assassinations and armed plots against the government. But in the past two decades some of its leaders have rejected revolutionary and violent methods (they claim completely), even suggesting that violence contradicts Islamic Sharia.

The Muslim Brotherhood's stated objectives now are the establishment of an Islamic democracy based on freedom, and the creation of a society with social justice and security for all citizens. It seeks an Egypt governed by Sharia law, while emphasizing the need to work within the institutions of democracy.

The Egyptian state allowed the Muslim Brotherhood to run for election, in alliance with other parties, in 1984 and 1987, without officially recognizing it. The Brotherhood contested in alliance with other parties (Wafd in 1984, Liberal and Socialist Labour in 1987) and scored impressive gains—initially 8 seats, then 36. However, partly due to internal conflicts, the Brotherhood was equivocal in condemning violent acts committed by other groups in the early 1990s. Such ambiguity about its ideology has undercut the Brotherhood's attempts to position itself as a moderate political alternative. In the 1990s the government arrested hundreds of Brotherhood members on the grounds that they were supporting terrorism.

Deciding how to deal with the Muslim Brotherhood is difficult. Egypt would be in a stronger position, however, if it acted from a position free from accusations of human rights abuses. Excluding one of the country's promi-

nent political organizations from public life is untenable in the long term.

Al-Jama'a al-Islamiyya and al-Jihad, which originated in the 1970s, have relied on violent tactics to secure their objective of imposing Sharia. The most gruesome attack was the massacre of 68 foreigners and Egyptians at a temple in Luxor in 1997 (the Muslim Brotherhood denounced the attack). Since then these groups have suffered ideological divisions. Some leaders now reject violence, while others defend it. The attacks on US embassies in Kenya and Tanzania in 1998 (both groups allegedly contributed to them) highlighted the threats extremist elements pose. Alleged links to al-Qaeda have further eroded their claims to political participation. They are not allowed to enter elections.

As the world seeks solutions to the threats posed by international terrorism, the Egyptian experience shows how difficult it is to distinguish between moderate and extremist groups. But opening the political sphere to the moderates can help to reduce the appeal of the extremists.

Source: Abed-Kotob 1995; Campagna 1996; Fahmy 1998; Gerges 2000.

Allowing political parties that espouse coercive ideologies to participate in elections might provide a democratic channel for expressing resentment, thereby reducing violence. The risk is that such parties, on gaining power, might then try to suppress cultural freedoms. Should the state ban parties that want to coercively impose Islamic Sharia law? Should a white-power group in Sweden be allowed to operate freely?

This Report has already argued that universal values of human rights and individual freedoms must not be sacrificed to claims of tradition or customary law. But repressing a party for its ideology risks undermining democratic processes and might encourage the excluded to turn to violence. The experience of several countries suggests four strategies to guide the actions of democratic states—strategies that non-democracies can learn from:

- Allowing normal democratic processes to function.
- Prosecuting hate crimes.
- Paying attention to school curricula.
- Helping communities come to terms with past hatred and violence.

Allowing normal democratic processes to function. Suppression of political rights on grounds of ideology seldom succeeds. In Algeria a military intervention in 1992 annulled the election of the Islamic Salvation Front (FIS) party. This led to the emergence of a more militant group, the Armed Islamist Group (GIA). The result: more than a decade of deadly violence and nearly 100,000 lives lost.[15] Political accommodation can split coercive movements between those prepared to participate in elections or government and those not (box 4.4).

Mainstream parties in Europe tend to avoid links with racist, anti-immigrant parties, but political realities have at times coaxed them into bringing extreme right parties into a coalition. Austria's extreme right Freedom Party (FPÖ) has been part of regional coalition governments since the 1970s. After winning 26.9% of the vote in 1999, it became a partner in the national coalition government. But this was on the condition that its leader, Jörg Haider, not be part of the government; he even stepped down as party chairman in 2000. Government policy remained moderate: Austrian immigration policy

Democratic accommodation can shed the hard light of reality on the fringe appeal of extremism

---

BOX 4.4

Algeria—discontent, democratization and violence

The Algerian civil war is often portrayed as a conflict between Islamic fundamentalists and the state. But the rise of intolerant and violent groups resulted from failed democratization. Accommodative strategies in recent years have yielded some initial positive results even as several other challenges remain.

After an economic collapse in the 1980s pressure for greater democratization increased. The National Liberation Front (FLN) government, which had ruled Algeria since independence, introduced constitutional changes in 1989 to legalize political parties and curtail the role of the military. It had also encouraged an Islamist movement by significantly increasing religious spending from 1982 to 1987. Beginning in 1988 the country prepared for its first multiparty election, and the government dramatically cut religious spending to dampen the Islamist movement's growing appeal. In the December 1991 elections the Islamic Salvation Front (FIS), which wanted to establish an Islamic state, won 47% of the vote in the first round. With the election outcome almost certain, the government halted

the electoral process in early 1992. Democracy had failed in Algeria.

While the failure had little to do with Islam, Islam was a major factor in the crisis. An armed Islamist movement had begun organizing in Algeria in 1990. Many groups, believing that democracy was not the route to an Islamic state, stayed out of the FIS. The FIS, arguing for democratic processes, at first marginalized violent groups. But it started losing credibility in the aftermath of the 1992 coup. By 1994, when armed groups opposing dialogue with the "apostate regime" (Hafez 2000, p. 577) united as the Armed Islamic Group (GIA), the FIS formed its own military wing—the Islamic Salvation Army (AIS).

The differences in ideology were substantial. The GIA targeted civilians; the AIS declared such methods un-Islamic and focused on military targets. The GIA considered violent *jihad* an Islamic imperative; the AIS viewed it as only one of many means to build an Islamic state. The GIA portrayed an uncompromising struggle against infidels and apostates; the AIS and FIS appealed to the president to restore democracy and political rights.

These varying interpretations of Islam and its role indicate why generalizations about Islam and Islamist movements in Algeria are unhelpful.

Since 1997, when the AIS negotiated a ceasefire with the military in return for a general amnesty, Algeria has made some moves towards reconciliation and democracy. In 1999 the government released political prisoners and passed a Law of Civil Reconciliation to extend amnesty to rebels who had not killed civilians, placed bombs in public places or committed rape. In elections in 2002 two Islamist-oriented parties earned seats in the National Assembly.

Algeria has a long road ahead. The FIS continues to be disqualified from elections. The GIA and the recently established Salafist Group for Preaching and Combat continue to threaten violence. Demands for cultural recognition by the Berbers are another source of tension. Algeria's experience exemplifies the argument presented throughout this Report: religion and ethnicity are not intrinsically causes of conflict, and democracy is a necessary but not sufficient condition for guaranteeing cultural freedoms.

Source: Hafez 2000; Middle East Institute 2003; Testas 2002; Tremlett 2002.

Difference is not a threat but a source of strength

Most societies in the world today include more than one culture, one community or one tradition. All too often in such a situation one element may seek to dominate the society as a whole. That approach can generate tension and conflict. It is in the interests of all to work together to build a society beneficial to all its members.

Northern Ireland and the European Union are particularly strong examples of how the existence of more than one culture can prove to be positive in the building and development of society through a process of conflict resolution.

It is now almost four decades since the beginnings of the civil rights movement in Northern Ireland, which has sought by peaceful means the same rights and opportunities for all the people living in Northern Ireland, irrespective of their background or religion. Throughout those years I have maintained that, when you have a divided people, violence has absolutely no role to play in healing the division or in solving the problems—it only deepens the division. The problem can be resolved only through peace, stability, agreement, consensus and partnership. There cannot be victory for one side or the other.

So long as the legitimate rights of each community in Northern Ireland were not accommodated together in a new political framework acceptable to all, the situation would continue to give rise to conflict and instability. There needed to be agreement.

That is the purpose of the 1998 Belfast Agreement. It represents an accommodation that protects and promotes the identities and rights of all political traditions, groups and individuals. No one is asked to yield cherished convictions or beliefs. Everyone is asked to respect the views and rights of others as equal to his or her own.

I also believe that the European Union is the best example of conflict prevention and conflict resolution in international history. It is important that we maintain and build on that record. European visionaries demonstrated that difference—whether of race, religion or nationality—is not a threat, but is natural, positive and a source of strength. It should never be the source of hatred or conflict. A fundamental principle of peace is respect for diversity.

I entered the European Parliament in 1979 on the occasion of the first direct election to the parliament by the voters of its then nine member states. I will soon be stepping down from elected public life, delighted in the knowledge that in those 25 years the European Union has progressed to the point that it will by then have expanded to include 25 member states. This will end the artificial division of our continent created after the Second World War and reunite our European family.

The European Parliament's location is in Strasbourg, on the River Rhine, on the border between France and Germany. When I first visited Strasbourg I walked across the bridge from Strasbourg in France to Kehl in Germany and reflected on the tens of millions of people who had been killed in the numerous wars waged for control of territory. The European Union has replaced those conflicts with co-operation between its people. It has transformed its wide range of traditions from a source of conflict into a source of unifying strength.

John Hume

John Hume, MP MEP
1998 Nobel Peace Prize Winner

did not become dramatically harsher, as had been feared. And in 2002 the FPÖ won only 10% of the vote, suffering from internal party divisions (see figure 4.2).

Democratic accommodation can shed the hard light of reality on the fringe appeal of extremism. Extreme right parties might initially show populism-driven electoral success, but it is not always easy to maintain the momentum. Many European extreme right parties, like the Denmark Progress Party (FRPd) or the German Republican Party (REP), openly contested elections but were rendered irrelevant when they received miniscule proportions of the vote. Others like the Social Movement Tricolour Flame (MS-FT) in Italy got barely any support (figure 4.3).

Non-democratic countries, by definition, have a narrow public space for political contests. This can encourage the growth of coercive movements, but it also limits the state's ability to confront them in a way that the public deems legitimate.

Prosecuting hate crimes. Failure to prosecute hate crimes only encourages coercive movements to advance their agenda through threats and violence. Legislation that specifically targets hate crimes is controversial. Critics ask why bigotry should be considered more reprehensible

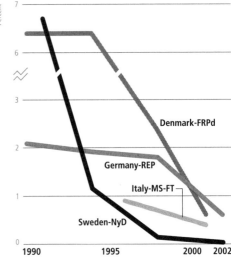

Figure 4.3 **Democratic participation can expose the fringe appeal of extreme right parties**

Share of vote in national parliamentary elections

Source: Electionworld.org 2004; Ignazi 2003; Jackman and Volpert 1996; Widfeldt 2004; Susning.nu 2004; Swedish Election Authority 2002.

than, say, greed, and claim that such laws come close to prosecuting thoughts not deeds, perilous territory for democracies.

The case for hate crime legislation rests on two premises. First, hate crimes have symbolic relevance—they are intended to send a message to an entire community and therefore, in a sense, threaten all its members. The crime is greater than the physical or verbal assault involved. Second, a potential victim can do little to prevent attack. Since it is religious or ethnic identity that motivates such crimes—often immutable characteristics—the threat is constant. Cultural liberty is about allowing individuals to make choices; hate crime is about coercing them into a straitjacket of someone else's design.

Having hate crime laws on the books is not enough. To identify potential threats countries need to collect data on hate crimes or xenophobic violence. The European Monitoring Centre on Racism and Xenophobia, which assists EU countries with standard procedures for collecting such data, undertakes comparative analysis for the region. States must also have the political will to take a stand against intolerance. Of the 191 member states of the United Nations, 56 states (29%) have not ratified the International Convention on the Prevention and Punishment of the Crime of Genocide (indicator table 30).

Paying attention to school curricula. States should ensure that religious schools are not exempt from state regulation and that their students receive a broad-based education. Some countries have made encouraging efforts in this direction. Pakistan recently sanctioned a $100 million programme for including secular subjects in the curricula of religious schools.[16] In Malaysia the government is introducing the J-QAF project to incorporate a comprehensive Islamic studies syllabus in the national education system; students will thus get both religious and secular education. In Indonesia since the early 20th century the Muhammadiyah and Nahdlatul Ulama movements have run schools that have the same syllabus as public schools in addition to their religious curriculum. The State University of Islamic Studies also promotes humanities and social sciences within Islamic education systems.

The curriculum of state schools also deserves attention. UNESCO has been engaged in several projects in Central America, western and southern Africa and southeastern Europe for the promotion of human rights in teacher

States must have the political will to take a stand against intolerance

---

BOX 4.5

United States—targeting intolerance and hatred

The United States has used a mix of strategies to respond to cultural extremism. These strategies have targeted intolerance, but they have not compromised fundamental rights and freedoms.

Protecting freedom of speech and expression
The United States targeted the Ku Klux Klan in the 1920s and American Nazis in the 1930s. But since then the evolution of the US legal system has been towards strongly defending the First Amendment to the Constitution, which guarantees freedom of speech and the right to assemble peaceably. A famous case during the 1970s involved the neo-Nazi National Socialist Party (NSPA), which demanded the right to march in Skokie, Illinois, a town with a large Jewish population. In 1978 the Illinois Supreme Court permitted the NSPA to march, arguing that "[s]peech can be restricted only when it interferes in a physical way with other legitimate activities" (Pehdazur 2001, p. 349).

Recording hate crimes
Yet the United States also has been recording hate crimes for a longer time than many other countries. In 1990 Congress enacted the Hate Crimes Statistics Act and amended it in 1994. Hate crimes are categorized according to the bias-motivation for a criminal act—race, religion, ethnicity, disability and sexual orientation. Law enforcement agencies have several guidelines to objectively determine whether a crime was motivated by a bias—clothing, drawings and symbols, oral and written comments, acts on religious holidays and so forth. Lately, debate has begun on extending the scope of biases considered as hate crimes. A bill was introduced in the Oregon State Senate to extend the law to eco-terrorist and anti-capitalist actions.

Prosecuting militants
In the United States criminal prosecutions and civil law suits have been pursued with vigour against violent racist groups, with long jail sentences handed down to their leaders. Consequently, several groups have become bankrupt and fallen into disarray in recent years—Aryan Nations, the Creativity Movement, Greater Ministries International. Others, like the Hammerskin Nation, have also suffered but continue to pose a threat.

Helping communities
Finally, the Department of Justice has tried to resolve hate crimes at the community level. It established the Community Relations Service in 1964 to provide several services targeted at reducing hate crime activity: mediation to resolve communitywide tensions; technical assistance and training for local officials, police officers and residents on how to recognize hate crimes and share information; public awareness programmes and planning for contingencies such as marches and demonstrations that might exacerbate tensions.

Source: ADL 2003; De Kadt 2004; DoJ 2001; FBI 1999; Levin 2001; Pehdazur 2001.

CONFRONTING MOVEMENTS FOR CULTURAL DOMINATION

To choke off coercive movements for cultural domination, states need to respond constructively, openly and legitimately to the forces that animate them

training programmes. The Asia-Pacific Centre of Education for International Understanding, in the Republic of Korea, develops education curricula to promote understanding of diverse cultures in the region. Cameroon's teacher training programmes include courses on tolerance and international understanding. Subjects like ethics and civics have become compulsory in primary and secondary education. Croatia has begun producing textbooks incorporating human rights education in both national (nursery, primary and secondary) and non-formal education programmes.

Helping communities come to terms with past hatred and violence. Coercive movements, often the product of entrenched historical antagonisms, cannot be wiped out unless these antagonisms are dealt with. South Africa's Truth and Reconciliation Commission set in motion successful efforts in this direction. The use of community institutions (like the Gacaca Courts in Rwanda) appears to have had some success in healing wounds in the community. Communities in Angola and Mozambique are using traditional purification rituals to help traumatized child soldiers re-establish relations with their families and larger communities. In Sweden joint projects between police and schools and youth centres have reduced ethnic tensions and provide alternative activities for youth.[17]

As countries like Afghanistan emerge from violent conflict, efforts to keep coercive movements at bay require strong state institutions (inclusive constitutions, fair legislative processes and independent judiciaries) and sound strategies for reintegration. Over several decades the United States has used such a mix of policies to effectively target racist groups and individuals. Criminal acts are met with force, but fundamental rights have also been protected (box 4.5).

* * *

Movements for cultural domination exist because they tap into people's real grievances and concerns. Wishing them away, pretending they do not exist or simply outlawing them only gives them more legitimacy to grow. To choke off coercive movements for cultural domination, states need to respond constructively, openly and legitimately to the forces that animate them.

CHAPTER 5

Globalization and cultural choice

"I do not want my house to be walled in on all sides and my windows to be stuffed. I want the cultures of all lands to be blown about my house as freely as possible. But I refuse to be blown off my feet by any."

—Mahatma Gandhi[1]

When historians write of the world's recent history, they are likely to reflect on two trends: the advance of globalization and the spread of democracy. Globalization has been the more contentious, because it has effects both good and bad, and democracy has opened space for people to protest the bad effects. So, controversies rage over the environmental, economic and social consequences of globalization. But there is another domain of globalization, that of culture and identity, which is just as controversial and even more divisive because it engages ordinary people, not just economists, government officials and political activists.

Globalization has increased contacts between people and their values, ideas and ways of life in unprecedented ways (feature 5.1). People are travelling more frequently and more widely. Television now reaches families in the deepest rural areas of China. From Brazilian music in Tokyo to African films in Bangkok, to Shakespeare in Croatia, to books on the history of the Arab world in Moscow, to the CNN world news in Amman, people revel in the diversity of the age of globalization.

For many people this new diversity is exciting, even empowering, but for some it is disquieting and disempowering. They fear that their country is becoming fragmented, their values lost as growing numbers of immigrants bring new customs and international trade and modern communications media invade every corner of the world, displacing local culture. Some even foresee a nightmarish scenario of cultural homogenization—with diverse national cultures giving way to a world dominated by Western values and symbols. The questions go deeper. Do economic growth and social progress have to mean adoption of dominant Western values? Is there only one model for economic policy, political institutions and social values?

The fears come to a head over investment, trade and migration policies. Indian activists protest the patenting of the neem tree by foreign pharmaceutical companies. Anti-globalization movements protest treating cultural goods the same as any other commodity in global trade and investment agreements. Groups in Western Europe oppose the entry of foreign workers and their families. What these protesters have in common is the fear of losing their cultural identity, and each contentious issue has sparked widespread political mobilization.

How should governments respond? This chapter argues that policies that regulate the advance of economic globalization—the movements of people, capital, goods and ideas—must promote, rather than quash, cultural freedoms. It looks at three policy challenges that are among the most divisive in today's public debates:

- *Indigenous people, extractive industries and traditional knowledge.* Controversy rages over the importance of extractive industries for national economic growth and the socio-economic and cultural exclusion and dislocation of indigenous people that often accompany mining activities. Indigenous people's traditional knowledge is recognized by the Convention on Biological Diversity but not by the global intellectual property rights regime as embodied in the World Intellectual Property Organization and the Trade-Related Aspects of Intellectual Property Rights agreement.
- *Trade in cultural goods.* International trade and investment negotiations have been divided over the question of a "cultural

Policies that regulate the advance of economic globalization must promote, rather than quash, cultural freedoms

Cross-border flows of investment and knowledge, films and other cultural goods, and people are not new phenomena. Indigenous people have struggled for centuries to maintain their identity and way of life against the tide of foreign economic investment and the new settlers that often come with it. As chapter 2 shows, new settlers have spread their culture, sometimes by design, often by failing to respect indigenous ways of life. Similarly, the free flow of films has been an essential part of the development of the industry since the early 20th century. And people have moved across national borders from the earliest times. International migration has risen in recent decades but is still below 3% of world population, no higher than it was when it last peaked 100 years ago.[1]

What makes these flows a stronger source of identity politics today? Are old problems worsening? Are new problems emerging? Or are people simply freer, with more capacity to claim their rights? For each case, the answer is different but contains an element of all three.

Indigenous people and flows of investment and knowledge

Globalization has accelerated the flows of investment that profoundly affect the livelihoods of many indigenous people. In the last 20 years more than 70 countries have strengthened legislation to promote investment in extractive industries such as oil, gas and mining. Foreign investment in these sectors is up sharply (figure 1). For example, investments in mining exploration and development in Africa doubled between 1990 and 1997.[2]

Because so many of the world's untapped natural resources are located in indigenous people's territories, the global spread of investments in mining and the survival of indigenous people are inextricably linked (see map 5.1 and table 5.1). These trends have increased pressure on indigenous people's territories, resulting in forcible displacement in Colombia, Ghana, Guyana, Indonesia, Malaysia, Peru and the Philippines.[3] If current trends continue, most large mines may end up being on the territory of indigenous people.[4]

Globalization has also heightened demand for knowledge as an economic resource. Indigenous people have a rich resource of traditional knowledge—about plants with

medicinal value, food varieties that consumers demand and other valuable knowledge. Entrepreneurs were quick to see the market potential if they could patent and sell this knowledge. So traditional knowledge is increasingly misappropriated, with many "inventions" falsely awarded patents. Examples include the medicinal properties of the sacred Ayahuasca plant in the Amazon basin (processed by indigenous communities for centuries); the Maca plant in Peru, which enhances fertility (known by Andean Indians when the Spanish arrived in the 16th century); and a pesticidal extract from the neem tree used in India for its antiseptic properties (common knowledge since ancient times).

Developing countries seldom have the resources to challenge false patents in foreign jurisdictions—indigenous people even less so. A March 2000 study concluded that 7,000 patents had been granted for the unauthorized use of traditional knowledge or the misappropriation of medicinal plants.[5]

But indigenous groups are increasingly assertive. Globalization has made it easier for indigenous people to organize, raise funds and network with other groups around the world, with greater political reach and impact than before. The United Nations declared 1995–2004 the International Decade for the World's Indigenous People, and in 2000 the Permanent Forum on Indigenous Issues was created. In August 2003 the Canadian government recognized the ownership claims of the Tlicho Indians over a diamond-rich area in the Northwest Territories. In October 2003 the Constitutional Court of South Africa ruled that indigenous

people had both communal land ownership and mineral rights over their territory and that attempts to dispossess them constituted racial discrimination. Indigenous people now own or control more than 16% of Australia, with the Indigenous Land Corporation expected to be fully funded with a A$1.3 billion capital base, to be used to purchase land for indigenous people unable to gain ownership by other means.[6]

Flows of cultural goods—films and other audiovisual products

The controversy over cultural goods in international trade and investment agreements has intensified because of exponential growth in the quantity of trade, increasing concentration of the film industry in Hollywood and the growing influence of films and entertainment on youth lifestyles.

World trade in cultural goods—cinema, photography, radio and television, printed matter, literature, music and visual arts—quadrupled, from $95 billion in 1980 to more than $380 billion in 1998.[7] About four-fifths of these flows originate in 13 countries.[8] Hollywood reaches 2.6 billion people around the world, and Bollywood 3.6 billion.[9]

In the film industry US productions regularly account for about 85% of film audiences worldwide.[10] In the audiovisual trade with just the European Union, the United States had an $8.1 billion surplus in 2000, divided equally between films and television rights.[11] Of 98 countries around the world with comparable data, only 8 produced more films than they imported annually in the 1990s.[12] China, India and the Philippines are among the largest producers in the number of films per year. But the evidence changes when revenue is considered. Of global production of more than 3,000 films a year Hollywood accounted for more than 35% of total industry revenues. Furthermore, in 1994–98, in 66 of 73 countries with data, the United States was the first or second major country of origin of imported films.[13]

The European film industry, by contrast, has been in decline over the past three decades. Production is down in Italy, which produced 92 films in 1998, and Spain, which produced 85, while remaining unchanged in the United Kingdom and Germany.[14] France is the exception. Production there increased to 183 films in 1998.[15] The share of domestic films

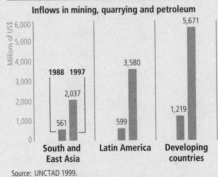

Figure 1 **Rapid increases in investments in extractive industries in developing countries, 1988–97**

Inflows in mining, quarrying and petroleum

South and East Asia: 1988 = 561, 1997 = 2,037
Latin America: 1988 = 599, 1997 = 3,580
Developing countries: 1988 = 1,219, 1997 = 5,671

(Millions of US$)

Source: UNCTAD 1999.

viewed between 1984 and 2001 declined dramatically in much of Europe, with the exception of France and Germany, where policies support the domestic film industry. For the same period, the share of US films increased across most of the continent (figure 2).

The international dominance of US films is just one aspect of the spread of Western consumer culture. New satellite communications technologies in the 1980s gave rise to a powerful new medium with global reach and to such global media networks as CNN. The number of television sets per thousand people worldwide more than doubled, from 113 in 1980 to 229 in 1995. It has grown to 243 since then.[16] Consumption patterns are now global. Market research has identified a "global elite", a global middle class that follows the same consumption style and prefers "global brands". Most striking are "global teens", who inhabit a "global space", a single pop culture world, soaking up the same videos and music and providing a huge market for designer running shoes, t-shirts and jeans.

Flows of people

Policies on immigration have become socially divisive in many countries. Debates are not just about jobs and competition for social welfare resources but about culture—whether immigrants should be required to adopt the language and values of their new society. Why are these issues more prominent today? What has globalization got to do with it?

Globalization is quantitatively and qualitatively reshaping international movements of people, with more migrants going to high-income countries and wanting to maintain their cultural identities and ties with their home countries (table 1).

People have always moved across borders, but the numbers have grown over the last three decades. The number of international migrants—people living outside their country of birth—grew from 76 million in 1960 to 154 million in 1990 and 175 million in 2000.[17] Technological advances make travel and communication easier, faster and cheaper. The price of a plane ticket from Nairobi to London fell from $24,000 in 1960 to $2,000 in 2000.[18] The telephone, the Internet and the global media bring the realities of life across the globe into the living room, making people aware of disparities in wages and living conditions—and eager to improve their prospects.

TABLE 1

Top 10 countries by share of migrant population, 2000
(Percent)

United Arab Emirates	68
Kuwait	49
Jordan	39
Israel	37
Singapore	34
Oman	26
Switzerland	25
Australia	25
Saudi Arabia	24
New Zealand	22

Source: UN 2003a.

Politics also influence the flow of people. Repression can push people to leave; so can greater openness. Political transitions in the former Soviet Union, Eastern Europe and the Baltics made it possible for many people to leave for the first time in decades. But more than the numeric increase, the structure of migration has changed radically.

- *Changing demographics.* For Western Europe, Australia and North America, the growth in migration in the last decade was almost entirely concentrated in flows from

Figure 2

Fewer domestic films, more US films: evolving film attendance, 1984–2001

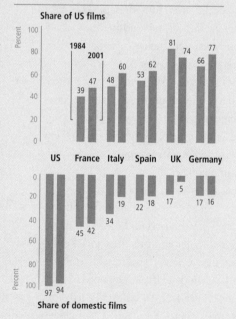

Share of US films

1984
2001

	US	France	Italy	Spain	UK	Germany
US films	39 / 47	48 / 60	53 / 62	81 / 74	66 / 77	
domestic films	97 / 94	45 / 42	34 / 19	22 / 18	17 / 5	17 / 16

Share of domestic films

Source: Cohen 2004.

poor to rich countries. In the 1990s the foreign-born population in more developed regions increased by 23 million.[19] Today, almost 1 in 10 people living in those countries was born elsewhere.[20]

- *Irregular migration* has reached unprecedented levels: up to 30 million people worldwide do not have legal residency status in the country where they live.[21]

- *Circular migration.* People who decide to migrate today are more likely to return to their place of birth, or to move on to a third country, than to stay in the first country to which they migrate. With cheaper communication and travel, migrants stay in closer touch with their home communities.

- *Diaspora network.* Having friends and family abroad makes migration easier. Diaspora networks provide shelter, work and assistance with bureaucracy. So migrants coming from the same country tend to concentrate where others have settled: 92% of Algerian immigrants to Europe live in France, and 81% of Greek immigrants in Germany.[22] Chinese illegal emigration has swelled the diaspora to some 30–50 million people.[23]

- *Remittances.* In little more than 10 years remittances to developing countries went from $30 billion in 1990 to nearly $80 billion in 2002.[24] Remittances sent from Salvadorans abroad amounted to 13.3% of El Salvador's GDP in 2000.[25]

- *Asylum seekers and refugees.* About 9% of the world's migrants are refugees (16 million people). Europe hosted more than 2 million political asylum seekers in 2000, four times more than North America.[26]

- *Feminization.* Women have always migrated as family members, but today more women are migrating alone for work abroad, leaving their families at home. For the Philippines, women made up 70% of migrant workers abroad in 2000.[27]

Source: ATSIA 2003; CSD and ICC 2002; Moody 2000; WIPO 2003d; World Bank 2004; Cohen 2004; Kapur and McHale 2003; IOM 2003b, 2003c, 2004; UN 2002a, 2002b, 2003a.

exception" for films and audiovisual goods, which would permit them to be treated differently from other goods.

- *Immigration*. Managing the inflow and integration of foreign migrants requires responding to anti-immigrant groups, who argue that the national culture is threatened, and to migrant groups, who demand respect for their ways of life.

The extreme positions in these debates often provoke regressive responses that are nationalistic, xenophobic and conservative: close the country off from all outside influences and preserve tradition. That defence of national culture comes at great costs to development and to human choice. This report argues that these extreme positions are not the way to protect local cultures and identities. There need not be a choice between protecting local identities and adopting open policies to global flows of migrants, foreign films and knowledge and capital. The challenge for countries around the world is to design country-specific policies that widen choices rather than narrow them by supporting and protecting national identities while also keeping borders open.

GLOBALIZATION AND MULTICULTURALISM

The impact of globalization on cultural liberty deserves special attention. Previous *Human Development Reports* have addressed sources of economic exclusion, such as trade barriers that keep markets closed to poor countries' exports, and of political exclusion, such as the weak voice of developing countries in trade negotiations. Removing such barriers will not itself eliminate a third type of exclusion: cultural exclusion. That requires new approaches based on multicultural policies.

Global flows of goods, ideas, people and capital can seem a threat to national culture in many ways. They can lead to the abandonment of traditional values and practices and the dismantling of the economic basis on which the survival of indigenous cultures depends. When such global flows lead to cultural exclusion, multicultural policies are needed to manage trade, immigration and investments in ways that recognize cultural differences and identities. And the exclusion of traditional knowledge

from global regimes for intellectual property needs to be explicitly recognized, as does the cultural impact of such goods as films and the cultural identity of immigrants.

The aim of multicultural policies is not to preserve tradition, however, but to protect cultural liberty and expand people's choices—in the ways people live and identify themselves—and not to penalize them for these choices. Preserving tradition can help to keep the options open, but people should not be bound in an immutable box called "a culture". Unfortunately, today's debates about globalization and the loss of cultural identity have often been argued in terms of upholding national sovereignty, preserving the ancient heritage of indigenous people and safeguarding national culture in the face of growing inflows of foreign people, films, music and other goods. But cultural identities are heterogeneous and evolving—they are dynamic processes in which internal inconsistencies and conflicts drive change (box 5.1).

Four principles should inform a strategy for multiculturalism in globalization:

- Defending tradition can hold back human development.
- Respecting difference and diversity is essential.
- Diversity thrives in a globally interdependent world when people have multiple and complementary identities and belong not only to a local community and a country but also to humanity at large.
- Addressing imbalances in economic and political power helps to forestall threats to the cultures of poorer and weaker communities.

DEFENDING TRADITION CAN HOLD BACK HUMAN DEVELOPMENT

The first principle is that tradition should not be confused with freedom of choice. As chapter 1 points out, "To argue for cultural diversity on the ground that this is what the different groups of people have inherited is clearly not reasoning based on cultural liberty". Furthermore, tradition can work against cultural freedom. "Cultural conservatism can discourage—or prevent—people from adopting a different lifestyle, indeed even from joining the lifestyle

The aim of multicultural policies is to protect cultural liberty and expand people's choices—in the ways people live and identify themselves—and not to penalize them for these choices

that others, from a different cultural background, standardly follow in the society in question." There is much to cherish in traditional values and practices, and much that is consonant with universal values of human rights. But there is also much that is challenged by universal ethics, such as inheritance laws that are biased against women, or decision-making procedures that are not participatory and democratic.

Taking the extreme position of preserving tradition at all cost can hold back human development. Some indigenous people fear that their ancient cultural practices are endangered by the inflow of foreign investment in extractive industries or that sharing traditional knowledge necessarily leads to its misuse. Some have reacted to violations of their cultural identity by shutting out all new ideas and change, trying to preserve tradition at all cost. Such reactions reduce not only cultural choices but also social and economic choices for indigenous people. Similarly, anti-immigrant groups often defend national identities in the name of tradition. This narrows their choices as well by shutting countries off from the socio-economic benefits of immigration, which brings new skills and workers to an economy. And defending national cultural industries through protectionism reduces the choices for consumers.

In no society are lifestyles or values static. Anthropologists have discarded concerns with reifying cultures and now see importance in how cultures change, continuously influenced by internal conflicts and contradictions (see box 5.1).

RESPECTING DIVERSITY

The second principle is that diversity is not an end in itself but, as chapter 1 points out, it promotes cultural liberty and enriches people's lives. It is an outcome of the freedoms people have and the choices they make. It also implies an opportunity to assess different options in making these choices. If local cultures disappear and countries become homogeneous, the scope for choice is reduced.

Much of the fear of a loss of national identity and culture comes from the belief that cultural diversity inevitably leads to conflict or to failed development. As chapter 2 explains, this is a myth:

BOX 5.1

Culture—paradigm shift in anthropology

For many years, defining cultural and social anthropology as the study of the cultural dimension of people would have raised few objections. "A culture" was understood as synonymous with what before had been called "a people".

During the past two decades, however, the concept of "culture", and by extension the idea of "cultural difference" and the underlying assumptions of homogeneity, holism and integrity, have been re-evaluated. Cultural difference is no longer viewed as a stable, exotic otherness. Self-other relations are increasingly considered to be matters of power and rhetoric rather than essence. And cultures are increasingly conceived of as reflecting processes of change and internal contradictions and conflicts.

But just as anthropologists were losing faith in the concept of coherent, stable and bounded cultural "wholes", the concept was being embraced by a wide range of culture builders worldwide. Anthropological works are increasingly being consulted by people trying to assign to groups the kinds of generalized cultural identities that anthropologists now find deeply problematic. Today, politicians, economists and the general public want culture defined in precisely the bounded, reified, essentialized and timeless fashion recently discarded by anthropologists.

Culture and cultural diversity have become political and juridical realities, as stated in the first Article of the UNESCO Universal Declaration on Cultural Diversity (2001): "cultural diversity is as necessary for humankind as biodiversity is for nature. In this sense, it is the common heritage of humanity and should be recognized and affirmed for the benefit of present and future generations". Many people have grasped at least part of the anthropological message: culture is there, it is learned, it permeates everyday life, it is important and it is far more responsible for differences among human groups than are genes.

Source: Preis 2004 citing Brumann 1999; Clifford 1988; Rosaldo 1989; Olwig, Fog and Hastrup 1997; UNESCO 2002.

---

it is not diversity that inevitably leads to conflict but the suppression of cultural identity and social, political and economic exclusion on the basis of culture that can spark violence and tensions. People may be fearful of diversity and its consequences, but it is opposition to diversity—as in the positions of anti-immigrant groups—that can polarize societies and that fuels social tensions.

DEVELOPING MULTIPLE AND COMPLEMENTARY IDENTITIES—LIVING LOCALLY AND GLOBALLY

The third principle is that globalization can expand cultural freedoms only if all people develop multiple and complementary identities as citizens of the world as well as citizens of a state and members of a cultural group. Just as a culturally diverse state can build unity on multiple and complementary identities (chapter 3), a culturally diverse world needs to do the same. As globalization proceeds, this means not only recognizing local and national identities but also strengthening commitments to being citizens of the world.

Today's intensified global interactions can function well only if governed by bonds of shared values, communication and commitment. Cooperation among people and nations with different interests is more likely when all are bound and motivated by shared values and commitments. Global culture is not about the English language or brand name sneakers—it is about universal ethics based on universal human rights and respect for the freedom, equality and dignity of all individuals (box 5.2).

Today's interactions also require respect for difference—respect for the cultural heritage of the thousands of cultural groups in the world. Some people believe that there are contradictions between the values of some cultural traditions and advances in development and democracy. As chapter 2 shows, there is no objective evidence for claiming that some cultures are "inferior" or "superior" for human progress and the expansion of human freedoms.

States develop national identities not only to unify the population but also to project an identity different from that of others. But unchanging notions of identity can lead to morbid mistrust of people and things foreign—to wanting to bar immigrants, fearing that they would not be loyal to their adopted country or its values, or wanting to block flows of cultural goods and ideas, fearing that homogenizing forces would destroy their national arts and heritage. But identities are seldom singular. Multiple and complementary identities are a reality in many countries—and people have a sense of belonging to the country as well as to a group or groups within it.

ADDRESSING ASYMMETRIC POWER

The fourth principle is that asymmetries in flows of ideas and goods need to be addressed, so that some cultures do not dominate others because of their economic power. The unequal economic and political powers of countries, industries and corporations cause some cultures to spread, others to wither. Hollywood's powerful film industry, with access to enor-

Multiple and complementary identities are a reality in many countries

---

BOX 5.2

Sources of global ethics

All cultures share a commonality of basic values that are the foundation of global ethics. That individuals can have multiple and complementary identities suggests that they can find these commonalities of values.

Global ethics are not the imposition of "Western" values on the rest of the world. To think so would be both artificially restrictive of the scope of global ethics and an insult to other cultures, religions and communities. The principal source of global ethics is the idea of human vulnerability and the desire to alleviate the suffering of every individual to the extent possible. Another source is the belief in the basic moral equality of all human beings. The injunction to treat others as you would want to be treated finds explicit mention in Buddhism, Christianity, Confucianism, Hinduism, Islam, Judaism, Taoism and Zoroastrianism, and it is implicit in the practices of other faiths.

It is on the basis of these common teachings across all cultures that states have come together to endorse the Universal Declaration of Human Rights, supported by the International Covenants on Civil and Political Rights and on Economic and Social Rights. Regional treaties, such as the European Convention for the Protection of Human Rights, the American Convention of Human Rights and the African Charter on Human and People's Rights, have taken similar initiatives. More recently, the UN's Millennium Declaration, adopted by the full membership of the General Assembly in 2000, recommitted itself to human rights, fundamental freedoms and respect for equal rights to all without distinction.

There are five core elements of global ethics.
- *Equity.* Recognizing the equality of all individuals regardless of class, race, gender, community or generation is the ethos of universal values. Equity also envelops the need to preserve the environment and natural resources that can be used by future generations.
- *Human rights and responsibilities.* Human rights are an indispensable standard of international conduct. The basic concern is to protect the integrity of all individuals from threats to freedom and equality. The focus on individual rights acknowledges their expression of equity between individuals, which outweighs any claims made on behalf of group and collective values. But with rights come duties: bonds without options are oppressive; options without bonds are anarchy.

- *Democracy.* Democracy serves multiple ends: providing political autonomy, safeguarding fundamental rights and creating conditions for the full participation of citizens in economic development. At the global level democratic standards are essential for ensuring participation and giving voice to poor countries, marginalized communities and discriminated against minorities.
- *Protection of minorities.* Discrimination against minorities occurs at several levels: non-recognition, denial of political rights, socio-economic exclusion and violence. Global ethics cannot be comprehensive unless minorities receive recognition and equal rights within a larger national and global community. The promotion of tolerance is central to the process.
- *Peaceful conflict resolution and fair negotiation.* Justice and fairness cannot be achieved by imposing pre-conceived moral principles. Resolution of disagreements must be sought through negotiations. All parties deserve a say. Global ethics does not mean a single path towards peace or development or modernization. It is a framework within which societies can find peaceful solutions to problems.

Source: World Commission on Culture and Development 1995; UN 2000a.

Indigenous peoples and development

Development divorced from its human or cultural context is growth without a soul. Economic development in its full flowering is part of a people's culture.

—World Commission on Culture
and Development 1995

Indigenous peoples are proponents and representatives of humanity's cultural diversity. Historically, however, indigenous peoples have been marginalized by dominant societies and have often faced assimilation and cultural genocide.

In the multicultural societies growing up around them, indigenous peoples seek an end to such marginalization and fringe dwelling. They have much to contribute to society, and they bring to both national and international debates valuable advice about the great issues facing humanity in this new millennium.

In May 2003 the Permanent Forum on Indigenous Issues stressed in its Second Session the importance of recognizing cultural diversity in development processes and the need for all development to be sustainable. Recommendation 8 of the Second Session calls for "instituting a legal framework that makes cultural, environmental and social impact assessment studies mandatory" (E/2003/43). The forum also expressed concern over development practices that do not take into account the characteristics of indigenous communities as groups, thus significantly undermining meaningful ways of participatory development.

Indigenous peoples have dynamic living cultures and seek their place in the modern world. They are not against development, but for too long they have been victims of development and now demand to be participants in—and to benefit from—a development that is sustainable.

Ole Henrik Magga
*Chairman of the UN Permanent
Forum on Indigenous Issues*

---

mous resources, can squeeze the Mexican film industry and other small competitors out of existence. Powerful corporations can outbid indigenous people in using land rich in resources. Powerful countries can outnegotiate weak countries in recognition of traditional knowledge in World Trade Organization (WTO) agreements. Powerful and exploitative employers can victimize defenceless migrants.

FLOWS OF INVESTMENT AND KNOWLEDGE— INCLUDING INDIGENOUS PEOPLE IN A GLOBALLY INTEGRATED WORLD

Indigenous people see globalization as a threat to their cultural identities, their control over territory and their centuries-old traditions of knowledge and artistic expression (see feature 5.1). They fear that the cultural significance of their territories and knowledge will go unrecognized—or that they will receive inadequate compensation for these cultural assets. In these situations globalization is often blamed.

One reaction is to opt out of the global economy and to oppose the flows of goods and ideas. Another is to preserve tradition for its own sake, without accounting for individual choice or democratic decision-making. But there are alternatives. Preserving cultural identity need not require staying out of the global economy. There are ways of ensuring the cultural and socio-economic inclusion of indigenous people based on respect for cultural traditions and the sharing of the economic benefits of resource use.

WHY DO SOME INDIGENOUS PEOPLE FEEL THREATENED?

Central to ensuring the inclusion of indigenous people in a global world are how national governments and international institutions deal with investments in indigenous territories and protect traditional knowledge. The historical territories of indigenous people are often rich in minerals and oil and gas deposits (map 5.1, table 5.1 and feature 5.1). That can set up the potential for conflict between promoting national economic growth through extractive industries and protecting the cultural identity and economic livelihood of indigenous people. The traditional knowledge, innovations and practices of indigenous people, developed over many generations and collectively owned by the community, can have practical uses in agriculture, forestry and health. Conflict can arise between recognizing collective ownership and following the modern intellectual property regime, which focuses on individual rights.

Extractive industries. The cultural identity and socio-economic equity of indigenous people can be threatened in several ways by the activities of extractive industries. First, there is inadequate recognition of the cultural significance of the land and territories that indigenous

TABLE 5.1
Indigenous population in Latin America
Percent

Country	Share of total population
Bolivia	71.0
Guatemala	66.0
Peru	47.0
Ecuador	38.0
Honduras	15.0
Mexico	14.0
Panama	10.0
Chile	8.0
El Salvador	7.0
Nicaragua	5.0
Colombia	1.8
Paraguay	1.5
Argentina	1.0
Venezuela	0.9
Costa Rica	0.8
Brazil	0.4
Uruguay	0.4

Source: De Ferranti and others 2003.

Map
5.1 **Much extractive and infrastructural activity in developing countries is in areas where indigenous people live**

Latin America, 2003

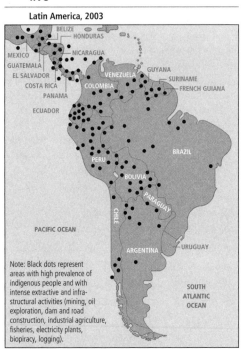

Note: Black dots represent areas with high prevalence of indigenous people and with intense extractive and infrastructural activities (mining, oil exploration, dam and road construction, industrial agriculture, fisheries, electricity plants, biopiracy, logging).

South-East Asia and Pacific, 2003

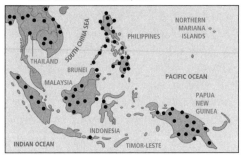

Source: Tebtebba and International Forum on Globalization 2003.

people inhabit. Indigenous people have strong spiritual connections to their land, which is why some of them oppose any investment in extractive industries within their territories. For instance, some groups of San Bushmen in Botswana oppose the exploration licences that the government has granted to Kalahari Diamonds Ltd.

Second, there is plausible concern about the impact of extractive industries on local livelihoods. When mineral extraction leads to the widespread displacement of communities and loss of their farmlands, it affects both their sense of cultural identity and their source of sustainable livelihood. The Lihir Gold Mine in Papua New Guinea has destroyed sacred sites of the

Lihirians and sharply reduced their ability to subsist by hunting game.

Third, indigenous groups complain about unfair exclusion from decision-making. And when consultations with local communities do occur, they often leave much to be desired. Keeping such concerns in mind, the World Bank used a new approach to support the Chad–Cameroon Pipeline project.[2] By law, net incomes were to be deposited in an offshore account to ensure annual publication of audits and reduce corruption. Further, 10% of revenues were earmarked for a Future Generations Fund. Civil society representatives and a member of the opposition were to be part of a monitoring board. The project had to comply with the Bank's safeguard policies on environmental assessments and resettlement. And two new national parks were planned to compensate for the loss of a small forest area. The project highlights the innovative steps international institutions are taking to build capacity and transparency and ensure targeted benefit sharing. But some indigenous groups believe that this has been inadequate. Fewer than 5% of the Bagyéli people affected by the pipeline were employed on the project. They received little compensation and few of the promised health care facilities.[3] In countries with very weak institutional structures, project partners face major challenges in effectively implementing well conceived projects. This does not mean that investments need to be stopped; rather, even greater efforts are needed.

Fourth, indigenous people feel cheated when their physical resources are misappropriated without adequate compensation. There was very limited involvement of local people on the Yanacocha gold mine in the Cajamarca region in Peru (a joint venture between Peruvian and US mining companies and the International Finance Corporation). Some of the tax revenues were to go to the indigenous inhabitants, but they received less than they were promised.[4] Ecuador is home to one of the largest confirmed oil reserves in Latin America. Companies pay about $30 million in taxes for a special Amazon development fund, but little of that money reaches the indigenous communities.[5]

These issues highlight the conflict between national sovereignty over resources and the special rights of indigenous people to their territories and the mineral resources they contain. For instance, Ecuador's Constitution does not give native Indians any rights to the oil and gas within their territories. While it is not necessary that such rights be constitutionally guaranteed, it is necessary that indigenous people have a say in the use of resources within their territories.

Traditional knowledge. The traditional knowledge of indigenous groups has attributes of communal ownership and sometimes has spiritual significance. Intellectual property regimes fail to recognize either the community ownership or spiritual significance of traditional knowledge. The laws protect the work of individual, identifiable authors or inventors and spell out how others can use their work. The Quechua Indians in Peru oppose the commercial exploitation of their traditional knowledge but can do little about it. The Maori in New Zealand believe that even when their knowledge is publicly disclosed, there is no automatic right to use it—that right must be determined collectively.

There is also a danger of wrongly awarding intellectual property rights, so that communities that have produced, preserved or developed traditional knowledge over several generations are not compensated for its use. To qualify for patent protection an invention must fulfil three strict criteria: it must be novel, not obvious and industrially useful. Since traditional knowledge does not always meet these criteria, the international intellectual property regime does not explicitly protect it. Researchers can appropriate traditional knowledge and apply for a patent, claiming to have invented a new product. Copyright protection can also be wrongly awarded for the appropriation.

Misappropriation of traditional knowledge need not be deliberate. Sometimes it arises from mistakenly treating traditional knowledge as part of the public domain, where intellectual property protection does not apply. Traditional knowledge, because it is known publicly within the community (and sometimes outside it), is more prone to appropriation without compensation to the community that developed it than are other types of intellectual property. The Sami Council of Scandinavia argues that even if its knowledge is publicly known, the public domain principle ignores obligations to the community.

The Convention on Biological Diversity recognizes traditional knowledge, in contrast to the global intellectual property rights regime administered under the World Intellectual Property Organization (WIPO) and the agreement on Trade-Related Aspects of Intellectual Property Rights (TRIPS). Article 8(j) stipulates that contracting parties must preserve and maintain the knowledge and innovations of indigenous and local communities. It also seeks the wider application of traditional knowledge "with the approval and involvement of the holders of such knowledge" and encourages "equitable sharing of the benefits". Article 10(c) of the convention encourages the "customary use of biological resources in accord with traditional cultural practices". The issue, then, is to find ways to reconcile the provisions of different international intellectual property regimes in order to protect traditional knowledge for the benefit of the indigenous community and promote its appropriate use within wider society.

POLICY OPTIONS AND CHALLENGES FOR PROTECTING RIGHTS AND SHARING BENEFITS

The solution is not to block flows of investment or knowledge or to preserve tradition for its own sake. Human development aims at expanding an individual's choices, through growth that favours the poor and through equitable socio-economic opportunities within a democratic framework that protects liberties. Addressing the concerns of indigenous people will require global, national and corporate policies that advance human development goals (box 5.3).

International institutions are already looking for ways to mitigate some of the problems. In 2001 the World Bank commissioned an extractive industries review to determine how such projects can assist in poverty reduction and sustainable development. Based on discussions with governments, non-governmental organizations, indigenous people's organizations, industry, labour unions and academia, the 2004 report recommends pro-poor public and corporate governance, effective social and environmental policies and respect for human

The solution is not to block flows of investment or knowledge or to preserve tradition for its own sake. Human development aims at expanding an individual's choices

Private companies and indigenous people can work together for development

Is it possible for private companies to work co-operatively with indigenous people and to gain in the process? Yes. Consider these examples.

Pilbara region, Australia

Hamersley Iron Pty Ltd has been exporting ore from the natural resource–rich Pilbara region since the mid-1960s. While Aboriginal populations remained concentrated in welfare-dependent towns, the company's need for skilled labour led to a massive influx into the region of non-indigenous people. The Aboriginal groups began to oppose the development of newer mines and demanded discussions on the company's activities on traditional lands. In 1992 Hamersley established the Aboriginal Training and Liaison Unit, to provide job training, increase business development in the area and improve infrastructure and living conditions while preserving the aboriginal heritage and culture. By 1997 the Gumala Aboriginal Corporation had signed joint venture agreements with Hamersley to develop newer mines. Aboriginal men

would receive training in operating machinery, and services would be contracted to the local communities. Hamersley would contribute more than A$60 million for these purposes.

Raglan project, Canada

After a 1975 agreement to settle land ownership issues in northern Quebec between indigenous groups and the provincial and federal governments, the Inuit received financial compensation to set up the Makivik Corporation as a heritage fund. In 1993 Makivik signed a Memorandum of Understanding with Falconbridge Ltd (later the Raglan Agreement) to guarantee benefits from planned mining projects in the region, including priority employment and contracts for the Inuit, profit sharing and environmental monitoring. Falconbridge will pay an estimated C$70 million to an Inuit trust fund over 18 years. Archaeological sites were also identified and marked as off limits to mining, and the rights of Inuit employees to hunt outside the Raglan site were assured.

Red Dog Mine, United States

In the 1970s the Inupiat people of Northwest Alaska successfully blocked Cominco Inc.'s interest in exploiting zinc-lead deposits at the Red Dog site. After several years of negotiations the Northwest Alaska Native Association (NANA) and Cominco signed an agreement in 1982 to allow mining to go forward. Cominco agreed to compensate the Inupiat through royalties, to include NANA representatives in an advisory committee, to employ indigenous people and to protect the environment. In lieu of taxes Red Dog would pay $70 million into the Northwest Arctic Borough over 24 years. By 1998 Cominco had invested $8.8 million in technical training almost entirely for NANA shareholders employed in the project. NANA has also monitored the impact on subsistence activities and forced efforts to reduce effluent flows into streams. Cominco has maintained a flexible work schedule that allows Inupiat employees to continue their traditional way of life.

Source: International Council on Metals and the Environment 1999.

rights. WIPO's General Assembly established an Intergovernmental Committee on Intellectual Property and Genetic Resources, Traditional Knowledge and Folklore in October 2000. It is reviewing mechanisms for protecting traditional knowledge while increasing the participation of indigenous people.

States and international institutions need to collaborate in continuing to adjust global rules and national laws in ways that more successfully take into account the concerns of indigenous people, giving them a genuine stake in the flows of investments, ideas and knowledge. Three measures are essential:

- Explicitly recognizing indigenous people's rights over their physical and intellectual property.
- Requiring consultations with indigenous communities and their participation for the use of any resource, thus ensuring informed consent.
- Empowering communities by developing strategies to share benefits.

Loans to companies or countries for projects that wrongly appropriate property must be withdrawn, and patents granted to others who

have misappropriated traditional knowledge should be revoked.

Recognizing rights. Many states have laws that explicitly recognize indigenous people's rights over their resources. In a 2002 report the UK Commission on Intellectual Property Rights argued that national legislation is needed to address specific circumstances. The Philippines has laws requiring informed consent for access to ancestral lands and indigenous knowledge and for equitable sharing of benefits. Guatemalan law promotes the wider use of traditional knowledge and cultural expressions by placing them under state protection. Bangladesh, the Philippines and the African Union recognize the customary practices of communities and the community-based rights to biological resources and associated traditional knowledge.

Requiring participation and consultation. Including the local community in decision-making is not only democratic—it also ensures against future disruption of projects. Having learned from the Yanacocha mine, the Antamina zinc and copper mine in Peru involved indigenous communities in decision-making at the start of operations in 2001. But consultations have to be meaningful. This requires carefully identifying the affected groups and providing full information about the likely costs and benefits of a project.

Consultations can also prevent the false appropriation of genetic resources and traditional knowledge. Countries now demand disclosure of the origin of plants and other genetic material before granting patents. The Andean Communities, Costa Rica and India, among others, include this provision in laws and regulations.

Documenting traditional knowledge is often essential for protecting it, as is being done by the Traditional Knowledge Digital Library in India and a similar initiative in China. Lao PDR has a Traditional Medicines Resource Centre. In Africa, where much traditional knowledge is oral, documentation would diminish possibilities for uncompensated exploitation of knowledge. But in Latin America some indigenous people worry that documentation, by making their knowledge more accessible, would facilitate exploitation.

Documentation does not prejudice rights. It preserves knowledge in written form and prevents others from claiming it as their own. WIPO has an Online Portal of Databases and Registries of Traditional and Genetic Resources for use by patent examiners. The Consultative Group on International Agricultural Research has linked its information to the portal. And India has contributed its Health Heritage Test Database.

Sharing benefits. Opportunities for benefit sharing in extractive industries are extensive, including education, training, preferential employment for local people, financial compensation, business opportunities and environmental commitments. In Papua New Guinea, where indigenous communities own 97% of the land, small mining projects have assisted in poverty alleviation. At the Bulolo mine a well planned closure allowed the mining company to use its infrastructure to develop a timber plantation—which remains financially viable 35 years after the mine was closed.[6] Companies in other countries have also had success involving local communities in decision-making and profit sharing.

While multilateral negotiations on protecting traditional knowledge within the intellectual property rights regime continue, countries are discovering ways of using existing systems to do so (box 5.4). Industrial designs protect carpets and headdresses in Kazakhstan. Geographical indications protect liquors and teas in Venezuela

Documenting traditional knowledge is often essential for protecting it

---

BOX 5.4

Using intellectual property rights to protect traditional knowledge

Respecting traditional knowledge does not mean keeping it from the world. It means using it in ways that benefit the communities from which it is drawn.

Australia's intellectual property rights laws do not cover traditional knowledge, but certification trademarks are used to identify and authenticate products or services provided by indigenous people. In the 1995 *Milpurrurru* case—Aboriginal designs were reproduced on carpets without prior consent—an Australian court judged that "cultural harm" had been caused due to trademark violation and awarded compensation of A$70,000 (WIPO 2003c). In the 1998 *Bulun Bulun* case a court judgement found that an indigenous person owed fiduciary obligations to his community and could not exploit indigenous art contrary to the community's customary law.

In Canada trademarks are used to protect traditional symbols, including food products, clothing and tourist services run by First Nations.

The Copyright Act protects tradition-based creations like woodcarvings, songs and sculptures. In 1999 the Snuneymuxw First Nation used the Trademarks Act to protect 10 religious petroglyphs (ancient rock paintings) from unauthorized reproduction and to stop the sale of goods bearing these images.

Other countries have explicitly recognized traditional knowledge and customary legal systems. Greenland retains its Inuit legal tradition within its Home Rule Government. Over the past 150 years written Inuit literature has documented cultural heritage. Cultural heritage is treated as dynamic and not restricted to traditional aspects alone. Both traditional and modern cultural expressions are respected and enjoy equal protection under law.

A more celebrated case involves the San Bushmen of southern Africa. An anthropologist noticed in 1937 that the San ate the Hoodia cactus to stave off hunger and thirst. Based on this knowledge the South African Council for Scientific and Industrial Research (CSIR) in 1995 patented the Hoodia cactus's appetite-suppressing element (P57). By 1998 revenues from the licensing fee for developing and marketing P57 as a slimming drug had risen to $32 million (Commission on Intellectual Property Rights 2002). When the San alleged biopiracy and threatened legal action in 2002, the CSIR agreed to share future royalties with the San.

Recognition of traditional culture can occur at the regional level as well. Article 136(g) of Decision 486 of the Commission of the Andean Community states that signs may not be registered as marks if they consist of the names of indigenous, Afro-American or local communities. The Colombian government used Article 136(g) to reject an application for registration of the term "Tairona", citing it as an invaluable heritage of the country—the Taironas inhabited Colombian territory in the pre-Hispanic period.

Source: Commission on Intellectual Property Rights 2002; WIPO 2003c.

and Viet Nam. Copyrights and trademarks are used for traditional art in Australia and Canada. In many cases these measures have resulted in monetary benefits for the community as well.

Discussions at WIPO are focusing on how to complement intellectual property provisions with unique national approaches. One proposal—the compensatory liability approach—envisages rights for both the patent owner and the owner of traditional knowledge. While the patent owner would have to seek a compulsory licence to use the traditional knowledge resource, the owner would also have the right to commercialize the patented invention after paying royalties to the patent owner. This mechanism avoids restricting scientific progress and makes benefit sharing economically significant.

By promoting flows of investments and knowledge, globalization can bring recognition to indigenous people who have developed their resources over the centuries. But national and international rules on global trade and investment must also account for the cultural sensitivities and customary property rights of indigenous people. Respecting cultural identity and promoting socio-economic equity through participation and benefit sharing are possible as long as decisions are made democratically—by

Globalization can bring recognition to indigenous people who have developed their resources over the centuries

states, by companies, by international institutions and by indigenous people.

FLOWS OF CULTURAL GOODS—WIDENING CHOICES THROUGH CREATIVITY AND DIVERSITY

During the 1994 countdown to the Uruguay Round of multilateral trade negotiations, a group of French movie producers, actors and directors was able to insert a "cultural exception" clause in trade rules, excluding cinema and other audiovisual goods from their provisions. The clause acknowledges the special nature of cultural goods as traded commodities. The Uruguay Round text provided a precedent for other trade agreements to allow countries to exempt cultural goods from trade agreements and adopt policies to protect such industries at home. Some exceptions for trade in cultural goods were written into the North American Free Trade Agreement (NAFTA) in 1994. In the acrimonious debates over the Multilateral Agreement on Investments in the OECD in 1998 the cultural exception was one of the most bitterly contested issues, propelling the collapse of negotiations (box 5.5).

At the preparatory meetings in Cancun for the Doha Round in 2003 negotiations reportedly foundered over the Singapore Issues—trade facilitation, transparency in government procurement, trade and investment, and trade and competition.[7] The United States had asked for a freeze on the extension of the cultural exception, to avoid bringing Internet-related audiovisual activities into the negotiations. The Free Trade Area of the Americas ministerial meeting in Miami in November 2003 faced similar challenges for cultural goods, and no clear agreement was reached.

So, whether to treat cultural goods like any other commercial good or to make them an exception has become a hotly contested issue in international trade negotiations. Positions remain polarized. On one side are those who consider cultural products as commercial as apples or cars and therefore subject to all the rules of international trade. On the other side are those who view cultural products as assets conveying values, ideas and meaning and therefore deserving of special treatment.

BOX 5.5

The debate on cultural goods and the Multilateral Agreement on Investments fiasco

After the Uruguay Round of trade negotiations ended in 1994, some countries wanted to set up a mechanism to liberalize, regulate and enforce global investment flows. This set the stage in 1998 for the Multilateral Agreement on Investments (MAI). The objective was to create a single multilateral regulatory framework to replace some 1,600 bilateral investment treaties. Among other provisions the MAI aimed at introducing the "national treatment" principle of non-discrimination to investment rules and foreign investors. Country of origin would have ceased to be a factor when applying rules on investment and trade in services in order to stop discrimination against foreign investment and facilitate its flows.

As the MAI was being negotiated within the OECD, though, a number of countries inserted exceptions and reservations that weakened the initiative. Concerned about the effect that MAI could have on cultural industries and fearing loss of leeway to subsidize or protect national industries, France introduced clauses for cultural industries. Motivated by a number of objections to the negotiations, including the treatment of cultural goods like any other merchandise, non-governmental groups in Australia, Canada, India, New Zealand, the United Kingdom and the United States joined the French government's campaign against the agreement. The initiative collapsed, demonstrating how contentious these issues are and complicating future talks on trade in services and investment that affect countries' cultural diversity.

Source: UNESCO 2000b, 2000c; Public Citizen 2004.

The cultural exception has mobilized public support that politicians find difficult to ignore. The cultural exception touches people's concerns that their national cultures might be swept away by the economic forces of the global market, threatening their cultural identity. The most extreme advocates of the cultural exception fear that foreign films and television programmes will spread foreign culture and eventually obliterate local cultures and traditional values.

No doubt nationalism, traditionalism and economic advantage motivate many who advocate banning foreign products. But are the fears of those who predict a narrowing of cultural choices justified? In fact, free flows of foreign products widen cultural choices and do not necessarily weaken commitment to the national culture. Teenagers the world over listen to rap, but that has not meant the death of classical music or local folk music traditions. Attempts to close off foreign influences have had limited impact. Not until 1998 did the Republic of Korea gradually start to lift a half-century-old ban on Japanese music and film. Yet it is very likely that Koreans had access to Japanese pop culture, particularly animation and *manga* (comic books), well before the ban was eased. Restricting foreign influence does not promote cultural freedom. But that does not mean that cultural goods are not different in some ways from other commercial goods.

Why are cultural goods different? Cultural goods convey ideas, symbols and lifestyles and are an intrinsic part of the identity of the community that produces them. There is little disagreement that cultural products need some public support to flourish. Subsidies for museums, ballet, libraries and other cultural products and services are widespread and accepted in all free market economies.

The disagreement is over whether films and audiovisual products are cultural goods or merely entertainment. While it can be debated whether cinema and television programmes have intrinsic artistic value, it is clear that they are cultural goods in that they are symbols of ways of life. Films and audiovisual products are powerful conveyors of lifestyles and carry social messages (see feature 5.1). They can have a powerful cultural impact. Indeed, they are contested precisely because of their impact on choices about identity.[8]

Why do cultural goods need public support? The reasons behind the arguments for public intervention have to do with the way cultural goods are consumed and produced. Both give advantage to large economies and large industries with access to large financial resources and lead to asymmetric flows of films and television programmes (figure 5.1).[9]

- *Cultural goods are experience goods.* Cultural products are consumed through experience: because of the subjective nature of these goods, consumers will not know whether they like the good until after they have consumed it. So prices will not reflect the quality of the product or the satisfaction it is likely to give to the consumer. Marketing campaigns, advertising and commercial reviews—amplified by word of mouth—are consumers' principal sources of information, giving a massive advantage to producers with greater command over resources for marketing and distribution. Many small local producers will struggle to access the market, particularly producers operating from developing countries.

Whether to treat cultural goods like any other commercial good has become a hotly contested issue

Figure 5.1 **Top-grossing films of all time at the international (non-US) box office were US films, April 2004**

Rank	US Films	Year	Country of origin	Total gross revenue (millions of US$)
1	Titanic	1997	US	1,235
2	Lord of the Rings: The Return of the King	2003	US	696
3	Harry Potter and the Sorcerer's Stone	2001	US	651
4	Harry Potter and the Chamber of Secrets	2002	US	604
5	Lord of the Rings: The Two Towers	2002	US	581
6	Jurassic Park	1993	US	563
7	Lord of the Rings: The Fellowship of the Ring	2001	US	547
8	Finding Nemo	2003	US	513
9	Independence Day	1996	US	505
10	Star Wars: Episode I: The Phantom Menace	1999	US	491
	Non-US Films			
44	Sen to Chihiro no kamikakushi	2001	Japan	254
69	The Full Monty	1997	UK	211
86	Four Weddings and a Funeral	1994	UK	191
96	Bridget Jones' Diary	2001	UK	183

Source: The Internet Movie Database 2004.

- *Large producers can benefit from economies of scale.* Smaller and less well financed producers are penalized in these markets because they cannot enjoy the economies of scale that characterize many cultural industries, especially films and other audiovisual products.[10] The cost of making a movie is the same whether it is shown one time or a million times. The more times it is shown, the higher the returns. When the film reaches a big market—thanks to large domestic demand, widespread understanding of the language spoken in the film and strong advertising campaigns—it is much likelier to become an international success. The same is true for other cultural goods. Countries and corporations with greater financial leverage can benefit from these economies of scale by capturing large markets and enjoying their exclusive advantages in markets with few other large producers (table 5.2).

POLICY OPTIONS AND CHALLENGES—
PROTECTION OR PROMOTION?

For these reasons, cultural products and creative activities, if left to the market, could wither and diversity could decline. What is the solution? Cultural protectionism and quotas? Or production subsidies?

Protection. As argued in past *Human Development Reports,* raising barriers to reduce flows of imports can be problematic, a conclusion that applies to trade in cultural goods as well. Trade barriers to reduce or block imports defeat the expansion of diversity and choice. Yet many countries have set production and broadcasting quotas for locally produced programmes on radio, television and films to guarantee a minimum market share. Hungary has a quota of 15% for national programmes on public channels.[11] And the Republic of Korea's screen quota system, based on minimum days of domestic projections each year, probably contributed to the increase in domestic market share and exports.

But aggressive quota-based policies have not always resulted in greater variety and choice. Some critics point out that high quotas make local producers depend more on quotas and less on holding production costs down. Some also argue that protection can reduce the quality of goods.[12]

Promotion. Some countries have successfully maintained healthy cultural industries while also keeping trade links open. Argentina and Brazil offer financial incentives to help domestic industries, including tax breaks. In Hungary 6% of television receipts go to the production of Hungarian films. France spends some $400 million a year to support its film industry, one of the few thriving in Europe, producing more than 180

TABLE 5.2
Policy choices for the promotion of the domestic film and audiovisual industry—market and industry size matter

	Advantages	Disadvantages	Policy solutions
Large producing countries (more than 200 productions)	Large home markets, expanding broadcasting audiences allow higher returns	Lowers market competition and the production of cultural and artistic films	Specialized taxation incentives to encourage independent film-makers and specialized distributors to make more films
Medium-size producing countries (from 20 to 199 productions)	State and legal financial support guarantee the existence of a national infrastructure and markets, allowing for a public sector role and higher quality films	National legal protectionism could impede international free film trade	New international legal frameworks to allow better and more balanced exchanges, expanding national production capacities
Small producing countries (fewer than 20 productions)	Creativity does not suffer from high technical and organizational competition or financial constraints; the very limited financing does not seek immediate returns	Small domestic markets reflect a structural lack of investment in the film industry, limiting the number of national productions; unfair asymmetric international trade practices also diminish domestic production	As with communications and computer technologies, digital technologies can create new and less expensive production opportunities, thus overcoming distribution and production bottlenecks

Source: Human Development Report Office based on UNESCO 200a.

films annually (box 5.6 and feature 5.1).[13, 14] The French-German worldwide success, *Le Fabuleux Destin d'Amélie Poulain,* shows the possibilities for cross-border co-productions.[15]

Studios and equipment can also be supported. Since 1996 the Egypt Film Society has built film studios with financing from a private-public partnership. Other developing economies are trying to do the same. As with all subsidies, there are challenges to make them work. Who should decide on the criteria for making grants? How should such decisions be made? The measures depend largely on the size of the domestic market (see table 5.2).

The 2001 Declaration on Cultural Diversity of the United Nations Educational, Scientific and Cultural Organization (UNESCO) set the stage for a number of international initiatives to encourage action in setting standards for cultural diversity, including the Round Table on Cultural Diversity and Biodiversity for Sustainable Development, the Summit on the Francophonie, the annual Meeting of the International Network on Cultural Policy and the UN resolution proclaiming 21 May as "World Day for Cultural Diversity for Dialogue and Development". Preparatory work has begun for a legally binding convention to secure the diversity of cultural expression.

The emergence or consolidation of cultural industries should also be supported. Cooperation can support development of the necessary infrastructure and skills to create domestic markets and help local cultural products reach global markets. Small business incubators can encourage small and medium-size companies in music, fashion and design. International funds could be mobilized to finance the translation of books and the subtitling or dubbing of local films in international languages. Skills in these fields could be formalized in business schools and through exchanges on the economics of cultural industries.

Cultural tourism and partnerships with the World Tourism Organization can disseminate advice to host communities. And partnerships with parliaments, ministries of culture and national statistical offices can gather best practices on cultural exchanges, data gathering and policy-making.

FLOWS OF PEOPLE—MULTIPLE IDENTITIES FOR GLOBAL CITIZENS

Almost half the people in Toronto and Los Angeles are foreign born, and more than a quarter are in Abidjan, London and Singapore (table 5.3). Driven by globalization, the number of migrants soared in the last decade, especially to the high-income countries of Western Europe, North America and Australia (figure 5.2). And with the growing availability of the Internet and the low cost of air travel, more immigrants are maintaining closer ties with their countries of origin (see feature 5.1). Globalization is not only bringing cultural groups together. It is altering the rules of engagement. Democratization and a growing respect for human rights are bringing increasing political freedom and a sense of entitlement to fair treatment and are legitimizing protest.

Immigration gives rise to an array of concerns on both sides. Receiving countries struggle with issues of cultural freedom. Should Muslim girls be allowed to wear headscarves to state schools in France (box 5.7)? Similar debates rage over whether education should be provided in Spanish in US schools or whether Sikh motorcyclists should be permitted to wear a turban instead of a standard helmet in Canada. Immigrants protest a lack of recognition for their cultural identities as well as discrimination in jobs, housing and education. In many countries these concerns are met by the counter-protests of local populations,

TABLE 5.3

Top 10 cities by share of foreign born population, 2000/01
Percent

Miami	59
Toronto	44
Los Angeles	41
Vancouver	37
New York City	36
Singapore	33
Sydney	31
Abidjan	30
London	28
Paris	23

Source: UN HABITAT 2004; U.S. Census Bureau 2004b; World Cities Project 2002; Australian Bureau of Statistics 2001; Statistics Canada 2004.

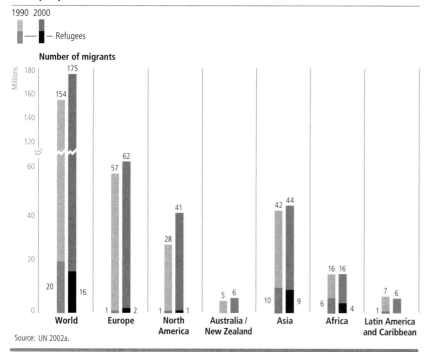

Figure 5.2 Unprecedented growth in international migration to Europe, North America, Australia and New Zealand, but refugees remain a small proportion, 1990–2000

1990 2000

— Refugees

Number of migrants

Source: UN 2002a.

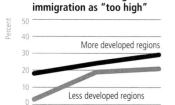

Figure 5.3 More and more governments (rich and poor) want to control immigration, 1976–2001

Governments viewing immigration as "too high"

More developed regions

Less developed regions

Governments adopting policies to reduce immigration

More developed regions

Less developed regions

1976   1986   2001

Source: UN 2002a.

who fear that their national identities and values are also being challenged. "They don't adopt our way of life and values", say those opposed to immigration. "Respect our way of life and our cultures and our human rights", retort immigrant communities and their allies.

One response would be to acknowledge diversity and promote the inclusion of immigrants, addressing both the social, economic and political exclusions they suffer and living mode exclusion, giving recognition to their identities. An alternative, advocated by anti-immigrant groups, would be to close countries to flows of people—reversing the trend of increasing diversity (figure 5.3). The political agenda of France's National Front Party, for example, proposes to turn back the flow of immigration, revoking family reunification programmes, expelling undocumented aliens, developing programmes to return immigrants to their countries of origin and giving citizens preference in employment, social assistance and other areas.[16] Italy's Northern League and National Alliance parties (both members of the ruling coalition) are introducing legislation to limit immigration to people who have an employment contract in Italy and to provide aid to countries to stop illegal immigration.[17]

But this choice between acknowledging diversity and closing the country to immigration may be a false one if national cultures are not really threatened by diversity.

DOES CULTURAL DIVERSITY THREATEN NATIONAL CULTURES?

Those fearing that immigrants threaten national values make three arguments: that immigrants do not "assimilate" but reject the core values of the country; that immigrant and local cultures clash, inevitably leading to social conflict and fragmentation; and that immigrant cultures are inferior and if allowed a foothold would undermine democracy and retard progress, a drain on economic and social development. Their solution is to manage diversity by reducing immigrant flows and acculturating immigrant communities.

Single or multiple identities. Underlying fears of losing national culture is an implicit belief that identities are singular. But people do not have single, fixed identities. They have multiple and often changing identities and loyalties. In the words of Long Litt-Woon, chairperson of the Drafting Group of the Council of Europe's Conference on Diversity and Cohesion: "I am often asked how long I have lived [in Norway]; '20 years', I say. The next remark often is 'Oh, you are almost Norwegian!' The assumption here is that I have become less Malaysian because it is common to think about identity as a zero sum game; if you have more of one identity, you have less of another. Identity is somehow imagined to be like a square box with a fixed size."[18]

Some groups of immigrants may want to retain their cultural identities. But that does not mean that they do not develop loyalties to their new country. People of Turkish ancestry in Germany may speak Turkish at home well into the second generation, but they also speak German. Mexicans in the United States may cheer for the Mexican football team but serve in the US Army.

Suspicions about the loyalties of immigrants have been common. But they are misplaced. Suspecting divided loyalties, the US and Canadian governments interned their citizens of Japanese descent during World War II. Yet soldiers of Japanese descent serving in the US

BOX 5.7

The headscarf dilemma in France

Should Muslim girls be allowed to wear head-scarves in state schools in France? Would that contradict the principles of secularism (*laïcité*) and respect for freedom of religion? Does this freedom require public spaces to be kept free of religious influence? Or would that constitute discrimination against the Muslim immigrant community? Or does the headscarf reflect sub-jugation of women by men? Few controversies have aroused as much passion—on both sides—and raised more penetrating challenges to ac-commodating cultural diversity in recent years.

The controversy dates to 1989, when a sec-ondary school expelled three young women who wore headscarves in class on the grounds that this violated French principles of secularism. This triggered massive public debate. The Council of State declared that the wearing of religious to-kens is not in itself incompatible with secular-ism as long as it did not have an "ostentatious or militant" character. The Ministry of Educa-tion appointed a special mediator to deal with future such incidents.

The controversy quieted down until De-cember 2002, when a girl in a predominantly im-migrant neighbourhood in Lyon appeared in school wearing a headscarf. The headscarf had been reduced nearly to a headband, covering nei-ther her forehead nor her ears. The principal

called in her parents and demanded that the girl stop wearing a headscarf to school. The par-ents protested that they had already accommo-dated French norms by reducing the headscarf to a headband. The mediator was called in but was unable to find an acceptable solution. Some teachers threatened to go on strike if the student were allowed to continue to wear the headscarf in school.

The affair quickly turned into a politicized debate. Members of the National Assembly on both the left and the right proposed a law ex-plicitly prohibiting the wearing of headscarves in schools and other public spaces. Leftist intellec-tuals quickly took positions for and against: ei-ther in defence of freedom of expression and against discrimination against Muslims, or in

Are you in favour of, or opposed to, a law banning signs or dress that conspicuously display religious affiliation? (21 January 2004)

Group	In favour (%)	Opposed (%)
All French	69	29
Left	66	33
Right	75	24
Muslims	42	53
Muslim women	49	43

Source: Zolberg 2003; Gutmann 1995; *The Economist* 2004b.

defence of secularism and values of gender equality, since it was thought that many girls were being intimidated into wearing the head-scarf. In 2003 the Ministry of Education and the National Assembly established a committee of en-quiry. In July an Independent Commission on the Application of Secularism in the Republic pro-posed a ban on the wearing of any obvious reli-gious symbols in schools, including the headscarf.

Ultimately, the legislation was passed, but opinions were divided. Positions did not fall as might be expected along typical divides: left–right, non-Muslim–Muslim, or women–men. Opinion polls taken just prior to the vote showed Muslim women equally divided for and against the new law (see table).

The case highlights the dilemmas that coun-tries face in trying to accommodate the religious and other cultural differences of immigrant com-munities. As in this case there are difficult trade-offs and complex arguments. Those who defend the ban argue that it is a defence of freedom—freedom of religion and freedom of women from subordination. But so do those who argue against the ban—freedom against discrimination and unequal opportunities. Such trade-offs of prin-ciples are particularly difficult in public educa-tion, which is intended to impart the values of the state.

---

and Canadian armies exhibited high levels of val-our and loyalty, becoming some of the most decorated heroes. In 1960 there were fears in the United States that a Roman Catholic President might have loyalties to the Pope beyond and above his loyalties to the United States, fears that President John F. Kennedy had to actively com-bat as a candidate in 1960.

Concerns about national identity are some-times also expressed through denunciations of im-migrant cultures as "inferior", with claims that allowing immigrants to flourish would retard the country's progress and development. But this Report has demonstrated how little foundation there is for the arguments of cultural determin-ism. To be sure, many immigrant groups—though by no means all groups or in all countries—do have high rates of unemployment and lower than average educational achievement. But the rea-sons have to do with the multiple disadvantages they suffer rather than any culturally determined

group characteristics—disadvantages that can be remedied with appropriate policies of inclu-sion, as chapter 3 proposes.

For most societies accommodating multiple identities does not happen overnight. It means coming to see as familiar differences that were once considered "alien". Social scientists call this a shifting and blurring of the boundaries that separate "us" and "not us". The confrontations in France over Muslim girls wearing headscarves to school or in the United States over instruction in Spanish in primary school are about people fighting to maintain boundaries as they have been drawn. Islam and Spanish are symbols of the "not us". Admitting them as part of "us" sug-gests giving in to the dangers seen looming ahead: communal conflict and loss of cultural identity.

In accommodating multiple identities, societies debate two questions: How different can we afford to be? How alike must we be? Accepting multiple identities is a major social transformation. But history shows that it does happen. Almost all European countries have undergone such a transformation. Today, being different is no longer the difference between being an Alsatien and being a Breton but between being a Sri Lankan and being a Scot, creating a broader category of "us".

Immigration supports economic growth and development. Closing doors to immigration is neither practical nor in the interest of national development. Far from being a drain on development, immigrants are a source of skills, labour, ideas and know-how. Economists have long argued that the gains from liberalizing migration dwarf those from removing barriers to world trade. From Indian technology entrepreneurs in Silicon Valley in the United States to West African nurses throughout Europe to Chinese investors in Australia to Filipino domestic workers in Saudi Arabia, immigrants' contributions to innovation, enterprise and skill are daily reminders of their value to society.

In today's knowledge economy countries compete by creating and attracting top talent. In 1990, for example, foreign-born students earned 62% of engineering doctorates in the United States, and more than 70% of foreign-born students who get doctorates in the United States stay in the United States.[19, 20] Often among the more entrepreneurial in society, immigrants invest in small businesses and rejuvenate urban neighbourhoods—in Europe they are creating commercial zones in abandoned areas to generate thousands of jobs.[21]

Today, countries of Western Europe and Japan, facing the prospect of aging and shrinking populations, are in dire need of fresh inflows of people. Western Europe's working age population is forecast to fall from 225 million in 1995 to 223 million by 2025.[22] According to UN Population Division estimates, Europe will have to double its intake of immigrants just to maintain its population size by 2050.[23]

Barriers to entry have not been removed for people as they have been for goods and capital. Yet migration has climbed rapidly in the 1990s, including undocumented migration that has proliferated in the 1990s, reaching almost 30 million people worldwide (see feature 5.1). Efforts to reverse the flows of people fight against the tide of globalization.[24] Significantly reducing immigration would require measures that are difficult to implement in democracies.

*POLICY OPTIONS AND CHALLENGES—
CULTURAL RECOGNITION AND SOCIO-ECONOMIC
AND POLITICAL INCLUSION*

Countries with historically large numbers of immigrants have followed two approaches to integration, differentialism and assimilation. Differentialism means maintaining clear boundaries between groups and respecting them as separate communities. Differentialist policies have typically been used when the state organizes immigration to fill temporary labour needs and does not expect migrants to become full members of the local community. Examples are guest workers in Germany in the 1960s and 1970s and domestic servants in Saudi Arabia today.

The other approach, assimilation, seeks to make immigrants become "more like us". The state and other institutions encourage immigrants to learn the predominant national language and adopt the social and cultural practices of the receiving community. By the time immigrants' children have passed through the primary institutions of the new society, especially public schools, they will be almost indistinguishable from the rest of the local community. The image of the US "melting pot" best represents this approach.

These two approaches, effective in earlier decades, are inadequate in diverse societies that need to build respect for differences and a commitment to unity. Culturally diverse societies are not predestined to disintegrate or to lose their national cultures and identities. But accommodating diversity requires efforts to build cohesion in managing immigration and the integration of migrants into society. Just as there are many ways in multi-ethnic states for ethnic minorities to feel pride in their own community as well as strong loyalty to the state, so too can immigrants become full members of their adopted countries and still maintain ties to their countries of origin. The challenge is to craft policies that integrate the objectives of unity and respect for difference and diversity. Differentialism does not build commitment to the country among

Closing doors to immigration is neither practical nor in the interest of national development

immigrants or provide adequate social protection. And guest worker programmes can be a source of exploitation and conflicts—"we wanted workers, but we got people" was the reaction of some (box 5.8). Assimilation does not accommodate difference or respect for diversity, nor does it explicitly address asymmetry.

Immigrants are more inclined today—and more able—than in the past to maintain close connections with family and community in their place of birth. Such connections are not new, but the influence on social, economic and political behaviour is different, thanks to the ease of modern communication and travel. Immigrants want to keep a foot in each world—one in their place of birth and the other in their adopted country.

Multiculturalism has recently become a third approach to incorporating immigrants, one that recognizes the value of diversity and supports multiple identities. It began in Canada in the early 1960s, when Prime Minister Pierre Trudeau articulated the idea in response to the challenges of a diverse population of indigenous people, French and English settlers and recent immigrants, with major divisions and inequalities among them. Australia introduced such a policy in the 1990s, after concluding that it was the only way to create cohesion amid diversity.

Multiculturalism is not only about recognizing different value systems and cultural practices within society—it is also about building a common commitment to core, non-negotiable values, such as human rights, rule of law, gender equality, and diversity and tolerance.[25] Australia describes this as "United in Diversity". Such a policy emphasizes not only the freedom of individuals to express and share their cultural values but also their obligations to abide by mutual civic obligations.

Although there is a historical sequence to these models of immigrant integration, at any one time countries use all three approaches. While not adopting multiculturalism as an explicit state policy, many countries are introducing elements of this approach as they struggle to manage growing diversity. The challenge involves addressing cultural exclusions along three dimensions, with a common theme of building unity and respecting difference:

- Addressing cultural exclusion by recognizing cultural identities (living mode exclusion).
- Addressing socio-economic exclusion (participation exclusion).
- Addressing exclusion from civic participation and citizenship rights (participation exclusion).

Addressing cultural exclusion by recognizing cultural identities. Immigrant communities might not suffer explicit discrimination and suppression of their way of life, but most

Multiculturalism is about building a common commitment to core, non-negotiable values

---

BOX 5.8

Temporary contracts—welcoming workers but not people does not work

As states struggle to control the flow of workers in the globalized labor market, many are experimenting with temporary migration programmes. Immigrants recruited under such programmes are not offered citizenship; they are expected to work for a set period of time and then to go back "home", making little impact on national culture and identity. Things rarely work that way, however.

Nearly every region at some time has recruited temporary workers to meet specific economic needs. In the 19th century hundreds of thousands of South Indians were recruited to the rubber plantations of Malaysia and to the sugar cane plantations of Trinidad and Tobago. In the United States an agricultural labour programme that started as a temporary solution to a shortage during World War II

became a labour recruitment programme lasting several decades. A number of European countries, including Germany and the Netherlands, experimented with "guest worker" programmes in the 1960s and early 1970s. More recently, Middle Eastern oil-producing states have turned to temporary labour for construction and other projects. South Africa continues to depend on temporary migrants to mine its natural resources and, in just the last few years, Mexico has designed a programme for 39,000 temporary workers from Guatemala to harvest coffee.

Such programmes have provided opportunities for many to work and earn, sending billions home in remittances. But these programmes have also created marginalized communities. In the now famous phrase used to describe the

European guest worker programme, "We recruited workers, but we got people."

Many temporary workers often decide to stay, despite government efforts to prevent this—and then bring their families, creating communities of the undocumented. But because they are excluded from the mainstream, they create ghetto communities—feeding anti-immigrant sentiments. Explicit legal restrictions and powerful informal social obstacles, such as physically segregated housing compounds, also prevent immigrants from participating fully in society.

These situations leave immigrants without protection from their home countries or their host countries. Legal residents without citizenship can be abused by employers and have little recourse to the legal or social services of the host country.

Source: Bach 2004.

---

do suffer from a lack of support to practice it. Perhaps more important, they often suffer from the rejection of values felt to be in conflict with core national values or from a social prejudice that their culture is inferior (see box 5.7).

Combating social prejudice and xenophobia is critical to building social harmony and unity in diverse societies. Greater respect and understanding for cultures can be fostered by providing positive and accurate images in the media, teaching the history of other cultures in schools and preparing museum exhibitions that demonstrate respect for cultural diversity and address socio-economic discrimination and inequalities (box 5.9).

Religion is the most contested of cultural identities. Greater recognition has enormous practical value, making it easier to obtain permits to build places of worship, establish burial grounds and hold celebrations. It also has great symbolic value, demonstrating respect for other cultures. The celebration of Eid at the White House in 1996 was a strong sign of respect for the millions of Muslims in the United States. Controversies arise over support to religion in secular states. As chapter 3 shows, secularism does not necessarily mean no involvement by the state in religion. The state can support religious

activity in ways that do not favour one religion over another, such as support to all religious schools. But the religions of immigrants are not always treated the same as the religion of the majority population.

Some of the most divisive issues of "us" and "not us" concern traditional or religious practices that are thought to contradict national values or human rights. Cultural recognition does not simply mean defending tradition. It means promoting cultural liberty and human development. And immigrant communities themselves need to challenge "traditional values" that conflict with core national values or human rights.

Addressing socio-economic inclusion. The 175 million people who live outside their countries of birth are a very mixed group. From highly skilled professionals to the young men and women who are smuggled across borders to work in sweat shops, they include people who have been in the country for decades and those who arrived only yesterday. And the ranks of "immigrant communities" that are politically mobilized expand beyond the 175 million to include the relatives and even friends of immigrants.

Not all immigrants suffer socio-economic exclusion. For those who do, that exclusion takes many different forms. The biggest problem is that in many countries the poverty of immigrant groups divides society. It gives rise to anti-immigrant movements and accusations that immigrants are unwilling or unable to be productive members of society, that they live together in ghettos with no interest in integrating with the rest of society. State support to address socio-economic exclusion of immigrant groups is therefore a critical part of building social harmony.

Education and language are the first step. Many countries have proactive programmes for integration that offer instruction in the country's national language. More controversial is the use of immigrants' mother tongues in schools and in official communication. No single formula is appropriate for all situations. But objections to the use of mother tongues are often more ideological than pragmatic. People learn better, respect laws and generally participate in the life of a community more fully if they can understand better. Learning the language of

Some of the most divisive issues of "us" and "not us" concern traditional or religious practices thought to contradict national values or human rights

---

BOX 5.9

How Berlin promotes respect for cultural difference

Berlin has earned a reputation in Germany as a pioneer in promoting the integration of immigrants. Berlin was the first among the federal states to establish an office to address obstacles to integration. In 1981 under the motto "Miteinander leben" (living with one another), the Commissioner's Office of the Berlin Senate for Migration and Integration established a campaign for tolerance, respect for others and understanding. It conducts outreach activities in neighbourhoods with a high proportion of immigrants and public information campaigns describing the basic principles of the policy. The office also provides counselling and legal consultations in 12 languages, helping immigrants find jobs and tackle discrimination. Together with non-governmental organizations, the office organizes regular training for the police on relations towards

immigrants and conducts annual surveys on local attitudes towards immigrants.

The Commissioner's Office builds capacity among immigrant organizations, helps immigrants organize into self-help groups and is a primary information source for people seeking advice on integration. Half of its €6.5 million annual budget goes to funding immigrant organizations and groups.

The Commissioner's Office has brought integration concerns to the attention of the media and the public. It has opened a direct channel of communication between immigrants and government. It has also focused on activities for both immigrant populations and ethnic Germans, showing that integration is a two-way process. Many other federal states have copied Berlin's example.

Source: IOM 2003c; European Union 2004; Independent Commission on Migration to Germany 2001.

---

the state is critical, but there will be lags in achieving proficiency.

Also controversial is the issue of social welfare protection for non-citizens, including undocumented residents. The fear—difficult to prove or disprove—is that social protection encourages more inflows of people, who in turn become dependent on the state. But the reality is that without welfare protection, the broader social consequences would be worse. And states have an obligation to protect and promote human rights—for all their residents.

Addressing exclusion from civic participation and citizenship rights. Many immigrants are not citizens. For that reason they are excluded from the bundle of obligations and rights that states and their citizens have to each other. Without such rights immigrants lack access to the jobs and services that help them become fully contributing members of society. They also lack protection from abuse. Naturalization is intended to be the answer, but most states are beginning to rethink their policies in response to rising flows, temporary and circular movements and transnational multiple identities.

Extending the civic rights traditionally associated with citizenship to non-citizens is a critical step, as is the recognition of dual nationality. Many countries, including Denmark, the Netherlands, Norway and Sweden, have extended voting rights to non-citizens in local elections. In other countries, like Belgium, such rights are likely to be extended soon. Some 30 countries now acknowledge dual nationality. But there are also contradictory trends of restrictions on access to long-term residence, naturalization and citizenship, and social services. For example, California recently made it impossible for immigrants without legal residence to acquire drivers' licences, effectively excluding them from many jobs and other activities essential in everyday life.

A globally interdependent world needs a new approach to citizenship for native residents and immigrants that incorporates the fundamental principles of human rights into a multicultural strategy for advancing human development—a strategy that benefits everyone.

*   *   *

States, communities, institutions and individuals all have to make choices:

- Should states seek to impose a homogenizing and unchanging national identity? Or should they celebrate diversity, helping to foster syncretic and evolving societies?
- Should communities protect tradition even if it narrows choice and freedoms? Or should they use their common knowledge and resources for exchange and mutual benefit?
- Should international institutions persist with rules that adhere to particular cultural and legal traditions? Or should they recognize, respect and promote the products and resources of other cultures, strengthening the legitimacy of institutions?
- Should individuals restrict themselves to singular identities? Or should they recognize themselves as part of an interlinked humanity?

Democracy and equitable growth are important in fostering cultural inclusion. But they are not enough. Multicultural policies for cultural inclusion—recognizing differences, supporting diversity and mitigating asymmetries of power—are also needed. Individuals have to shed rigid identities if they are to become part of a diverse society. International institutions have to respect other cultural traditions and create enabling conditions for developing local cultural resources. Poor countries and marginalized communities have to be given a greater voice in negotiations involving their cultures and rights and fair compensation for the use of their resources. Only under these circumstances will multiple and complementary identities evolve across national boundaries. Only then will identity and freedom flourish in a culturally diverse world.

Extending the civic rights traditionally associated with citizenship to non-citizens is a critical step, as is the recognition of dual nationality

Notes

Chapter 1

1. Smith 1976.
2. Kymlicka and Norman 2000; Benhabib 2002; Kymlicka 1990; Stepan 2001; Taylor 1992.
3. Fraser and Honneth 2003.
4. Hart 1955, pp. 175–91.
5. Sen 2004c.
6. Sen 2004c.
7. Sandel 1998.
8. Sandel 1998.
9. Crowley 1987.
10. Sen 1999, 2001.
11. Appiah 1996, p. 84.
12. This section is drawn from Sen 2002.
13. As quoted in Mokyr 1983, p. 291.
14. This section is drawn from Sen 2004b.
15. Harrison and Huntington 2000, p. xiii.
16. Kymlicka and Norman 2000; Stepan 2001; Young 2000.
17. Sen 2003.
18. Aston 1972.
19. Mandela 1994, p. 21.
20. Okin 1999.

Chapter 2

1. Kymlicka 1996.
2. HDRO calculations based on CIA 2003.
3. Statistics Canada 2004.
4. Kymlicka 2004.
5. UNDP 2003e.
6. Dragoljub 2000.
7. Gurr 2000.
8. While there is no internationally agreed on definition of indigenous people, a widely accepted understanding of indigenous people may be found in UNDP 2004a.
9. UNDP 2004c.
10. Stavenhagen 2004.
11. Minority Rights Group International 2003.
12. Bell-Fiakoff 1993, pp. 110–21; Kiernan 1999; *The Bangkok Post* 2000; 2001. The vast majority of this reduction in numbers was from introduced diseases. The extent of intent is unclear, and it appears to be more of a case of non-prevention.
13. Indigenous Australia 2003.
14. During 1992.
15. UN 2002a.
16. HDRO calculations based on Wanner 2002. Total refers to 15 European countries with data: Austria, Belgium, Denmark, Finland, France, Germany, Iceland, Italy, Liechtenstein, Luxembourg, Netherlands, Norway, Spain, Sweden and Switzerland.
17. *The Guardian* 2001.
18. Migration Information Source 2003.
19. UN 2002a.
20. UN 2002a.
21. Kelso and Vasagar 2002.
22. Statistical feature 1, *The state of human development,* in this volume.
23. Statistical feature 1, *The state of human development,* in this volume.
24. Statistical feature 1, *The state of human development,* in this volume.
25. Statistical feature 1, *The state of human development,* in this volume.
26. Calculations based on the Polity IV Project 2003.
27. Kymlicka 2004.
28. Wikipedia 2004.
29. Zolberg 2004.
30. Human Rights Watch 2002.
31. Human Rights Watch 2002.
32. International Federation of Human Rights 2003.
33. Zolberg 2004.
34. UNESCO 2003b.
35. UNESCO 2003b.
36. Calculations based on UNESCO 2000c.
37. SIL International 2004b.
38. The Minorities at Risk (MAR) Project 2003.
39. Calculations based on the Minorities at Risk (MAR) Project 2003.
40. Human Rights Watch 2003.
41. Libanio 2004.
42. Kanyinga 2003.
43. Fraenkel 2003.
44. Premdas 2003.
45. Calculations based on the Minorities at Risk (MAR) Project 2003.
46. UNDP 2000c.
47. Dragoljub 2000.
48. Alvim 2002.
49. Bryld and others 2003.
50. UNDP 2003e.
51. UNDP 2000c.
52. Kymlicka 2004.
53. Kymlicka 2004.
54. Arizpe 2004.
55. Sen 2004b.
56. Huntington 1996.
57. Sen 2004b.
58. Sen 2004b.
59. See, for example, Inglehart 1997.
60. Sen 2004b
61. Inglehart and Baker 2000; Sen 2004b.
62. Barro and McLeary 2003.
63. Sen 2004b.
64. Sen 2004b.
65. See, for example, Etounga-Manguelle 2000.

66. Sen 2004b.
67. Indicator table 13.
68. UNDP 2003b.
69. Sen 2004b.
70. Stepan and Robertson 2003, pp. 30–44.
71. Sen 2004b.
72. Stepan and Robertson 2003. Countries with average GDP per capita under $1,500.
73. UNDP 2003a.
74. UNDP 2003a.
75. Not counting the peoples of former European colonies.
76. Marshall and Gurr 2003.
77. Huntington 1996.
78. Stewart 2003.
79. Cohen 1974; Alexander and McGregor 2000; Ranger 1983; Turton 1997, pp. 77–94.
80. Collier and Hoeffler 2001.
81. Justiniano 2004.
82. Stewart 2003.
83. Stewart 2002.
84. See, for example, Easterley and Levine 1997, pp. 1203–50.
85. See, for example, Easterley and Levine 1997, pp. 1203–50.
86. Snodgrass 1995.
87. The Economist 2002a.
88. Kapur and McHale 2003, pp. 48–57.
89. Kapur and McHale 2003, pp. 48–57.
90. "Charter oath" as cited in Sen 2004b.
91. Sen 2004b.
92. UNDP 2003a.
93. Florida and Gates 2002, pp. 32–35.

Chapter 3
1. Benhabib 1996.
2. Kymlicka and Norman 2000.
3. Moncrieffe 2004, pp 32–33, has an interesting discussion of the founding ideology of the revolutionary movement in Cuba, which argues that the racial problem was subsumed within the general battle against social injustice in all is manifestations.
4. Sheth 2004.
5. Okin 1999.
6. Moncrieffe 2004.
7. Prashad 2001.
8. Kymlicka 1996.
9. Young 2000.
10. Requejo 2001.
11. Young 1999.
12. Snyder 2000, p. 327.
13. Martínez-Herrera 2002, pp. 1–22.
14. Alfred 1995.
15. Watts 1998.
16. ILO 2003.
17. ILO 2003.
18. Luter and Deschouwer 1999.
19. Fleiner 2003.
20. Moncrieffe 2004.
21. O'Leary 2004.
22. O'Leary 2004.
23. Boix 1999, pp. 609–24.
24. Nagel 2004.
25. O'Leary 2004.
26. Cohn 1996; Kaviraj 1992; Hansen 2001; Corbridge and Harriss 2000; Dirks 2004.
27. Phillips 2001.
28. Care 1999.
29. Schacher 2001.
30. Tetley 1999.
31. Dirks 2004.
32. Kuruk 2002.
33. Thompson 2001.

34. Haffajee 1999.
35. Zorzi 2002.
36. This was unequivocally shown by the European Court of Human Rights in the Belgian linguistic case (de Varennes 1996, pp. 291–300).
37. Dutcher 1982.
38. Cummings and Tamayo 1994.
39. Ndoye 2003.
40. Patrinos and Velez 1996.
41. Patrinos and Velez 1996.
42. India 2004.
43. Ndoye 2003.
44. Matiki 2003.
45. Moeketsi 1999.
46. Temu 2000.
47. Eades 2004, pp. 23 and 113–33.
48. De Varennes 1996, pp. 291–300.
49. Chua 2003.
50. Duncan, Jefferis and Molutsi 2000.
51. Moyo 2004.
52. Psacharopoulos and Patrinos 1994.
53. UNICEF 2004.
54. United Nations Association of Great Britain and Northern Ireland 2004.
55. UNICEF 2004.
56. Psacharopoulos and Patrinos 1994.
57. Miguel 1999.
58. Alesina, Baqir and Easterly 1997.
59. Luttmer 1997.
60. Yashar 2004.
61. Sheth 2004.
62. For instance, in the Surat District of Gujarat in the 1960s about 80% of primary school teachers were members of tribal groups. This enabled members of the tribal groups in the district to access political power in Gujarat. They have become members of the legislative assembly and members of Parliament (which was mechanically possible through quotas) and also ministers and chief minister of the state. This political power was then used to acquire other linkages.
63. Sabbagh 2004.

Feature 3.1
1. Kymlicka 2004.
2. Kymlicka 2004.
3. Stepan, Linz and Yadav 2004.
4. Breytenbach 2000.
5. Keating 2002.
6. Linz and Stepan 1996.
7. Stepan 2001.
8. Bhargava 2004.
9. Stepan, Linz and Yadav 2004.

Chapter 4
1. CPS 2002; DUMC 2002; EUMC 2002; FBI 2002; SSS 2002. The number for the United States does not include hate crimes motivated by sexual orientation or disability.
2. RAND Corporation 2004.
3. Engineer 2004. Casualties include numbers killed and injured. For 1954–94 the data are from Home Ministry records. For 1995–2002 the data are from newspaper accounts.
4. Noting the threat posed by extremist organizations, in August 2001 Pakistan banned the Lashkar-e-Jhangvi. In January 2002 it banned the Sipah-e-Sahaba and Tehreek-i-Jafariya (*South Asia Monitor* 2003).
5. Symonds 2003.
6. ADL 2003.
7. Mudde 2000.
8. Eatwell 2000.
9. Arjomand 1989, cited in De Kadt 2004, p. 23.

10. Sands 2003. Estimates are those of Pakistan's Minister of Education, Zubaida Jalal.
11. Macan-Markar 2004.
12. Entzinger 2003; Meyer 2001.
13. Kaldor and Muro 2003, p. 179.
14. *The Economist* 2003a, p. 19.
15. Testas 2002.
16. AFP 2004.
17. Widfeldt 2001.

Chapter 5
1. Gandhi 1921.
2. World Bank 2002.
3. Tebtebba and Forest Peoples Programme 2003.
4. World Bank 2002.
5. Forero 2003; *The New York Times* 2003.
6. World Bank 2004.
7. European Union 2003.
8. In the United States, for example, these have become some of the strongest export sectors, providing much needed export revenues at a time when the country is facing a ballooning trade deficit.
9. Assuming a $3 admission price, an estimated 1 in every 10 people around the world saw the film *Titanic.* Moreover, its titanic $200 million production cost is dwarfed by its revenues: over $1.8 billion worldwide of which $1.2 billion came from abroad (Internet Movie Database 2004). Such cost structures often create very high entry costs in domestic—let alone international—markets that justify public intervention.
10. Extensive literature on this matter and more details on the theory behind how the industry works can be found in Vogel 2001.
11. Cohen 2004.
12. The quality of French audiovisual programming deteriorated rapidly after the introduction of a heavy system of quotas for national content (Cohen 2004).
13. Riding 2003.
14. Cohen 2004.
15. Cross-subsidization initiatives like this are already raising concerns by some groups, who often attack them on nationalistic grounds (Buck 2004).

16. Front National 2004.
17. Lega Nord 2004.
18. Council of Europe 2000.
19. Bhagwati 2003, pp. 98–104.
20. IOM 2003c.
21. Niessen 2000.
22. Geddes 2002.
23. UN 2000b.
24. *The Economist* 2002a.
25. IOM 2003a.

Feature 5.1
1. IOM 2003b.
2. ATSIA 2003.
3. World Bank 2004.
4. CSD and ICC 2002.
5. Moody 2000.
6. WIPO 2003d.
7. UNESCO 2000a.
8. UNESCO 2000b.
9. Mishra 2003.
10. UNESCO 2000a.
11. Riding 2003.
12. UNESCO 2000a.
13. UNESCO 2000a.
14. Cohen 2004.
15. Cohen 2004.
16. World Bank 2003.
17. UN 2003a.
18. IOM 2003b.
19. UN 2002a.
20. UN 2002a.
21. IOM 2004.
22. Wanner 2002.
23. IOM 2003c.
24. Kapur and McHale 2003, pp. 48–57.
25. UN 2002b.
26. UN 2002b.
27. IOM 2003c.

Bibliographic note

Chapter 1 draws on Agarwal 1994; Ambedkar 2002; Appadurai 1996; Appiah 1996; Appiah and Gates 1995; Arizpe 2000; Aston 1972; Avrami, Mason, and De La Torre 2000; Basu 1992; Benhabib 1996, 2002; Blau 1993, 2001; Crowley 1987; Fraser 1995, 1997; Fraser and Honneth 2003; Goody 1996; Granovetter 1985; Greif 1994; Gutmann 1994, 1995; Gutmann and Thompson 1996; Habermas 1975, 1996; Harrison and Huntington 2000; Hart 1955; Huntington 1996; Kymlicka 1990; Kymlicka and Norman 2000; Lenoir 1989; Linz and Stepan 1996; Mandela 1994; Mansbridge 1998; Mokyr 1983; Nussbaum 1995; Nussbaum and Glover 1995; Okin 1999; Ostrom 1990, 1998; Pattanaik 1998; Platteau 2000; Putnam 1993; Putnam, Leonardi, and Nanetti 1993; Rodgers, Gore, and Figueirdo 1995; Runciman 1966; Sandel 1998; Sen 1984, 1999, 2001, 2002, 2004a, 2003, 2004c, Forthcoming; Silver 1995; Smith 1976; Stepan 2001; Taylor 1992; Throsby 1999; Townsend 1979; UN 2000a; UNESCO 1998, 2000c; Weber 1976; and Young 2000.

Chapter 2 draws on Afrikanska Språk 2004; Alexander and McGregor 2000; Alvim 2002; Ansari 2002; *The Arizona Republic* 2003; Arizpe 2004; *The Associated Press* 2003; Australian Bureau of Statistics 2004; *The Bangkok Post* 2000, 2001; Barro and McCleary 2003; Bell-Fiakoff 1993; Bengwayan 2003; Bird 2003; Brindis and others 2002; Bromley 1974; CIA 2003; Cohen 1974; Collier and Hoeffler 2001; Davenport 2004; Discover France 2000; Douglas 1988; Dragoljub 2000; During 1992, 1993; Easterley and Levine 1997; Etounga-Manguelle 2000; France, Ministère de Jeunesse, Éducation et Recherche 2004; FBI 2004; Florida and Gates 2002; Fraenkel 2003; Fukuda-Parr 2001; Goldstone 1998; *The Guardian* 2001; Gurr 1993, 2000; Human Rights Watch 2002, 2003; Huntington 1996; IOE 2003; IOM 2003c; India, Ministry of Personnel 2002; India, Office of the Registrar General 2004; Indigenous Australia 2003; Inglehart 1997; Inglehart and Wayne 2000; International Federation of Human Rights 2003; Jacobs 2003; Justiniano 2004; Justino and Litchfield 2003; Kanyinga 2003; Kapur and McHale 2003; Kelso and Vasagar 2002; Kiernan 1999; Kymlicka 2004; Lavery 2004; Libanio 2004; Linz and Stepan 1996; Marshall 2000; Marshall and Gurr 2003; Mexico, Ministry of Health 2004; Migration Information Source 2003; The Minorities at Risk Project 2003; Minority Rights Group International 2003; NARAL Pro Choice 2004; *The New York Times* 2003; Nicaragua Network 2004; Opondo 2004; The Pew Research Center 2003; The Polity IV Project 2003; Ponzio 2004; Premdas 2003; Ranger 1983; Rutter 1998; Schwenken 2003; Sen 2002, 2004b; SIL International 2004b; Smith 1986, 1991; Snodgrass 1995; Stamatopoulou 2002; Statistics Canada 2004; Statistics Sweden 2004; Stavenhagen 2004; Stepan and Robertson 2003; Stepanov 2004; Stewart 2002, 2003; Third World Network 2003; Turton 1997; UN 2002a, 2003b, 2004; UNDP 2000a, 2000b, 2000c, 2002a, 2002b, 2003a, 2003b, 2003c, 2003e, 2004a, 2004b, 2004c; UNESCO 2000c; 2003b, 2004a; Valdés 2002; WHO 2001; Walden 2000; Wanner 2002; Wikipedia 2004; World Values Survey 2004; World Bank 2004; and Zolberg 2004.

Chapter 3 draws on Addison and Rahman 2001; Alesina, Baquir, and Easterly 1997; Austin and O'Neill 2000; Awakuni and Mio 2000; Bangura 2004; Baqir and Easterly 1997; Bardhan 1997; Baron and Diermeier 2001; Barry 2001; Bauböck 2001;

Bauböck and Rundell 1998; Benhabib 1996; Bgoya and others 1997; Bhargava 2004; Bird 2003; Boix 1999; Boothroyd 2004; Boulle 1984; Bowen and Derek 1998; Breytenbach 2000; Brint and Renéo 2001; Brock-Utne 2002; Brown and Ganguly 1997; Bryld and others 2003; Burnley 2001; Buvollen 2002; Caballero 2003; Care 1999; Carens 2000; Chua 2003; Cohn 1996; Congleton 2000; Congleton, Kyriacou and Bacaria 1999; Conversi 2002; Corbridge and Harriss 2000; CRIP 2004; Cummings and Tamayo 1994; De Varennes 1996; Delgado-Moreira 2000; D'Ercole and Salvini 2003; Dirks 2004; Donders 2003; Doomernik 2001; Duncan and Molutsi 2000; Dunleavy and O'Leary 1987; Dutcher 1982; Eades 2004; *The Economist* 2004a; Edgerton 1996; Elazar 1998; Engineer 2003; Fafunwa 1990; Feldman 2002; Fleiner 2003; Fossas 1999; Fraser 1989; Funke 2001; Gill 2001; Giovarelli and Akmatova 2002; Goodman 2004; Griffiths and Nerenberg 2002; Grillo 1998; Grin 2003; Halfin 2002; Hammer and Schulz 2003; Hansen 2001; Harding and Narayan 2000; Harris and Reilly 1998; Hastrup 2001; Helwege 1995; Hoodfar and Pazira 2003; ILO 2001, 2003; Indian and Northern Affairs Canada 2004; India, Ministry of Education 2004; Jarkko and Smith 2001; Jefferis and Molutsi 2000; Jomo 2004; Jureidini 2001; Kanbur 2001; Kaviraj 1992; Kearns and Sarat 1997, 1999; Keating 2002; Kertzer and Arel 2002; Klaus 2003; Knop 2002; Knowles and Amit-Talai 1996; Kuruk 2002; Kymlicka 1990, 1996, 1998, 2001, 2004; Kymlicka and Norman 2000; Leibfried and Rieger 2003; Lewis 1998, 2003; Lewis and Miller 2003; Licha 2002; Linz and Stepan 1978; Linz and Yadav 2004; Ljiphart 1984; Lott 1998; Loury 2001; Lukes and Joppke 1999; Luter and Deschouwer 1999; Luttmer 1997; Macedo 2000; Malhotra 2002; Martínez-Herrera 2002; Matiki 2003; Mazrui 1996; McRae 1974; Medrano 2002; Mehrotra and Delamonica Forthcoming; Miguel 1999; Modood and Werbner 1997; Mody 2003; Moeketsi 1999; Moghadam 2004; Moncrieffe 2004; Moya 2002; Moyo 2004; Myerson 1991; Nagel 2004; National Commission on Indigenous Peoples 2004a, 2004b; Ndoye 2003; Neville 2001; Ocampo 2001; Office of Personnel Management 2003; Okin 1999; O'Leary 2004, Forthcoming; Parekh 2000; Patrinos and Velez 1996; Patterson and Susser 2001; Phillips 2001; Prah 2000, 2004; Prashad 2001; Preis 2004; Psacharopoulos and Patrinos 1994; Reiss 2002; Renshon 2001; Requejo 2001; Richey 2003; Rotimi 2001; Rubin 2004; Rudolph 2001; Russell 2002; Sabbagh 2004; Sarat and Simon 2003; Schacher 2001; Schultz and Mwabo 1998; Schulze 1999; Sepúlveda 2003; Sheth 2004; SIL International 2004a; South Africa, Ministry of Labour 2004; Snyder 2000; Stepan 2001; Subirats 2003; Taiaiake 1995; Tauli-Corpus 2004; Temu 2000; Tetley 1999; Thompson 2001; Tran 2000; UN 1994; UNDP 2003d; UNICEF 2001, 2004; United Nations Association of Great Britain and Northern Ireland 2004; U.S. Census Bureau 2004b; U.S. Department of Labor 2004; Van der Westhuizen 2002; Vuchelen 2003; Watts 1998, 1999, 2002; Willett 1998; World Bank 2003; Wright 2001; Yashar 2004; Young 1999, 2000; and Zorzi 2002.

Chapter 4 draws on Abed-Kotob 1995; Abuza 2002; ADL 2003; AFP 2004; Arjomand 1989; Barraclough 1998; Berman 2003; Bhavnani and Backer 2000; Brumberg 2002; Byman and others 2001; Campagna 1996; Caplan 1987; Chicuecue 1997; CNN 2003; Conner 1986; Cornell and Spector 2002; CPS 2002; De Kadt 2004; DUMC 2002; Eatwell 2000; *The Economist* 2000,

2003a, 2003b; Electionworld.org 2004; Engineer 2004; Entelis 2002; Entzinger 2003; Esman 1986; EUMC 2002; Fahmy 1998; FBI 1999, 2002; Gerges 2000; Godmer and Kestel 2001; Grove and Carter 1999; Gurr 1993; Hafez 2000; Haubrich 2003; HinduUnity.org 2004; Hoffman 1998-99; Honwana 1999; Iganski 2002; Ignazi 2003; IRR 2003; Jackman and Volpert 1996; Jeness 2002; Kaldor and Muro 2003; Kogacioglu 2003; Koh 2002; Leone and Angrig 2003; Levin 2001; Levin and McDevitt 1999; Mabry 1998; Macan-Markar 2004; Mamdani 2001; Martínez-Herrera 2002; Marty and Appleby 1991, 1993, 1995; Mayer 2001; Meyer 2001; Middle East Institute 2003; The Minorities at Risk Project 2003; Moreau Yousafazai, and Hussain 2003; Mudde 2000; Pehdazur 2001; Prah 2004; RAND Corporation 2004; Roberts 2002; Rotar 2002; Rubin 2004; Sands 2003; SATP 2004; Scott 2003; Sen 2004a; Shain 1994-95; Shain and Barth 2003; Sheffer 1986, 1993; Sivan 2003; *South Asia Monitor* 2003; SSS 2002; Stern 2000, 2003; Susning.nu 2004; Swedish Election Authority 2002; Symonds 2003; Testas 2002; Tremlett 2002; UNESCO 2001; U.S. Department of Justice 2001; Van Holsteyn 2003; Wahlbeck 2002; Wanandi 2002; Wedgwood 2002; Widfeldt 2001, 2004; Moreau, Yousafzai and Hussain 2003; Zelkina 1999; and Zhao 1998.

Chapter 5 draws on Aleinikoff and Klusmeyer 2000; ATSIA 2003; Australian Bureau of Statistics 2001; Bach 2004; Bhagwati 2003; Brucker and others 2001; Brumann 1999; Buck 2004; CBD 2002; Clifford 1988; Cohen 2004; Commission on Intellectual Property Rights 2002; Coombe 1998; Council of Europe 2000; Coussey 2000; CSD and ICC 2002; De Ferranti and others 2003; Department of Immigration and Multicultural and Indigenous Affairs 2003; Doomernik 2001; Droege and Soete 2001; *The Economist* 2002a, 2002b, 2004b; European Union 2003; European Union 2004; Fermin 2001; *Financial Times* 2004; Forero 2003; Front National 2004; Garson and Loizillon 2003; Geddes 2002; Ghosh 2003; Graeme 2003; Independent Commission on Migration to Germany 2001; Inglis 2004; International Council on Metals and the Environment 1999; The Internet Movie Database 2004; IOM 2003a, 2003b, 2003c, 2004; Kongolo 2001; Koopmans 2002; Kymlicka 2003; Lega Nord 2004; McPhail 2000; Mgbeoji 2001; Mishra 2003; Moody 2000; Niessen Jan 2000; Norchi 2000; OECD 2003; Olwig and Hastrup 1997; Ostergard and Altman 2001; Papademetriou 2003; Preis 2004; Public Citizen 2004; Riding 2003; Rodwin 2002; Rosaldo 1989; Salomon and Sengupta 2003; Sen 2004a; Stalker 2002; Statistics Canada 2004; Stavenhagen 2004; Tebtebba and Forest Peoples Programme 2003; Tebtebba and International Forum on Globalization 2003; UIS 2001; UN 2000b, 2002a, 2002b, 2003a; UNCTAD 1999; UNDP 1999; UNESCO 2000a, 2000b, 2000c, 2002, 2003a, 2003c, 2004b; UN HABITAT forthcoming; U.S. Census Bureau 2004a; WIPO 2003b, 2003c, 2003d, 2004; World Bank 2002, 2004; World Commission on Culture and Development 1995; Yashar 2004; and Zolberg 2001, 2004.

Bibliography

Background papers

Conceptual studies

Arizpe, Lourdes. 2004. "Notes on Cultural Policies and Best Practices in Cultural Diversity."

Bach, Robert. 2004. "Migration."

Cohen, Elie. 2004. "Économie de L'Exception Culturelle."

De Kadt, Emanuel. 2004. "Curbing Coercive Identities."

Deere, Carolyn. 2003. "Building Inclusive Societies: Managing Diversity."

Dirks, Nicholas. 2004. "Colonial and Postcolonial Histories: Comparative Reflections on the Legacies of Empire."

Kymlicka, Will. 2004. "Culturally Responsive Policies."

O'Leary, Brendan. 2004. "Building Inclusive States."

Sabbagh, Daniel. 2004. "Affirmative Action Policies: An International Perspective."

Sen, Amartya. 2004a. "Cultural Freedom and Human Development."

Stavenhagen, Rodolfo. 2004. "Indigenous Peoples in Comparative Perspective."

Stepan, Alfred, Juan J. Linz, and Yogendra Yadav. 2004. ""Nation State" or "State Nation"?: Conceptual Reflections and Some Spanish, Belgian and Indian Data."

UNDP (United Nations Development Programme). 2004. "BCPR (Bureau for Crisis Prevention and Recovery) Geneva: Contribution to HDR2004."

Regional studies

Bhargava, Rajeev. 2004. "Inclusion and Exclusion in South Asia: The Role of Religion."

Jomo, K. S., with Wee Chong Hui 2004. "Affirmative Action and Exclusion in Malaysia: Ethnic and Regional Inequalities in a Multicultural Society."

Moghadam, Valentine. 2004. "Cultural Traditions and Gender Equality in the Arab Region."

Moncrieffe, Joy. 2004. "Ethnic Diversity and State Response in the Caribbean."

Moyo, Sam. 2004. "Dominance of Ethnic and Racial Groups: The African Experience."

Prah, Kwesi Kwaa. 2004. "African Wars and Ethnic Conflict—Rebuilding Failed States."

Rubin, Barnett R. 2004. "Central Asia: Wars and Ethnic Conflicts—Rebuilding Failed States."

Sheth, D. L. 2004. "Caste, Ethnicity and Exclusion in South Asia: The Role of Affirmative Action Policies in Building Inclusive Societies."

Yashar, Deborah. 2004. "Citizenship and Ethnic Politics in Latin America: Building Inclusive Societies."

Zolberg, Aristide. 2004. "The Democratic Management of Cultural Differences: Building Inclusive Societies in Western Europe and North America."

References

Abed-Kotob, Sana. 1995. "The Accommodationists Speak: Goals and Strategies of the Muslim Brotherhood of Egypt." *International Journal of Middle East Studies* 27(3): 321–39.

Abuza, Zachary. 2002. "Tentacles of Terror: Al Qaeda's Southeast Asian Network." *Contemporary Southeast Asia* 24(3): 427–65.

Addison, T., and A. Rahman. 2001. "Why is So Little Spent on Educating the Poor?" Discussion Paper 2001/29. World Institute for Development Economics Research, Helsinki.

ADL (Anti-Defamation League). 2003. "Extremism in America." [http://www.adl.org/learn/ext_us/]. December 2003.

AFP (Agence France Presse). 2004. "Pakistan Approves 100 Million Dollars to Reform Religious Schools." 7 January.

Afrikanska Språk. 2004. "Small and Endangered Languages of Africa: A Bibliographical Survey." Stockholm. [http://www.african.gu.se/research/elbiblio.html]. February 2004.

Agarwal, Bina. 1994. *A Field Of One's Own; Gender and Land Rights in South Asia.* Cambridge: Cambridge University Press.

Aleinikoff, T. Alexander, and Douglas Klusmeyer, eds. 2000. *From Migrants to Citizens: Membership in a Changing World.* Washington, DC: Brookings Institution Press.

Alesina, Alberto, Reza Baqir, and William Easterly. 1997. *Public Goods and Ethnic Divisions.* NBER Working Paper 6009. Washington, DC: National Bureau of Economic Research.

Alexander, J., and J. McGregor. 2000. "Ethnicity and the Politics of Conflict: The Case of Matabeleland." In S. F. Nafziger and R. Vayrynen, eds. *War, Hunger and Displacement: The Origin of Human Emergencies.* Oxford: Oxford University Press.

Alfred, Taiaiake. 1995. *Heeding the Voices of Our Ancestors: Mohawk Politics and the Rise of Native Nationalism.* Toronto: Oxford University Press.

Alvim, Marta. 2002. "Mixed Race, Mixed Feeling." Los Angeles. [http://www.brazil.com/cvmar02.com]. February 2004.

Ambedkar, B. R. 2002. "Basic Features of the Indian Constitution." In Valerian Rodriguez, ed. *The Essential Writings of B.R. Ambedkar.* New Delhi: Oxford University Press.

Ansari, Humayun. 2002. "Muslims in Britain." Minority Rights Group International, London. [http://www.minorityrights.org/admin/Download/Pdf/muslimsinbritain.pdf]. February 2004.

Appadurai, Arjun. 1996. *Modernity at Large: Cultural Dimensions of Globalization.* Minneapolis: University of Minnesota Press.

Appiah, K. Anthony. 1996. "Race, Culture, Identity: Misunderstood Connections." In K. Anthony Appiah and Amy Gutmann, eds. *Color Consciousness: The Political Morality of Race.* Princeton: Princeton University Press.

Appiah, K. Anthony, and Henry Gates. 1995. *Identities.* Chicago: University Chicago Press.

Arizpe, Lourdes. 2000. "Cultural Heritage and Globalization." In Erica Avrami, Randall Mason, and Marta De La Torre, eds. *Values and Heritage Conservation.* Los Angeles: Getty Conservation Institute.

The Arizona Republic. 2003. "English-Only Latinos on the Rise." 5 May. [http://www.azcentral.com/arizonarepublic/news/articles/0505speakingspanish.html]. February 2004.

Arjomand, Said Amir. 1989. "The Emergence of Islamic Political Ideologies." In James A. Beckford and Thomas Luckman, eds. *The Changing Face of Religion.* London: Sage.

The Associated Press. 2003. "Falun Gong Turns to International Courts in Campaign Against Chinese Leadership." 26 September. [http://www.rickross.com/reference/fa_lun_gong/falun282.html]. February 2004.

Aston, W. G. 1972. *Nihongi: Chronicles of Japan from the Earliest Time to A.D. 697.* Tokyo: Tuttle.

ATSIA (Office of Aboriginal and Torres Strait Islander Affairs, Department of Immigration and Multicultural and Indigenous Affairs, Australia). 2003. "Land and Native Title." [http://www.minister.immi.gov.au/atsia/facts/pdf/land.pdf]. December 2003.

Austin, Dennis, and Michael O'Neill, eds. 2000. *Democracy and Cultural Diversity.* Oxford: Oxford University Press.

Australian Bureau of Statistics. 2004. "Indigenous Health: Greater Risks, Shorter Life Expectancy." Canberra. [http://www.abs.gov.au/Ausstats/abs@.nsf/Lookup/39A210FEEAE928D4CA256AB7007FBBFE]. February 2004.

Australian Bureau of Statistics, Community Relations Commission, Census Statistics. 2001. "The People of New South Wales." [http://www.crc.nsw.gov.au/statistics/Nsw/SydneyStatisticalDivision4pp.pdf]. March 2004.

Avrami, Erica, Randall Mason, and Marta De La Torre, eds. 2000. *Values and Heritage Conservation.* Los Angeles: Getty Conservation Institute.

Awakuni, Gene, and Jeffery Scott Mio. 2000. *Resistance to Multiculturalism: Issues and Interventions.* Philadelphia and London: Brunner/Mazel.

The Bangkok Post. 2000. "Australia's Aboriginal Genocides." 10 September.

———. 2001. "The Genocide of Native Americans." 29 July.

Bangura, Yusuf. 2004. "Ethnic Structure, Inequality and Governance of the Public Sector." United Nations Research Institute for Social Development, Geneva.

Bardhan, Pranab. 1997. "Method in the Madness? A Political Economy Analysis of the Ethnic Conflicts in Less Developed Countries." *World Development* 25(9): 1381–98.

Baron, David P., and Daniel Diermeier. 2001. "Elections, Governments and Parliaments in Proportional Representation Systems." *The Quarterly Journal of Economics* 116(3): 933–67.

Barraclough, Steven. 1998. "Al-Azhar: Between the Government and the Islamists." *The Middle East Journal* 52(2): 236–49.

Barro, Robert J., and Rachel M. McCleary. 2003. "Religion and Economic Growth." Cambridge, Mass. [http://post.economics.harvard.edu/faculty/barro/papers/Religion_and_Economic_Growth.pdf]. March 2004.

Barry, Brian. 2001. *Culture and Equality: An Egalitarian Critique of Multiculturalism.* Cambridge: Polity.

Basu, Alaka. 1992. *Culture, the Status of Women and Demographic Behaviour.* Oxford: Clarendon Press.

Bauböck, Rainer, and John Rundell, eds. 1998. *Blurred Boundaries: Migration, Ethnicity and Citizenship.* Aldershot: Ashgate.

Bauböck, Rainer. 2001. "Multinational Federalism: Territorial or Cultural Autonomy?" Willy Brandt Series of Working Papers. School of International Migration and Ethnic Relations. Malmö University, Malmö, Sweden. [http://racoon.mah.se/Forsk.nsf/0/2e9cc319839b3a2dc1256cf5005a4f8e/$FILE/Workingpaper201.pdf]. February 2004.

Bell-Fiakoff, Andrew. 1993. "A Brief History of Ethnic Cleansing." *Foreign Affairs* 72(3): 110–21.

Bengwayan, Michael A. 2003. "Intellectual and Cultural Property Rights of Indigenous and Tribal Peoples in Asia." Minority Rights Group International, London.

Benhabib, Seyla, ed. 1996. *Democracy and Difference: Contesting the Boundaries of the Political.* Princeton: Princeton University Press.

Benhabib, Seyla. 2002. *The Claims of Culture: Equality and Diversity in the Global Era.* Princeton: Princeton University Press.

Berman, Eli. 2003. *Hamas, Taliban and the Jewish Underground: An Economist's View of Radical Religious Militias.* NBER Working Paper 10004. Cambridge, Mass.: National Bureau of Economic Research. [http://www.nber.org/papers/w10004]. January 2004.

Bgoya, W., N. Billany, M. Lujanen, R. Noonan, T. Paajanen, and E. Syrjanen. 1997. "The Economics of Publishing Educational Materials in Africa." Working Group on Books and Learning Materials, Perspectives on African Book Development. The Association for the Development of Education in Africa, London.

Bhagwati, Jagdish. 2003. "Borders Beyond Control." *Foreign Affairs* 82(1): 98–104.

Bhavnani, Ravi, and David Backer. 2000. "Localized Ethnic Conflict and Genocide: Accounting for Differences in Rwanda and Burundi." *Journal of Conflict Resolution* 44(3): 283–306.

Bird, Karen. 2003. "The Political Representation of Women and Ethnic Minorities in Established Democracies: A Framework for Comparative Research." Paper presented at the Academy for Migration Studies in Denmark, Aalborg University, 11 November, Aalborg, Denmark. [http://www.socsci.mcmaster.ca/polisci/emplibrary/amidpaper.pdf]. February 2004.

Blau, Judith. 1993. *Social Contracts and Economic Markets.* New York: Plenum.

Blau, Judith, ed. 2001. *The Blackwell Companion to Sociology.* Oxford: Blackwell.

Boix, Charles. 1999. "Setting the Rules of the Game. The Choice of Electoral Systems in Advanced Democracies." *American Political Science Review* 93: 609–24.

Boothroyd, David. 2004. "United Kingdom Election Results." London. [http://www.election.demon.co.uk/ge2001.html]. February 2004.

Boulle, L. J. 1984. *South Africa and the Consociational Option: A Constitutional Analysis.* Cape Town: Juta.

Bowen, W., and B. Derek. 1998. *The Shape of the River: Long-Term Consequences of Considering Race in College and University Admissions.* Princeton: Princeton University Press.

Breytenbach, W. J. 2000. "Democracy in South Africa: What Kind and Is It Consolidating?" Bureau for Economic Research. University of Stellenbosch, Johannesburg. [http://www.kas.org.za/Publications/SeminarReports/ConsolidatingDemocracy/Consolidating%20Democracy.pdf]. February 2004.

Brindis, C. D., A. K. Driscoll, M. A. Biggs, and L. T. Valderrama. 2002. "Fact Sheet on Latino Youth: Immigrant Generation." Center for Reproductive Health Research and Policy. Department of Obstetrics, Gynecology and Reproductive Health Sciences and the Institute for Health Policy Studies. University of California at San Francisco, San Francisco. [http://reprohealth.ucsf.edu/articles/Latino.imm.pdf]. February 2004.

Brint, Michael, and Lukic Renéo, eds. 2001. *Culture, Politics and Nationalism in the Age of Globalization.* Aldershot: Ashgate.

Brock-Utne, Birgit. 2002. "Language, Democracy and Education in Africa." Discussion Paper 15. Nordiska Afrikainstitut. Uppsala, Sweden.

Bromley, Yulian. 1974. *Soviet Ethnology and Anthropology Today.* The Hague: Mouton.

Brown, Michael E., and Sumit Ganguly, eds. 1997. *Government Policies and Ethnic Relations in Asia and the Pacific.* Cambridge, Mass. and London: MIT Press.

Brucker, Herbert, Gil Epstein, Barry McCormick, Gilles Saint-Paul, Alessandra Venturini, and Klaus Zimmermann. 2001. "Managing Migration in the European Welfare State." Third European Conference of the Fondazione Rodolfo Debenedetti "Immigration Policy and the Welfare State," June, Trieste, Italy. [http://www.frdb.org/images/customer/copy_0_paper1_23jun01.pdf]. February 2004.

Brumann, Christoph. 1999. "Writing for Culture. Why a Successful Concept Should not be Discarded." *Current Anthropology* 40.

Brumberg, Daniel. 2002. "Islamists and the Politics of Consensus." *Journal of Democracy* 13(3): 109–15.

Bryld, Erik, Heather Bryant, Nanako Tsukahara, Leela Sthapit, and Mayline Py. 2003. "Rural Urban Linkages (RLL) Under the Rural Urban Partnership Programme (RUPP): A Case of Affirmative Action for Dalits in Nepal." United Nations Development Programme, Kathmandu.

Buck, Tobias. 2004. "Brussels Call for Bigger Budget Will Irk Rich States." *Financial Times.* 9 January.

Burnley, Ian H. 2001. *The Impact of Immigration on Australia: A Demographic Approach.* South Melbourne and Oxford: Oxford University Press.

Buvollen, Hans Petter. 2002. "Cultural and Legal Barriers to Justice in Guatemala." UNDP Access to Justice Workshop, 1 March, Oslo. [http://www.undp.org/governance/cd/documents/34.pdf]. February 2002.

Byman, Daniel L., Peter Chalk, Bruce Hoffman, William Rosenau and David Brannan. 2001. *Trends in Outside Support for Insurgent Movements.* Santa Monica, Calif.: RAND.

Caballero, Gonzalo. 2003. "The Dynamics of the Spanish Institutional Evolution Towards Economic, Social and Political Decentralization, 1950–2000: Markets, Democracy and Federalism for Economic Development." Paper presented at the 2003 European Association for Evolutionary Political Economy Conference, 7 November, Maastricht, Netherlands. [http://eaepe.infonomics.nl/papers/caballero.pdf]. March 2004.

Campagna, Joel. 1996. "From Accommodation to Confrontation: The Muslim Brotherhood in the Mubarak Years." *Journal of International Affairs* 50(1): 278–304.

Caplan, Lionel. 1987. *Studies in Religious Fundamentalism.* Houndsmills and London: Macmillan.

Care, Jennifer Corrin. 1999. "Conflict Between Customary Laws and Human Rights in the South Pacific." Paper presented at the 12th Commonwealth Law Conference, 1 September, Kuala Lumpur. [http://www.mlj.com.my/articles/JenniferCorrin-Care.htm]. February 2004.

Carens, Joseph H. 2000. *Culture, Citizenship and Community: A Contextual Exploration of Justice as Evenhandedness.* Oxford: Oxford University Press.

CBD (Convention on Biological Diversity). 2002. "Traditional Knowledge and the Convention on Biological Diversity." [http://www.biodiv.org/programmes/socio-eco/traditional/]. February 2004.

Chicuecue, Noel Muchenga. 1997. "Reconciliation: The Role of Truth Commissions and Alternative Ways of Healing." *Development in Practice* 7(4): 483–86.

Chua, Amy. 2003. *World on Fire: How Exporting Free Market Democracy Breeds Ethnic Hatred and Global Instability.* New York: Doubleday.

CIA (Central Intelligence Agency). 2003. "The World Factbook 2003." Washington, DC. [http://www.cia.gov/cia/publications/factbook/]. February 2004.

Clifford, James. 1988. *The Predicament of Culture: Twentieth-Century Ethnography, Literature and Art.* Cambridge, Mass.: Harvard University Press.

CNN. 2003. "U.S. Court Rebukes Bush Over Gitmo." 18 December. [http://www.cnn.com/2003/LAW/12/18/court.gitmo/index.html]. February 2004.

Cohen, Abner. 1974. *Two-Dimensional Man: An Essay on the Anthropology of Power and Symbolism in Complex Society.* Berkeley, Calif.: University of California Press.

Cohn, B. 1996. *Colonialism and Its Forms of Knowledge: The British in India.* Princeton: Princeton University Press.

Collier, Paul, and Anke Hoeffler. 2001. "Greed and Grievance in Civil War." World Bank, Washington, DC. [http://www.worldbank.org/research/conflict/papers/greedgrievance_23oct.pdf]. February 2004.

Commission on Intellectual Property Rights. 2002. "Integrating Intellectual Property Rights and Development Policy: Report of the Commission on Intellectual Property Rights." London. [http://www.iprcommission.org/graphic/documents/final_report.htm]. February 2004.

Congleton, Roger D. 2000. "A Political Efficiency Case for Federalism in Multinational States: Controlling Ethnic Rent-Seeking." In G. Galeotti, P. Slamon, and R. Wintrobe, eds. *Competition and Structure: The Political Economy of Collective Decisions: Essays in Honor of Albert Breton.* New York: Cambridge University Press.

Congleton, Roger D., Andreas Kyriacou, and Jordi Bacaria. 1999. "Political and Economic Origins of Asymmetric Federalism: A Model of Endogenous Centralization." [http://selene.uab.es/jbacaria/Economia_Aplicada/asymfed3.pdf]. March 2004.

Conner, Walker. 1986. "The Impact of Homelands Upon Diasporas." In Gabriel Sheffer, ed. *Modern Diaspora in International Politics.* New York: St. Martin's Press.

Conversi, Daniele, ed. 2002. *Ethnonationalism in the Contemporary Word: Walker Connor and the Study of Nationalism.* London: Routledge.

Coombe, Rosemary J. 1998. "Intellectual Property, Human Rights and Sovereignty: New Dilemmas in International Law Posed by the Recognition of Indigenous Knowledge and the Conservation of Biodiversity." *Indiana Journal of Global Legal Studies* 6(1): 59–115.

Corbridge, Stuart, and John Harriss. 2000. *Reinventing India.* Cambridge: Polity Press.

Cornell, Svante E., and Regine A. Spector. 2002. "Central Asia: More than Islamic Extremists." *The Washington Quarterly* 25(1): 193–206.

Council of Europe. 2000. "Conference on Diversity and Cohesion: New Challenges for the Integration of Immigrants and Minorities." [http://www.coe.int/T/E/Social_Cohesion/Migration/Documentation/Publications_and_reports/Reports_and_proceedings/20001201_CDMG(2000)35_ProceedingsNamur.asp]. March 2004.

Coussey, Mary. 2000. "Framework of Integration Policies." Directorate General III–Social Cohesion, Directorate of Social Affairs and Health. Council of Europe, Brussels.

CPS (Crown Prosecution Service). 2002. "Racist Incident Monitoring Annual Report 2001–2002." London. [http://www.cps.gov.uk/Home/CPSPublications/Scheme/reports.htm]. January 2004.

CRIP (Curriculum Reform Implementation Project). 2004. "Curriculum Reform in Papua New Guinea." Port Moresby. [http://www.pngcurriculumreform.ac.pg/text/CURRICULUM%20REFORM%20IN%20PAPUA%20NEW%20GUINEA.pdf]. February 2004.

Crowley, B. 1987. *The Self, the Individual and the Community.* Oxford: Clarendon Press.

CSD (Commission on Sustainable Development Indigenous Peoples' Caucus) and ICC (Inuit Circumpolar Conference). 2002. "Dialogue Paper by Indigenous People." Preparatory Committee for the World Summit on Sustainable Development First Substantive Session, New York. [http://www.treatycouncil.org/new_page_5241221.htm]. March 2004.

Cummings, S. M., and S. Tamayo. 1994. "Language and Education in Latin America: An Overview." Human Resources Development and Operations Policy Working Papers. World Bank, Washington, DC.

Davenport, Christian. 2004. "Minorities At Risk: Dataset Users Manual 030703." The Minorities At Risk (MAR) Project. Center for International Development and Conflict Management. University of Maryland, Baltimore. [http://www.cidcm.umd.edu/inscr/mar/margene/MAR-codebook_040903.doc]. February 2004.

De Ferranti, David, Guillermo Perry, Francisco H. G. Ferreira, and Michael Walton. 2003. "Inequality in Latin America and the Caribbean: Breaking with History?" World Bank, Washington, DC.

De Varennes, F. 1996. "Law, Language and the Multiethnic State." *Language and Communication* 16(3): 291-300.

Delgado-Moreira, Juan M. 2000. *Multicultural Citizenship of the European Union.* Aldershot: Ashgate.

Department of Immigration and Multicultural and Indigenous Affairs, Australia. 2003. "Multicultural Australia: United in Diversity." Canberra. [http://www.immi.gov.au/multicultural/australian/index.htm]. February 2004.

D'Ercole, Marco Mira, and Andrea Salvini. 2003. "Towards Sustainable Development: The Role of Social Protection." Social, Employment and Migration Working Papers. Organization for Economic Cooperation and Development, Geneva. [http://www.oecd.org/dataoecd/19/2/16362056.pdf]. February 2004.

Directorate of Social Affairs and Health. 2000. "Diversity and Cohesion: New Challenges for the Integration of Immigrants and Minorities." Council of Europe, Strasbourg, France. [http://www.social.coe.int/en/cohesion/action/publi/migrants/EDéfis.pdf]. February 2004.

Discover France. 2000. "French National Holidays, Festivals, Religious Celebrations." Paris. [http://www.discoverfrance.net/France/DF_holidays.shtml]. March 2004.

Donders, Yvonne. 2003. *Towards a Right to Cultural Identity?* Antwerpen and Oxford: Intersentia.

Doomernik, Jeroen. 2001. "Immigration, Multiculturalism and the Nation State in Western Europe." Paper presented at the United Nations Research Institute for Social Development Conference on Racism and Public Policy, 3 September, Durban, South Africa. [http://www.unrisd.org/unrisd/website/projects.nsf/(httpProjectsForResearchHome-en)/CE2B1BCD4B5F5D3A80256B4900530E39?OpenDocument]. February 2004.

Douglas, W. A. 1988. "A Critique of Recent Trends in the Analysis of Ethnonationalism." *Ethnic and Racial Studies* 11(2): 192-206.

Dragoljub, Ackovic. 2000. "Roma in Serbia: Introducing Romany Language and Culture into Primary Schools." Minority Rights Group International, London.

Droege, Susanne, and Birgit Soete. 2001. "Trade-Related Intellectual Property Rights, North-South Trade, and Biological Diversity." *Environmental and Resource Economics* 19(2): 149-63.

DUMC (Dutch Monitoring Centre on Racism and Xenophobia). 2002. "Racial Violence and Violence Incited by the Extreme Right 2001 and 2002." Rotterdam, The Netherlands. [http://www.lbr.nl/internationaal/DUMC/publicatie/ar_racial_violence2001.pdf]. January 2004.

Duncan, T., K. Jefferis, and P. Molutsi. 2000. "Botswana: Social Development in a Resource-Rich Country." In Santosh Mehrotra and Jolly Richard, eds. *Development with a Human Face: Experiences in Social Achievement and Economic Growth.* Oxford: Oxford University Press.

Dunleavy, Patrick, and Brendan O'Leary. 1987. *Theories of the State: The Politics of Liberal Democracy.* Basingstoke: MacMillan Education.

During, A. T. 1992. "Guardians of the Land: Indigenous Peoples and the Health of the Earth." Worldwatch Paper 112. Worldwatch Institute. Washington, DC. [http://www.worldwatch.org/pubs/paper/112.html/]. February 2004.

———. 1993. *Supporting Indigenous Peoples in State of the World 1993: A Worldwatch Institute Report on Progress Toward a Sustainable Society.* New York: W.W. Norton.

Dutcher, N. 1982. "The Use of First and Second Languages in Primary Education." Working Paper. World Bank, Education Department Washington, DC.

Eades, D. 2004. "Participation in a Second Language and Second Dialect Speakers in the Legal System." *Annual Review of Applied Linguistics* 23: 113-33.

Easterley, William, and Ross Levine. 1997. "Africa's Growth Tragedy: Policies and Ethnic Divisions." *The Quarterly Journal of Economics* 112(4): 1203-250.

Eatwell, Roger. 2000. "The Rebirth of the 'Extreme Right' in Western Europe?" *Parliamentary Affairs* 53(3): 407-25.

The Economist. 2000. "Sri Lanka Backs Away from Devolution." 10 August.

———. 2002a. "Survey on Migration." 2 November.

———. 2002b. "The Best of Reasons." 31 October.

———. 2003a. "Ends, Means and Barbarity: Special Report on Torture." 11 January.

———. 2003b. "Religion, Politics and Moderation." 17 May.

———. 2004a. "Africa's Engine." Survey: Sub-Saharan Africa. 15 January.

———. 2004b. "The War of the Headscarves." 7 February.

Edgerton, Susan Huddleston. 1996. *Translating the Curriculum: Multiculturalism into Cultural Studies.* New York and London: Routledge.

Elazar, Daniel. 1998. *Constitutionalizing Globalization.* Lanham, Maryland: Rowman & Littlefield.

Electionworld.org. 2004. "Elections Around the World." [http://www.electionworld.org/]. February 2004.

Engineer, Asghar Ali. 2003. "Uniform Civil Code or Legal Pluralism." Institute of Islamic Studies and Center for Study of Society and Secularism, Mumbai. [http://ecumene.org/IIS/csss114.htm]. February 2004.

———. 2004. *Communal Riots After Independence: A Comprehensive Account.* New Delhi: Shipra.

Entelis, John P. 2002. "Morocco: Democracy Denied." *Le Monde Diplomatique.* 1 October. [http://mondediplo.com/2002/10/13morocco]. February 2004.

Entzinger, Han. 2003. "Nationale Identiteit en burgerschap." *Civis Mundi* 42(1): 22-26.

Esman, Milton J. 1986. "Diasporas and International Relations." In Gabriel Sheffer, ed. *Modern Diaspora in International Politics.* New York: St. Martin's Press.

Etounga-Manguelle, Daniel. 2000. "Does Africa Need a Cultural Adjustment Program?" In Lawrence E. Harrison and Samuel P. Huntington, eds. *Culture Matters.* New York: Basic Books.

EUMC (European Monitoring Centre on Racism and Xenophobia). 2002. "Racism and Xenophobia in the EU Member States: Trends, Developments and Good Practice in 2002." Annual Report 2002, Part 2. Vienna. [http://eumc.eu.int/eumc/index.php?fuseaction=content.dsp_cat_content&catid=3fb38ad3e22bb]. January 2004.

European Union. 2003. "The Doha Development Agenda: Outcome of the WTO Ministerial, European Parliament Resolution on the 5th Ministerial Conference of the WTO in Cancun." [http://europa.eu.int/comm/trade/issues/newround/doha_da/epr250903_en.htm]. March 2004.

———. 2004. "The Commissioner of Foreign Affairs of the Berlin Senate (Die Auslanderbeauftagte des Senats von Berlin)." Berlin. [http://europa.eu.int/comm/employment_social/fundamental_rights/pdf/legisln/mslegln/de_berlin_en.pdf]. March 2004.

Fafunwa, B. 1990. "Using National Languages in Education: A Challenge to African Educators." In *African Thoughts on the Prospects of Education for All.* Paris: UNESCO Publishing.

Fahmy, Ninette S. 1998. "The Performance of the Muslim Brotherhood in the Egyptian Syndicates: An Alternative Formula for Reform?" *The Middle East Journal* 52(4): 551-62.

FBI (Federal Bureau of Investigation). 1999. "Hate Crime Data Collection Guidelines." Washington, DC. [http://www.fbi.gov/ucr/ucr.htm#hate]. April 2004.

———. 2002. "Hate Crime Statistics 2002." Washington, DC. [http://www.fbi.gov/ucr/ ucr.htm#hate]. January 2004.

———. 2004. "Uniform Crime Reports: Hate Crime Statistics." Washington, DC. [http://www.fbi.gov/ucr/ucr.htm#hate]. February 2004.

Feldman, Leonard C. 2002. "Redistribution, Recognition and the State: The Irreducibly Political Dimension of Injustice." *Political Theory* 30(3): 410–40.

Fermin, Alfons. 2001. "The Justification of Mandatory Integration Programmes for New Immigrants." European Research Centre on Migration and Ethnic Relations, Utrecht.

Financial Times. 2004. "French Filmmakers Fear for L'Exception Culturelle." 9 January.

Fleiner, Thomas, ed. 2003. *Multicultural Federalism: The Swiss Case*. Fribourg, Switzerland: The Institute of Federalism.

Florida, Richard, and Gary Gates. 2002. "Technology and Tolerance: Diversity and High Tech Growth." *The Brookings Review* 20(1): 32–35.

Forero, Juan. 2003. "Seeking Balance: Growth vs. Culture in Amazon." *The New York Times*. 10 December.

Fossas, Enric. 1999. "Asymmetry and Pluriantionality in Spain." Working Paper, Universitat Autònoma de Barcelona. [http://www.diba.es/icps/working_papers/docs/Wp_i_167.pdf]. March 2004.

Fraenkel, Jon. 2003. "Ethnic Structure, Inequality and Public Sector Governance in the Fiji Islands." Ethnic Conflict, Inequality and Public Sector Governance Country Studies. United Nations Research Institute for Social Development, Geneva.

France, Ministère de Jeunesse, Éducation et Recherche. 2004. "Bulletin Officiel: Calendrier des Fêtes Légales." [http://www.education.gouv.fr/bo/2004/4/MENA0302913C.htm]. March 2004.

Fraser, Nancy, and Axel Honneth. 2003. *Redistribution or Recognition? A Political-Philosophical Exchange*. London: Verso Books.

Fraser, Nancy. 1989. *Unruly Practices: Power, Discourse and Gender in Contemporary Social Theory*. Cambridge: Polity.

———. 1995. "From Redistribution to Recognition? Dilemmas of Justice in a 'Postsocialist' Age." *New Left Review* 212: 68–93.

———. 1997. *Justice Interrupts: Critical Reflections on the 'Postsocialist' Condition*. New York: Routledge.

Front National. 2004. "Nos Propositions: Identite." [http://www.frontnational.com/doc_prop_identite.php]. March 2004.

Fukuda-Parr, Sakiko. 2001. "In Search of Indicators of Culture and Development: Review of Progress and Proposals for Next Steps." Text for the *World Culture Report*. New York. [http://www.undp.org/hdro/events/rioforum/fukudaparr2.pdf]. February 2004.

Funke, Hajo. 2001. "Europe at the Threshold: Fairness or Fortress? Racism, Public Policy and Anti-racist Concepts." Paper presented at the United Nations Research Institute for Social Development Conference on Racism and Public Policy, 3 September, Durban. [http://www.unrisd.org/unrisd/website/projects.nsf/(httpProjectsForResearchHome-en)/CE2B1BCD4B5F5D3A80256B4900530E39?OpenDocument]. February 2004.

Gandhi, Mohandas. 1921. "English Learning." *Young India*. 1 June.

Garson, Jean-Pierre, and Anais Loizillon. 2003. "Changes and Challenges, Europe and Migration from 1950 to Present." Paper presented at the conference jointly organized by the European Commision and the Organisation for Economic Cooperation and Develoment, "The Economic and Social Aspects of Migration", 21–22 January, Brussels. [http://www.oecd.org/dataoecd/15/3/15516948.pdf]. February 2004.

Geddes, Andrew. 2002. "Europe's Ageing Workforce." *BBC Online*. 20 June. [http://news.bbc.co.uk/1/hi/world/europe/2053581.stm]. February 2004.

Gerges, Fawaz A. 2000. "The End of the Islamist Insurgency in Egypt?: Costs and Prospects." *The Middle East Journal* 54(4): 592–612.

Ghosh, Bimal. 2003. "Elusive Protection, Uncertain Lands: Migrants' Access to Human Rights." International Organization for Migration, Geneva.

Gill, Emily R. 2001. *Becoming Free: Autonomy and Diversity in the Liberal Polity*. Lawrence: University Press of Kansas.

Giovarelli, Renée, and Cholpon Akmatova. 2002. "Local Institutions that Enforce Customary Law in the Kyrgyz Republic and their Impact on Women's Rights." Agriculture and Rural Development E-Paper. World Bank, Washington, DC.

Godmer, Laurent, and Laurent Kestel. 2001. "Extremism and Democratic Coalitions: The Institutional Integration of Extreme Right Parties in the Regional Parliaments of Germany, Austria and France." Paper presented at the European Consortium for Political Research Conference, 6 April, Grenoble, France. [http://www.essex.ac.uk/ecpr/events/jointsessions/paperarchive/grenoble.asp?section=14]. February 2004.

Goldstone, Leo. 1998. "Cultural Statistics." In Ruth Towse, ed. *A Handbook of Cultural Economics*. Cheltenham, UK: Edward Elgar. [https://dspace.ubib.eur.nl/retrieve/1351/TOWSE+EBOOK_pages0189-0194.pdf]. February 2004.

Goodman, Diane J. 2004. *Promoting Diversity and Social Justice: Educating People From Privileged Groups*. Thousand Oaks, Calif. and London: Sage.

Goody, Jack. 1996. *The East in the West*. Cambridge: Cambridge University Press.

Graeme, Hugo. 2003. "Circular Migration: Keeping Development Rolling." Migration Policy Institute, Washington, DC. [http://www.migrationinformation.org/Feature/display.cfm?ID=129]. February 2004.

Granovetter, Mark. 1985. "Economic Action and Social Structure: The Problem of Embeddedness." *American Journal of Sociology* 91: 481–510.

Greif, Avner. 1994. "Cultural Beliefs and Organization of Society: A Historical and Theoretical Reflection on Collectivist and Individualist Societies." *Journal of Political Economy* 102: 912–50.

Griffiths, Ann L., and Karl Nerenberg, eds. 2002. *Handbook of Federal Countries, 2002*. Montreal and Kingston: McGill-Queen's University Press.

Grillo, R. D. 1998. *Pluralism and the Politics of Difference: State, Culture and Ethnicity in Comparative Perspective*. Oxford: Clarendon Press.

Grin, Francois. 2003. *Language Policy Evaluation and the European Charter for Regional or Minority Languages*. Berkeley, Calif.: University of California Press.

Grove, A. K., and N. A. Carter. 1999. "Not All Blarney is Cast in Stone: International Cultural Conflict in Northern Ireland." *Political Psychology* 20(4): 725–65.

The Guardian. 2001. "The Truth of Multicultural Britain." 25 November.

Gurr, Ted Robert. 1993. *Minorities At Risk: A Global View of Ethnopolitical Conflicts*. Washington, DC: United States Institute for Peace Press.

———. 2000. *People Versus States*. Washington, DC: United States Institute for Peace Press.

Gutmann, Amy, and Dennis Thompson. 1996. *Democracy and Disagreement*. Cambridge, Mass.: Harvard University Press.

Gutmann, Amy, ed. 1994. *Multiculturalism*. Princeton: Princeton University Press.

Gutmann, Amy. 1995. "Challenges of Multiculturalism in Democratic Education." Princeton. [http://www.ed.uiuc.edu/EPS/PES-Yearbook/95_docs/gutmann.html. February 2004.

Habermas, Juergen. 1975. *Legitimation Crisis*. Boston: Beacon Press.

———. 1996. *Between Facts and Norms: Contributions to a Discourse Theory of Law and Democracy*. Cambridge, Mass.: MIT Press.

Hafez, Mohammed M. 2000. "Armed Islamist Movements and Political Violence in Algeria." *The Middle East Journal* 54(4): 572–91.

Haffajee, Ferial. 1999. "South Africa: Blending Tradition and Change." *UNESCO Courier*. November. [http://www.unesco.org/courier/1999_11/uk/dossier/txt23.htm].

Halfin, Igal, ed. 2002. *Language and Revolution: Making Modern Political Identities.* London and Portland: Frank Cass.

Hammer, Juliane, and Helena Lindholm Schulz. 2003. *The Palestinian Diaspora: Formation of Identities and Politics of Homeland.* London: Routledge.

Hansen, Thomas Blom. 2001. *The Saffron Wave: Democracy and Hindu Nationalism in Modern India.* Oxford: Oxford University Press.

Harding, Sandra, and Uma Narayan, eds. 2000. *Decentering the Center: Philosophy for a Multicultural, Postcolonial and Feminist World.* Bloomington: Indiana University Press.

Harris, Peter, and Ben Reilly. 1998. "Democracy and Deep-Rooted Conflict: Options for Negotiators." International Institute for Democracy and Electoral Assistance, Stockholm.

Harrison, Lawrence E., and Samuel P. Huntington, eds. 2000. *Culture Matters: How Values Shape Human Progress.* New York: Basic Books.

Hart, H. L. A. 1955. "Are There Any Natural Rights?" *The Philosophical Review* 64: 175–91.

Hastrup, Kirsten, ed. 2001. *Legal Cultures and Human Rights: The Challenge of Diversity.* The Hague and London: Kluwer Law Interantional.

Haubrich, Dirk. 2003. "September 11, Anti-Terror Laws and Civil Liberties: Britain, France and Germany Compared." *Government and Opposition* 38(1): 1–28.

Helwege, Ann. 1995. "Poverty in Latin America: Back to the Abyss?" *Journal of Interamerican Studies and World Affairs* 37(3): 99–123.

HinduUnity.org. 2004. "HinduUnity.org: Promoting and Supporting the Ideals of the Bajrang Dal—V.H.P., Youth Wing Bharat." [http://hinduunity.org/aboutus.html]. April 2004.

Hoffman, Bruce. 1998–99. "Revival of Religious Terrorism Begs for Broad U.S. Policy." *Rand Review* 22(2). [http://www.rand.org/publications/randreview/issues/rr.winter98.9/methods.html. December 2003.

Honwana, Alcinda. 1999. "Non-Western Concepts of Mental Health." [http://earlybird.qeh.ox.ac.uk/rfgexp/rsp_tre/student/nonwest/toc.htm]. March 2004.

Hoodfar, Homa, and Nelofer Pazira. 2003. "Building Civil Societies: A Guide for Social and Political Activism." Santa Cruz, Calif. [http://www2.ucsc.edu/globalinterns/cpapers/hoodfar.pdf]. February 2004.

Human Rights Watch. 2002. "Human Rights Watch Statement: Freedom of Religion—On the Occasion of the OSCE Human Dimension Implementation." New York. [http://www.hrw.org/press/2002/09/osce-religion0912.htm]. February 2004.

———. 2003. "Nationality and Statelessness." New York. [http://www.hrw.org/campaigns/race/nationality.htm]. February 2004.

Huntington, Samuel P. 1996. *The Clash of Civilizations and the Remaking the World Order.* New York: Simon and Schuster.

Iganski, Paul. 2002. "Hate Crimes Hurt More, But Should They Be More Harshly Punished." In Paul Iganski, ed. *The Hate Debate: Should Hate Be Punished as a Crime?* London: Profile Books.

Ignazi, Piero. 2003. *Extreme Right Parties in Western Europe.* New York: Oxford University Press.

ILO (International Labour Organization). 2001. "Vietnam Desk Review." Project to Promote ILO Policy on Indigenous and Tribal Peoples (Convention 169), Geneva.

———. 2003. *ILO Convention on Indigenous and Tribal Peoples: A Manual.* Geneva.

Independent Commission on Migration to Germany. 2001. "Structuring Immigration, Fostering Integration." Berlin. [http://www.eng.bmi.bund.de/Annex/en_14626/Download_Summary.pdf]. February 2004.

Indian and Northern Affairs Canada. 2004. "Aboriginal Customary Law." Ottawa. [http://www.ainc-inac.gc.ca/pr/pub/matr/acl_e.html]. February 2004.

India, Ministry of Education. 2004. Personal communication on human resource development. March. New Delhi.

India, Ministry of Personnel. 2002. "Holidays to be Observed in Government Offices During the Year 2002." Department of Personnel and Training, New Delhi. [http://persmin.nic.in/circular/jcm3.html#6]. February 2004.

India, Office of the Registrar General. 2004. "Census of India." New Delhi. [http://www.censusindia.net/]. March 2004.

Indigenous Australia. 2003. "What is Cultural Heritage?" [http://www.dreamtime.net.au/indigenous/culture.cfm]. February 2004.

Inglehart, Ronald. 1997. *Modernization and Postmodernization: Cultural, Economic, and Political Change in 43 Societies.* Princeton: Princeton University Press.

Inglehart, Ronald, and Wayne Baker. 2000. "Modernization, Cultural Change, and the Persistence of Traditional Values." *American Sociological Review* 65: 19-51.

Inglis, Christine. 2004. "Multiculturalism: New Policy Responses to Diversity." Policy Paper No. 4. United Nations Educational, Scientific and Cultural Organization, Paris.

International Council on Metals and the Environment. 1999. "Mining and Indigenous Peoples: Case Studies." Ottawa.

International Federation of Human Rights. 2003. "Discrimination Against Religious Minorities in Iran." Paris. [http://www.fidh.org/asie/rapport/2003/ir0108a.pdf]. February 2004.

The Internet Movie Database. 2004. "International All-Time Box Office Chart." [http://us.imdb.com/Charts/intltopmovies]. March 2004.

IOE (International Organisation of Employers). 2003. "Migration in Europe: Political, Social and Economic Dimensions." Background Document. London. [http://www.ioe-emp.org/ioe_emp/pdf/migration_IOE_Moscow.pdf]. February 2004.

IOM (International Organization for Migration). 2003a. "Integration of Migrants: The IOM Approach." Geneva. [http://www.iom.si/pdf/Integration%20master.pdf]. February 2004.

———. 2003b. "Migration in a World of Global Change. New Strategies and Policies for New Realities." IOM Migration Policy and Research. Geneva.

———. 2003c. "World Migration Report 2003: Managing Migration Challenges and Responses for People on the Move." Geneva.

———. 2004. "Assisted Returns Service." [http://www.iom.int/en/who/main%5Fservice%5Fareas%5Fassisted.shtml]. March 2004.

IRR (Institute of Race Relations). 2003. "Norway: Progress Party (FrP)." [http://www.irr.org.uk/europe/norway.html]. December 2003.

Jackman, Robert W., and Karin Volpert. 1996. "Conditions Favouring Parties of the Extreme Right in Western Europe." *British Journal of Political Science* 26(1): 501-21.

Jacobs, Dirk. 2003. "The Arab European League: The Rapid Growth of a Radical Immigrant Movement." Paper presented at the European Consortium for Political Research Conference, 18 September, Marburg, Germany. [http://www.essex.ac.uk/ecpr/events/generalconference/marburg/papers/21/5/Jacobs.pdf]. February 2004.

Jarkko, Lars, and Tom W. Smith. 2001. "National Pride in Cross-National Perspective." National Opinion Research Center. University of Chicago, Chicago. [http://spitswww.uvt.nl/web/iric/papers/pap1e1.doc]. February 2004.

Jeness, Valerie. 2002. "Contours of Hate Crime Politics and Law in the United States." In Paul Iganski, ed. *The Hate Debate: Should Hate be Punished as a Crime?* London: Profile Books.

Jureidini, Ray. 2001. "Migrant Workers and Xenophobia in the Middle East." Keynote address at the United Nations Research Institute for Social Development Conference on Racism and Public Policy, 3 September, Durban. [http://www.unrisd.org/80256B3C005BCCF9/httpNetITFrame?ReadForm&parent unid=8EAB85CCEBB1C65480256B6D00578762&parent

doctype=paper&netitpath=http://www.unrisd.org/unpublished_/specialevents_/djureidi/content.htm]. February 2004.

Justiniano, Freddy. 2004. "Correspondence on the Political Situation in Bolivia and Ecuador." United Nations Development Programme, Regional Bureau for Latin America and the Caribbean, New York. March 2004.

Justino, Patricia, and Julie Litchfield. 2003. "Economic Exclusion and Discrimination: The Experience of Minorities and Indigenous Peoples." Minority Rights Group International, London. [http://www.minorityrights.org/admin/Download/pdf/IP_EconomicExclusion_JustinoLitchfield.pdf]. February 2004.

Kaldor, Mary, and Diego Muro. 2003. "Religious and Nationalist Militant Groups." In H. Anheier, M. Glasius, and M. Kaldor, eds. *Global Civil Society 2003.* Oxford: Oxford University Press.

Kanbur, Ravi. 2001. "Economic Policy, Distribution and Poverty: Nature of Disagreements." Cornell University, Ithaca, New York. [http://people.cornell.edu/pages/sk145/papers/Disagreements.pdf]. February 2004.

Kanyinga, Karuti. 2003. "Ethnic Structure, Inequality and Governance of the Public Sector in Kenya." Ethnic Structure, Inequality and Public Sector Governance Country Studies. United Nations Research Institute for Social Development, Geneva.

Kapur, Devesh, and John McHale. 2003. "Migration's New Payoff." *Foreign Policy* 139: 48–57.

Kaviraj, Sudipto. 1992. "The Imaginary Institution of India." In Partha Chatterjee and Gyanendra Pandey, eds. *Subaltern Studies VII.* New Delhi: Oxford University Press.

Kearns, Thomas R., and Austin Sarat. 1997. *Identities, Politics and Rights.* Ann Arbor: University of Michigan Press.

———. 1999. *Cultural Pluralism, Identity Politics and the Law.* Ann Arbor: University of Michigan Press.

Keating, Michael. 2002. "Plurinational Democracy in a Post-Sovereign Order." Queen's Papers on Europeanisation. Institute of European Studies. Queen's University of Belfast, Belfast. [http://www.qub.ac.uk/ies/onlinepapers/poe1-02.pdf]. February 2004.

Kelso, Paul, and Jeevan Vasagar. 2002. "Muslims Reject Image of Separate Society." *The Guardian.* 17 June.

Kertzer, David I., and Dominique Arel, eds. 2002. *Census and Identity: The Politics of Race, Ethnicity and Language in National Censuses.* Cambridge: Cambridge University Press.

Kiernan, Ben. 1999. "Sur La Notion de Génocide." *Le Débat.* 1 March.

Klaus, David. 2003. "The Use of Indigenous Languages in Early Basic Education in Papua New Guinea: A Model for Elsewhere?" *Language and Education: An International Journal* 17(2).

Knop, Karen. 2002. *Diversity and Self-Determination in International Law.* Cambridge: Cambridge University Press.

Knowles, Caroline, and Vered Amit-Talai. 1996. *Re-situating Identities: The Politics of Race, Ethnicity and Culture.* Orchard Park, New York: Broadview Press.

Kogacioglu, Dicle. 2003. "Dissolution of Political Parties by the Constitutional Court in Turkey: Judicial Delimitation of the Political Domain." *International Sociology* 18(1): 258–76.

Koh, Harold Hongju. 2002. "The Case against Military Commissions." *The American Journal of International Law* 96(2): 337–44.

Kongolo, Tshimanga. 2001. "Towards a More Balanced Coexistence of Traditional Knowledge and Pharmaceuticals Protection in Africa." *Journal of World Trade* 35(2): 349–61.

Koopmans, Ruud. 2002. "Good Intentions Sometimes Make Bad Policies: A Comparison of Dutch and German Integration Policies." *Migrantenstudies* 18: 87–92.

Kuruk, Paul. 2002. "African Customary Law and the Protection of Folklore." Bulletin Volume XXXVI Number 2. United Nations Educational, Scientific and Cultural Organization, Paris.

Kymlicka, Will, and Wayne Norman, eds. 2000. *Citizenship in Diverse Societies.* Oxford: Oxford University Press.

Kymlicka, Will. 1990. *Contemporary Political Philosophy: An Introduction.* Oxford: Clarendon.

———. 1996. *Multicultural Citizenship: A Liberal Theory of Minority Rights.* Oxford: Clarendon.

———. 1998. *Finding Our Way: Rethinking Ethnocultural Relations in Canada.* Toronto and Oxford: Oxford University Press.

———. 2001. *Politics in the Vernacular: Nationalism, Multiculturalism and Citizenship.* Oxford: Oxford University Press.

———. 2003. "Immigration, Citizenship, Multiculturalism: Exploring the Links." *The Political Quarterly* 74(1): 195–208.

Lavery, David. 2004. "Universal Language: American Film and Monoculture at Century's End." Paper presented at the annual conference of the South Central Modern Language Association, 31 October, Dallas. [http://mtsu32.mtsu.edu:11072/Writing/Universal%20Language.htm]. February 2004.

Lega Nord. 2004. "Stop Ai Clandestini." [http://www.leganord.org/a_2_docpolitici_clandestini.htm]. March 2004.

Leibfried, Stephan, and Elmar Rieger. 2003. *Limits of Globalization: Welfare States and the World Economy.* Cambridge: Polity.

Lenoir, Rene. 1989. *Les Exclus: Un Francais sur Dix.* Paris: Editions de Seuil.

Leone, Richard C., and Greg Angrig Jr., eds. 2003. *The War on Our Freedoms: Civil Liberties in an Age of Terrorism.* New York: Century Foundation and Public Affairs Books.

Levin, Brian. 2001. "Extremism and the Constitution: How America's Legal Evolution Affects the Response to Extremism." *The American Behavioral Scientist* 45(4): 714–55.

Levin, Jack, and Jack McDevitt. 1999. "Hate Crimes." In *Encyclopedia of Violence, Peace and Conflict.* San Diego: Academic Press. [http://www.violence.neu.edu/publication4.html]. January 2004.

Lewis, Bernard. 1998. *The Multiple Identities of the Middle East.* London: Weidenfeld and Nicholson.

Lewis, Justin, and Toby Miller, eds. 2003. *Critical Cultural Policy Studies: A Reader.* Malden, Mass. and Oxford: Blackwell.

Lewis, Peter. 2003. "Nigeria: Elections in a Fragile Regime." *Journal of Democracy* 14(3).

Libanio, José Carlos. 2004. Correspondence on the Share of Afro-Brazilian Cabinet Members. March. Sao Paolo.

Licha, Isabel. 2002. "Citizen Participation and Local Government in Latin America: Advances, Challenges and Best Practices." Paper presented at the Citizenship Participation in the Context of Fiscal Decentralization Conference, 2 September, Kobe. [http://www.adb.org/Documents/Events/2002/Citizen_Participation/Overview_LAC.pdf]. February 2004.

Linz, Juan J., and Alfred Stepan, eds. 1978. *The Breakdown of Democratic Regimes.* Baltimore: The Johns Hopkins University Press.

Linz, Juan J., and Alfred Stepan. 1996. *Problems of Democratic Transition and Consolidation: Southern Europe, South America and Post-Communist Europe.* Baltimore and London: The Johns Hopkins University Press.

Ljiphart, Arend. 1984. "Proportionality by Non-PR Methods: Ethnic Representation in Belgium, Cyprus, Lebanon, New Zealand, West Gemany and Zimbabwe." In A. Ljiphart and B. Grofman, eds. *Choosing an Electoral System: Issues and Alternatives.* New York: Praeger.

Lott, Juanita Tamayo. 1998. *Asian Americans: From Racial Category to Multiple Identities.* Walnut Creek, Calif., and London: Altamira Press.

Loury, Glenn. 2001. "Racial Justice and Affirmative Action Policies: The Superficial Morality of Colour-Blindness in the United States." Paper presented at the United Nations Research Institute for Social Development Conference on Racism and Public Policy, 3 September, Durban. [http://www.unrisd.org/80256B3C005BCCF9/httpNetITFrame?ReadForm&parentunid=0A3B836D101A5A4580256B6D005

78931&parentdoctype=paper&netitpath=http://www.
unrisd.org/unpublished_/specialevents_/dloury/content.htm].
February 2004.

Lukes, Steven, and Christian Joppke. 1999. *Multicultural Questions*. Oxford: Oxford University Press.

Luter, Kurt Richard, and Kris Deschouwer, eds. 1999. *Party Elites in Divided Societies: Political Parties in Consociational Democracy*. London: Routledge.

Luttmer, E. 1997. "Group Loyalty and the Taste for Redistribution." *Journal of Political Economy* 109(3): 500–28.

Mabry, Tristan James. 1998. "Modernization, Nationalism and Islam: An Examination of Ernest Gellner's Writings on Muslim Society with Reference to Indonesia and Malaysia." *Ethnic and Racial Studies* 21(1): 64–88.

Macan-Markar, Marwaan. 2004. "Thailand: Amid Violence, Final Bell Tolls for Islamic Schools." Inter Press Service. 20 February.

Macedo, Stephen. 2000. *Diversity and Distrust: Civic Education in a Multicultural Democracy*. Cambridge, Mass. and London: Harvard University Press.

Malhotra, Anshu. 2002. *Gender, Caste and Religious Identities: Restructuring Class in Colonial Punjab*. Oxford and New Delhi: Oxford University Press.

Mamdani, Mahmood. 2001. *When Victims Become Killers: Colonialism, Nativism, and the Genocide in Rwanda*. Princeton: Princeton University Press.

Mandela, Nelson. 1994. *A Long Walk to Freedom*. Boston: Little, Brown and Co.

Mansbridge, Jane. 1998. *Beyond Self-Interest*. Chicago: Chigaco University Press.

Marshall, Monty G., and Ted Robert Gurr. 2003. *Peace and Conflict: A Global Survey of Armed Conflicts, Self-Determination Movements and Democracy*. Baltimore: Center for International Development and Conflict Management.

Marshall, Paul, ed. 2000. *Religious Freedom in the World: A Global Report on Freedom and Persecution*. Nashville: Broadman & Holman Publishers.

Martínez-Herrera, Enric. 2002. "Nationalist Extremism and Outcomes of State Policies in the Basque Country, 1979–2001." *International Journal on Multicultural Societies* 4(1): 1–22.

Marty, Martin E., and R. Scott Appleby, eds. 1991. *Fundamentalisms Observed*. Chicago and London: University of Chicago Press.

———. 1993. *Fundamentalisms and the State: Remaking Polities, Economies, and Militance*. Chicago and London: University of Chicago Press.

———. 1995. *Fundamentalisms Comprehended*. Chicago and London: University of Chicago Press.

Matiki, A. J. 2003. "Linguistic Exclusion and the Opinions of Malawian Legislators." *Language Policy* 2(2): 133–52.

Mayer, Jean-François. 2001. "Cults, Violence and Religious Terrorism: An International Perspective." *Studies in Conflict and Terrorism* 24(5): 361–76.

Mazrui, A. 1996. "Perspectives: The Muse of Modernity and the Quest for Development." In P. Altbach and S. Hassan, eds. *The Muse of Modernity: Essays on Culture as Development in Africa*. Trenton: Africa World Press.

McPhail, Kathryn. 2000. "How Oil, Gas, and Mining Projects Can Contribute to Development." *Finance and Development* 37(4): 46–49.

McRae, Kenneth D., ed. 1974. *Consociational Democracy: Political Accommodation in Segmented Societies*. Toronto: McClelland and Stewart.

Medrano, Juan Díez. 2002. "Thematic Introduction." *International Journal on Multicultural Societies* 4(1). [http://www.unesco.org/most/vl4n1intro.htm]. February 2004.

Mehrotra, Santosh, and Enrique Delamonica. Forthcoming. *Public Spending for the Poor: Getting the Fundamentals Right. In Social and Macroeconomic Policy*. Oxford: Oxford University Press.

Meyer, Thomas. 2001. *Identity Mania. Fundamentalism and the Politicization of Cultural Differences*. London and New York: Zed Books.

Mexico, Ministry of Health. 2004. "Mexico National Health Programme, 2001–2006." Mexico City. [http://www.gob.mx/wb2/egobierno/egob_Programa_Nacional_de_Salud]. February 2004.

Mgbeoji, Ikechi. 2001. "Patents and Traditional Knowledge of the Uses of Plants: Is a Communal Patent Regime Part of the Solution to the Scourge of Biopiracy?" *Indiana Journal of Global Legal Studies* 9(1): 163–86.

Middle East Institute. 2003. "Algeria." [http://www.mideasti.org/countries/countries.php?name=algeria]. March 2004.

Migration Information Source. 2003. "Canada: Policy Legacies, New Directions and Future Challenges." Washington, DC. [http://www.migrationinformation.org/Profiles/display.cfm?ID=20]. February 2004.

Miguel. T. 1999. "Ethnic Diversity and School Funding in Kenya." Economics Working Papers Archive. Washington University, St. Louis.

The Minorities at Risk (MAR) Project. 2003. *MARGene: Minorities At Risk Data Generation and Management Program*. Center for International Development and Conflict Management, University of Maryland, Baltimore. [http://www. cidcm.umd.edu/inscr/mar/data.htm]. February 2004.

Minority Rights Group International. 2003. "Indigenous Peoples and Poverty: The Cases of Bolivia, Guatemala, Honduras and Nicaragua." Executive Summary. London. [http://www.minorityrights.org/Dev/mrg_dev_title12_LatinAmerica/mrg_dev_title12_LatinAmerica_8.htm]. February 2004.

Mishra, Pankaj. 2003. "Hurray for Bollywood." *The New York Times*. 28 February.

Modood, Tariq, and Pnina Werbner, eds. 1997. *The Politics of Multiculturalism in the New Europe: Racism, Identity and Community*. London: Zed Books.

Mody, Anjali. 2003. "It Is About Equality, Not Uniformity." *The Hindu*. 10 August.

Moeketsi, R. 1999. *Discourse in a Multilingual and Multicultural Courtroom: A Court Interpreter's Guide*. Pretoria: J. L. Van Schaik.

Mokyr, Joel. 1983. *Why Ireland Starved: A Quantitative and Analytical History of the Irish Economy, 1800–1850*. London: Allen and Unwin.

Moody, R. 2000. "The Decade of Destruction: How the Mining Companies Betrayed their Promised Greening." [http://www.minesandcommunities.org/Company/decade.htm]. March 2004.

Moreau, Ron, Sami Yousafzai, and Zahid Hussain, with Michael Hirsh. 2003. "Holy War 101." *Newsweek*. 1 December.

Moya, Paula M. 2002. *Learning From Experience: Minority Identities, Multicultural Struggles*. Berkeley: University of California Press.

Mudde, Cas. 2000. *The Ideology of the Extreme Right*. Manchester: Manchester University Press.

Myerson, Roger B. 1991. "Proportional Representation, Approval Voting and Coalitionally Straightforward Elections." Discussion Paper 928. Center for Mathematical Studies in Economics and Management Science. Northwestern University, Chicago. [http://www.kellogg.nwu.edu/research/math/dps/928.pdf]. February 2004.

Nagel, Jack H. 2004. "Stormy Passage to a Safe Harbour? Proportional Representation in New Zealand." In Henry Miller, ed. *Making Every Vote Count: Reassessing Canada's Electoral System*. Peterborough, Ontario: Broadview Press.

NARAL Pro Choice. 2004. "Clinic Violence and Intimidation." [http://www.naral.org/facts/terrorism.cfm]. February 2004.

National Commission on Indigenous Peoples. 2004a. "Latest News." Manila. [http://www.ncip.gov.ph/news/newsdisplay.php?articleid=66]. February 2004.

———. 2004b. "Republic Act 8371." Manila. [http://www.ncip. gov.ph/indexmain.php]. February 2004.

Ndoye, Mamadou. 2003. "Bilingualism, Language Policies and Educational Strategies in Africa." International Institute for Education Planning. United Nations Educational, Scientific and Cultural Organization, Paris.

Neville, Alexander. 2001. "Language, Education and Race Relations." Paper presented at the United Nations Research Institute on Sustainable Development Conference on Racism and Public Policy, 3 September, Durban. [http://www. unrisd.org/unrisd/website/projects.nsf/(httpProjectsForResearchHome-en)/CE2B1BCD4B5F5D3A80256B4900530E39 ?OpenDocument]]. February 2004.

The New York Times. 2003. "Just As Mexican Movies Become Chic Again, the Government Pulls Its Support." 11 December.

Nicaragua Network. 2004. "CAFTA: A Shotgun Wedding?" [http://www.nicanet.org/alerts/cafta_negociations_2.htm]. February 2004.

Niessen Jan. 2000. "Diversity and Cohesion: New Challenges for the Integration of Immigrants and Minorities." Council of Europe, Strasbourg.

Norchi, Charles H. 2000. "Indigenous Knowledge as Intellectual Property." *Policy Sciences* 33(3/4): 387–98.

Nussbaum, Martha. 1995. *Women and Human Development: The Capabilities Approach.* Cambridge: Cambridge University Press.

Nussbaum, Martha, and Jonathan Glover, eds. 1995. *Women, Culture and Development.* Oxford: Clarendon Press.

Ocampo, José Antonio. 2001. "Rethinking the Development Agenda." Paper presented at the American Economic Associations Annual Meeting, 5 January, New Orleans. [http://www.undp.org/rblac/documents/poverty/ rethinking_dev_agenda.pdf]. February 2004.

OECD (Organisation for Economic Co-operation and Development). 2003. Trends in International Migration, Annual Report 2003 Edition. Paris: SOPEMI. [http://www.oecd.org/ document/17/0,2340,en_2649_33931_28703185_1_1_1_1,00. html]. February 2004.

Office of Personnel Management. 2003. "2003 Federal Holidays." Washington, DC. [http://www.opm.gov/fedhol/2003.asp]. February 2004.

Okin, Susan Moller, ed. 1999. *Is Multiculturalism Bad for Women.* Princeton: Princeton University Press.

O'Leary, Brendan. Forthcoming. "Multi-National Federalism, Power-Sharing, Federacy and the Kurds of Iraq." In Brendan O'Leary, John McGarry, and Khaled Salih, eds. *The Future of Iraq and Kurdistan.* Philadelphia: University of Pennsylvania Press.

Olwig, Karen Fog, and Kirsten Hastrup, eds. 1997. *Siting Culture. The Shifting Anthropological Object.* New York: Routledge.

Opondo, Abiero. 2004. "Ethnicity: A Cause of Political Instability in Africa?" [http://129.194.252.80/catfiles/2731.pdf]. February 2004.

Ostergard Jr., Robert L., Matthew Tubin, and Jordan Altman. 2001. "Stealing from the Past: Globalisation, Strategic Formation and the Use of Indigenous Intellectual Property in the Biotechnology Industry." *Third World Quarterly* 22(4): 643–56.

Ostrom, Elinor. 1990. *Governing the Commons: The Evolution of Institutions for Collective Action.* Cambridge: Cambridge University Press.

———. 1998. *The Comparative Study of Public Economies.* Memphis: P.K. Seidman Foundation.

Papademetriou, Demetrios. 2003. "Policy Considerations for Immigrant Integration." Migration Policy Institute, Washington, DC. February 2004.

Parekh, Bhikhu. 2000. *Rethinking Multiculturalism: Cultural Diversity and Political Theory.* Basingstoke: Palgrave.

Patrinos, H., and E. Velez. 1996. "Costs and Benefits of Bilingual Education in Guatemala: A Partial Analysis." Human Capital Development Working Paper 74. World Bank, Washington, DC.

Pattanaik, Prasanta. 1998. "Cultural Indicators of Well-Being: Some Conceptual Issues." In *World Culture Report: Culture, Creativity and Markets.* Paris: UNESCO Publishing.

Patterson, Thomas C., and Ida Susser, eds. 2001. *Cultural Diversity in the United States: A Critical Reader.* Oxford: Blackwell.

Pehdazur, Ami. 2001. "Struggling with the Challenges of Right-Wing Extremism and Terrorism within Democratic Boundaries: A Comparative Analysis." *Studies in Conflict and Terrorism* 24(5): 339–59.

The Pew Research Center. 2003. "Globalization With Few Discontents." Washington, DC. [http://www.globalpolicy.org/ globaliz/cultural/2003/0603globalopinion.htm]. February 2004.

Phillips, Anne. 2001. "Multiculturalism, Universalism and the Claims of Democracy." Programme Paper Number 7. Democracy, Governance and Human Rights. United Nations Research Institute for Social Development, Geneva. [http://www.unrisd.org/unrisd/website/projects.nsf/ (httpProjectsForResearchHome-en)/CE2B1BCD4B5F5D3A 80256B4900530E39?OpenDocument]. February 2004.

Platteau, Jean-philippe. 2000. *Institutions, Social Norms and Economic Development.* Amsterdam: Harwood Academic Publishers.

The Polity IV Project. 2003. *Political Regime Characteristics and Transitions, 1800–2002.* Center for International Development and Conflict Management, University of Maryland, Baltimore. [http://www.cidcm.umd.edu/inscr/polity]. February 2004.

Ponzio, Richard. 2004. "Solomon Island's Ethnic Difference Not the Cause of Conflict." United Nations Development Programme, Solomon Islands, Honiara.

Prah, Kwesi Kwaa. 2000. *African Languages for the Mass Education of Africans.* Cape Town: CASAS.

Prashad, Vijay. 2001. "Cataracts of Silence: Race on the Edge of Indian Thought." Paper presented at the United Nations Research Institute for Social Development Conference on Racism and Public Policy, 3 September, Durban. [http://www. unrisd.org/unrisd/website/projects.nsf/(httpProjectsFor ResearchHome-en)/CE2B1BCD4B5F5D3A80256B4900530E39 ?OpenDocument]. February 2004.

Preis, Ann-Belinda. 2004. "Culture—Paradigm Shift in Anthropology." United Nations Educational, Scientific and Cultural Organization, Paris.

Premdas, Ralph. 2003. "Ethnic Conflict, Inequality and Public Sector Governance in A Multi-Ethnic State: The Case of Trinidad and Tobago." Ethnic Conflict, Inequality and Public Sector Governance Country Studies. United Nations Research Institute for Social Development, Geneva.

Psacharopoulos, G., and H. Patrinos. 1994. "Indigenous People and Poverty in Latin America." In G. Psacharopoulos and H. Patrinos, eds. *Indigenous People and Poverty in Latin America.* Washington, DC: World Bank.

Public Citizen. 2004. "Global Trade Watch: Promoting Democracy by Challenging Corporate Globalization." [http://www. citizen.org/trade]. March 2004.

Putnam, Robert, R. Leonardi, and R. Y. Nanetti. 1993. *Making Democracy Work: Civic Traditions in Modern Italy.* Princeton: Princeton University Press.

Putnam, Robert. 1993. "The Prosperous Community: Social Capital and Public Life." *American Prospect* 13: 35–42.

RAND Corporation. 2004. *Correspondence on Terrorist Groups 1996–2003.* March. Arlington.

Ranger, T. 1983. "The Invention of Tradition in Colonial Africa." In E. Hobsbawm and T. Ranger, eds. *The Invention of Tradition.* Cambridge: Canto.

Reilly, Benjamin. 2002. "Internal Conflict and Regional Security in Asia and the Pacific." *Pacific Review* 14 (1): 10–11.

Reiss, Timothy. 2002. *Against Autonomy: Global Dialectics of Cultural Exchange.* Stanford: Stanford University Press.

Renshon, Stanley A., ed. 2001. *One America? Political Leadership, National Identity and the Dilemmas of Diversity.* Washington, DC: Georgetown University Press.

Requejo, Ferran. 2001. "Federalism and the Quality of Democracy in Plurinational Contexts: Present Shortcomings and Possible Improvements." Paper presented at the European Consortium for Political Science Research Conference, 6 April, Grenoble, France. [http://www.essex.ac.uk/ecpr/events/jointsessions/paperarchive/grenoble/ws4/requejo.pdf]. February 2004.

Richey, W. 2003. "Affirmative Action's Evaluation: How the Debate has Changed Since the 1970s." *The Christian Science Monitor.* 28 March.

Riding, Alan. 2003. "Filmmakers Seek Protection from U.S. Dominance." *The New York Times.* 5 February.

Roberts, Adam. 2002. "Counter-Terrorism. Armed Force and the Laws of War." *Survival* 44(1): 7–32.

Rodgers, Gerry, Charles Gore, and Jose B. Figueiredo, eds. 1995. *Social Exclusion: Rhetoric, Reality, Responses.* Geneva: International Institute for Labour Studies.

Rodwin, Victor G. 2002. "World Cities Project." New York University, International Longevity Center, New York [http://www.nyu.edu/projects/rodwin/world_cp.htm]. March 2004.

Rosaldo, Renato. 1989. *Culture and Truth: The Remaking of Social Analysis.* Boston: Beacon Press.

Rotar', Igor'. 2002. "Under the Green Banner: Islamic Radicals in Russia and the Former Soviet Union." *Religion, State & Society* 30(2): 89–153.

Rotimi, Suberu. 2001. *Federalism and Ethnic Conflict in Nigeria.* Washington, DC: United States Institute of Peace Press.

Rudolph, Susanne H. 2001. "Living With Difference in India: Legal Pluralism and Legal Universalism in Historical Context." In Gerald James Larson, ed. *Religion and Personal Law in Secular India: A Call to Judgment.* Bloomington and Indianapolis: Indiana University Press.

Runciman, W. G. 1966. *Relative Deprivation and Social Justice.* London: Routledge.

Russell, Cheryl. 2002. *Racial and Ethnic Diversity: Asians, Blacks, Hispanics, Native Americans and Whites.* Ithaca: New Strategist Publications.

Rutter, Terri L. 1998. "Study Finds 'Life Gap' in the United States." *Harvard Public Health Review* Fall 1998. [http://www.hsph.harvard.edu/review/life_gap.shtml]. February 2004.

Salomon, Margot E., and Arjun Sengupta. 2003. "The Right to Development: Obligations of States and the Rights of Minorities and Indigenous Peoples." Minority Rights Group International, London. [http://www.minorityrights.org/]. February 2004.

Sandel, Michael. 1998. *Liberalism and the Limits of Justice.* Cambridge: Cambridge University Press.

Sands, David R. 2003. "Effort to Rein in Madrassas Begun; Educator Predicts 10 Years of Work." *The Washington Times.* 7 November.

Sarat, Austin, and Jonathan Simon, eds. 2003. *Cultural Analysis, Cultural Studies and the Law: Moving Beyond Legal Realism.* Durham: Duke University Press.

SATP (South Asia Terrorism Portal). 2004. "Sectarian Violence in Pakistan." [http://www.satp.org/satporgtp/countries/pakistan/database/sect-killing.htm]. March 2004.

Schacher, Ayelet. 2001. *Multicultural Jurisdictions: Cultural Differences and Women's Rights.* Cambridge: Cambridge University Press.

Schoorl, J. J., and Friesen, W. 2000. "Restoration of Law and Order by Regional Intervention Force Allows for the Return of the Displaced." [http://www.db.idpproject.org/Sites/idpSurvey.nsf/wViewSingleEnv/Solomon+IslandsProfile+Summary]. February 2004.

Schultz, Paul T., and Germano Mwabo. 1998. "Labor Unions and the Distribution of Wages and Employment in South Africa." *Industrial and Labor Relations Review* 51(4).

Schulze, Karl. 1999. *The Constitution, Multiculturalism and Our Changing Form of Government: A Guide for the Future.* London: Minerva.

Schwenken, Helen. 2003. "RESPECT for All: The Political Self-Organization of Female Migrant Domestic Workers in the European Union." Refuge 21(3): 45–52. [http://www.uni-kassel.de/fb5/globalisation/docs/diss/schwenken_refuge_2003.pdf]. February 2004.

Scott, Rachel. 2003. "An 'Official' Islamic Response to the Egyptian Al-Jihad Movement." *Journal of Political Ideologies* 8(1): 39–61.

Sen, Amartya. 1984. *Resources, Values and Development.* Cambridge, Mass.: Harvard University Press.

———. 1999. *Reason Before Identity.* Oxford: Oxford University Press.

———. 2001. "Other People." *The New Republic.* 18 December.

———. 2002. "Civilizational Imprisonments: How to Misunderstand Everybody in the World." *The New Republic.* 10 June.

———. 2003. "Democracy and its Global Roots." *The New Republic.* 6 October.

———. 2004a. "Cultural Freedom and Human Development."

———. 2004b. "How Does Culture Matter?" In Vijayendra Rao and Michael Walton, eds. *Culture and Public Action: A Cross-Disciplinary Dialogue on Development Policy.* Stanford, Calif.: Stanford University Press.

———. 2004c. "Elements of a Theory of Human Rights." *Philosophy and Public Affairs* 32(Fall).

———. Forthcoming. *Identity and Innocence.* New York: Norton.

Sepúlveda, Magdalena M. 2003. *The Nature of Obligations Under the International Covenant on Economic, Social and Cultural Rights.* Antwerpen and Oxford: Intersentia.

Shain, Yossi, and Aharon Barth. 2003. "Diasporas and International Relations Theory." *International Organization* 57(3): 449–79.

Shain, Yossi. 1994–95. "Ethnic Diasporas and U.S. Foreign Policy." *Political Science Quarterly* 109(5): 811–41.

Sheffer, Gabriel. 1986. "A New Field of Study: Modern Diasporas in International Politics." In Gabriel Sheffer, ed. *Modern Diaspora in International Politics.* New York: St. Martin's Press.

———. 1993. "Ethnic Diasporas: A Threat to their Hosts?" In Myron Weiner, ed. *International Migration and Security.* Boulder: Westview Press.

SIL International. 2004a. *Ethnologue: Languages of the World.* Houston.

———. 2004b. "HDR2004 Comments and Contributions from SIL International." Washington, DC and Houston. [http://www.sil.org/sildc/index.htm]. February 2004.

Silver, Hilary. 1995. "Reconceptualizing Social Disadvantage: Three Paradigms of Social Exclusion." In Gerry Rodgers, Charles Gore, and Jose B. Figueiredo, eds. *Social Exclusion; Rhetoric, Reality, Responses.* Geneva: International Institute for Labour Studies.

Sivan, Emmanuel. 2003. "The Clash Within Islam." *Survival* 45(1): 25–44.

Smith, Adam. 1976 [1776]. *An Inquiry into the Nature and Causes of the Wealth of Nations,* eds. Campbell, R. H. and A. S. Skinner. Oxford: Clarendon Press.

Smith, Anthony. 1986. *The Ethnic Origin of Nations.* Oxford: Blackwell.

———. 1991. "The Nation: Invented, Imagined, Reconstructed." *Millennium Journal of International Studies* 20: 353–68.

Snodgrass, Donald R. 1995. "Successful Economic Development in a Multi-ethnic Society: The Malaysian Case." The Harvard Institute for International Development, Cambridge, Mass. [http://www.hiid.harvard.edu/pub/pdfs/503.pdf]. February 2004.

Snyder, Jack. 2000. *From Voting to Violence: Democraticization and Nationalist Conflict.* New York: W.W. Norton.

South Africa, Ministry of Labour. 2004. "South Africa Employment Equity Act." No. 55, Section 20(5). Pretoria. [http://www.labour.gov.za/docs/legislation/eea/]. February 2004.

South Asia Monitor. 2003. "Musharraf Bans Resurfacing Militant Groups, Orders Crackdown." [http://www.southasiamonitor.org/pak/2003/nov/16head4.htm]. April 2004.

SSS (Swedish Security Service). 2002. "Offences Related to National Internal Security." Stockholm. [http://www.sakerhetspolisen.se/Publikationer/brott_2002.pdf]. January 2004.

Stalker, Peter. 2002. "Migration Trends and Migration Policy in Europe." *International Migration* 40(5): 151–79.

Stamatopoulou, Elsa. 2002. "Cultural Politics or Cultural Rights: UN Human Rights Responses." Office of the High Commissioner on Human Rights, New York.

Statistics Canada. 2004. Proportion of Foreign-Born Population, Census Metropolitan Areas. Ottawa. [http://www.statcan.ca/english/Pgdb/demo46b.htm]. February 2004.

Statistics Sweden. 2004. Population Statistics. Stockholm. [http://www.scb.se/templates/Product____25799.asp]. February 2004.

Stepan, Alfred. 2001. *Arguing Comparative Politics.* Oxford: Oxford University Press.

Stepan, Alfred, and Graeme Robertson. 2003. "An 'Arab' More than a 'Muslim' Electoral Gap." *Journal of Democracy* 14(3): 30–44.

Stepanov, Valery. 2004. "Russian Experience in the North Indigenous Statistics." PFII/2004/WS.1/5. Department of Social and Economic Affairs. United Nations, New York.

Stern, Jessica. 2000. "Pakistan's Jihad Culture." *Foreign Affairs* 79(6): 115–26.

———. 2003. "The Protean Enemy." *Foreign Affairs* 82(4): 27–40.

Stewart, Frances. 2002. "Horizontal Inequalities: A Neglected Dimension of Development." Queen Elizabeth House Working Paper S81, Oxford. [http://www2.qeh.ox.ac.uk/research/wpaction.html?jor_id=239]. February 2004.

———. 2003. "Conflict and the Millennium Development Goals." Background Paper for *Human Development Report 2003.* United Nations Development Programme, New York.

Stiefel, Leanna, Amy Ellen Schwartz, and Dylan Conger. 2003. "Language Proficiency and Home Languages of Students in New York City Elementary and Middle Schools." New York University, Taub Urban Research Center, New York. [http://urban.nyu.edu/education/nyclanguage.pdf]. February 2004.

Subirats, Joan. 2003. "Nations Without States in Europe." Paper presented at the King Juan Carlos I of Spain Center at New York University, 8 April, New York. [http://www.nyu.edu/pages/kjc/lectures/nations_without_states3.doc]. February 2004.

Susning.nu. 2004. "Ny demokrati." [http://susning.nu/Ny_demokrati]. March 2004.

Swedish Election Authority. 2002. "Resultat Övriga Riksdagsvalen Komplettering." [http://www.val.se/utils/pdf/tillagg_ovriga.pdf]. March 2004.

Symonds, Peter. 2003. "The Political Origins and Outlook of Jemaah Islamiyah, Part I." [http://www.wsws.org/articles/2003/nov2003/jis1-n12.shtml]. March 2004.

Tauli-Corpus, Victoria. 2004. "Land Rights in the Philippines." Indigenous Peoples' International Centre for Policy Research and Education (Tebtebba), Baguio City, Philippines.

Taylor, Charles. 1992. "The Politics of Recognition." In *Multiculturalism and the "Politics of Recognition."* Princeton: Princeton University Press.

Tebtebba and Forest Peoples Programme. 2003. *Extracting Promises: Indigenous Peoples, Extractive Industries & the World Bank.* Baguio City, Philippines.

Tebtebba and International Forum on Globalization. 2003. "Globalization: Effects on Indigenous Peoples." [http://www.tebtebba.org/]. March 2004.

Temu, A. 2000. "The Development of National Language: A Survey of Kiswahili in Tanzania." In Kwesi Kwaa Prah, ed. *Between Distinction and Extinction: The Harmonization and Standardization of African Languages.* Cape Town: CASAS.

Testas, Abdelaziz. 2002. "The Roots of Algeria's Religious and Ethnic Violence." *Studies in Conflict and Terrorism* 25(3): 161–83.

Tetley, William Q. C. 1999. "Mixed Jurisdictions: Common Law Versus Civil Law (Codified and Uncodified)." International Institute for the Unification of Private Law, Rome. [http://www.unidroit.org/english/publications/review/articles/1999-3.htm]. February 2004.

Third World Network. 2003. "More than 200 Organizations from 35 Nations Challenge US Patent on Neem." [http://www.twnside.org.sg/title/neem-ch.htm]. February 2004.

Thompson, Charles D. 2001. *Maya Identities and the Violence of Place: Borders Bleed.* Aldershot: Ashgate.

Throsby, David. 1999. "Cultural Capital." *Journal of Cultural Economics* 23: 3–12.

Townsend, Peter. 1979. *Poverty in the United Kingdom.* London: Penguin Books.

Tran, Luan-Vu N. 2000. *Human Rights and Federalism: A Comparative Study on Freedom, Democracy and Cultural Diversity.* The Hague and London: Martinus Nijhoff.

Tremlett, Giles. 2002. "Death and Dissent as Algeria Goes to the Polls." *The Guardian.* 31 May.

Turton, D. 1997. "War and Ethnicity: Global Connections and Local Violence in North East Africa and Former Yugoslavia." *Oxford Development Studies* 25: 77–94.

UN (United Nations). 1994. "General Comment No. 23 (50) (Article 27)." United Nations Document CCPR/C/21/Rev.1/Add.5. Adopted at the 50th Session of the Human Rights Committee, 6 April, New York.

———. 2000a. "Millennium Declaration." A/RES/55/2, 18 September. New York. [http://www.un.org/millennium/declaration/ares552e.pdf]. March 2003.

———. 2000b. "Replacement Migration: Is It a Solution to Declining and Ageing Populations?" Department of Economic and Social Affairs, Population Division. New York. [http://www.un.org/esa/population/publications/migration/migration.htm]. March 2004.

———. 2002a. "International Migration Report 2002." Department of Economic and Social Affairs, Population Division. New York. [http://www.un.org/esa/population/publications/ittmig2002/2002ITTMIGTEXT22-11.pdf]. February 2004.

———. 2002b. "International Migration Report Website." [http://www.un.org/esa/population/publications/ittmig2002/ittmigrep2002.htm]. March 2004.

———. 2003a. "Trends in Total Migrant Stock by Sex. 1960–2000." 2003 Revision to the International Migration Report 2002. Department of Economic and Social Affairs, Population Division. New York.

———. 2003b. *World Population Prospects 1950–2050: The 2002 Revision.* Department of Economic and Social Affairs, Population Division, New York

———. 2004. "Data Collection Pertaining to Indigenous Peoples: Issues and Challenges." PFII/2004/WA.1/13. Department of Economic and Social Affairs. New York.

UNCTAD (United Nations Conference on Trade and Development). 1999. *World Investment Report.* Geneva.

UNDP (United Nations Development Programme). 1999. *Human Development Report 1999: Globalization with a Human Face.* New York: Oxford University Press.

———. 2000a. *Human Development Report 2000: Human Rights and Human Development.* New York: Oxford University Press.

———. 2000b. "Namibia Human Development Report 2000/2001: Gender and Violence in Namibia." Windhoek.

———. 2000c. "South Africa Human Development Report 2000: Transformation for Human Development." Pretoria. [http://www.undp.org.za/sahdr2000/sahdr20002.html]. February 2004.

———. 2002a. *Human Development Report 2002: Deepening Democracy in a Fragmented World.* New York: Oxford University Press.

———. 2002b. "Situacíon Del Desarrollo Human En Las Comarcas Indígenas." Panama City.

———. 2003a. *Arab Human Development Report 2003: Building a Knowledge Society.* Amman.

———. 2003b. *Human Development Report 2003: Millennium Development Goals: A Compact Among Nations to End Human Poverty.* New York: Oxford University Press.

———. 2003c. "Indonesia." Crisis Prevention and Recovery Unit. Jakarta.

———. 2003d. "Report of the United Nations Development Programme to the 59th Session of the United Nations Commission on Human Rights." E/CN.4/2003/128. New York. [http://www.unhchr.ch/huridocda/huridoca.nsf]. February 2004.

———. 2003e. "Roma Human Development Report: The Roma in Central and Eastern Europe: Avoiding the Dependency Trap." Bratislava. [http://www.roma.undp.sk]. February 2004.

———. 2004a. "About Indigenous Peoples: A Definition." New York. [http://www.undp.org/csopp/cso/NewFiles/paboutdef.html]. February 2004.

———. 2004b. "UNDP and Indigenous Peoples: A Policy of Engagement." Civil Society Organization, Bureau for Resources and Strategic Partnerships. New York. [http://www.undp.org/cso/policies.html]. February 2004.

UNESCO (United Nations Educational, Scientific and Cultural Organization). 1998. *World Culture Report: Culture, Creativity and Markets.* Paris: UNESCO Publishing.

———. 2000a. "A Survey on National Cinematography." Culture Sector, Division of Creativity, Cultural Industries and Copyright. Paris.

———. 2000b. "Study of International Flows of Cultural Goods between 1980 and 1998." Paris.

———. 2000c. *World Culture Report: Cultural Diversity, Conflict and Pluralism.* Paris: UNESCO Publishing.

———. 2001. "Synthesis of Reports by Member States in the Context of the Permanent System of Reporting on Education for Peace, Human Rights, Democracy, International Understanding and Tolerance, General Conference 31st Session." 31 C/INF.5. Paris.

———. 2002. "Universal Declaration on Cultural Diversity." Cultural Diversity Series No. 1. Paris.

———. 2003a. "Desirability of Drawing Up an International Standard-Setting Instrument on Cultural Diversity, General Conference 32nd Session." 32 C/52. Paris.

———. 2003b. "Language Vitality and Endangerment." Paper presented at the "International Expert Meeting on the UNESCO Programme: Safeguarding Languages," 10 March, Paris. [http://portal.unesco.org/culture/en/ev.php@URL_ID=9105&URL_DO=DO_TOPIC&URL_SECTION=201.html]. February 2004.

———. 2003c. "Preliminary Draft International Convention for the Safeguarding of the Intangible Cultural Heritage, General Conference 32nd Session." 32 C/26. Paris.

———. 2004a. "Culture, Trade and Globalization." Paris. [http://www.unesco.org/culture/industries/trade/index.shtml]. March 2004.

———. 2004b. "What Was the Draft Multilateral Agreement on Investments (MAI)?" [http://www.unesco.org/culture/industries/trade/html_eng/question20.shtml#20]. March 2004.

UNESCO (United Nations Educational, Scientific and Cultural Organization)–UIS (Institute of Statistics). 2001. "Fast Facts: Did You Know? International Trade in Cultural Goods." Paris. [http://www.uis.unesco.org]. February 2004.

UN HABITAT (United Nations Human Settlements Programme). Forthcoming. *State of the World's Cities Report 2004.* Draft chapter on transnational migration. Nairobi.

UNICEF (United Nations Children's Fund). 2001. *State of the World's Children 2001.* New York.

———. 2004. "Ensuring the Rights of Indigenous Children." *Innocenti Digest* 11. Innocenti Research Center, Rome. [http://www.unicef.org/irc]. February 2004.

United Nations Association of Great Britain and Northern Ireland. 2004. "Help For Brazil's Indians." London and New York. [http://www.una-uk.org/Environment/brazil2.html]. February 2004.

U.S. Census Bureau. 2004a. "Adding Diversity From Abroad: The Foreign-Born Population 2000." Washington, DC. [http://www.census.gov/population/pop-profile/2000/chap17.pdf]. February 2004.

———. 2004b. "United States Census 2000." [http://www.census.gov/]. March 2004.

U.S. Department of Justice. 2001. "Hate Crime: The Violence of Intolerance." [http://www.usdoj.gov/crs/ pubs/htecrm.htm]. April 2004.

U.S. Department of Labor. 2004. "Latest Numbers." Bureau of Labor Statistics. [http://www.bls.gov/]. March 2004.

Valdés, Julio Carranza. 2002. "Cultural Development Indicators: Towards a New Dimension of Human Well-Being." Paper presented at the International Symposium for Cultural Statistics, 21 October, Montréal. [http://www.colloque2002symposium.gouv.qc.ca/PDF/Carranza_paper_Symposium.pdf]. February 2004.

Van Beetz, Freek. 2000. "The Legal Instruments Required in the Strategy for a Successful Integration Policy in the Netherlands." Paper presented at the Strategies for Implementing Integration Policies Conference, 4 May, Prague.

Van der Westhuizen, Janis. 2002. *Adapting to Globalization: Malaysia, South Africa, and the Challenges of Ethnic Redistribution with Growth.* Westport: Praeger.

Van Holsteyn, Joop J. M. 2003. "Beating a Dead Horse? The Dutch State and the Defense of Democracy Against Right-Wing Extremism." Paper presented at the European Consortium for Political Research Conference, 28 March, Edinburgh. [http://www.essex.ac.uk/ecpr/events/jointsessions/paperarchive/edinburgh.asp?section=4]. February 2004.

Vogel, H. L. 2001. *Entertainment Industry Economics: A Guide for Financial Analysis.* Cambridge: Cambridge University Press.

Vuchelen, Jef. 2003. "Electoral Systems and the Effects of Political Events on the Stock Market: The Belgian Case." *Economics and Politics* 15(1): 85–102.

Wahlbeck, Osten. 2002. "The Concept of Diaspora as an Analytical Tool in the Study of Refugee Communities." *Journal of Ethnic and Migration Studies* 28(2): 221–38.

Walden, Bello. 2000. "2000: A Year of Global Protest Against Globalization." New York. [http://www.globalpolicy.org]. February 2004.

Wanandi, Jusuf. 2002. "Islam in Indonesia: Its History, Development and Future Challenges." *Asia-Pacific Review* 9(2): 104–12.

Wanner, Philippe. 2002. "Migration Trends in Europe." European Population Papers Series No. 7. European Population Committee. Council of Europe, Strasbourg. [http://www.coe.int/t/e/social_cohesion/population/No_7_Migration_trends_in_Europe.pdf]. February 2004.

Watts, Ronald L. 1998. "Federal Systems and Accommodation of Distinct Groups: A Comparative Survey of International Arrangements for Aboriginal Peoples." Institute of Intergovernmental Relations. Queen's University, Kingston, Ontario. [http://www.iigr.ca/pdf/publications/146_Federal_Systems_and_Acco.pdf]. February 2004.

———. 1999. *Comparing Federal Systems.* Montreal and Kingston: McGill-Queen's University Press.

———. 2002. "The Relevance Today of the Federal Idea." Paper presented at the International Conference on Federalism, 27 August, St. Gallen. [http://www.forumfed.org/federalism/Watts.asp?lang=en]. February 2004.

Weatherall, Kimberlee. 2001. "Culture, Autonomy and Djulibinya-murr: Individual and Community in the Construction of Rights to Traditional Designs." *Modern Law Review* 64(2): 215–42.

Weber, Max. 1976 [1930]. *The Protestant Ethics and the Spirit of Capitalism,* republished with a new introduction by Anthony Giddens. London: Allen and Unwin.

Wedgwood, Ruth. 2002. "Al Qaeda, Terrorism, and Military Commissions." *The American Journal of International Law* 96(2): 328–37.

WHO (World Health Organization). 2001. "International Decade of the World's Indigenous People." Report by the Secretariat. Geneva. [http://www.who.int/gb/EB_WHA/PDF/WHA54/ea5433.pdf]. February 2004.

Widfeldt, Anders. 2001. "Responses to the Extreme Right in Sweden: The Diversified Approach." Working Paper 10. Keele European Parties Research Unit, Keele. [http://www.keele.ac.uk/depts/spire/Working%20Papers/KEPRU/KEPRU%20Working%20papers.htm]. February 2004.

———. 2004. Correspondence on the vote shares of European extreme right parties between 1990 and 2003. February. Aberdeen.

Wikipedia. 2004. "Religious Persecution." Tampa. [http://en.wikipedia.org/wiki/Religious_persecution]. February 2004.

Willett, Cynthia, ed. 1998. *Theorizing Multiculturalism: A Guide to the Current Debate.* Cambridge, Mass. and Oxford: Blackwell.

WIPO (World Intellectual Property Organization). 2003a. "Composite Study on the Protection of Traditional Knowledge." WIPO/GRTKF/IC/5/8. Intergovernmental Committee on Intellectual Property and Genetic Resources, Traditional Knowledge and Folklore. Geneva.

———. 2003b. "Consolidated Analysis of the Legal Protection of Traditional Cultural Expressions." WIPO/GRTKF/IC/5/3. Intergovernmental Committee on Intellectual Property and Genetic Resources, Traditional Knowledge and Folklore. Geneva.

———. 2003c. "Information on National Experiences with the Intellectual Property Protection of Traditional Knowledge." WIPO/GRTKF/IC/5/INF/2. Intergovernmental Committee on Intellectual Property and Genetic Resources, Traditional Knowledge and Folklore. Geneva.

———. 2003d. "Intergovernmental Committee on Intellectual Property and Genetic Resources, Traditional Knowledge and Folklore Fifth Session Report." WIPO/GRTKF/IC/5/15. Intergovernmental Committee on Intellectual Property and Genetic Resources, Traditional Knowledge and Folklore. Geneva.

———. 2004. "Revised Version of Traditional Knowledge: Policy and Legal Options." WIPO/GRTKF/IC/6/4 Rev. Intergovernmental Committee on Intellectual Property and Genetic Resources, Traditional Knowledge and Folklore. Geneva.

World Bank. 2002. *World Development Report 2003: Sustainable Development in a Dynamic World.* New York: Oxford University Press.

———. 2003. *World Development Indicators 2003.* Washington, DC.

———. 2004. "Striking a Better Balance: Extractive Industries Review Final Report." Washington, DC.

World Commission on Culture and Development. 1995. "Our Creative Diversity: Report of the World Commission on Culture and Development." Paris.

World Values Survey. 2004. "World Values Survey." [http://www.worldvaluessurvey.org]. February 2004.

Wright, Sue. 2001. "Language and Power: Background to the Debate on Linguistic Rights." International Journal on Multicultural Societies 3(1). [http://www.unesco.org/most/l3n1wri.htm]. February 2004.

Young, Crawford, ed. 1999. *The Accommodation of Cultural Diversity: Case Studies.* Basingstoke: MacMillan Press.

Young, Iris Marion. 2000. *Inclusion and Democracy.* Oxford: Oxford University Press.

Zelkina, Anna. 1999. "Islam and Security in the New States of Central Asia: How Genuine is the Islamic Threat?" *Religion, State & Society* 27(3/4): 355–72.

Zhao, Susheng. 1998. "A State-Led Nationalism: The Patriotic Education Campaign in Post-Tiananmen China." *Communist and Post-Communist Studies* 31(3): 287–302.

Zolberg, Aristide. 2001. "Introduction." In Aristide Zolberg and Peter Benda, eds. *Global Migrants, Global Refugees.* New York: Berghahn Books.

Zorzi, Christine. 2002. "The 'Irrecognition' of Aboriginal Customary Law." Lawyers Information Network, Melbourne. [http://www.link.asn.au/downloads/papers/indeginous/p_in_09.pdf]. February 2004.

HUMAN DEVELOPMENT INDICATORS

People are the real wealth of nations. Indeed, the basic purpose of development is to enlarge human freedoms. The process of development can expand human capabilities by expanding the choices that people have to live full and creative lives. And people are both the beneficiaries of such development and the agents of the progress and change that bring it about. This process must benefit all individuals equitably and build on the participation of each of them. This approach to development—human development—has been advocated by every *Human Development Report* since the first in 1990.

The range of capabilities that individuals can have, and the choices that can help to expand them, are potentially infinite and vary by individual. However, public policy is about setting priorities, and two criteria are helpful in identifying the most important capabilities for assessing meaningful global progress in achieving human well-being, the purpose of this Report. First, these capabilities must be universally valued. Second, they must be basic to life, in the sense that their absence would foreclose many other choices. For these reasons *Human Development Report* focuses on four important capabilities: to lead a long and healthy life, to be knowledgeable, to have access to the resources needed for a decent standard of living and to participate in the life of the community.

The ideas behind this development paradigm are not new—they are at least as old as Aristotle. Aristotle argued that "wealth is evidently not the good we are seeking; for it is merely useful and for the sake of something else." Immanuel Kant similarly asserted that human beings should be seen as ends in themselves, rather than as a means to other ends. And parallel ideas are reflected in the writings of Adam Smith, Robert Malthus and John Stuart Mill—to name just a few.

But for a long time development policy debates seemed to forget this simple, yet profound truth. Caught up with the rise and fall of national incomes, economists often lost sight of the real end of development—people's well-being. Economic growth is merely a means—albeit an important one—for achieving this end.

Measuring human development

It is easier to measure national incomes than human development. And many economists would argue that national income is a good indicator of human well-being. While there is evidently a strong relationship, since economic growth is an important means to human development, human outcomes do not depend on economic growth and levels of national income alone. They also depend on how these resources are used—whether for developing weapons or producing food, building palaces or providing clean water. And human outcomes such as

democratic participation in decision-making or equal rights for men and women do not depend on incomes. For these reasons the Report presents an extensive set of indicators (33 tables and almost 200 indicators) on important human outcomes achieved in countries around the world, such as life expectancy at birth or under-five mortality rates, which reflect the capability to survive, or literacy rates, which reflect the capability to learn. They also include indicators on important means for achieving these capabilities, such as access to clean water, and on equity in achievement, such as the gaps between men and women in schooling or political participation.

While this rich array of indicators provides measures for evaluating progress in human development in its many dimensions, policymakers also need a summary measure to evaluate progress, particularly one that focuses more sharply on human well-being than on income. For this purpose *Human Development Reports* have since their inception published the human development index, later complemented by indices looking specifically at gender (gender-related development index and gender empowerment measure) and poverty (human poverty index; table 1). These indices give an overview of some basic dimensions of human development, but they must be complemented by looking at their underlying data and other indicators.

TABLE 1
HDI, HPI-1, HPI-2, GDI—same components, different measurements

Index	Longevity	Knowledge	Decent standard of living	Participation or exclusion
Human development index (HDI)	Life expectancy at birth	• Adult literacy rate • Combined gross enrolment ratio for primary, secondary and tertiary schools	GDP per capita (PPP US$)	—
Human poverty index for developing countries (HPI-1)	Probability at birth of not surviving to age 40	Adult literacy rate	Deprivation in economic provisioning, measured by: • Percentage of people without sustainable access to an improved water source • Percentage of children under five underweight for age	—
Human poverty index for high-income OECD countries (HPI-2)	Probability at birth of not surviving to age 60	Percentage of adults lacking functional literacy skills	Percentage of people living below the income poverty line (50% of median adjusted disposable household income)	Long-term unemployment rate (12 months or more)
Gender-related development index (GDI)	Female and male life expectancy at birth	• Female and male adult literacy rates • Female and male combined gross enrolment ratio for primary, secondary and tertiary schools	Estimated female and male earned income	—

Human development index

The human development index (HDI) focuses on three measurable dimensions of human development: living a long and healthy life, being educated and having a decent standard of living (see *Technical note 1*). Thus it combines measures of life expectancy, school enrolment, literacy and income to allow a broader view of a country's development than does income alone.

Although the HDI is a useful starting point, it is important to remember that the concept of human development is much broader and more complex than any summary measure can capture, even when supplemented by other indices. The HDI is not a comprehensive measure. It does not include important aspects of human development, notably the ability to participate in the decisions that affect one's life and to enjoy the respect of others in the community. A person can be rich, healthy and well educated, but without this ability human development is impeded. The omission of this dimension of human development from the HDI has been highlighted since the first *Human Development Reports*—and drove the creation of a human freedom index in 1991 and a political freedom index in 1992. Neither measure survived past its first year, a testament to the difficulty of adequately quantifying such complex aspects of human development.

This difficulty does not make the many aspects of participation, such as political freedom and equal respect in the community, any less important to human development than the dimensions included in the HDI. In fact, these issues have been explored extensively in *Human Development Reports*. *Human Development Report 2002* dealt with democracy and its importance to human development. This year's report introduces a related and vitally important aspect of human development: cultural liberty. Leading a full life includes being free to follow different cultural practices and traditions without facing discrimination or disadvantage in participating politically, economically or socially.

The HDI clearly illustrates the distinction between income and human well-being. By measuring average achievements in health, education and income, the HDI can give a more complete picture of the state of a country's development than can incomes alone. Bolivia, with a much lower GDP per capita than

Guatemala, has achieved a higher HDI because it has done more to translate that income into human development (figure 1). Tanzania, one of the world's poorest countries, has an HDI comparable to that of Guinea, a country almost four times richer. Conversely, countries at the same level of income have large differences in HDI—Viet Nam has roughly the same income as Pakistan but a much higher HDI, due to its higher life expectancy and literacy (figure 2). Indicator table 1 highlights these differences in another way by comparing HDI ranks with ranks in GDP per capita (last column). Sri Lanka ranks 96 of 177 countries in HDI, much higher than its GDP rank of 112. These examples highlight the importance of policies that translate wealth into human development. In particular, well designed public policy and provision of services by governments, local communities and civil society can advance human development even without high levels of income or economic growth.

This does not mean, however, that economic growth is unimportant. Economic growth is an important means to human development, and when growth stagnates over a prolonged

period, it becomes difficult to sustain progress in human development.

Gender-related development index

The HDI measures average achievements in a country, but it does not incorporate the degree of gender imbalance in these achievements. Two countries with the same average level of adult literacy (say 30%) may have different disparities in rates between men and women (one could have a rate of 28% for women and 32% for men while the other could have a rate of 20% for women and 40% for men). Such differences in disparities would not be reflected in the HDI for the two countries. The gender-related development index (GDI), introduced in *Human Development Report 1995,* measures achievements in the same dimensions using the same indicators as the HDI but captures inequalities in achievement between women and men. It is simply the HDI adjusted downward for gender inequality. The greater the gender disparity in basic human development, the lower is a country's GDI relative to its HDI. The countries with the worst disparities between their GDI and HDI values are Saudi Arabia, Oman, Pakistan,

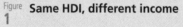

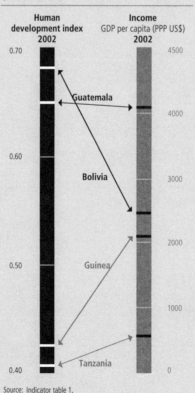

Figure 1

Same HDI, different income

Source: Indicator table 1.

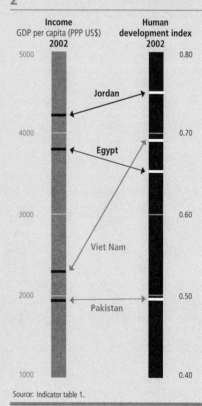

Figure 2

Same income, different HDI

Source: Indicator table 1.

Yemen and India, indicating a need for greater attention to gender equality. Sweden, Denmark, Australia, Latvia and Bulgaria have the closest correspondence between HDI and GDI. Full results and ranks are in indicator table 24.

Gender empowerment measure
The HDI does not include a measure of participation, an aspect of human development that is central to gender equity. The gender empowerment measure (GEM) reveals whether women take an active part in economic and political life. It focuses on gender inequality in key areas of economic and political participation and decision-making. It tracks the share of seats in parliament held by women; of female legislators, senior officials and managers; and of female professional and technical workers—and the gender disparity in earned income, reflecting economic independence. Differing from the GDI, the GEM exposes inequality in opportunities in selected areas. It has been calculated for 78 countries (for full results and ranking, see indicator table 25). The top three countries are Norway, Sweden and Denmark, which have opened significant opportunities for women to participate in economic and political life. But all countries can do more to expand the opportunities for women: only nine countries have GEM values higher than 0.8 (out of 1)—most have a long way to go to achieve full empowerment of women.

Human poverty index
The HDI measures the average progress of a country in human development. *Human Development Report 1997* introduced the human poverty index (HPI), which focuses on the proportion of people below a threshold level in basic dimensions of human development, much as the poverty headcount measures the proportion of people below an income threshold. The human poverty index for developing countries (HPI-1) uses different variables than the index for high-income OECD countries (HPI-2), as shown in table 1. Indicator tables 3 and 4, respectively, give the full results and rankings of these indices. As with the HDI, these indices provide a more complete view of poverty because they go beyond measures of income poverty. For developing countries Barbados, Uruguay, Chile, Costa Rica and Cuba rank highest, with human poverty levels of 5% or lower. Burkina Faso, Niger,

Mali, Ethiopia and Zimbabwe have the highest human poverty levels of the countries in the index—all above 50%.

For high-income OECD countries HPI-2 shows a different picture from that shown by the HDI. These countries tend to have very similar HDI values, because of their high overall levels of development. But when variables and dimensions of deprivation are used that are specifically adapted to the situation in these countries and to the different meaning of poverty there (such as social exclusion), there are substantial differences. For the 17 countries with data, human poverty as measured by HPI-2 varies from 6.5% in Sweden to 15.8% in the United States. And there are large differences between HDI and HPI-2 ranks: Australia ranks 3rd in the HDI but 14th in the HPI-2. Luxembourg ranks 15th in the HDI but 7th in the HPI-2, reflecting differences in how well these countries have distributed the overall human development achieved.

Trends in human development
Progress in human development during the 20th century was dramatic and unprecedented. Between 1960 and 2000 life expectancy in developing countries increased from 46 to 63 years.[1] Mortality rates for children under five were more than halved.[2] Between 1975, when one of every two adults could not read, and 2000 the

share of illiterate people was almost halved.[3] Real per capita incomes more than doubled, from $2,000 to $4,200.[4] But despite this impressive progress, massive human deprivation remains. More than 800 million people suffer from undernourishment (table 2). Some 100 million children who should be in school are not, 60 million of them girls. More than a billion people survive on less than $1 a day. Some 1.8 billion people live in countries where political regimes do not fully accommodate democratic, political and civil freedoms.[5] And about 900 million people belong to ethnic, religious, racial or linguistic groups that face discrimination.[6]

The Millennium Development Goals
Recognizing these problems, world leaders at the United Nations Millennium Summit in September 2000 expressed an unprecedented determination to end world poverty. They declared their commitment not only to the people of their own countries but to the people of the world. The 189 countries at the summit adopted the Millennium Declaration, committing themselves to do their utmost to achieve key objectives of humanity in the 21st century, including eradicating poverty, promoting human dignity and achieving peace, democracy and environmental sustainability. Stemming from the Declaration were the Millennium Development Goals—a set of 8 goals,

TABLE 2
Eliminating poverty: massive deprivation remains, 2000
(Millions)

Region	Living on less than $1 (PPP US$) a day	Total population under-nourished [a]	Primary age children not in school	Primary age girls not in school	Children under age five dying each year	People without access improved water sources	People without access to adequate sanitation
Sub-Saharan Africa	323	185	44	23	5	273	299
Arab States	8	34	7	4	1	42	51
East Asia and the Pacific	261	212	14	7	1	453	1,004
South Asia	432	312	32	21	4	225	944
Latin America and the Caribbean	56	53	2	1	0	72	121
Central & Eastern Europe & CIS	21	33	3	1	0	29	..
World	1,100	831	104	59	11	1,197	2,742

a. 1998–2000.
Source: World Bank 2003a, 2004f; UNESCO 2003; UN 2003.

Figure
3

Not enough progress toward the Millennium Development Goals

Poverty: Proportion of people living on less than $1 a day (%)

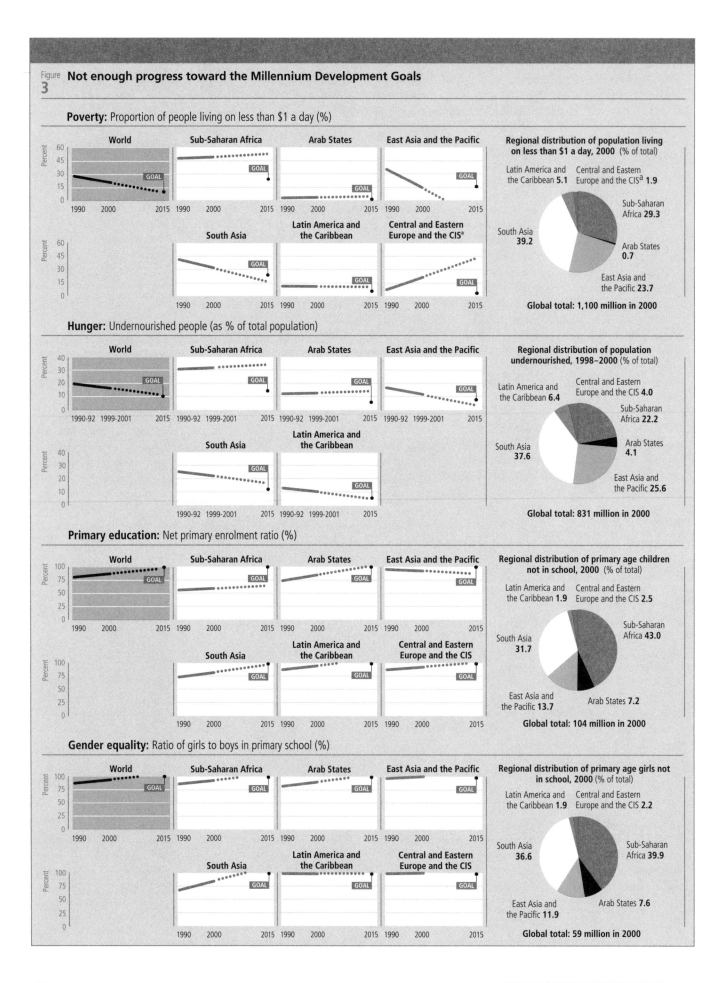

Hunger: Undernourished people (as % of total population)

Primary education: Net primary enrolment ratio (%)

Gender equality: Ratio of girls to boys in primary school (%)

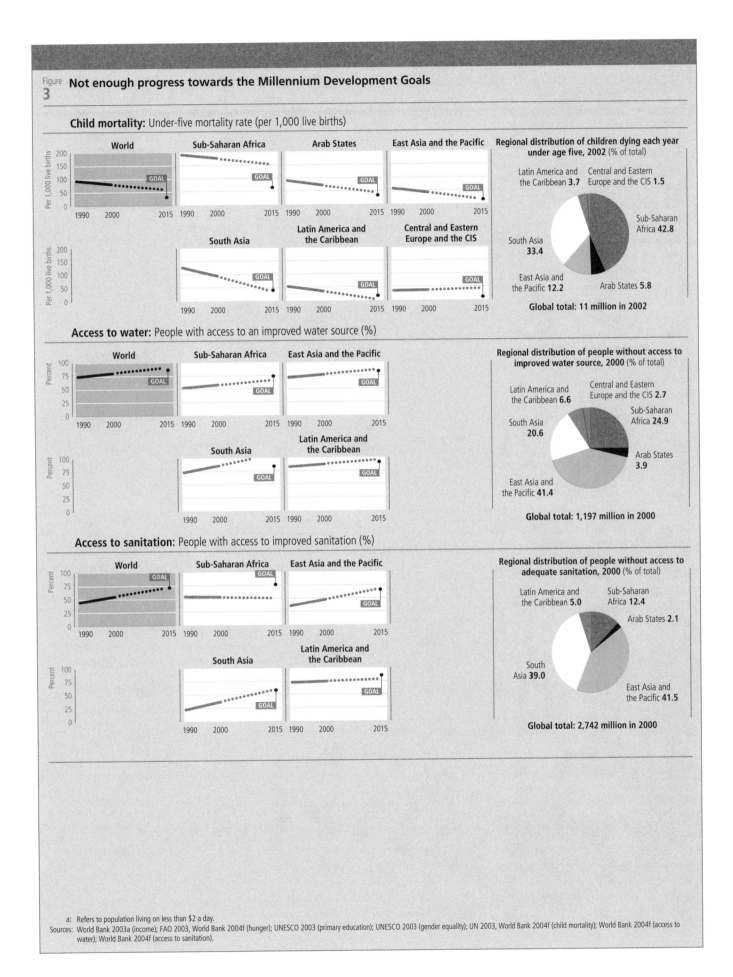

Figure
3

Not enough progress towards the Millennium Development Goals

Child mortality: Under-five mortality rate (per 1,000 live births)

World | Sub-Saharan Africa | Arab States | East Asia and the Pacific

South Asia | Latin America and the Caribbean | Central and Eastern Europe and the CIS

Regional distribution of children dying each year under age five, 2002 (% of total)

Latin America and the Caribbean **3.7**
Central and Eastern Europe and the CIS **1.5**
Sub-Saharan Africa **42.8**
South Asia **33.4**
East Asia and the Pacific **12.2**
Arab States **5.8**

Global total: 11 million in 2002

Access to water: People with access to an improved water source (%)

World | Sub-Saharan Africa | East Asia and the Pacific

South Asia | Latin America and the Caribbean

Regional distribution of people without access to improved water source, 2000 (% of total)

Latin America and the Caribbean **6.6**
Central and Eastern Europe and the CIS **2.7**
South Asia **20.6**
Sub-Saharan Africa **24.9**
Arab States **3.9**
East Asia and the Pacific **41.4**

Global total: 1,197 million in 2000

Access to sanitation: People with access to improved sanitation (%)

World | Sub-Saharan Africa | East Asia and the Pacific

South Asia | Latin America and the Caribbean

Regional distribution of people without access to adequate sanitation, 2000 (% of total)

Latin America and the Caribbean **5.0**
Sub-Saharan Africa **12.4**
Arab States **2.1**
South Asia **39.0**
East Asia and the Pacific **41.5**

Global total: 2,742 million in 2000

a: Refers to population living on less than $2 a day.
Sources: World Bank 2003a (income); FAO 2003, World Bank 2004f (hunger); UNESCO 2003 (primary education); UNESCO 2003 (gender equality); UN 2003, World Bank 2004f (child mortality); World Bank 2004f (access to water); World Bank 2004f (access to sanitation).

18 targets and 48 indicators—that establish concrete, time-bound targets for advancing development and reducing poverty by 2015 or earlier (see Index to Millennium Development Goal indicators at the end of this feature).

As *Human Development Report 2003* argued, human development and the Millennium Development Goals share a common motivation and vital commitment to promoting human well-being. The progress of countries and regions on the Millennium Development Goals since 1990 highlights a key aspect of development over the past decade: rapid progress for some, but reversals for an unprecedented number of other countries (figure 3). The picture that emerges is increasingly one of two very different groups of countries: those that have benefited from development, and those that have been left behind (tables 3–5).

An examination of regional progress on selected Millennium Development Goals reveals several noteworthy trends (see figure 3). East Asia and the Pacific stands out as being on track for all the goals for which trend data are available. The number of people living on less than $1 a day in the region was almost halved during the 1990s. South Asia is also making rapid progress on a number of goals. But despite the impressive pace of these two regions, which together account for almost half the world's population, human development is proceeding too slowly. Only two of the goals, halving income poverty and halving the proportion of people without access to safe water, will be met at the pace of progress of the last decade, and progress on the others, hunger reduction and access to sanitation, is nearly on track (figure 4). But even progress on these goals is driven mainly by the rapid development of China and India.

Other regions, particularly Sub-Saharan Africa, are performing much less well. At the current pace Sub-Saharan Africa will not meet the goal for universal primary education until 2129 or the goal for reducing child mortality by two-thirds until 2106—100 years away, rather than the 11 called for by the goals. In three of the goals—hunger, income poverty and access to sanitation—no date can be set because the situation in the region is worsening, not improving.

The unprecedented reversals of the 1990s
Looking beyond regional averages reveals many tragic reversals. An unprecedented number of countries saw development slide backwards in the 1990s. In 46 countries people are poorer today than in 1990. In 25 countries more people go hungry today than a decade ago.

These reversals can also be seen clearly in the HDI. This is particularly troubling—in previous decades, virtually no country experienced a decline in the HDI. The index has moved steadily upward, though usually slowly because three of its key components—literacy, school enrolment and life expectancy—take time to change. So when the HDI falls, that indicates crisis. Countries are depleting their

---

TABLE 3
Progress and setbacks: child mortality
(Per 1,000 live births)

Country	1990	2002	Change
Best performers			
Bhutan	166	94	−72
Guinea	240	169	−71
Bangladesh	144	77	−67
Egypt	104	41	−63
Lao, PDR	163	100	−63
Eritrea	147	89	−58
Worst performers			
Iraq	50	125	75
Botswana	58	110	52
Zimbabwe	80	123	43
Swaziland	110	149	39
Cameroon	139	166	27
Kenya	97	122	25

Source: UNICEF 2003b.

TABLE 4
Progress and setbacks: primary education
(Net primary enrolment ratio, percent)

Country	1990/91	2001/02	Change
Best performers			
Dominican Republic	58	97	39
Guinea	25	61	36
Kuwait	49	85	36
Morocco	57	88	32
Mauritania	35	67	31
Malawi	50	81	31
Worst performers			
Angola	58	30	−28
Azerbaijan	101	80	−21
Congo, Dem. Rep.	54	35	−20
United Arab Emirates	100	81	−19
Myanmar	99	82	−18
Nepal	85	70	−14

Source: Indicator table 11.

TABLE 5
Progress and setbacks: income poverty
(People living under the national poverty line, percent)

Country	Year	Share	Year	Share	Change[a] (percentage points)
Good performers					
Azerbaijan	1995	68.1	2001	49.6	−18.5
Uganda	1993	55.0	1997	44.0	−11.0
India	1993–94	36.0	1999–2000	28.6	−7.4
Jordan	1991	15.0	1997	11.7	−3.3
Cambodia	1993–94	39.0	1997	36.1	−2.9
Guatemala	1989	57.9	2000	56.2	−1.7
Bangladesh	1995–96	51.0	2000	49.8	−1.2
Poor performers					
Zimbabwe	1990–91	25.8	1995–96	34.9	9.1
Morocco	1990–91	13.1	1998–99	19.0	5.9
Pakistan	1993	28.6	1998–99	32.6	4.0
Hungary	1993	14.5	1997	17.3	2.8

Note: Comparisons should not be made across countries because national poverty lines vary considerably.
a. A minus sign indicates an improvement—less poverty.
Source: World Bank 2004f.

TABLE 6
Countries experiencing a drop in the human development index, 1980s and 1990s

Period	Number	Countries
1980–90	3	Democratic Republic of Congo, Rwanda, Zambia
1990–2002	20	Bahamas, Belize, Botswana, Cameroon, Central African Republic, Congo, Democratic Republic of Congo, Côte d'Ivoire, Kazakhstan,[a] Kenya, Lesotho, Moldova,[a] Russian Federation,[a] South Africa, Swaziland, Tajikistan,[a] Tanzania,[a] Ukraine,[a] Zambia, Zimbabwe

a. Country does not have HDI data for 1980–90, so drop may have begun before 1990.
Source: Indicator table 2.

Figure
4

Timeline: when will the Millennium Development Goals be achieved if progress does not accelerate?

Years		Poverty	Hunger	Primary education	Gender equality	Child mortality	Access to water	Access to sanitation
	Achieved	Arab States[a]		East Asia & the Pacific	East Asia & the Pacific		Central & Eastern Europe & the CIS[a]	
		East Asia & the Pacific		Latin America & the Caribbean[a]	Latin America & the Caribbean[a]			
				Central & Eastern Europe & the CIS[a]	Central & Eastern Europe & the CIS[a]			
					World[a]			
2000		South Asia	East Asia & the Pacific		South Asia		South Asia	
		World			Arab States		World	
			Latin America & the Caribbean	Arab States	Sub-Saharan Africa	Latin America & the Caribbean	Latin America & the Caribbean	
2015			World	World		East Asia & the Pacific	East Asia & the Pacific	East Asia & the Pacific
			South Asia	South Asia		South Asia	Sub-Saharan Africa	World
						Arab States		South Asia
						World		Latin America & the Caribbean
2100				Sub-Saharan Africa		Sub-Saharan Africa		
2150						Central & Eastern Europe & the CIS		
2200		Latin America & the Caribbean						
	Reversal	Sub-Saharan Africa	Arab States					Sub-Saharan Africa
		Central & Eastern Europe & the CIS	Sub-Saharan Africa					

a. Region is considered achieved as it has low human poverty (below 10%) in most recent year for the relevant goal (See technical note 2)

Source: Calculated on the basis of figure 3.

basis for development—their people, who are their real wealth.

Since 1990, 20 countries have suffered a reversal in the HDI. By contrast, only 3 (of 113 countries with available data) saw their HDI decline in the 1980s (table 6). The reversals in these countries, together with stagnation in others, do much to explain the overall deceleration in HDI progress in the last decade (figure 5). Of the 20 countries experiencing reversals, 13 are in Sub-Saharan Africa. Much of this is due to the HIV/AIDS epidemic and its massive impact on life expectancy. The other reversals are mainly in countries in the Commonwealth of Independent States (CIS), many of which started on a downward trend in the mid-1980s, reflected in the data as a drop in incomes and HDI between 1990 and 1995. The region's HDI started to improve again in the later half of the 1990s.

The drop in many countries' HDI signals a problem; looking at key indicators of progress towards the Millennium Development Goals reveals its depth. Without significant changes, countries experiencing reversals or stagnation have little chance of achieving the goals.

Priority countries

For each goal there are countries where the situation is particularly urgent—where failed progress is combined with brutally low starting levels. These *top priority* countries are in greatest need of the world's attention, resources and commitments (see *Technical note 2*). In *high priority* countries the situation is less desperate, but progress is still insufficient. These countries are either making progress from low levels of development or achieving slow (or negative) progress from higher levels.

There are 27 top priority countries that are failing in several goals: 21 in Sub-Saharan Africa, 3 in the Arab States and 1 each in East Asia and Pacific, South Asia and Latin America and the Caribbean (figure 6). In these countries development is failing across the board. They require the world's attention and resources if they are to achieve the Millennium Development Goals. Another 27 high priority countries face serious challenges across the goals. Again, Sub-Saharan Africa has the greatest number, at 17, and Central and Eastern Europe and the CIS and the Arab States have 3 each, East Asia and the Pacific has 2, and South Asia and Latin America and the Caribbean have 1 each.

Grouping countries into top priority, high priority and other categories is useful, but such efforts should be viewed with caution. The underlying data for individual goals are often measured imprecisely, and some country classifications will change as the data improve. Moreover, many countries are missing too much data for individual goals to be given proper overall classifications. Thus some of the 30 countries in the "other" category would be top or high priority countries if the underlying data were more complete. (Examples include Kyrgyzstan and Pakistan.) In addition, the classification criteria used here are plausible but only one among many reasonable choices.

No single factor can explain the predicaments of the top and high priority countries. But 24 of these 54 countries also saw incomes fall during the decade. And the countries from Sub-Saharan Africa tend to share common features. Many are landlocked or have a large portion of their populations living far from a coast. In addition, most are small—only four have more than 40 million people. Being far from world markets and having a small economy make it much harder to diversify from primary commodities to less volatile exports with more value added. Indeed, primary commodities account for more than two-thirds of exports in 16 of the 23 top or high priority Sub-Saharan countries with data. Many of the region's priority countries also have other serious concerns: in 22 countries more than 5% of the population has HIV/AIDS, and in 9 countries there were violent conflicts in the 1990s.

In other regions top priority countries face other challenges. Many countries in the CIS, for example—while also facing some of the structural problems affecting Sub-Saharan Africa—are trying to make the transition to a market economy, a process that has been much more successful in Central and Eastern Europe. In the Arab States constraints are unrelated to income, deriving instead from a failure to convert income into human development and progress towards the goals.

So what needs to be done to achieve the Millennium Development Goals? No matter how that question is answered, the top priority and high priority countries must be front and centre. The issues they face and ways to resolve them were considered in detail in *Human Development Report 2003*.

1. Calculated on the basis of life expectancy data from UN 2003. 2. UNICEF 2003b. 3. UNESCO Institute for Statistics 2003a. 4. Calculated on the basis of GDP per capita (PPP US$) data from World Bank 2004f. 5. Polity IV 2002. 6. Chapter 2.

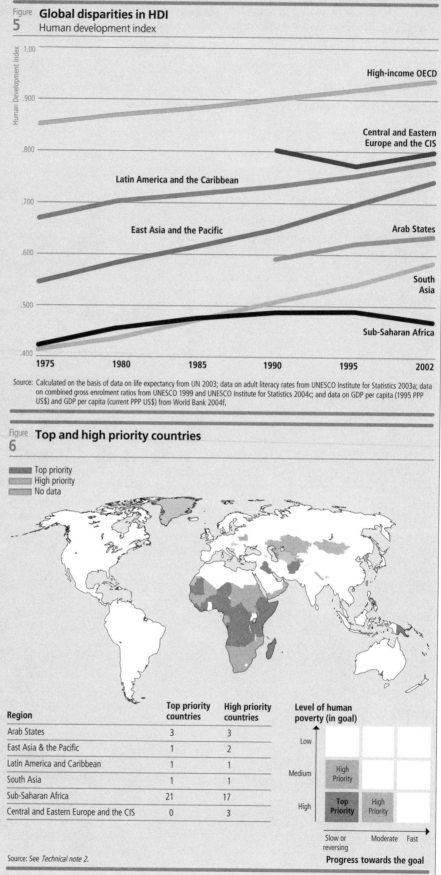

Figure 5

Global disparities in HDI
Human development index

Source: Calculated on the basis of data on life expectancy from UN 2003; data on adult literacy rates from UNESCO Institute for Statistics 2003a; data on combined gross enrolment ratios from UNESCO 1999 and UNESCO Institute for Statistics 2004c; and data on GDP per capita (1995 PPP US$) and GDP per capita (current PPP US$) from World Bank 2004f.

Figure 6

Top and high priority countries

Top priority
High priority
No data

Region	Top priority countries	High priority countries
Arab States	3	3
East Asia & the Pacific	1	2
Latin America and Caribbean	1	1
South Asia	1	1
Sub-Saharan Africa	21	17
Central and Eastern Europe and the CIS	0	3

Level of human poverty (in goal)

Source: See *Technical note 2*.

Index to Millennium Development Goal indicators in the indicator tables

Goals and targets	Indicators for monitoring progress	Indicator table
Goal 1 Eradicate extreme poverty and hunger *Target 1* Halve, between 1990 and 2015, the proportion of people whose income is less than $1 a day	1. Proportion of population below $1 (PPP) a day 2. Poverty gap ratio (incidence × depth of poverty) 3. Share of poorest quintile in national consumption	3 14
Target 2 Halve, between 1990 and 2015, the proportion of people who suffer from hunger	4. Prevalence of underweight children under five years of age 5. Proportion of population below minimum level of dietary energy consumption	3, 7 7[1], 33[1]
Goal 2 Achieve universal primary education *Target 3* Ensure that, by 2015, children everywhere, boys and girls alike, will be able to complete a full course of primary schooling	6. Net enrolment ratio in primary education 7. Proportion of pupils starting grade 1 who reach grade 5 8. Literacy rate of 15- to 24-year-olds	11, 33 11 11
Goal 3 Promote gender equality and empower women *Target 4* Eliminate gender disparity in primary and secondary education, preferably by 2005, and to all levels of education no later than 2015	9. Ratio of girls to boys in primary, secondary and tertiary education 10. Ratio of literate women to men ages 15–24 11. Share of women in wage employment in the non-agricultural sector[4] 12. Proportion of seats held by women in national parliaments	26[2] 26[3] 25, 29
Goal 4 Reduce child mortality *Target 5* Reduce by two thirds, between 1990 and 2015, the under-five mortality rate	13. Under-five mortality rate 14. Infant mortality rate 15. Proportion of one-year-old children immunized against measles	9, 33 9 6
Goal 5 Improve maternal health *Target 6* Reduce by three quarters, between 1990 and 2015, the maternal mortality ratio	16. Maternal mortality ratio 17. Proportion of births attended by skilled health personnel	9 6

Goal 6 Combat HIV/AIDS, malaria and other diseases
Target 7
Have halted by 2015 and begun to reverse the spread of HIV/AIDS
	18. HIV prevalence among pregnant women ages 15–24[5]
	19. Condom use rate of the contraceptive prevalence rate
	    19a. Condom use at last high-risk sex
	    19b. Percentage of 15- to 24-year-olds with comprehensive correct knowledge of HIV/AIDS
	20. Ratio of school attendance of orphans to school attendance of non-orphans ages 10–14
		
		8

Target 8 Have halted by 2015 and begun to reverse the incidence of malaria and other major diseases	21. Prevalence and death rates associated with malaria 22. Proportion of population in malaria-risk areas using effective malaria prevention and treatment measures 23. Prevalence and death rates associated with tuberculosis 24. Proportion of tuberculosis cases detected and cured under directly observed treatment, short course (DOTS)	8[6] 8[7] 8[8] 8
Goal 7 Ensure environmental sustainability *Target 9* Integrate the principles of sustainable development into country policies and programmes and reverse the loss of environmental resources	25. Proportion of land area covered by forest 26. Ratio of area protected to maintain biological diversity to surface area 27. Energy use (kilograms of oil equivalent) per $1 GDP (PPP)	 21[9]

Goals and targets	Indicators for monitoring progress	Indicator table
Goal 7, continued *Target 9, continued*	28. Carbon dioxide emissions per capita and consumption of ozone-depleting chlorofluorocarbons (ODP tons) 29. Proportion of population using solid fuels	21 [10]
Target 10 Halve by 2015 the proportion of people without sustainable access to safe drinking water and sanitation	30. Proportion of population with sustainable access to an improved water source, urban and rural 31. Proportion of population with access to improved sanitation, urban and rural	7 [11], 33 [11] 7 [12]
Target 11 By 2020 to have achieved a significant improvement in the lives of at least 100 million slum dwellers	32. Proportion of households with access to secure tenure	

Goal 8 Develop a global partnership for development

Target 12 Develop further an open, rule-based, predictable, non-discriminatory trading and financial system Includes a commitment to good governance, development, and poverty reduction—both nationally and internationally	*Official development assistance* 33. Net ODA, total and to least developed countries, as a percentage of OECD/DAC donors' gross national income GNI 34. Proportion of total bilateral, sector-allocable ODA of OECD/DAC donors to basic social services (basic education, primary health care, nutrition, safe water and sanitation) 35. Proportion of bilateral ODA of OECD/DAC donors that is untied	16 [13] 16 16
Target 13 Address the special needs of the least developed countries Includes: tariff and quota-free access for least-developed countries' exports; enhanced programme of debt relief for HIPCs and cancellation of official bilateral debt; and more generous ODA for countries committed to poverty reduction	36. ODA received in landlocked countries as proportion of their gross national incomes 37. ODA received in small island developing States as proportion of their gross national incomes *Market access* 38. Proportion of total developed country imports (by value and excluding arms) from developing countries and from the least developed countries, admitted free of duties	
Target 14 Address the special needs of landlocked countries and small island developing States	39. Average tariffs imposed by developed countries on agricultural products and textiles and clothing from developing countries 40. Agricultural support estimate for OECD countries as a percentage of their gross domestic product	17
Target 15 Deal comprehensively with the debt problems of developing countries through national and international measures in order to make debt sustainable in the long term	41. Proportion of ODA provided to help build trade capacity *Debt sustainability* 42. Total number of countries that have reached their HIPC decision points and number that have reached their HIPC completion points (cumulative) 43. Debt relief committed under HIPC Debt Initiative [14] 44. Debt service as a percentage of exports of goods and services	18
Target 16 In cooperation with developing countries, develop and implement strategies for decent and productive work for youth	45. Unemployment rate of 15- to 24-year-olds, male and female and total	20 [15]
Target 17 In cooperation with pharmaceutical companies, provide access to affordable essential drugs in developing countries	46. Proportion of population with access to affordable essential drugs on a sustainable basis	6
Target 18 In cooperation with the private sector, make available the benefits of new technologies, especially information and communications	47. Telephone lines and cellular subscribers per 100 people 48a. Personal computers in use per 100 people 48b. Internet users per 100 people	12 [16] 12

Note: Millennium Development Goal (MDG) indicators are identified in the indicator tables by the symbol **MDG** in orange above the relevant columns.
1. Tables 7 and 33 present this indicator as undernourished people as percent of total population. **2.** Table presents female enrolment ratio as percent of male ratio for primary, secondary and tertiary education levels separately. **3.** Table presents data on female youth literacy rate as percent of male rate. **4.** Table 27 includes data on female employment by economic activity. **5.** Table 8 presents HIV prevalence among people ages 15–49. **6.** Table includes data on malaria cases per 100,000 people. **7.** Table includes data on children under age five with insecticide-treated bed nets and children under age five with fever treated with anti-malarial drugs. **8.** Table includes data on tuberculosis cases per 100,000 people. **9.** Table presents this indicator as GDP per unit of energy use (1995 PPP US$ per kilogram of oil equivalent). **10.** Table includes data on carbon dioxide emissions per capita. **11.** Tables 7 and 33 include data on population with sustainable access to an improved water source for urban and rural combined. **12.** Table includes data on population with sustainable access to improved sanitation for urban and rural combined. **13.** Table includes data on official development assistance (ODA) to least developed countries as percent of total ODA. **14.** Table 17 includes data on bilateral debt relief pledges to the HIPC trust fund and gross bilateral debt forgiveness. **15.** Table includes data on unemployment rate of 15- to 24-year-olds as total and female rate as percent of male rate for OECD countries only. **16.** Table presents telephone lines and cellular subscribers separately.

The human development index (HDI) is a composite index that measures the average achievements in a country in three basic dimensions of human development: a long and healthy life, as measured by life expectancy at birth; knowledge, as measured by the adult literacy rate and the combined gross enrolment ratio for primary, secondary and tertiary schools; and a decent standard of living, as measured by GDP per capita in purchasing power parity (PPP) US dollars. The index is constructed using indicators that are currently available globally, and a methodology that is simple and transparent (see *Technical note 1*).

While the concept of human development is much broader than any single composite index can measure, the HDI offers a powerful alternative to income as a summary measure of human well-being. It provides a useful entry point into the rich information contained in the subsequent indicator tables on different aspects of human development.

Country coverage

The HDI in this Report, presented in indicator table 1, refers to 2002. It covers 175 UN member countries, along with Hong Kong, China (SAR) and the Occupied Palestinian Territories. As a result of improvements in data availability, two countries—Timor-Leste and Tonga—are included in the HDI table for the first time.

Data availability affects the HDI country coverage. To enable cross-country comparisons, the HDI is, to the extent possible, calculated based on data from leading international data agencies available when the Report was prepared (see *Data sources* below). But for a number of countries data are missing for one or more of the four HDI components.

In response to the desire of countries to be included in the HDI table, and striving to include as many UN member countries as possible, the Human Development Report Office has made special efforts in a number of cases to obtain an estimate from other international, regional or national sources when data are lacking from the primary international data agencies for one or two of the HDI components for a country. In a very few cases, the Human Development Report Office has produced an estimate. These estimates from sources other than the primary international agencies (see descriptions below) are documented in the footnotes to indicator table 1. They are often of varying

quality and reliability and are not presented in other indicator tables showing similar data.

Owing to a lack of comparable data, 16 UN member countries cannot be included in the HDI. For these countries basic human development indicators are presented in table 33.

Data sources

Life expectancy at birth. The life expectancy estimates are from the *2002 Revision* of *World Population Prospects* (UN 2003). They are prepared biannually by the United Nations Population Division on the basis of data from national population censuses and surveys. In the *2002 Revision,* the United Nations Population Division made significant adjustments to further incorporate the demographic impact of the HIV/AIDS epidemic. It anticipates a more serious and prolonged impact of the epidemic in the most affected countries than previous revisions did. The impact of the disease is explicitly modeled for 53 countries, up from the 45 considered in the *2000 Revision* (UN 2001).

The life expectancy estimates published by the United Nations Population Division are five-year averages. The life expectancy estimates for 2002 shown in indicator table 1 and those underlying indicator table 2 are obtained through linear interpolation based on these five-year averages.

Adult literacy rate. The adult literacy rate is defined as the percentage of people ages 15 and above who can, with understanding, both read and write a short simple statement related to their everyday life. Literacy data using this definition are usually collected during national population censuses, generally conducted every 5 or 10 years, or from household surveys.

This report uses data on adult literacy rates from the United Nations Educational, Scientific and Cultural Organization (UNESCO) Institute for Statistics (UIS) March 2004 Assessment (UNESCO Institute for Statistics 2004a), which combines direct national estimates with UIS estimates. The national estimates, made available to UIS only recently, are obtained from national censuses or surveys between 1995 and 2004. The UIS estimates, produced in July 2002, were based on national data collected before 1995.

Many high-income OECD countries, having attained universal primary schooling for their populations, no longer collect literacy statistics in national population censuses or household surveys and thus are not included in the UNESCO

data. In calculating the HDI, a literacy rate of 99.0% is applied for those countries.

In collecting literacy data, many countries estimate the number of literate people based on self-reported data. Some use educational attainment data as a proxy, but measures of school attendance or grade completion may differ. Because definitions and data collection methods vary across countries, literacy estimates should be used with caution (UNDP 2000, box 2, p. 143).

The UIS, in collaboration with other partners, is actively pursuing an alternative methodology for measuring literacy, the Literacy Assessment and Monitoring Programme (LAMP; see box 5 in *Note on statistics*). LAMP seeks to go beyond the current simple categories of literate and illiterate by providing information on a continuum of literacy skills.

For details on both the 2002 UIS estimation methods and the new literacy data collection methodology, see http://www.uis.unesco.org/.

Combined gross enrolment ratio for primary, secondary and tertiary schools. Gross enrolment ratios are produced by the UNESCO Institute for Statistics based on enrolment data collected from national governments (usually from administrative sources) and population data from the United Nations Population Division's *2002 Revision* of *World Population Prospects* (UN 2003). The ratios are calculated by dividing the number of students enrolled in all levels of schooling by the total population in the official age group corresponding to these levels. The tertiary age group is set to five cohorts immediately following on the end of upper secondary school in all countries.

Countries are usually asked to report numbers of students enrolled at the beginning of the academic year in each level of education as defined by the International Standard Classification of Education (ISCED). A revised version of ISCED was introduced in 1997, which led to some changes in the classifications of national programmes of education. These changes, however, have less impact on the estimation of combined gross enrolment ratios for primary, secondary and tertiary schools.

Though intended as a proxy for educational attainment, the combined gross enrolment ratio does not reflect the quality of education outcomes. Even when used to capture access to education opportunities, it can hide important differences among countries because of differences in the age range corresponding to a level of education and in the duration of education programmes. Such factors as grade repetition can also create distortions in the data.

Measures such as mean years of schooling of a population or school life expectancy more adequately capture education outcomes and ideally would replace gross enrolment ratios in the HDI. However, such data are not yet regularly available for a sufficient number of countries. Expanding the coverage and quality of such data should be a priority for the international statistical community.

As currently defined, the combined gross enrolment ratio does not take into account students enrolled in other countries. Current data for many smaller countries, such as Luxembourg and Seychelles, where many people pursue tertiary education abroad, could significantly underrepresent actual access to education or the educational attainment of a population and thus lead to a lower HDI value. For instance, the combined gross enrolment ratio for Luxembourg is estimated at 75% but rises to 85% when students enrolled abroad are taken into account.[1] Though the differences in the resulting HDI values are small (0.933 and 0.944, respectively), the HDI ranking of Luxembourg would change from 15 to 4 due to the small differences in the HDI values among the high human development countries. However, data on such a revised gross enrolment ratio are not widely available for other countries and so cannot yet be used in the HDI.

GDP per capita (PPP US$). To compare standards of living across countries GDP per capita needs to be converted into purchasing power parity (PPP) terms that eliminate differences in national price levels. The GDP per capita (PPP US$) data for the HDI are provided for 163 countries by the World Bank based on price data from the latest International Comparison Program (ICP) surveys and GDP in local currency from national accounts data.

The ICP survey covered 118 countries for which PPPs have been estimated directly by extrapolating from the latest benchmark results. For countries not included in the benchmark

surveys, estimates are made using econometric regression. For countries not covered by the World Bank, PPP estimates provided by the Penn World Tables of the University of Pennsylvania are used.[2]

In a limited number of cases where reliable PPP estimates are not available from the two international sources, the Human Development Report Office has worked with regional and national agencies to obtain a PPP estimate for a country. For example, in the case of Cuba, a technical team of national and international experts has been formed to explore different methodologies for obtaining a better PPP estimate. The results of this effort will be reflected in future Reports.

Though much progress has been made in recent decades, the current PPP data set suffers a number of deficiencies, including lack of universal coverage, of timeliness of the data and of uniformity in the quality of results from different regions and countries. Filling gaps in country coverage using econometric regression requires strong assumptions, and extrapolation over time means that the results become increasingly weak as the distance lengthens between the reference survey year and the current year.

The importance of PPPs in economic analysis underlines the need for improvement in PPP data. A new Millennium Round of the ICP has been established and promises much improved PPP data for economic policy analysis, including international poverty assessment (*Note on statistics,* box 6).

Comparisons over time and across editions of the Report

The HDI is an important tool for monitoring long-term trends in human development. To facilitate trend analysis across countries, the HDI is calculated at five-year intervals for the period 1975–2002. These estimates, presented in indicator table 2, are based on a consistent methodology and on comparable trend data available when the Report is prepared.

As international data agencies continually improve their data series, including updating

historical data periodically, the year-to-year changes in the HDI values and rankings across editions of the *Human Development Report* often reflect revisions to data—both specific to a country and relative to other countries—rather than real changes in a country. In addition, occasional changes in country coverage could also affect the HDI ranking of a country, even when a consistent methodology is used to calculate the HDI. As a result, a country's HDI rank could drop considerably between two consecutive Reports, but when comparable, revised data are used to reconstruct the HDI for recent years, the HDI rank and value may actually show an improvement.

For these reasons HDI trend analyses should not be based on data from different editions of the Report. Indicator table 2 provides up-to-date HDI trend data based on consistent data and methodology. For HDI values and ranks recalculated for 2001 (the reference year of the HDI in *Human Development Report 2003*) based on data and country coverage comparable to this year's Report, see http://hdr.undp.org/.

HDI for high human development countries
The HDI in this Report is constructed to compare country achievements across all levels of human development. The indicators currently used in the HDI yield very small differences among the top HDI countries, and thus the top of the HDI rankings often reflects only the very small differences in these underlying indicators. For these high-income countries an alternative index—the human poverty index (shown in indicator table 4 and discussed in Statistical feature 1, *The state of human development*)—can better reflect the extent of human deprivation that still exists among these populations and help direct the focus of public policies.

For further discussions on the use and limitations of the HDI, see Statistical feature 1, *The state of human development*.

1. Statec 2004.
2. Aten, Heston and Summers 2001, 2002.

1 Human development index

HDI rank [a]		Life expectancy at birth (years) 2002	Adult literacy rate (% ages 15 and above) 2002 [b]	Combined gross enrolment ratio for primary, secondary and tertiary schools (%) 2001/02 [c]	GDP per capita (PPP US$) 2002	Life expectancy index	Education index	GDP index	Human development index (HDI) value 2002	GDP per capita (PPP US$) rank minus HDI rank [d]
High human development										
1	Norway	78.9	.. [e]	98 [f]	36,600	0.90	0.99	0.99	0.956	1
2	Sweden	80.0	.. [e]	114 [g, h]	26,050	0.92	0.99	0.93	0.946	19
3	Australia	79.1	.. [e]	113 [g, h]	28,260	0.90	0.99	0.94	0.946	9
4	Canada	79.3	.. [e]	95 [f]	29,480	0.90	0.98	0.95	0.943	5
5	Netherlands	78.3	.. [e]	99 [f]	29,100	0.89	0.99	0.95	0.942	6
6	Belgium	78.7	.. [e]	111 [f, g]	27,570	0.90	0.99	0.94	0.942	7
7	Iceland	79.7	.. [e]	90 [f]	29,750	0.91	0.96	0.95	0.941	1
8	United States	77.0	.. [e]	92 [h]	35,750	0.87	0.97	0.98	0.939	-4
9	Japan	81.5	.. [e]	84 [h]	26,940	0.94	0.94	0.93	0.938	6
10	Ireland	76.9	.. [e]	90 [f]	36,360	0.86	0.96	0.98	0.936	-7
11	Switzerland	79.1	.. [e]	88 [f]	30,010	0.90	0.95	0.95	0.936	-4
12	United Kingdom	78.1	.. [e]	113 [f, g]	26,150	0.88	0.99	0.93	0.936	8
13	Finland	77.9	.. [e]	106 [f, g]	26,190	0.88	0.99	0.93	0.935	6
14	Austria	78.5	.. [e]	91 [f]	29,220	0.89	0.96	0.95	0.934	-4
15	Luxembourg	78.3	.. [e]	75 [f, i]	61,190 [j]	0.89	0.91	1.00	0.933	-14
16	France	78.9	.. [e]	91 [f]	26,920	0.90	0.96	0.93	0.932	0
17	Denmark	76.6	.. [e]	96 [f]	30,940	0.86	0.98	0.96	0.932	-12
18	New Zealand	78.2	.. [e]	101 [g, h]	21,740	0.89	0.99	0.90	0.926	6
19	Germany	78.2	.. [e]	88 [h]	27,100	0.89	0.95	0.94	0.925	-5
20	Spain	79.2	97.7 [e, f, k]	92 [h]	21,460	0.90	0.97	0.90	0.922	5
21	Italy	78.7	98.5 [e, f, k]	82 [f]	26,430	0.89	0.93	0.93	0.920	-3
22	Israel	79.1	95.3	92	19,530	0.90	0.94	0.88	0.908	5
23	Hong Kong, China (SAR)	79.9	93.5 [f, k]	72	26,910	0.91	0.86	0.93	0.903	-6
24	Greece	78.2	97.3 [e, f, k]	86 [f]	18,720	0.89	0.95	0.87	0.902	5
25	Singapore	78.0	92.5 [l]	87 [m]	24,040	0.88	0.91	0.92	0.902	-3
26	Portugal	76.1	92.5 [e, f, k]	93 [f]	18,280	0.85	0.97	0.87	0.897	6
27	Slovenia	76.2	99.7 [e]	90 [f]	18,540	0.85	0.96	0.87	0.895	3
28	Korea, Rep. of	75.4	97.9 [e, f, k]	92 [h]	16,950	0.84	0.97	0.86	0.888	9
29	Barbados	77.1	99.7 [f, n]	88 [f]	15,290	0.87	0.95	0.84	0.888	11
30	Cyprus	78.2	96.8 [l]	74 [f]	18,360 [f]	0.89	0.89	0.87	0.883	1
31	Malta	78.3	92.6	77 [f]	17,640	0.89	0.87	0.86	0.875	3
32	Czech Republic	75.3	.. [e]	78 [h]	15,780	0.84	0.92	0.84	0.868	7
33	Brunei Darussalam	76.2	93.9 [l]	73	19,210 [f, o]	0.85	0.87	0.88	0.867	-5
34	Argentina	74.1	97.0	94 [h]	10,880	0.82	0.96	0.78	0.853	14
35	Seychelles	72.7 [m]	91.9 [l]	85	18,232 [p, q]	0.80	0.90	0.87	0.853	-2
36	Estonia	71.6	99.8 [e, l]	96 [f]	12,260	0.78	0.98	0.80	0.853	10
37	Poland	73.8	99.7 [e, f, k]	90 [h]	10,560	0.81	0.96	0.78	0.850	13
38	Hungary	71.7	99.3 [e, f, k]	86 [h]	13,400	0.78	0.95	0.82	0.848	3
39	Saint Kitts and Nevis	70.0 [r]	97.8 [r]	97 [f]	12,420	0.75	0.98	0.80	0.844	6
40	Bahrain	73.9	88.5	79	17,170	0.81	0.85	0.86	0.843	-4
41	Lithuania	72.5	99.6 [e, l]	90 [f]	10,320	0.79	0.96	0.77	0.842	10
42	Slovakia	73.6	99.7 [e, l]	74 [h]	12,840	0.81	0.91	0.81	0.842	1
43	Chile	76.0	95.7 [l]	79 [f]	9,820	0.85	0.90	0.77	0.839	11
44	Kuwait	76.5	82.9	76 [f]	16,240 [q]	0.86	0.81	0.85	0.838	-6
45	Costa Rica	78.0	95.8	69	8,840 [q]	0.88	0.87	0.75	0.834	14
46	Uruguay	75.2	97.7	85 [h]	7,830	0.84	0.94	0.73	0.833	16
47	Qatar	72.0	84.2 [f, l]	82	19,844 [f, s]	0.78	0.83	0.88	0.833	-21
48	Croatia	74.1	98.1 [l]	73	10,240	0.82	0.90	0.77	0.830	4
49	United Arab Emirates	74.6	77.3	68	22,420 [f, q]	0.83	0.74	0.90	0.824	-26
50	Latvia	70.9	99.7 [e, l]	87 [f]	9,210	0.76	0.95	0.75	0.823	6

HDI rank [a]		Life expectancy at birth (years) 2002	Adult literacy rate (% ages 15 and above) 2002 [b]	Combined gross enrolment ratio for primary, secondary and tertiary schools (%) 2001/02 [c]	GDP per capita (PPP US$) 2002	Life expectancy index	Education index	GDP index	Human development index (HDI) value 2002	GDP per capita (PPP US$) rank minus HDI rank [d]
51	Bahamas	67.1	95.5 [f, k]	74 [f, t]	17,280 [f]	0.70	0.88	0.86	0.815	-16
52	Cuba	76.7	96.9	78	5,259 [f, s, u]	0.86	0.91	0.66	0.809	39
53	Mexico	73.3	90.5 [l]	74 [h]	8,970	0.81	0.85	0.75	0.802	5
54	Trinidad and Tobago	71.4	98.5	64	9,430	0.77	0.87	0.76	0.801	1
55	Antigua and Barbuda	73.9 [r]	85.8 [f, n]	69 [r]	10,920	0.82	0.80	0.78	0.800	-8
Medium human development										
56	Bulgaria	70.9	98.6	76 [f]	7,130	0.77	0.91	0.71	0.796	10
57	Russian Federation	66.7	99.6 [e]	88 [h]	8,230	0.69	0.95	0.74	0.795	3
58	Libyan Arab Jamahiriya	72.6	81.7	97 [h]	7,570 [v]	0.79	0.87	0.72	0.794	6
59	Malaysia	73.0	88.7 [l]	70 [h]	9,120	0.80	0.83	0.75	0.793	-2
60	Macedonia, TFYR	73.5	96.0 [w, x]	70 [f]	6,470	0.81	0.87	0.70	0.793	15
61	Panama	74.6	92.3	73 [f]	6,170	0.83	0.86	0.69	0.791	18
62	Belarus	69.9	99.7 [e]	88	5,520	0.75	0.95	0.67	0.790	24
63	Tonga	68.4	98.8 [l]	82	6,850 [q]	0.72	0.93	0.71	0.787	5
64	Mauritius	71.9	84.3 [l]	69	10,810	0.78	0.79	0.78	0.785	-15
65	Albania	73.6	98.7 [l]	69 [f]	4,830	0.81	0.89	0.65	0.781	31
66	Bosnia and Herzegovina	74.0	94.6	64 [y]	5,970 [f, o]	0.82	0.84	0.68	0.781	15
67	Suriname	71.0	94.0 [w, x]	74 [h]	6,590 [p, q]	0.77	0.87	0.70	0.780	6
68	Venezuela	73.6	93.1	71	5,380	0.81	0.86	0.67	0.778	21
69	Romania	70.5	97.3 [l]	68 [f]	6,560	0.76	0.88	0.70	0.778	5
70	Ukraine	69.5	99.6 [e]	84	4,870	0.74	0.94	0.65	0.777	25
71	Saint Lucia	72.4	94.8 [f, n]	74	5,300	0.79	0.88	0.66	0.777	19
72	Brazil	68.0	86.4 [l]	92 [h]	7,770	0.72	0.88	0.73	0.775	-9
73	Colombia	72.1	92.1	68	6,370 [q]	0.78	0.84	0.69	0.773	4
74	Oman	72.3	74.4	63	13,340	0.79	0.71	0.82	0.770	-32
75	Samoa (Western)	69.8	98.7	69	5,600 [q]	0.75	0.89	0.67	0.769	10
76	Thailand	69.1	92.6 [l]	73 [f]	7,010	0.74	0.86	0.71	0.768	-9
77	Saudi Arabia	72.1	77.9	57	12,650 [q]	0.79	0.71	0.81	0.768	-33
78	Kazakhstan	66.2	99.4 [e]	81	5,870	0.69	0.93	0.68	0.766	4
79	Jamaica	75.6	87.6 [f, n]	75 [h]	3,980	0.84	0.83	0.61	0.764	28
80	Lebanon	73.5	86.5 [f, k]	78	4,360	0.81	0.84	0.63	0.758	21
81	Fiji	69.6	92.9 [f, l]	73 [h]	5,440	0.74	0.86	0.67	0.758	7
82	Armenia	72.3	99.4 [e, l]	72	3,120	0.79	0.90	0.57	0.754	33
83	Philippines	69.8	92.6 [l]	81 [h]	4,170	0.75	0.89	0.62	0.753	22
84	Maldives	67.2	97.2	78	4,798 [f, p, q]	0.70	0.91	0.65	0.752	13
85	Peru	69.7	85.0 [z]	88 [h]	5,010	0.74	0.86	0.65	0.752	7
86	Turkmenistan	66.9	98.8 [f, l]	81 [f, t]	4,300 [f]	0.70	0.93	0.63	0.752	16
87	St. Vincent & the Grenadines	74.0	83.1 [f, n]	64	5,460	0.82	0.77	0.67	0.751	0
88	Turkey	70.4	86.5 [l]	68 [h]	6,390	0.76	0.80	0.69	0.751	-12
89	Paraguay	70.7	91.6 [z]	72 [h]	4,610 [q]	0.76	0.85	0.64	0.751	9
90	Jordan	70.9	90.9	77 [h]	4,220	0.76	0.86	0.62	0.750	14
91	Azerbaijan	72.1	97.0 [w, x]	69	3,210	0.78	0.88	0.58	0.746	23
92	Tunisia	72.7	73.2	75 [h]	6,760	0.79	0.74	0.70	0.745	-23
93	Grenada	65.3 [f, n]	94.4 [f, n]	65 [f]	7,280	0.67	0.85	0.72	0.745	-28
94	China	70.9	90.9 [l]	68 [f]	4,580	0.76	0.83	0.64	0.745	5
95	Dominica	73.1 [n]	76.4 [f, n]	74 [f]	5,640	0.80	0.76	0.67	0.743	-11
96	Sri Lanka	72.5	92.1	65 [h]	3,570	0.79	0.83	0.60	0.740	16
97	Georgia	73.5	100.0 [e, w, x]	69	2,260	0.81	0.89	0.52	0.739	29
98	Dominican Republic	66.7	84.4	77 [h]	6,640 [q]	0.70	0.82	0.70	0.738	-27
99	Belize	71.5	76.9 [l]	71 [f]	6,080	0.78	0.75	0.69	0.737	-19
100	Ecuador	70.7	91.0 [l]	72 [f, aa]	3,580	0.76	0.85	0.60	0.735	11

HDI rank [a]		Life expectancy at birth (years) 2002	Adult literacy rate (% ages 15 and above) 2002 [b]	Combined gross enrolment ratio for primary, secondary and tertiary schools (%) 2001/02 [c]	GDP per capita (PPP US$) 2002	Life expectancy index	Education index	GDP index	Human development index (HDI) value 2002	GDP per capita (PPP US$) rank minus HDI rank [d]
101	Iran, Islamic Rep. of	70.1	77.1 [f, k,z]	69	6,690	0.75	0.74	0.70	0.732	-31
102	Occupied Palestinian Territories	72.3	90.2 [m]	79	.. [ab]	0.79	0.86	0.52	0.726	21
103	El Salvador	70.6	79.7	66	4,890 [q]	0.76	0.75	0.65	0.720	-9
104	Guyana	63.2	96.5 [f, n]	75 [f]	4,260 [q]	0.64	0.89	0.63	0.719	-1
105	Cape Verde	70.0	75.7	73 [h]	5,000 [q]	0.75	0.75	0.65	0.717	-12
106	Syrian Arab Republic	71.7	82.9	59	3,620	0.78	0.75	0.60	0.710	4
107	Uzbekistan	69.5	99.3 [e]	76	1,670	0.74	0.91	0.47	0.709	35
108	Algeria	69.5	68.9	70 [h]	5,760 [q]	0.74	0.69	0.68	0.704	-25
109	Equatorial Guinea	49.1	84.2 [f, k]	58	30,130 [f,q]	0.40	0.76	0.95	0.703	-103
110	Kyrgyzstan	68.4	97.0 [w, ac]	81	1,620	0.72	0.92	0.46	0.701	33
111	Indonesia	66.6	87.9	65 [h]	3,230	0.69	0.80	0.58	0.692	2
112	Viet Nam	69.0	90.3 [f, l]	64	2,300	0.73	0.82	0.52	0.691	12
113	Moldova, Rep. of	68.8	99.0 [e]	62	1,470	0.73	0.87	0.45	0.681	36
114	Bolivia	63.7	86.7 [l]	86 [h]	2,460	0.64	0.86	0.53	0.681	6
115	Honduras	68.8	80.0 [l]	62 [f, aa]	2,600 [q]	0.73	0.74	0.54	0.672	3
116	Tajikistan	68.6	99.5 [e, l]	73	980	0.73	0.90	0.38	0.671	45
117	Mongolia	63.7	97.8 [l]	70	1,710	0.64	0.89	0.47	0.668	21
118	Nicaragua	69.4	76.7 [z]	65 [h]	2,470 [q]	0.74	0.73	0.54	0.667	1
119	South Africa	48.8	86.0	77	10,070 [q]	0.40	0.83	0.77	0.666	-66
120	Egypt	68.6	55.6 [f, l]	76 [f, t]	3,810	0.73	0.62	0.61	0.653	-12
121	Guatemala	65.7	69.9	56 [h]	4,080 [q]	0.68	0.65	0.62	0.649	-15
122	Gabon	56.6	71.0 [w, x]	74 [h]	6,590	0.53	0.72	0.70	0.648	-50
123	São Tomé and Principe	69.7	83.1 [m]	62	1,317 [f,s]	0.75	0.76	0.43	0.645	29
124	Solomon Islands	69.0	76.6 [m]	50 [m]	1,590 [q]	0.73	0.68	0.46	0.624	21
125	Morocco	68.5	50.7	57	3,810	0.72	0.53	0.61	0.620	-17
126	Namibia	45.3	83.3	71	6,210 [q]	0.34	0.79	0.69	0.607	-48
127	India	63.7	61.3 [l]	55 [f]	2,670 [q]	0.64	0.59	0.55	0.595	-10
128	Botswana	41.4	78.9	70	8,170	0.27	0.76	0.73	0.589	-67
129	Vanuatu	68.6	34.0 [m]	59	2,890 [q]	0.73	0.42	0.56	0.570	-13
130	Cambodia	57.4	69.4	59	2,060 [q]	0.54	0.66	0.50	0.568	1
131	Ghana	57.8	73.8	46	2,130 [q]	0.55	0.65	0.51	0.568	-3
132	Myanmar	57.2	85.3	48	1,027 [v]	0.54	0.73	0.39	0.551	26
133	Papua New Guinea	57.4	64.6 [f, k]	41	2,270 [q]	0.54	0.57	0.52	0.542	-8
134	Bhutan	63.0	47.0 [w, x]	.. [ad]	1,969 [f,s]	0.63	0.48	0.50	0.536	0
135	Lao People's Dem. Rep.	54.3	66.4	59	1,720	0.49	0.64	0.47	0.534	2
136	Comoros	60.6	56.2	45	1,690 [q]	0.59	0.53	0.47	0.530	4
137	Swaziland	35.7	80.9	61	4,550	0.18	0.74	0.64	0.519	-37
138	Bangladesh	61.1	41.1	54	1,700	0.60	0.45	0.47	0.509	1
139	Sudan [ae]	55.5	59.9	36	1,820 [q]	0.51	0.52	0.48	0.505	-3
140	Nepal	59.6	44.0	61	1,370	0.58	0.50	0.44	0.504	11
141	Cameroon	46.8	67.9 [z]	56 [h]	2,000	0.36	0.64	0.50	0.501	-9
Low human development										
142	Pakistan	60.8	41.5 [f, l]	37 [f]	1,940	0.60	0.40	0.49	0.497	-7
143	Togo	49.9	59.6	67	1,480 [q]	0.41	0.62	0.45	0.495	5
144	Congo	48.3	82.8	48 [h]	980	0.39	0.71	0.38	0.494	17
145	Lesotho	36.3	81.4 [z]	65	2,420 [q]	0.19	0.76	0.53	0.493	-24
146	Uganda	45.7	68.9	71	1,390 [q]	0.34	0.70	0.44	0.493	4
147	Zimbabwe	33.9	90.0	58 [h]	2,400 [f]	0.15	0.79	0.53	0.491	-25
148	Kenya	45.2	84.3	53	1,020	0.34	0.74	0.39	0.488	11
149	Yemen	59.8	49.0	53 [f]	870	0.58	0.50	0.36	0.482	16
150	Madagascar	53.4	67.3 [f, k]	45	740	0.47	0.60	0.33	0.469	20
151	Nigeria	51.6	66.8	45 [f, t]	860	0.44	0.59	0.36	0.466	15

1 Human development index

HDI rank [a]	Life expectancy at birth (years) 2002	Adult literacy rate (% ages 15 and above) 2002 [b]	Combined gross enrolment ratio for primary, secondary and tertiary schools (%) 2001/02 [c]	GDP per capita (PPP US$) 2002	Life expectancy index	Education index	GDP index	Human development index (HDI) value 2002	GDP per capita (PPP US$) rank minus HDI rank [d]
152 Mauritania	52.3	41.2	44	2,220 q	0.45	0.42	0.52	0.465	-25
153 Haiti	49.4	51.9	52 f, t	1,610 q	0.41	0.52	0.46	0.463	-9
154 Djibouti	45.8	65.5 f, k	24	1,990 q	0.35	0.52	0.50	0.454	-21
155 Gambia	53.9	37.8 f, k	45 h	1,690 q	0.48	0.40	0.47	0.452	-15
156 Eritrea	52.7	56.7 f, k	33	890 q	0.46	0.49	0.36	0.439	8
157 Senegal	52.7	39.3	38 h	1,580	0.46	0.39	0.46	0.437	-11
158 Timor-Leste	49.3	58.6 f, m	75	.. af	0.41	0.64	0.26	0.436	19
159 Rwanda	38.9	69.2	53	1,270 q	0.23	0.64	0.42	0.431	-6
160 Guinea	48.9	41.0 w, x	29 f	2,100 q	0.40	0.37	0.51	0.425	-30
161 Benin	50.7	39.8	52 h	1,070	0.43	0.44	0.40	0.421	-5
162 Tanzania, U. Rep. of	43.5	77.1	31 f	580	0.31	0.62	0.29	0.407	12
163 Côte d'Ivoire	41.2	49.7 f, k	42	1,520	0.27	0.47	0.45	0.399	-16
164 Zambia	32.7	79.9	45	840	0.13	0.68	0.36	0.389	3
165 Malawi	37.8	61.8	74 h	580	0.21	0.66	0.29	0.388	9
166 Angola	40.1	42.0 w, ac	30 f	2,130 q	0.25	0.38	0.51	0.381	-38
167 Chad	44.7	45.8	35 f	1,020 q	0.33	0.42	0.39	0.379	-8
168 Congo, Dem. Rep. of the	41.4	62.7 f, k	27 f, aa	650 q	0.27	0.51	0.31	0.365	4
169 Central African Republic	39.8	48.6 z	31	1,170 q	0.25	0.43	0.41	0.361	-15
170 Ethiopia	45.5	41.5	34	780 q	0.34	0.39	0.34	0.359	-1
171 Mozambique	38.5	46.5	41	1,050 q	0.22	0.45	0.39	0.354	-14
172 Guinea-Bissau	45.2	39.6 f, k	37 f	710 q	0.34	0.39	0.33	0.350	-1
173 Burundi	40.8	50.4	33	630 q	0.26	0.45	0.31	0.339	0
174 Mali	48.5	19.0 f, l	26 f	930	0.39	0.21	0.37	0.326	-11
175 Burkina Faso	45.8	12.8 f, l	22 h	1,100 q	0.35	0.16	0.40	0.302	-20
176 Niger	46.0	17.1	19	800 q	0.35	0.18	0.35	0.292	-8
177 Sierra Leone	34.3	36.0 w, x	45 f	520	0.16	0.39	0.28	0.273	-1
Developing countries	64.6	76.7	60	4,054	0.66	0.71	0.62	0.663	..
Least developed countries	50.6	52.5	43	1,307	0.43	0.49	0.42	0.446	..
Arab States	66.3	63.3	60	5,069	0.69	0.61	0.65	0.651	..
East Asia and the Pacific	69.8	90.3	65	4,768	0.75	0.83	0.64	0.740	..
Latin America and the Caribbean	70.5	88.6	81	7,223	0.76	0.86	0.72	0.777	..
South Asia	63.2	57.6	54	2,658	0.64	0.57	0.55	0.584	..
Sub-Saharan Africa	46.3	63.2	44	1,790	0.35	0.56	0.48	0.465	..
Central & Eastern Europe & CIS	69.5	99.3	79	7,192	0.74	0.93	0.72	0.796	..
OECD	77.1	..	87	24,904	0.87	0.94	0.92	0.911	..
High-income OECD	78.3	..	93	29,000	0.89	0.97	0.95	0.935	..
High human development	77.4	..	89	24,806	0.87	0.95	0.92	0.915	..
Medium human development	67.2	80.4	64	4,269	0.70	0.75	0.63	0.695	..
Low human development	49.1	54.3	40	1,184	0.40	0.50	0.41	0.438	..
High income	78.3	..	92	28,741	0.89	0.97	0.94	0.933	..
Middle income	70.0	89.7	71	5,908	0.75	0.84	0.68	0.756	..
Low income	59.1	63.6	51	2,149	0.57	0.59	0.51	0.557	..
World	66.9	..	64	7,804	0.70	0.76	0.73	0.729	..

Note: Aggregates for columns 5-8 are based on all data in the table. For detailed notes on the data, see Statistical feature 2, *Note to table 1: About this year's human development index.*
a. The HDI rank is determined using HDI values to the fifth decimal point. b. Data refer to estimates produced by UNESCO Institute for Statistics in July 2002, unless otherwise specified. Due to differences in methodology and timeliness of underlying data, comparisons across countries and over time should be made with caution. c. Data refer to the 2001/02 school year, unless otherwise specified. Data for some countries may refer to national or UNESCO Institute for Statistics estimates. For details, see http://www.uis.unesco.org/. Because data are from different sources, comparisons across countries should be made with caution. d. A positive figure indicates that the HDI rank is higher than the GDP per capita (PPP US$) rank, a negative the opposite. e. For purposes of calculating the HDI, a value of 99.0% was applied. f. Data refer to a year other than that specified. g. For purposes of calculating the HDI, a value of 100% was applied. h. Preliminary UNESCO Institute for Statistics estimate, subject to further revision. i. The ratio is an underestimate, as many secondary and tertiary students pursue their studies in nearby countries (see Statistical feature 2, *Note to table 1: About this year's human development index*). j. For purposes of calculating the HDI, a value of $40,000 (PPP US$) was applied. k. UNESCO Institute for Statistics 2003a. Data are subject to further revision. l. Census data. m. Data are from national sources. n. Data are from the Secretariat of the Caribbean Community, based on national sources. o. World Bank 2003b. p. Preliminary World Bank estimate, subject to further revision. q. Estimate based on regression. r. Data are from the Secretariat of the Organization of Eastern Caribbean States, based on national sources. s. Aten, Heston, and Summers 2002. Data differ from the standard definition. t. Data refer to the 1999/2000 school year. They were provided by the UNESCO Institute for Statistics for *Human Development Report 2001* (see UNESCO Institute for Statistics 2001). u. Efforts to produce a more accurate and recent estimate are ongoing (see Statistical feature 2, *Note to table 1: About this year's human development index*). v. Aten, Heston, and Summers 2001. Data differ from the standard definition. w. Data refer to a year or period other than that specified, differ from the standard definition or refer to only part of a country. x. UNICEF 2003b. y. UNDP 2002a. z. Survey data. aa. UNESCO Institute for Statistics 2003b. ab. In the absence of an estimate of GDP per capita (PPP US$), the Human Development Report Office estimate of $2,302, derived using the value of GDP in US dollars and the weighted average ratio of PPP US dollars to US dollars in the Arab States, was used. ac. UNICEF 2000. ad. Because the combined gross enrolment ratio was unavailable, the Human Development Report Office estimate of 49% was used. ae. Estimates are based primarily on information for northern Sudan. af. The estimated value of $478 was used (UNDP 2002b).
Source: Column 1: UN 2003, unless otherwise noted; column 2: UNESCO Institute for Statistics 2004a, unless otherwise noted; column 3: UNESCO Institute for Statistics 2004c, unless otherwise noted; column 4: World Bank 2004f, unless otherwise noted; aggregates calculated for the Human Development Report Office by the World Bank; column 5: calculated on the basis of data in column 1; column 6: calculated on the basis of data in columns 2 and 3; column 7: calculated on the basis of data in column 4; column 8: calculated on the basis of data in columns 5-7; see technical note 1 for details; column 9: calculated on the basis of data in columns 4 and 8.

2 Human development index trends

HDI rank	1975	1980	1985	1990	1995	2000	2002
High human development							
1 Norway	0.866	0.886	0.897	0.911	0.935	0.954	0.956
2 Sweden	0.863	0.873	0.885	0.895	0.928	0.943	0.946
3 Australia	0.847	0.864	0.877	0.892	0.932	0.942	0.946
4 Canada	0.869	0.885	0.908	0.928	0.933	0.939	0.943
5 Netherlands	0.865	0.877	0.891	0.907	0.927	0.938	0.942
6 Belgium	0.845	0.862	0.876	0.897	0.927	0.940	0.942
7 Iceland	0.862	0.885	0.895	0.913	0.919	0.939	0.941
8 United States	0.866	0.886	0.899	0.914	0.926	0.935	0.939
9 Japan	0.854	0.879	0.894	0.910	0.924	0.934	0.938
10 Ireland	0.810	0.825	0.844	0.869	0.893	0.926	0.936
11 Switzerland	0.878	0.889	0.895	0.909	0.918	0.932	0.936
12 United Kingdom	0.845	0.853	0.862	0.883	0.921	0.932	0.936
13 Finland	0.839	0.859	0.876	0.899	0.913	0.933	0.935
14 Austria	0.842	0.856	0.870	0.893	0.913	0.931	0.934
15 Luxembourg	0.838	0.850	0.856	0.882	0.908	0.928	0.933
16 France	0.852	0.867	0.880	0.902	0.919	0.929	0.932
17 Denmark	0.872	0.881	0.889	0.897	0.912	0.929	0.932
18 New Zealand	0.847	0.853	0.867	0.874	0.904	0.921	0.926
19 Germany	..	0.860	0.868	0.887	0.911	..	0.925
20 Spain	0.836	0.853	0.867	0.885	0.903	0.917	0.922
21 Italy	0.841	0.856	0.865	0.887	0.904	0.915	0.920
22 Israel	0.794	0.818	0.839	0.857	0.880	0.907	0.908
23 Hong Kong, China (SAR)	0.760	0.799	0.826	0.862	0.879	..	0.903
24 Greece	0.832	0.847	0.860	0.870	0.875	0.894	0.902
25 Singapore	0.724	0.761	0.784	0.821	0.859	..	0.902
26 Portugal	0.785	0.800	0.823	0.847	0.876	0.892	0.897
27 Slovenia	..	..	..	..	0.852	0.883	0.895
28 Korea, Rep. of	0.705	0.741	0.779	0.817	0.852	0.878	0.888
29 Barbados	0.804	0.827	0.837	0.851	0.859	0.888	0.888
30 Cyprus	..	0.791	0.812	0.835	0.855	0.880	0.883
31 Malta	0.726	0.763	0.789	0.824	0.850	0.873	0.875
32 Czech Republic	..	..	..	..	0.843	0.856	0.868
33 Brunei Darussalam	..	..	..	..	..	..	0.867
34 Argentina	0.784	0.799	0.808	0.810	0.832	0.854	0.853
35 Seychelles	..	..	..	..	..	..	0.853
36 Estonia	..	..	..	0.817	0.796	0.839	0.853
37 Poland	..	..	..	0.802	0.816	0.843	0.850
38 Hungary	0.777	0.793	0.807	0.807	0.810	0.837	0.848
39 Saint Kitts and Nevis	..	..	..	..	..	..	0.844
40 Bahrain	..	0.746	0.779	0.808	0.825	0.835	0.843
41 Lithuania	..	..	..	0.823	0.789	0.829	0.842
42 Slovakia	..	..	..	..	..	..	0.842
43 Chile	0.703	0.738	0.761	0.784	0.814	0.835	0.839
44 Kuwait	0.761	0.776	0.778	..	0.810	0.834	0.838
45 Costa Rica	0.745	0.770	0.774	0.791	0.810	0.829	0.834
46 Uruguay	0.759	0.779	0.785	0.803	0.816	..	0.833
47 Qatar	..	..	..	..	..	..	0.833
48 Croatia	..	..	..	0.806	0.798	0.823	0.830
49 United Arab Emirates	0.744	0.777	0.785	0.805	0.803	..	0.824
50 Latvia	..	0.795	0.807	0.807	0.765	0.808	0.823

HDI rank	1975	1980	1985	1990	1995	2000	2002
51 Bahamas	..	0.809	0.820	0.825	0.812	..	0.815
52 Cuba	..	..	..	..	..	..	0.809
53 Mexico	0.688	0.734	0.753	0.761	0.776	0.800	0.802
54 Trinidad and Tobago	0.735	0.768	0.786	0.791	0.793	0.806	0.801
55 Antigua and Barbuda	..	..	..	..	..	..	0.800
Medium human development							
56 Bulgaria	..	0.768	0.788	0.795	0.784	0.791	0.796
57 Russian Federation	..	..	..	0.813	0.771	..	0.795
58 Libyan Arab Jamahiriya	..	..	..	..	..	..	0.794
59 Malaysia	0.614	0.657	0.693	0.720	0.759	0.789	0.793
60 Macedonia, TFYR	..	..	..	..	..	..	0.793
61 Panama	0.708	0.735	0.746	0.748	0.771	0.791	0.791
62 Belarus	..	..	..	0.785	0.752	0.775	0.790
63 Tonga	..	..	..	..	..	..	0.787
64 Mauritius	..	0.658	0.689	0.723	0.747	0.775	0.785
65 Albania	..	..	0.691	0.702	0.702	0.740	0.781
66 Bosnia and Herzegovina	..	..	..	..	..	..	0.781
67 Suriname	..	..	..	..	..	..	0.780
68 Venezuela	0.716	0.730	0.739	0.759	0.768	0.776	0.778
69 Romania	..	..	..	0.771	0.769	0.773	0.778
70 Ukraine	..	..	..	0.798	0.751	0.762	0.777
71 Saint Lucia	..	..	..	..	..	..	0.777
72 Brazil	0.644	0.680	0.695	0.714	0.739	0.771	0.775
73 Colombia	0.661	0.689	0.706	0.727	0.751	0.771	0.773
74 Oman	0.493	0.546	0.640	0.696	0.733	0.761	0.770
75 Samoa (Western)	..	..	..	..	0.741	0.762	0.769
76 Thailand	0.613	0.651	0.676	0.707	0.742	..	0.768
77 Saudi Arabia	0.602	0.656	0.671	0.707	0.741	0.764	0.768
78 Kazakhstan	..	..	..	0.767	0.725	0.744	0.766
79 Jamaica	0.687	0.695	0.699	0.726	0.737	0.752	0.764
80 Lebanon	..	..	..	0.673	0.732	0.752	0.758
81 Fiji	0.659	0.683	0.698	0.722	0.744	0.751	0.758
82 Armenia	..	..	..	0.751	0.708	..	0.754
83 Philippines	0.653	0.686	0.692	0.719	0.735	..	0.753
84 Maldives	..	..	..	..	..	..	0.752
85 Peru	0.642	0.672	0.696	0.706	0.733	..	0.752
86 Turkmenistan	..	..	..	..	..	..	0.752
87 St. Vincent & the Grenadines	..	..	..	..	..	..	0.751
88 Turkey	0.590	0.614	0.651	0.683	0.713	..	0.751
89 Paraguay	0.667	0.701	0.708	0.719	0.738	0.751	0.751
90 Jordan	..	0.639	0.663	0.682	0.707	0.741	0.750
91 Azerbaijan	..	..	..	..	..	..	0.746
92 Tunisia	0.516	0.574	0.623	0.656	0.696	0.734	0.745
93 Grenada	..	..	..	..	..	..	0.745
94 China	0.523	0.557	0.593	0.627	0.683	0.721	0.745
95 Dominica	..	..	..	..	..	..	0.743
96 Sri Lanka	0.613	0.648	0.674	0.698	0.719	..	0.740
97 Georgia	..	..	..	..	..	..	0.739
98 Dominican Republic	0.617	0.648	0.670	0.678	0.699	0.731	0.738
99 Belize	..	0.707	0.717	0.747	0.768	0.773	0.737
100 Ecuador	0.630	0.674	0.696	0.710	0.719	..	0.735

HDI rank		1975	1980	1985	1990	1995	2000	2002
101	Iran, Islamic Rep. of	0.565	0.569	0.610	0.649	0.693	0.723	0.732
102	Occupied Palestinian Territories	..	..	..	..	..	..	0.726
103	El Salvador	0.590	0.590	0.610	0.648	0.686	0.713	0.720
104	Guyana	0.677	0.683	0.679	0.697	0.706	0.724	0.719
105	Cape Verde	..	..	..	0.623	0.675	..	0.717
106	Syrian Arab Republic	0.534	0.576	0.611	0.635	0.663	0.683	0.710
107	Uzbekistan	..	..	..	..	0.687	..	0.709
108	Algeria	0.504	0.554	0.603	0.642	0.664	0.693	0.704
109	Equatorial Guinea	..	..	0.483	0.504	0.528	0.670	0.703
110	Kyrgyzstan	..	..	..	..	..	..	0.701
111	Indonesia	0.467	0.529	0.582	0.623	0.662	0.680	0.692
112	Viet Nam	..	..	..	0.610	0.649	0.686	0.691
113	Moldova, Rep. of	..	..	..	0.736	0.684	0.673	0.681
114	Bolivia	0.512	0.548	0.580	0.603	0.635	0.670	0.681
115	Honduras	0.517	0.568	0.599	0.624	0.646	..	0.672
116	Tajikistan	..	..	0.719	0.719	0.651	0.655	0.671
117	Mongolia	..	..	0.650	0.656	0.629	0.658	0.668
118	Nicaragua	0.565	0.576	0.584	0.589	0.624	0.643	0.667
119	South Africa	0.655	0.672	0.697	0.729	0.735	0.690	0.666
120	Egypt	0.438	0.487	0.539	0.577	0.608	..	0.653
121	Guatemala	0.510	0.546	0.559	0.583	0.613	0.642	0.649
122	Gabon	..	..	..	..	..	..	0.648
123	São Tomé and Principe	..	..	..	..	..	..	0.645
124	Solomon Islands	..	..	..	..	..	..	0.624
125	Morocco	0.429	0.474	0.510	0.542	0.571	0.603	0.620
126	Namibia	..	..	..	..	0.667	0.625	0.607
127	India	0.411	0.437	0.476	0.514	0.548	0.579	0.595
128	Botswana	0.503	0.574	0.633	0.675	0.666	0.620	0.589
129	Vanuatu	..	..	..	..	..	..	0.570
130	Cambodia	..	..	..	..	0.540	0.551	0.568
131	Ghana	0.439	0.467	0.481	0.511	0.532	0.560	0.568
132	Myanmar	..	..	..	..	..	..	0.551
133	Papua New Guinea	0.423	0.444	0.465	0.482	0.522	0.540	0.542
134	Bhutan	..	..	..	..	..	..	0.536
135	Lao People's Dem. Rep.	..	..	0.422	0.449	0.485	0.520	0.534
136	Comoros	..	0.479	0.498	0.501	0.509	0.521	0.530
137	Swaziland	0.516	0.544	0.565	0.611	0.606	0.548	0.519
138	Bangladesh	0.345	0.363	0.388	0.417	0.445	0.497	0.509
139	Sudan	0.344	0.372	0.394	0.427	0.465	0.492	0.505
140	Nepal	0.291	0.330	0.372	0.418	0.455	0.488	0.504
141	Cameroon	0.415	0.462	0.504	0.519	0.508	..	0.501
Low human development								
142	Pakistan	0.346	0.373	0.405	0.444	0.473	..	0.497
143	Togo	0.396	0.445	0.445	0.474	0.486	0.491	0.495
144	Congo	0.451	0.497	0.541	0.532	0.530	0.487	0.494
145	Lesotho	0.457	0.499	0.517	0.544	0.549	0.513	0.493
146	Uganda	..	..	0.395	0.395	0.404	..	0.493
147	Zimbabwe	0.547	0.572	0.629	0.617	0.571	0.511	0.491
148	Kenya	0.445	0.490	0.515	0.540	0.524	0.496	0.488
149	Yemen	..	..	..	0.392	0.435	0.469	0.482
150	Madagascar	0.400	0.433	0.429	0.436	0.443	0.469	0.469
151	Nigeria	0.324	0.385	0.401	0.430	0.455	..	0.466

HDI rank		1975	1980	1985	1990	1995	2000	2002
152	Mauritania	0.339	0.362	0.382	0.387	0.423	0.449	0.465
153	Haiti	..	0.443	0.459	0.455	0.448	..	0.463
154	Djibouti	..	..	..	..	0.450	0.452	0.454
155	Gambia	0.283	..	..	..	0.418	0.448	0.452
156	Eritrea	..	..	..	..	0.410	0.430	0.439
157	Senegal	0.315	0.332	0.359	0.382	0.398	0.425	0.437
158	Timor-Leste	..	..	..	..	..	..	0.436
159	Rwanda	0.341	0.386	0.397	0.351	0.341	0.413	0.431
160	Guinea	..	..	..	..	..	..	0.425
161	Benin	0.288	0.324	0.351	0.356	0.381	0.406	0.421
162	Tanzania, U. Rep. of	..	..	..	0.413	0.406	0.403	0.407
163	Côte d'Ivoire	0.382	0.416	0.428	0.429	0.410	0.402	0.399
164	Zambia	0.466	0.474	0.485	0.466	0.418	0.389	0.389
165	Malawi	0.315	0.347	0.360	0.368	0.408	0.395	0.388
166	Angola	..	..	..	..	..	..	0.381
167	Chad	0.260	0.260	0.301	0.326	0.335	0.363	0.379
168	Congo, Dem. Rep. of the	0.410	0.418	0.425	0.414	0.380	..	0.365
169	Central African Republic	0.334	0.351	0.373	0.375	0.366	..	0.361
170	Ethiopia	..	..	0.281	0.305	0.319	0.345	0.359
171	Mozambique	..	0.298	0.286	0.310	0.318	0.342	0.354
172	Guinea-Bissau	0.254	0.262	0.282	0.311	0.339	0.354	0.350
173	Burundi	0.282	0.306	0.332	0.338	0.311	0.325	0.339
174	Mali	0.232	0.262	0.269	0.288	0.309	..	0.326
175	Burkina Faso	0.239	0.262	0.287	0.302	0.312	0.323	0.302
176	Niger	0.237	0.257	0.250	0.259	0.265	0.279	0.292
177	Sierra Leone	..	..	..	..	..	..	0.273

Note: The human development index values in this table were calculated using a consistent methodology and data series. They are not strictly comparable with those in earlier *Human Development Reports*. For detailed discussion, see Statistical feature 2, *Note to table 1: About this year's human development index.*

Source: Columns 1-6: calculated on the basis of data on life expectancy from UN 2003; data on adult literacy rates from UNESCO Institute for Statistics 2003a; data on combined gross enrolment ratios from UNESCO 1999 and UNESCO Institute for Statistics 2004c; and data on GDP per capita (1995 PPP US$) and GDP per capita (current PPP US$) from World Bank 2004f; *column 7:* column 8 of table 1.

3 Human and income poverty
Developing countries

HDI rank		Human poverty index (HPI-1) Rank	Value (%)	Probability at birth of not surviving to age 40 [a, †] (% of cohort) 2000-05	Adult illiteracy rate [b, †] (% ages 15 and above) 2002	Population without sustainable access to an improved water source [†] (%) 2000	MDG Children under weight for age [†] (% under age 5) 1995-2002 [c]	MDG Population below income poverty line (%) $1 a day [d] 1990-2002 [c]	$2 a day [e] 1990-2002 [c]	National poverty line 1990-2001 [c]	HPI-1 rank minus income poverty rank [f]
High human development											
23	Hong Kong, China (SAR)	..	..	1.8	6.5 [g]	..	..	..	..	..	..
25	Singapore	6	6.3	1.9	7.5 [h]	0	14 [i]	..	..	..	..
28	Korea, Rep. of	..	..	3.4	2.1 [g]	8	..	<2	<2	..	..
29	Barbados	1	2.5	2.6	0.3	0	6 [i]	..	..	..	..
30	Cyprus	..	..	2.9	3.2 [h]	0	..	..	..	..	..
33	Brunei Darussalam	..	..	2.8	6.1 [h]	..	..	..	..	..	..
34	Argentina	..	..	5.1	3.0	..	5	3.3	14.3	..	..
35	Seychelles	..	..	..	8.1 [h]	..	6 [i]	..	..	..	..
39	Saint Kitts and Nevis	..	..	..	..	2	..	..	..	..	..
40	Bahrain	..	..	4.0	11.5	..	9	..	..	..	..
43	Chile	3	4.1	4.1	4.3 [h]	7	1	<2	9.6	17.0	1
44	Kuwait	..	..	2.6	17.1	..	10	..	..	..	..
45	Costa Rica	4	4.4	3.7	4.2	5	5	2.0	9.5	22.0	-10
46	Uruguay	2	3.6	4.4	2.3	2	5	<2	3.9	..	0
47	Qatar	..	..	5.1	15.8 [h, j]	..	6	..	..	..	..
49	United Arab Emirates	..	..	3.4	22.7	..	14	..	..	..	..
51	Bahamas	..	..	16.0	4.5 [g]	3	..	..	..	..	..
52	Cuba	5	5.0	4.1	3.1	9	4	..	..	..	..
53	Mexico	12	9.1	7.6	9.5 [h]	12	8	9.9	26.3	10.1 [k]	-12
54	Trinidad and Tobago	8	7.7	9.1	1.5	10	7 [i]	12.4	39.0	21.0	-17
55	Antigua and Barbuda	..	..	..	..	9	10 [i]	..	..	..	..
Medium human development											
58	Libyan Arab Jamahiriya	29	15.3	4.5	18.3	28	5	..	..	..	..
59	Malaysia	..	..	4.2	11.3 [h]	..	12	<2	9.3	15.5 [k]	..
61	Panama	9	7.7	6.8	7.7	10	7	7.2	17.6	37.3	-11
63	Tonga	..	..	8.9	1.2 [h]	0	..	..	..	..	..
64	Mauritius	16	11.3	4.6	15.7 [h]	0	15	..	..	..	..
67	Suriname	..	..	6.5	..	18	13	..	..	..	..
68	Venezuela	11	8.5	5.9	6.9	17	5 [i]	15.0	32.0	31.3 [k]	-20
71	Saint Lucia	..	..	5.7	..	2	14 [i]	..	..	..	..
72	Brazil	18	11.8	11.5	13.6 [h]	13	6	8.2	22.4	17.4	-7
73	Colombia	10	8.1	8.4	7.9	9	7	8.2	22.6	64.0	-13
74	Oman	50	31.5	5.0	25.6	61	24	..	..	..	..
75	Samoa (Western)	..	..	6.6	1.3	1	..	..	..	..	..
76	Thailand	22	13.1	10.2	7.4 [h]	16	19 [i]	<2	32.5	13.1	15
77	Saudi Arabia	30	15.8	5.2	22.1	5	14	..	..	..	..
79	Jamaica	13	9.2	4.9	12.4	8	6	<2	13.3	18.7	9
80	Lebanon	14	9.5	4.3	13.5 [g]	0	3	..	..	..	..
81	Fiji	42	21.3	5.4	7.1 [h, j]	53	8 [i]	..	..	..	..
83	Philippines	28	15.0	7.4	7.4 [h]	14	28	14.6	46.4	36.8	-5
84	Maldives	17	11.4	10.2	2.8	0	30	..	..	..	..
85	Peru	23	13.2	10.2	15.0 [l]	20	7	18.1	37.7	49.0	-19
87	St. Vincent & the Grenadines	..	..	3.9	..	7	..	..	..	..	..
88	Turkey	19	12.0	8.0	13.5 [h]	18	8	<2	10.3	..	12
89	Paraguay	15	10.6	8.0	8.4 [l]	22	5	14.9	30.3	21.8	-16
90	Jordan	7	7.2	6.6	9.1	4	5	<2	7.4	11.7	3
92	Tunisia	39	19.2	4.9	26.8	20	4	<2	6.6	7.6	28
93	Grenada	..	..	..	..	5	..	..	..	..	..
94	China	24	13.2	7.1	9.1 [h]	25	11	16.6	46.7	4.6	-14
95	Dominica	..	..	..	..	3	5 [i]	..	..	..	..
96	Sri Lanka	36	18.2	5.1	7.9	23	29	6.6	45.4	25.0	11
98	Dominican Republic	26	13.7	14.6	15.6	14	5	<2	<2	28.6	18

HDI rank	Human poverty index (HPI-1) Rank	Human poverty index (HPI-1) Value (%)	Probability at birth of not surviving to age 40 [a,†] (% of cohort) 2000-05	Adult illiteracy rate [b,†] (% ages 15 and above) 2002	Population without sustainable access to an improved water source [†] (%) 2000	MDG Children under weight for age [†] (% under age 5) 1995-2002[c]	MDG Population below income poverty line (%) $1 a day [d] 1990-2002[c]	$2 a day [e] 1990-2002[c]	National poverty line 1990-2001[c]	HPI-1 rank minus income poverty rank [f]
99 Belize	33	16.7	11.3	23.1 [h]	8	6 [i]	..	..	..	..
100 Ecuador	20	12.0	10.3	9.0 [h]	15	15	17.7	40.8	35.0	-20
101 Iran, Islamic Rep. of	31	16.4	7.0	22.9 [g,j,l]	8	11	<2	7.3	..	21
102 Occupied Palestinian Territories	..	..	5.2	..	14	4	..	..	..	..
103 El Salvador	34	17.0	9.9	20.3	23	12	31.1	58.0	48.3	-21
104 Guyana	21	12.9	17.6	1.4 [g]	6	14	<2	6.1	35.0	14
105 Cape Verde	40	19.7	7.6	24.3	26	14 [i]	..	..	..	..
106 Syrian Arab Republic	25	13.7	5.7	17.1	20	7	..	..	..	..
108 Algeria	43	21.9	9.3	31.1	11	6	<2	15.1	12.2	30
109 Equatorial Guinea	54	32.7	36.4	15.8 [g]	56	19	..	..	..	..
111 Indonesia	35	17.8	10.8	12.1	22	26	7.5	52.4	27.1	7
112 Viet Nam	41	20.0	10.7	9.7 [h,j]	23	33	17.7	63.7	50.9	-5
114 Bolivia	27	14.4	16.0	13.3 [h]	17	10	14.4	34.3	62.7	-5
115 Honduras	32	16.6	13.8	20.0 [h]	12	17	23.8	44.4	53.0	-17
117 Mongolia	38	19.1	13.0	2.2 [h]	40	13	13.9	50.0	36.3	4
118 Nicaragua	37	18.3	10.3	23.3 [l]	23	10	45.1	79.9	47.9	-31
119 South Africa	52	31.7	44.9	14.0	14	12	7.1	23.8	..	20
120 Egypt	47	30.9	8.6	44.4 [h,j]	3	11	3.1	43.9	16.7	20
121 Guatemala	44	22.5	14.1	30.1	8	24	16.0	37.4	56.2	1
122 Gabon	..	..	28.1	..	14	12	..	..	..	..
123 São Tomé and Principe	..	..	10.0	..	..	13	..	..	..	..
124 Solomon Islands	..	..	6.8	..	29	21 [i]	..	..	..	..
125 Morocco	56	34.5	9.4	49.3	20	9	<2	14.3	19.0	36
126 Namibia	64	37.7	52.3	16.7	23	24	34.9	55.8	..	-5
127 India	48	31.4	15.3	38.7 [h]	16	47	34.7	79.9	28.6	-12
128 Botswana	76	43.5	61.9	21.1	5	13	23.5	50.1	..	11
129 Vanuatu	..	..	7.3	..	12	20 [i]	..	..	..	..
130 Cambodia	74	42.6	24.0	30.6	70	45	34.1	77.7	36.1	3
131 Ghana	46	26.0	25.8	26.2	27	25	44.8	78.5	39.5	-23
132 Myanmar	45	25.4	24.6	14.7	28	35	..	..	..	..
133 Papua New Guinea	62	37.0	19.0	35.4 [g]	58	35 [i]	..	..	37.5	..
134 Bhutan	..	..	17.3	..	38	19	..	..	..	..
135 Lao People's Dem. Rep.	66	40.3	27.9	33.6	63	40	26.3	73.2	38.6	1
136 Comoros	49	31.4	18.1	43.8	4	25	..	..	..	..
137 Swaziland	..	..	70.5	19.1	..	10	..	..	40.0	..
138 Bangladesh	72	42.2	17.3	58.9	3	48	36.0	82.8	49.8	-3
139 Sudan	51	31.6	27.6	40.1	25	17	..	..	..	..
140 Nepal	69	41.2	19.3	56.0	12	48	37.7	82.5	42.0	-7
141 Cameroon	61	36.9	44.2	32.1 [l]	42	21	17.1	50.6	40.2	8
Low human development										
142 Pakistan	71	41.9	17.8	58.5 [h,j]	10	38	13.4	65.6	32.6	24
143 Togo	65	38.0	37.9	40.4	46	25	..	..	32.3 [k]	..
144 Congo	53	31.9	39.3	17.2	49	14	..	..	..	..
145 Lesotho	85	47.9	68.1	18.6 [l]	22	18	36.4	56.1	..	6
146 Uganda	60	36.4	41.1	31.1	48	23	..	..	44.0	..
147 Zimbabwe	91	52.0	74.8	10.0	17	13	36.0	64.2	34.9	12
148 Kenya	63	37.5	49.5	15.7	43	21	23.0	58.6	52.0	4
149 Yemen	67	40.3	19.1	51.0	31	46	15.7	45.2	41.8	15
150 Madagascar	58	35.9	29.0	32.7 [g]	53	33	49.1	83.3	71.3	-20
151 Nigeria	57	35.1	34.9	33.2	38	36 [i]	70.2	90.8	34.1	-27

| HDI rank | | Human poverty index (HPI-1) | | Probability at birth of not surviving to age 40 [a,†] (% of cohort) 2000-05 | Adult illiteracy rate [b,†] (% ages 15 and above) 2002 | Population without sustainable access to an improved water source [†] (%) 2000 | MDG Children under weight for age [†] (% under age 5) 1995-2002[c] | MDG Population below income poverty line (%) | | | HPI-1 rank minus income poverty rank [f] |
		Rank	Value (%)					$1 a day [d] 1990-2002[c]	$2 a day [e] 1990-2002[c]	National poverty line 1990-2001[c]	
152	Mauritania	87	48.3	30.5	58.8	63	32	25.9	63.1	46.3	18
153	Haiti	68	41.1	37.3	48.1	54	17	..	..	65.0 [k]	..
154	Djibouti	55	34.3	42.9	34.5 [g]	0	18	..	..	45.1	..
155	Gambia	81	45.8	29.6	62.2 [g]	38	17	59.3	82.9	64.0	-7
156	Eritrea	70	41.8	27.5	43.3 [g]	54	44	..	..	53.0	..
157	Senegal	77	44.1	27.7	60.7	22	23	26.3	67.8	33.4	9
158	Timor-Leste	..	..	33.0	..	..	43	..	..	..	..
159	Rwanda	78	44.7	54.3	30.8	59	27	35.7	84.6	51.2	3
160	Guinea	..	..	35.9	..	52	23	..	..	40.0	..
161	Benin	80	45.7	34.6	60.2	37	23	..	..	33.0	..
162	Tanzania, U. Rep. of	59	36.0	46.4	22.9	32	29	19.9	59.7	35.7	3
163	Côte d'Ivoire	79	45.0	51.7	50.3 [g]	19	21	15.5	50.4	36.8	24
164	Zambia	90	50.4	70.1	20.1	36	28	63.7	87.4	72.9	-2
165	Malawi	83	46.8	59.6	38.2	43	25	41.7	76.1	65.3	1
166	Angola	..	..	49.2	..	62	31	..	..	..	..
167	Chad	88	49.6	42.9	54.2	73	28	..	..	64.0	..
168	Congo, Dem. Rep. of the	75	42.9	47.2	37.3 [g]	55	31	..	..	..	..
169	Central African Republic	84	47.7	55.3	51.4 [l]	30	24	66.6	84.0	..	-7
170	Ethiopia	92	55.5	43.3	58.5	76	47	26.3	80.7	44.2	20
171	Mozambique	89	49.8	56.0	53.5	43	26	37.9	78.4	69.4	6
172	Guinea-Bissau	86	48.0	41.3	60.4 [g]	44	25	..	..	48.7	..
173	Burundi	82	45.8	50.5	49.6	22	45	58.4	89.2	..	-5
174	Mali	93	58.9	35.3	81.0 [h,j]	35	33	72.8	90.6	63.8	-2
175	Burkina Faso	95	65.5	43.4	87.2 [h,j]	58	34	44.9	81.0	45.3	9
176	Niger	94	61.4	38.7	82.9	41	40	61.4	85.3	63.0 [k]	3
177	Sierra Leone	..	..	57.5	..	43	27	57.0	74.5	68.0 [k]	..

† Denotes indicators used to calculate the human poverty index (HPI-1). For further details, see technical note 1.
a. Data refer to the probability at birth of not surviving to age 40, multiplied by 100. They are medium-variant projections for the period specified. b. Data refer to estimates produced by UNESCO Institute for Statistics in July 2002, unless otherwise specified. Due to differences in methodology and timeliness of underlying data, comparisons across countries and over time should be made with caution. c. Data refer to the most recent year available during the period specified. d. Poverty line is equivalent to $1.08 (1993 PPP US$). e. Poverty line is equivalent to $2.15 (1993 PPP US$). f. Income poverty refers to the percentage of the population living on less than $1 a day. All countries with an income poverty rate of less than 2% were given equal rank. The rankings are based on countries for which data are available for both indicators. A positive figure indicates that the country performs better in income poverty than in human poverty, a negative the opposite. g. UNESCO Institute for Statistics 2003a. Data are subject to revision. h. Census data. i. Data refer to a year or period other than that specified, differ from the standard definition or refer to only part of a country. j. Data refer to a year between 1995 and 1999. k. Data refer to a period other than that specified. l. Survey data.
Source: Column 1: determined on the basis of the HPI-1 values in column 2; column 2: calculated on the basis of data in columns 3-6, see technical note 1 for details; column 3: UN 2003; column 4: UNESCO Institute for Statistics 2004a; columns 5 and 6: UNICEF 2003b; columns 7-9: World Bank 2004f; column 10: calculated on the basis of data in columns 1 and 7.

HPI-1 ranks for 95 developing countries				
1 Barbados	18 Brazil	38 Mongolia	58 Madagascar	78 Rwanda
2 Uruguay	19 Turkey	39 Tunisia	59 Tanzania, U. Rep. of	79 Côte d'Ivoire
3 Chile	20 Ecuador	40 Cape Verde	60 Uganda	80 Benin
4 Costa Rica	21 Guyana	41 Viet Nam	61 Cameroon	81 Gambia
5 Cuba	22 Thailand	42 Fiji	62 Papua New Guinea	82 Burundi
6 Singapore	23 Peru	43 Algeria	63 Kenya	83 Malawi
7 Jordan	24 China	44 Guatemala	64 Namibia	84 Central African Republic
8 Trinidad and Tobago	25 Syrian Arab Republic	45 Myanmar	65 Togo	85 Lesotho
9 Panama	26 Dominican Republic	46 Ghana	66 Lao People's Dem. Rep.	86 Guinea-Bissau
10 Colombia	27 Bolivia	47 Egypt	67 Yemen	87 Mauritania
11 Venezuela	28 Philippines	48 India	68 Haiti	88 Chad
12 Mexico	29 Libyan Arab Jamahiriya	49 Comoros	69 Nepal	89 Mozambique
13 Jamaica	30 Saudi Arabia	50 Oman	70 Eritrea	90 Zambia
14 Lebanon	31 Iran, Islamic Rep.	51 Sudan	71 Pakistan	91 Zimbabwe
15 Paraguay	32 Honduras	52 South Africa	72 Bangladesh	92 Ethiopia
16 Mauritius	33 Belize	53 Congo	73 Iraq	93 Mali
17 Maldives	34 El Salvador	54 Equatorial Guinea	74 Cambodia	94 Niger
	35 Indonesia	55 Djibouti	75 Congo, Dem. Rep. of the	95 Burkina Faso
	36 Sri Lanka	56 Morocco	76 Botswana	
	37 Nicaragua	57 Nigeria	77 Senegal	

4 Human and income poverty
OECD, Central & Eastern Europe & CIS

HDI rank		Human poverty index (HPI-2) [a] Rank	Value (%)	Probability at birth of not surviving to age 60 [b, †] (% of cohort) 2000-05	People lacking functional literacy skills [†] (% ages 16-65) 1994-98 [c]	Long-term unemployment [d, †] (% of labour force) 2002	Population below income poverty line (%) 50% of median income [e, †] 1990-2000 [f]	$11 a day 1994-95 [f, g]	$4 a day 1996-99 [f, h]	HPI-2 rank minus income poverty rank [i]
High human development										
1	Norway	2	7.1	8.3	8.5	0.2	6.4	4.3	..	-1
2	Sweden	1	6.5	7.3	7.5	1.1	6.5	6.3	..	-3
3	Australia	14	12.9	8.8	17.0	1.3	14.3	17.6	..	-2
4	Canada	12	12.2	8.7	16.6	0.7	12.8	7.4	..	-3
5	Netherlands	3	8.2	8.7	10.5	0.8	7.3	7.1	..	-2
6	Belgium	13	12.4	9.4	18.4 [j]	3.4	8.0	..	..	7
7	Iceland	..	..	7.6	..	0.4	..	..	..	..
8	United States	17	15.8	12.6	20.7	0.5	17.0	13.6	..	0
9	Japan	10	11.1	7.5	.. [k]	1.7	11.8 [l]	..	..	-1
10	Ireland	16	15.3	9.3	22.6	1.2	12.3	..	..	4
11	Switzerland	..	..	9.1	..	0.6	9.3	..	..	..
12	United Kingdom	15	14.8	8.9	21.8	1.2	12.5	15.7	..	2
13	Finland	4	8.4	10.2	10.4	2.2	5.4	4.8	..	3
14	Austria	..	..	9.5	..	0.8	8.0	..	..	..
15	Luxembourg	7	10.5	9.7	.. [k]	0.7 [m]	6.0	0.3	..	5
16	France	8	10.8	10.0	.. [k]	3.0	8.0	9.9	..	2
17	Denmark	5	9.1	11.0	9.6	0.8	9.2	..	..	-4
18	New Zealand	..	..	9.8	18.4	0.7	..	..	..	..
19	Germany	6	10.3	9.2	14.4	4.1	8.3	7.3	..	-2
20	Spain	9	11.0	8.8	.. [k]	4.6	10.1	..	..	-1
21	Italy	11	11.6	8.6	.. [k]	5.3	12.7	..	..	-3
22	Israel	..	..	7.4	..	..	13.5	..	..	..
24	Greece	..	..	9.1	..	5.0	..	..	..	..
26	Portugal	..	..	11.7	48.0	1.8	..	..	..	..
27	Slovenia	..	..	11.8	42.2	..	8.2	..	<1	..
31	Malta	..	..	7.7	..	..	..	..	..	..
32	Czech Republic	..	..	12.2	15.7	3.7	4.9	..	<1	..
36	Estonia	..	..	20.4	..	..	12.4	..	18	..
37	Poland	..	..	15.6	42.6	9.6	8.6	..	10	..
38	Hungary	..	..	19.6	33.8	2.6	6.7	..	<1	..
41	Lithuania	..	..	19.5	..	..	..	..	17	..
42	Slovakia	..	..	15.2	..	11.1	7.0	..	8	..
48	Croatia	..	..	14.5	..	..	..	..	..	..
50	Latvia	..	..	21.4	..	..	..	..	28	..
Medium human development										
56	Bulgaria	..	..	18.6	..	..	..	..	22	..
57	Russian Federation	..	..	28.9	..	..	18.8	..	53	..
60	Macedonia, TFYR	..	..	13.3	..	..	..	..	..	..
62	Belarus	..	..	22.8	..	..	..	..	..	..
65	Albania	..	..	11.3	..	..	..	..	..	..
66	Bosnia and Herzegovina	..	..	13.7	..	..	..	..	..	..
69	Romania	..	..	20.3	..	..	8.1	..	23	..
70	Ukraine	..	..	23.0	..	..	..	..	25	..
78	Kazakhstan	..	..	27.0	..	..	..	..	62	..
82	Armenia	..	..	14.9	..	..	..	..	..	..

HDI rank		Human poverty index (HPI-2)[a]		Probability at birth of not surviving to age 60[b, †] (% of cohort) 2000-05	People lacking functional literacy skills[†] (% ages 16-65) 1994-98[c]	Long-term unemployment[d, †] (% of labour force) 2002	Population below income poverty line (%)			HPI-2 rank minus income poverty rank[i]
		Rank	Value (%)				50% of median income[e, †] 1990-2000[f]	$11 a day 1994-95[f, g]	$4 a day 1996-99[f, h]	
86	Turkmenistan	..	..	24.8	..	..	..	..	..	..
91	Azerbaijan	..	..	18.5	..	..	..	..	..	..
97	Georgia	..	..	16.2	..	..	..	..	..	..
107	Uzbekistan	..	..	21.8	..	..	..	..	..	..
110	Kyrgyzstan	..	..	23.7	..	..	..	..	88	..
113	Moldova, Rep. of	..	..	22.8	..	..	..	..	82	..
116	Tajikistan	..	..	22.8	..	..	..	..	..	..

† Denotes indicators used to calculate the human poverty index (HPI-2). For further details, see technical note 1.

Note: This table includes Israel and Malta, which are not OECD member countries, but excludes the Republic of Korea, Mexico and Turkey, which are. For the human poverty index and related indicators for these countries, see table 3.

a. The human poverty index (HPI-2) is calculated for selected high-income OECD countries only. b. Data refer to the probability at birth of not surviving to age 60, multiplied by 100. They are medium-variant projections for the period specified. c. Based on scoring at level 1 on the prose literacy scale of the International Adult Literacy Survey. Data refer to the most recent year available during the period specified. More recent data will be available shortly. d. Data refer to unemployment lasting 12 months or longer. e. Poverty line is measured at 50% of equivalent median adjusted disposable household income. f. Data refer to the most recent year available during the period specified. g. Based on the US poverty line, $11 (1994 PPP US$) a day per person for a family of three. h. Poverty line is $4 (1990 PPP US$) a day. i. Income poverty refers to the percentage of the population living on less than 50% of the median adjusted disposible household income. A positive figure indicates that the country performs better in income poverty than in human poverty, a negative the opposite. j. Data refer to Flanders. k. For purposes of calculating the HPI-2, an estimate of 15.1%, the unweighted average of countries with available data, was applied. l. Smeeding 1997. m. Data are based on small samples and should be treated with caution.

Source: Column 1: determined on the basis of HPI-2 values in column 2; *column 2:* calculated on the basis of data in columns 3-6; see technical note 1 for details; *column 3:* calculated on the basis of survival data from UN 2003; *column 4:* OECD and Statistics Canada 2000, unless otherwise noted; *column 5:* calculated on the basis of data on long-term unemployment and labour force from OECD 2004d; *column 6:* LIS 2004; *column 7:* Smeeding, Rainwater, and Burtless 2000; *column 8:* Milanovic 2002; *column 9:* calculated on the basis of data in columns 1 and 6.

HPI-2 ranks for 17 selected OECD countries

1	Sweden	7	Luxembourg	13	Belgium
2	Norway	8	France	14	Australia
3	Netherlands	9	Spain	15	United Kingdom
4	Finland	10	Japan	16	Ireland
5	Denmark	11	Italy	17	United States
6	Germany	12	Canada		

5 Demographic trends

HDI rank	Total population (millions) 1975	2002[b]	2015[b]	Annual population growth rate 1975-2002	2002-15[b]	Urban population (% of total)[a] 1975	2002[b]	2015[b]	Population under age 15 (% of total) 2002[b]	2015[b]	Population age 65 and above (% of total) 2002[b]	2015[b]	Total fertility rate (births per woman) 1970-75[c]	2000-05[c]
High human development														
1 Norway	4.0	4.5	4.7	0.4	0.3	68.2	77.6	86.4	19.7	16.6	15.2	18.0	2.2	1.8
2 Sweden	8.2	8.9	9.0	0.3	0.1	82.7	83.3	84.3	17.9	15.7	17.4	21.4	1.9	1.6
3 Australia	13.9	19.5	21.7	1.3	0.8	85.9	91.6	94.9	20.1	17.3	12.5	15.5	2.5	1.7
4 Canada	23.1	31.3	34.1	1.1	0.7	75.6	80.1	84.0	18.4	14.8	12.8	16.4	2.0	1.5
5 Netherlands	13.7	16.1	16.8	0.6	0.3	56.9	65.4	71.4	18.4	16.4	13.8	17.4	2.1	1.7
6 Belgium	9.8	10.3	10.5	0.2	0.1	94.5	97.2	97.5	17.2	15.5	17.3	19.5	1.9	1.7
7 Iceland	0.2	0.3	0.3	1.0	0.6	86.6	92.7	94.1	23.0	18.7	11.5	13.5	2.8	2.0
8 United States	220.2	291.0	329.7	1.0	1.0	73.7	79.8	83.6	21.6	20.3	12.2	14.2	2.0	2.1
9 Japan	111.5	127.5	127.2	0.5	(.)	56.8	65.3	67.7	14.3	13.0	18.2	26.0	2.1	1.3
10 Ireland	3.2	3.9	4.4	0.8	0.9	53.6	59.6	63.6	20.9	20.3	11.3	13.4	3.8	1.9
11 Switzerland	6.3	7.2	7.0	0.5	-0.2	55.7	67.6	68.7	16.2	12.6	16.4	22.0	1.8	1.4
12 United Kingdom	55.4	59.1	61.3	0.2	0.3	82.7	89.0	90.2	18.7	15.9	15.9	17.8	2.0	1.6
13 Finland	4.7	5.2	5.3	0.4	0.1	58.3	61.0	62.1	17.8	15.8	15.3	20.3	1.6	1.7
14 Austria	7.6	8.1	8.1	0.3	-0.1	65.3	65.8	67.2	16.2	12.4	15.8	19.5	2.0	1.3
15 Luxembourg	0.4	0.4	0.5	0.8	1.2	73.7	91.6	94.1	19.0	17.6	13.4	14.4	2.0	1.7
16 France	52.7	59.8	62.8	0.5	0.4	72.9	76.1	79.0	18.6	17.8	16.2	18.5	2.3	1.9
17 Denmark	5.1	5.4	5.4	0.2	0.1	82.1	85.2	86.8	18.5	16.3	15.0	19.2	2.0	1.8
18 New Zealand	3.1	3.8	4.2	0.8	0.6	82.8	85.8	87.0	22.6	19.3	11.9	14.6	2.8	2.0
19 Germany	78.7	82.4	82.5	0.2	(.)	81.2	87.9	90.0	15.2	13.2	17.1	20.8	1.6	1.4
20 Spain	35.6	41.0	41.2	0.5	(.)	69.6	76.4	78.1	14.3	13.2	17.0	19.2	2.9	1.2
21 Italy	55.4	57.5	55.5	0.1	-0.3	65.6	67.3	69.2	14.1	12.3	18.7	22.3	2.3	1.2
22 Israel	3.4	6.3	7.8	2.3	1.6	86.6	91.6	92.4	27.9	24.8	9.9	11.4	3.8	2.7
23 Hong Kong, China (SAR)	4.4	7.0	7.9	1.7	0.9	89.7	100.0	100.0	15.7	12.9	11.0	13.6	2.9	1.0
24 Greece	9.0	11.0	10.9	0.7	(.)	55.3	60.6	65.2	14.7	13.2	18.2	20.9	2.3	1.3
25 Singapore	2.3	4.2	4.7	2.3	0.9	100.0	100.0	100.0	21.1	12.9	7.6	13.1	2.6	1.4
26 Portugal	9.1	10.0	10.0	0.4	(.)	27.7	54.1	60.9	16.6	15.3	16.0	18.0	2.7	1.5
27 Slovenia	1.7	2.0	1.9	0.5	-0.2	42.4	50.8	52.6	15.0	12.1	14.6	18.5	2.2	1.1
28 Korea, Rep. of	35.3	47.4	49.7	1.1	0.4	48.0	80.1	83.0	20.3	15.5	7.8	11.9	4.3	1.4
29 Barbados	0.2	0.3	0.3	0.3	0.3	40.8	51.1	59.1	20.0	16.4	10.0	11.1	2.7	1.5
30 Cyprus	0.6	0.8	0.9	1.0	0.6	45.2	69.0	71.6	22.1	18.9	11.8	14.9	2.5	1.9
31 Malta	0.3	0.4	0.4	0.9	0.4	80.4	91.4	93.7	19.4	17.0	12.5	18.0	2.1	1.8
32 Czech Republic	10.0	10.2	10.1	0.1	-0.1	63.7	74.2	75.7	15.7	13.2	13.9	18.6	2.2	1.2
33 Brunei Darussalam	0.2	0.3	0.5	2.9	2.0	62.0	75.5	82.8	30.6	25.4	2.9	4.4	5.4	2.5
34 Argentina	26.0	38.0	43.4	1.4	1.0	81.0	89.9	92.2	27.3	24.4	9.9	11.0	3.1	2.4
35 Seychelles	0.1	0.1	0.1	1.2	0.7	33.3	49.8	53.3	..	..	..	..	..	..
36 Estonia	1.4	1.3	1.2	-0.3	-1.1	67.6	69.4	71.4	16.7	14.2	15.8	18.2	2.2	1.2
37 Poland	34.0	38.6	38.2	0.5	-0.1	55.4	61.8	64.0	17.9	14.6	12.5	14.8	2.3	1.3
38 Hungary	10.5	9.9	9.3	-0.2	-0.5	52.8	64.7	70.0	16.4	13.3	14.8	17.4	2.1	1.2
39 Saint Kitts and Nevis	(.)	(.)	(.)	-0.3	-0.3	35.0	32.4	32.5	..	..	..	..	..	..
40 Bahrain	0.3	0.7	0.9	3.5	1.8	85.8	89.9	91.4	29.2	23.2	2.7	3.9	5.9	2.7
41 Lithuania	3.3	3.5	3.2	0.2	-0.6	55.7	66.8	67.5	19.0	16.0	14.5	16.4	2.3	1.3
42 Slovakia	4.7	5.4	5.4	0.5	0.1	46.3	57.2	60.8	18.4	15.4	11.5	13.6	2.5	1.3
43 Chile	10.3	15.6	18.0	1.5	1.1	78.4	86.6	90.2	27.8	23.6	7.5	9.8	3.6	2.4
44 Kuwait	1.0	2.4	3.4	3.3	2.4	83.8	96.2	96.9	26.1	22.6	1.4	3.5	6.9	2.7
45 Costa Rica	2.1	4.1	5.0	2.6	1.6	42.5	60.1	66.8	30.4	23.9	5.5	7.4	4.3	2.3
46 Uruguay	2.8	3.4	3.7	0.7	0.6	83.4	92.4	94.4	24.6	22.5	13.1	13.7	3.0	2.3
47 Qatar	0.2	0.6	0.7	4.7	1.3	84.8	91.8	93.6	26.6	21.7	1.5	4.6	6.8	3.2
48 Croatia	4.3	4.4	4.3	0.1	-0.3	45.1	58.6	64.6	16.9	16.5	16.3	17.8	2.0	1.7
49 United Arab Emirates	0.5	2.9	3.6	6.5	1.5	83.6	85.0	87.2	25.8	20.8	1.3	4.2	6.4	2.8
50 Latvia	2.5	2.3	2.1	-0.2	-0.9	65.4	66.3	66.3	16.5	13.0	15.8	18.3	2.0	1.1

HDI rank		Total population (millions)			Annual population growth rate 1975-		Urban population (% of total)[a]			Population under age 15 (% of total)		Population age 65 and above (% of total)		Total fertility rate (births per woman)	
		1975	2002[b]	2015[b]	2002	2002-15[b]	1975	2002[b]	2015[b]	2002[b]	2015[b]	2002[b]	2015[b]	1970-75[c]	2000-05[c]
51	Bahamas	0.2	0.3	0.4	1.8	0.9	73.4	89.2	91.6	29.0	24.5	5.5	8.3	3.4	2.3
52	Cuba	9.3	11.3	11.5	0.7	0.2	64.2	75.5	78.1	20.3	16.3	10.2	14.4	3.5	1.6
53	Mexico	59.1	102.0	119.6	2.0	1.2	62.8	75.2	78.8	32.8	26.4	5.0	6.8	6.5	2.5
54	Trinidad and Tobago	1.0	1.3	1.3	0.9	0.3	63.0	75.0	79.7	23.3	19.7	6.9	10.0	3.5	1.6
55	Antigua and Barbuda	0.1	0.1	0.1	0.6	0.4	34.2	37.4	43.4	..	..	..	..	..	..
Medium human development															
56	Bulgaria	8.7	8.0	7.2	-0.3	-0.8	57.5	69.4	74.0	14.8	12.6	16.3	18.0	2.2	1.1
57	Russian Federation	134.2	144.1	133.4	0.3	-0.6	66.4	73.3	74.3	16.5	13.7	13.2	14.3	2.0	1.1
58	Libyan Arab Jamahiriya	2.4	5.4	6.9	3.0	1.8	60.9	86.0	89.0	31.3	28.7	3.7	5.5	7.6	3.0
59	Malaysia	12.3	24.0	29.6	2.5	1.6	37.7	63.3	71.0	33.2	27.2	4.3	6.1	5.2	2.9
60	Macedonia, TFYR	1.7	2.0	2.2	0.7	0.4	50.6	59.4	62.0	22.0	20.0	10.4	12.2	3.0	1.9
61	Panama	1.7	3.1	3.8	2.1	1.6	49.0	56.8	61.7	31.2	27.5	5.7	7.5	4.9	2.7
62	Belarus	9.4	9.9	9.4	0.2	-0.4	50.3	70.5	75.2	17.1	14.1	14.2	14.3	2.3	1.2
63	Tonga	0.1	0.1	0.1	0.4	0.9	24.4	33.2	38.2	37.1	31.4	5.9	5.2	5.5	3.7
64	Mauritius	0.9	1.2	1.3	1.1	0.8	43.4	43.1	47.3	25.3	21.0	6.2	8.2	3.2	1.9
65	Albania	2.4	3.1	3.4	1.0	0.7	32.7	43.2	51.2	28.5	22.9	6.2	8.1	4.7	2.3
66	Bosnia and Herzegovina	3.7	4.1	4.3	0.4	0.3	31.3	43.9	51.1	17.6	14.1	10.8	13.6	2.6	1.3
67	Suriname	0.4	0.4	0.5	0.6	0.7	49.5	75.4	81.6	31.0	27.0	5.3	6.2	5.3	2.5
68	Venezuela	12.7	25.2	31.2	2.5	1.6	75.8	87.4	90.0	33.0	27.6	4.6	6.6	4.9	2.7
69	Romania	21.2	22.4	21.6	0.2	-0.3	42.8	54.5	56.4	17.1	15.4	13.9	14.8	2.6	1.3
70	Ukraine	49.0	48.9	44.4	(.)	-0.7	58.3	67.2	68.9	16.5	13.2	14.6	16.1	2.2	1.2
71	Saint Lucia	0.1	0.1	0.2	1.3	0.7	23.6	30.1	36.8	30.4	26.0	5.4	6.2	5.7	2.3
72	Brazil	108.1	176.3	202.0	1.8	1.0	61.2	82.4	88.4	28.3	24.1	5.4	7.5	4.7	2.2
73	Colombia	25.4	43.5	52.2	2.0	1.4	60.0	76.0	81.3	32.1	27.0	4.9	6.5	5.0	2.6
74	Oman	0.9	2.8	3.9	4.1	2.7	19.6	77.0	82.6	37.2	36.0	2.1	3.0	7.2	5.0
75	Samoa (Western)	0.2	0.2	0.2	0.6	1.1	21.1	22.2	24.7	40.8	35.5	4.5	4.4	5.7	4.1
76	Thailand	41.3	62.2	69.6	1.5	0.9	23.8	31.6	36.7	25.6	22.0	5.8	8.1	5.0	1.9
77	Saudi Arabia	7.3	23.5	32.7	4.4	2.5	58.3	87.2	91.1	39.1	34.5	2.7	3.4	7.3	4.5
78	Kazakhstan	14.1	15.5	15.3	0.3	-0.1	52.2	55.8	58.2	26.0	21.4	7.5	8.4	3.5	2.0
79	Jamaica	2.0	2.6	3.0	1.0	1.0	44.1	52.1	54.2	30.8	25.8	7.1	7.7	5.0	2.4
80	Lebanon	2.8	3.6	4.2	1.0	1.2	67.0	87.2	90.1	29.6	24.0	6.2	6.5	4.9	2.2
81	Fiji	0.6	0.8	0.9	1.4	0.8	36.7	51.0	60.1	32.7	27.6	3.7	5.8	4.2	2.9
82	Armenia	2.8	3.1	3.0	0.3	-0.3	63.0	64.6	64.2	21.4	14.4	9.2	9.9	3.0	1.2
83	Philippines	42.0	78.6	96.3	2.3	1.6	35.6	60.2	69.2	36.6	29.9	3.7	4.9	6.0	3.2
84	Maldives	0.1	0.3	0.4	3.0	2.8	18.1	28.4	35.2	43.1	39.6	3.2	3.1	7.0	5.3
85	Peru	15.2	26.8	32.0	2.1	1.4	61.5	73.5	78.0	33.6	27.5	5.0	6.5	6.0	2.9
86	Turkmenistan	2.5	4.8	5.8	2.4	1.5	47.6	45.1	50.0	34.6	27.4	4.5	4.6	6.2	2.7
87	St. Vincent & the Grenadines	0.1	0.1	0.1	0.8	0.5	27.0	57.2	68.6	31.1	26.0	6.7	7.1	5.5	2.2
88	Turkey	41.0	70.3	82.1	2.0	1.2	41.6	65.8	71.9	30.7	25.0	5.7	6.7	5.2	2.4
89	Paraguay	2.7	5.7	7.7	2.9	2.2	39.0	56.6	64.3	38.8	34.2	3.6	4.3	5.7	3.8
90	Jordan	1.9	5.3	7.0	3.7	2.1	57.8	78.9	81.1	38.0	31.6	3.0	4.0	7.8	3.6
91	Azerbaijan	5.7	8.3	9.5	1.4	1.0	51.5	50.2	51.3	30.1	23.5	6.1	5.9	4.3	2.1
92	Tunisia	5.7	9.7	11.1	2.0	1.0	49.9	63.4	68.1	28.5	22.6	5.9	6.7	6.2	2.0
93	Grenada	0.1	0.1	0.1	-0.5	-0.3	32.6	40.0	49.5	..	..	..	..	..	..
94	China	927.8[d]	1,294.9[d]	1,402.3[d]	1.2[d]	0.6[d]	17.4	37.7	49.5	23.7	19.4	7.1	9.4	4.9	1.8
95	Dominica	0.1	0.1	0.1	0.3	0.2	55.3	71.7	76.2	..	..	..	..	..	..
96	Sri Lanka	13.5	18.9	20.6	1.3	0.7	22.0	21.0	22.5	25.0	21.3	6.9	9.3	4.1	2.0
97	Georgia	4.9	5.2	4.7	0.2	-0.7	49.5	52.2	51.6	19.2	15.2	13.8	14.9	2.6	1.4
98	Dominican Republic	5.0	8.6	10.1	2.0	1.2	45.7	58.9	64.6	32.5	28.3	4.6	6.4	5.6	2.7
99	Belize	0.1	0.3	0.3	2.3	1.8	50.2	48.2	51.8	37.9	31.1	4.4	4.8	6.3	3.2
100	Ecuador	6.9	12.8	15.2	2.3	1.3	42.4	61.3	67.6	33.1	27.1	5.0	6.6	6.0	2.8

5 Demographic trends

HDI rank		Total population (millions)			Annual population growth rate		Urban population (% of total)[a]			Population under age 15 (% of total)		Population age 65 and above (% of total)		Total fertility rate (births per woman)	
		1975	2002[b]	2015[b]	1975-2002	2002-15[b]	1975	2002[b]	2015[b]	2002[b]	2015[b]	2002[b]	2015[b]	1970-75[c]	2000-05[c]
101	Iran, Islamic Rep. of	33.4	68.1	81.4	2.6	1.4	45.8	65.9	73.9	32.6	26.8	4.5	4.9	6.4	2.3
102	Occupied Palestinian Territories	1.3	3.4	5.3	3.7	3.3	59.6	70.8	75.6	46.1	42.1	3.4	3.0	7.7	5.6
103	El Salvador	4.1	6.4	7.6	1.6	1.3	41.5	59.3	64.2	35.1	29.4	5.3	6.5	6.1	2.9
104	Guyana	0.7	0.8	0.8	0.1	(.)	30.0	37.1	44.2	30.0	25.5	5.1	6.6	4.9	2.3
105	Cape Verde	0.3	0.5	0.6	1.8	1.8	21.4	55.1	64.8	39.9	32.6	4.4	3.5	7.0	3.3
106	Syrian Arab Republic	7.5	17.4	23.0	3.1	2.2	45.1	50.1	52.4	38.3	32.2	3.0	3.6	7.5	3.3
107	Uzbekistan	14.0	25.7	30.7	2.3	1.4	39.1	36.8	37.0	34.5	26.2	4.9	5.0	6.3	2.4
108	Algeria	16.0	31.3	38.1	2.5	1.5	40.3	58.3	65.3	33.5	27.4	4.2	4.9	7.4	2.8
109	Equatorial Guinea	0.2	0.5	0.7	2.8	2.5	27.1	47.1	58.2	43.6	43.0	3.9	3.6	5.7	5.9
110	Kyrgyzstan	3.3	5.1	5.9	1.6	1.2	37.9	34.0	35.4	32.6	26.4	6.3	5.9	4.7	2.6
111	Indonesia	134.4	217.1	250.4	1.8	1.1	19.3	44.5	57.8	29.9	25.3	5.1	6.4	5.2	2.4
112	Viet Nam	48.0	80.3	94.7	1.9	1.3	18.9	25.2	32.4	31.7	25.3	5.4	5.5	6.7	2.3
113	Moldova, Rep. of	3.8	4.3	4.2	0.4	-0.1	35.8	45.9	50.0	21.2	16.5	9.7	10.9	2.6	1.4
114	Bolivia	4.8	8.6	10.8	2.2	1.7	41.3	62.9	69.0	39.0	32.8	4.4	5.3	6.5	3.8
115	Honduras	3.0	6.8	8.8	3.0	2.0	32.1	45.2	51.3	40.7	33.5	3.6	4.5	7.1	3.7
116	Tajikistan	3.4	6.2	7.3	2.2	1.2	35.5	25.0	24.4	37.4	28.5	4.8	4.6	6.8	3.1
117	Mongolia	1.4	2.6	3.1	2.1	1.4	48.7	56.7	59.5	33.2	26.6	3.8	4.1	7.3	2.4
118	Nicaragua	2.5	5.3	7.0	2.8	2.1	48.9	56.9	62.8	41.9	34.9	3.1	3.8	6.8	3.7
119	South Africa	25.8	44.8	44.3	2.0	-0.1	48.0	56.5	62.7	33.2	29.2	3.9	6.0	5.4	2.6
120	Egypt	39.3	70.5	90.0	2.2	1.9	43.5	42.1	44.9	35.2	31.7	4.6	5.4	5.7	3.3
121	Guatemala	6.0	12.0	16.2	2.6	2.3	36.7	45.9	51.9	43.0	37.4	3.6	3.9	6.5	4.4
122	Gabon	0.6	1.3	1.6	2.9	1.8	40.0	83.1	89.1	41.0	35.0	4.6	4.3	5.3	4.0
123	São Tomé and Principe	0.1	0.2	0.2	2.4	2.3	27.3	37.7	40.3	40.2	36.4	4.5	3.8	5.4	4.0
124	Solomon Islands	0.2	0.5	0.6	3.2	2.5	9.1	16.2	20.9	42.9	36.5	2.6	3.4	7.2	4.4
125	Morocco	17.3	30.1	36.5	2.0	1.5	37.8	56.8	64.8	31.8	27.9	4.4	5.1	6.9	2.7
126	Namibia	0.9	2.0	2.2	2.8	0.9	20.6	31.9	39.8	43.2	37.5	3.7	4.6	6.6	4.6
127	India	620.7	1,049.5	1,246.4	1.9	1.3	21.3	28.1	32.2	33.3	27.7	5.1	6.3	5.4	3.0
128	Botswana	0.8	1.8	1.7	2.8	-0.3	12.8	51.1	57.5	39.8	37.4	2.7	4.5	6.7	3.7
129	Vanuatu	0.1	0.2	0.3	2.7	2.2	15.7	22.4	28.6	40.6	34.9	3.4	4.0	6.1	4.1
130	Cambodia	7.1	13.8	18.4	2.5	2.2	10.3	18.0	26.1	41.9	37.4	2.9	3.6	5.5	4.8
131	Ghana	9.9	20.5	26.4	2.7	1.9	30.1	45.0	51.1	40.1	34.9	3.3	4.1	6.9	4.1
132	Myanmar	30.2	48.9	55.8	1.8	1.0	23.9	28.9	37.6	32.3	26.8	4.6	5.9	5.8	2.9
133	Papua New Guinea	2.9	5.6	7.2	2.5	1.9	11.9	13.2	14.5	41.2	34.0	2.4	2.8	6.1	4.1
134	Bhutan	1.2	2.2	3.0	2.3	2.5	3.5	8.2	12.6	41.8	37.8	4.3	4.5	5.9	5.0
135	Lao People's Dem. Rep.	3.0	5.5	7.3	2.2	2.1	11.1	20.2	27.4	42.0	36.8	3.5	3.7	6.2	4.8
136	Comoros	0.3	0.7	1.0	3.2	2.6	21.2	34.4	43.0	42.3	38.5	2.4	3.0	7.1	4.9
137	Swaziland	0.5	1.1	1.1	2.7	(.)	14.0	23.4	27.0	43.7	39.7	3.3	4.6	6.9	4.5
138	Bangladesh	75.2	143.8	181.4	2.4	1.8	9.9	23.9	29.6	38.3	31.9	3.2	3.8	6.2	3.5
139	Sudan	16.7	32.9	41.4	2.5	1.8	18.9	38.0	49.3	39.7	34.8	3.5	4.4	6.7	4.4
140	Nepal	13.4	24.6	32.0	2.3	2.0	5.0	14.6	20.5	40.2	35.6	3.7	4.2	5.8	4.3
141	Cameroon	7.6	15.7	18.9	2.7	1.4	26.9	50.6	59.9	42.4	37.8	3.7	4.1	6.3	4.6
Low human development															
142	Pakistan	70.3	149.9	204.5	2.8	2.4	26.4	33.7	39.5	41.5	38.1	3.7	4.0	6.3	5.1
143	Togo	2.3	4.8	6.4	2.8	2.2	16.3	34.5	43.3	43.9	40.3	3.1	3.5	7.1	5.3
144	Congo	1.5	3.6	5.2	3.2	2.8	34.8	53.1	59.3	46.8	46.2	2.9	2.8	6.3	6.3
145	Lesotho	1.1	1.8	1.7	1.7	-0.4	10.8	17.8	21.0	39.9	38.2	4.7	5.4	5.7	3.8
146	Uganda	10.8	25.0	39.3	3.1	3.5	8.3	12.2	14.2	50.1	49.7	2.6	2.3	7.1	7.1
147	Zimbabwe	6.1	12.8	13.0	2.7	0.1	19.6	34.5	41.4	43.1	39.6	3.4	4.2	7.6	3.9
148	Kenya	13.6	31.5	36.9	3.1	1.2	12.9	38.2	51.8	42.1	36.5	2.9	3.4	8.1	4.0
149	Yemen	6.9	19.3	30.7	3.8	3.6	14.8	25.3	31.3	48.7	47.2	2.3	2.2	8.4	7.0
150	Madagascar	7.9	16.9	24.0	2.8	2.7	16.4	26.3	30.7	44.6	41.7	3.0	3.1	6.6	5.7
151	Nigeria	54.9	120.9	161.7	2.9	2.2	23.4	45.9	55.5	44.6	40.6	3.1	3.4	6.9	5.4

HDI rank	Total population (millions)			Annual population growth rate 1975-		Urban population (% of total) [a]			Population under age 15 (% of total)		Population age 65 and above (% of total)		Total fertility rate (births per woman)	
	1975	2002 [b]	2015 [b]	2002	2002-15 [b]	1975	2002 [b]	2015 [b]	2002 [b]	2015 [b]	2002 [b]	2015 [b]	1970-75 [c]	2000-05 [c]
152 Mauritania	1.4	2.8	4.0	2.5	2.7	20.3	60.5	73.9	43.2	41.7	3.3	3.5	6.5	5.8
153 Haiti	4.9	8.2	9.7	1.9	1.3	21.7	36.9	45.5	39.1	35.1	3.9	4.5	5.8	4.0
154 Djibouti	0.2	0.7	0.8	4.3	1.5	61.6	83.3	87.6	43.0	40.3	3.2	3.8	7.2	5.7
155 Gambia	0.6	1.4	1.9	3.4	2.2	17.0	26.1	27.8	40.9	36.6	3.5	4.4	6.5	4.7
156 Eritrea	2.1	4.0	5.9	2.4	3.0	12.7	19.5	26.5	45.5	41.7	2.1	2.4	6.5	5.4
157 Senegal	4.8	9.9	13.2	2.7	2.2	34.2	48.9	57.9	43.5	39.0	2.4	2.7	7.0	5.0
158 Timor-Leste	0.7	0.7	1.1	0.3	2.8	8.9	7.6	9.5	39.3	30.2	2.8	3.8	6.2	3.8
159 Rwanda	4.4	8.3	10.6	2.3	1.9	4.0	16.6	40.5	45.2	43.5	2.5	2.9	8.3	5.7
160 Guinea	4.1	8.4	11.2	2.7	2.3	16.3	34.2	44.2	44.0	41.5	2.9	3.1	7.0	5.8
161 Benin	3.0	6.6	9.1	2.8	2.5	21.9	43.8	53.5	45.6	42.1	2.7	2.8	7.1	5.7
162 Tanzania, U. Rep. of	16.2	36.3	45.9	3.0	1.8	10.1	34.4	46.8	45.3	40.2	2.3	2.7	6.8	5.1
163 Côte d'Ivoire	6.8	16.4	19.8	3.3	1.5	32.1	44.4	51.0	41.8	37.3	3.2	3.9	7.4	4.7
164 Zambia	5.1	10.7	12.7	2.8	1.3	34.8	35.4	40.8	46.5	44.7	3.0	3.2	7.8	5.6
165 Malawi	5.2	11.9	15.2	3.0	1.9	7.7	15.9	22.2	46.2	44.9	3.5	3.6	7.4	6.1
166 Angola	6.2	13.2	19.3	2.8	2.9	17.4	34.9	44.9	47.5	47.9	2.7	2.6	6.6	7.2
167 Chad	4.1	8.3	12.1	2.6	2.9	15.6	24.5	31.1	46.7	46.5	3.1	2.8	6.7	6.7
168 Congo, Dem. Rep. of the	23.9	51.2	74.2	2.8	2.8	29.5	31.2	39.7	46.8	47.2	2.6	2.6	6.5	6.7
169 Central African Republic	2.1	3.8	4.6	2.3	1.4	33.7	42.2	50.3	43.1	40.4	4.0	4.0	5.7	4.9
170 Ethiopia	33.1	69.0	93.8	2.7	2.4	9.5	15.4	19.8	45.7	43.1	2.9	3.2	6.8	6.1
171 Mozambique	10.6	18.5	22.5	2.1	1.5	8.7	34.5	48.5	44.0	41.2	3.2	3.5	6.6	5.6
172 Guinea-Bissau	0.7	1.4	2.1	3.0	2.9	16.0	33.2	43.5	47.1	46.9	3.1	2.8	7.1	7.1
173 Burundi	3.7	6.6	9.8	2.2	3.1	3.2	9.6	14.6	46.9	45.8	2.9	2.5	6.8	6.8
174 Mali	6.3	12.6	19.0	2.6	3.1	16.2	31.6	40.9	49.2	48.7	2.4	2.1	7.1	7.0
175 Burkina Faso	6.1	12.6	18.6	2.7	3.0	6.3	17.4	23.2	48.9	47.7	2.7	2.4	7.8	6.7
176 Niger	4.8	11.5	18.3	3.3	3.6	10.6	21.6	29.7	50.0	49.7	2.0	1.9	8.1	8.0
177 Sierra Leone	2.9	4.8	6.4	1.8	2.3	21.4	38.1	47.6	44.2	44.1	2.9	3.0	6.5	6.5
Developing countries	2,961.2 T	4,936.9 T	5,868.2 T	1.9	1.3	26.4	41.4	48.6	32.2	28.2	5.2	6.4	5.4	2.9
Least developed countries	353.7 T	700.9 T	941.9 T	2.5	2.3	14.7	26.1	33.4	42.9	40.1	3.1	3.3	6.6	5.1
Arab States	143.4 T	296.6 T	389.7 T	2.7	2.1	41.7	54.2	58.8	37.1	33.5	3.7	4.3	6.7	3.8
East Asia and the Pacific	1,310.5 T	1,917.6 T	2,124.6 T	1.4	0.8	20.4	40.2	51.0	25.8	21.4	6.5	8.4	5.0	2.0
Latin America and the Caribbean	317.9 T	530.2 T	622.5 T	1.9	1.2	61.2	76.2	80.8	31.1	26.3	5.6	7.3	5.1	2.5
South Asia	842.1 T	1,480.3 T	1,805.3 T	2.1	1.5	21.3	29.6	34.3	34.8	29.6	4.7	5.6	5.6	3.3
Sub-Saharan Africa	305.8 T	641.0 T	843.1 T	2.7	2.1	21.0	35.0	42.4	44.3	41.9	3.0	3.3	6.8	5.4
Central & Eastern Europe & CIS	366.6 T	408.9 T	398.4 T	0.4	-0.2	56.8	62.8	63.7	19.5	16.3	12.2	13.2	2.5	1.4
OECD	925.6 T	1,148.1 T	1,227.7 T	0.8	0.5	67.3	75.7	79.0	20.2	17.9	13.3	16.0	2.5	1.8
High-income OECD	766.2 T	911.6 T	962.9 T	0.6	0.4	69.9	77.3	80.4	18.2	16.5	14.8	18.0	2.2	1.7
High human development	972.3 T	1,201.3 T	1,282.0 T	0.8	0.5	68.9	77.1	80.3	20.0	17.8	13.4	16.2	2.5	1.8
Medium human development	2,678.4 T	4,165.2 T	4,759.1 T	1.6	1.0	28.1	42.2	49.3	29.3	24.8	6.0	7.4	4.9	2.4
Low human development	354.5 T	755.8 T	1,021.6 T	2.8	2.3	19.4	32.4	39.9	44.6	42.1	3.0	3.2	6.8	5.6
High income	782.0 T	941.2 T	997.7 T	0.7	0.4	70.1	77.8	80.9	18.3	16.6	14.6	17.7	2.2	1.7
Middle income	1,847.5 T	2,720.7 T	3,027.9 T	1.4	0.8	35.7	52.8	61.0	26.3	22.3	7.0	8.6	4.5	2.1
Low income	1,437.1 T	2,560.8 T	3,169.0 T	2.1	1.6	20.7	31.2	37.5	37.0	32.8	4.3	5.0	5.9	3.7
World	4,068.1 T [e]	6,225.0 T [e]	7,197.2 T [e]	1.6	1.1	37.2	47.8	53.5	29.4	26.1	7.1	8.3	4.5	2.7

a. Because data are based on national definitions of what constitutes a city or metropolitan area, cross-country comparisons should be made with caution. b. Data refer to medium-variant projections. c. Data refer to estimates for the period specified. d. Population estimates include Taiwan, province of China. e. Data refer to the total world population according to UN 2003. The total population of the 177 countries included in the main indicator tables was estimated to be 4,063 million in 1975, and projected to be 6,217 million in 2002 and 7,188 million in 2015.

Source: Columns 1-3, 13 and 14: UN 2003; column 4: calculated on the basis of columns 1 and 2; column 5: calculated on the basis of columns 2 and 3; columns 6-8: UN 2004h; columns 9 and 10: calculated on the basis of data on population under age 15 and total population from UN 2003; columns 11 and 12: calculated on the basis of data on population ages 65 and above and total population from UN 2003.

6 Commitment to health: resources, access and services

HDI rank	Health expenditure			One-year-olds fully immunized (MDG)		Oral rehydration therapy use rate (%) 1994-2002 c	Contra-ceptive prevalence rate a (%) 1995-2002 c	MDG Births attended by skilled health personnel (%) 1995-2002 c	Physicians (per 100,000 people) 1990-2003 c	MDG Population with sustainable access to affordable essential drugs b (%) 1999
	Public (% of GDP) 2001	Private (% of GDP) 2001	Per capita (PPP US$) 2001	Against tuberculosis (%) 2002	Against measles (%) 2002					
High human development										
1 Norway	6.9	1.2	2,920	..	88	..	..	100 d	367	95-100
2 Sweden	7.5	1.3	2,270	..	94	..	..	100 d	287	95-100
3 Australia	6.2	3.0	2,532	..	94	..	..	100	247	95-100
4 Canada	6.8	2.8	2,792	..	96	..	75	98	187	95-100
5 Netherlands	5.7	3.3	2,612	..	96	..	..	100	328	95-100
6 Belgium	6.4	2.5	2,481	..	75	..	..	100 d	419	95-100
7 Iceland	7.6	1.6	2,643	..	88	..	..	..	352	95-100
8 United States	6.2	7.7	4,887	..	91	..	76	99	279	95-100
9 Japan	6.2	1.8	2,131	..	98	..	56	100	202	95-100 '
10 Ireland	4.9	1.6	1,935	90	73	..	..	100	239	95-100
11 Switzerland	6.3	4.7	3,322	..	79	..	82	..	350	95-100
12 United Kingdom	6.2	1.4	1,989	..	83	..	84 e	99	164	95-100
13 Finland	5.3	1.7	1,845	99	96	..	..	100 d	311	95-100
14 Austria	5.6	2.5	2,259	..	78	..	51	100 d	323	95-100
15 Luxembourg	5.4	0.6	2,905	..	91	..	..	100 d	254	95-100
16 France	7.3	2.3	2,567	83	85	..	..	99 d	330	95-100
17 Denmark	7.0	1.5	2,503	..	99	..	..	100 d	366	95-100
18 New Zealand	6.4	1.9	1,724	..	85	..	75	100	219	95-100
19 Germany	8.1	2.7	2,820	..	89	..	..	100 d	363	95-100
20 Spain	5.4	2.2	1,607	..	97	..	81	..	329	95-100
21 Italy	6.3	2.1	2,204	..	70	..	60	..	607	95-100
22 Israel	6.0	2.7	1,839	..	95	..	..	99 d	375	95-100
23 Hong Kong, China (SAR)	..	..	..	..	..	..	..	..	160	..
24 Greece	5.2	4.1	1,522	88	88	..	..	..	438	95-100
25 Singapore	1.3	2.6	993	98	91	..	62	100	140	95-100
26 Portugal	6.4	2.9	1,618	82	87	..	..	100	318	95-100
27 Slovenia	6.3	2.1	1,545	98	94	..	..	100 d	219	95-100
28 Korea, Rep. of	2.7	3.3	948	89	97	..	81	100	180	95-100
29 Barbados	4.3	2.2	940	..	92	..	..	91	137	95-100
30 Cyprus	3.9	4.3	941	..	86	..	..	100	269	95-100
31 Malta	6.0	2.8	813	..	65	..	..	98 d	291	95-100
32 Czech Republic	6.7	0.6	1,129	97	..	..	72	99	342	80-94
33 Brunei Darussalam	2.5	0.6	638	99	99	..	..	99	99	95-100
34 Argentina	5.1	4.4	1,130	99	97	..	..	98	304	50-79
35 Seychelles	4.1	1.9	770	99	98	..	..	..	132	80-94
36 Estonia	4.3	1.2	562	99	95	..	..	..	313	95-100
37 Poland	4.4	1.7	629	95	98	..	..	99 d	220	80-94
38 Hungary	5.1	1.7	914	99	99	..	..	..	355	95-100
39 Saint Kitts and Nevis	3.2	1.6	576	99	99	..	..	99	117	50-79
40 Bahrain	2.9	1.3	664	..	99	..	62	98	169	95-100
41 Lithuania	4.2	1.8	478	99	98	..	47	..	403	80-94
42 Slovakia	5.1	0.6	681	98	99	..	..	..	326	95-100
43 Chile	2.9	3.9	792	94	95	..	..	100	115	80-94
44 Kuwait	3.0	0.8	612	..	99	..	50	98	160	95-100
45 Costa Rica	4.9	2.3	562	91	94	..	..	98	160	95-100
46 Uruguay	5.1	5.9	971	99	92	..	..	100	387	50-79
47 Qatar	2.3	0.8	782	99	99	..	43	98	220	95-100
48 Croatia	7.3	1.6	726	99	95	..	..	100	238	95-100
49 United Arab Emirates	2.6	0.8	921	98	94	..	28	96	177	95-100
50 Latvia	3.4	3.1	509	99	98	..	48	100	291	80-94

HDI rank		Health expenditure			One-year-olds fully immunized	MDG	Oral rehydration therapy use rate (%)	Contra-ceptive prevalence rate [a] (%)	MDG Births attended by skilled health personnel (%)	Physicians (per 100,000 people)	MDG Population with sustainable access to affordable essential drugs [b] (%)
		Public (% of GDP) 2001	Private (% of GDP) 2001	Per capita (PPP US$) 2001	Against tuberculosis (%) 2002	Against measles (%) 2002	1994-2002[c]	1995-2002[c]	1995-2002[c]	1990-2003[c]	1999
51	Bahamas	3.2	2.4	1,220	..	92	..	..	99 [d]	163	80-94
52	Cuba	6.2	1.0	229	99	98	..	73	100	596	95-100
53	Mexico	2.7	3.4	544	99	96	..	67	86	156	80-94
54	Trinidad and Tobago	1.7	2.2	388	..	88	6	38	96	75	50-79
55	Antigua and Barbuda	3.4	2.2	614	..	99	..	..	100	105	50-79
Medium human development											
56	Bulgaria	3.9	0.9	303	98	90	..	42	..	344	80-94
57	Russian Federation	3.7	1.7	454	97	98	..	..	99	420	50-79
58	Libyan Arab Jamahiriya	1.6	1.3	239	99	91	..	40	94	120	95-100
59	Malaysia	2.1	1.8	345	99	92	..	..	97	68	50-79
60	Macedonia, TFYR	5.8	1.0	331	91	98	..	..	97	219	50-79
61	Panama	4.8	2.2	458	92	79	7	..	90	121	80-94
62	Belarus	4.8	0.7	464	99	99	..	50	100	450	50-79
63	Tonga	3.4	2.1	223	99	90	..	..	92	35	95-100
64	Mauritius	2.0	1.4	323	87	84	..	..	99	85	95-100
65	Albania	2.4	1.3	150	94	96	48	58	99	137	50-79
66	Bosnia and Herzegovina	2.8	4.8	268	91	89	11	48	100	145	80-94
67	Suriname	5.7	3.8	398	..	73	24	42	85	50	95-100
68	Venezuela	3.8	2.3	386	90	78	10	..	94	200	80-94
69	Romania	5.2	1.4	460	99	98	..	64	98	189	80-94
70	Ukraine	2.9	1.4	176	98	99	..	68	100	299	50-79
71	Saint Lucia	2.9	1.6	272	95	97	..	..	100	58	50-79
72	Brazil	3.2	4.4	573	99	93	18	77	88	206	0-49
73	Colombia	3.6	1.9	356	85	89	..	77	86	94	80-94
74	Oman	2.4	0.6	343	98	99	88	24	95	137	80-94
75	Samoa (Western)	4.7	1.0	199	98	99	..	..	100	34	95-100
76	Thailand	2.1	1.6	254	99	94	..	72	99	30	95-100
77	Saudi Arabia	3.4	1.2	591	98	97	..	32	91	153	95-100
78	Kazakhstan	1.9	1.2	204	99	95	20	66	99	345	50-79
79	Jamaica	2.9	4.0	253	90	86	2	66	95	85	95-100
80	Lebanon	3.4	8.8	673	..	96	30	61	89	274	80-94
81	Fiji	2.7	1.3	224	99	88	..	..	100	34	95-100
82	Armenia	3.2	4.6	273	97	91	40	61	97	287	0-49
83	Philippines	1.5	1.8	169	75	73	28	47	58	115	50-79
84	Maldives	5.6	1.1	263	98	99	..	..	70	78	50-79
85	Peru	2.6	2.1	231	90	95	29	69	59	103	50-79
86	Turkmenistan	3.0	1.1	245	99	88	31	62	97	300	50-79
87	St. Vincent & the Grenadines	3.8	2.2	358	90	99	..	..	100	88	80-94
88	Turkey	3.6	1.5	294	77	82	15	64	81	123	95-100
89	Paraguay	3.1	4.9	332	65	82	..	57	71	49	0-49
90	Jordan	4.5	5.0	412	..	95	..	56	97	205	95-100
91	Azerbaijan	1.1	0.5	48	99	97	27	55	84	359	50-79
92	Tunisia	4.9	1.6	463	97	94	..	..	90	70	50-79
93	Grenada	3.8	1.5	445	..	94	..	..	99	81	95-100
94	China	2.0	3.4	224	77	79	29	84	76	164	80-94
95	Dominica	4.3	1.7	312	98	98	..	..	100	49	80-94
96	Sri Lanka	1.8	1.9	122	99	99	..	..	97	43	95-100
97	Georgia	1.4	2.2	108	91	73	33	41	96	463	0-49
98	Dominican Republic	2.2	3.9	353	99	92	22	65	98	190	50-79
99	Belize	2.4	2.9	278	97	89	..	..	83	102	80-94
100	Ecuador	2.3	2.3	177	99	80	..	66	69	145	0-49

HDI rank		Health expenditure			MDG One-year-olds fully immunized		Oral rehydration therapy use rate	Contra- ceptive prevalence rate [a]	MDG Births attended by skilled health personnel	Physicians (per 100,000 people)	MDG Population with sustainable access to affordable essential drugs [b]
		Public (% of GDP) 2001	Private (% of GDP) 2001	Per capita (PPP US$) 2001	Against tuberculosis (%) 2002	Against measles (%) 2002	(%) 1994- 2002 [c]	(%) 1995- 2002 [c]	(%) 1995- 2002 [c]	1990- 2003 [c]	(%) 1999
101	Iran, Islamic Rep. of	2.8	3.6	422	99	99	..	73	90	110	80-94
102	Occupied Palestinian Territories	..	..	..	96	94	43	..	97	84	..
103	El Salvador	3.7	4.3	376	92	93	..	60	90	126	80-94
104	Guyana	4.2	1.1	215	91	95	7	37	86	26	0-49
105	Cape Verde	3.8	0.7	165	92	85	..	53	89	17	80-94
106	Syrian Arab Republic	2.4	3.0	427	99	98	..	..	76 [d]	142	80-94
107	Uzbekistan	2.7	0.9	91	98	97	19	67	96	293	50-79
108	Algeria	3.1	1.0	169	98	81	24	64	92	85	95-100
109	Equatorial Guinea	1.2	0.8	106	73	51	..	..	65	25	0-49
110	Kyrgyzstan	1.9	2.1	108	99	98	13	60	98	272	50-79
111	Indonesia	0.6	1.8	77	77	76	5	57	64	16	80-94
112	Viet Nam	1.5	3.7	134	97	96	20	78	70	54	80-94
113	Moldova, Rep. of	2.9	2.9	112	99	94	19	62	99	271	50-79
114	Bolivia	3.5	1.8	125	94	79	40	53	69	76	50-79
115	Honduras	3.2	2.9	153	94	97	..	62	56	87	0-49
116	Tajikistan	1.0	2.3	43	98	84	20	34	71	212	0-49
117	Mongolia	4.6	1.8	122	98	98	32	67	97	278	50-79
118	Nicaragua	3.8	4.0	158	84	98	18	69	67	62	0-49
119	South Africa	3.6	5.1	652	94	78	..	56	84	25	80-94
120	Egypt	1.9	2.0	153	98	97	..	56	61	218	80-94
121	Guatemala	2.3	2.5	199	96	92	15	38	41	109	50-79
122	Gabon	1.7	1.9	197	89	55	..	33	86	..	0-49
123	São Tomé and Principe	1.5	0.7	22	99	85	25	29	79	47	0-49
124	Solomon Islands	4.7	0.3	133	76	78	..	..	85	13	80-94
125	Morocco	2.0	3.1	199	90	96	..	50	40	49	50-79
126	Namibia	4.7	2.2	342	83	68	8	..	78	29	80-94
127	India	0.9	4.2	80	81	67	..	48 [f]	43	51	0-49
128	Botswana	4.4	2.2	381	99	90	..	40	94	29	80-94
129	Vanuatu	2.3	1.6	107	90	44	..	..	89	12	..
130	Cambodia	1.8	10.0	184	63	52	..	24	32	16	0-49
131	Ghana	2.8	1.9	60	91	81	22	22	44	9	0-49
132	Myanmar	0.4	1.7	26	80	75	11	33	56	30	50-79
133	Papua New Guinea	3.9	0.5	144	71	71	..	26	53	6	80-94
134	Bhutan	3.6	0.4	64	83	78	..	..	24	5	80-94
135	Lao People's Dem. Rep.	1.7	1.4	51	65	55	20	32	19	61	50-79
136	Comoros	1.9	1.2	29	90	71	22	26	62	7	80-94
137	Swaziland	2.3	1.1	167	95	72	7	28	70	15	95-100
138	Bangladesh	1.6	2.0	58	95	77	49	54	12	23	50-79
139	Sudan	0.7	2.8	39	48	49	13	..	86 [d]	16	0-49
140	Nepal	1.5	3.6	63	85	71	11	39	11	5	0-49
141	Cameroon	1.2	2.1	42	77	62	23	19	60	7	50-79
Low human development											
142	Pakistan	1.0	3.0	85	67	57	19	28	20	68	50-79
143	Togo	1.4	1.5	45	84	58	15	26	49	6	50-79
144	Congo	1.4	0.8	22	51	37	13	..	..	25	50-79
145	Lesotho	4.3	1.2	101	83	70	10	30	60	7	80-94
146	Uganda	3.4	2.5	57	96	77	..	23	39	5	50-79
147	Zimbabwe	2.8	3.4	142	80	58	50	54	73	6	50-79
148	Kenya	1.7	6.2	114	91	78	30	39	44	14	0-49
149	Yemen	1.6	3.0	69	74	65	..	21	22	22	50-79
150	Madagascar	1.3	0.7	20	73	61	30	19	46	9	50-79
151	Nigeria	0.8	2.6	31	54	40	24	15	42	27	0-49

		Health expenditure			MDG One-year-olds fully immunized		Oral rehydration therapy use rate (%)	Contra- ceptive prevalence rate [a] (%)	MDG Births attended by skilled health personnel (%)	Physicians (per 100,000 people)	MDG Population with sustainable access to affordable essential drugs [b] (%)
		Public (% of GDP) 2001	Private (% of GDP) 2001	Per capita (PPP US$) 2001	Against tuberculosis (%) 2002	Against measles (%) 2002	1994- 2002 [c]	1995- 2002 [c]	1995- 2002 [c]	1990- 2003 [c]	1999
HDI rank											
152	Mauritania	2.6	1.0	45	98	81	..	8	57	14	50-79
153	Haiti	2.7	2.4	56	71	53	..	27	24	25	0-49
154	Djibouti	4.1	2.9	90	52	62	..	..	..	13	80-94
155	Gambia	3.2	3.3	78	99	90	27	10	55	4	80-94
156	Eritrea	3.7	2.0	36	91	84	30	8	21	5	50-79
157	Senegal	2.8	2.0	63	70	54	33	13	58	10	50-79
158	Timor-Leste	5.8	4.0	..	83	47	7	..	24	..	..
159	Rwanda	3.1	2.5	44	99	69	4	13	31	2	0-49
160	Guinea	1.9	1.6	61	71	54	21	6	35	13	80-94
161	Benin	2.1	2.4	39	94	78	35	19	66	10	50-79
162	Tanzania, U. Rep. of	2.1	2.3	26	88	89	21	25	36	4	50-79
163	Côte d'Ivoire	1.0	5.2	127	66	56	25	15	63	9	80-94
164	Zambia	3.0	2.7	52	92	85	28	34	43	7	50-79
165	Malawi	2.7	5.1	39	78	69	..	31	56	..	0-49
166	Angola	2.8	1.6	70	82	74	7	6	45	5	0-49
167	Chad	2.0	0.6	17	67	55	36	8	16	3	0-49
168	Congo, Dem. Rep. of the	1.5	1.9	12	55	45	11	31	61	7	..
169	Central African Republic	2.3	2.2	58	70	35	34	28	44	4	50-79
170	Ethiopia	1.4	2.1	14	76	52	..	8	6	3	50-79
171	Mozambique	4.0	1.9	47	78	58	27	6	44	2	50-79
172	Guinea-Bissau	3.2	2.7	37	70	47	13	8	35	17	0-49
173	Burundi	2.1	1.5	19	84	75	10	16	25	1	0-49
174	Mali	1.7	2.7	30	73	33	22	8	41	4	50-79
175	Burkina Faso	1.8	1.2	27	72	46	37	12	31	4	50-79
176	Niger	1.4	2.3	22	47	48	38	14	16	3	50-79
177	Sierra Leone	2.6	1.7	26	70	60	29	4	42	9	0-49
Developing countries		..	..	..	80	72	..	..	55	..	..
Least developed countries		..	..	..	76	62	..	..	33	..	..
Arab States		..	..	..	86	82	..	..	67	..	..
East Asia and the Pacific		..	..	..	79	79	..	..	73	..	..
Latin America and the Caribbean		..	..	..	95	91	..	..	83	..	..
South Asia		..	..	..	81	68	..	..	37	..	..
Sub-Saharan Africa		..	..	..	73	58	..	..	42	..	..
Central & Eastern Europe & the CIS		..	..	..	97	96	..	..	97	..	..
OECD		..	..	..	..	90	..	..	95	..	..
High-income OECD		..	..	..	..	90	..	..	99	..	..
High human development		..	..	..	..	92	..	..	97	..	..
Medium human development		..	..	..	84	78	..	..	62	..	..
Low human development		..	..	..	71	57	..	..	35	..	..
High income		..	..	..	..	90	..	..	99	..	..
Middle income		..	..	..	87	86	..	..	80	..	..
Low income		..	..	..	77	64	..	..	41	..	..
World		..	..	..	81 [g]	75 [g]	..	..	58 [g]	..	..

a. Data usually refer to married women ages 15-49; the actual age range covered may vary across countries. b. The data on access to essential drugs are based on statistical estimates received from World Health Organization (WHO) country and regional offices and regional advisers and through the World Drug Situation Survey carried out in 1998-99. These estimates represent the best information available to the WHO Department of Essential Drugs and Medicines Policy to date and are currently being validated by WHO member states. The department assigns the estimates to four groupings: very low access (0-49%), low access (50-79%), medium access (80-94%) and good access (95-100%). These groupings, used here in presenting the data, are often employed by the WHO in interpreting the data, as the actual estimates may suggest a higher level of accuracy than the data afford. c. Data refer to the most recent year available during the period specified. d. Data refer to a year or period other than that specified, differ from the standard definition or refer to only part of a country. e. Excluding Northern Ireland. f. Excluding the state of Tripura. g. Data refer to the world aggregate from UNICEF 2003b.

Source: Columns 1-3: WHO 2004b; columns 4-6 and 8: UNICEF 2003b; column 7: UN 2004g; column 9: WHO 2004d; column 10: WHO 2004a.

7 Water, sanitation and nutritional status

HDI rank		MDG Population with sustainable access to improved sanitation (%)		MDG Population with sustainable access to an improved water source (%)		MDG Undernourished people (% of total population)		MDG Children under weight for age (% under age 5)	Children under height for age (% under age 5)	Infants with low birthweight (%)
		1990	2000	1990	2000	1990/92 [a]	1999/2001 [a]	1995-2002 [b]	1995-2002 [b]	1998-2002 [b]
High human development										
1	Norway	..	..	100	100	..	..	..	..	5
2	Sweden	100	100	100	100	..	..	..	..	4
3	Australia	100	100	100	100	..	..	..	..	7
4	Canada	100	100	100	100	..	..	..	..	6
5	Netherlands	100	100	100	100	..	..	..	..	..
6	Belgium	..	..	..	..	..	..	..	..	8 [c]
7	Iceland	..	..	..	..	..	..	..	..	4
8	United States	100	100	100	100	..	..	1 [c]	2 [c]	8
9	Japan	..	..	..	..	..	..	..	..	8
10	Ireland	..	..	..	..	..	..	..	..	6
11	Switzerland	100	100	100	100	..	..	..	..	6
12	United Kingdom	100	100	100	100	..	..	..	..	8
13	Finland	100	100	100	100	..	..	..	..	4
14	Austria	100	100	100	100	..	..	..	..	7
15	Luxembourg	..	..	..	..	..	..	..	..	8
16	France	..	..	..	..	..	..	..	..	7
17	Denmark	..	..	..	100	..	..	..	..	5
18	New Zealand	..	..	..	..	..	..	..	..	6
19	Germany	..	..	..	..	..	..	..	..	7
20	Spain	..	..	..	..	..	..	..	..	6 [c]
21	Italy	..	..	..	..	..	..	..	..	6
22	Israel	..	..	..	..	..	..	..	..	8
23	Hong Kong, China (SAR)	..	..	..	..	..	..	..	..	..
24	Greece	..	..	..	..	..	..	..	..	8
25	Singapore	100	100	100	100	..	..	14 [c]	11 [c]	8
26	Portugal	..	..	..	..	..	..	..	..	8
27	Slovenia	..	..	100	100	..	..	..	..	6
28	Korea, Rep. of	..	63	..	92	..	..	..	..	4
29	Barbados	..	100	..	100	..	..	6 [c]	7 [c]	10 [c]
30	Cyprus	100	100	100	100	..	..	..	..	..
31	Malta	100	100	100	100	..	..	..	..	6
32	Czech Republic	..	..	..	..	..	..	1 [c]	2 [c]	7
33	Brunei Darussalam	..	..	..	..	..	..	..	..	10
34	Argentina	82	..	94	..	..	..	5	12	7
35	Seychelles	..	..	..	..	..	..	6 [c]	5 [c]	..
36	Estonia	..	..	..	..	..	4	..	..	4
37	Poland	..	..	..	..	..	..	..	..	6
38	Hungary	99	99	99	99	..	..	2 [c]	3 [c]	9
39	Saint Kitts and Nevis	..	96	..	98	..	..	..	..	9
40	Bahrain	..	..	..	..	..	..	9	10	8
41	Lithuania	..	..	..	..	..	..	..	..	4
42	Slovakia	..	100	..	100	..	5	..	..	7
43	Chile	97	96	90	93	8	4	1	2	5
44	Kuwait	..	..	..	..	22	4	10	24	7
45	Costa Rica	..	93	..	95	7	6	5	6	7
46	Uruguay	..	94	..	98	6	3	5	8	8
47	Qatar	..	..	..	..	..	..	6	8	10
48	Croatia	..	..	..	..	..	12	1	1	6
49	United Arab Emirates	..	..	..	..	4	..	14	17	15 [c]
50	Latvia	..	..	..	..	..	6	..	..	5

HDI rank		MDG Population with sustainable access to improved sanitation (%)		MDG Population with sustainable access to an improved water source (%)		MDG Undernourished people (% of total population)		MDG Children under weight for age (% under age 5)	Children under height for age (% under age 5)	Infants with low birthweight (%)
		1990	2000	1990	2000	1990/92 [a]	1999/2001 [a]	1995-2002 [b]	1995-2002 [b]	1998-2002 [b]
51	Bahamas	..	100	..	97	..	..	..	..	7
52	Cuba	..	98	..	91	8	11	4	5	6
53	Mexico	70	74	80	88	5	5	8	18	9
54	Trinidad and Tobago	99	99	91	90	13	12	7 [c]	5 [c]	23
55	Antigua and Barbuda	..	95	..	91	..	..	10 [c]	7 [c]	8
Medium human development										
56	Bulgaria	..	100	..	100	..	16	..	..	10
57	Russian Federation	..	..	..	99	..	4	3	13	6
58	Libyan Arab Jamahiriya	97	97	71	72	..	..	5	15	7 [c]
59	Malaysia	..	..	..	..	3	..	12	..	10
60	Macedonia, TFYR	..	..	..	..	..	10	6	7	5
61	Panama	..	92	..	90	20	26	7	14	10 [c]
62	Belarus	..	..	..	100	..	3	..	..	5
63	Tonga	..	..	..	100	..	..	..	..	0
64	Mauritius	100	99	100	100	6	5	15	10	13
65	Albania	..	91	..	97	..	4	14	32	3
66	Bosnia and Herzegovina	..	..	..	..	..	8	4	10	4
67	Suriname	..	93	..	82	13	11	13	10	13
68	Venezuela	..	68	..	83	11	18	5 [c]	13 [c]	7
69	Romania	..	53	..	58	..	..	6 [c]	8 [c]	9
70	Ukraine	..	99	..	98	..	4	3	15	5
71	Saint Lucia	..	89	..	98	..	..	14 [c]	11 [c]	8
72	Brazil	71	76	83	87	12	9	6	11	10 [c]
73	Colombia	83	86	94	91	17	13	7	14	9
74	Oman	84	92	37	39	..	..	24	23	8
75	Samoa (Western)	..	99	..	99	..	..	..	..	4 [c]
76	Thailand	79	96	80	84	28	19	19 [c]	16 [c]	9
77	Saudi Arabia	..	100	..	95	4	3	14	20	11 [c]
78	Kazakhstan	..	99	..	91	..	22	4	10	8
79	Jamaica	99	99	93	92	14	9	6	6	9
80	Lebanon	..	99	..	100	3	3	3	12	6
81	Fiji	..	43	..	47	..	..	8 [c]	3 [c]	10
82	Armenia	..	..	..	..	..	51	3	13	7
83	Philippines	74	83	87	86	26	22	28	30	20
84	Maldives	..	56	..	100	..	..	30	25	22
85	Peru	60	71	74	80	40	11	7	25	11 [c]
86	Turkmenistan	..	..	..	..	..	7	12	22	6
87	St. Vincent & the Grenadines	..	96	..	93	..	..	..	..	10
88	Turkey	87	90	79	82	..	3	8	16	16
89	Paraguay	93	94	63	78	18	13	5	11	9 [c]
90	Jordan	98	99	97	96	4	6	5	8	10 [c]
91	Azerbaijan	..	81	..	78	..	21	7	13	11
92	Tunisia	76	84	75	80	..	..	4	12	7
93	Grenada	..	97	..	95	..	..	..	..	9
94	China	29 [d]	40	71	75	17	11	11	16	6
95	Dominica	..	83	..	97	..	..	5 [c]	6 [c]	10
96	Sri Lanka	85	94	68	77	29	25	29	14	22
97	Georgia	..	100	..	79	..	26	3	12	6
98	Dominican Republic	66	67	83	86	27	25	5	6	14
99	Belize	..	50	..	92	..	..	6 [c]	..	6
100	Ecuador	70	86	71	85	8	4	15	27	16

HDI rank		Population with sustainable access to improved sanitation (%)		Population with sustainable access to an improved water source (%)		Undernourished people (% of total population)		Children under weight for age (% under age 5)	Children under height for age (% under age 5)	Infants with low birthweight (%)
		MDG		MDG		MDG		MDG	MDG	
		1990	2000	1990	2000	1990/92 [a]	1999/2001 [a]	1995-2002 [b]	1995-2002 [b]	1998-2002 [b]
101	Iran, Islamic Rep. of	..	83	..	92	5	5	11	15	7
102	Occupied Palestinian Territories	..	100	..	86	..	..	4	9	9
103	El Salvador	73	82	66	77	12	14	12	23	13
104	Guyana	..	87	..	94	21	14	14	11	12
105	Cape Verde	..	71	..	74	..	..	14 [c]	16 [c]	13
106	Syrian Arab Republic	..	90	..	80	5	4	7	18	6
107	Uzbekistan	..	89	..	85	..	26	19	31	7
108	Algeria	..	92	..	89	5	6	6	18	7
109	Equatorial Guinea	..	53	..	44	..	..	19	39	13
110	Kyrgyzstan	..	100	..	77	..	7	11	25	7 [c]
111	Indonesia	47	55	71	78	9	6	26	..	10 [c]
112	Viet Nam	29	47	55	77	27	19	33	36	9
113	Moldova, Rep. of	..	99	..	92	..	12	3	10	5
114	Bolivia	52	70	71	83	26	22	10	26	9
115	Honduras	61	75	83	88	23	20	17	29	14
116	Tajikistan	..	90	..	60	..	71	..	..	15
117	Mongolia	..	30	..	60	34	38	13	25	8
118	Nicaragua	76	85	70	77	30	29	10	20	13
119	South Africa	86	87	86	86	..	..	12	25	15
120	Egypt	87	98	94	97	5	3	11	21	12
121	Guatemala	70	81	76	92	16	25	24	46	13
122	Gabon	..	53	..	86	11	7	12	21	14
123	São Tomé and Principe	..	..	..	..	..	..	13	29	..
124	Solomon Islands	..	34	..	71	..	..	21 [c]	27 [c]	13 [c]
125	Morocco	58	68	75	80	6	7	9	24	11 [c]
126	Namibia	33	41	72	77	20	7	24	24	16 [c]
127	India	16	28	68	84	25	21	47	46	30
128	Botswana	60	66	93	95	18	24	13	23	10
129	Vanuatu	..	100	..	88	..	..	20 [c]	19 [c]	6
130	Cambodia	..	17	..	30	43	38	45	45	11
131	Ghana	61	72	53	73	35	12	25	26	11
132	Myanmar	..	64	..	72	10	7	35	34	15
133	Papua New Guinea	82	82	40	42	25	27	35 [c]	..	11 [c]
134	Bhutan	..	70	..	62	..	..	19	40	15
135	Lao People's Dem. Rep.	..	30	..	37	29	22	40	41	14
136	Comoros	98	98	88	96	..	..	25	42	25
137	Swaziland	..	..	..	..	10	12	10	30	9
138	Bangladesh	41	48	94	97	35	32	48	45	30
139	Sudan	58	62	67	75	31	25	17	..	31
140	Nepal	20	28	67	88	18	17	48	51	21
141	Cameroon	77	79	51	58	33	27	21	35	11
Low human development										
142	Pakistan	36	62	83	90	26	19	38	37	19 [c]
143	Togo	37	34	51	54	33	25	25	22	15
144	Congo	..	..	..	51	37	30	14	19	..
145	Lesotho	..	49	..	78	27	25	18	46	14
146	Uganda	..	79	45	52	23	19	23	39	12
147	Zimbabwe	56	62	78	83	43	39	13	27	11
148	Kenya	80	87	45	57	44	37	21	35	11
149	Yemen	32	38	..	69	35	33	46	52	32 [c]
150	Madagascar	36	42	44	47	35	36	33	49	14
151	Nigeria	53	54	53	62	13	8	36 [c]	43 [c]	12

HDI rank		Population with sustainable access to improved sanitation (%) MDG		Population with sustainable access to an improved water source (%) MDG		Undernourished people (% of total population) MDG		Children under weight for age (% under age 5) MDG	Children under height for age (% under age 5)	Infants with low birthweight (%)
		1990	2000	1990	2000	1990/92 [a]	1999/2001 [a]	1995-2002 [b]	1995-2002 [b]	1998-2002 [b]
152	Mauritania	30	33	37	37	14	10	32	35	42
153	Haiti	23	28	53	46	65	49	17	23	21
154	Djibouti	..	91	..	100	..	..	18	26	..
155	Gambia	..	37	..	62	22	27	17	19	17
156	Eritrea	..	13	..	46	..	61	44	38	21 [c]
157	Senegal	57	70	72	78	23	24	23	25	18
158	Timor-Leste	..	..	..	..	..	..	43	47	10
159	Rwanda	..	8	..	41	43	41	27	41	9
160	Guinea	55	58	45	48	40	28	23	26	12
161	Benin	20	23	..	63	20	16	23	31	16
162	Tanzania, U. Rep. of	84	90	38	68	35	43	29	44	13
163	Côte d'Ivoire	46	52	80	81	18	15	21	25	17
164	Zambia	63	78	52	64	45	50	28	47	10
165	Malawi	73	76	49	57	49	33	25	49	16
166	Angola	..	44	..	38	61	49	31	45	12
167	Chad	18	29	..	27	58	34	28	29	17 [c]
168	Congo, Dem. Rep. of the	..	21	..	45	31	75	31	38	12
169	Central African Republic	24	25	48	70	50	44	24	39	14
170	Ethiopia	8	12	25	24	..	42	47	52	15
171	Mozambique	..	43	..	57	69	53	26	44	14 [c]
172	Guinea-Bissau	44	56	..	56	..	..	25	30	22
173	Burundi	87	88	69	78	49	70	45	57	16
174	Mali	70	69	55	65	25	21	33	38	23
175	Burkina Faso	..	29	..	42	22	17	34	37	19
176	Niger	15	20	53	59	42	34	40	40	17
177	Sierra Leone	..	66	..	57	46	50	27	34	..
Developing countries		..	51	..	78	21	17	..	..	..
Least developed countries		..	44	..	62	35	37	..	..	..
Arab States		..	83	..	86	13	13	..	..	..
East Asia and the Pacific		..	48	..	76	..	..	..	..	..
Latin America and the Caribbean		72	77	82	86	14	11	..	..	..
South Asia		22	37	72	85	26	22	..	..	..
Sub-Saharan Africa		54	53	52	57	31	32	..	..	..
Central & Eastern Europe & CIS		..	..	..	93	..	10	..	..	..
OECD		..	..	..	..	..	..	..	..	..
High-income OECD		..	..	..	..	..	..	..	..	..
High human development		..	..	..	..	..	..	..	..	..
Medium human development		..	51	..	82	19	14	..	..	..
Low human development		44	51	57	62	30	31	..	..	..
High income		..	..	..	..	..	..	..	..	..
Middle income		..	61	..	82	..	10	..	..	..
Low income		30	43	..	76	26	24	..	..	..
World		..	61 [e]	..	82 [e]	..	..	..	..	..

a. Data refer to the average for the years specified. b. Data refer to the most recent year available during the period specified. c. Data refer to a year or period other than that specified, differ from the standard definition or refer to only part of the country. d. Data from the World Bank 2004f. e. Data refer to the world aggregate from UNICEF 2003b.

Source: Columns 1 and 3: UN 2004d, based on a joint effort by the United Nations Children's Fund and the World Health Organization; column 2, 4, 7-9: UNICEF 2003b, based on a joint effort by the United Nations Children's Fund and the World Health Organization; columns 5 and 6: FAO 2003.

... TO LEAD A LONG AND HEALTHY LIFE ...

	HIV prevalence[a] (% ages 15-49) 2003	MDG Condom use at last high-risk sex[b] (% ages 15-24) Women 1996-2002[h]	Men 1996-2002[h]	MDG Malaria cases[c] (per 100,000 people) 2000	MDG Children under age 5 With insecticide-treated bed nets (%) 1999-2001[h]	With fever treated with anti-malarial drugs (%) 1999-2001[h]	MDG Tuberculosis cases Per 100,000 people[e] 2002	Detected under DOTS (%)[f] 2002	Cured under DOTS (%)[g] 2001	Prevalence of smoking[d] (% of adults) Women 2000	Men 2000
HDI rank											
High human development											
1 Norway	0.1 [0.0-0.2]	..	..	..	..	..	5	26	87	32	31
2 Sweden	0.1 [0.0-0.2]	..	..	..	..	..	4	59	62	19	19
3 Australia	0.1 [0.1-0.2]	..	..	..	..	..	6	25	66	18	21
4 Canada	0.3 [0.2-0.5]	72	72	..	..	..	5	52	67	23	27
5 Netherlands	0.2 [0.1-0.4]	..	..	..	..	..	7	54	..	29	37
6 Belgium	0.2 [0.1-0.3]	..	..	..	..	..	11	64	64	26	30
7 Iceland	0.2 [0.1-0.3]	..	..	..	..	..	3	48	67	..	..
8 United States	0.6 [0.3-1.1]	65	65	..	..	..	4	87	70	22	26
9 Japan	<0.1 [<0.2]	..	..	..	..	..	44	33	75	13	53
10 Ireland	0.1 [0.0-0.3]	..	..	..	..	..	13	..	..	31	32
11 Switzerland	0.4 [0.2-0.6]	..	..	..	..	..	8	..	..	28	39
12 United Kingdom	0.1 [0.1-0.2]	..	..	..	..	..	12	..	..	26	27
13 Finland	<0.1 [<0.2]	..	..	..	..	..	10	..	..	20	27
14 Austria	0.3 [0.1-0.4]	..	..	..	..	..	12	41	64	19	30
15 Luxembourg	0.2 [0.1-0.4]	..	..	..	..	..	11	69	..	..	..
16 France	0.4 [0.2-0.7]	..	..	..	..	..	14	..	..	30	39
17 Denmark	0.2 [0.1-0.3]	..	..	..	..	..	13	..	..	29	32
18 New Zealand	<0.1 [<0.2]	..	..	..	..	..	11	48	9	25	25
19 Germany	0.1 [0.1-0.2]	..	..	..	..	..	8	52	67	31	39
20 Spain	0.7 [0.3-1.1]	33	49	..	..	..	30	..	..	25	42
21 Italy	0.5 [0.2-0.8]	..	..	..	..	..	6	63	40	17	32
22 Israel	0.1 [0.1-0.2]	..	..	..	..	..	9	58	79	24	33
23 Hong Kong, China (SAR)	0.1 [<0.2]	..	..	..	..	..	95	51	78	..	..
24 Greece	0.2 [0.1-0.3]	..	..	..	..	..	22	..	..	29	47
25 Singapore	0.2 [0.1-0.5]	..	..	..	..	..	44	39	88	3	27
26 Portugal	0.4 [0.2-0.7]	..	..	..	..	..	37	94	78	7	30
27 Slovenia	<0.1 [<0.2]	18	17	..	..	..	25	68	82	20	30
28 Korea, Rep. of	<0.1 [<0.2]	..	..	9	..	..	138	..	..	5	65
29 Barbados	1.5 [0.4-5.4]	..	..	..	..	..	20	24	..	..	..
30 Cyprus	..	..	..	..	..	..	6	46	92	..	..
31 Malta	0.2 [0.1-0.3]	..	..	..	..	..	5	44	100	..	..
32 Czech Republic	0.1 [<0.2]	..	..	..	..	..	13	57	73	22	36
33 Brunei Darussalam	<0.1 [<0.2]	..	..	..	..	..	58	121	56	..	..
34 Argentina	0.7 [0.3-1.1]	..	..	1	..	..	61	51	64	34	47
35 Seychelles	..	..	..	..	..	..	52	60	67	..	..
36 Estonia	1.1 [0.4-2.1]	..	..	..	..	..	59	61	64	20	44
37 Poland	0.1 [0.0-0.2]	..	..	..	..	..	36	55	77	25	44
38 Hungary	0.1 [0.0-0.2]	..	..	..	..	..	37	39	46	27	44
39 Saint Kitts and Nevis	..	..	..	..	..	..	14	49	..	..	..
40 Bahrain	0.2 [0.1-0.3]	..	..	..	..	..	68	12	87	..	..
41 Lithuania	0.1 [<0.2]	..	..	..	..	..	73	62	75	16	51
42 Slovakia	<0.1 [<0.2]	..	..	..	..	..	28	35	87	30	55
43 Chile	0.3 [0.2-0.5]	18	33	..	..	..	20	112	83	18	26
44 Kuwait	..	..	..	..	..	..	53	..	..	2	30
45 Costa Rica	0.6 [0.3-1.0]	..	..	42	..	..	19	79	72	7	29
46 Uruguay	0.3 [0.2-0.5]	..	..	..	..	..	37	70	85	14	32
47 Qatar	..	..	..	..	..	..	70	39	60	..	..
48 Croatia	<0.1 [<0.2]	..	..	..	..	..	74	..	..	32	34
49 United Arab Emirates	..	..	..	..	..	..	26	25	62	1	18
50 Latvia	0.6 [0.3-1.0]	66	69	..	..	..	83	78	73	13	49

HDI rank		HIV prevalence [a] (% ages 15-49) 2003	MDG Condom use at last high-risk sex [b] (% ages 15-24) Women 1996-2002 [h]	Men 1996-2002 [h]	MDG Malaria cases [c] (per 100,000 people) 2000	MDG Children under age 5 With insecticide-treated bed nets (%) 1999-2001 [h]	With fever treated with anti-malarial drugs (%) 1999-2001 [h]	MDG Tuberculosis cases Per 100,000 people [e] 2002	Detected under DOTS (%) [f] 2002	Cured under DOTS (%) [g] 2001	Prevalence of smoking [d] (% of adults) Women 2000	Men 2000
51	Bahamas	3.0 [1.8-4.9]	..	..	..	..	..	60	50	64	..	..
52	Cuba	0.1 [<0.2]	..	..	..	..	..	14	91	93	26	48
53	Mexico	0.3 [0.1-0.4]	57	57	8	..	..	44	73	83	18	51
54	Trinidad and Tobago	3.2 [1.2-8.3]	..	..	1	..	..	19	..	..	8	42
55	Antigua and Barbuda	..	..	..	..	..	..	8	92	100	..	..
Medium human development												
56	Bulgaria	<0.1 [<0.2]	..	..	..	..	..	60	43	87	24	49
57	Russian Federation	1.1 [0.6-1.9]	..	..	1	..	..	181	6	67	10	63
58	Libyan Arab Jamahiriya	0.3 [0.1-0.6]	..	..	2	..	..	20	..	..	..	..
59	Malaysia	0.4 [0.2-0.7]	..	..	57	..	..	120	78	79	4	49
60	Macedonia, TFYR	<0.1 [<0.2]	..	..	..	..	..	54	37	88	32	40
61	Panama	0.9 [0.5-1.5]	..	..	36	..	..	50	88	65	20	56
62	Belarus	0.5 [0.2-0.8]	..	..	..	..	..	125	..	..	5	55
63	Tonga	..	..	..	..	..	..	41	164	92	..	..
64	Mauritius	..	..	26	1 [i]	..	..	137	25	93	3	45
65	Albania	..	..	..	..	..	..	41	24	98	18	60
66	Bosnia and Herzegovina	<0.1 [<0.2]	..	..	..	..	..	65	47	98	..	..
67	Suriname	1.7 [0.5-5.8]	..	..	2,954	3	..	103	..	..	..	..
68	Venezuela	0.7 [0.4-1.2]	..	..	94	..	..	54	65	80	39	42
69	Romania	<0.1 [<0.2]	..	..	..	..	..	189	41	78	25	62
70	Ukraine	1.4 [0.7-2.3]	..	..	..	..	..	143	..	..	19	51
71	Saint Lucia	..	..	..	..	..	..	21	72	50	..	..
72	Brazil	0.7 [0.3-1.1]	32	59	344	..	..	94	10	67	29	38
73	Colombia	0.7 [0.4-1.2]	29	..	250	1	..	69	9	85	21	24
74	Oman	0.1 [0.0-0.2]	..	..	27	..	..	13	106	90	2	16
75	Samoa (Western)	..	..	..	..	..	..	44	75	77	..	..
76	Thailand	1.5 [0.8-2.8]	..	..	130	..	..	179	73	75	3	44
77	Saudi Arabia	..	..	..	32	..	..	59	37	77	1	22
78	Kazakhstan	0.2 [0.1-0.3]	65	28	(.)	..	..	149	93	78	7	60
79	Jamaica	1.2 [0.6-2.2]	38	..	..	..	..	9	68	78	..	..
80	Lebanon	0.1 [0.0-0.2]	69	69	..	..	..	15	68	91	35	46
81	Fiji	0.1 [0.0-0.2]	..	..	..	..	..	43	66	85	..	..
82	Armenia	0.1 [0.1-0.2]	..	43	4	..	..	106	28	90	1	64
83	Philippines	<0.1 [<0.2]	..	..	15	..	..	540	58	88	11	54
84	Maldives	..	..	..	..	..	..	46	92	97	..	..
85	Peru	0.5 [0.3-0.9]	19	..	258	..	..	246	84	90	16	42
86	Turkmenistan	<0.1 [<0.2]	..	..	1	..	..	125	36	75	1	27
87	St. Vincent & the Grenadines	..	..	..	..	..	..	41	0	80	..	..
88	Turkey	<0.1 [<0.2]	..	..	17	..	..	50	..	..	24	65
89	Paraguay	0.5 [0.2-0.8]	79	..	124	..	..	109	8	86	6	24
90	Jordan	..	..	..	3	..	..	6	72	86	10	48
91	Azerbaijan	<0.1 [<0.2]	..	..	19	1	1	109	43	66	1	30
92	Tunisia	<0.1 [<0.2]	..	..	1	..	..	26	92	90	8	62
93	Grenada	..	..	..	..	..	..	8	..	..	..	..
94	China	0.1 [0.1-0.2]	..	..	1	..	..	272	27	96	4	67
95	Dominica	..	..	..	..	..	..	23	36	100	..	..
96	Sri Lanka	<0.1 [<0.2]	..	44	1,110	..	..	73	79	80	2	26
97	Georgia	0.2 [0.1-0.4]	0	..	5	..	..	99	50	67	15	61
98	Dominican Republic	1.7 [0.9-3.0]	12	48	6	..	..	125	43	85	17	24
99	Belize	2.4 [0.8-6.9]	..	..	657	..	..	55	117	66	..	..
100	Ecuador	0.3 [0.1-0.5]	..	..	728	..	..	210	31	82	17	46

HDI rank		HIV prevalence [a] (% ages 15-49) 2003	Condom use at last high-risk sex [b] (% ages 15-24) Women 1996-2002 [h]	Men 1996-2002 [h]	Malaria cases [c] (per 100,000 people) 2000	Children under age 5 With insecticide-treated bed nets (%) 1999-2001 [h]	With fever treated with anti-malarial drugs (%) 1999-2001 [h]	Tuberculosis cases Per 100,000 people [e] 2002	Detected under DOTS (%) [f] 2002	Cured under DOTS (%) [g] 2001	Prevalence of smoking [d] (% of adults) Women 2000	Men 2000
101	Iran, Islamic Rep. of	0.1 [0.1-0.2]	..	..	27	..	..	37	60	84	3	27
102	Occupied Palestinian Territories	..	..	..	..	..	..	38	..	..	..	..
103	El Salvador	0.7 [0.3-1.1]	..	..	11	..	..	83	57	88	12	38
104	Guyana	2.5 [0.8-7.7]	..	..	3,074	8	3	157	11	90	..	..
105	Cape Verde	..	..	..	..	..	..	352	31	42	..	..
106	Syrian Arab Republic	<0.1 [<0.2]	..	..	(.)	..	..	54	42	81	10	51
107	Uzbekistan	0.1 [0.0-0.2]	..	..	1	..	..	134	24	76	9	49
108	Algeria	0.1 [<0.2]	..	..	2 [i]	..	..	51	114	84	7	44
109	Equatorial Guinea	..	..	..	2,744 [j]	1	49	362	..	..	..	..
110	Kyrgyzstan	0.1 [<0.2]	..	..	(.)	..	..	164	45	81	16	60
111	Indonesia	0.1 [0.0-0.2]	..	..	920	0	4	609	30	86	4	59
112	Viet Nam	0.4 [0.2-0.7]	..	..	95	16	7	263	82	93	4	51
113	Moldova, Rep. of	0.2 [0.1-0.3]	..	..	..	..	..	233	19	66	18	46
114	Bolivia	0.1 [0.0-0.2]	8	22	378	..	..	312	75	82	18	43
115	Honduras	1.8 [1.0-3.2]	..	..	541	..	..	98	114	86	11	36
116	Tajikistan	<0.1 [<0.2]	..	..	303	2	69	169	3	..	..	..
117	Mongolia	<0.1 [<0.2]	..	..	..	..	..	270	69	87	26	68
118	Nicaragua	0.2 [0.1-0.3]	17	..	402	..	..	83	85	83	..	..
119	South Africa	[17.8-24.3]	20	..	143	..	..	366	96	65	11	42
120	Egypt	<0.1 [<0.2]	..	..	(.)	..	..	38	53	82	2	35
121	Guatemala	1.1 [0.6-1.8]	..	..	386	1	..	108	45	85	18	38
122	Gabon	8.1 [4.1-15.3]	33	48	2,148 [k]	..	..	307	73	49	..	..
123	São Tomé and Principe	..	..	..	..	23	61	308	..	..	..	..
124	Solomon Islands	..	..	..	15,172	..	..	126	57	89	..	..
125	Morocco	0.1 [0.0-0.2]	..	..	(.)	..	..	100	83	87	2	35
126	Namibia	21.3 [18.2-24.7]	..	..	1,502	..	..	478	76	68	35	65
127	India	[0.4-1.3]	40	51	7	..	..	344	31	85	3	29
128	Botswana	37.3 [35.5-39.1]	75	88	48,704	..	..	338	73	78	..	..
129	Vanuatu	..	..	..	3,260	..	..	147	37	88	..	..
130	Cambodia	2.6 [1.5-4.4]	43	..	476	..	..	734	52	92	8	66
131	Ghana	3.1 [1.9-5.0]	20	33	15,344	..	61	371	41	42	4	28
132	Myanmar	1.2 [0.6-2.2]	..	..	224	..	..	176	73	81	22	44
133	Papua New Guinea	0.6 [0.3-1.0]	..	..	1,688	..	..	543	15	67	28	46
134	Bhutan	..	..	..	285	..	..	205	31	93	..	..
135	Lao People's Dem. Rep.	0.1 [<0.2]	..	..	759	..	..	359	43	77	15	41
136	Comoros	..	..	..	1,930	9	63	121	..	..	..	..
137	Swaziland	38.8 [37.2-40.4]	..	..	2,835	0	26	769	31	36	2	25
138	Bangladesh	[<0.2]	..	..	40	..	..	447	32	84	24	54
139	Sudan	2.3 [0.7-7.2]	..	..	13,934	0	50	346	33	80	1	24
140	Nepal	0.3 [0.2-0.5]	..	52	33	..	..	271	64	88	29	48
141	Cameroon	6.9 [4.8-9.8]	16	31	2,900 [k]	1	66	238	60	62	..	..
Low human development												
142	Pakistan	0.1 [0.0-0.2]	..	..	58	..	..	379	13	77	9	36
143	Togo	4.1 [2.7-6.4]	22	41	7,701 [k]	2	60	688	6	55	..	..
144	Congo	4.9 [2.1-11.0]	12	..	5,880	..	..	435	69	66	..	..
145	Lesotho	28.9 [26.3-31.7]	..	..	0 [i]	..	..	449	61	71	1	39
146	Uganda	4.1 [2.8-6.6]	44	62	46	0	..	550	47	56	17	52
147	Zimbabwe	24.6 [21.7-27.8]	42	69	5,410	..	..	452	46	71	1	34
148	Kenya	6.7 [4.7-9.6]	14	43	545	3	65	579	49	80	32	67
149	Yemen	0.1 [0.0-0.2]	..	..	15,160 [i]	..	..	145	49	80	29	60
150	Madagascar	1.7 [0.8-2.7]	13	..	..	0	61	407	62	69	..	..
151	Nigeria	5.4 [3.6-8.0]	21	38	30	..	..	565	12	79	2	15

HDI rank		HIV prevalence [a] (% ages 15-49) 2003	MDG Condom use at last high-risk sex [b] (% ages 15-24) Women 1996-2002 [h]	Men 1996-2002 [h]	MDG Malaria cases [c] (per 100,000 people) 2000	MDG Children under age 5 With insecticide-treated bed nets (%) 1999-2001 [h]	With fever treated with anti-malarial drugs (%) 1999-2001 [h]	MDG Tuberculosis cases Per 100,000 people [e] 2002	Detected under DOTS (%) [f] 2002	Cured under DOTS (%) [g] 2001	Prevalence of smoking [d] (% of adults) Women 2000	Men 2000
152	Mauritania	0.6 [0.3-1.1]	..	..	11,150 [i]	..	..	437	..	..	..	..
153	Haiti	5.6 [2.5-11.9]	19	30	15 [i]	..	12	392	41	75	9	11
154	Djibouti	..	..	..	715 [i]	..	..	1,161	45	78	..	..
155	Gambia	1.2 [0.3-4.2]	..	..	17,340 [k]	15	55	325	73	71	2	34
156	Eritrea	2.7 [0.9-7.3]	..	..	3,479	..	4	480	14	80	..	..
157	Senegal	0.8 [0.4-1.7]	..	..	11,925	2	36	438	54	53	..	..
158	Timor-Leste	..	..	..	..	..	..	734	59	73	..	..
159	Rwanda	5.1 [3.4-7.6]	23	55	6,510	5	13	598	29	..	4	7
160	Guinea	3.2 [1.2-8.2]	17	32	75,386	..	..	375	54	74	44	60
161	Benin	1.9 [1.1-3.3]	19	34	10,697 [l]	7	60	131	98	79	..	..
162	Tanzania, U. Rep. of	8.8 [6.4-11.9]	21	31	1,207 [i]	2	53	472	43	81	12	50
163	Côte d'Ivoire	7.0 [4.9-10.0]	25	56	12,152	1	58	634	25	73	2	42
164	Zambia	16.5 [13.5-20.0]	33	42	34,204	1	58	588	40	75	10	35
165	Malawi	14.2 [11.3-17.7]	32	38	25,948	3	27	462	36	70	9	20
166	Angola	3.9 [1.6-9.4]	..	..	8,773	2	63	398	91	66	..	..
167	Chad	4.8 [3.1-7.2]	3	2	197 [i]	1	32	388	42	..	..	24
168	Congo, Dem. Rep. of the	4.2 [1.7-9.9]	13	..	2,960 [i]	1	45	594	52	77	6	..
169	Central African Republic	13.5 [8.3-21.2]	..	..	2,207 [m]	2	69	438	49	61	..	..
170	Ethiopia	[3.9-8.5]	17	30	556 [j]	..	3	508	33	76	..	..
171	Mozambique	12.2 [9.4-15.7]	..	..	18,115	..	..	547	45	77	..	..
172	Guinea-Bissau	..	..	..	2,421 [i]	7	58	316	43	51	..	..
173	Burundi	6.0 [4.1-8.8]	..	..	48,098	1	31	531	28	80	..	..
174	Mali	1.9 [0.6-5.9]	14	30	4,008 [k]	..	..	695	15	50	..	..
175	Burkina Faso	4.2 [2.7-6.5]	41	55	619	..	..	272	18	65	..	..
176	Niger	1.2 [0.7-2.3]	..	..	1,693 [k]	1	48	386	..	..	..	..
177	Sierra Leone	..	..	..	..	2	61	628	36	80	..	..
	Developing countries	1.2 [1.0-1.6]	..	..	..	..	..	307	..	..	..	..
	Least developed countries	3.4 [2.6-4.8]	..	..	..	..	..	449	..	..	..	..
	Arab States	0.3 [0.1-0.5]	..	..	..	..	..	131	..	..	..	..
	East Asia and the Pacific	0.2 [0.1-0.3]	..	..	..	..	..	313	..	..	..	..
	Latin America and the Caribbean	0.7 [0.4-1.0]	..	..	..	..	..	92	..	..	..	..
	South Asia	0.6 [0.3-1.0]	..	..	..	..	..	343	..	..	..	..
	Sub-Saharan Africa	7.7 [6.3-9.7]	..	..	..	..	..	495	..	..	..	..
	Central & Eastern Europe & CIS	0.6 [0.3-0.9]	..	..	..	..	..	132	..	..	..	..
	OECD	0.3 [0.2-0.5]	..	..	..	..	..	25	..	..	..	..
	High-income OECD	..	..	..	..	..	..	21	..	..	..	..
	High human development	0.3 [0.2-0.5]	..	..	..	..	..	26	..	..	..	..
	Medium human development	0.7 [0.5-1.0]	..	..	..	..	..	278	..	..	..	..
	Low human development	5.0 [4.0-6.6]	..	..	..	..	..	480	..	..	..	..
	High income	0.3 [0.2-0.5]	..	..	..	..	..	22	..	..	..	..
	Middle income	0.7 [0.5-0.8]	..	..	..	..	..	197	..	..	..	..
	Low income	1.8 [1.2-2.9]	..	..	..	..	..	405	..	..	..	..
	World	1.1 [0.9-1.5]	..	..	..	..	..	257	..	..	..	..

a. Data refer to point and range estimates based on new estimation models developed by the Joint United Nations Programme on HIV/AIDS (UNAIDS). Range estimates are presented in square brackets. b. Because of data limitations, comparisons across countries should be made with caution. Data for some countries may refer to only part of the country or differ from the standard definition. c. Data refer to malaria cases reported to the World Health Organization (WHO) and may represent only a fraction of the true number in a country. d. The age range varies across countries but in most is 18 and older or 15 and older. e. Data refer to the prevalence of all forms of tuberculosis. f. Calculated by dividing the new smear-positive cases of tuberculosis detected under the directly observed treatment, short course (DOTS) case detection and treatment strategy by the estimated annual incidence of new smear-positive cases. Values can exceed 100% because of intense case detection in an area with a backlog of chronic cases, overreporting (for example, double counting), overdiagnosis or underestimation of incidence (WHO 2003). g. Data refer to the percentage of new smear-positive cases registered for treatment under the DOTS case detection and treatment strategy in 2001 that were successfully treated. h. Data refer to the most recent year available during the period specified. i. Data refer to 1999. j. Data refer to 1995. k. Data refer to 1998. l. Data refer to 1997. m. Data refer to 1994.

Source: Column 1: UNAIDS 2004; aggregates calculated for the Human Development Report Office by the UNAIDS; *columns 2 and 3:* UNICEF 2003b, based on data from a joint effort by the United Nations Children's Fund (UNICEF), UNAIDS and the WHO; *column 4:* UN 2004e, based on data from the WHO; *columns 5 and 6:* UNICEF 2003b; *columns 7-9:* WHO 2004e; *columns 10 and 11:* World Bank 2004f, based on data from the WHO and the National Tobacco Information Online System.

		Life expectancy at birth (years)		MDG Infant mortality rate (per 1,000 live births)		MDG Under-five mortality rate (per 1,000 live births)		Probability at birth of surviving to age 65 [a]		MDG Maternal mortality [b]	
								Female (% of cohort)	Male (% of cohort)	Ratio reported (per 100,000 live births)	Ratio adjusted (per 100,000 live births)
HDI rank		1970-75 [c]	2000-05 [c]	1970	2002	1970	2002	2000-05 [c]	2000-05 [c]	1985-2002 [d]	2000
High human development											
1	Norway	74.4	78.9	13	4	15	4	90.8	83.5	6	16
2	Sweden	74.7	80.1	11	3	15	3	91.6	86.1	5	2
3	Australia	71.7	79.2	17	6	20	6	90.7	83.8	..	8
4	Canada	73.2	79.3	19	5	23	7	90.1	83.9	..	6
5	Netherlands	74.0	78.3	13	5	15	5	89.7	83.5	7	16
6	Belgium	71.4	78.8	21	5	29	6	90.4	82.5	..	10
7	Iceland	74.3	79.8	13	3	14	4	90.7	85.9	..	0
8	United States	71.5	77.1	20	7	26	8	86.4	78.1	8	17
9	Japan	73.3	81.6	14	3	21	5	93.0	85.0	8	10
10	Ireland	71.3	77.0	20	6	27	6	89.0	82.0	6	5
11	Switzerland	73.8	79.1	15	5	18	6	91.0	82.9	5	7
12	United Kingdom	72.0	78.2	18	5	23	7	89.4	83.2	7	13
13	Finland	70.7	78.0	13	4	16	5	91.1	79.9	6	6
14	Austria	70.6	78.5	26	5	33	5	90.7	81.6	..	4
15	Luxembourg	70.7	78.4	19	5	26	5	89.8	82.7	0	28
16	France	72.4	79.0	18	4	24	6	91.0	80.2	10	17
17	Denmark	73.6	76.6	14	4	19	4	86.5	79.8	10	5
18	New Zealand	71.7	78.3	17	6	20	6	88.3	82.6	15	7
19	Germany	71.0	78.3	22	4	26	5	90.2	81.7	8	8
20	Spain	72.9	79.3	27	4	34	6	92.2	82.3	0	4
21	Italy	72.1	78.7	30	4	33	6	91.4	82.4	7	5
22	Israel	71.6	79.2	24	6	27	6	90.5	86.2	5	17
23	Hong Kong, China (SAR)	72.0	79.9	..	..	..	..	92.3	84.4	..	..
24	Greece	72.3	78.3	38	5	54	5	91.5	82.3	1	9
25	Singapore	69.5	78.1	22	3	27	4	90.5	83.3	6	30
26	Portugal	68.0	76.2	53	5	62	6	89.3	77.4	8	5
27	Slovenia	69.8	76.3	25	4	29	5	88.7	76.2	17	17
28	Korea, Rep. of	62.6	75.5	43	5	54	5	89.0	73.9	20	20
29	Barbados	69.4	77.2	40	12	54	14	89.0	82.2	0	95
30	Cyprus	71.4	78.3	29	5	33	6	90.8	83.9	0	47
31	Malta	70.6	78.4	25	5	32	5	90.2	85.5	..	0
32	Czech Republic	70.1	75.4	21	4	24	5	88.3	74.8	3	9
33	Brunei Darussalam	68.3	76.3	58	6	78	6	87.9	84.8	0	37
34	Argentina	67.1	74.2	59	16	71	19	85.3	72.3	41	82
35	Seychelles	..	..	..	12	..	16	..	..	..	..
36	Estonia	70.5	71.7	21	10	26	12	83.7	59.9	46	63
37	Poland	70.5	73.9	32	8	36	9	86.5	68.8	4	13
38	Hungary	69.3	71.9	36	8	39	9	82.6	62.7	5	16
39	Saint Kitts and Nevis	..	..	..	20	..	24	..	..	130	..
40	Bahrain	63.3	74.0	55	13	75	16	84.8	78.1	46	28
41	Lithuania	71.3	72.7	23	8	28	9	84.9	62.8	13	13
42	Slovakia	70.0	73.7	25	8	29	9	86.5	68.9	16	3
43	Chile	63.4	76.1	78	10	98	12	86.3	76.8	23	31
44	Kuwait	67.0	76.6	49	9	59	10	87.2	82.3	5	5
45	Costa Rica	67.8	78.1	62	9	83	11	88.3	81.1	29	43
46	Uruguay	68.7	75.3	48	14	57	15	85.8	73.2	26	27
47	Qatar	62.1	72.2	45	11	65	16	80.3	72.8	5	7
48	Croatia	69.6	74.2	34	7	42	8	86.3	71.1	2	8
49	United Arab Emirates	62.2	74.7	61	8	83	9	86.6	80.0	3	54
50	Latvia	70.1	71.0	21	17	26	21	82.8	59.2	25	42

HDI rank		Life expectancy at birth (years)		MDG Infant mortality rate (per 1,000 live births)		MDG Under-five mortality rate (per 1,000 live births)		Probability at birth of surviving to age 65[a] Female (% of cohort)	Male (% of cohort)	MDG Maternal mortality[b] Ratio reported (per 100,000 live births)	Ratio adjusted (per 100,000 live births)
		1970-75[c]	2000-05[c]	1970	2002	1970	2002	2000-05[c]	2000-05[c]	1985-2002[d]	2000
51	Bahamas	66.5	67.1	38	13	49	16	69.6	56.8	..	60
52	Cuba	70.7	76.7	34	7	43	9	85.1	79.1	30	33
53	Mexico	62.4	73.4	79	24	110	29	82.1	71.5	79	83
54	Trinidad and Tobago	65.9	71.3	49	17	57	20	78.8	67.5	70	160
55	Antigua and Barbuda	..	..	..	12	..	14	..	..	150	..
Medium human development											
56	Bulgaria	71.0	70.9	28	14	32	16	83.2	64.9	15	32
57	Russian Federation	69.7	66.8	29	18	36	21	78.0	48.4	37	67
58	Libyan Arab Jamahiriya	52.8	72.8	105	16	160	19	81.5	73.4	77	97
59	Malaysia	63.0	73.1	46	8	63	8	83.9	73.3	30	41
60	Macedonia, TFYR	67.5	73.6	85	22	120	26	84.1	75.8	15	23
61	Panama	66.2	74.7	46	19	68	25	85.1	76.3	70	160
62	Belarus	71.5	70.1	22	17	27	20	81.6	56.4	14	35
63	Tonga	62.6	68.6	..	16	..	20	73.0	69.9	..	..
64	Mauritius	62.9	72.0	64	17	86	19	82.4	66.6	21	24
65	Albania	67.7	73.7	68	26	82	30	87.7	80.1	20	55
66	Bosnia and Herzegovina	67.5	74.0	60	15	82	18	85.2	74.1	10	31
67	Suriname	64.0	71.1	..	31	..	40	79.6	68.4	110	110
68	Venezuela	65.7	73.7	47	19	61	22	83.5	73.2	60	96
69	Romania	69.2	70.5	46	19	57	21	81.5	63.7	34	49
70	Ukraine	70.1	69.7	22	16	27	20	81.1	56.5	18	35
71	Saint Lucia	65.3	72.5	..	17	..	19	77.4	71.2	30	..
72	Brazil	59.5	68.1	95	30	135	36	76.5	59.7	160	260
73	Colombia	61.6	72.2	69	19	108	23	80.8	70.9	78	130
74	Oman	52.1	72.4	126	11	200	13	82.4	75.4	23	87
75	Samoa (Western)	56.1	70.0	106	20	160	25	78.2	65.1	..	130
76	Thailand	61.0	69.3	74	24	102	28	79.9	62.4	36	44
77	Saudi Arabia	53.9	72.3	118	23	185	28	81.1	75.7	..	23
78	Kazakhstan	64.4	66.3	..	61	..	76	76.7	53.1	50	210
79	Jamaica	69.0	75.7	49	17	64	20	85.4	78.9	97	87
80	Lebanon	65.0	73.5	45	28	54	32	83.6	77.2	100	150
81	Fiji	60.6	69.8	50	17	61	21	75.1	67.3	38	75
82	Armenia	72.5	72.4	..	30	..	35	85.4	70.3	22	55
83	Philippines	58.1	70.0	60	29	90	38	78.0	69.9	170	200
84	Maldives	51.4	67.4	157	58	255	77	69.5	69.5	350	110
85	Peru	55.4	69.8	115	30	178	39	77.0	68.0	190	410
86	Turkmenistan	60.7	67.1	..	76	..	98	74.2	60.6	9	31
87	St. Vincent & the Grenadines	61.6	74.1	..	22	..	25	84.2	78.6	93	..
88	Turkey	57.9	70.5	150	36	201	42	81.0	71.0	130	70
89	Paraguay	65.9	70.9	57	26	76	30	79.8	71.4	190	170
90	Jordan	56.5	71.0	77	27	107	33	77.3	71.2	41	41
91	Azerbaijan	69.0	72.2	..	74	..	105	81.3	68.0	25	94
92	Tunisia	55.6	72.8	135	21	201	26	84.6	75.2	69	120
93	Grenada	..	..	..	20	..	25	..	..	1	..
94	China	63.2	71.0	85	31	120	39	81.3	72.7	53	56
95	Dominica	..	..	..	13	..	15	..	..	67	..
96	Sri Lanka	65.1	72.6	65	17	100	19	84.6	73.5	92	92
97	Georgia	69.2	73.6	36	24	46	29	85.6	69.2	67	32
98	Dominican Republic	59.7	66.7	91	32	128	38	72.0	62.3	230	150
99	Belize	67.6	71.4	56	34	77	40	77.9	72.5	140	140
100	Ecuador	58.8	70.8	87	25	140	29	78.6	70.3	160	130

HDI rank		Life expectancy at birth (years)		MDG Infant mortality rate (per 1,000 live births)		MDG Under-five mortality rate (per 1,000 live births)		Probability at birth of surviving to age 65[a] Female (% of cohort)	Male (% of cohort)	MDG Maternal mortality[b] Ratio reported (per 100,000 live births)	Ratio adjusted (per 100,000 live births)
		1970-75[c]	2000-05[c]	1970	2002	1970	2002	2000-05[c]	2000-05[c]	1985-2002[d]	2000
101	Iran, Islamic Rep. of	55.3	70.3	122	35	191	42	79.5	71.8	37	76
102	Occupied Palestinian Territories	56.6	72.4	..	23	..	25	81.6	75.1	..	100
103	El Salvador	58.2	70.7	111	33	162	39	77.6	67.3	120	150
104	Guyana	60.0	63.2	81	54	101	72	67.1	54.8	190	170
105	Cape Verde	57.5	70.2	..	29	..	38	79.5	68.1	76	150
106	Syrian Arab Republic	57.0	71.9	90	23	129	28	80.0	74.7	110	160
107	Uzbekistan	64.2	69.7	..	52	..	68	76.9	65.7	34	24
108	Algeria	54.5	69.7	143	39	234	49	76.9	72.8	140	140
109	Equatorial Guinea	40.5	49.1	165	101	281	152	44.2	39.2	..	880
110	Kyrgyzstan	63.1	68.6	111	52	146	61	77.2	61.5	44	110
111	Indonesia	49.2	66.8	104	33	172	45	72.5	64.2	380	230
112	Viet Nam	50.3	69.2	55	30	81	39	77.2	68.8	95	130
113	Moldova, Rep. of	64.8	68.9	46	27	61	32	76.4	60.2	44	36
114	Bolivia	46.7	63.9	147	56	243	71	68.0	60.0	390	420
115	Honduras	53.8	68.9	116	32	170	42	73.4	65.4	110	110
116	Tajikistan	63.4	68.8	78	53	111	72	75.4	66.2	45	100
117	Mongolia	53.8	63.9	..	58	..	71	67.4	57.6	160	110
118	Nicaragua	55.1	69.5	113	32	165	41	75.2	66.5	120	230
119	South Africa	53.7	47.7	..	52	..	65	37.4	24.9	150	230
120	Egypt	52.1	68.8	157	35	235	41	78.0	67.9	84	84
121	Guatemala	53.7	65.8	115	36	168	49	70.5	59.0	190	240
122	Gabon	48.7	56.6	..	60	..	91	52.0	48.6	520	420
123	São Tomé and Principe	56.5	69.9	..	75	..	118	79.1	68.9	..	..
124	Solomon Islands	55.6	69.2	71	20	99	24	76.0	70.2	550	130
125	Morocco	52.9	68.7	119	39	184	43	77.1	69.4	230	220
126	Namibia	49.9	44.3	104	55	155	67	30.8	24.7	270	300
127	India	50.3	63.9	127	67	202	93	67.5	61.9	540	540
128	Botswana	56.1	39.7	99	80	142	110	21.7	17.3	330	100
129	Vanuatu	54.0	68.8	107	34	160	42	73.1	66.3	68	130
130	Cambodia	40.3	57.4	..	96	..	138	56.9	47.6	440	450
131	Ghana	49.9	57.9	112	57	190	100	55.8	50.1	210	540
132	Myanmar	49.3	57.3	122	77	179	109	58.9	47.7	230	360
133	Papua New Guinea	44.7	57.6	106	70	147	94	51.5	45.0	370	300
134	Bhutan	43.2	63.2	156	74	267	94	66.1	61.1	260	420
135	Lao People's Dem. Rep.	40.4	54.5	145	87	218	100	52.9	47.8	530	650
136	Comoros	48.9	60.8	159	59	215	79	61.8	55.3	..	480
137	Swaziland	47.3	34.4	132	106	196	149	15.2	11.0	230	370
138	Bangladesh	45.2	61.4	145	51	239	77	61.1	57.9	380	380
139	Sudan	43.6	55.6	104	64	172	94	54.6	48.3	550	590
140	Nepal	43.3	59.9	165	66	250	91	57.6	56.4	540	740
141	Cameroon	45.7	46.2	127	95	215	166	36.8	31.7	430	730
Low human development											
142	Pakistan	49.0	61.0	120	83	181	107	61.9	60.0	530	500
143	Togo	45.5	49.7	128	79	216	141	42.6	36.9	480	570
144	Congo	55.0	48.2	100	81	160	108	37.5	31.1	..	510
145	Lesotho	49.5	35.1	128	64	190	87	19.2	8.5	..	550
146	Uganda	46.3	46.2	100	82	170	141	33.5	30.6	510	880
147	Zimbabwe	56.0	33.1	86	76	138	123	8.3	9.2	700	1,100
148	Kenya	50.9	44.6	96	78	156	122	30.6	26.1	590	1,000
149	Yemen	39.8	60.0	194	79	303	107	60.0	54.5	350	570
150	Madagascar	44.9	53.6	109	84	180	136	51.5	46.7	490	550
151	Nigeria	44.0	51.5	120	110	201	183	44.5	42.0	..	800

HDI rank		Life expectancy at birth (years)		MDG Infant mortality rate (per 1,000 live births)		MDG Under-five mortality rate (per 1,000 live births)		Probability at birth of surviving to age 65 [a] Female (% of cohort)	Male (% of cohort)	MDG Maternal mortality [b] Ratio reported (per 100,000 live births)	Ratio adjusted (per 100,000 live births)
		1970-75 [c]	2000-05 [c]	1970	2002	1970	2002	2000-05 [c]	2000-05 [c]	1985-2002 [d]	2000
152	Mauritania	43.4	52.5	150	120	250	183	50.5	44.4	750	1,000
153	Haiti	48.5	49.5	148	79	221	123	36.1	34.5	520	680
154	Djibouti	41.0	45.7	160	100	241	143	37.1	33.2	74	730
155	Gambia	38.0	54.1	183	91	319	126	51.3	45.8	..	540
156	Eritrea	44.3	52.7	..	47	..	89	43.7	35.4	1,000	630
157	Senegal	41.8	52.9	164	79	279	138	52.5	40.0	560	690
158	Timor-Leste	40.0	49.5	..	89	..	126	44.0	39.1	..	660
159	Rwanda	44.6	39.3	124	96	209	183	24.1	22.7	1,100	1,400
160	Guinea	37.3	49.1	197	109	345	169	42.8	40.3	530	740
161	Benin	44.0	50.6	149	93	252	156	47.8	38.8	500	850
162	Tanzania, U. Rep. of	46.5	43.3	129	104	218	165	29.2	26.1	530	1,500
163	Côte d'Ivoire	45.4	41.0	158	102	239	176	25.5	24.8	600	690
164	Zambia	49.7	32.4	109	108	181	192	10.6	11.3	650	750
165	Malawi	41.0	37.5	189	114	330	183	21.3	19.7	1,100	1,800
166	Angola	38.0	40.1	180	154	300	260	31.1	26.4	..	1,700
167	Chad	39.0	44.7	..	117	..	200	36.4	32.4	830	1,100
168	Congo, Dem. Rep. of the	45.8	41.8	148	129	245	205	31.4	27.9	950	990
169	Central African Republic	43.0	39.5	149	115	248	180	24.0	21.0	1,100	1,100
170	Ethiopia	41.8	45.5	160	114	239	171	35.8	32.3	870	850
171	Mozambique	41.1	38.1	163	125	278	197	26.3	19.8	1,100	1,000
172	Guinea-Bissau	36.5	45.3	..	130	..	211	39.4	33.7	910	1,100
173	Burundi	43.9	40.9	138	114	233	190	26.6	25.1	..	1,000
174	Mali	38.2	48.6	225	122	400	222	41.0	37.3	580	1,200
175	Burkina Faso	41.2	45.7	163	107	290	207	34.5	32.1	480	1,000
176	Niger	38.2	46.2	197	156	330	265	39.9	37.6	590	1,600
177	Sierra Leone	35.0	34.2	206	165	363	284	23.5	19.4	1,800	2,000
	Developing countries	55.5	64.7	108	61	166	89	69.2	62.0	..	..
	Least developed countries	43.8	50.7	150	99	244	157	44.7	40.7	..	..
	Arab States	51.9	66.4	128	48	197	62	72.5	65.6	..	..
	East Asia and the Pacific	60.5	69.9	84	32	122	42	79.0	70.0	..	..
	Latin America and the Caribbean	61.1	70.6	86	27	123	34	78.7	66.5	..	..
	South Asia	49.8	63.3	129	69	206	95	66.4	61.4	..	..
	Sub-Saharan Africa	45.2	46.1	139	108	231	178	36.1	32.0	..	..
	Central & Eastern Europe & CIS	69.2	69.6	34	18	43	22	80.6	58.8	..	..
	OECD	70.4	77.2	40	11	53	14	88.1	78.7	..	..
	High-income OECD	71.6	78.4	22	5	28	7	89.5	80.9	..	..
	High human development	70.7	77.5	32	9	42	11	88.4	78.9	..	..
	Medium human development	57.8	67.3	102	45	154	61	74.3	65.2	..	..
	Low human development	45.0	49.1	138	104	225	164	41.2	38.5	..	..
	High income	71.6	78.4	22	5	28	7	89.5	80.9	..	..
	Middle income	62.9	70.1	85	30	121	37	79.5	68.4	..	..
	Low income	48.7	59.2	126	80	202	120	59.1	54.1	..	..
	World	59.8	66.9	96	56	146	81	72.9	64.4	..	..

a. Data refer to the probability at birth of surviving to age 65, multiplied by 100. b. Annual number of deaths of women from pregnancy-related causes. The reported column shows figures reported by national authorities. The adjusted column shows results of adjusted figures based on reviews by the United Nations Children's Fund (UNICEF), World Health Organization (WHO) and United Nations Population Fund (UNFPA) to account for well-documented problems of underreporting and misclassification. c. Data refer to estimates for the period specified. d. Data refer to the most recent year available during the period specified.
Source: Columns 1, 2, 7 and 8: UN 2003; columns 3 and 5: UNICEF 2004; columns 4, 6, 9 and 10: UNICEF 2003b.

10 Commitment to education: public spending

HDI rank	Public expenditure on education [a] As % of GDP		Public expenditure on education [a] As % of total government expenditure		Public expenditure on education by level [b] (% of all levels) Pre-primary and primary		Public expenditure on education by level [b] (% of all levels) Secondary		Public expenditure on education by level [b] (% of all levels) Tertiary	
	1990[c]	1999-2001[d]	1990[c]	1999-2001[d]	1990[c]	1999-2001[d]	1990[c]	1999-2001[d]	1990[c]	1999-2001[d]
High human development										
1 Norway	7.1	6.8	14.6	16.2	39.5	48.3	24.7	20.6 [e]	15.2	25.4
2 Sweden	7.4	7.6	13.8	..	47.7	33.8	19.6	37.7	13.2	28.0
3 Australia	5.1	4.6	14.8	13.8	2.2	35.4	57.4	40.1	32.0	22.9
4 Canada	6.5	5.2	14.2	..	..	..	62.2	..	28.6	35.7
5 Netherlands	6.0	5.0	14.8	10.4	21.5	33.7	37.7	39.7	32.1	26.5
6 Belgium	5.0	5.8 [e]	..	11.6	23.3	33.3 [e]	42.9	45.0 [e]	16.5	19.2 [e]
7 Iceland	5.4	6.0 [e]	..	..	59.5	..	25.6	..	14.9	..
8 United States	5.2	5.6	12.3	15.5	..	39.2	..	34.5	..	26.3
9 Japan	..	3.6	..	10.5	..	37.8	..	39.8	..	15.1
10 Ireland	5.2	4.3	10.2	13.5	37.8	30.9	40.1	34.1	20.4	30.3
11 Switzerland	5.1	5.6	18.7	..	49.9	35.3	25.1	39.0	19.7	23.1
12 United Kingdom	4.9	4.6	..	..	29.7	34.4	43.8	48.4	19.6	17.2
13 Finland	5.6	6.3	11.9	12.2	27.9	27.0	39.4	40.0	23.9	32.9
14 Austria	5.4	5.9	7.6	11.0	23.7	27.0	46.6	45.0	19.1	24.0
15 Luxembourg	3.0	4.1	10.4	8.5 [e]	..	..	..	..	..	..
16 France	5.4	5.7	..	11.4	27.3	31.2	40.7	49.8	13.8	17.6
17 Denmark	..	8.3	..	15.3	..	29.6	..	36.7	..	30.0
18 New Zealand	6.2	6.6	..	..	30.5	30.6	25.3	40.1	37.4	24.7
19 Germany	..	4.6	..	9.9	..	22.8	..	49.0	..	24.5
20 Spain	4.4	4.4	9.4	..	29.3	35.4	45.0	41.8	15.4	22.8
21 Italy	3.1	5.0	..	9.5	33.0	33.8	63.2	48.7	..	16.4
22 Israel	6.3	7.3	11.3	..	43.0	45.2	31.3	29.7	16.2	17.9
23 Hong Kong, China (SAR)	..	4.1	..	21.9	26.6	25.1	38.8	32.7	30.8	33.2
24 Greece	2.5	3.8	..	7.0	34.1	30.2	45.1	40.7	19.5	24.0
25 Singapore	..	..	..	..	29.6	..	36.5	..	29.3	..
26 Portugal	4.2	5.8	..	12.7	44.6	35.2	32.5	43.0	16.3	18.1
27 Slovenia	..	..	..	..	..	..	..	..	..	..
28 Korea, Rep. of	3.5	3.6	22.4	17.4	44.4	42.3	34.1	37.3	7.4	13.5
29 Barbados	7.8	6.5	22.2	16.7	37.5	33.4 [e]	37.6	33.9	19.2	29.9
30 Cyprus	3.5	5.6	11.3	..	38.5	32.6	50.3	50.3	3.8	17.1
31 Malta	4.3	4.9 [e]	8.3	..	25.1	..	44.7	..	14.6	..
32 Czech Republic	..	4.4	..	9.7	..	26.4	..	50.5	..	19.3
33 Brunei Darussalam	..	..	..	9.1 [e]	24.1	..	26.1	..	9.5	..
34 Argentina	1.1	4.6 [e]	10.9	13.7 [e]	3.4	43.3 [e]	44.9	35.6 [e]	46.7	18.4 [e]
35 Seychelles	7.8	7.5 [e]	14.8	..	28.2	..	40.7	..	9.5	..
36 Estonia	..	7.4	..	..	..	44.5	..	34.1	..	16.8
37 Poland	..	5.4	..	12.2	42.8	44.8	17.5	38.0	22.0	16.0
38 Hungary	5.8	5.1	7.8	14.1	55.4	32.0	23.9	38.8	15.2	21.6
39 Saint Kitts and Nevis	2.7	7.7	..	14.7	..	28.5	..	31.5	..	21.2
40 Bahrain	4.2	..	14.6	..	..	..	45.8	..	..	..
41 Lithuania	4.6	..	13.8	..	..	..	..	..	..	..
42 Slovakia	5.1	4.1	..	13.8	..	25.8	..	51.3	..	20.5
43 Chile	2.5	3.9	10.4	17.5	60.1	51.2	17.3	34.3	20.3	14.5
44 Kuwait	4.8	..	3.4	..	53.4	..	13.6	..	16.0	..
45 Costa Rica	4.4	4.7	20.8	21.1	..	50.1	..	30.7	..	19.2
46 Uruguay	3.0	2.5	15.9	11.8	37.5	39.2	30.3	31.5	22.6	29.2
47 Qatar	3.5	..	..	..	..	..	..	..	..	..
48 Croatia	..	4.2 [e]	..	..	..	..	..	..	..	..
49 United Arab Emirates	1.9	..	14.6	..	..	51.9	..	46.4	..	..
50 Latvia	3.8	5.9	10.8	..	11.2	33.3	56.3	48.7	11.6	16.3

		Public expenditure on education [a]			Public expenditure on education by level [b] (% of all levels)					
		As % of GDP		As % of total government expenditure		Pre-primary and primary		Secondary		Tertiary	
HDI rank		1990 [c]	1999-2001 [d]	1990 [c]	1999-2001 [d]	1990 [c]	1999-2001 [d]	1990 [c]	1999-2001 [d]	1990 [c]	1999-2001 [d]
51	Bahamas	4.0	..	17.8	..	..	..	..	..	..	..
52	Cuba	..	8.5	12.3	16.8	25.7	39.4	39.0	36.4	14.4	17.1
53	Mexico	3.6	5.1	12.8	22.6	32.3	48.6	29.6	34.4	16.5	14.5
54	Trinidad and Tobago	3.6	4.0	11.6	16.7 [e]	42.5	59.6 [e]	36.8	32.3 [e]	11.9	3.7 [e]
55	Antigua and Barbuda	..	3.2	..	..	..	36.9 [e]	..	37.3 [e]	..	15.1 [e]
Medium human development											
56	Bulgaria	5.2	..	..	..	70.7	..	..	..	13.9	..
57	Russian Federation	3.5	3.1	..	10.6	..	..	..	..	..	..
58	Libyan Arab Jamahiriya	..	2.7	..	..	..	17.8 [e]	..	14.2 [e]	..	52.7
59	Malaysia	5.2	7.9	18.3	20.0	34.3	28.1	34.4	34.5	19.9	32.1
60	Macedonia, TFYR	..	4.1 [e]	..	..	..	..	..	..	..	..
61	Panama	4.7	4.3	20.9	7.5 [e]	37.0	40.8 [e]	23.3	33.9 [e]	21.3	25.3 [e]
62	Belarus	4.9	6.0	..	..	57.7	..	16.2	..	14.4	..
63	Tonga	..	5.0	..	14.0 [e]	..	49.2 [f]	..	28.9	..	..
64	Mauritius	3.5	3.3	11.8	13.3	37.7	32.0	36.4	38.3	16.6	15.6
65	Albania	5.8	..	..	..	..	..	..	..	..	..
66	Bosnia and Herzegovina	..	..	..	..	..	..	..	..	..	..
67	Suriname	8.1	..	..	..	60.5	..	14.5	..	8.8	..
68	Venezuela	3.0	..	12.0	..	23.5	..	4.5	..	40.7	..
69	Romania	2.8	3.5 [e]	7.3	..	52.1	..	22.1	..	9.6	..
70	Ukraine	5.2	4.2	19.7	15.0	54.9	..	15.0	..	15.1	..
71	Saint Lucia	..	7.3 [e]	..	20.7 [e]	48.2	..	23.3	..	12.8	..
72	Brazil	..	4.0	..	10.4	..	38.7	..	37.6	..	21.6
73	Colombia	2.5	4.4	16.0	18.0 [e]	39.3	47.0	30.9	33.1	20.7	19.9
74	Oman	3.1	4.2 [e]	11.1	..	54.1	36.4 [e, f]	37.0	51.4 [e]	7.4	1.8 [e]
75	Samoa (Western)	3.4	4.5 [e]	10.7	14.6	52.6	43.0	25.2	23.8	0.0	33.2
76	Thailand	3.5	5.0	20.0	31.0	56.2	42.3	21.6	20.5	14.6	21.7
77	Saudi Arabia	6.5	..	17.8	..	78.8	..	..	..	21.2	..
78	Kazakhstan	3.2	..	17.6	..	..	..	..	..	..	..
79	Jamaica	4.7	6.3	12.8	12.3	37.4	36.8	33.2	33.8	21.1	19.2
80	Lebanon	..	2.9	..	11.1	..	..	..	..	..	..
81	Fiji	4.6	5.5 [e]	..	19.4 [e]	..	35.0 [e, f]	..	48.9 [e]	..	16.0 [e]
82	Armenia	7.0	3.2	20.5	..	..	..	..	..	..	29.8
83	Philippines	2.9	3.2	10.1	..	..	60.6	..	21.9	..	13.7
84	Maldives	4.0	..	10.0	..	..	..	..	..	..	..
85	Peru	2.2	3.3	..	21.1	..	..	..	..	..	..
86	Turkmenistan	4.3	..	21.0	..	..	..	..	..	..	..
87	St. Vincent & the Grenadines	6.4	9.3	13.8	13.4 [e]	..	48.9	..	25.5	..	5.2
88	Turkey	2.2	3.7	..	..	58.1	37.8 [e, f]	29.4	30.1	..	32.2
89	Paraguay	1.1	4.7 [e]	9.1	11.2 [e]	..	53.9 [e]	22.6	29.0 [e]	25.8	17.1 [e]
90	Jordan	8.4	4.6	17.1	20.6	..	51.7	62.4	48.3	35.1	..
91	Azerbaijan	..	3.5	23.5	23.1	..	..	..	..	..	8.3
92	Tunisia	6.0	6.8 [e]	13.5	17.4 [e]	39.8	33.3 [e, f]	36.4	45.0 [e]	18.5	21.7 [e]
93	Grenada	5.1	..	13.2	..	64.1	..	31.7	..	0.0	..
94	China	2.3	..	12.8	..	..	..	..	..	..	..
95	Dominica	..	5.0 [e]	..	..	..	64.4 [e]	..	30.1 [e]	..	..
96	Sri Lanka	2.6	1.3	8.1	..	..	..	84.3	..	13.4	..
97	Georgia	..	2.5	..	13.1	..	..	..	..	..	..
98	Dominican Republic	..	2.4	..	13.2	..	46.3 [e]	..	18.9 [e]	..	10.9
99	Belize	4.7	6.2	18.5	20.9	61.0	44.9	20.2	35.1	8.1	16.2
100	Ecuador	2.8	1.0 [e]	17.2	8.0 [e]	34.4	45.3 [e]	34.2	44.5 [e]	18.3	9.1 [e]

| HDI rank | | Public expenditure on education [a] | | | | Public expenditure on education by level [b] (% of all levels) | | | | | |
| | | As % of GDP | | As % of total government expenditure | | Pre-primary and primary | | Secondary | | Tertiary | |
		1990 [c]	1999-2001 [d]	1990 [c]	1999-2001 [d]	1990 [c]	1999-2001 [d]	1990 [c]	1999-2001 [d]	1990 [c]	1999-2001 [d]
101	Iran, Islamic Rep. of	4.1	5.0	22.4	21.7	33.2	26.8	39.2	36.3	13.6	18.5
102	Occupied Palestinian Territories	..	..	..	..	..	..	..	..	..	..
103	El Salvador	1.9	2.5 e	16.6	19.4 e	..	61.2 e	..	20.8 e	..	6.7
104	Guyana	3.4	4.1 e	4.4	8.6 e	..	..	..	..	..	..
105	Cape Verde	..	..	..	..	..	..	..	..	..	..
106	Syrian Arab Republic	4.1	4.0	17.3	11.1	38.5	..	28.2	39.2	21.3	..
107	Uzbekistan	..	..	20.4	..	..	..	..	..	..	..
108	Algeria	5.3	..	21.1	..	..	..	..	..	..	..
109	Equatorial Guinea	..	0.5	..	1.6	..	39.1 e	..	30.7 e	..	30.1 e
110	Kyrgyzstan	8.3	3.1	22.5	18.6	8.5	..	57.9	..	10.0	..
111	Indonesia	1.0	1.3	..	9.8	..	37.8	..	38.8	..	23.4
112	Viet Nam	..	..	7.5	..	..	..	..	..	..	..
113	Moldova, Rep. of	..	4.0	..	15.0	..	..	..	..	..	..
114	Bolivia	2.3	6.0	..	18.4	..	38.1	..	19.0	..	26.6
115	Honduras	..	..	..	..	..	..	..	..	..	..
116	Tajikistan	9.7	2.4	24.7	..	6.9	..	57.0	..	9.1	..
117	Mongolia	12.1	6.5 e	17.6	..	13.9	..	48.8	..	14.5	..
118	Nicaragua	3.4	..	9.7	13.8	..	47.5 f	..	..	..	..
119	South Africa	6.2	5.7	..	..	75.6	47.2	..	31.3	21.5	14.5
120	Egypt	3.7	..	..	..	..	..	..	..	..	..
121	Guatemala	1.4	1.7	11.8	11.4	31.1	..	12.9	..	21.2	..
122	Gabon	..	3.9 e	..	..	..	35.6 e	..	38.9 e	..	25.5 e
123	São Tomé and Principe	..	..	..	..	..	..	..	..	..	..
124	Solomon Islands	..	3.5 e	..	15.4 e	..	..	..	..	..	..
125	Morocco	5.3	5.1	26.1	..	34.8	48.0 f	48.9	51.5	16.2	0.3
126	Namibia	7.6	7.9	..	21.0	..	59.0	..	27.2	..	12.0
127	India	3.9	4.1	12.2	12.7	38.9	38.4	27.0	40.1	14.9	20.3
128	Botswana	6.7	2.1	17.0	25.6	..	53.2	..	23.8	..	18.6
129	Vanuatu	4.6	10.5	..	26.7	59.8	27.9	26.6	57.4	3.4	10.5
130	Cambodia	..	2.0	..	15.3	..	75.5	..	11.2	..	5.0
131	Ghana	3.2	4.1 e	24.3	..	29.2	..	34.3	..	11.0	..
132	Myanmar	..	1.3	..	18.1 e	..	46.6 e, f	..	27.0 e	..	26.4
133	Papua New Guinea	..	2.3 e	..	17.5 e	..	71.4 e	..	24.3 e	..	4.3 e
134	Bhutan	..	5.2	..	12.9	..	..	..	..	..	..
135	Lao People's Dem. Rep.	..	3.2	..	10.6	..	46.9	..	19.0	..	12.6
136	Comoros	..	..	..	..	42.4	..	28.2	..	17.3	..
137	Swaziland	5.7	5.5	19.5	..	31.2	37.7	24.5	31.1	26.0	22.4
138	Bangladesh	1.5	2.3	10.3	15.8	45.6	45.1 f	42.2	43.8	8.7	11.1
139	Sudan	0.9	..	2.8	..	..	..	..	..	..	..
140	Nepal	2.0	3.4	8.5	13.9	48.2	59.2 f	15.7	23.1	23.3	12.1
141	Cameroon	3.2	5.4	19.6	22.1	70.5	..	..	..	29.5	..
Low human development											
142	Pakistan	2.6	1.8 e	7.4	7.8 e	..	..	..	..	..	..
143	Togo	5.5	4.8	26.4	23.2	30.4	48.6 e	25.8	29.3	29.0	17.4
144	Congo	5.0	3.2	14.4	12.6	..	32.7	..	27.3	..	32.6
145	Lesotho	6.1	10.0	12.2	18.4	..	49.3	..	27.7	..	16.7
146	Uganda	1.5	2.5 e	11.5	..	..	..	..	..	..	..
147	Zimbabwe	..	10.4 e	..	..	54.1	..	28.6	..	12.3	..
148	Kenya	6.7	6.2 e	17.0	22.3 e	50.3	..	18.8	..	21.6	..
149	Yemen	..	10.0 e	..	32.8	..	..	..	..	..	..
150	Madagascar	2.1	2.5	..	..	49.1	48.0 f	35.6	33.0	..	11.9 e
151	Nigeria	0.9	..	..	..	..	..	..	..	..	..

10 Commitment to education: public spending

HDI rank		Public expenditure on education[a]				Public expenditure on education by level[b] (% of all levels)					
		As % of GDP		As % of total government expenditure		Pre-primary and primary		Secondary		Tertiary	
		1990[c]	1999-2001[d]	1990[c]	1999-2001[d]	1990[c]	1999-2001[d]	1990[c]	1999-2001[d]	1990[c]	1999-2001[d]
152	Mauritania	..	3.6 [e]	..	..	33.3	54.5 [e, f]	37.7	31.4 [e]	24.9	14.1 [e]
153	Haiti	1.4	..	20.0	..	53.1	..	19.0	..	9.1	..
154	Djibouti	..	..	10.5	..	58.0	..	21.7	..	11.5	..
155	Gambia	3.8	2.7 [e]	14.6	14.2 [e]	41.6	..	21.2	..	17.8	..
156	Eritrea	..	2.7	..	..	..	45.8 [f]	..	10.0	..	..
157	Senegal	3.9	3.2 [e]	26.9	..	43.9	..	25.7	..	24.0	..
158	Timor-Leste	..	..	..	..	..	..	..	..	..	..
159	Rwanda	..	2.8 [e]	..	..	..	48.7 [e]	..	16.7 [e]	..	34.7 [e]
160	Guinea	..	1.9 [e]	..	25.6 [e]	..	..	..	..	..	..
161	Benin	..	3.3 [e]	..	..	..	57.4 [e]	..	25.5 [e]	..	16.4 [e]
162	Tanzania, U. Rep. of	3.2	..	11.4	..	..	..	..	..	..	..
163	Côte d'Ivoire	..	4.6	..	21.5	..	42.4 [e]	..	32.5 [e]	..	25.1 [e]
164	Zambia	2.4	1.9	8.7	..	..	..	..	..	..	..
165	Malawi	3.3	4.1 [e]	11.1	..	44.7	..	13.1	..	20.2	..
166	Angola	3.9	2.8 [e]	10.7	..	96.3	..	..	..	3.7	..
167	Chad	..	2.0 [e]	..	..	..	..	..	25.9 [e]	..	16.6 [e]
168	Congo, Dem. Rep. of the	..	..	..	..	..	..	..	..	..	..
169	Central African Republic	2.2	..	..	..	..	..	..	..	..	..
170	Ethiopia	3.4	4.8	9.4	13.8	53.9	..	28.1	..	12.1	..
171	Mozambique	3.9	2.4 [e]	12.0	..	49.8	..	15.7	..	9.9	..
172	Guinea-Bissau	..	2.1	..	4.8	..	..	..	..	..	..
173	Burundi	3.4	3.6 [e]	16.7	20.7 [e]	46.8	38.0	29.1	35.0	22.0	26.9
174	Mali	..	2.8 [e]	..	..	..	45.7 [e]	..	39.7 [e]	..	14.6 [e]
175	Burkina Faso	2.7	..	..	..	..	..	..	..	..	..
176	Niger	3.2	2.3	18.6	..	..	49.2 [f]	..	24.5	..	16.2
177	Sierra Leone	..	..	..	..	..	..	..	..	..	..

Note: As a result of limitations in the data and methodological changes, comparisons of education expenditure data across countries and over time must be made with caution. For detailed notes on the data see http://www.uis.unesco.org/.

a. Data refer to total public expenditure on education, including current and capital expenditure. See the definitions of statistical terms. b. Data refer to current public expenditure on education. Data may not be strictly comparable between 1990 and 1999-2001 as a result of methodological changes. Expenditures by level may not sum to 100 as a result of rounding or the omission of the categories expenditures in postsecondary education and expenditures not allocated by level. c. Data may not be comparable between countries as a result of differences in method of data collection. d. Data refer to the most recent year available during the period specified. e. Data refer to a UNESCO Institute for Statistics estimate where no national estimate is available. f. Data refer to primary school expenditure only.
Source: Columns 1, 3 and 5: UNESCO Institute for Statistics 2003c; columns 2, 4 and 7-10: UNESCO Institute for Statistics 2004b; column 6: calculated on the basis of data on public expenditure on education by pre-primary and primary levels from UNESCO Institute for Statistics 2004b.

11 Literacy and enrolment

		Adult literacy rate [a] (% ages 15 and above)		MDG Youth literacy rate [a] (% ages 15-24)		MDG Net primary enrolment ratio [b] (%)		Net secondary enrolment ratio [b, c] (%)		MDG Children reaching grade 5 (% of grade 1 students)		Tertiary students in science, math and engineering (% of all tertiary students)
HDI rank		1990	2002	1990	2002	1990/91	2001/02 [d]	1990/91	2001/02 [d]	1990/91	2000/01 [d]	1994-97 [e]
High human development												
1	Norway	..	..	..	..	100	101 [f]	88	95 [f]	100	..	18
2	Sweden	..	..	..	..	100	102 [g]	85	99 [g]	100	..	31
3	Australia	..	..	..	..	99	96 [g]	79	88 [g]	..	..	32
4	Canada	..	..	..	..	98	100 [f]	89	98 [f]	..	..	..
5	Netherlands	..	..	..	..	95	100 [f]	84	90 [f]	..	100 [h]	20
6	Belgium	..	..	..	..	96	101 [f]	87	..	..	..	..
7	Iceland	..	..	..	..	101	101 [f]	..	82 [f]	..	99 [h]	20
8	United States	..	..	..	..	97	93 [g]	85	85 [g]	..	..	..
9	Japan	..	..	..	..	100	101 [g]	97	101 [g]	100	..	23
10	Ireland	..	..	..	..	90	94 [f]	80	82 [f]	100	98 [h]	30
11	Switzerland	..	..	..	..	84	99 [f]	80	88 [f]	80	99	31
12	United Kingdom	..	..	..	..	100	101 [f]	81	95 [f]	..	..	29
13	Finland	..	..	..	..	98	100 [f]	93	95 [f]	100	100	37
14	Austria	..	..	..	..	88	91 [f]	..	88 [f]	..	..	28
15	Luxembourg	..	..	..	..	81	96 [f]	..	80 [f]	..	99	..
16	France	..	..	..	..	101	100 [f]	..	92 [f]	96	98 [i]	25
17	Denmark	..	..	..	..	98	99 [h]	87	89 [h]	94	100 [h]	21
18	New Zealand	..	..	..	..	101	98 [g]	85	92 [f]	92	..	21
19	Germany	..	..	..	..	84	83 [g]	..	88 [g]	..	..	31
20	Spain	96.3	..	99.6	..	103	104 [g]	..	94 [g]	..	..	31
21	Italy	97.7	..	99.8	..	103	100 [f]	..	88 [h]	..	96	28
22	Israel	91.4	95.3	98.7	99.5	92	100	..	89	..	99	..
23	Hong Kong, China (SAR)	89.7	..	98.2	..	..	98	..	72	100	..	..
24	Greece	94.9	..	99.5	..	95	95 [f]	83	85 [f]	100	..	..
25	Singapore	88.8	92.5 [j]	99.0	99.5 [j]	96	..	..	..	..	..	..
26	Portugal	87.2	..	99.5	..	102	..	..	85 [f]	..	..	31
27	Slovenia	99.6	99.7	99.8	99.8	104	93 [f]	..	96 [f]	..	..	29
28	Korea, Rep. of	95.9	..	99.8	..	104	101 [g]	86	89 [g]	99	100	34
29	Barbados	99.4	99.7	99.8	99.8	80	103	..	87	..	95	21
30	Cyprus	94.3	96.8 [i]	99.7	99.8 [i]	87	95 [f]	69	88 [f]	100	99 [h]	17
31	Malta	88.4	92.6	97.5	98.7	97	98 [f]	78	80 [f]	99	99 [h]	13
32	Czech Republic	..	..	..	..	87	88 [g]	..	89 [g]	..	97	34
33	Brunei Darussalam	85.5	93.9 [i]	97.9	99.1 [i]	90	..	..	..	..	93	6
34	Argentina	95.7	97.0	98.2	98.6	94	108 [g]	..	81 [g]	..	93	30
35	Seychelles	..	91.9 [i]	..	99.1 [i]	..	106	..	98	..	91	..
36	Estonia	99.8	99.8 [i]	99.8	99.8 [i]	100	98 [f]	..	92 [f]	..	99 [h]	32
37	Poland	99.6	..	99.8	..	97	98 [g]	76	91 [g]	98	99	..
38	Hungary	99.1	..	99.7	..	91	91 [g]	75	92 [g]	98	..	32
39	Saint Kitts and Nevis	..	..	..	..	..	102 [f]	..	106 [f]	..	90 [h]	..
40	Bahrain	82.1	88.5	95.6	98.6	99	91	85	81	89	99	..
41	Lithuania	99.3	99.6 [j]	99.8	99.7 [j]	..	97 [f]	..	92 [f]	..	..	38
42	Slovakia	..	99.7 [j]	..	99.6 [j]	..	87 [g]	..	87 [g]	..	..	43
43	Chile	94.0	95.7 [i]	98.1	99.0 [i]	88	89 [f]	55	75 [f]	..	100 [h]	43
44	Kuwait	76.7	82.9	87.5	93.1	49	85	..	77	..	..	23
45	Costa Rica	93.9	95.8	97.4	98.4	87	91	37	51	82	94	18
46	Uruguay	96.5	97.7	98.7	99.1	92	90 [g]	..	72 [g]	94	89	24
47	Qatar	77.0	84.2 [j,k]	90.3	94.8 [j,k]	89	94	70	78	64	..	..
48	Croatia	96.9	98.1 [i]	99.6	99.6 [i]	74	88	57	86	..	..	38
49	United Arab Emirates	71.0	77.3	84.7	91.4	100	81	58	72	80	97	27
50	Latvia	99.8	99.7 [i]	99.8	99.7 [i]	92	91 [f]	..	89 [f]	..	..	29

HDI rank		Adult literacy rate [a] (% ages 15 and above)		MDG Youth literacy rate [a] (% ages 15-24)		MDG Net primary enrolment ratio [b] (%)		Net secondary enrolment ratio [b, c] (%)		MDG Children reaching grade 5 (% of grade 1 students)		Tertiary students in science, math and engineering (% of all tertiary students)
		1990	2002	1990	2002	1990/91	2001/02 [d]	1990/91	2001/02 [d]	1990/91	2000/01 [d]	1994-97 [e]
51	Bahamas	94.4	..	96.5	..	90	86	..	79	..	..	..
52	Cuba	95.1	96.9	99.3	99.8	92	96	69	83	92	95 [h]	21
53	Mexico	87.3	90.5 [j]	95.2	96.6 [j]	100	101 [g]	45	60 [g]	80	90	31
54	Trinidad and Tobago	96.8	98.5	99.6	99.8	91	94	..	68	..	98 [h]	41
55	Antigua and Barbuda	..	..	..	..	..	..	..	..	..	..	..
Medium human development												
56	Bulgaria	97.2	98.6	99.4	99.7	86	93 [f]	63	86 [f]	91	..	25
57	Russian Federation	99.2	99.6	99.8	99.8	99	..	..	..	..	..	49
58	Libyan Arab Jamahiriya	68.1	81.7	91.0	97.0	96	..	..	..	..	..	..
59	Malaysia	80.7	88.7 [j]	94.8	97.2 [j]	94	95 [g]	..	69 [g]	98	..	..
60	Macedonia, TFYR	..	..	..	..	94	93 [f]	..	82 [f]	..	..	38
61	Panama	89.0	92.3	95.3	97.0	92	99	50	62	..	89	27
62	Belarus	99.5	99.7	99.8	99.8	86	94	..	78	..	..	33
63	Tonga	..	98.8 [j]	..	99.2 [j]	92	105	83	72 [f]	90	83	..
64	Mauritius	79.8	84.3 [j]	91.1	94.5 [j]	95	93	..	62	98	99	17
65	Albania	77.0	98.7 [j]	94.8	99.4 [j]	95	97 [f]	..	74 [f]	..	..	22
66	Bosnia and Herzegovina	..	94.6	..	99.6	..	..	..	..	..	..	..
67	Suriname	..	..	..	..	78	97 [g]	..	63 [g]	..	..	..
68	Venezuela	88.9	93.1	96.0	98.2	88	92	19	57	86	96	..
69	Romania	97.1	97.3 [j]	99.3	97.8 [j]	81	93 [f]	..	80 [f]	..	..	32
70	Ukraine	99.4	99.6	99.8	99.9	80	82	..	91	98	..	..
71	Saint Lucia	..	..	..	..	95	103	..	70	..	97	..
72	Brazil	82.0	86.4 [j]	91.8	94.2 [j]	86	97 [g]	15	72 [g]	..	..	23
73	Colombia	88.4	92.1	94.9	97.2	68	87	..	54	62	61	31
74	Oman	54.7	74.4	85.6	98.5	69	75	..	68	97	96	31
75	Samoa (Western)	98.0	98.7	99.0	99.5	112	95	..	61	..	94	..
76	Thailand	92.4	92.6 [j]	98.1	98.0 [j]	76	86	..	..	..	94 [i]	21
77	Saudi Arabia	66.2	77.9	85.4	93.5	59	59	31	53	83	94	18
78	Kazakhstan	98.8	99.4	99.8	99.8	88	90	..	84	..	..	42
79	Jamaica	82.2	87.6	91.2	94.5	96	95 [g]	64	75 [g]	..	90	20
80	Lebanon	80.3	..	92.1	..	78	90	..	..	..	94	17
81	Fiji	88.6	92.9 [j, k]	97.8	99.3 [j, k]	105	100 [g]	..	76 [g]	..	88	..
82	Armenia	97.5	99.4 [j]	99.5	99.8 [j]	..	85	..	85	..	..	33
83	Philippines	91.7	92.6 [j]	97.3	95.1 [j]	96	93 [g]	..	56 [g]	..	79	..
84	Maldives	94.8	97.2	98.1	99.2	87	96	..	31 [h]	..	..	..
85	Peru	85.5	85.0 [l]	94.5	96.6 [l]	88	100 [g]	..	66 [f]	..	86	..
86	Turkmenistan	..	98.8 [j, k]	..	99.8 [j, k]	..	..	..	..	..	..	..
87	St. Vincent & the Grenadines	..	..	..	..	..	92	..	52	..	85 [h]	..
88	Turkey	77.9	86.5 [j]	92.7	95.5 [j]	89	88 [g]	42	..	98	..	22
89	Paraguay	90.3	91.6 [l]	95.6	96.3 [l]	93	92 [g]	26	50 [g]	70	77	22
90	Jordan	81.5	90.9	96.7	99.4	94	91 [g]	..	80 [g]	..	98 [i]	27
91	Azerbaijan	..	..	..	..	101	80	..	76	..	..	..
92	Tunisia	59.1	73.2	84.1	94.3	94	97 [g]	..	68 [g]	87	95	27
93	Grenada	..	..	..	..	..	84 [f]	..	46 [f]	..	..	..
94	China	78.3	90.9 [j]	95.3	98.9 [j]	97	93 [f]	..	..	86	99 [i]	53
95	Dominica	..	..	..	..	..	91 [f]	..	84 [f]	..	85	..
96	Sri Lanka	88.7	92.1	95.1	97.0	90	105 [g]	..	..	94	..	29
97	Georgia	..	..	..	..	97	91	..	71 [i]	..	..	48
98	Dominican Republic	79.4	84.4	87.5	91.7	58	97 [g]	..	41 [g]	..	66	25
99	Belize	89.1	76.9 [j]	96.0	84.2 [j]	94	96 [f]	31	60 [f]	67	81 [h]	..
100	Ecuador	87.6	91.0 [j]	95.5	96.4 [j]	98	102	..	50	..	78	..

HDI rank	Adult literacy rate [a] (% ages 15 and above)		Youth literacy rate [a] (% ages 15-24) **MDG**		Net primary enrolment ratio [b] (%) **MDG**		Net secondary enrolment ratio [b,c] (%)		Children reaching grade 5 (% of grade 1 students) **MDG**		Tertiary students in science, math and engineering (% of all tertiary students)
	1990	2002	1990	2002	1990/91	2001/02 [d]	1990/91	2001/02 [d]	1990/91	2000/01 [d]	1994-97 [e]
101 Iran, Islamic Rep. of	63.2	..	86.3	..	92	87	..	..	90	94	36
102 Occupied Palestinian Territories	..	..	..	..	..	95	..	81	..	..	10
103 El Salvador	72.4	79.7	83.8	88.9	73	89	..	46	..	67	20
104 Guyana	97.2	..	99.8	..	89	98 [h]	67	75 [h]	93	95 [i]	25
105 Cape Verde	63.8	75.7	81.5	89.1	94	101 [g]	..	53 [g]	..	93	..
106 Syrian Arab Republic	64.8	82.9	79.9	95.2	92	98	43	39	96	92	31
107 Uzbekistan	98.7	99.3	99.6	99.7	78	..	..	..	..	..	..
108 Algeria	52.9	68.9	77.3	89.9	93	95 [g]	54	62 [g]	95	96	50
109 Equatorial Guinea	73.3	..	92.7	..	91	85	..	26 [h]	..	33	..
110 Kyrgyzstan	..	..	..	..	92	90	..	..	..	..	..
111 Indonesia	79.5	87.9	95.0	98.0	97	92 [g]	39	47 [h]	84	89	28
112 Viet Nam	90.4	90.3 [j,k]	94.1	..	90	94	..	65	..	89	..
113 Moldova, Rep. of	97.5	99.0	99.8	99.8	89	78	..	68	..	..	44
114 Bolivia	78.1	86.7 [j]	92.6	97.3 [j]	91	94 [g]	29	67 [f]	..	78	..
115 Honduras	68.1	80.0 [j]	79.7	88.9 [j]	90	87	..	..	..	..	26
116 Tajikistan	98.2	99.5 [i]	99.8	99.8 [i]	77	105	..	79	..	..	23
117 Mongolia	97.8	97.8 [i]	98.9	97.7 [j]	90	87	..	71	..	..	25
118 Nicaragua	62.7	76.7 [l]	68.2	86.2 [l]	72	82 [g]	..	37 [g]	46	54	31
119 South Africa	81.2	86.0	88.5	91.8	88	90	..	62 [f]	75	65 [h]	18
120 Egypt	47.1	55.6 [j,k]	61.3	73.2 [j,k]	84	90	..	81	..	99 [h]	15
121 Guatemala	61.0	69.9	73.4	80.1	64	85 [g]	..	28 [g]	..	56	..
122 Gabon	..	..	..	..	86	78 [f]	..	..	..	100	..
123 São Tomé and Principe	..	..	..	..	..	98	..	..	..	61	..
124 Solomon Islands	..	..	..	..	83	..	..	..	85	..	..
125 Morocco	38.7	50.7	55.3	69.5	57	88	..	31 [f]	75	84	29
126 Namibia	74.9	83.3	87.4	92.3	83	78	..	38	..	94	4
127 India	49.3	61.3 [i]	64.3	..	..	83 [f]	..	..	..	59 [h]	25
128 Botswana	68.1	78.9	83.3	89.1	85	81	29	55 [f]	97	89	27
129 Vanuatu	..	..	..	..	71	93	..	28	..	95	..
130 Cambodia	62.0	69.4	73.5	80.3	67	86	..	21	..	70	23
131 Ghana	58.5	73.8	81.8	92.2	52	60	..	32	80	..	..
132 Myanmar	80.7	85.3	88.2	91.4	99	82	..	35	..	60	37
133 Papua New Guinea	56.6	..	68.6	..	66	77	..	23	59	60	..
134 Bhutan	..	..	..	..	..	..	..	..	..	91	..
135 Lao People's Dem. Rep.	56.5	66.4	70.1	79.3	63	83	..	31	..	62	..
136 Comoros	53.8	56.2	56.7	59.0	57	55 [h]	..	..	..	..	..
137 Swaziland	71.6	80.9	85.1	91.2	77	77	..	32	76	74	22
138 Bangladesh	34.2	41.1	42.0	49.7	71	87	19	44	..	65	..
139 Sudan	45.8	59.9	65.0	79.1	43	46 [h]	..	..	94	84 [i]	..
140 Nepal	30.4	44.0	46.6	62.7	85	70 [f]	..	..	..	78	14
141 Cameroon	57.9	67.9 [l]	81.1	..	74	..	..	..	..	81 [i]	..
Low human development											
142 Pakistan	35.4	41.5 [j,k]	47.4	53.9 [j,k]	35	..	..	..	..	..	..
143 Togo	44.2	59.6	63.5	77.4	75	95	18	27 [h]	51	84	11
144 Congo	67.1	82.8	92.5	97.8	79	..	..	..	63	..	..
145 Lesotho	78.0	81.4 [l]	87.2	.. [l]	73	84	..	22	71	67	13
146 Uganda	56.1	68.9	70.1	80.2	53	..	..	14 [f]	..	..	15
147 Zimbabwe	80.7	90.0	93.9	97.6	86	83 [g]	..	40 [g]	..	..	23
148 Kenya	70.8	84.3	89.8	95.8	74	70	..	24	..	..	..
149 Yemen	32.7	49.0	50.0	67.9	52	67 [f]	..	35 [h]	..	86 [h]	6
150 Madagascar	58.0	..	72.2	..	65	69	..	11 [i]	22	34	20
151 Nigeria	48.7	66.8	73.6	88.6	60	..	..	..	..	..	41

HDI rank		Adult literacy rate [a] (% ages 15 and above)		MDG Youth literacy rate [a] (% ages 15-24)		MDG Net primary enrolment ratio [b] (%)		Net secondary enrolment ratio [b, c] (%)		MDG Children reaching grade 5 (% of grade 1 students)		Tertiary students in science, math and engineering (% of all tertiary students)
		1990	2002	1990	2002	1990/91	2001/02 [d]	1990/91	2001/02 [d]	1990/91	2000/01 [d]	1994-97 [e]
152	Mauritania	34.8	41.2	45.8	49.6	35	67	..	15	75	55	..
153	Haiti	39.7	51.9	54.8	66.2	22	..	..	..	..	..	..
154	Djibouti	53.0	..	73.2	..	31	34	..	17	87	86	..
155	Gambia	25.6	..	42.2	..	48	73 g	..	28 g	..	70 i	..
156	Eritrea	46.4	..	60.9	..	16	43	..	21	..	..	..
157	Senegal	28.4	39.3	40.1	52.9	47	58 g	..	..	85	68	..
158	Timor-Leste	..	..	..	..	..	..	..	20 f	..	..	..
159	Rwanda	53.3	69.2	72.7	84.9	67	84	7	..	60	40	..
160	Guinea	..	..	..	..	25	61	..	12 i	59	84 h	42
161	Benin	26.4	39.8	40.4	55.5	45	71 h	..	20 f	55	84 h	18
162	Tanzania, U. Rep. of	62.9	77.1	83.1	91.6	50	54	..	..	79	78	39
163	Côte d'Ivoire	38.5	..	52.6	59.9 k	46	63	..	..	73	69 i	..
164	Zambia	68.2	79.9	81.2	89.2	79	66	..	20	..	77	..
165	Malawi	51.8	61.8	63.2	72.5	50	81 g	..	29 g	64	54	..
166	Angola	..	..	..	..	58	30 h	..	..	..	..	..
167	Chad	27.7	45.8	48.0	69.9	36	58	..	8 f	53	45	14
168	Congo, Dem. Rep. of the	47.5	..	68.9	..	54	35 i	..	12 i	55	..	..
169	Central African Republic	33.2	48.6 l	52.1	58.5 l	53	..	..	..	24	..	..
170	Ethiopia	28.6	41.5	43.0	57.4	23	46	..	15	..	61	36
171	Mozambique	33.5	46.5	48.8	62.8	45	60	..	11	33	52	46
172	Guinea-Bissau	27.2	..	44.1	..	38	45 h	..	..	..	38 i	..
173	Burundi	37.0	50.4	51.6	66.1	53	53	..	8	62	64	..
174	Mali	18.8	19.0 j, k	27.6	24.2 j, k	20	38 i	5	..	73	84	..
175	Burkina Faso	16.3	12.8 j, k	24.9	19.4 j, k	26	35 g	..	8 f	70	64	19
176	Niger	11.4	17.1	17.0	24.5	24	34	6	5	62	71	..
177	Sierra Leone	..	..	..	..	41	..	..	..	..	..	..
Developing countries		67.3	76.7	85.5	88.1	..	..	..	..	..	..	..
Least developed countries		43.0	52.5	54.9	64.3	..	..	..	..	..	..	..
Arab States		50.8	63.3	68.4	81.2	..	..	..	..	..	..	..
East Asia and the Pacific		79.8	90.3	95.1	98.0	..	..	..	..	..	..	..
Latin America and the Caribbean		85.0	88.6	92.7	94.8	..	..	..	..	..	..	..
South Asia		47.0	57.6	..	..	..	..	..	..	..	..	..
Sub-Saharan Africa		50.8	63.2	66.8	76.8	..	..	..	..	..	..	..
Central & Eastern Europe & CIS		98.7	99.3	99.7	99.6	..	..	..	..	..	..	..
OECD		..	..	..	..	..	..	..	..	..	..	..
High-income OECD		..	..	..	..	..	..	..	..	..	..	..
High human development		..	..	..	..	..	..	..	..	..	..	..
Medium human development		71.8	80.4	90.5	93.0	..	..	..	..	..	..	..
Low human development		42.5	54.3	59.0	69.3	..	..	..	..	..	..	..
High income		..	..	..	..	..	..	..	..	..	..	..
Middle income		81.6	89.7	93.7	96.3	..	..	..	..	..	..	..
Low income		53.3	63.6	..	..	..	..	..	..	..	..	..
World		..	..	..	..	..	..	..	..	..	..	..

a. Data refer to estimates produced by UNESCO Institute for Statistics in July 2002, unless otherwise specified. Due to differences in methodology and timeliness of underlying data, comparisons across countries and over time should be made with caution. b. The net enrolment ratio is the ratio of enrolled children of the official age for the education level indicated to the total population of that age. Net enrolment ratios exceeding 100% reflect discrepancies between these two data sets. c. Enrolment ratios are based on the new International Standard Classification of Education, adopted in 1997 (UNESCO 1997), and so may not be strictly comparable with those for earlier years. d. Data on net enrolment ratios refer to the 2001/02 school year, and data on children reaching grade 5 to the 2000/01 school year, unless otherwise specified. Data for some countries may refer to national or UNESCO Institute for Statistics estimates. For details, see http://www.uis.unesco.org/. Because data are from different sources, comparisons across countries should be made with caution. e. Data refer to the most recent year available during the period specified. f. Data refer to the 2000/01 school year. g. Preliminary UNESCO Institute for Statistics estimate, subject to further revision. h. Data refer to the 1999/2000 school year. i. Data refer to the 1998/99 school year. j. Census data. k. Data refer to a year between 1995 and 1999. l. Survey data.

Source: Columns 1 and 3: UNESCO Institute for Statistics 2003a; columns 2 and 4: UNESCO Institute for Statistics 2004a; columns 5-10: UNESCO Institute for Statistics 2004c; column 11: calculated on the basis of data on tertiary students from UNESCO 1999.

12 Technology: diffusion and creation

HDI rank	MDG Telephone mainlines [a] (per 1,000 people)		MDG Cellular subscribers [a] (per 1,000 people)		MDG Internet users (per 1,000 people)		Patents granted to residents (per million people)	Receipts of royalties and licence fees (US$ per person)	Research and development (R&D) expenditures (% of GDP)	Researchers in R&D (per million people)
	1990	2002	1990	2002	1990	2002	2000	2002	1996-2002 [b]	1990-2001 [b]
High human development										
1 Norway	502	734	46	844	7.1	502.6	88	37.9	1.6	4,377
2 Sweden	681	736	54	889	5.8	573.1	235	169.7	4.6	5,186
3 Australia	456	539	11	640	5.9	481.7	68	15.5	1.5	3,439
4 Canada	565	635	22	377	3.7	512.8	36	54.0	1.9	2,978
5 Netherlands	464	618	5	745	3.3	506.3	177	122.1	1.9	2,572
6 Belgium	393	494	4	786	(.)	328.3	73	86.4 [c]	2.0	2,953
7 Iceland	510	653	39	906	0.0	647.9	7	0.1	3.0	6,639
8 United States	547	646	21	488	8.0	551.4	298	151.7	2.8	4,099
9 Japan	441	558	7	637	0.2	448.9	884	81.8	3.1	5,321
10 Ireland	281	502	7	763	0.0	270.9	9	63.6	1.2	2,190
11 Switzerland	574	744	18	789	5.8	351.0	188	..	2.6	3,592
12 United Kingdom	441	591	19	841	0.9	423.1	71	130.4	1.9	2,666
13 Finland	534	523	52	867	4.0	508.9	5	107.5	3.4	7,110
14 Austria	418	489	10	786	1.3	409.4	138	13.6	1.9	2,313
15 Luxembourg	481	797	2	1,061	0.0	370.0	145	274.8	..	..
16 France	495	569	5	647	0.5	313.8	174	54.2	2.2	2,718
17 Denmark	567	689	29	833	1.0	512.8	59	..	2.1	3,476
18 New Zealand	434	448	16	622	0.0	484.4	145	23.0	1.0	2,197
19 Germany	441	651	4	727	1.4	411.9	205	45.7	2.5	3,153
20 Spain	316	506	1	824	0.1	156.3	42	9.0	1.0	1,948
21 Italy	388	481	5	939	0.2	352.4	82	9.4	1.1	1,128
22 Israel	343	453	3	955	1.1	301.4	75	61.7	5.0	1,563
23 Hong Kong, China (SAR)	450	565	24	942	0.0	430.1	6	28.4 [c]	0.4	93
24 Greece	389	491	0	845	0.0	154.7	(.)	1.1	0.7	1,400
25 Singapore	346	463	17	796	0.0	504.4	27	..	2.1	4,052
26 Portugal	243	421	1	825	0.0	193.5	5	3.1	0.8	1,754
27 Slovenia	211	506	0	835	0.0	375.8	93	3.8	1.6	2,258
28 Korea, Rep. of	306	489	2	679	0.2	551.9	490	17.4	3.0	2,880
29 Barbados	281	494	0	361	0.0	111.5	0	1.9	..	..
30 Cyprus	419	688	5	584	0.0	293.7	0	3.2	0.3	400
31 Malta	360	523	0	699	0.0	303.0	54	3.2	..	96 [d]
32 Czech Republic	158	362	0	849	0.0	256.3	26	4.4	1.3	1,466
33 Brunei Darussalam	136	256	7	401 [c]	0.0	102.3 [c]	..	..	..	..
34 Argentina	93	219	(.)	178	0.0	112.0	4	0.5	0.4	684
35 Seychelles	124	269	0	553	0.0	145.2	..	..	..	..
36 Estonia	204	351	0	650	0.0	327.7	1	3.7	0.7	1,947
37 Poland	86	295 [c]	0	363	0.0	230.0	24	0.9	0.7	1,473
38 Hungary	96	361	(.)	676	0.0	157.6	18	35.3	0.9	1,440
39 Saint Kitts and Nevis	237	500	0	106	0.0	212.8	..	..	..	..
40 Bahrain	191	261	10	579	0.0	245.6	..	..	..	..
41 Lithuania	212	270	0	475	0.0	144.4	24	0.1	0.6	2,303
42 Slovakia	135	268	0	544	0.0	160.4	15	..	0.6	1,774
43 Chile	66	230	1	428	0.0	237.5	2	0.4	0.5	419
44 Kuwait	188	204	12	519	0.0	105.8	..	0.0	0.2	212
45 Costa Rica	101	251	0	111	0.0	193.1	0	0.4	0.2	530 [d]
46 Uruguay	134	280	0	193	0.0	119.0 [c]	2	0.0	0.2	276
47 Qatar	220	286	9	433	0.0	113.4	..	..	..	591 [d]
48 Croatia	172	417	(.)	535	0.0	180.4	26	19.1	1.0	1,187
49 United Arab Emirates	224	291	19	647	0.0	313.2	0	..	..	..
50 Latvia	234	301	0	394	0.0	133.1	40	1.5	0.4	1,078

HDI rank		MDG Telephone mainlines [a] (per 1,000 people)		MDG Cellular subscribers [a] (per 1,000 people)		MDG Internet users (per 1,000 people)		Patents granted to residents (per million people)	Receipts of royalties and licence fees (US$ per person)	Research and development (R&D) expenditures (% of GDP)	Researchers in R&D (per million people)
		1990	2002	1990	2002	1990	2002	2000	2002	1996-2002 [b]	1990-2001 [b]
51	Bahamas	274	406	8	390	0.0	192.3	..	..	..	..
52	Cuba	31	51 [c]	0	2	0.0	10.7 [c]	0	..	0.6	489
53	Mexico	65	147	1	255	0.0	98.5	1	0.5	0.4	225
54	Trinidad and Tobago	141	250	0	278	0.0	106.0	0	..	0.1	456
55	Antigua and Barbuda	253	488	0	490	0.0	128.2	0	0.0 [c]	..	..
Medium human development											
56	Bulgaria	242	368	0	333	0.0	80.8	18	0.5	0.5	1,167
57	Russian Federation	140	242	0	120	0.0	40.9	99	1.0	1.2	3,494
58	Libyan Arab Jamahiriya	48	118 [c]	0	13	0.0	22.5	..	..	..	361
59	Malaysia	89	190	5	377	0.0	319.7	..	0.5	0.4	160
60	Macedonia, TFYR	148	271	0	177	0.0	48.4	17	1.6	..	387
61	Panama	93	122	0	189	0.0	41.4 [c]	0	0.0	0.4	95
62	Belarus	154	299	0	47	0.0	81.6	35	0.1	..	1,893
63	Tonga	46	113	0	34	0.0	29.2	..	..	..	..
64	Mauritius	52	270	2	288	0.0	99.1	..	0.0	0.3	360
65	Albania	13	71	0	276	0.0	3.9	0	..	..	..
66	Bosnia and Herzegovina	..	237	0	196	0.0	26.2	0	..	..	..
67	Suriname	92	164	0	225	0.0	41.6	..	..	..	..
68	Venezuela	76	113	(.)	256	0.0	50.6	1	0.0	0.4	193
69	Romania	102	194	0	236	0.0	101.5	38	0.1	0.4	879
70	Ukraine	136	216	0	84	0.0	18.0	99	0.1	0.9	2,118
71	Saint Lucia	129	320	0	89	0.0	82.4 [c]	0	..	..	..
72	Brazil	65	223	(.)	201	0.0	82.2	0	0.6	1.1	323
73	Colombia	69	179	0	106	0.0	46.2	(.)	0.1	0.2	101
74	Oman	60	92	2	183	0.0	70.9	..	..	..	4
75	Samoa (Western)	26	57	0	15	0.0	22.2	..	..	..	..
76	Thailand	24	105	1	260	0.0	77.6	3	0.1	0.1	74
77	Saudi Arabia	77	151	1	228	0.0	64.6	(.)	0.0	..	..
78	Kazakhstan	80	130	0	64	0.0	15.7	72	0.0	0.3	716
79	Jamaica	45	169	0	533	0.0	228.4	0	2.3	..	8 [d]
80	Lebanon	155	199	0	227	0.0	117.1	0	..	..	..
81	Fiji	58	119	0	110	0.0	61.0	..	..	..	50 [d]
82	Armenia	157	143	0	19	0.0	15.8	31	..	..	1,313
83	Philippines	10	42	0	191	0.0	44.0	(.)	(.)	..	156
84	Maldives	29	102	0	149	0.0	53.4	..	12.4	..	..
85	Peru	26	66	(.)	86	0.0	93.5	(.)	0.1	0.1	229
86	Turkmenistan	60	77	0	2	0.0	1.7 [c]	0	..	..	..
87	St. Vincent & the Grenadines	124	234	0	85	0.0	59.8	0	0.0 [c]	..	..
88	Turkey	121	281	1	347	0.0	72.8	(.)	0.0	0.6	306
89	Paraguay	27	47	0	288	0.0	17.3	..	32.1	0.0	166
90	Jordan	72	127	(.)	229	0.0	57.7	..	..	6.3	1,948
91	Azerbaijan	86	113	0	107	0.0	36.9	0	..	0.4	2,799
92	Tunisia	37	117	(.)	52	0.0	51.7	..	1.7	0.5	336
93	Grenada	177	316	2	71	0.0	141.5	0	0.0 [c]	..	..
94	China	6	167	(.)	161	0.0	46.0	5	0.1	1.1	584
95	Dominica	164	304	0	120	0.0	160.3	0	0.0 [c]	..	..
96	Sri Lanka	7	47	(.)	49	0.0	10.6	0	..	0.2	191
97	Georgia	99	131	0	102	0.0	14.9	49	1.1	0.3	2,421
98	Dominican Republic	48	110	(.)	207	0.0	36.4	..	..	..	..
99	Belize	92	114	0	188	0.0	108.9	0	0.0	..	..
100	Ecuador	48	110	0	121	0.0	41.6	0	..	0.1	83

12 Technology: diffusion and creation

		Telephone mainlines [a] (per 1,000 people)		Cellular subscribers [a] (per 1,000 people)		Internet users (per 1,000 people)		Patents granted to residents (per million people)	Receipts of royalties and licence fees (US$ per person)	Research and development (R&D) expenditures (% of GDP)	Researchers in R&D (per million people)
		MDG		MDG		MDG					
HDI rank		1990	2002	1990	2002	1990	2002	2000	2002	1996-2002 [b]	1990-2001 [b]
101	Iran, Islamic Rep. of	40	187	0	33	0.0	48.5	4	..	..	590
102	Occupied Palestinian Territories	..	87	0	93	0.0	30.4	..	..	..	..
103	El Salvador	24	103	0	138	0.0	46.5	..	0.2	(.)	47
104	Guyana	20	92	0	99	0.0	142.2	..	45.0	..	..
105	Cape Verde	24	160	0	98	0.0	36.4	..	1.2	..	..
106	Syrian Arab Republic	41	123	0	23	0.0	12.9	3	..	0.2	29
107	Uzbekistan	69	66	0	7	0.0	10.9	16	..	..	1,754
108	Algeria	32	61	(.)	13	0.0	16.0	0	..	..	..
109	Equatorial Guinea	4	17	0	63	0.0	3.6	..	..	..	..
110	Kyrgyzstan	72	77	0	10	0.0	29.8	13	0.5	0.2	581
111	Indonesia	6	37	(.)	55	0.0	37.7	0	..	..	130 [d]
112	Viet Nam	1	48	0	23	0.0	18.5	(.)	..	..	274
113	Moldova, Rep. of	106	161	0	77	0.0	34.1	47	0.3	0.6	329
114	Bolivia	28	68	0	105	0.0	32.4	..	0.2	0.3	123
115	Honduras	17	48	0	49	0.0	25.2	(.)	0.0	..	73
116	Tajikistan	45	37	0	2	0.0	0.5	3	0.1	..	660
117	Mongolia	32	53	0	89	0.0	20.6	32	0.0 [c]	..	531
118	Nicaragua	13	32	0	38	0.0	16.8	1	..	0.1	73
119	South Africa	93	107	(.)	304	0.0	68.2	0	1.0	..	992
120	Egypt	30	110	(.)	67	0.0	28.2	1	0.5	0.2	493
121	Guatemala	21	71	(.)	131	0.0	33.3	(.)	0.0	..	103 [d]
122	Gabon	22	25	0	215	0.0	19.2	..	..	..	..
123	São Tomé and Principe	19	41	0	13	0.0	72.8	..	..	..	..
124	Solomon Islands	15	15	0	2	0.0	5.0	..	..	..	..
125	Morocco	16	38	(.)	209	0.0	23.6	0	0.4	..	..
126	Namibia	39	65	0	80	0.0	26.7	..	1.9	..	..
127	India	6	40	0	12	0.0	15.9	0	(.)	..	157
128	Botswana	21	87	0	241	0.0	29.7 [c]	0	..	..	..
129	Vanuatu	18	33	0	24	0.0	34.6	..	..	..	..
130	Cambodia	(.)	3	0	28	0.0	2.2	..	..	..	..
131	Ghana	3	13	0	21	0.0	7.8	0	..	..	..
132	Myanmar	2	7	0	1	0.0	0.5	..	(.) [c]	..	..
133	Papua New Guinea	8	11	0	3	0.0	13.7	..	..	..	..
134	Bhutan	4	28	0	0	0.0	14.5	..	..	..	..
135	Lao People's Dem. Rep.	2	11	0	10	0.0	2.7	..	..	..	..
136	Comoros	8	13	0	0	0.0	4.2	..	..	..	..
137	Swaziland	17	34	0	66	0.0	19.4	0	0.1	..	..
138	Bangladesh	2	5	0	8	0.0	1.5	..	(.)	..	51
139	Sudan	3	21	0	6	0.0	2.6	0	..	..	..
140	Nepal	3	14	0	1	0.0	3.4	..	..	..	..
141	Cameroon	3	7	0	43	0.0	3.8	..	..	..	3
Low human development											
142	Pakistan	8	25	(.)	8	0.0	10.3	(.)	(.)	..	69
143	Togo	3	10	0	35	0.0	41.0	..	(.) [c]	..	102
144	Congo	7	7	0	67	0.0	1.5	..	..	..	33
145	Lesotho	7	13	0	45	0.0	9.7	0	5.9	..	..
146	Uganda	2	2	0	16	0.0	4.0	0	(.)	0.8	24
147	Zimbabwe	13	25	0	30	0.0	43.0	(.)	..	..	..
148	Kenya	8	10	0	37	0.0	12.5	(.)	0.2 [c]	..	..
149	Yemen	11	28	0	21	0.0	5.1	..	..	..	..
150	Madagascar	3	4	0	10	0.0	3.5	0	(.)	0.1	15
151	Nigeria	3	5	0	13	0.0	3.5	..	..	..	15 [d]

HDI rank	MDG Telephone mainlines [a] (per 1,000 people)		MDG Cellular subscribers [a] (per 1,000 people)		MDG Internet users (per 1,000 people)		Patents granted to residents (per million people)	Receipts of royalties and licence fees (US$ per person)	Research and development (R&D) expenditures (% of GDP)	Researchers in R&D (per million people)
	1990	2002	1990	2002	1990	2002	2000	2002	1996-2002 [b]	1990-2001 [b]
152 Mauritania	3	12	0	92	0.0	3.7	..	..	..	..
153 Haiti	7	16	0	17	0.0	9.6	..	..	..	..
154 Djibouti	11	15	0	23	0.0	6.9	..	..	..	..
155 Gambia	7	29	0	75	0.0	18.8	0	..	..	..
156 Eritrea	..	9	0	0	0.0	2.3	..	..	..	..
157 Senegal	6	22	0	55	0.0	10.4	..	..	(.)	2
158 Timor-Leste	..	0	..	0.0	..	..	..	..		
159 Rwanda	2	3	0	14	0.0	3.1	..	0.0	..	30 [d]
160 Guinea	2	3	0	12	0.0	4.6	..	(.)	..	..
161 Benin	3	9	0	32	0.0	7.4	..	(.) [c]	..	174 [d]
162 Tanzania, U. Rep. of	3	5	0	22	0.0	2.3	0	0.0	..	..
163 Côte d'Ivoire	6	20	0	62	0.0	5.5	..	(.)	..	..
164 Zambia	8	8	0	13	0.0	4.8	0	..	..	..
165 Malawi	3	7	0	8	0.0	2.6	(.)	0.0	..	..
166 Angola	8	6	0	9	0.0	2.9	..	0.3 [c]	..	..
167 Chad	1	2	0	4	0.0	1.9	..	..	..	..
168 Congo, Dem. Rep. of the	1	(.)	0	11	0.0	0.9	..	..	..	..
169 Central African Republic	2	2	0	3	0.0	1.3	..	..	..	47
170 Ethiopia	3	5	0	1	0.0	0.7	0	0.0	..	..
171 Mozambique	3	5	0	14	0.0	2.7	0	0.0 [c]	..	..
172 Guinea-Bissau	6	9	0	0	0.0	4.0	..	..	..	..
173 Burundi	1	3	0	7	0.0	1.2	..	0.0	..	21 [d]
174 Mali	1	5	0	5	0.0	2.4	..	(.) [c]	..	..
175 Burkina Faso	2	5	0	8	0.0	2.1	..	..	0.2	16
176 Niger	1	2	0	1	0.0	1.3	..	..	..	..
177 Sierra Leone	3	5	0	14	0.0	1.6	0	..	..	..
Developing countries	29	96	(.)	101	(.)	40.9	..	0.3	0.6 [e]	384 [f]
Least developed countries	3	7	0	10	0.0	2.8	..	(.)	..	..
Arab States	79	81	(.)	85	0.0	28.0	..	0.2	..	..
East Asia and the Pacific	18	142	(.)	159	(.)	60.9	..	0.5	1.6	607 [f]
Latin America and the Caribbean	89	166	(.)	191	0.0	81.2	1	0.8	0.5 [e]	285 [f]
South Asia	7	41	(.)	13	0.0	14.9	..	(.)	..	160 [f]
Sub-Saharan Africa	5	15	(.)	39	0.0	9.6	..	0.1	..	..
Central & Eastern Europe & CIS	120	226	(.)	189	0.0	71.8	30	1.7	1.0	2,289 [f]
OECD	365	516	10	588	2.6	383.1	290	68.4	2.6	2,908 [f]
High-income OECD	439	590	13	650	3.2	450.5	360	85.6	2.6	3,483 [f]
High human development	290	507	10	582	2.5	382.6	253	66.4	2.6	2,890 [f]
Medium human development	24	111	(.)	104	0.0	37.3	3	0.2	..	555 [f]
Low human development	4	11	(.)	15	0.0	5.9	..	(.)	..	..
High income	420	584	13	653	3.1	445.8	350	82.9	2.6	3,449 [f]
Middle income	49	168	(.)	176	0.0	59.5	5	0.5	0.7 [e]	751 [f]
Low income	6	28	(.)	17	0.0	13.0	..	(.)	..	..
World	81	175	2	184	0.5	99.4	48	12.9	2.5	1,096 [f]

a. Telephone mainlines and cellular subscribers combined form an indicator for Millennium Development Goal 8; see Index to Millennium Development Goal indicators in Statistical feature 1, *The state of human development*. b. Data refer to the most recent year available during the period specified. c. Data refer to 2001. d. Data refer to a year prior to 1990. e. Data refer to 1999. f. Data refer to 1996.
Source: Columns 1-6: ITU 2004; *column 7:* calculated on the basis of data on patents granted to residents from WIPO 2004 and data on population from UN 2003; *column 8:* calculated on the basis of data on population from UN 2003 and data on receipts of royalties and licence fees from World Bank 2004f, based on data from the International Monetary Fund; *columns 9 and 10:* World Bank 2004f, based on data from the United Nations Educational, Scientific and Cultural Organization; aggregates calculated for the Human Development Report Office by the World Bank.

13 Economic performance

HDI rank		GDP US$ billions 2002	GDP PPP US$ billions 2002	GDP per capita US$ 2002	GDP per capita PPP US$ 2002	GDP per capita annual growth rate (%) 1975-2002	GDP per capita annual growth rate (%) 1990-2002	GDP per capita Highest value during 1975-2002 (PPP US$)	Year of highest value	Average annual change in consumer price index (%) 1990-2002	Average annual change in consumer price index (%) 2001-02
High human development											
1	Norway	190.5	166.1	41,974	36,600	2.8	3.0	36,750	2001	2.2	1.3
2	Sweden	240.3	232.5	26,929	26,050	1.5	2.0	26,050	2002	1.8	2.1
3	Australia	409.4	555.7	20,822	28,260	1.9	2.6	28,260	2002	2.3	3.0
4	Canada	714.3	924.7	22,777	29,480	1.5	2.2	29,480	2002	1.8	2.2
5	Netherlands	417.9	469.9	25,886	29,100	1.9	2.2	29,100	2002	2.5	3.5
6	Belgium	245.4	284.9	23,749	27,570	1.9	1.8	27,570	2002	1.9	1.6
7	Iceland	8.4	8.4	29,749	29,750	1.7	2.1	30,600	2001	3.1	5.2
8	United States	10,383.1	10,308.0 [a]	36,006	35,750 [a]	2.0	2.0	35,750	2002	2.6	1.6
9	Japan	3,993.4	3,425.1	31,407	26,940	2.6	1.0	26,940	2002	0.5	-0.9
10	Ireland	121.4	142.5	30,982	36,360	4.4	6.8	36,360	2002	2.6	4.7
11	Switzerland	267.4	218.8	36,687	30,010	0.9	0.4	30,230	2001	1.4	0.6
12	United Kingdom	1,566.3	1,549.1	26,444	26,150	2.1	2.4	26,150	2002	2.7	1.6
13	Finland	131.5	136.1	25,295	26,190	2.0	2.5	26,190	2002	1.6	0.8
14	Austria	204.1	235.2	25,356	29,220	2.1	1.9	29,230	2001	2.1	1.8
15	Luxembourg	21.0	27.2	47,354	61,190	4.0	3.7	61,190	2002	2.0	2.1
16	France	1,431.3	1,601.4	24,061	26,920	1.7	1.6	26,920	2002	1.6	1.9
17	Denmark	172.9	166.3	32,179	30,940	1.6	2.1	30,940	2002	2.1	2.4
18	New Zealand	58.6	85.6	14,872	21,740	1.0	2.1	21,740	2002	1.9	2.7
19	Germany	1,984.1	2,235.8	24,051	27,100	2.0	1.3	27,190	2001	2.1	1.3
20	Spain	653.1	878.0	15,961	21,460	2.2	2.3	21,460	2002	3.6	3.1
21	Italy	1,184.3	1,524.7	20,528	26,430	2.0	1.5	26,430	2002	3.4	2.5
22	Israel	103.7	128.2	15,792	19,530	2.0	1.8	21,330	2000	8.3	5.6
23	Hong Kong, China (SAR)	161.5	182.6	23,800	26,910	4.4	2.2	26,910	2002	4.1	-3.0
24	Greece	132.8	199.0	12,494	18,720	1.1	2.2	18,720	2002	7.7	3.6
25	Singapore	87.0	100.1	20,886	24,040	5.0	3.8	24,650	2000	1.5	-0.4
26	Portugal	121.6	186.1	11,948	18,280	2.9	2.5	18,280	2002	4.2	3.5
27	Slovenia	22.0	36.4	11,181	18,540	..	4.2 [b]	18,540 [b]	2002	19.8 [b]	3.0
28	Korea, Rep. of	476.7	807.3	10,006	16,950	6.1	4.7	16,950	2002	4.7	2.8
29	Barbados	2.5	4.1	9,423	15,290	1.2	1.6	15,900	2000	2.4	0.2
30	Cyprus	10.1	13.8 [c]	13,210	18,150 [c]	4.7	3.2	18,360 [b]	2001	3.4	2.8
31	Malta	3.9	7.0	9,748	17,640	4.4	3.6	18,610	2000	2.9	1.7
32	Czech Republic	69.5	161.1	6,808	15,780	..	1.4	15,780 [b]	2002	6.7 [b]	1.8
33	Brunei Darussalam	..	..	..	..	..	..	..	..	..	..
34	Argentina	102.0	412.7	2,797	10,880	0.4	1.7	13,440	1998	7.2	25.9
35	Seychelles	0.7	..	8,320	..	3.0	2.6	..	..	2.2	0.2
36	Estonia	6.5	16.6	4,792	12,260	-0.2 [b]	2.3	12,260 [b]	2002	16.7 [b]	3.6
37	Poland	189.0	407.7	4,894	10,560	..	4.2	10,560 [b]	2002	21.0	1.9
38	Hungary	65.8	136.1	6,481	13,400	1.0	2.4	13,400	2002	18.0	5.5
39	Saint Kitts and Nevis	0.4	0.6	7,745	12,420	5.3 [b]	3.5	12,420 [b]	2002	3.4 [b]	..
40	Bahrain	7.7	12.0	11,007	17,170	1.1 [b]	1.5	17,170 [b]	2002	0.7 [b]	..
41	Lithuania	13.8	35.8	3,977	10,320	..	-0.3	11,820 [b]	1990	22.7 [b]	0.4
42	Slovakia	23.7	69.0	4,403	12,840	0.3 [b]	2.1	12,840 [b]	2002	8.3 [b]	3.3
43	Chile	64.2	153.1	4,115	9,820	4.1	4.4	9,820	2002	7.7	2.5
44	Kuwait	35.4	37.8	15,193	16,240	-1.2 [b]	-1.7 [b]	29,180 [b]	1975	1.9	1.4
45	Costa Rica	16.8	34.9	4,271	8,840	1.2	2.7	9,650	1999	14.6	9.2
46	Uruguay	12.1	26.3	3,609	7,830	1.3	1.4	9,680	1998	27.5	14.0
47	Qatar	17.5	..	28,634	..	..	..	..	..	2.6	1.0
48	Croatia	22.4	45.7	5,025	10,240	..	2.1	10,240 [b]	2002	61.3	2.0
49	United Arab Emirates	71.0	..	22,051	..	-2.8	(.)	47,790 [b]	1975	..	..
50	Latvia	8.4	21.5	3,595	9,210	-0.5	0.2	11,050	1989	21.7 [b]	2.0

HDI rank	GDP US$ billions 2002	GDP PPP US$ billions 2002	GDP per capita US$ 2002	GDP per capita PPP US$ 2002	GDP per capita annual growth rate (%) 1975-2002	GDP per capita annual growth rate (%) 1990-2002	GDP per capita Highest value during 1975-2002 (PPP US$)	Year of highest value	Average annual change in consumer price index (%) 1990-2002	Average annual change in consumer price index (%) 2001-02
51 Bahamas	4.8 d	5.1 d	15,797 d	16,690 d	1.5 b	0.1 b	17,930 b	1989	2.0	2.2
52 Cuba	..	..	..	..	..	3.5 b	..	..	..	..
53 Mexico	637.2	904.6	6,320	8,970	0.9	1.4	9,240	2000	17.7	5.0
54 Trinidad and Tobago	9.6	12.3	7,384	9,430	0.8	2.9	9,430	2002	5.4 b	..
55 Antigua and Barbuda	0.7	0.8	10,449	10,920	4.3 b	2.6	10,920 b	2002	..	..

Medium human development

HDI rank	GDP US$ billions 2002	GDP PPP US$ billions 2002	GDP per capita US$ 2002	GDP per capita PPP US$ 2002	GDP per capita annual growth rate (%) 1975-2002	GDP per capita annual growth rate (%) 1990-2002	GDP per capita Highest value during 1975-2002 (PPP US$)	Year of highest value	Average annual change in consumer price index (%) 1990-2002	Average annual change in consumer price index (%) 2001-02
56 Bulgaria	15.5	56.8	1,944	7,130	0.1 b	(.)	7,890 b	1988	94.0	5.8
57 Russian Federation	346.5	1,185.6	2,405	8,230	..	-2.4	11,030 b	1989	75.2 b	15.8
58 Libyan Arab Jamahiriya	19.1	..	3,512	..	..	..	..	..	..	..
59 Malaysia	94.9	221.7	3,905	9,120	4.0	3.6	9,280	2000	3.3	1.8
60 Macedonia, TFYR	3.8	13.2	1,860	6,470	..	-0.7	7,350 b	1991	6.5 b	0.1
61 Panama	12.3	18.1	4,182	6,170	1.0	2.5	6,510	2000	1.1	1.0
62 Belarus	14.3	54.8	1,441	5,520	..	0.2	5,520 b	2002	258.0 b	42.5
63 Tonga	0.1	0.7	1,347	6,850	1.9 b	2.2	6,850 b	2002	3.9	10.4
64 Mauritius	4.5	13.1	3,740	10,810	4.6 b	4.0	10,810 b	2002	6.6	6.7
65 Albania	4.8	15.2	1,535	4,830	0.3 b	6.0	4,830 b	2002	21.6 b	7.8
66 Bosnia and Herzegovina	5.6	..	1,362	..	..	18.0 b	..	..	..	..
67 Suriname	1.0	..	2,199	..	-0.8	0.5	..	..	88.0 b	..
68 Venezuela	94.3	135.1	3,760	5,380	-1.0	-1.0	7,810	1977	43.2	22.4
69 Romania	45.7	146.2	2,052	6,560	-1.1 b	0.1	6,810 b	1990	85.5	22.5
70 Ukraine	41.5	237.3	851	4,870	-6.6 b	-6.0	9,550 b	1989	116.7 b	..
71 Saint Lucia	0.7	0.8	4,124	5,300	3.7 b	0.2	5,850 b	1998	2.6	1.6
72 Brazil	452.4	1,355.0	2,593	7,770	0.8	1.3	7,770	2002	134.1	8.4
73 Colombia	80.9	278.6	1,850	6,370	1.5	0.4	6,720	1997	18.3	3.2
74 Oman	20.3	33.8	8,002	13,340	2.2	0.9	13,710	2001	-0.1	-0.7
75 Samoa (Western)	0.3	1.0	1,484	5,600	..	3.2 b	.. b	..	3.7	8.1
76 Thailand	126.9	431.9	2,060	7,010	5.2	2.9	7,080	1996	4.3	0.6
77 Saudi Arabia	188.5	276.9	8,612	12,650	-2.5	-0.6	23,980	1977	0.7	-0.5
78 Kazakhstan	24.6	87.4	1,656	5,870	..	-0.7	5,920 b	1990	45.6 b	5.9
79 Jamaica	7.9	10.4	3,008	3,980	0.4	-0.1	4,060	1991	19.7	7.1
80 Lebanon	17.3	19.4	3,894	4,360	3.6 b	3.1	4,520 b	1997	..	..
81 Fiji	1.9	4.5	2,281	5,440	0.9	1.8	5,610	1999	3.2	0.8
82 Armenia	2.4	9.6	771	3,120	..	1.7	3,460 b	1990	44.7 b	1.1
83 Philippines	78.0	333.5	975	4,170	0.2	1.1	4,460	1982	7.6	3.1
84 Maldives	0.6	..	2,182	..	..	4.7 b	..	..	5.6	0.9
85 Peru	56.5	134.1	2,113	5,010	-0.6	2.2	5,740	1981	20.9	0.2
86 Turkmenistan	7.7	20.1 c	1,601	4,250 c	-4.4 b	-3.2	7,130 b	1992	..	..
87 St. Vincent & the Grenadines	0.4	0.6	3,082	5,460	3.3	1.1	5,490	2000	2.0	0.8
88 Turkey	183.7	444.8	2,638	6,390	1.8	1.3	6,470	2000	75.5	45
89 Paraguay	5.5	25.4	1,000	4,610	0.7	-0.5	5,270	1981	12.0	10.5
90 Jordan	9.3	21.8	1,799	4,220	0.3	0.9	5,100	1987	3.1	1.8
91 Azerbaijan	6.1	26.2	745	3,210	..	0.2 b	3,580 b	1992	109.1 b	2.8
92 Tunisia	21.0	66.2	2,149	6,760	2.1	3.1	6,760	2002	4.0	2.8
93 Grenada	0.4	0.7	4,060	7,280	3.7 b	2.7	7,700 b	2000	2.3 b	..
94 China	1,266.1	5,860.9	989	4,580	8.2	8.6	4,580	2002	6.7	-0.6
95 Dominica	0.2	0.4	3,438	5,640	3.3 b	1.4	6,180 b	2000	1.7	-0.1
96 Sri Lanka	16.6	67.7	873	3,570	3.4	3.4	3,590	2000	9.8	9.6
97 Georgia	3.4	11.7	656	2,260	-5.2	-3.9	6,910	1985	17.7 b	5.6
98 Dominican Republic	21.7	57.2	2,514	6,640	1.9	4.2	6,640	2002	8.3	5.2
99 Belize	0.8	1.5	3,332	6,080	2.8	1.7	6,080	2002	1.7	2.2
100 Ecuador	24.3	45.9	1,897	3,580	0.1	(.)	3,690	1988	38.6	12.5

HDI rank		GDP US$ billions 2002	GDP PPP US$ billions 2002	GDP per capita US$ 2002	GDP per capita PPP US$ 2002	GDP per capita annual growth rate (%) 1975-2002	GDP per capita annual growth rate (%) 1990-2002	GDP per capita Highest value during 1975-2002 (PPP US$)	Year of highest value	Average annual change in consumer price index (%) 1990-2002	Average annual change in consumer price index (%) 2001-02
101	Iran, Islamic Rep. of	108.2	438.3	1,652	6,690	-0.4	2.2	8,290	1976	23.6	14.3
102	Occupied Palestinian Territories	3.4	..	1,051	..	..	-4.9 [b]	..	..	..	..
103	El Salvador	14.3	31.4	2,226	4,890	0.2	2.3	5,330	1978	7.2	1.9
104	Guyana	0.7	3.3	937	4,260	0.6	4.1	4,400	1997	5.8 [b]	5.3
105	Cape Verde	0.6	2.3	1,345	5,000	3.0 [b]	3.4	5,000 [b]	2002	4.9	1.5
106	Syrian Arab Republic	20.8	61.5	1,224	3,620	0.9	1.8	3,630	1998	5.1	-1.8
107	Uzbekistan	7.9	42.1	314	1,670	-1.5 [b]	-0.9	1,850 [b]	1991	..	..
108	Algeria	55.9	180.4	1,785	5,760	-0.2	0.3	6,190	1985	14.0	1.4
109	Equatorial Guinea	2.1	14.0 [c]	4,394	29,780 [c]	12.7 [b]	20.8	30,130 [b]	2001	..	..
110	Kyrgyzstan	1.6	8.1	320	1,620	-3.6 [b]	-3.2	2,530 [b]	1990	18.7 [b]	2.1
111	Indonesia	172.9	682.9	817	3,230	4.2	2.1	3,430	1997	14.0	12.7
112	Viet Nam	35.1	185.4	436	2,300	5.0 [b]	5.9	2,300 [b]	2002	2.9 [b]	3.8
113	Moldova, Rep. of	1.6	6.2	382	1,470	-5.4 [b]	-6.9	3,890 [b]	1990	18.5 [b]	5.1
114	Bolivia	7.8	21.6	886	2,460	-0.4	1.1	2,650	1978	7.5	0.9
115	Honduras	6.6	17.7	966	2,600	0.1	0.3	2,820	1979	17.2	7.7
116	Tajikistan	1.2	6.1	193	980	-9.0 [b]	-8.1	2,730 [b]	1988	..	..
117	Mongolia	1.1	4.2	457	1,710	-0.3 [b]	0.2	2,110 [b]	1989	39.0 [b]	..
118	Nicaragua	4.0	13.2	749	2,470	-2.9	1.5	5,250	1977	27.1 [b]	..
119	South Africa	104.2	456.8	2,299	10,070	-0.7	(.)	12,410	1981	8.1	10.0
120	Egypt	89.9	252.6	1,354	3,810	2.8	2.5	3,810	2002	7.5	2.7
121	Guatemala	23.3	48.9	1,941	4,080	0.1	1.3	4,170	1980	9.4	8.0
122	Gabon	5.0	8.7	3,780	6,590	-1.5	-0.2	11,560	1976	4.6 [b]	..
123	São Tomé and Principe	0.1	..	326	..	-0.6 [b]	-0.4	..	..	..	..
124	Solomon Islands	0.2	0.7	541	1,590	1.6	-2.4	2,580	1996	10.8 [b]	..
125	Morocco	36.1	112.9	1,218	3,810	1.3	0.8	3,810	2002	3.3	2.8
126	Namibia	2.9	12.3	1,463	6,210	-0.2 [b]	0.9	8,940 [b]	1980	9.5	11.3
127	India	510.2	2,799.6	487	2,670	3.3	4.0	2,670	2002	8.3	4.4
128	Botswana	5.3	14.0	3,080	8,170	5.1	2.5	8,170	2002	9.8	8.0
129	Vanuatu	0.2	0.6	1,138	2,890	0.2 [b]	-0.1	3,860 [b]	1984	2.7	..
130	Cambodia	4.0	25.7	321	2,060	..	4.1 [b]	2,060 [b]	2002	4.7 [b]	3.2
131	Ghana	6.2	43.1	304	2,130	0.3	1.8	2,130	2002	27.4	14.8
132	Myanmar	..	..	..	..	1.8 [b]	5.7 [b]	..	..	25.4	57.1
133	Papua New Guinea	2.8	12.2	523	2,270	0.4	0.5	2,840	1994	10.0	11.8
134	Bhutan	0.6	..	695	..	4.0 [b]	3.6	..	..	8.4 [b]	..
135	Lao People's Dem. Rep.	1.7	9.5	304	1,720	3.3 [b]	3.8	1,720 [b]	2002	30.0	10.6
136	Comoros	0.3	1.0	437	1,690	-1.0 [b]	-1.4	2,140 [b]	1985	..	..
137	Swaziland	1.2	4.9	1,091	4,550	1.8	0.1	4,690	1998	9.2	12.0
138	Bangladesh	47.6	230.0	351	1,700	1.9	3.1	1,700	2002	5.0	4.9
139	Sudan	13.5	59.5	412	1,820	0.9	3.1	1,820	2002	66.8 [b]	..
140	Nepal	5.5	33.1	230	1,370	2.1	2.3	1,410	2001	7.4	-0.9
141	Cameroon	9.1	31.5	575	2,000	-0.6	-0.1	2,810	1986	5.5	2.8
Low human development											
142	Pakistan	59.1	281.3	408	1,940	2.6	1.1	1,980	2000	8.6	3.3
143	Togo	1.4	7.0	291	1,480	-1.2	-0.7	2,180	1980	7.2	3.1
144	Congo	3.0	3.6	825	980	(.)	-1.6	1,290	1996	7.9 [b]	4.6
145	Lesotho	0.7	4.3	402	2,420	3.2	2.4	2,420	2002	9.0 [b]	33.1
146	Uganda	5.8	34.1	236	1,390	2.6 [b]	3.9	1,390 [b]	2002	8.5	-0.3
147	Zimbabwe	8.3	30.5 [c]	639	2,370 [c]	(.)	-0.8	3,060 [b]	1998	36.1	140.1
148	Kenya	12.3	31.9	393	1,020	0.3	-0.6	1,180	1990	13.3	2.0
149	Yemen	10.0	16.2	537	870	..	2.5	870 [b]	2002	32.6 [b]	..
150	Madagascar	4.4	12.2	268	740	-1.6	-0.9	1,250	1975	16.8	15.9
151	Nigeria	43.5	113.6	328	860	-0.6	-0.3	1,070	1977	27.8	12.9

		GDP		GDP per capita		GDP per capita annual growth rate (%)		GDP per capita Highest value during 1975-2002 (PPP US$)	Year of highest value	Average annual change in consumer price index (%)	
HDI rank		US$ billions 2002	PPP US$ billions 2002	US$ 2002	PPP US$ 2002	1975-2002	1990-2002			1990-2002	2001-02
152	Mauritania	1.0	6.2	348	2,220	0.3	1.6	2,220	2002	5.7	3.8
153	Haiti	3.4	13.3	415	1,610	-2.3	-3.0	3,050	1980	19.8	9.9
154	Djibouti	0.6	1.4	861	1,990	-4.6 b	-3.8	.. b	..	..	..
155	Gambia	0.4	2.4	257	1,690	-0.2	(.)	2,070	1986	4.0 b	..
156	Eritrea	0.6	3.8	150	890	..	1.5 b	1,010 b	1998	..	..
157	Senegal	5.0	15.8	503	1,580	-0.1	1.2	1,640	1976	4.6	2.2
158	Timor-Leste	0.4	..	497	..	..	..	..	..	..	..
159	Rwanda	1.7	10.4	212	1,270	-0.6	0.3	1,420	1983	13.3 b	2.5
160	Guinea	3.2	16.2	415	2,100	1.5 b	1.7	2,100 b	2002	..	..
161	Benin	2.7	7.0	411	1,070	0.6	2.1	1,070	2002	7.2 b	2.5
162	Tanzania, U. Rep. of	9.4	20.4	267	580	0.6 b	0.7	580 b	2002	17.8	4.6
163	Côte d'Ivoire	11.7	25.1	707	1,520	-2.0	-0.1	2,680	1978	6.3	3.1
164	Zambia	3.7	8.6	361	840	-2.1	-1.2	1,470	1976	52.7 b	..
165	Malawi	1.9	6.2	177	580	0.2	1.1	640	1979	32.6	14.7
166	Angola	11.2	28.0	857	2,130	-1.5 b	-0.1	2,850 b	1992	563.0	108.9
167	Chad	2.0	8.5	240	1,020	(.)	-0.5	1,100	1977	7.7	5.2
168	Congo, Dem. Rep. of the	5.7	33.7	111	650	0.0	..	2,400	1975	693.8	24.9
169	Central African Republic	1.0	4.5	274	1,170	-1.5	-0.2	1,670	1977	4.6	2.9
170	Ethiopia	6.1	52.6	90	780	0.2 b	2.3	780 b	2002	4.0	1.6
171	Mozambique	3.6	19.3	195	1,050	2.0 b	4.5	1,050 b	2002	26.6	16.8
172	Guinea-Bissau	0.2	1.0	141	710	-0.3	-2.2	1,070	1997	27.5	-0.6
173	Burundi	0.7	4.5	102	630	-0.9	-3.9	930	1991	15.3	-1.4
174	Mali	3.4	10.5	296	930	-0.2	1.7	930 b	2002	4.6	5.0
175	Burkina Faso	3.1	13.0	264	1,100	1.1	1.6	1,100	2002	4.9	2.2
176	Niger	2.2	9.1	190	800	-1.9	-0.8	1,360	1979	5.4	2.6
177	Sierra Leone	0.8	2.7	150	520	-3.3	-5.9	1,120	1982	24.5	-3.3
Developing countries		6,189.3 T	19,848.5 T	1,264	4,054	2.3	2.8	..	..	..	..
Least developed countries		204.7 T	897.7 T	298	1,307	0.5 b	1.4	..	..	..	..
Arab States		712.3 T	1,466.3 T	2,462	5,069	0.1	1.0	..	..	..	..
East Asia and the Pacific		2,562.6 T	9,046.9 T	1,351	4,768	5.9	5.4	..	..	..	..
Latin America and the Caribbean		1,676.1 T	3,796.1 T	3,189	7,223	0.7	1.3	..	..	..	..
South Asia		757.1 T	3,898.7 T	516	2,658	2.4	3.2	..	..	..	..
Sub-Saharan Africa		303.5 T	1,157.4 T	469	1,790	-0.8	(.)	..	..	..	..
Central & Eastern Europe & CIS		971.1 T	2,914.7 T	2,396	7,192	-1.5 b	-0.9	..	..	..	..
OECD		26,298.9 T	28,491.5 T	22,987	24,904	2.0	1.7	..	..	..	..
High-income OECD		25,129.9 T	26,368.2 T	27,638	29,000	2.1	1.7	..	..	..	..
High human development		26,924.9 T	29,435.4 T	22,690	24,806	2.0	1.7	..	..	..	..
Medium human development		4,659.1 T	17,763.5 T	1,120	4,269	1.7	2.1	..	..	..	..
Low human development		233.9 T	860.0 T	322	1,184	0.1 e	0.3 e	..	..	..	..
High income		25,767.9 T	27,115.7 T	27,312	28,741	2.1	1.7	..	..	..	..
Middle income		5,138.5 T	16,174.9 T	1,877	5,908	1.4	2.0	..	..	..	..
Low income		1,123.9 T	5,359.9 T	451	2,149	2.2 e	2.3 e	..	..	..	..
World		31,927.2 T	48,151.1 T	5,174	7,804	1.3	1.2	..	..	..	..

a. In theory, for the United States the value of GDP in PPP US dollars should be the same as that in US dollars, but practical issues arising in the calculation of the PPP US dollar GDP prevent this. b. Data refer to a period shorter than that specified. c. Data refer to 2001. d. Data refer to 2000. e. India's growth rate accounts for most of the difference in average annual growth rates of low income and low human development countries.
Source: Columns 1 and 2: World Bank 2004f, aggregates calculated for the Human Development Report Office by the World Bank; columns 3 and 4: calculated on the basis of GDP and population data from World Bank 2004f, aggregates calculated for the Human Development Report Office by the World Bank; columns 5 and 6: World Bank 2004b, aggregates calculated for the Human Development Report Office by the World Bank using least squares method; columns 7 and 8: based on GDP per capita PPP US$ time series from World Bank 2004f; columns 9 and 10: calculated on the basis of data on the consumer price index from World Bank 2004f.

14 Inequality in income or consumption

			MDG Share of income or consumption (%)				Inequality measures		
HDI rank		Survey year	Poorest 10%	Poorest 20%	Richest 20%	Richest 10%	Richest 10% to poorest 10% [a]	Richest 20% to poorest 20% [a]	Gini index [b]
High human development									
1	Norway	2000 [c]	3.9	9.6	37.2	23.4	6.1	3.9	25.8
2	Sweden	2000 [c]	3.6	9.1	36.6	22.2	6.2	4.0	25.0
3	Australia	1994 [c]	2.0	5.9	41.3	25.4	12.5	7.0	35.2
4	Canada	1998 [c]	2.5	7.0	40.4	25.0	10.1	5.8	33.1
5	Netherlands	1994 [c]	2.8	7.3	40.1	25.1	9.0	5.5	32.6
6	Belgium	1996 [c]	2.9	8.3	37.3	22.6	7.8	4.5	25.0
7	Iceland	..	..	..	..	..	..	..	..
8	United States	2000 [c]	1.9	5.4	45.8	29.9	15.9	8.4	40.8
9	Japan	1993 [c]	4.8	10.6	35.7	21.7	4.5	3.4	24.9
10	Ireland	1996 [c]	2.8	7.1	43.3	27.6	9.7	6.1	35.9
11	Switzerland	1992 [c]	2.6	6.9	40.3	25.2	9.9	5.8	33.1
12	United Kingdom	1999 [c]	2.1	6.1	44.0	28.5	13.8	7.2	36.0
13	Finland	2000 [c]	4.0	9.6	36.7	22.6	5.6	3.8	26.9
14	Austria	1997 [c]	3.1	8.1	38.5	23.5	7.6	4.7	30.0
15	Luxembourg	2000 [c]	3.5	8.4	38.9	23.8	6.8	4.6	30.8
16	France	1995 [c]	2.8	7.2	40.2	25.1	9.1	5.6	32.7
17	Denmark	1997 [c]	2.6	8.3	35.8	21.3	8.1	4.3	24.7
18	New Zealand	1997 [c]	2.2	6.4	43.8	27.8	12.5	6.8	36.2
19	Germany	2000 [c]	3.2	8.5	36.9	22.1	6.9	4.3	28.3
20	Spain	1990 [c]	2.8	7.5	40.3	25.2	9.0	5.4	32.5
21	Italy	2000 [c]	2.3	6.5	42.0	26.8	11.6	6.5	36.0
22	Israel	1997 [c]	2.4	6.9	44.3	28.2	11.7	6.4	35.5
23	Hong Kong, China (SAR)	1996 [c]	2.0	5.3	50.7	34.9	17.8	9.7	43.4
24	Greece	1998 [c]	2.9	7.1	43.6	28.5	10.0	6.2	35.4
25	Singapore	1998 [c]	1.9	5.0	49.0	32.8	17.7	9.7	42.5
26	Portugal	1997 [c]	2.0	5.8	45.9	29.8	15.0	8.0	38.5
27	Slovenia	1998/99 [c]	3.6	9.1	35.7	21.4	5.9	3.9	28.4
28	Korea, Rep. of	1998 [c]	2.9	7.9	37.5	22.5	7.8	4.7	31.6
29	Barbados	..	..	..	..	..	..	..	..
30	Cyprus	..	..	..	..	..	..	..	..
31	Malta	..	..	..	..	..	..	..	..
32	Czech Republic	1996 [c]	4.3	10.3	35.9	22.4	5.2	3.5	25.4
33	Brunei Darussalam	..	..	..	..	..	..	..	..
34	Argentina [d]	2001 [c]	1.0	3.1	56.4	38.9	39.1	18.1	52.2
35	Seychelles	..	..	..	..	..	..	..	..
36	Estonia	2000 [c]	1.9	6.1	44.0	28.5	14.9	7.2	37.2
37	Poland	1999 [e]	2.9	7.3	42.5	27.4	9.3	5.8	31.6
38	Hungary	1999 [e]	2.6	7.7	37.5	22.8	8.9	4.9	24.4
39	Saint Kitts and Nevis	..	..	..	..	..	..	..	..
40	Bahrain	..	..	..	..	..	..	..	..
41	Lithuania	2000 [e]	3.2	7.9	40.0	24.9	7.9	5.1	31.9
42	Slovakia	1996 [c]	3.1	8.8	34.8	20.9	6.7	4.0	25.8
43	Chile	2000 [c]	1.2	3.3	62.2	47.0	40.6	18.7	57.1
44	Kuwait	..	..	..	..	..	..	..	..
45	Costa Rica	2000 [c]	1.4	4.2	51.5	34.8	25.1	12.3	46.5
46	Uruguay [d]	2000 [c]	1.8	4.8	50.1	33.5	18.9	10.4	44.6
47	Qatar	..	..	..	..	..	..	..	..
48	Croatia	2001 [e]	3.4	8.3	39.6	24.5	7.3	4.8	29.0
49	United Arab Emirates	..	..	..	..	..	..	..	..
50	Latvia	1998 [c]	2.9	7.6	40.3	25.9	8.9	5.3	32.4

HDI rank		Survey year	Share of income or consumption (%)				Inequality measures		
			MDG				**Richest 10% to poorest 10%** [a]	**Richest 20% to poorest 20%** [a]	**Gini index** [b]
			Poorest 10%	Poorest 20%	Richest 20%	Richest 10%			
51	Bahamas	..	..	..	..	..	..	..	..
52	Cuba	..	..	..	..	..	..	..	..
53	Mexico	2000 [c]	1.0	3.1	59.1	43.1	45.0	19.3	54.6
54	Trinidad and Tobago	1992 [c]	2.1	5.5	45.9	29.9	14.4	8.3	40.3
55	Antigua and Barbuda	..	..	..	..	..	..	..	..
Medium human development									
56	Bulgaria	2001 [c]	2.4	6.7	38.9	23.7	9.9	5.8	31.9
57	Russian Federation	2000 [e]	1.8	4.9	51.3	36.0	20.3	10.5	45.6
58	Libyan Arab Jamahiriya	..	..	..	..	..	..	..	..
59	Malaysia	1997 [c]	1.7	4.4	54.3	38.4	22.1	12.4	49.2
60	Macedonia, TFYR	1998 [e]	3.3	8.4	36.7	22.1	6.8	4.4	28.2
61	Panama	2000 [c]	0.7	2.4	60.3	43.3	62.3	24.7	56.4
62	Belarus	2000 [e]	3.5	8.4	39.1	24.1	6.9	4.6	30.4
63	Tonga	..	..	..	..	..	..	..	..
64	Mauritius	..	..	..	..	..	..	..	..
65	Albania	2002 [e]	3.8	9.1	37.4	22.4	5.9	4.1	28.2
66	Bosnia and Herzegovina	2001 [e]	3.9	9.5	35.8	21.4	5.4	3.8	26.2
67	Suriname	..	..	..	..	..	..	..	..
68	Venezuela	1998 [c]	0.6	3.0	53.4	36.3	62.9	17.9	49.1
69	Romania	2000 [e]	3.3	8.2	38.4	23.6	7.2	4.7	30.3
70	Ukraine	1999 [e]	3.7	8.8	37.8	23.2	6.4	4.3	29.0
71	Saint Lucia	1995 [c]	2.0	5.2	48.3	32.5	16.2	9.2	42.6
72	Brazil	1998 [c]	0.5	2.0	64.4	46.7	85.0	31.5	59.1
73	Colombia	1999 [c]	0.8	2.7	61.8	46.5	57.8	22.9	57.6
74	Oman	..	..	..	..	..	..	..	..
75	Samoa (Western)	..	..	..	..	..	..	..	..
76	Thailand	2000 [e]	2.5	6.1	50.0	33.8	13.4	8.3	43.2
77	Saudi Arabia	..	..	..	..	..	..	..	..
78	Kazakhstan	2001 [e]	3.4	8.2	39.6	24.2	7.1	4.8	31.3
79	Jamaica	2000 [e]	2.7	6.7	46.0	30.3	11.4	6.9	37.9
80	Lebanon	..	..	..	..	..	..	..	..
81	Fiji	..	..	..	..	..	..	..	..
82	Armenia	1998 [e]	2.6	6.7	45.1	29.7	11.5	6.8	37.9
83	Philippines	2000 [e]	2.2	5.4	52.3	36.3	16.5	9.7	46.1
84	Maldives	..	..	..	..	..	..	..	..
85	Peru	2000 [c]	0.7	2.9	53.2	37.2	49.9	18.4	49.8
86	Turkmenistan	1998 [e]	2.6	6.1	47.5	31.7	12.3	7.7	40.8
87	St. Vincent & the Grenadines	..	..	..	..	..	..	..	..
88	Turkey	2000 [e]	2.3	6.1	46.7	30.7	13.3	7.7	40.0
89	Paraguay	1999 [c]	0.6	2.2	60.2	43.6	70.4	27.3	56.8
90	Jordan	1997 [e]	3.3	7.6	44.4	29.8	9.1	5.9	36.4
91	Azerbaijan	2001 [e]	3.1	7.4	44.5	29.5	9.7	6.0	36.5
92	Tunisia	2000 [e]	2.3	6.0	47.3	31.5	13.4	7.9	39.8
93	Grenada	..	..	..	..	..	..	..	..
94	China	2001 [e]	1.8	4.7	50.0	33.1	18.4	10.7	44.7
95	Dominica	..	..	..	..	..	..	..	..
96	Sri Lanka	1995 [e]	3.5	8.0	42.8	28.0	7.9	5.3	34.4
97	Georgia	2001 [e]	2.3	6.4	43.6	27.9	12.0	6.8	36.9
98	Dominican Republic	1998 [c]	2.1	5.1	53.3	37.9	17.7	10.5	47.4
99	Belize	..	..	..	..	..	..	..	..
100	Ecuador	1998 [e]	0.9	3.3	58.0	41.6	44.9	17.3	43.7

			MDG Share of income or consumption (%)				Inequality measures		
HDI rank		Survey year	Poorest 10%	Poorest 20%	Richest 20%	Richest 10%	Richest 10% to poorest 10% [a]	Richest 20% to poorest 20% [a]	Gini index [b]
101	Iran, Islamic Rep. of	1998 [e]	2.0	5.1	49.9	33.7	17.2	9.7	43.0
102	Occupied Palestinian Territories	..	..	..	..	..	..	..	..
103	El Salvador	2000 [c]	0.9	2.9	57.1	40.6	47.4	19.8	53.2
104	Guyana	1999 [e]	1.3	4.5	49.7	33.8	25.9	11.1	43.2
105	Cape Verde	..	..	..	..	..	..	..	..
106	Syrian Arab Republic	..	..	..	..	..	..	..	..
107	Uzbekistan	2000 [e]	3.6	9.2	36.3	22.0	6.1	4.0	26.8
108	Algeria	1995 [e]	2.8	7.0	42.6	26.8	9.6	6.1	35.3
109	Equatorial Guinea	..	..	..	..	..	..	..	..
110	Kyrgyzstan	2001 [e]	3.9	9.1	38.3	23.3	6.0	4.2	29.0
111	Indonesia	2002 [e]	3.6	8.4	43.3	28.5	7.8	5.2	34.3
112	Viet Nam	1998 [e]	3.6	8.0	44.5	29.9	8.4	5.6	36.1
113	Moldova, Rep. of	2001 [e]	2.8	7.1	43.7	28.4	10.2	6.2	36.2
114	Bolivia	1999 [e]	1.3	4.0	49.1	32.0	24.6	12.3	44.7
115	Honduras	1999 [c]	0.9	2.7	58.9	42.2	49.1	21.5	55.0
116	Tajikistan	1998 [e]	3.2	8.0	40.0	25.2	8.0	5.0	34.7
117	Mongolia	1998 [e]	2.1	5.6	51.2	37.0	17.8	9.1	44.0
118	Nicaragua	2001 [c]	1.2	3.6	59.7	45.0	36.1	16.8	55.1
119	South Africa	1995 [e]	0.7	2.0	66.5	46.9	65.1	33.6	59.3
120	Egypt	1999 [e]	3.7	8.6	43.6	29.5	8.0	5.1	34.4
121	Guatemala	2000 [c]	0.9	2.6	64.1	48.3	55.1	24.4	48.3
122	Gabon	..	..	..	..	..	..	..	..
123	São Tomé and Principe	..	..	..	..	..	..	..	..
124	Solomon Islands	..	..	..	..	..	..	..	..
125	Morocco	1998/99 [e]	2.6	6.5	46.6	30.9	11.7	7.2	39.5
126	Namibia	1993 [c]	0.5	1.4	78.7	64.5	128.8	56.1	70.7
127	India	1999/2000 [e]	3.9	8.9	41.6	27.4	7.0	4.7	32.5
128	Botswana	1993 [e]	0.7	2.2	70.3	56.6	77.6	31.5	63.0
129	Vanuatu	..	..	..	..	..	..	..	..
130	Cambodia	1997 [e]	2.9	6.9	47.6	33.8	11.6	6.9	40.4
131	Ghana	1999 [e]	2.1	5.6	46.6	30.0	14.1	8.4	30.0
132	Myanmar	..	..	..	..	..	..	..	..
133	Papua New Guinea	1996 [e]	1.7	4.5	56.5	40.5	23.8	12.6	50.9
134	Bhutan	..	..	..	..	..	..	..	..
135	Lao People's Dem. Rep.	1997 [e]	3.2	7.6	45.0	30.6	9.7	6.0	37.0
136	Comoros	..	..	..	..	..	..	..	..
137	Swaziland	1994 [c]	1.0	2.7	64.4	50.2	49.7	23.8	60.9
138	Bangladesh	2000 [e]	3.9	9.0	41.3	26.7	6.8	4.6	31.8
139	Sudan	..	..	..	..	..	..	..	..
140	Nepal	1995/96 [e]	3.2	7.6	44.8	29.8	9.3	5.9	36.7
141	Cameroon	2001 [e]	2.3	5.6	50.9	35.4	15.7	9.1	44.6
Low human development									
142	Pakistan	1998/99 [e]	3.7	8.8	42.3	28.3	7.6	4.8	33.0
143	Togo	..	..	..	..	..	..	..	..
144	Congo	..	..	..	..	..	..	..	..
145	Lesotho	1995 [e]	0.5	1.5	66.5	48.3	105.0	44.2	63.2
146	Uganda	1999 [e]	2.3	5.9	49.7	34.9	14.9	8.4	43.0
147	Zimbabwe	1995 [e]	1.8	4.6	55.7	40.3	22.0	12.0	56.8
148	Kenya	1997 [e]	2.3	5.6	51.2	36.1	15.6	9.1	44.5
149	Yemen	1998 [e]	3.0	7.4	41.2	25.9	8.6	5.6	33.4
150	Madagascar	2001 [e]	1.9	4.9	53.5	36.6	19.2	11.0	47.5
151	Nigeria	1996/97 [e]	1.6	4.4	55.7	40.8	24.9	12.8	50.6

		Survey year	MDG Share of income or consumption (%)				Inequality measures		
HDI rank			Poorest 10%	Poorest 20%	Richest 20%	Richest 10%	Richest 10% to poorest 10% [a]	Richest 20% to poorest 20% [a]	Gini index [b]
152	Mauritania	2000 [e]	2.5	6.2	45.7	29.5	12.0	7.4	39.0
153	Haiti	..	..	..	..	..	..	..	..
154	Djibouti	..	..	..	..	..	..	..	..
155	Gambia	1998 [e]	1.5	4.0	55.2	38.0	25.4	13.8	38.0
156	Eritrea	..	..	..	..	..	..	..	..
157	Senegal	1995 [e]	2.6	6.4	48.2	33.5	12.8	7.5	41.3
158	Timor-Leste	..	..	..	..	..	..	..	..
159	Rwanda	1983/85 [e]	4.2	9.7	39.1	24.2	5.8	4.0	28.9
160	Guinea	1994 [e]	2.6	6.4	47.2	32.0	12.3	7.3	40.3
161	Benin	..	..	..	..	..	..	..	..
162	Tanzania, U. Rep. of	1993 [e]	2.8	6.8	45.5	30.1	10.8	6.7	38.2
163	Côte d'Ivoire	1998 [e]	2.2	5.5	51.1	35.9	16.2	9.2	45.2
164	Zambia	1998 [e]	1.1	3.3	56.6	41.0	36.6	17.3	52.6
165	Malawi	1997 [e]	1.9	4.9	56.1	42.2	22.7	11.6	50.3
166	Angola	..	..	..	..	..	..	..	..
167	Chad	..	..	..	..	..	..	..	..
168	Congo, Dem. Rep. of the	..	..	..	..	..	..	..	..
169	Central African Republic	1993 [e]	0.7	2.0	65.0	47.7	69.2	32.7	61.3
170	Ethiopia	2000 [e]	3.9	9.1	39.4	25.5	6.6	4.3	30.0
171	Mozambique	1996/97 [e]	2.5	6.5	46.5	31.7	12.5	7.2	39.6
172	Guinea-Bissau	1993 [e]	2.1	5.2	53.4	39.3	19.0	10.3	47.0
173	Burundi	1998 [e]	1.7	5.1	48.0	32.8	19.3	9.5	33.3
174	Mali	1994 [e]	1.8	4.6	56.2	40.4	23.1	12.2	50.5
175	Burkina Faso	1998 [e]	1.8	4.5	60.7	46.3	26.2	13.6	48.2
176	Niger	1995 [e]	0.8	2.6	53.3	35.4	46.0	20.7	50.5
177	Sierra Leone	1989 [e]	0.5	1.1	63.4	43.6	87.2	57.6	62.9

Note: Because the underlying household surveys differ in method and in type of data collected, the distribution data are not strictly comparable across countries.

a. Data show the ratio of the income or consumption share of the richest group to that of the poorest. Because of rounding, results may differ from ratios calculated using the income or consumption shares in columns 2-5.
b. The Gini index measures inequality over the entire distribution of income or consumption. A value of 0 represents perfect equality, and a value of 100 perfect inequality. c. Survey based on income. d. Data refer to urban areas only. e. Survey based on consumption.

Source: Columns 1-5 and 8: World Bank 2004a; *columns 6 and 7:* calculated on the basis of income or consumption data from World Bank 2004a.

15 Structure of trade

HDI rank		Imports of goods and services (% of GDP)		Exports of goods and services (% of GDP)		Primary exports (% of merchandise exports)		Manufactured exports (% of merchandise exports)		High-technology exports (% of manufactured exports)		Terms of trade (1980 = 100)[a]
		1990	2002	1990	2002	1990	2002	1990	2002	1990	2002	2001
High human development												
1	Norway	34	27	40	41	67	74	33	22	12	22	123
2	Sweden	28	37	29	43	16	13	83	81	13	16	103
3	Australia	17	22	17	20	73	65	24	29	8	16	86
4	Canada	26	39 [b]	26	44 [b]	36	30	59	63	14	14	93
5	Netherlands	51	56	54	62	37	26	59	74	16	28	105
6	Belgium	69	78	71	82	..	17 [b]	..	79 [b]	..	11 [b]	..
7	Iceland	33	38	34	40	91	85	8	14	10	6	..
8	United States	11	14	10	10	22	14	74	81	33	32	114
9	Japan	9	10	10	11	3	3	96	93	24	24	126
10	Ireland	52	83 [b]	57	98 [b]	26	8	70	88	41	41	96
11	Switzerland	36	38	36	44	6	7	94	93	12	21	..
12	United Kingdom	27	28	24	26	19	16	79	79	24	31	100
13	Finland	24	30	23	38	17	14	83	85	8	24	107
14	Austria	38	51	40	52	12	13	88	82	8	15	..
15	Luxembourg	100	127	104	145	..	12 [b]	..	86 [b]	..	19 [b]	..
16	France	22	25	21	27	23	16	77	81	16	21	..
17	Denmark	31	39	36	45	35	29	60	66	15	22	..
18	New Zealand	27	32	27	33	75	68	23	28	4	10	117
19	Germany	25	32	25	35	10	9	89	86	11	17	106
20	Spain	20	30	16	28	24	21 [b]	75	78	6	7	123
21	Italy	20	26	20	27	11	10	88	88	8	9	125
22	Israel	45	46	35	37	13	7	87	93	10	20	122
23	Hong Kong, China (SAR)	124	142	133	151	4	5	95	95	..	17	100
24	Greece	28	27	18	21	46	47 [b]	54	52 [b]	2	10 [b]	76
25	Singapore	..	..	..	..	27	11	72	85	40	60	75
26	Portugal	39	41 [b]	33	31 [b]	19	13 [b]	80	86	4	7	..
27	Slovenia	..	56	..	58	..	10	..	90	..	5	..
28	Korea, Rep. of	30	39	29	40	6	8	94	92	18	32	84
29	Barbados	52	55	49	52	55	47	43	50	..	16	..
30	Cyprus	57	..	52	..	45	45	55	55	6	3	..
31	Malta	99	89	85	88	4	4 [b]	96	96 [b]	45	62 [b]	..
32	Czech Republic	43	67	45	65	..	10	..	89	..	14	..
33	Brunei Darussalam	..	..	..	..	100	..	(.)	12	..	4	..
34	Argentina	5	13	10	28	71	66 [b]	29	31	..	7	81
35	Seychelles	67	81	62	78	..	..	(.)	5	..	..	..
36	Estonia	..	94	..	84	..	28	..	72	..	12	..
37	Poland	22	31	29	28	36	18	59	82	..	3	285
38	Hungary	29	67	31	64	35	11	63	86	..	25	85
39	Saint Kitts and Nevis	83	71	52	46	..	27 [b]	..	73 [b]	..	(.) [b]	..
40	Bahrain	95	65	116	81	91	87 [b]	9	13 [b]	..	(.) [b]	..
41	Lithuania	61	60	52	54	..	41 [b]	..	58 [b]	..	5 [b]	..
42	Slovakia	36	80	27	73	..	15	..	85	..	3	..
43	Chile	31	32	35	36	87	80 [b]	11	18 [b]	5	3 [b]	39
44	Kuwait	58	40	45	48	94	..	6	..	3	..	..
45	Costa Rica	41	47	35	42	66	37	27	63	..	37	122
46	Uruguay	18	20	24	22	61	63	39	37	..	3	102
47	Qatar	..	..	..	..	84	89	16	10	..	0	..
48	Croatia	..	55	..	46	..	27	..	73	..	12	..
49	United Arab Emirates	40	..	65	..	54	..	46	4 [b]	..	2 [b]	..
50	Latvia	49	56	48	45	..	41	..	59	..	4	..

HDI rank		Imports of goods and services (% of GDP)		Exports of goods and services (% of GDP)		Primary exports (% of merchandise exports)		Manufactured exports (% of merchandise exports)		High-technology exports (% of manufactured exports)		Terms of trade (1980 = 100) [a]
		1990	2002	1990	2002	1990	2002	1990	2002	1990	2002	2001
51	Bahamas	..	..	..	..	..	57 c	..	37 b	..	1 b	..
52	Cuba	..	18 c	..	16 c	..	90 b	..	10 b	..	29 b	..
53	Mexico	20	29	19	27	56	16	43	84	8	21	33
54	Trinidad and Tobago	29	43	45	47	73	54 b	27	46 b	..	3 b	..
55	Antigua and Barbuda	87	68	89	60	..	..	..	..	..	..	..
Medium human development												
56	Bulgaria	37	60	33	53	..	37 c	..	61 b	..	3 b	..
57	Russian Federation	18	24	18	35	..	69	..	22	..	13	..
58	Libyan Arab Jamahiriya	31	36	40	48	95	..	5	..	0	..	..
59	Malaysia	72	97	75	114	46	19 b	54	79	38	58	..
60	Macedonia, TFYR	36	57	26	38	..	30 b	..	70 b	..	1 b	..
61	Panama	34	29	38	28	78	88	21	12	..	1	86
62	Belarus	44	74	46	70	..	33	..	64	..	4	..
63	Tonga	65	58 b	34	13 b	..	..	21	4 c	0	0 c	..
64	Mauritius	71	57	64	61	34	27	66	73	1	2	109
65	Albania	23	43	15	19	..	14	..	86	..	1	..
66	Bosnia and Herzegovina	..	59	..	26	..	..	..	..	..	..	..
67	Suriname	44	45	42	21	26	22 c	74	78 c	..	(.) c	..
68	Venezuela	20	17	39	29	90	89 b	10	13	4	3	55
69	Romania	26	41	17	35	26	18	73	81	2	3	..
70	Ukraine	29	52	28	56	..	32	..	67	..	5	..
71	Saint Lucia	84	59	73	55	..	76	28	24	..	8	..
72	Brazil	7	14	8	16	47	44 b	52	54 b	7	19 b	136
73	Colombia	15	21	21	20	74	62	25	38	..	7	83
74	Oman	31	35	53	57	94	84	5	15	2	2	..
75	Samoa (Western)	..	82 c	..	33 c	..	..	4	..	0	..	..
76	Thailand	42	57	34	65	36	22 b	63	74 b	21	31 b	60
77	Saudi Arabia	32	23	41	41	93	91 b	7	10	..	(.)	..
78	Kazakhstan	..	46	..	47	..	81 b	..	19 b	..	10 b	..
79	Jamaica	52	60	48	39	31	27 c	69	64	..	(.)	..
80	Lebanon	100	41	18	14	..	31 b	..	69 b	..	3 b	..
81	Fiji	67	65 b	62	71 b	63	55	36	44	12	1	..
82	Armenia	46	47	35	30	..	39	..	61	..	2	..
83	Philippines	33	49	28	49	31	8	38	50	..	65	96
84	Maldives	64	67	24	88	..	..	..	38	..	0	..
85	Peru	14	17	16	16	82	79	18	21	..	2	39
86	Turkmenistan	..	47 b	..	47 b	..	92 c	..	7 c	..	5 c	..
87	St. Vincent & the Grenadines	77	59	66	48	..	91	..	9	..	0	..
88	Turkey	18	30	13	30	32	15	68	84	1	2	89
89	Paraguay	39	43	33	31	..	84 b	10	15	(.)	3	147
90	Jordan	93	67	62	46	..	32	51	68	1	3	113
91	Azerbaijan	39	51	44	44	..	93	..	6	..	8	..
92	Tunisia	51	49	44	45	31	19 b	69	82	2	4	81
93	Grenada	63	57	42	47	..	..	20	24	..	8	..
94	China	14	26	18	29	27	10	72	90	..	23	..
95	Dominica	81	63	55	55	..	..	32	54	..	8	..
96	Sri Lanka	38	43	29	36	42	25	54	74	1	1	..
97	Georgia	46	39	40	27	..	65 b	..	35 b	..	38 b	..
98	Dominican Republic	44	35	34	26	..	..	..	34 b	..	1 b	58
99	Belize	62	74 b	64	55 b	..	..	15	1	..	0	..
100	Ecuador	32	31	33	24	98	90	2	10	(.)	7	43

		Imports of goods and services (% of GDP)		Exports of goods and services (% of GDP)		Primary exports (% of merchandise exports)		Manufactured exports (% of merchandise exports)		High-technology exports (% of manufactured exports)		Terms of trade (1980 = 100) [a]
HDI rank		1990	2002	1990	2002	1990	2002	1990	2002	1990	2002	2001
101	Iran, Islamic Rep. of	24	29	22	31	..	91	..	9	..	3	..
102	Occupied Palestinian Territories	..	47	..	12	..	..	..	..	..	..	..
103	El Salvador	31	41	19	27	62	41	38	58	..	6	103
104	Guyana	80	106	63	93	..	78	..	22	..	7	..
105	Cape Verde	44	68	13	31	..	..	..	96 [b]	..	1 [b]	100
106	Syrian Arab Republic	28	28	28	37	64	90 [c]	36	7	..	1	..
107	Uzbekistan	48	34	29	38	..	..	..	..	..	..	..
108	Algeria	25	26	23	36	97	98 [c]	3	2 [c]	..	4 [c]	60
109	Equatorial Guinea	70	..	32	..	..	..	..	..	..	..	..
110	Kyrgyzstan	50	43	29	39	..	67	..	33	..	6	..
111	Indonesia	24	29	25	35	65	44 [b]	35	54	1	16	..
112	Viet Nam	45	60	36	56	..	..	..	..	..	..	..
113	Moldova, Rep. of	51	79	49	54	..	69	..	31	..	4	..
114	Bolivia	24	27	23	22	95	78 [b]	5	17	..	7	53
115	Honduras	40	53	36	37	91	74	9	26	..	2	87
116	Tajikistan	35	72	28	58	..	87 [c]	..	13 [c]	..	42 [c]	..
117	Mongolia	53	81	24	67	..	64	..	36	..	(.)	..
118	Nicaragua	46	49	25	23	92	80	8	19	..	5	56
119	South Africa	19	31	24	34	..	37	..	63	..	5	83
120	Egypt	33	23	20	16	57	47	42	35	..	1	46
121	Guatemala	25	28	21	16	76	65	24	35	..	7	73
122	Gabon	31	39	46	59	..	98 [c]	..	2 [c]	..	7 [c]	46
123	São Tomé and Principe	72	95	14	44	..	..	..	..	..	..	..
124	Solomon Islands	73	..	47	..	..	..	..	..	..	..	..
125	Morocco	32	37	26	32	48	35 [b]	52	66	..	11	114
126	Namibia	67	49	52	48	..	47 [b]	..	52 [b]	..	1 [b]	..
127	India	9	16	7	15	28	22 [b]	71	75	2	5	136
128	Botswana	50	37	55	51	..	9 [b]	..	91 [b]	..	(.) [b]	137
129	Vanuatu	77	..	49	..	..	86 [c]	13	8 [c]	20	1 [c]	..
130	Cambodia	13	67	6	59	..	..	..	..	..	..	..
131	Ghana	26	55	17	43	..	85 [c]	..	16 [b]	..	3 [b]	53
132	Myanmar	5	..	3	..	..	..	..	..	..	..	..
133	Papua New Guinea	49	..	41	..	89	98 [c]	10	2 [c]	..	19 [c]	..
134	Bhutan	32	39	28	22	..	..	..	..	..	..	..
135	Lao People's Dem. Rep.	25	..	11	..	..	..	..	..	..	..	..
136	Comoros	35	31	14	15	..	..	..	8 [c]	..	1 [c]	91
137	Swaziland	74	100	75	91	..	53 [b]	..	76	..	1	100
138	Bangladesh	14	19	6	14	..	8 [b]	77	92 [b]	(.)	(.) [b]	68
139	Sudan	..	13	..	15	..	97	..	3	..	7	..
140	Nepal	22	29	11	16	..	..	83	67 [c]	..	(.) [c]	..
141	Cameroon	17	28	20	27	91	93	9	7	3	1	102
Low human development												
142	Pakistan	23	19	16	19	21	14	79	85	(.)	1	77
143	Togo	45	50	33	33	89	50 [b]	9	43	..	1	89
144	Congo	46	54	54	81	..	..	..	..	..	..	84
145	Lesotho	109	107	16	51	..	..	..	..	..	..	76
146	Uganda	19	27	7	12	..	92	..	8	..	12	..
147	Zimbabwe	23	22	23	24	68	62	31	38	2	3	118
148	Kenya	31	30	26	27	71	76	29	24	4	10	91
149	Yemen	20	39	14	38	..	..	..	..	..	..	..
150	Madagascar	28	23	17	16	85	..	14	..	8	..	140
151	Nigeria	29	44	43	38	..	100 [c]	..	(.) [c]	..	(.) [c]	48

HDI rank		Imports of goods and services (% of GDP)		Exports of goods and services (% of GDP)		Primary exports (% of merchandise exports)		Manufactured exports (% of merchandise exports)		High-technology exports (% of manufactured exports)		Terms of trade (1980 = 100) [a]
		1990	2002	1990	2002	1990	2002	1990	2002	1990	2002	2001
152	Mauritania	61	68	46	39	..	..	..	..	..	..	135
153	Haiti	20	36	18	13	15	..	85	..	14	..	45
154	Djibouti	..	63 [c]	..	45 [c]	44	..	8	..	0	..	..
155	Gambia	72	72	60	54	..	82 [c]	..	17 [c]	..	3 [c]	55
156	Eritrea	..	85	..	29	..	..	..	..	..	..	..
157	Senegal	30	41	25	31	77	49	23	51	..	4	91
158	Timor-Leste	..	..	..	..	..	..	..	..	..	..	..
159	Rwanda	14	25	6	8	..	98 [b]	..	3	..	1	138
160	Guinea	31	30	31	24	..	72 [b]	..	28 [b]	..	(.) [b]	..
161	Benin	26	26	14	14	..	94 [b]	..	6 [b]	..	(.) [b]	101
162	Tanzania, U. Rep. of	37	24	13	17	..	83 [b]	..	17 [b]	..	2 [b]	..
163	Côte d'Ivoire	27	30	32	48	..	85 [c]	..	21	..	3	90
164	Zambia	37	42	36	29	..	86	..	14	..	2	48
165	Malawi	33	43	24	25	95	90 [b]	5	10 [b]	(.)	3 [b]	62
166	Angola	21	70	39	77	100	..	(.)	..	0	..	..
167	Chad	28	65	13	12	..	..	..	..	..	..	94
168	Congo, Dem. Rep. of the	29	21	30	18	..	..	..	..	..	..	..
169	Central African Republic	28	17	15	12	..	..	..	..	..	..	40
170	Ethiopia	12	34	8	16	..	86	..	14	..	..	..
171	Mozambique	36	38	8	24	..	91 [b]	..	8 [b]	..	3 [b]	50
172	Guinea-Bissau	37	77	10	45	..	..	..	..	..	..	57
173	Burundi	28	19	8	7	..	..	..	1 [b]	..	2 [b]	31
174	Mali	34	41	17	32	..	..	2	..	..	..	90
175	Burkina Faso	24	22	11	9	..	81 [b]	..	19 [b]	..	7 [b]	166
176	Niger	22	25	15	16	..	95 [b]	..	3 [b]	..	8 [b]	..
177	Sierra Leone	24	40	22	18	..	..	..	..	..	..	..
Developing countries		23	30	24	33	..	..	61	73	..	20	..
Least developed countries		23	34	14	23	..	..	..	..	..	..	..
Arab States		38	30	38	36	..	..	20	17 [b]	..	2	..
East Asia and the Pacific		33	45	34	49	..	..	75	86	..	28	..
Latin America and the Caribbean		12	19	14	21	65	40	34	48 [b]	7	16	..
South Asia		14	20	11	19	..	..	71	56	..	4	..
Sub-Saharan Africa		26	35	27	34	..	..	..	35 [c]	..	4 [c]	..
Central & Eastern Europe & CIS		25	40	25	42	..	..	..	55	..	11	..
OECD		18	21	18	21	20	16	78	81	18	22	..
High-income OECD		18	21	18	21	19	16	79	81	18	23	..
High human development		19	22	19	22	20	16	78	82	18	22	..
Medium human development		19	27	20	30	..	..	50	57	..	18	..
Low human development		27	30	23	26	..	..	..	29 [c]	..	1 [c]	..
High income		19	22	19	22	19	15	79	82	18	23	..
Middle income		19	28	20	32	..	..	48	60	..	19	..
Low income		19	25	17	25	..	..	49	58	..	9	..
World		19	23	19	24	..	..	74	78	18	21	..

a. The ratio of the export price index to the import price index measured relative to the base year 1980. A value of more than 100 means that the price of exports has risen relative to the price of imports. b. Data refer to 2001. c. Data refer to 2000.

Source: Columns 1-10: World Bank 2004f, based on data from United Nations Conference on Trade and Development and the International Monetary Fund; aggregates calculated for the Human Development Report Office by the World Bank; *column 11:* calculated on the basis of data on terms of trade from World Bank 2004f.

16 Rich country responsibilities: aid

		Net official development assistance (ODA) disbursed			ODA per capita of donor country (2001 US$)		MDG ODA to least developed countries [b] (% of total)		MDG ODA to basic social services [c] (% of total)		MDG Untied bilateral ODA (% of total)	
		Total [a] (US$ millions)	MDG As % of GNI									
HDI rank		2002	1990 [d]	2002	1990	2002	1990	2002	1995/96	2001/02	1990	2002
1	Norway	1,517	1.17	0.89	283	333	44	37	10.7	15.1	61	99
2	Sweden	1,848	0.91	0.83	170	207	39	32	14.2	11.8	87	79
3	Australia	916	0.34	0.26	45	47	18	19	5.9	17.7	33	57
4	Canada	2,011	0.44	0.28	80	64	30	17	8.9	22.4	47	61
5	Netherlands	3,068	0.92	0.81	164	190	33	35	11.7	26.7	56	89
6	Belgium	996	0.46	0.43	83	97	41	33	9.2	20.4	..	..
8	United States	13,140	0.21	0.13	58	46	19	23	19.0	27.0	..	..
9	Japan	9,731	0.31	0.23	87	76	19	20	2.0	4.8	89	83
10	Ireland	360	0.16	0.40	17	93	37	53	0.5	30.8	..	100
11	Switzerland	863	0.32	0.32	109	118	43	27	6.5	19.8	78	95
12	United Kingdom	4,581	0.27	0.31	52	78	32	23	24.4	29.9	..	100
13	Finland	434	0.65	0.35	122	83	38	33	8.9	14.3	31	82
14	Austria	488	0.11	0.26	20	61	36	33	2.6	14.7	32	69
15	Luxembourg	139	0.21	0.77	68	316	39	40	..	..	..	..
16	France	5,125	0.60	0.38	111	86	32	30	..	..	64	92
17	Denmark	1,540	0.94	0.96	213	286	39	33	13.1	7.8	..	82
18	New Zealand	110	0.23	0.22	24	28	19	25	1.7	8.3	100	76
19	Germany	4,980	0.42	0.27	90	60	28	25	8.8	10.3	62	87
20	Spain	1,559	0.20	0.26	21	38	20	15	8.3	11.5	..	60
21	Italy	2,157	0.31	0.20	50	37	41	45	7.3	10.7	22	..
24	Greece	253	..	0.21	..	23	..	13	19.3	3.9	..	14
26	Portugal	293	0.24	0.27	17	28	70	37	4.2	3.1	..	33
DAC		58,274 T	0.33	0.23	72	65	28	26	8.1	17.3	68	85

Note: DAC is the Development Assistance Committee of the Organisation for Economic Co-operation and Development (OECD).
a. Some non-DAC countries and areas also provide ODA. According to OECD 2004e, net ODA disbursed in 2002 by the Czech Republic, Estonia, Iceland, Israel, the Republic of Korea, Kuwait, Poland, Saudi Arabia, Slovakia, Turkey and the United Arab Emirates and other small donors, including Taiwan (province of China), Estonia, Latvia and Lithuania, totalled $3,201 million. China also provides aid but does not disclose the amount. b. Includes imputed multilateral flows that make allowance for contributions through multilateral organizations. These are calculated using the geographic distribution of disbursements for the year specified. c. Data refer to the average for the years specified, and refer to the percentage of sector-allocable ODA. d. Data for individual countries (but not the DAC average) include forgiveness of non-ODA claims.
Source: Columns 1-7: OECD 2004b, aggregates calculated for the Human Development Report Office by the Organisation for Economic Co-operation and Development (OECD); columns 8-11: UN 2004e, aggregates calculated for the Human Development Report Office by the OECD.

17 Rich country responsibilities: debt relief and trade

		Debt relief			Trade				
						Goods imports			
					From developing countries		From least developed countries		
		Bilateral pledges to the HIPC trust fund [a]	Gross bilateral debt forgiveness	Average tariff barriers and non-tariff equivalents [b]	Total	Share of total imports	Total	Share of total imports	
		(US$ millions)	(US$ millions)		(US$ millions)	(%)	(US$ millions)	(%)	
HDI rank		2003	1990-2002	2000	2002	2002	2002	2002	
1	Norway	127	237	32.0	9,357	18	233	0.4	
2	Sweden	109	121	10.0	11,374	14	247	0.3	
3	Australia	14	77	13.4	38,187	41	183	0.2	
4	Canada	165	1,471	10.2	52,879	21	805	0.3	
5	Netherlands	242	1,915	9.6	60,389	30	1,164	0.6	
6	Belgium	64	711	9.9	43,845	19	5,469	2.4	
8	United States	750	8,482	7.4	598,695	48	13,621	1.1	
9	Japan	256	4,170	13.0	217,224	59	3,181	0.9	
10	Ireland	25	..	9.9	15,114	20	308	0.4	
11	Switzerland	93	311	22.2	14,567	14	192	0.2	
12	United Kingdom	436	2,493	9.8	90,787	23	2,872	0.7	
13	Finland	51	156	10.1	6,956	13	301	0.6	
14	Austria	50	369	10.0	12,116	13	291	0.3	
15	Luxembourg	4	..	..	377	2	7	(.)	
16	France	258	13,549	9.8	81,259	23	4,856	1.4	
17	Denmark	80	377	9.8	9,329	14	360	0.5	
18	New Zealand	2	..	12.1	8,810	33	45	0.2	
19	Germany	333	6,034	9.9	98,168	19	4,095	0.8	
20	Spain	165	1,092	9.7	63,993	31	2,965	1.4	
21	Italy	217	1,775	9.7	71,139	24	2,547	0.9	
24	Greece	17	..	9.8	15,222	28	218	0.4	
26	Portugal	24	470	9.8	10,058	18	649	1.2	

Note: This table presents data for members of the Development Assistance Committee (DAC) of the Organisation for Economic Co-operation and Development (OECD).

a. The Debt Initiative for Heavily Indebted Poor Countries (HIPC) is a mechanism for debt relief, jointly overseen by the International Monetary Fund and the World Bank. Bilateral and multilateral creditors have provided debt relief through this framework since 1996. Includes pledges through the European Union. b. This measure is an aggregate measure of trade barriers towards developing countries. It measures monetary barriers (tariffs) as well as quotas and subsidies, in manufactures, textiles, agricultural products, and fuels, weighted by endogeneity-corrected import volume.

Source: Column 1: IMF and IDA 2004; column 2: Calculated on the basis of data on debt cancellation from OECD 2004f; column 3: Roodman 2004; columns 4-7: Calculations based on import data from UN 2004a.

OECD country support to domestic agriculture
(% of GDP)

	MDG	
	1990	2002 [a]
Australia	0.8	0.3
Canada	1.7	0.8
Czech Republic	..	1.7
European Union [b]	2.2	1.3
Hungary	..	2.8
Iceland	4.6	1.6
Japan	1.7	1.4
Korea	8.7	4.5
Mexico	2.9	1.4
New Zealand	0.5	0.3
Norway	3.2	1.5
Poland	..	1.3
Slovak Republic	..	1.6
Switzerland	3.3	2.0
Turkey	4.3	4.1
United States	1.2	0.9
OECD	1.8	1.2

a. Provisional data. b. No data are available for individual member countries of the European Union. The member countries in 2002 were Austria, Belgium, Denmark, Finland, France, Germany, Greece, Ireland, Italy, Luxembourg, the Netherlands, Portugal, Spain, Sweden and the United Kingdom. Austria, Finland and Sweden joined in 1995 and thus are not included in the data for 1990.

Source: OECD 2004a.

18 Flows of aid, private capital and debt

	Official development assistance (ODA) received [a] (net disbursements)				Net foreign direct investment inflows [b] (% of GDP)		Other private flows [b, c] (% of GDP)		MDG Total debt service			
	Total (US$ millions)	Per capita (US$)	As % of GDP						As % of GDP		As % of exports of goods and services	
HDI rank	2002	2002	1990	2002	1990	2002	1990	2002	1990	2002	1990	2002
High human development												
22 Israel	754.0 [d]	119.6 [d]	2.6	0.7 [d]	0.3	1.6	..	..	..	..	..	..
23 Hong Kong, China (SAR)	4.0 [d]	0.6 [d]	0.1	(.) [d]	..	7.9	..	..	..	..	..	..
24 Greece	..	..	..	..	1.2	(.)	..	..	..	..	..	..
25 Singapore	7.4 [d]	1.8 [d]	(.)	(.) [d]	15.1	7.0	..	..	..	..	..	..
26 Portugal	..	..	..	..	3.7	3.5	..	..	..	..	..	..
27 Slovenia	170.9	86.1	..	0.8	..	8.5	..	..	..	..	..	..
28 Korea, Rep. of	-81.7 [d]	-1.7 [d]	(.)	(.) [d]	0.3	0.4	..	..	..	..	..	..
29 Barbados	3.4	12.8	0.2	0.1	0.7	0.7	..	..	..	..	..	..
30 Cyprus	49.6 [d]	62.3 [d]	0.7	0.5 [d]	2.3	6.1	..	..	..	..	..	..
31 Malta	11.3	28.8	0.2	0.3	2.0	-11.0	..	..	..	..	..	..
32 Czech Republic	392.7 [d]	38.3 [d]	(.) [d]	0.6 [d]	..	13.4	..	1.5	..	6.5	..	9.5
33 Brunei Darussalam	-1.7 [d]	-5.0 [d]	..	..	..	..	..	..	..	..	..	..
34 Argentina	0.1	(.)	0.1	(.)	1.3	0.8	-1.5	-0.1	4.4	5.7	37.0	18.3
35 Seychelles	7.9	97.8	9.8	1.1	5.5	8.8	-1.7	-0.3	5.9	2.1	9.0	2.6
36 Estonia	68.9 [d]	51.5 [d]	..	1.1 [d]	..	4.4	..	20.0	..	12.0	..	13.7
37 Poland	1,159.8 [d]	30.0 [d]	2.2 [d]	0.6 [d]	0.2	2.2	(.)	0.5	1.6	7.1	4.9	22.5
38 Hungary	471.5 [d]	47.5 [d]	0.2 [d]	0.7 [d]	0.9	1.3	-1.4	-1.0	12.8	22.6	34.3	33.9
39 Saint Kitts and Nevis	28.6	683.8	5.1	8.0	30.7	22.7	-0.3	4.7	1.9	10.7	2.9	22.6
40 Bahrain	70.6	99.5	3.2	0.9	..	..	..	..	..	..	..	..
41 Lithuania	146.9 [d]	42.4 [d]	..	1.1 [d]	..	5.2	..	0.3	..	9.3	..	16.6
42 Slovakia	189.4 [d]	35.1 [d]	(.) [d]	0.8 [d]	..	16.9	..	6.1	..	14.3	..	19.3
43 Chile	-22.6	-1.5	0.3	(.)	2.2	2.7	5.1	1.7	9.1	12.0	25.9	32.9
44 Kuwait	4.6 [d]	1.9 [d]	(.)	(.) [d]	0.0	(.)	..	..	..	..	..	..
45 Costa Rica	5.3	1.3	4.0	(.)	2.8	3.9	-2.5	-0.4	8.8	4.0	23.9	8.9
46 Uruguay	13.4	4.0	0.6	0.1	0.0	1.5	-2.1	-0.6	10.6	10.6	40.8	40.0
47 Qatar	2.2 [d]	3.7 [d]	(.)	(.)	..	..	..	..	..	..	..	..
48 Croatia	166.5	37.5	..	0.7	..	4.4	..	11.7	..	13.5	..	25.9
49 United Arab Emirates	4.2 [d]	1.4 [d]	(.)	(.)	..	..	..	..	..	..	..	..
50 Latvia	86.4 [d]	37.1 [d]	..	1.0 [d]	..	4.5	..	1.3	..	7.7	..	15.8
51 Bahamas	5.3 [d]	17.2 [d]	0.1	..	-0.6	5.2 [e]	..	..	..	..	..	..
52 Cuba	61.0	5.4	..	..	..	..	..	..	..	..	..	..
53 Mexico	135.5	1.3	0.1	(.)	1.0	2.3	2.7	-0.7	4.3	6.8	20.7	23.2
54 Trinidad and Tobago	-7.2	-5.6	0.4	-0.1	2.2	7.6	-3.5	0.0	8.9	2.8	19.3	5.7
55 Antigua and Barbuda	14.0	192.1	1.2	1.9	..	..	..	..	..	..	..	..
Medium human development												
56 Bulgaria	381.3 [d]	47.9 [d]	0.1 [d]	2.5 [d]	..	3.9	..	1.3	..	8.8	..	15.9
57 Russian Federation	1,300.9 [d]	9.0 [d]	(.) [d]	0.4 [d]	..	0.9	..	1.4	..	4.1	..	11.3
58 Libyan Arab Jamahiriya	10.4 [d]	1.9 [d]	0.1	0.1	..	..	..	..	..	..	..	..
59 Malaysia	85.9	3.6	1.1	0.1	5.3	3.4	-4.2	1.7	9.8	8.5	12.6	7.3
60 Macedonia, TFYR	276.6	135.2	..	7.3	..	2.0	..	0.9	..	6.3	..	15.8
61 Panama	35.3	11.5	1.9	0.3	2.6	0.5	-0.1	1.0	6.5	13.6	6.2	19.7
62 Belarus	39.4 [d]	4.0 [d]	..	0.3 [d]	..	1.7	..	-0.1	..	1.4	..	2.1
63 Tonga	22.3	217.2	26.3	16.4	0.2	1.8	-0.1	0.0	1.7	2.0	2.9	5.9
64 Mauritius	23.9	19.8	3.7	0.5	1.7	0.6	1.9	-1.6	6.5	5.5	8.8	8.2
65 Albania	317.0	100.9	0.5	6.6	..	2.8	..	(.)	..	1.2	..	3.4
66 Bosnia and Herzegovina	587.4	142.3	..	10.5	..	5.2	..	0.1	..	2.8	..	6.9
67 Suriname	11.6	26.9	15.5	1.2	..	..	..	..	..	..	..	..
68 Venezuela	57.1	2.3	0.2	0.1	0.9	0.7	-1.2	-2.5	10.3	7.9	23.3	25.6
69 Romania	700.8 [d]	31.3 [d]	0.6 [d]	1.5 [d]	0.0	2.5	(.)	4.4	(.)	6.8	0.3	18.6
70 Ukraine	483.8 [d]	9.9 [d]	0.4 [d]	1.2 [d]	..	1.7	..	-3.1	..	7.8	..	13.7

HDI rank	Official development assistance (ODA) received [a] (net disbursements) Total (US$ millions) 2002	Per capita (US$) 2002	As % of GDP 1990	As % of GDP 2002	Net foreign direct investment inflows [b] (% of GDP) 1990	(% of GDP) 2002	Other private flows [b, c] (% of GDP) 1990	(% of GDP) 2002	Total debt service As % of GDP 1990	As % of GDP 2002	MDG Total debt service As % of exports of goods and services 1990	As % of exports of goods and services 2002
71 Saint Lucia	33.5	226.5	3.1	5.1	11.3	3.4	-0.2	4.5	1.6	4.0	2.1	7.2
72 Brazil	375.9	2.1	(.)	0.1	0.2	3.7	-0.1	-1.5	1.8	11.4	22.2	68.9
73 Colombia	441.0	10.1	0.2	0.5	1.2	2.5	-0.4	-1.3	9.7	8.6	40.9	40.2
74 Oman	40.8	14.7	0.6	0.2	1.4	0.2	-3.8	-5.8	7.0	8.6	12.3	14.2 [f]
75 Samoa (Western)	37.8	214.2	42.6	14.5	5.9	0.5	0.0	0.0	4.9	3.0	5.8	10.8 [e]
76 Thailand	295.5	4.8	0.9	0.2	2.9	0.7	2.3	-2.3	6.2	15.6	16.9	23.1
77 Saudi Arabia	26.9	1.1	(.)	(.)	..	..	..	..	..	..	..	..
78 Kazakhstan	188.3	12.2	..	0.8	..	10.5	..	7.5	..	16.7	..	34.4
79 Jamaica	24.3	9.2	5.9	0.3	3.0	6.1	-1.0	0.7	14.4	10.7	26.9	18.4
80 Lebanon	455.8	126.8	8.9	2.6	0.2	1.5	0.2	26.3	3.5	12.7	3.3	51.0
81 Fiji	34.1	41.0	3.8	1.8	6.9	4.1	-1.2	-0.3	7.9	1.5	12.0	5.9
82 Armenia	293.5	95.5	..	12.4	..	4.7	..	-0.1	..	3.1	..	8.8
83 Philippines	559.7	7.1	2.9	0.7	1.2	1.4	0.2	3.1	8.1	11.8	27.0	20.2
84 Maldives	27.5	88.9	9.8	4.4	2.6	1.9	0.5	2.3	4.1	3.5	4.8	4.5
85 Peru	491.3	18.4	1.5	0.9	0.2	4.2	0.1	1.3	1.8	5.9	10.8	32.8
86 Turkmenistan	40.5	8.5	..	0.5	..	1.3	..	..	..	..	..	..
87 St. Vincent & the Grenadines	4.8	40.1	7.8	1.3	3.9	5.3	0.0	2.1	2.2	3.7	2.9	7.6
88 Turkey	635.8	9.0	0.8	0.3	0.5	0.6	0.8	3.6	4.9	15.0	29.4	46.8
89 Paraguay	56.7	9.9	1.1	1.0	1.5	-0.4	-0.2	1.0	6.2	5.9	12.4	10.5
90 Jordan	534.3	100.3	22.1	5.7	0.9	0.6	5.3	-0.9	15.6	6.3	20.4	8.7
91 Azerbaijan	349.4	42.1	..	5.7	..	22.9	..	-1.3	..	3.1	..	6.5
92 Tunisia	475.0	48.8	3.2	2.3	0.6	3.8	-1.6	4.0	11.6	6.8	24.5	13.5
93 Grenada	9.5	117.5	6.3	2.3	5.8	9.9	0.1	23.3	1.5	6.2	3.1	13.6
94 China	1,475.8	1.1	0.6	0.1	1.0	3.9	1.3	-0.2	2.0	2.4	11.7	8.2
95 Dominica	29.9	381.7	11.9	12.1	7.8	5.8	-0.1	0.7	3.5	4.5	5.6	7.9
96 Sri Lanka	344.0	18.2	9.1	2.1	0.5	1.5	0.1	-0.2	4.8	4.3	13.8	9.8
97 Georgia	312.6	60.4	..	9.2	..	4.9	..	-0.5	..	3.8	..	11.0
98 Dominican Republic	156.7	18.2	1.4	0.7	1.9	4.4	(.)	1.8	3.3	3.1	10.4	6.4
99 Belize	22.2	88.6	7.6	2.6	4.3	3.0	1.4	9.0	5.0	22.3	7.5	36.5
100 Ecuador	216.0	16.9	1.6	0.9	1.2	5.2	0.6	3.4	10.5	9.0	32.5	28.7
101 Iran, Islamic Rep. of	115.8	1.7	0.1	0.1	-0.3	(.)	(.)	0.7	0.5	1.3	3.2	4.1
102 Occupied Palestinian Territories	1,616.5	470.9	..	47.6	..	..	..	..	..	..	..	..
103 El Salvador	233.5	36.4	7.2	1.6	(.)	1.5	0.1	8.5	4.3	3.2	15.3	7.7
104 Guyana	64.8	84.9	42.6	9.0	2.0	6.1	-4.1	-0.1	74.5	10.8	..	10.7 [g, h]
105 Cape Verde	92.2	203.1	31.8	15.0	0.1	2.4	(.)	0.2	1.7	3.5	4.8	7.6
106 Syrian Arab Republic	80.8	4.7	5.6	0.4	0.6	1.1	-0.1	(.)	9.7	1.2	21.8	3.0
107 Uzbekistan	189.4	7.4	..	2.4	..	0.8	..	-1.0	..	9.2	..	24.3
108 Algeria	361.0	11.5	0.2	0.6	(.)	1.9	-0.7	-0.1	14.2	7.5	63.4	..
109 Equatorial Guinea	20.2	42.0	46.0	1.0	8.4	15.3	0.0	0.0	3.9	0.2	12.1	..
110 Kyrgyzstan	186.0	36.7	..	11.6	..	0.3	..	-3.7	..	10.8	..	25.3
111 Indonesia	1,308.1	6.0	1.5	0.8	1.0	-0.9	1.6	-3.2	8.7	9.8	33.3	24.8
112 Viet Nam	1,276.8	15.9	2.9	3.6	2.8	4.0	0.0	-1.8	2.7	3.4	..	6.0 [g, i]
113 Moldova, Rep. of	141.7	33.2	..	8.7	..	6.8	..	-2.1	..	14.1	..	19.9
114 Bolivia	681.0	78.8	11.2	8.7	0.6	8.7	-0.5	-1.0	7.9	6.1	38.6	27.7 [g, j]
115 Honduras	434.9	64.1	14.7	6.6	1.4	2.2	1.0	-0.6	12.8	6.0	35.3	12.3 [g, h]
116 Tajikistan	168.4	27.2	..	13.9	..	0.7	..	-1.6	..	6.5	..	10.2
117 Mongolia	208.5	81.5	..	18.6	..	7.0	..	(.)	..	4.7	..	6.7
118 Nicaragua	517.5	97.0	32.9	12.9	0.0	4.3	2.0	0.8	1.6	3.8	3.9	11.7 [g, j]
119 South Africa	656.8	14.7	..	0.6	..	0.7	..	(.)	..	4.5	..	12.5
120 Egypt	1,286.1	18.2	12.6	1.4	1.7	0.7	-0.2	-0.2	7.1	2.3	20.4	10.3

HDI rank		Official development assistance (ODA) received [a] (net disbursements)				Net foreign direct investment inflows [b] (% of GDP)		Other private flows [b, c] (% of GDP)		MDG Total debt service			
		Total (US$ millions)	Per capita (US$)	As % of GDP						As % of GDP		As % of exports of goods and services	
		2002	2002	1990	2002	1990	2002	1990	2002	1990	2002	1990	2002
121	Guatemala	248.7	20.7	2.6	1.1	0.6	0.5	-0.1	-0.2	2.8	1.8	12.6	7.5
122	Gabon	71.9	55.1	2.2	1.4	1.2	2.5	0.5	0.3	3.0	8.3	6.4	11.7
123	São Tomé and Principe	26.0	166.0	95.0	51.8	0.0	6.0	-0.2	0.0	4.9	12.1	34.0	31.8 g, h
124	Solomon Islands	26.3	56.8	21.7	11.0	4.9	-2.8	-1.5	-1.1	5.5	2.4	11.9	6.9 e
125	Morocco	636.2	21.2	4.1	1.8	0.6	1.2	1.2	-1.1	6.9	10.2	21.5	23.9
126	Namibia	135.1	68.9	5.2	4.7	..	..	..	..	..	..	..	..
127	India	1,462.7	1.4	0.4	0.3	0.1	0.6	0.5	0.4	2.6	2.6	31.9	14.9
128	Botswana	37.6	21.2	3.9	0.7	2.5	0.7	-0.5	(.)	2.8	1.1	4.3	2.0
129	Vanuatu	27.5	133.0	33.0	11.7	8.7	6.4	-0.1	0.0	1.6	0.9	2.1	1.0 f
130	Cambodia	486.9	35.3	3.7	12.2	0.0	1.3	0.0	0.0	2.7	0.5	..	0.8
131	Ghana	652.8	31.9	9.6	10.6	0.3	0.8	-0.3	-0.4	6.2	3.4	36.8	8.0 g, h
132	Myanmar	120.5	2.5	..	..	..	..	..	..	..	..	18.4	2.9 f, g, i
133	Papua New Guinea	203.3	36.4	12.8	7.2	4.8	1.8	1.5	-3.4	17.2	9.9	37.2	12.7 f
134	Bhutan	73.5	33.5	16.5	12.4	0.6	0.1	-0.9	0.0	1.8	1.1	5.5	4.6
135	Lao People's Dem. Rep.	278.3	50.3	17.3	16.6	0.7	1.5	0.0	0.0	1.1	2.7	8.7	9.0 f, g, i
136	Comoros	32.5	43.5	17.3	12.7	0.2	0.6	0.0	0.0	0.4	1.9	2.3	.. g, i
137	Swaziland	24.7	23.1	6.1	2.1	3.4	3.8	-0.5	0.0	5.3	1.7	5.7	1.7
138	Bangladesh	912.8	6.3	7.0	1.9	(.)	0.1	0.2	0.2	2.5	1.5	25.8	7.3
139	Sudan	350.9	10.7	6.2	2.6	0.0	4.7	0.0	0.0	0.4	0.2	8.7	0.8 g, i
140	Nepal	365.5	14.9	11.7	6.6	0.0	0.2	-0.4	(.)	1.9	1.8	15.7	8.8
141	Cameroon	631.9	40.2	4.0	7.0	-1.0	1.0	-0.1	-0.5	4.6	3.9	20.5	.. g, h
	Low human development												
142	Pakistan	2,143.7	14.3	2.8	3.6	0.6	1.4	-0.2	-0.8	4.8	4.8	21.3	17.8
143	Togo	51.0	10.6	16.0	3.7	1.1	5.4	0.3	0.0	5.3	0.9	11.9	2.5 g, i
144	Congo	419.8	115.5	7.8	13.9	0.0	11.0	-3.6	0.0	19.0	0.8	35.3	1.0 g, i
145	Lesotho	76.4	42.5	23.0	10.7	2.8	11.3	(.)	-1.1	3.8	9.4	4.2	11.8
146	Uganda	637.9	25.5	15.5	11.0	0.0	2.6	0.4	(.)	3.4	1.4	81.4	7.1 g, j
147	Zimbabwe	200.6	15.6	3.9	2.4	-0.1	0.3	1.1	-0.4	5.4	0.7	23.1	..
148	Kenya	393.1	12.5	13.9	3.2	0.7	0.4	0.8	-0.1	9.2	3.7	35.4	13.6 g, i
149	Yemen	583.7	30.2	8.4	5.8	-2.7	1.1	3.3	0.0	3.5	1.7	5.6	3.3 g, i
150	Madagascar	372.6	22.0	12.9	8.5	0.7	0.2	-0.5	0.0	7.2	1.7	45.5	9.9 g, h
151	Nigeria	313.8	2.6	0.9	0.7	2.1	2.9	-0.4	-1.5	11.7	3.4	22.6	8.6
152	Mauritania	355.4	126.6	23.3	36.7	0.7	1.2	-0.1	0.4	14.3	6.6	29.8	.. g, j
153	Haiti	155.7	18.9	5.9	4.5	0.0	0.2	0.0	0.0	1.2	0.8	11.0	..
154	Djibouti	77.8	112.3	46.4	13.0	(.)	0.6	-0.1	0.0	3.6	2.0	..	..
155	Gambia	60.5	43.6	31.3	17.0	0.0	12.0	-2.4	-0.1	11.9	5.4	22.2	.. g, h
156	Eritrea	230.4	57.7	..	35.9	..	3.3	..	0.0	..	1.4	..	4.7
157	Senegal	448.8	45.5	14.4	8.9	1.0	1.9	-0.2	(.)	5.7	4.3	20.0	12.6 g, h
158	Timor-Leste	219.8	297.6	..	56.6	..	..	..	..	..	..	..	..
159	Rwanda	356.1	43.1	11.3	20.6	0.3	0.2	-0.1	0.0	0.8	1.3	14.2	14.9 g, h
160	Guinea	249.6	29.9	10.4	7.8	0.6	0.0	-0.7	(.)	6.0	4.2	20.0	13.6 g, h
161	Benin	220.3	33.6	14.5	8.2	3.4	1.5	(.)	0.0	2.1	2.3	8.2	9.6 g, i
162	Tanzania, U. Rep. of	1,232.8	34.0	27.5	13.1	0.0	2.6	0.1	-0.3	4.2	1.5	32.9	8.9 g, i
163	Côte d'Ivoire	1,068.8	65.3	6.4	9.1	0.4	2.0	0.1	-1.0	11.7	7.1	35.4	14.1 g, i
164	Zambia	640.6	59.9	14.6	17.3	6.2	5.3	-0.3	-0.3	6.2	8.3	14.9	27.1 g, h
165	Malawi	377.1	31.8	26.8	19.8	1.2	0.3	0.1	0.0	7.1	1.9	29.3	7.6 g, h
166	Angola	421.4	32.0	2.6	3.7	-3.3	11.7	5.6	1.0	3.2	7.7	8.1	10.0 g, i

HDI rank	Official development assistance (ODA) received [a] (net disbursements) Total (US$ millions) 2002	Per capita (US$) 2002	As % of GDP 1990	As % of GDP 2002	Net foreign direct investment inflows [b] (% of GDP) 1990	(% of GDP) 2002	Other private flows [b, c] (% of GDP) 1990	(% of GDP) 2002	MDG Total debt service As % of GDP 1990	As % of GDP 2002	As % of exports of goods and services 1990	As % of exports of goods and services 2002
167 Chad	233.0	27.9	18.0	11.6	0.5	45.0	(.)	(.)	0.7	1.5	4.4	.. [g, h]
168 Congo, Dem. Rep. of the	806.7	15.8	9.6	14.1	-0.2	0.6	-0.1	0.0	3.7	16.2	..	.. [g, i]
169 Central African Republic	59.8	15.7	16.8	5.7	(.)	0.4	(.)	0.0	2.0	0.1	13.2	.. [g, i]
170 Ethiopia	1,306.7	18.9	11.8	21.6	0.1	1.2	-0.7	-0.1	2.7	1.8	39.0	9.7 [g, h]
171 Mozambique	2,057.6	111.0	40.7	57.2	0.4	11.3	1.0	-0.7	3.2	2.1	26.2	6.1 [g, j]
172 Guinea-Bissau	59.4	41.0	52.7	29.2	0.8	0.5	(.)	0.0	3.4	7.3	31.0	.. [g, h]
173 Burundi	172.1	26.1	23.3	23.9	0.1	0.0	-0.5	-0.3	3.7	3.2	43.4	59.0 [g, i]
174 Mali	472.1	37.4	19.9	14.0	0.2	3.0	(.)	0.0	2.8	2.7	12.3	7.0 [g, j]
175 Burkina Faso	472.7	37.4	10.6	15.1	(.)	0.3	(.)	0.0	1.1	1.7	6.8	16.0 [g, j]
176 Niger	298.5	25.9	16.0	13.7	1.6	0.4	0.4	-0.4	4.0	1.3	17.4	.. [g, h]
177 Sierra Leone	353.4	74.2	9.4	45.1	5.0	0.6	0.6	0.0	3.3	2.9	10.1	.. [g, h]
Developing countries	55,150.0 T	8.8	1.5	0.7	1.0	2.5	0.4	-0.1	3.5	4.8	19.9	17.8
Least developed countries	17,282.3 T	24.7	11.7	8.9	0.1	2.9	0.4	..	2.7	2.3	16.2	7.7
Arab States	7,015.6 T	24.2	2.7	0.8	0.9	0.6	-0.1	0.5	4.0	2.3	14.9	6.7
East Asia and the Pacific	7,724.0 T	3.9	..	0.3	2.3	3.6	0.6	-0.3	3.0	3.4	17.9	12.1
Latin America and the Caribbean	5,063.1 T	8.6	0.4	0.3	0.7	2.7	0.5	-0.6	4.0	8.2	23.7	30.8
South Asia	6,851.4 T	4.5	1.1	0.7	(.)	0.6	0.3	0.3	2.6	2.5	19.5	11.9
Sub-Saharan Africa	17,854.0 T	26.3	..	..	..	2.4	0.2	-0.3	3.8	4.1	20.4	10.6
Central & Eastern Europe & CIS	7,140.0 T	31.2	..	..	..	3.5	(.)	1.5	0.5	7.3	13.5	17.0
OECD	..	..	..	..	1.0 [k]	1.9 [k]	..	..	..	..	..	..
High-income OECD	..	..	..	..	1.0 [k]	1.9 [k]	..	..	..	..	..	..
High human development	476.3 T	..	..	..	1.0 [k]	2.0 [k]	..	..	..	..	..	..
Medium human development	26,070.9 T	6.5	1.2	0.5	0.7	2.2	0.3	0.1	2.9	5.5	18.5	16.7
Low human development	17,379.9 T	24.2	8.5	7.4	0.5	2.9	0.3	-0.5	6.2	4.0	21.6	11.1
High income	88.0 T	..	..	..	1.0 [k]	1.9 [k]	..	..	..	..	..	..
Middle income	18,288.2 T	7.4	0.9	0.3	0.9	2.7	0.3	0.3	3.0	6.3	17.9	18.1
Low income	29,622.2 T	11.8	3.5	2.5	0.4	1.2	0.5	-0.5	4.2	3.9	27.0	15.0
World	61,567.8 T	9.7	..	..	1.0 [k]	2.0 [k]	..	..	..	..	..	..

Note: This table presents data for countries included in Parts I and II of the Development Assistance Committee's (DAC) list of aid recipients (OECD 2004e). The denominator conventionally used when comparing official development assistance and total debt service to the size of the economy is GNI, not GDP (see the definitions of statistical terms). GDP is used here, however, to allow comparability throughout the table. With few exceptions the denominators produce similar results.

a. ODA receipts are total net ODA flows from DAC countries as well as Czech Republic, Iceland, Israel, the Republic of Korea, Kuwait, Poland, Saudi Arabia, Slovakia, Turkey and the United Arab Emirates and other small donors, including Taiwan (province of China), Estonia, Latvia and Lithuania. A negative value indicates that the repayment of ODA loans exceeds the amount of ODA received. Aggregates do not include net official aid. See the definitions of statistical terms. b. A negative value indicates that the capital flowing out of the country exceeds that flowing in. c. Other private flows combine non-debt-creating portfolio equity investment flows, portfolio debt flows and bank and trade-related lending. See the definitions of statistical terms. d. Data refer to net official aid. See the definitions of statistical terms. e. Data refer to 2000. f. Data refer to 2001. g. Country included in the Debt Initiative for Heavily Indebted Poor Countries (HIPCs). h. Decision point reached under the HIPC Initiative. i. Decision and completion points not yet reached under the HIPC Initiative. j. Completion point reached under the HIPC Initiative. k. Data used to calculate the aggregate include countries not shown in table.

Source: Column 1: OECD 2004f; aggregates calculated for the Human Development Report Office by the Organisation for Economic Co-operation and Development (OECD); *column 2:* calculated on the basis of data on ODA from OECD 2004f; aggregates calculated for the Human Development Report Office by the OECD; *columns 3 and 4:* calculated on the basis of data on ODA from OECD 2004f and data on GDP from World Bank 2004f; *columns 5, 6, 11 and 12:* World Bank 2004f; aggregates calculated for the Human Development Report Office by the World Bank; *columns 7 and 8:* calculated on the basis of data on portfolio investment (bonds and equity), bank and trade-related lending and GDP data from World Bank 2004f; *columns 9 and 10:* calculated on the basis of data on total debt service and GDP from World Bank 2004f.

19 Priorities in public spending

HDI rank	Public expenditure on education[a] (% of GDP)		Public expenditure on health[b] (% of GDP)		Military expenditure[c] (% of GDP)		Total debt service[d] (% of GDP)	
	1990[e]	1999-2001[f]	1990	2001	1990	2002	1990	2002
High human development								
1 Norway	7.1	6.8	6.4	6.8	2.9	2.1	..	..
2 Sweden	7.4	7.6	7.6	7.4	2.6	1.9	..	..
3 Australia	5.1	4.6	5.3	6.2	2.1	1.9	..	..
4 Canada	6.5	5.2	6.8	6.8	2.0	1.2	..	..
5 Netherlands	6.0	5.0	5.7	5.7	2.5	1.6	..	..
6 Belgium	5.0	5.8 [g]	6.6	6.4	2.4	1.3	..	..
7 Iceland	5.4	6.0 [g]	6.8	7.6	0.0	0.0	..	..
8 United States	5.2	5.6	4.7	6.2	5.3	3.4	..	..
9 Japan	..	3.6	4.6	6.2	0.9	1.0	..	..
10 Ireland	5.2	4.3	4.8	4.9	1.2	0.7	..	..
11 Switzerland	5.1	5.6	5.7	6.4	1.8	1.1	..	..
12 United Kingdom	4.9	4.6	5.1	6.3	4.0	2.4	..	..
13 Finland	5.6	6.3	6.4	5.3	1.6	1.2	..	..
14 Austria	5.4	5.9	5.2	5.5	1.0	0.8	..	..
15 Luxembourg	3.0	4.1	5.7	5.4	0.9	0.9	..	..
16 France	5.4	5.7	6.7	7.3	3.5	2.5	..	..
17 Denmark	..	8.3	7.0	7.0	2.0	1.6	..	..
18 New Zealand	6.2	6.6	5.8	6.4	1.9	1.1	..	..
19 Germany	..	4.6	5.9	8.1	2.8 [h]	1.5	..	..
20 Spain	4.4	4.4	5.2	5.4	1.8	1.2	..	..
21 Italy	3.1	5.0	6.3	6.3	2.1	2.1	..	..
22 Israel	6.3	7.3	3.8	6.0	12.2	9.2	..	..
23 Hong Kong, China (SAR)	..	4.1	1.6	..	..	..	..	..
24 Greece	2.5	3.8	4.7	5.2	4.7	4.3	..	..
25 Singapore	..	..	1.0	1.3	4.9	5.2	..	..
26 Portugal	4.2	5.8	4.1	6.3	2.7	2.1	..	..
27 Slovenia	..	..	..	6.3	..	1.5	..	..
28 Korea, Rep. of	3.5	3.6	1.8	2.6	3.7	2.7	..	..
29 Barbados	7.8	6.5	5.0	4.3	..	..	..	..
30 Cyprus	3.5 [i]	5.6	..	3.9	5.0	1.6	..	..
31 Malta	4.3	4.9 [g]	..	6.0	0.9	0.9	..	..
32 Czech Republic	..	4.4	4.8	6.7	..	2.1	..	6.5
33 Brunei Darussalam	..	..	1.6	2.5	6.7 [j]	7.0	..	..
34 Argentina	1.1	4.6 [g]	4.2	5.1	1.3	1.2	4.4	5.7
35 Seychelles	7.8	7.5 [g]	3.6	4.1	4.0	1.7	5.9	2.1
36 Estonia	..	7.4	1.9	4.3	..	1.9	..	12.0
37 Poland	..	5.4	4.8	4.6	2.7	1.9	1.6	7.1
38 Hungary	5.8	5.1	..	5.1	2.8	1.8	12.8	22.6
39 Saint Kitts and Nevis	2.7	7.7	2.7	3.2	..	..	1.9	10.7
40 Bahrain	4.2	..	..	2.9	5.1	3.9	..	..
41 Lithuania	4.6	..	3.0	4.2	..	1.8	..	9.3
42 Slovakia	5.1	4.1	5.0	5.1	..	1.9	..	14.3
43 Chile	2.5	3.9	2.2	3.1	4.3	3.9	9.1	12.0
44 Kuwait	4.8	..	4.0	3.5	48.5	10.4	..	..
45 Costa Rica	4.4	4.7	6.7	4.9	0.0	0.0	8.8	4.0
46 Uruguay	3.0	2.5	2.0	5.1	2.5	1.7	10.6	10.6
47 Qatar	3.5	..	..	2.2	..	..	..	..
48 Croatia	..	4.2 [g]	9.5	7.3	..	2.5	..	13.5
49 United Arab Emirates	1.9	..	0.8	2.6	6.2	3.7	..	..
50 Latvia	3.8	5.9	2.7	3.4	..	1.8	..	7.7

HDI rank	Public expenditure on education [a] (% of GDP)		Public expenditure on health [b] (% of GDP)		Military expenditure [c] (% of GDP)		Total debt service [d] (% of GDP)	
	1990 [e]	1999-2001 [f]	1990	2001	1990	2002	1990	2002
51 Bahamas	4.0	..	2.8	3.2	..	..	..	..
52 Cuba	..	8.5	4.9	6.2	..	..	..	..
53 Mexico	3.6	5.1	1.8	2.7	0.5	0.5	4.3	6.8
54 Trinidad and Tobago	3.6	4.0	2.5	1.7	..	..	8.9	2.8
55 Antigua and Barbuda	..	3.2	2.8	3.4	..	..	..	..
Medium human development								
56 Bulgaria	5.2	..	4.1	3.9	3.5	2.7	..	8.8
57 Russian Federation	3.5	3.1	2.5	3.7	12.3 [k]	4.0	..	4.1
58 Libyan Arab Jamahiriya	..	2.7	..	1.6	..	2.4	..	..
59 Malaysia	5.2	7.9	1.5	2.0	2.6	2.4	9.8	8.5
60 Macedonia, TFYR	..	4.1 [g]	9.2	5.8	..	2.8	..	6.3
61 Panama	4.7	4.3	4.6	4.8	1.3	..	6.5	13.6
62 Belarus	4.9	6.0	2.5	4.8	..	1.4	..	1.4
63 Tonga	..	5.0	3.7	3.4	..	..	1.7	2.0
64 Mauritius	3.5	3.3	..	2.0	0.3	0.2	6.5	5.5
65 Albania	5.8	..	3.3	2.4	5.9	1.2	..	1.2
66 Bosnia and Herzegovina	..	..	..	2.8	..	..	..	2.8
67 Suriname	8.1	..	3.5	5.7	..	..	..	..
68 Venezuela	3.0	..	2.5	3.7	1.8 [j]	1.4	10.3	7.9
69 Romania	2.8	3.5 [g]	2.8	5.2	4.6	2.3	(.)	6.8
70 Ukraine	5.2	4.2	3.0	2.9	..	2.9	..	7.8
71 Saint Lucia	..	7.3 [g]	2.1	2.9	..	..	1.6	4.0
72 Brazil	..	4.0	3.0	3.2	1.9	1.6	1.8	11.4
73 Colombia	2.5	4.4	1.2	3.6	2.2	4.2	9.7	8.6
74 Oman	3.1	4.2 [g]	2.0	2.4	16.5	12.3	7.0	8.6
75 Samoa (Western)	3.4	4.5 [g]	2.8	4.8	..	..	4.9	3.0
76 Thailand	3.5	5.0	0.9	2.1	2.3	1.4	6.2	15.6
77 Saudi Arabia	6.5	..	..	3.4	12.8	9.8	..	..
78 Kazakhstan	3.2	..	3.2	1.9	..	1.0	..	16.7
79 Jamaica	4.7	6.3	2.6	2.9	..	..	14.4	10.7
80 Lebanon	..	2.9	..	..	7.6	4.7	3.5	12.7
81 Fiji	4.6	5.5 [g]	2.0	2.7	2.3	1.8	7.9	1.5
82 Armenia	7.0	3.2	..	3.2	..	2.7	..	3.1
83 Philippines	2.9	3.2	1.5	1.5	1.4	1.0	8.1	11.8
84 Maldives	4.0	..	3.6	5.6	..	..	4.1	3.5
85 Peru	2.2	3.3	1.3	2.6	..	1.5	1.8	5.9
86 Turkmenistan	4.3	..	4.0	3.0	..	..	..	..
87 St. Vincent & the Grenadines	6.4	9.3	4.4	3.8	..	..	2.2	3.7
88 Turkey	2.2	3.7	2.2	..	3.5	4.9	4.9	15.0
89 Paraguay	1.1	4.7 [g]	0.7	3.0	1.2	0.9	6.2	5.9
90 Jordan	8.4	4.6	3.6	4.5	9.9	8.4	15.6	6.3
91 Azerbaijan	..	3.5	2.7	..	..	2.0	..	3.1
92 Tunisia	6.0	6.8 [g]	3.0	4.9	2.0	..	11.6	6.8
93 Grenada	5.1	..	3.3	3.8	..	..	1.5	6.2
94 China	2.3	..	2.2	2.0	2.7	2.5	2.0	2.4
95 Dominica	..	5.0 [g]	3.9	4.3	..	..	3.5	4.5
96 Sri Lanka	2.6	1.3	1.5	1.8	2.1	3.1	4.8	4.3
97 Georgia	..	2.5	3.0	1.4	..	0.9	..	3.8
98 Dominican Republic	..	2.4	1.6	2.2	..	..	3.3	3.1
99 Belize	4.7	6.2	2.2	2.3	1.2	..	5.0	22.3
100 Ecuador	2.8	1.0 [g]	1.5	2.3	1.9	2.8	10.5	9.0

		Public expenditure on education [a] (% of GDP)		Public expenditure on health [b] (% of GDP)		Military expenditure [c] (% of GDP)		Total debt service [d] (% of GDP)	
HDI rank		1990 [e]	1999-2001 [f]	1990	2001	1990	2002	1990	2002
101	Iran, Islamic Rep. of	4.1	5.0	1.5	2.7	2.9	4.0	0.5	1.3
102	Occupied Palestinian Territories	..	..	..	..	..	..	..	..
103	El Salvador	1.9	2.5 [g]	1.4	3.7	2.7	0.8	4.3	3.2
104	Guyana	3.4	4.1 [g]	2.9	4.2	0.9	..	74.5	10.8
105	Cape Verde	..	..	..	3.8	..	0.7	1.7	3.5
106	Syrian Arab Republic	4.1	4.0	0.4	2.4	6.9	6.1	9.7	1.2
107	Uzbekistan	..	..	4.6	2.7	..	..	..	9.2
108	Algeria	5.3	..	3.0	3.1	1.5	3.7	14.2	7.5
109	Equatorial Guinea	..	0.5	1.0	1.2	..	..	3.9	0.2
110	Kyrgyzstan	8.3	3.1	4.7	1.9	..	1.5	..	10.8
111	Indonesia	1.0	1.3	0.6	0.6	1.8	1.2	8.7	9.8
112	Viet Nam	..	..	0.9	1.5	7.9	..	2.7	3.4
113	Moldova, Rep. of	..	4.0	4.4	2.8	..	0.4	..	14.1
114	Bolivia	2.3	6.0	2.1	3.5	2.4	1.7	7.9	6.1
115	Honduras	..	..	3.3	3.2	..	0.8	12.8	6.0
116	Tajikistan	9.7	2.4	4.9	1.0	..	1.4	..	6.5
117	Mongolia	12.1	6.5 [g]	6.4	4.6	5.7	2.3	..	4.7
118	Nicaragua	3.4	..	7.0	3.8	4.0 [j]	1.4	1.6	3.8
119	South Africa	6.2	5.7	3.1	3.6	3.8	1.6	..	4.5
120	Egypt	3.7	..	1.8	1.9	3.9	2.7	7.1	2.3
121	Guatemala	1.4	1.7	1.8	2.3	1.5	0.6	2.8	1.8
122	Gabon	..	3.9 [g]	2.0	1.7	..	..	3.0	8.3
123	São Tomé and Principe	..	..	..	1.5	..	..	4.9	12.1
124	Solomon Islands	..	3.5 [g]	5.0	4.7	..	..	5.5	2.4
125	Morocco	5.3	5.1	0.9	2.0	4.1	4.3	6.9	10.2
126	Namibia	7.6	7.9	3.7	4.7	5.6 [j]	2.9	..	..
127	India	3.9	4.1	0.9	0.9	2.7	2.3	2.6	2.6
128	Botswana	6.7	2.1	1.7	4.4	4.1	4.0	2.8	1.1
129	Vanuatu	4.6	10.5	2.6	2.2	..	..	1.6	0.9
130	Cambodia	..	2.0	..	1.7	3.1	2.7	2.7	0.5
131	Ghana	3.2	4.1 [g]	1.3	2.8	0.4	0.6	6.2	3.4
132	Myanmar	..	1.3	1.0	0.4	3.4	..	..	..
133	Papua New Guinea	..	2.3 [g]	3.1	3.9	2.1	..	17.2	9.9
134	Bhutan	..	5.2	1.7	3.6	..	..	1.8	1.1
135	Lao People's Dem. Rep.	..	3.2	0.0	1.7	..	..	1.1	2.7
136	Comoros	..	..	2.9	1.9	..	..	0.4	1.9
137	Swaziland	5.7	5.5	1.9	2.3	2.1	..	5.3	1.7
138	Bangladesh	1.5	2.3	0.7	1.5	1.0	1.1	2.5	1.5
139	Sudan	0.9	..	0.7	0.6	3.6	2.8	0.4	0.2
140	Nepal	2.0	3.4	0.8	1.5	0.9	1.4	1.9	1.8
141	Cameroon	3.2	5.4	0.9	1.2	1.5	1.4	4.6	3.9
Low human development									
142	Pakistan	2.6	1.8 [g]	1.1	1.0	5.8	4.7	4.8	4.8
143	Togo	5.5	4.8	1.4	1.5	3.1	..	5.3	0.9
144	Congo	5.0	3.2	1.5	1.4	..	..	19.0	0.8
145	Lesotho	6.1	10.0	2.6	4.3	4.5	2.7	3.8	9.4
146	Uganda	1.5	2.5 [g]	..	3.4	3.0	2.4	3.4	1.4
147	Zimbabwe	..	10.4 [g]	3.2	2.8	4.5	3.2	5.4	0.7
148	Kenya	6.7	6.2 [g]	2.4	1.7	2.9	1.7	9.2	3.7
149	Yemen	..	10.0 [g]	1.1	1.5	8.5	7.1	3.5	1.7
150	Madagascar	2.1	2.5	..	1.3	1.2	..	7.2	1.7
151	Nigeria	0.9	..	1.0	0.8	0.9	1.1	11.7	3.4

19 Priorities in public spending

HDI rank		Public expenditure on education[a] (% of GDP)		Public expenditure on health[b] (% of GDP)		Military expenditure[c] (% of GDP)		Total debt service[d] (% of GDP)	
		1990[e]	1999-2001[f]	1990	2001	1990	2002	1990	2002
152	Mauritania	..	3.6 [g]	..	2.6	3.8	1.9	14.3	6.6
153	Haiti	1.4	..	1.2	2.7	..	..	1.2	0.8
154	Djibouti	..	..	..	4.1	6.3	..	3.6	2.0
155	Gambia	3.8	2.7 [g]	2.2	3.2	1.1	0.9	11.9	5.4
156	Eritrea	..	2.7	..	3.7	..	23.5	..	1.4
157	Senegal	3.9	3.2 [g]	0.7	2.8	2.0	1.5	5.7	4.3
158	Timor-Leste	..	..	..	5.8	..	0.0	..	..
159	Rwanda	..	2.8 [g]	1.7	3.1	3.7	3.3	0.8	1.3
160	Guinea	..	1.9 [g]	2.0	1.9	2.4 [i]	2.9	6.0	4.2
161	Benin	..	3.3 [g]	1.6	2.1	1.8	..	2.1	2.3
162	Tanzania, U. Rep. of	3.2	..	1.6	2.0	2.0 [j]	1.5	4.2	1.5
163	Côte d'Ivoire	..	4.6	1.5	1.0	1.3	..	11.7	7.1
164	Zambia	2.4	1.9	2.6	3.0	3.7	..	6.2	8.3
165	Malawi	3.3	4.1 [g]	..	2.7	1.3	..	7.1	1.9
166	Angola	3.9	2.8 [g]	1.4	2.8	5.8	3.7	3.2	7.7
167	Chad	..	2.0 [g]	..	2.0	..	1.4	0.7	1.5
168	Congo, Dem. Rep. of the	..	..	..	1.5	..	..	3.7	16.2
169	Central African Republic	2.2	..	..	2.3	1.6 [i]	1.0	2.0	0.1
170	Ethiopia	3.4	4.8	0.9	1.4	8.5	5.2	2.7	1.8
171	Mozambique	3.9	2.4 [g]	3.6	4.0	10.1	2.4	3.2	2.1
172	Guinea-Bissau	..	2.1	1.1	3.2	..	..	3.4	7.3
173	Burundi	3.4	3.6 [g]	1.1	2.1	3.4	7.6	3.7	3.2
174	Mali	..	2.8 [g]	1.6	1.7	2.1	..	2.8	2.7
175	Burkina Faso	2.7	..	1.0	2.0	3.0	1.8	1.1	1.7
176	Niger	3.2	2.3	..	1.4	..	1.1	4.0	1.3
177	Sierra Leone	..	..	..	2.6	1.4	2.2	3.3	2.9

a. Data refer to total public expenditure on education, including current and capital expenditures. b. Data for some countries may differ slightly from data presented in table 6 from WHO 2004b. c. As a result of a number of limitations in the data, comparisons of military expenditure data over time and across countries should be made with caution. For detailed notes on the data see SIPRI 2003. d. For aggregates, see table 18. e. Data may not be comparable between countries as a result of differences in methods of data collection. f. Data refer to the most recent year available during the period specified. g. Data refer to UNESCO Institute for Statistics estimate when national estimate is not available. h. Data refer to the Federal Republic of Germany before reunification. i. Data refer to the Office of Greek Education only. j. Data refer to 1991. k. Data refer to the former Soviet Union.

Source: Column 1: Calculated on the basis of GDP and public expenditure data from UNESCO Institute for Statistics 2003c; *column 2:* UNESCO Institute for Statistics 2004b; *columns 3 and 4:* World Bank 2004f; *columns 5 and 6:* SIPRI 2004a; *columns 7 and 8:* calculated on the basis of data on GDP and total debt service from World Bank 2004f.

20 Unemployment in OECD countries

		Unemployment rate			MDG Youth unemployment rate		Long-term unemployment [a]	
	Unemployed people (thousands)	Total (% of labour force)	Average annual (% of labour force)	Female (% of male rate)	Total (% of labour force ages 15-24) [b]	Female (% of male rate)	(% of total unemployment)	
							Women	Men
HDI rank	2002	2002	1992-2002	2002	2002	2002	2002	2002
High human development								
1 Norway	94.3	4.0	4.4	89	11.5	85	3.9	8.3
2 Sweden	176.2	4.0	6.4	84	12.8	86	18.2	23.1
3 Australia	631.3	6.3	8.1	94	12.4	87	17.1	25.9
4 Canada	1,276.2	7.6	9.0	88	13.7	77	8.8	10.3
5 Netherlands	169.9	2.3	4.8	128	5.9	87	26.4	26.9
6 Belgium	329.9	7.3	8.4	125	15.7	95	53.6	45.9
7 Iceland	5.3	3.3	3.6	82	7.2	46	13.3	9.5
8 United States	8,388.7	5.8	5.4	95	12.0	87	8.1	8.9
9 Japan	3,586.6	5.4	3.8	91	10.0	76	22.4	36.2
10 Ireland	82.1	4.4	9.6	81	7.7	74	18.0	35.9
11 Switzerland	131.4	3.1	3.3	109	5.7	54	24.5	19.3
12 United Kingdom	1,508.5	5.2	7.3	77	11.0	68	17.1	26.9
13 Finland	236.9	9.1	12.5	100	20.7	97	21.2	27.3
14 Austria	229.5	5.3	5.3	96	6.3	94	23.3	16.4
15 Luxembourg	5.8	3.0	2.8	188	7.0	168	26.5 [c]	28.6 [c]
16 France	2,442.8	9.0	10.8	128	20.2	125	35.2	32.2
17 Denmark	129.4	4.5	6.1	102	7.1	59	22.4	17.2
18 New Zealand	102.5	5.2	7.1	106	11.4	98	11.5	16.9
19 Germany	3,396.0	8.1	7.9	95	9.7	70	50.3	46.0
20 Spain	2,082.9	11.4	14.6	203	22.2	149	44.5	34.3
21 Italy	2,163.2	9.1	10.8	177	26.3	139	60.1	58.2
24 Greece	435.7	10.0	10.1	236	25.7	181	55.7	47.1
26 Portugal	272.3	5.1	5.5	146	11.5	143	36.2	34.8
28 Korea, Rep. of	708.0	3.1	3.5	73	8.1	70	1.2	3.1
32 Czech Republic	374.1	7.3	6.0	153	16.0	115	51.1	50.3
37 Poland	3,430.8	19.9	14.4 [d]	109	43.9	102	52.0	45.1
38 Hungary	238.8	5.9	8.7	88	12.6	90	41.7	47.0
42 Slovakia	487.0	18.6	15.1 [e]	101	37.4	91	61.2	58.5
53 Mexico	548.6	2.7	3.5	104	4.9	124	0.4	1.2
Medium human development								
86 Turkey	2,473.0	10.3	7.7	91	19.5	87	36.4	27.3
OECD [f]	36,137.5 T	6.9	6.9	107	13.1	94	30.9	28.5

a. Data refer to unemployment lasting 12 months or longer. b. The age range for the youth labour force may be 16-24 for some countries. c. Data are based on a small sample and must be treated with caution. d. Data refer to the average annual rate in 1993-2002. e. Data refer to the average annual rate in 1994-2002. f. Aggregates for the group of Organisation for Economic Co-operation and Development (OECD) countries are from OECD 2004c.
Source: Columns 1, 2 and 5: OECD 2004c; columns 3, 4 and 6: calculated on the basis of data on male and female unemployment rates from OECD 2004c; columns 7 and 8: OECD 2004d.

21 Energy and the environment

		Traditional fuel consumption (% of total energy requirements)	Electricity consumption per capita (kilowatt-hours)		MDG GDP per unit of energy use (1995 PPP US$ per kg of oil equivalent)		MDG Carbon dioxide emissions Per capita (metric tons)		Share of world total (%)	Ratification of environmental treaties [a] Cartagena Protocol on Biosafety	Framework Convention on Climate Change	Kyoto Protocol to the Framework Convention on Climate Change [b]	Convention on Biological Diversity
HDI rank		2001	1980	2001	1980	2001	1980	2000	2000				
High human development													
1	Norway	5.1 c	22,400 c	29,290 c	4.4	5.5	9.5	11.1	0.2	●	●	●	●
2	Sweden	33.1	11,700	17,355	3.4	4.0	8.6	5.3	0.2	●	●	●	●
3	Australia	7.9	6,599	11,205	3.4	4.2	13.8	18.0	1.4		●	○	●
4	Canada	4.6	14,243	18,212	2.4	3.2	17.1	14.2	1.8	○	●	●	●
5	Netherlands	1.1	4,560	6,905	3.7	5.2	10.8	8.7	0.6	●	●	●	●
6	Belgium	1.5	5,177	8,818	3.6	4.3	13.3	10.0	0.4	○	●	●	●
7	Iceland	0.0	13,838	28,260	2.8	2.3	8.2	7.7	(.)	○	●	●	●
8	United States	4.0	10,336	13,241	2.6	4.0	20.4	19.8	23.1		●	○	○
9	Japan	1.2	4,944	8,203	5.1	5.8	7.9	9.3	4.9	●	●	●	●
10	Ireland	1.1	3,106	6,417	4.1	7.0	7.4	11.1	0.2	●	●	●	●
11	Switzerland	6.8 d	5,878 d	8,499 d	7.0	7.0	6.5	5.4	0.2	●	●	●	●
12	United Kingdom	0.5	5,022	6,631	4.1	5.8	10.3	9.6	2.3	●	●	●	●
13	Finland	24.7	8,372	16,273	2.8	3.6	11.9	10.3	0.2	○	●	●	●
14	Austria	13.3	4,988	8,110	5.6	6.8	6.9	7.6	0.3	●	●	●	●
15	Luxembourg	1.6	10,879	15,602	1.9	5.0	28.9	19.4	(.)	●	●	●	●
16	France	5.7 e	4,633 e	8,351 e	4.8	5.3	9.0	6.2	1.5 e	●	●	●	●
17	Denmark	11.5	5,059	8,173	4.9	7.3	12.3	8.4	0.2	●	●	●	●
18	New Zealand	6.3	7,270	10,366	4.9	4.0	5.6	8.3	0.1	○	●	●	●
19	Germany	2.3	..	7,207	3.7	5.6	..	9.6	3.2	●	●	●	●
20	Spain	3.9	2,906	5,986	6.2	6.0	5.3	7.0	1.2	●	●	●	●
21	Italy	2.0 f	3,364 f	5,770 f	6.5	7.8	6.6	7.4	1.8 f	●	●	●	●
22	Israel	0.0	3,187	6,591	5.6	..	5.4	10.0	0.3		●		●
23	Hong Kong, China (SAR)	0.4	2,449	6,127	10.2	9.9	3.2	5.0	0.1	–	–	–	–
24	Greece	5.0	2,413	5,082	7.5	5.8	5.4	8.5	0.4	○	●	●	●
25	Singapore	0.1	2,836	8,010	3.4	2.9	12.5	14.7	0.2		●		●
26	Portugal	9.7	1,750	4,539	8.4	6.4	2.8	5.9	0.2	○	●	●	●
27	Slovenia	7.5	..	6,372	..	4.5	..	7.3	0.1	●	●	●	●
28	Korea, Rep. of	1.9	1,051	6,632	3.8	3.5	3.3	9.1	1.8	○	●	●	●
29	Barbados	5.9	1,333	3,086	..	..	2.7	4.4	(.)		●	●	●
30	Cyprus	1.3	1,692	4,679	4.5	5.0	5.2	8.5	(.)		●	●	●
31	Malta	..	1,627	4,932	6.4	8.3	2.7	7.2	(.)		●	●	●
32	Czech Republic	2.1	..	6,368	..	3.2	..	11.6	0.5	●	●	●	●
33	Brunei Darussalam	0.0	2,430	8,459	3.5	..	35.5	..	(.)		●		●
34	Argentina	3.9	1,413	2,453	7.3	6.8	3.8	3.9	0.6	○	●	●	●
35	Seychelles	..	794	2,481	..	..	1.5	2.8	(.)	○	●	●	●
36	Estonia	19.0	..	5,777	1.9	2.8	..	11.7	0.1	●	●	●	●
37	Poland	5.2	3,419	3,595	..	3.9	12.8	7.8	1.2	●	●	●	●
38	Hungary	4.0	2,920	3,886	3.3	4.7	7.7	5.4	0.2	●	●	●	●
39	Saint Kitts and Nevis	50.0	..	2,500	..	..	..	..	(.)	●	●		●
40	Bahrain	0.0	4,784	10,350	1.4	1.5	23.4	29.1	0.1		●		●
41	Lithuania	15.1	..	3,095	..	3.7	..	3.4	(.)	●	●	●	●
42	Slovakia	1.8	..	5,273	..	3.1	..	6.6	0.1	●	●	●	●
43	Chile	16.2	1,054	2,851	4.9	5.6	2.5	3.9	0.2	○	●	●	●
44	Kuwait	0.0	6,849	15,309	2.3	2.2	18.0	21.9	0.2		●		●
45	Costa Rica	30.1	964	1,727	8.9	8.3	1.1	1.4	(.)	○	●	●	●
46	Uruguay	39.1	1,163	2,380	7.6	9.7	2.0	1.6	(.)	○	●	●	●
47	Qatar	0.0	10,616	16,677	..	..	56.3	69.5	0.2		●	●	●
48	Croatia	6.4	..	3,455	..	4.7	..	4.4	0.1	●	●	○	●
49	United Arab Emirates	0.0	6,204	13,948	..	..	34.8	21.0	0.2		●		●
50	Latvia	48.7	..	2,617	32.7	4.1	..	2.5	(.)	●	●	●	●

		Traditional fuel consumption (% of total energy requirements)	Electricity consumption per capita (kilowatt-hours)		GDP per unit of energy use (1995 PPP US$ per kg of oil equivalent)		Carbon dioxide emissions Per capita (metric tons)		Share of world total (%)	Cartagena Protocol on Biosafety	Framework Convention on Climate Change	Kyoto Protocol to the Framework Convention on Climate Change[b]	Convention on Biological Diversity
HDI rank		2001	1980	2001	1980	2001	1980	2000	2000				
51	Bahamas	..	4,062	5,407	..	..	38.0	5.9	(.)	●	●	●	●
52	Cuba	24.5	1,029	1,363	..	..	3.2	2.8	0.1	●	●	●	●
53	Mexico	15.0	999	2,228	4.9	5.3	3.7	4.3	1.8	●	●	●	●
54	Trinidad and Tobago	0.7	1,900	4,219	2.0	1.3	15.4	20.5	0.1	●	●	●	●
55	Antigua and Barbuda	..	984	1,375	..	..	2.3	5.2	(.)	●	●	●	●
Medium human development													
56	Bulgaria	5.3	4,371	4,681	1.5	2.5	8.5	5.2	0.2	●	●	●	●
57	Russian Federation	3.4	..	6,081	1.5	1.6	..	9.9	5.9		●	○	●
58	Libyan Arab Jamahiriya	1.2	1,588	4,021	..	..	8.8	10.9	0.2		●		●
59	Malaysia	2.3	740	3,039	4.3	3.6	2.0	6.2	0.6	●	●	●	●
60	Macedonia, TFYR	9.6	..	3,338	..	..	..	5.5	(.)	○	●		●
61	Panama	20.2	930	1,770	6.1	5.1	1.8	2.2	(.)	●	●	●	●
62	Belarus	5.8	..	3,340	..	1.9	..	5.9	0.2	●	●		●
63	Tonga	0.0	109	356	..	..	0.4	1.2	(.)	●	●		●
64	Mauritius	30.4	482	1,592	..	..	0.6	2.4	(.)	●	●	●	●
65	Albania	6.3	1,204	1,743	2.7	6.4	1.8	0.9	(.)		●		●
66	Bosnia and Herzegovina	7.4	..	2,303	..	4.8	..	4.8	0.1		●		●
67	Suriname	6.7	4,442	4,359	..	..	6.7	5.0	(.)		●		●
68	Venezuela	2.6	2,379	3,659	2.7	2.4	6.0	6.5	0.7	●	●	●	●
69	Romania	11.7	3,061	2,345	..	3.4	8.6	3.8	0.4	●	●	●	●
70	Ukraine	1.1	..	3,465	..	1.4	..	6.9	1.4	●	●	○	●
71	Saint Lucia	..	504	1,816	..	..	1.0	..	(.)		●	●	●
72	Brazil	35.7	1,145	2,122	6.7	6.2	1.5	1.8	1.3	●	●	●	●
73	Colombia	19.1	726	1,010	6.5	7.9	1.4	1.4	0.2	●	●	●	●
74	Oman	..	847	5,119	7.5	3.0	5.3	8.2	0.1	●	●	●	●
75	Samoa (Western)	33.3	252	600	..	..	0.6	0.8	(.)	●	●	●	●
76	Thailand	15.9	340	1,804	4.8	4.8	0.9	3.3	0.8		●	●	●
77	Saudi Arabia	(.)	1,969	6,018	5.6	2.0	14.0	18.1	1.5		●		●
78	Kazakhstan	..	..	3,964	..	1.7	..	8.1	0.5		●	○	●
79	Jamaica	8.5	834	2,539	2.7	2.1	4.0	4.2	(.)	○	●	●	●
80	Lebanon	1.0	1,056	3,025	..	3.2	2.1	3.5	0.1		●	●	●
81	Fiji	32.1	489	633	..	..	1.2	0.9	(.)	●	●	●	●
82	Armenia	1.1	..	1,413	..	3.3	..	1.1	(.)		●	●	●
83	Philippines	33.4	373	599	8.3	6.8	0.8	1.0	0.3	○	●	●	●
84	Maldives	0.0	25	420	..	..	0.3	1.8	(.)	●	●	●	●
85	Peru	25.4	579	874	7.2	9.4	1.4	1.1	0.1	○	●	●	●
86	Turkmenistan	..	..	1,908	..	1.3	..	7.5	0.1		●	●	●
87	St. Vincent & the Grenadines	..	276	780	..	..	0.4	..	(.)	●	●	○	●
88	Turkey	11.7	554	1,849	5.2	4.9	1.7	3.3	0.9	●	●		●
89	Paraguay	28.7	233	1,124	6.7	6.1	0.5	0.7	(.)	●	●	●	●
90	Jordan	2.0	366	1,507	5.4	3.7	2.2	3.2	0.1	●	●	●	●
91	Azerbaijan	0.0	..	2,422	..	1.7	..	3.6	0.1		●	●	●
92	Tunisia	10.4	434	1,106	6.5	7.0	1.5	1.9	0.1	●	●	●	●
93	Grenada	0.0	281	1,168	..	..	0.5	2.1	(.)	●	●	●	●
94	China	7.8	307	1,139	1.2	4.2	1.5	2.2	11.5	○	●	●	●
95	Dominica	..	149	1,038	..	..	0.5	1.4	(.)		●		●
96	Sri Lanka	34.8	113	354	5.1	7.3	0.2	0.6	(.)	○	●	●	●
97	Georgia	27.2	..	1,379	6.0	4.2	..	1.2	(.)		●	●	●
98	Dominican Republic	11.3	582	1,233	5.4	5.7	1.1	3.0	0.1		●	●	●
99	Belize	31.3	370	669	..	..	1.3	3.3	(.)	●	●	●	●
100	Ecuador	22.5	423	865	2.6	4.4	1.7	2.0	0.1	●	●	●	●

HDI rank		Traditional fuel consumption (% of total energy requirements) 2001	Electricity consumption per capita (kilowatt-hours) 1980	Electricity consumption per capita (kilowatt-hours) 2001	MDG GDP per unit of energy use (1995 PPP US$ per kg of oil equivalent) 1980	GDP per unit of energy use 2001	MDG Carbon dioxide emissions Per capita (metric tons) 1980	Per capita 2000	Share of world total (%) 2000	Ratification of environmental treaties [a] Cartagena Protocol on Biosafety	Framework Convention on Climate Change	Kyoto Protocol to the Framework Convention on Climate Change [b]	Convention on Biological Diversity
101	Iran, Islamic Rep. of	0.1	570	1,985	4.5	3.0	3.0	4.9	1.3	●	●		●
102	Occupied Palestinian Territories	..	..	..	..	..	..	..	..				
103	El Salvador	39.9	336	661	4.0	6.2	0.5	1.1	(.)	●	●	●	●
104	Guyana	47.6	545	1,189	..	..	2.3	2.1	(.)		●	●	●
105	Cape Verde	..	55	102	..	..	0.4	0.3	(.)		●		●
106	Syrian Arab Republic	0.0	433	1,528	4.3	3.5	2.2	3.3	0.2		●		●
107	Uzbekistan	0.0	..	1,971	..	0.7	..	4.8	0.5		●	●	●
108	Algeria	8.4	381	866	7.6	5.0	3.5	2.9	0.4	○	●		●
109	Equatorial Guinea	75.0	83	49	..	..	0.3	0.4	(.)		●		●
110	Kyrgyzstan	0.0	..	2,396	..	3.2	..	0.9	(.)		●	●	●
111	Indonesia	24.8	94	469	3.3	3.7	0.6	1.3	1.1	○	●	○	●
112	Viet Nam	32.5	78	389	..	4.0	0.3	0.7	0.2	●	●	●	●
113	Moldova, Rep. of	2.2	..	1,572	..	1.7	..	1.5	(.)	●	●	●	●
114	Bolivia	23.6	292	469	5.1	4.3	0.8	1.3	(.)	●	●	●	●
115	Honduras	62.1	259	650	4.4	4.6	0.6	0.7	(.)	○	●	●	●
116	Tajikistan	..	..	2,499	..	1.7	..	0.6	(.)	●	●	●	●
117	Mongolia	3.3	1,119	1,308	..	..	4.1	3.1	(.)	●	●	●	●
118	Nicaragua	54.6	363	485	5.3	..	0.7	0.7	(.)	●	●	●	●
119	South Africa	12.9 g	3,181 g	4,313 g	4.2	3.5	7.7	7.4	1.4	●	●	●	●
120	Egypt	12.6	433	1,129	5.0	4.5	1.1	2.2	0.6	●	●	○	●
121	Guatemala	65.3	245	481	6.5	5.7	0.7	0.9	(.)	●	●	●	●
122	Gabon	21.3	766	1,214	3.1	4.2	8.9	2.8	(.)	●	●	●	●
123	São Tomé and Principe	..	96	118	..	..	0.5	0.6	(.)		●		●
124	Solomon Islands	66.7	93	71	..	..	0.4	0.4	(.)		●	●	●
125	Morocco	2.5	254	569	10.6	9.0	0.8	1.3	0.2	○	●	●	●
126	Namibia	.. h	.. h	.. h	..	9.3	..	1.0	(.)	○	●	●	●
127	India	24.3	173	561	3.1	4.4	0.5	1.1	4.4	●	●	●	●
128	Botswana	.. h	.. h	.. h	..	..	1.1	2.3	(.)	●	●	●	●
129	Vanuatu	50.0	171	4,813	..	..	0.5	0.4	(.)		●	●	●
130	Cambodia	95.1	15	18	..	..	(.)	(.)	(.)	●	●	●	●
131	Ghana	84.5	450	404	4.4	4.3	0.2	0.3	(.)		●	●	●
132	Myanmar	81.1	44	118	..	..	0.1	0.2	(.)	○	●	●	●
133	Papua New Guinea	68.6	406	255	..	..	0.6	0.5	(.)		●	●	●
134	Bhutan	84.1	17	241	..	..	(.)	0.5	(.)	●	●	●	●
135	Lao People's Dem. Rep.	81.6	68	130	..	..	0.1	0.1	(.)		●	●	●
136	Comoros	..	26	26	..	..	0.1	0.1	(.)		●	●	●
137	Swaziland	.. h	.. h	.. h	..	..	0.8	0.4	(.)		●	●	●
138	Bangladesh	63.6	30	115	9.7	9.7	0.1	0.2	0.1	●	●	●	●
139	Sudan	80.1	47	81	2.3	3.3	0.2	0.2	(.)		●	●	●
140	Nepal	88.0	17	63	2.4	3.5	(.)	0.1	(.)	○	●	●	●
141	Cameroon	71.6	168	226	4.4	4.2	0.4	0.4	(.)	●	●	●	●
Low human development													
142	Pakistan	26.6	176	479	3.5	3.8	0.4	0.8	0.4	○	●	●	●
143	Togo	88.6	74	125	6.6	4.2	0.2	0.4	(.)	○	●	●	●
144	Congo	65.6	98	137	1.9	3.3	0.2	0.5	(.)	○	●	●	●
145	Lesotho	.. h	.. h	.. h	..	..	..	..	..	●	●	●	●
146	Uganda	95.0	28	66	..	..	0.1	0.1	(.)	●	●	●	●
147	Zimbabwe	68.6	1,020	950	2.5	2.8	1.3	1.2	0.1	○	●		●
148	Kenya	70.6	109	140	1.6	1.8	0.4	0.3	(.)	●	●		●
149	Yemen	3.2	..	164	..	3.8	..	0.5	(.)		●		●
150	Madagascar	84.4	49	51	..	..	0.2	0.1	(.)	●	●	●	●
151	Nigeria	82.3	108	154	1.3	1.1	1.0	0.3	0.1	●	●		●

HDI rank		Traditional fuel consumption (% of total energy requirements) 2001	Electricity consumption per capita (kilowatt-hours) 1980	2001	MDG GDP per unit of energy use (1995 PPP US$ per kg of oil equivalent) 1980	2001	MDG Carbon dioxide emissions Per capita (metric tons) 1980	2000	Share of world total (%) 2000	Ratification of environmental treaties [a] Cartagena Protocol on Biosafety	Framework Convention on Climate Change	Kyoto Protocol to the Framework Convention on Climate Change [b]	Convention on Biological Diversity
152	Mauritania	36.9	60	61	..	..	0.4	1.2	(.)	○	●		●
153	Haiti	54.0	58	67	6.5	5.8	0.1	0.2	(.)	●	●	●	●
154	Djibouti	..	416	286	..	..	1.0	0.6	(.)	○	●	●	●
155	Gambia	71.4	70	95	..	..	0.2	0.2	(.)	○	●		●
156	Eritrea	77.8	..	61	..	..	..	0.1	(.)		●		●
157	Senegal	72.5	115	151	3.6	4.3	0.5	0.4	(.)		●		●
158	Timor-Leste	..	..	..	..	..	..	..	..				
159	Rwanda	92.8	32	23	..	..	0.1	0.1	(.)	○	●		●
160	Guinea	90.6	85	97	..	..	0.2	0.2	(.)	○	●		●
161	Benin	81.9	37	75	2.0	2.9	0.1	0.3	(.)	○	●		●
162	Tanzania, U. Rep. of	92.8	41	85	..	1.2	0.1	0.1	(.)	●	●	●	●
163	Côte d'Ivoire	75.1	220	233	4.6	3.7	0.6	0.7	(.)		●		●
164	Zambia	87.1	1,125	598	1.3	1.2	0.6	0.2	(.)		●	○	●
165	Malawi	86.6	66	76	..	..	0.1	0.1	(.)	○	●	●	●
166	Angola	79.2	214	125	2.9	2.2	0.8	0.5	(.)		●		●
167	Chad	97.8	10	12	..	..	(.)	(.)	(.)	○	●		●
168	Congo, Dem. Rep. of the	94.6	161	93	5.3	1.9	0.1	0.1	(.)		●		●
169	Central African Republic	87.5	29	29	..	..	(.)	0.1	(.)	○	●		●
170	Ethiopia	95.2	..	30	..	2.2	(.)	0.1	(.)	●	●		●
171	Mozambique	90.5	364	70	..	..	0.3	0.1	(.)	●	●		●
172	Guinea-Bissau	66.7	18	43	..	..	0.7	0.2	(.)		●		●
173	Burundi	96.6	12	73	..	..	(.)	(.)	(.)		●	●	●
174	Mali	88.3	15	34	..	..	0.1	0.1	(.)	●	●	●	●
175	Burkina Faso	91.7	16	24	..	..	0.1	0.1	(.)	●	●		●
176	Niger	77.3	39	41	..	..	0.1	0.1	(.)	○	●	○	●
177	Sierra Leone	92.0	62	55	..	..	0.2	0.1	(.)		●		●
	Developing countries	21.4	388	1,035	3.3	4.2	1.3	1.9	36.9	-	-	-	-
	Least developed countries	84.1	83	95	..	3.7	0.1	0.2	0.4	-	-	-	-
	Arab States	5.9	626	1,783	5.1	3.4	3.0	4.1	4.5	-	-	-	-
	East Asia and the Pacific	10.9	329	1,194	1.9	4.2	1.4	2.3	17.6	-	-	-	-
	Latin America and the Caribbean	21.4	1,019	1,888	5.7	5.7	2.4	2.7	5.6	-	-	-	-
	South Asia	23.4	171	554	3.5	4.3	0.5	1.1	6.3	-	-	-	-
	Sub-Saharan Africa	62.6	434	495	3.0	2.4	1.0	0.8	1.9	-	-	-	-
	Central & Eastern Europe & CIS	4.0	3,284	3,326	..	2.0	..	7.3	12.2	-	-	-	-
	OECD	4.5	5,761	8,503	3.6	4.7	11.0	10.9	51.0	-	-	-	-
	High-income OECD	4.1	6,698	10,105	3.5	4.7	12.2	12.5	46.2	-	-	-	-
	High human development	4.5	5,700	8,520	3.6	4.7	10.9	10.9	52.8	-	-	-	-
	Medium human development	13.4	387	1,022	2.6	3.7	1.3	2.3	38.7	-	-	-	-
	Low human development	75.8	157	218	2.4	2.2	0.4	0.3	1.0	-	-	-	-
	High income	4.0	6,614	10,030	3.5	4.7	12.2	12.4	47.8	-	-	-	-
	Middle income	9.3	667	1,541	2.7	3.7	2.3	3.4	37.6	-	-	-	-
	Low income	43.5	166	400	3.1	3.6	0.5	0.9	8.5	-	-	-	-
	World	10.7	1,573	2,361	3.2	4.2	3.4	3.8	100.0 [i]	-	-	-	-

● Ratification, acceptance, approval, accession or succession. ○ Signature.

a. Information is as of 24 March 2004. The Cartagena Protocol on Biosafety was signed in Cartagena in 2000, the United Nations Framework Convention on Climate Change in New York in 1992, the Kyoto Protocol to the United Nations Framework Convention on Climate Change in Kyoto in 1997 and the Convention on Biological Diversity in Rio de Janeiro in 1992. b. Has not yet entered into force. c. Includes Svalbard and Jan Mayen Islands. d. Includes Liechtenstein. e. Includes Monaco. f. Includes San Marino. g. Data refer to the South African Customs Union, which includes Botswana, Lesotho, Swaziland and Namibia. h. Included in the data for South Africa. i. Data refer to the world aggregate from CDIAC 2004. Data refer to total carbon dioxide emissions, including those of countries not shown in the main indicator tables as well as emissions not included in national totals, such as those from bunker fuels and oxidation of non-fuel hydrocarbon products.

Source: Column 1: Calculated on the basis of data on traditional fuel consumption and total energy requirements from UN 2004c; *columns 2-3:* UN 2004b; *columns 4-7:* World Bank 2004f; aggregates calculated for the Human Development Report Office by the World Bank; *column 8:* calculated on the basis of data on carbon dioxide emissions from CDIAC 2004; *columns 9-12:* UN 2004f.

22 Refugees and armaments

		Internally displaced people (thousands)	Refugees [a]		Conventional arms transfers [b] (1990 prices)				Total armed forces	
			By country of asylum (thousands)	By country of origin [d] (thousands)	Imports (US$ millions)		Exports			Index (1985 = 100)
							US$ millions	Share [e] (%)	Thousands	
HDI rank		2003 [a, c]	2003	2003	1994	2003	2003	1999-2003	2002	2002
High human development										
1	Norway	0	56	(.)	99	(.)	150	1	27	72
2	Sweden	0 [f]	142 [f]	(.)	258	23	186	1	34	52
3	Australia	0 [f]	59 [f]	(.)	263	485	30	(.)	51	72
4	Canada	0	133	(.)	333	94	556	1	52	63
5	Netherlands	0 [f]	148 [f]	(.)	143	132	268	1	50	47
6	Belgium	0 [f]	13 [f]	(.)	52	27	6	(.)	39	43
7	Iceland	0	(.)	(.)	..	..	(.)	0	..	..
8	United States	0	453	(.)	725	515	4,385	34	1,414	66
9	Japan	0	2	(.)	596	210	(.)	0	240	99
10	Ireland	0	6	(.)	48	2	(.)	0	11	77
11	Switzerland	0	49	(.)	113	41	35	(.)	28	138
12	United Kingdom	0	277	(.)	38	555	525	5	210	63
13	Finland	0	13	(.)	179	125	10	(.)	32	87
14	Austria	0 [f]	14 [f]	(.)	65	55	2	(.)	35	63
15	Luxembourg	0 [f]	1 [f]	..	(.)	1	..	..	1	129
16	France	0 [f]	132 [f]	(.)	6	120	1,753	7	260	56
17	Denmark	0 [f]	74 [f]	(.)	66	7	3	(.)	23	77
18	New Zealand	0 [f]	6 [f]	(.)	16	71	(.)	0	9	70
19	Germany	0	960	(.)	..	69	1,549	6	296	62
20	Spain	0	6	(.)	636	97	124	(.)	178	56
21	Italy	0	12	(.)	151	348	277	2	217	56
22	Israel	0 [f]	4 [f]	(.)	829	318	212	1	162	114
23	Hong Kong, China (SAR)	0	2	..	..	..	..	..	..	..
24	Greece	0 [f]	3 [f]	(.)	1,262	1,957	(.)	(.)	178	88
25	Singapore	0	(.)	(.)	171	121	(.)	(.)	61	110
26	Portugal	0 [f]	(.) [f]	(.)	433	68	(.)	0	44	60
27	Slovenia	0	2	1	11	14	..	..	9	..
28	Korea, Rep. of	0	(.)	(.)	665	299	36	(.)	686	115
29	Barbados	..	..	(.)	..	..	..	..	1	60
30	Cyprus	0	(.)	(.)	46	(.)	(.)	0	10	100
31	Malta	0 [f]	(.) [f]	..	(.)	(.)	..	..	2	263
32	Czech Republic	0	2	6	(.)	111	48	(.)	49	24
33	Brunei Darussalam	..	..	(.)	(.)	(.)	..	..	7	171
34	Argentina	0	3	(.)	177	127	(.)	(.)	70	65
35	Seychelles	..	..	(.)	..	..	..	..	1	42
36	Estonia	0	(.)	1	15	16	(.)	0	6	..
37	Poland	0	2	14	8	420	89	(.)	163	51
38	Hungary	0	7	2	4	(.)	(.)	0	33	32
39	Saint Kitts and Nevis	..	..	..	..	..	..	..	..	..
40	Bahrain	0 [f]	0 [f]	(.)	10	(.)	(.)	(.)	11	382
41	Lithuania	0	(.)	1	(.)	(.)	(.)	(.)	14	..
42	Slovakia	0	(.)	(.)	30	(.)	(.)	(.)	26	..
43	Chile	0	(.)	1	113	156	(.)	(.)	81	80
44	Kuwait	0	2	(.)	37	21	(.)	0	16	129
45	Costa Rica	0	14	(.)	(.)	(.)	..	..	..	..
46	Uruguay	0	(.)	(.)	8	(.)	(.)	(.)	24	75
47	Qatar	0	(.)	(.)	10	10	(.)	(.)	12	207
48	Croatia	13	4	215	57	(.)	(.)	(.)	51	..
49	United Arab Emirates	0	(.)	(.)	554	922	(.)	0	42	97
50	Latvia	0	(.)	2	12	29	(.)	0	6	..

	Internally displaced people (thousands) 2003 [a,c]	Refugees [a] By country of asylum (thousands) 2003	By country of origin [d] (thousands) 2003	Conventional arms transfers [b] (1990 prices) Imports (US$ millions) 1994	Imports 2003	Exports US$ millions 2003	Exports Share [e] (%) 1999-2003	Total armed forces Thousands 2002	Total armed forces Index (1985 = 100) 2002
51 Bahamas	..	..	..	(.)	(.)	..	..	1	180
52 Cuba	0	1	3	..	..	..	..	46	28
53 Mexico	0	6	(.)	118	43	..	..	193	149
54 Trinidad and Tobago	..	..	(.)	(.)	(.)	..	..	3	129
55 Antigua and Barbuda	..	..	..	..	..	..	..	(.)	200
Medium human development									
56 Bulgaria	0	4	1	(.)	2	18	(.)	68	46
57 Russian Federation	368	10	67	40	(.)	6,980	30	..	..
58 Libyan Arab Jamahiriya	0	12	1	(.)	(.)	23	(.)	76	104
59 Malaysia	0	(.)	(.)	376	242	(.)	(.)	100	91
60 Macedonia, TFYR	0	(.)	5	27	(.)	..	..	12	..
61 Panama	0	1	(.)	(.)	(.)	..	..	..	..
62 Belarus	0	1	3	(.)	(.)	60	1	80	..
63 Tonga	..	..	(.)	(.)	(.)	..	..	..	..
64 Mauritius	0 [f]	0 [f]	(.)	(.)	(.)	..	..	..	..
65 Albania	0	(.)	2	(.)	1	..	..	27	67
66 Bosnia and Herzegovina	327	23	167	(.)	(.)	(.)	(.)	20	..
67 Suriname	0 [f]	0 [f]	(.)	(.)	(.)	..	..	2	100
68 Venezuela	0	(.)	(.)	1	(.)	..	..	82	168
69 Romania	0	2	6	25	46	22	(.)	99	52
70 Ukraine	0	3	58	..	..	234	2	302	..
71 Saint Lucia	..	..	..	..	..	..	..	..	..
72 Brazil	0	3	(.)	225	87	(.)	(.)	288	104
73 Colombia	2,040	(.)	16	39	48	..	..	158	239
74 Oman	0	0	(.)	173	14	(.)	0	42	143
75 Samoa (Western)	..	..	..	..	..	..	..	..	..
76 Thailand	0	119	(.)	661	163	5	(.)	306	130
77 Saudi Arabia	0	241	(.)	991	487	(.)	0	200	319
78 Kazakhstan	0	16	4	(.)	62	(.)	(.)	60	..
79 Jamaica	..	..	(.)	(.)	(.)	..	..	3	133
80 Lebanon	0	3	19	13	(.)	(.)	(.)	72	413
81 Fiji	..	..	(.)	4	(.)	..	..	4	130
82 Armenia	0	239	6	310	(.)	..	..	45	..
83 Philippines	0	(.)	(.)	71	8	..	..	106	92
84 Maldives	..	..	..	(.)	(.)	..	..	...	..
85 Peru	0	1	2	121	(.)	(.)	(.)	110	86
86 Turkmenistan	0	14	1	..	..	..	..	18	..
87 St. Vincent & the Grenadines	..	..	..	..	..	..	..	..	..
88 Turkey	0	2	147	1,250	504	61	(.)	515	82
89 Paraguay	0	(.)	(.)	(.)	4	..	..	19	129
90 Jordan	0	1	1	5	258	(.)	0	100	143
91 Azerbaijan	576	(.)	248	25	(.)	..	..	72	..
92 Tunisia	0	(.)	2	32	(.)	..	..	35	100
93 Grenada	..	..	..	..	..	..	..	..	..
94 China	0	299	100	142	2,548	404	2	2,270	58
95 Dominica	..	..	..	..	..	..	..	..	..
96 Sri Lanka	386	(.)	81	53	8	..	..	158	731
97 Georgia	260	4	10	(.)	(.)	(.)	(.)	18	..
98 Dominican Republic	..	..	(.)	(.)	76	..	..	25	110
99 Belize	0	1	(.)	(.)	(.)	..	..	1	183
100 Ecuador	0	6	(.)	(.)	(.)	..	..	60	140

HDI rank		Internally displaced people (thousands) 2003 [a,c]	Refugees [a] By country of asylum (thousands) 2003	Refugees [a] By country of origin [d] (thousands) 2003	Conventional arms transfers [b] (1990 prices) Imports (US$ millions) 1994	Imports 2003	Exports US$ millions 2003	Exports Share [e] (%) 1999-2003	Total armed forces Thousands 2002	Total armed forces Index (1985 = 100) 2002
101	Iran, Islamic Rep. of	0	985	57	376	323	(.)	0	520	85
102	Occupied Palestinian Territories	0	0 [g]	326 [g]	5	(.)	..	..	..	..
103	El Salvador	0	(.)	4	(.)	(.)	..	..	17	40
104	Guyana	..	..	(.)	(.)	(.)	..	..	2	24
105	Cape Verde	..	..	(.)	(.)	(.)	..	..	1	16
106	Syrian Arab Republic	0	4	16	44	15	(.)	0	319	79
107	Uzbekistan	0	45	4	(.)	(.)	510	1	52	..
108	Algeria	0	169	4	156	513	..	..	137	80
109	Equatorial Guinea	..	..	(.)	(.)	(.)	..	..	2	105
110	Kyrgyzstan	0	6	2	(.)	9	76	(.)	11	..
111	Indonesia	0	(.)	8	559	333	20	(.)	297	107
112	Viet Nam	0	15	331	(.)	7	..	..	484	47
113	Moldova, Rep. of	0	(.)	6	2	(.)	(.)	(.)	7	..
114	Bolivia	0	1	(.)	7	(.)	..	..	32	114
115	Honduras	0	(.)	(.)	..	..	..	..	8	50
116	Tajikistan	0	3	59	24	(.)	..	..	6	..
117	Mongolia	0 [f]	0 [f]	(.)	..	..	..	..	9	28
118	Nicaragua	0	(.)	4	..	..	(.)	0	14	22
119	South Africa	0	27	(.)	19	13	23	(.)	60	56
120	Egypt	0	89	1	1,976	504	(.)	(.)	443	100
121	Guatemala	0	1	4	3	(.)	..	..	31	99
122	Gabon	0	14	(.)	..	..	..	..	5	196
123	São Tomé and Principe	0	0	(.)	..	..	..	..	..	..
124	Solomon Islands	..	..	..	..	..	..	..	..	..
125	Morocco	0	2	1	131	(.)	..	..	196	132
126	Namibia	0	20	1	3	5	..	..	9	..
127	India	0	165	3	561	3,621	(.)	(.)	1,298	103
128	Botswana	0	3	(.)	(.)	(.)	..	..	9	225
129	Vanuatu	..	..	..	..	..	..	..	..	..
130	Cambodia	0	(.)	17	71	(.)	(.)	0	125	357
131	Ghana	0	44	13	10	(.)	..	..	7	46
132	Myanmar	0 [f]	0 [f]	141	3	31	..	..	444	239
133	Papua New Guinea	0	7	(.)	1	(.)	..	..	3	97
134	Bhutan	..	..	114	..	..	..	..	..	..
135	Lao People's Dem. Rep.	0 [f]	0 [f]	2	(.)	(.)	..	..	29	54
136	Comoros	0 [f]	0 [f]	(.)	..	..	..	..	..	..
137	Swaziland	0	1	(.)	(.)	(.)	..	..	..	..
138	Bangladesh	0	20	1	51	(.)	..	..	137	150
139	Sudan	0 [f]	328 [f]	567	(.)	(.)	..	..	117	207
140	Nepal	0	134	1	(.)	5	..	..	51	204
141	Cameroon	0	59	2	(.)	(.)	..	..	23	316
Low human development										
142	Pakistan	0	1,124	10	687	611	(.)	(.)	620	128
143	Togo	0	12	8	3	(.)	..	..	10	264
144	Congo	0	91	24	(.)	(.)	..	..	10	115
145	Lesotho	0 [f]	0 [f]	(.)	(.)	(.)	..	..	2	100
146	Uganda	0	231	24	(.)	19	..	..	55	275
147	Zimbabwe	0	13	(.)	(.)	23	..	..	36	88
148	Kenya	0	239	(.)	12	(.)	..	..	24	178
149	Yemen	0	62	1	4	30	..	..	67	104
150	Madagascar	0 [f]	0 [f]	(.)	..	..	..	..	14	64
151	Nigeria	0	9	19	75	51	..	..	79	84

HDI rank		Internally displaced people (thousands) 2003 [a, c]	Refugees [a] By country of asylum (thousands) 2003	By country of origin [d] (thousands) 2003	Conventional arms transfers [b] (1990 prices) Imports (US$ millions) 1994	Imports 2003	Exports US$ millions 2003	Exports Share [e] (%) 1999-2003	Total armed forces Thousands 2002	Index (1985 = 100) 2002
152	Mauritania	0	(.)	26	27	(.)	..	..	16	185
153	Haiti	..	..	(.)	..	..	..	..	..	..
154	Djibouti	0	27	(.)	(.)	(.)	..	..	10	327
155	Gambia	0	7	(.)	..	..	..	..	1	160
156	Eritrea	0	4	11	14	180	(.)	0	172	..
157	Senegal	0	21	8	1	(.)	..	..	9	93
158	Timor-Leste	0	(.)	..	..	..	..	..	..	..
159	Rwanda	0	37	66	(.)	(.)	..	..	70	1,346
160	Guinea	0	184	1	(.)	(.)	..	..	10	98
161	Benin	0	5	(.)	(.)	6	..	..	5	102
162	Tanzania, U. Rep. of	0	650	(.)	2	(.)	..	..	27	67
163	Côte d'Ivoire	38	76	47	(.)	22	..	..	17	129
164	Zambia	0	227	(.)	(.)	(.)	..	..	22	133
165	Malawi	0	3	(.)	1	(.)	(.)	(.)	5	100
166	Angola	0	13	313	96	(.)	(.)	(.)	100	202
167	Chad	0	146	46	8	(.)	..	..	30	249
168	Congo, Dem. Rep. of the	0	234	428	(.)	(.)	..	..	81	170
169	Central African Republic	0	45	35	..	..	..	..	3	111
170	Ethiopia	0	130	26	(.)	(.)	..	..	253	116
171	Mozambique	0	(.)	(.)	(.)	(.)	..	..	11	70
172	Guinea-Bissau	0	8	(.)	(.)	(.)	..	..	9	108
173	Burundi	100	41	525	(.)	(.)	..	..	46	875
174	Mali	0	10	(.)	(.)	(.)	..	..	7	151
175	Burkina Faso	0	(.)	1	..	..	..	..	10	255
176	Niger	0	(.)	(.)	(.)	(.)	..	..	5	241
177	Sierra Leone	0	61	78	1	(.)	..	..	13	419
	Developing countries	..	6,726 T	..	..	..	..	..	14,203 T	91
	Least developed countries	..	2,717 T	..	..	..	..	..	2,033 T	174
	Arab States	..	1,074 T	..	..	..	..	..	2,282 T	84
	East Asia and the Pacific	..	444 T	..	..	..	..	..	6,012 T	80
	Latin America and the Caribbean	..	38 T	..	..	..	..	..	1,268 T	94
	South Asia	..	2,428 T	..	..	..	..	..	2,834 T	112
	Sub-Saharan Africa	..	2,740 T	..	..	..	..	..	1,283 T	152
	Central & Eastern Europe & the CIS	..	678 T	..	..	..	..	..	1,253 T	19
	OECD	..	2,580 T	..	..	..	..	..	5,092 T	70
	High-income OECD	..	2,561 T	..	..	..	..	..	4,112 T	70
	High human development	..	2,610 T	..	..	..	..	..	5,208 T	71
	Medium human development	..	3,147 T	..	..	..	..	..	10,455 T	62
	Low human development	..	3,712 T	..	..	..	..	..	1,847 T	148
	High income	..	2,571 T	..	..	..	..	..	4,444 T	72
	Middle income	..	2,807 T	..	..	..	..	..	8,411 T	52
	Low income	..	4,591 T	..	..	..	..	..	6,191 T	116
	World	5,081 [h]	9,970 T	..	19,253 T [i]	18,679 T [i]	18,680 T [i]	..	19,045 T	69

a. Data refer to the end of 2003 unless otherwise specified. Provisional data subject to change. b. Data are as of 25 February 2004. Figures are trend indicator values, which are an indicator only of the volume of international arm transfers, not of the actual financial value of such transfers. Published reports of arms transfers provide partial information, as not all transfers are fully reported. The estimates presented are conservative and may understate actual transfers of conventional weapons. c. Persons who are displaced within their country and to whom the United Nations High Commissioner for Refugees (UNHCR) extends protection or assistance, generally pursuant to a special request by a competent organ of the United Nations. A zero indicates that the indicator has a value of zero, is not available or is not applicable. d. The country of origin for many refugees is unavailable or unreported. These data may therefore be underestimates. e. Calculated using the 1999-2003 totals for all countries and non-state actors with exports of major conventional weapons as defined in SIPRI 2004b. f. Refers to the end of 2002. g. Palestinian refugees under the mandate of the United Nations Relief and Works Agency for Palestine Refugees in the Near East (UNRWA) in Jordan, Occupied Palestinian Territories, the Syrian Arab Republic or Lebanon are not included. Data refer to the Gaza Strip. h. Data refer to the world aggregate from UNHCR 2004. i. Data refer to the world aggregate from SIPRI 2004b. It includes all countries and non-state actors with transfers of major conventional weapons as defined in SIPRI 2004b.

Source: Columns 1-3: UNHCR 2004; columns 4-6: SIPRI 2004b; column 7: calculated on the basis of data on weapons transfers from SIPRI 2004b; column 8: IISS 2003; column 9: calculated on the basis of data on armed forces from IISS 2003.

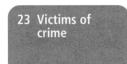

23 Victims of crime

		People victimized by crime[a] (% of total population)					
	Year[b]	Total crime[c]	Property crime[d]	Robbery	Sexual assault[e]	Assault	Bribery (corruption)[f]
National							
Australia	1999	30.1	13.9	1.2	1.0	2.4	0.3
Austria	1995	18.8	3.1	0.2	1.2	0.8	0.7
Belgium	1999	21.4	7.7	1.0	0.3	1.2	0.3
Canada	1999	23.8	10.4	0.9	0.8	2.3	0.4
Denmark	1999	23.0	7.6	0.7	0.4	1.4	0.3
England and Wales	1999	26.4	12.2	1.2	0.9	2.8	0.1
Finland	1999	19.1	4.4	0.6	1.1	2.1	0.2
France	1999	21.4	8.7	1.1	0.7	1.4	1.3
Italy	1991	24.6	12.7	1.3	0.6	0.2	..
Japan	1999	15.2	3.4	0.1	0.1	0.1	(.)
Malta	1996	23.1	10.9	0.4	0.1	1.1	4.0
Netherlands	1999	25.2	7.4	0.8	0.8	1.0	0.4
New Zealand	1991	29.4	14.8	0.7	1.3	2.4	..
Northern Ireland	1999	15.0	6.2	0.1	0.1	2.1	0.2
Poland	1999	22.7	9.0	1.8	0.2	1.1	5.1
Portugal	1999	15.5	7.5	1.1	0.2	0.4	1.4
Scotland	1999	23.2	7.6	0.7	0.3	3.0	..
Slovenia	2000	21.2	7.7	1.1	0.8	1.1	2.1
Sweden	1999	24.7	8.4	0.9	1.1	1.2	0.1
Switzerland	1999	18.2	4.5	0.7	0.6	1.0	0.2 [g]
United States	1999	21.1	10.0	0.6	0.4	1.2	0.2
Major city							
Asunción (Paraguay)	1995	34.4	16.7	6.3	1.7	0.9	13.3
Baku (Azerbaijan)	1999	8.3	2.4	1.6	0.0	0.4	20.8
Beijing (China)	1991	19.0	2.2	0.5	0.6	0.6	..
Bishkek (Kyrgyzstan)	1995	27.8	11.3	1.6	2.2	2.1	19.3
Bogotá (Colombia)	1996	54.6	27.0	11.5	4.8	2.5	19.5
Bratislava (Slovakia)	1996	36.0	20.8	1.2	0.4	0.5	13.5
Bucharest (Romania)	1999	25.4	10.8	1.8	0.4	0.6	19.2
Budapest (Hungary)	1999	32.1	15.6	1.8	0.9	0.8	9.8
Buenos Aires (Argentina)	1995	61.1	30.8	6.4	6.4	2.3	30.2
Cairo (Egypt)	1991	28.7	12.1	2.2	1.8	1.1	..
Dar es Salaam (Tanzania, U. Rep. of)	1991	..	23.1	8.2	6.1	1.7	..
Gaborone (Botswana)	1996	31.7	19.7	2.0	0.7	3.2	2.8
Jakarta (Indonesia)	1995	20.9	9.4	0.7	1.3	0.5	29.9
Johannesburg (South Africa)	1995	38.0	18.3	4.7	2.7	4.6	6.9
Kampala (Uganda)	1995	40.9	20.6	2.3	5.1	1.7	19.5
Kiev (Ukraine)	1999	29.1	8.9	2.5	1.2	1.5	16.2
La Paz (Bolivia)	1995	39.8	18.1	5.8	1.5	2.0	24.4
Manila (Philippines)	1995	10.6	3.3	1.5	0.1	0.1	4.3
Maputo (Mozambique)	2001	40.6	29.3	7.6	2.2	3.2	30.5
Minsk (Belarus)	1999	23.6	11.1	1.4	1.4	1.3	20.6
Moscow (Russian Federation)	1999	26.3	10.9	2.4	1.2	1.1	16.6
Mumbai (India)	1995	31.8	6.7	1.3	3.5	0.8	22.9
New Delhi (India)	1995	30.5	6.1	1.0	1.7	0.8	21.0
Prague (Czech Republic)	1999	34.1	21.6	0.5	0.9	1.1	5.7
Riga (Latvia)	1999	26.5	9.4	2.8	0.5	1.9	14.3

		People victimized by crime[a] (% of total population)					
	Year[b]	Total crime[c]	Property crime[d]	Robbery	Sexual assault[e]	Assault	Bribery (corruption)[f]
Rio de Janeiro (Brazil)	1995	44.0	14.7	12.2	7.5	3.4	17.1
San José (Costa Rica)	1995	40.4	21.7	8.9	3.5	1.7	9.2
Skopje (Macedonia, TFYR)	1995	21.1	9.4	1.1	0.3	0.7	7.4
Sofia (Bulgaria)	1999	27.2	16.1	1.5	0.1	0.6	16.4
Tallinn (Estonia)	1999	41.2	22.5	6.3	3.3	3.7	9.3
Tbjlisi (Georgia)	1999	23.6	11.1	1.8	0.4	0.9	16.6
Tirana (Albania)	1999	31.7	11.2	2.9	1.2	0.7	59.1
Tunis (Tunisia)	1991	37.5	20.1	5.4	1.5	0.4	..
Ulaanbaatar (Mongolia)	1999	41.8	20.0	4.5	1.4	2.1	21.3
Vilnius (Lithuania)	1999	31.0	17.8	3.2	2.0	1.4	22.9
Zagreb (Croatia)	1999	14.3	4.4	0.5	0.8	0.5	9.5

a. Data refer to victimization as reported in the International Crime Victims Survey. b. Surveys were conducted in 1992, 1995, 1996-97 and 2000-01. Data refer to the year preceding the survey. c. Data refer to people victimized by 1 or more of 11 crimes recorded in the survey: robbery, burglary, attempted burglary, car theft, car vandalism, bicycle theft, sexual assault, theft from car, theft of personal property, assault and threats and theft of motorcycle or moped. d. Includes car theft, theft from car, burglary with entry and attempted burglary. e. Data refer to women only. f. Data refer to people who have been asked or expected to pay a bribe by a government official. g. Data refer to 1995.

Source: *Columns 1-7:* UNODC 2004.

24 Gender-related development index

HDI rank		Gender-related development index (GDI)		Life expectancy at birth (years) 2002		Adult literacy rate (% ages 15 and above) 2002[a]		Combined gross enrolment ratio for primary, secondary and tertiary level schools (%) 2001/02[b]		Estimated earned income (PPP US$) 2002[c]		HDI rank minus GDI rank[d]
		Rank	Value	Female	Male	Female	Male	Female	Male	Female	Male	
High human development												
1	Norway	1	0.955	81.8	75.9	.. [e]	.. [e]	102 [f, g]	94 [g]	31,356	42,340	0
2	Sweden	2	0.946	82.5	77.5	.. [e]	.. [e]	124 [f, h]	104 [f, h]	23,781	28,700	0
3	Australia	3	0.945	82.0	76.4	.. [e]	.. [e]	114 [f, h]	111 [f, h]	23,643	33,259	0
4	Canada	4	0.941	81.9	76.6	.. [e]	.. [e]	96 [g]	93 [g]	22,964	36,299	0
5	Netherlands	5	0.938	81.0	75.6	.. [e]	.. [e]	99 [g]	100 [f, g]	20,358	38,266	0
6	Belgium	7	0.938	81.8	75.6	.. [e]	.. [e]	115 [f, g]	107 [f, g]	18,528	37,180	-1
7	Iceland	6	0.938	81.9	77.6	.. [e]	.. [e]	95 [g]	86 [g]	22,716	36,043	1
8	United States	8	0.936	79.8	74.2	.. [e]	.. [e]	96 [h]	89 [h]	27,338	43,797	0
9	Japan	12	0.932	85.0	77.8	.. [e]	.. [e]	83 [h]	85 [h]	16,977	37,208	-3
10	Ireland	14	0.929	79.5	74.3	.. [e]	.. [e]	94 [g]	87 [g]	21,056	52,008	-4
11	Switzerland	11	0.932	82.3	75.9	.. [e]	.. [e]	86 [g]	90 [g]	20,459	40,769	0
12	United Kingdom	9	0.934	80.6	75.6	.. [e]	.. [e]	119 [f, g]	107 [f, g]	19,807	32,984	3
13	Finland	10	0.933	81.4	74.3	.. [e]	.. [e]	111 [f, g]	102 [f, g]	21,645	30,970	3
14	Austria	17	0.924	81.4	75.3	.. [e]	.. [e]	92 [g]	91 [g]	15,410	43,169	-3
15	Luxembourg	16	0.926	81.3	75.0	.. [e]	.. [e]	75 [g, i]	74 [g, i]	33,517	88,803 [i]	-1
16	France	15	0.929	82.7	75.1	.. [e]	.. [e]	93 [g]	90 [g]	19,923	33,950	1
17	Denmark	13	0.931	79.0	74.1	.. [e]	.. [e]	99 [k]	92 [k]	26,074	36,161	4
18	New Zealand	18	0.924	80.7	75.7	.. [e]	.. [e]	107 [f, h]	96 [h]	18,168	26,481	0
19	Germany	19	0.921	81.1	75.1	.. [e]	.. [e]	88 [h]	89 [h]	18,763	35,885	0
20	Spain	20	0.916	82.7	75.8	96.9 [e]	98.7 [e]	95 [h]	89 [h]	13,209	29,971	0
21	Italy	21	0.914	81.9	75.5	98.1 [e]	98.9 [e]	84 [g]	81 [g]	16,702	36,959	0
22	Israel	22	0.906	80.9	77.0	93.4	97.3	94	89	14,201	26,636	0
23	Hong Kong, China (SAR)	23	0.898	82.7	77.2	89.6 [l]	96.9 [l]	70	73	18,805	33,776	0
24	Greece	25	0.894	80.9	75.7	96.1 [m]	98.6 [m]	88 [g]	84 [g]	10,892	25,601	-1
25	Singapore	28	0.884	80.2	75.8	88.6 [m]	96.6 [m]	75 [k, n]	76 [k, n]	15,822	31,927	-3
26	Portugal	24	0.894	79.5	72.5	90.3 [e]	95.2 [e]	97 [g]	90 [g]	13,084	24,373	2
27	Slovenia	26	0.892	79.7	72.5	99.6 [e]	99.7 [e]	94 [g]	86 [g]	14,084	22,832	1
28	Korea, Rep. of	29	0.882	79.2	71.7	96.6 [e, l]	99.2 [e, l]	85 [h]	98 [h]	10,747	23,226	-1
29	Barbados	27	0.884	79.4	74.4	99.7 [e]	99.7 [e]	93 [g]	84 [g]	11,634	19,116	2
30	Cyprus	30	0.875	80.5	75.9	95.1 [m]	98.6 [m]	75 [g]	74 [g]	11,223 [o]	23,916 [o]	0
31	Malta	31	0.866	80.6	75.8	93.4	91.8	77 [g]	77 [g]	9,654	26,160	0
32	Czech Republic	32	0.865	78.6	72.0	.. [e]	.. [e]	79 [h]	78 [h]	11,322	20,370	0
33	Brunei Darussalam	..	..	78.8	74.1	91.4 [m]	96.3 [m]	75	72	..	..	..
34	Argentina	36	0.841	77.6	70.5	97.0	97.0	98 [h]	90 [h]	5,662	15,431	-3
35	Seychelles	..	..	..	..	92.3 [m]	91.4 [m]	86	85	..	..	..
36	Estonia	33	0.852	76.7	66.3	99.8 [e, m]	99.8 [e, m]	101 [f, g]	92 [g]	9,777	15,571	1
37	Poland	34	0.848	77.9	69.7	99.7 [e, l]	99.8 [e, l]	93 [h]	87 [h]	8,120	13,149	1
38	Hungary	35	0.847	75.9	67.6	99.2 [e]	99.5 [e]	89 [h]	84 [h]	10,307	17,465	1
39	Saint Kitts and Nevis	..	..	..	..	..	..	111 [f, g]	85 [g]	..	..	..
40	Bahrain	39	0.832	75.8	72.4	84.2	91.5	82	77	7,961	23,505	-2
41	Lithuania	37	0.841	77.5	67.4	99.6 [e, m]	99.6 [e, m]	93 [g]	87 [g]	8,419	12,518	1
42	Slovakia	38	0.840	77.5	69.6	99.7 [e, m]	99.7 [e, m]	75 [h]	73 [h]	10,127	15,617	1
43	Chile	40	0.830	78.9	72.9	95.6 [m]	95.8 [m]	79 [g]	80 [g]	5,442	14,256	0
44	Kuwait	42	0.827	78.9	74.8	81.0	84.7	81 [k]	71 [k]	7,116	20,979	-1
45	Costa Rica	44	0.823	80.5	75.7	95.9	95.7	70	69	4,698	12,197	-2
46	Uruguay	41	0.829	78.8	71.5	98.1	97.3	90 [h]	81 [h]	5,367	10,304	2
47	Qatar	..	..	75.3	70.4	82.3 [m, p]	84.9 [m, p]	84	79	..	..	..
48	Croatia	43	0.827	78.0	70.2	97.1 [m]	99.3 [e, m]	74	72	7,453	13,374	1
49	United Arab Emirates	..	..	77.3	73.2	80.7	75.6	72	65	..	..	..
50	Latvia	45	0.823	76.1	65.4	99.7 [e, m]	99.8 [e, m]	92 [g]	83 [g]	7,685	11,085	0

HDI rank		Gender-related development index (GDI)		Life expectancy at birth (years) 2002		Adult literacy rate (% ages 15 and above) 2002 [a]		Combined gross enrolment ratio for primary, secondary and tertiary level schools (%) 2001/02 [b]		Estimated earned income (PPP US$) 2002 [c]		HDI rank minus GDI rank [d]
		Rank	Value	Female	Male	Female	Male	Female	Male	Female	Male	
51	Bahamas	46	0.813	70.4	63.9	96.3 [l]	94.6 [l]	77 [k, n]	72 [k, n]	13,375	20,700	0
52	Cuba	..	..	78.6	74.7	96.8	97.0	78	77	..	..	..
53	Mexico	50	0.792	76.3	70.3	88.7 [m]	92.6 [m]	74 [h]	73 [h]	4,915	12,967	-3
54	Trinidad and Tobago	47	0.795	74.5	68.5	97.9	99.0 [e]	65	63	5,916	13,095	1
55	Antigua and Barbuda	..	..	..	..	..	..	..	..	..	..	..
Medium human development												
56	Bulgaria	48	0.795	74.6	67.4	98.1	99.1 [e]	77 [g]	75 [g]	5,719	8,627	1
57	Russian Federation	49	0.794	73.0	60.7	99.5 [e]	99.7 [e]	92 [h]	85 [h]	6,508	10,189	1
58	Libyan Arab Jamahiriya	..	..	75.3	70.7	70.7	91.8	100 [f, h]	93 [h]			..
59	Malaysia	52	0.786	75.6	70.7	85.4 [m]	92.0 [m]	72 [h]	69 [h]	5,219	13,157	-1
60	Macedonia, TFYR	..	..	75.7	71.3	..	..	70 [g]	70 [g]	4,599	8,293	..
61	Panama	53	0.785	77.3	72.2	91.7	92.9	75 [k]	71 [k]	3,958	7,847	-1
62	Belarus	51	0.789	75.2	64.7	99.6 [e]	99.8 [e]	90	86	4,405	6,765	2
63	Tonga	..	..	69.0	67.9	98.9 [m]	98.8 [m]	83	82	..	..	..
64	Mauritius	55	0.775	75.7	68.3	80.5 [m]	88.2 [m]	68	70	5,827	15,897	-1
65	Albania	54	0.778	76.6	70.8	98.3 [m]	99.2 [e, m]	70 [g]	67 [g]	3,442	6,185	1
66	Bosnia and Herzegovina	..	..	76.6	71.2	91.1	98.4	..	..	..	..	..
67	Suriname	..	..	73.6	68.4	..	..	79 [h]	69 [h]	..	..	..
68	Venezuela	58	0.770	76.6	70.8	92.7	93.5	74	69	3,125	7,550	-2
69	Romania	56	0.775	74.2	67.0	96.3 [m]	98.4 [m]	70 [g]	67 [g]	4,837	8,311	1
70	Ukraine	57	0.773	74.6	64.5	99.5 [e]	99.8 [e]	86	83	3,429	6,493	1
71	Saint Lucia	..	..	74.0	70.7	..	..	77	70	..	..	..
72	Brazil	60	0.768	72.5	63.9	86.5 [m]	86.2 [m]	94 [h]	90 [h]	4,594	10,879	-1
73	Colombia	59	0.770	75.2	69.0	92.2	92.1	70	67	4,429	8,420	1
74	Oman	68	0.747	74.3	70.9	65.4	82.0	63	62	4,056	18,239	-7
75	Samoa (Western)	..	..	73.3	66.8	98.4	98.9	71	68	..	..	..
76	Thailand	61	0.766	73.4	65.2	90.5 [m]	94.9 [m]	72 [g]	74 [g]	5,284	8,664	1
77	Saudi Arabia	72	0.739	73.6	71.0	69.5	84.1	57	58	3,825	18,616	-9
78	Kazakhstan	63	0.761	71.8	60.7	99.2 [e]	99.7 [e]	82	80	4,247	7,156	1
79	Jamaica	62	0.762	77.7	73.6	91.4	83.8	78 [h]	72 [h]	3,169	4,783	3
80	Lebanon	64	0.755	75.0	71.8	81.0 [l]	92.4 [l]	79	77	2,552	8,336	2
81	Fiji	69	0.747	71.4	68.0	91.4 [m, p]	94.5 [m, p]	73 [h]	73 [h]	2,838	7,855	-2
82	Armenia	65	0.752	75.5	68.9	99.2 [e, m]	99.7 [e, m]	75	69	2,564	3,700	3
83	Philippines	66	0.751	71.9	67.9	92.7 [m]	92.5 [m]	82 [h]	81 [h]	3,144	5,326	3
84	Maldives	..	..	66.8	67.7	97.2	97.3	78	78	..	..	..
85	Peru	74	0.736	72.3	67.2	80.3 [q]	91.3 [q]	88 [h]	88 [h]	2,105	7,875	-4
86	Turkmenistan	67	0.748	70.3	63.7	98.3 [m, p]	99.3 [e, m, p]	81 [k, n]	81 [k, n]	3,274 [o]	5,212 [o]	4
87	St. Vincent & the Grenadines	..	..	75.5	72.5	..	..	66	63	..	..	..
88	Turkey	70	0.746	73.1	67.9	78.5 [m]	94.4 [m]	62 [h]	74 [h]	4,757	7,873	2
89	Paraguay	75	0.736	73.0	68.5	90.2 [q]	93.1 [q]	72 [h]	72 [h]	2,175	6,641	-2
90	Jordan	76	0.734	72.4	69.6	85.9	95.5	77 [h]	76 [h]	1,896	6,118	-2
91	Azerbaijan	..	..	75.4	68.6	..	..	67	70	2,322	4,044	..
92	Tunisia	77	0.734	74.8	70.7	63.1	83.1	75 [h]	74 [h]	3,615	9,933	-2
93	Grenada	..	..	..	..	..	..	57 [g]	73 [g]	..	..	..
94	China	71	0.741	73.2	68.8	86.5 [m]	95.1 [m]	64 [k]	69 [k]	3,571	5,435	5
95	Dominica	..	..	..	..	..	..	75 [g]	72 [g]	..	..	..
96	Sri Lanka	73	0.738	75.8	69.8	89.6	94.7	66 [r]	64 [r]	2,570	4,523	4
97	Georgia	..	..	77.5	69.4	..	..	70	68	1,325	3,283	..
98	Dominican Republic	78	0.728	69.2	64.4	84.4	84.3	81 [h]	73 [h]	3,491	9,694	0
99	Belize	80	0.718	73.1	70.0	77.1 [m]	76.7 [m]	72 [g]	71 [g]	2,376	9,799	-1
100	Ecuador	79	0.721	73.4	68.2	89.7 [m]	92.3 [m]	71 [g, s]	73 [g, s]	1,656	5,491	1

HDI rank		Gender-related development index (GDI)		Life expectancy at birth (years) 2002		Adult literacy rate (% ages 15 and above) 2002 [a]		Combined gross enrolment ratio for primary, secondary and tertiary level schools (%) 2001/02 [b]		Estimated earned income (PPP US$) 2002 [c]		HDI rank minus GDI rank [d]
		Rank	Value	Female	Male	Female	Male	Female	Male	Female	Male	
101	Iran, Islamic Rep. of	82	0.713	71.7	68.8	70.4 [l, p, q]	83.5 [l, p, q]	65	72	2,835	9,946	-1
102	Occupied Palestinian Territories	..	..	73.9	70.7	..	..	81	78	..	..	..
103	El Salvador	84	0.709	73.6	67.6	77.1	82.4	65	66	2,602	7,269	-2
104	Guyana	81	0.715	66.4	60.1	98.2 [l]	99.0 [l]	75 [k]	75 [k]	2,439	6,217	2
105	Cape Verde	83	0.709	72.7	66.9	68.0	85.4	72 [h]	73 [h]	3,229	7,034	1
106	Syrian Arab Republic	88	0.689	73.0	70.5	74.2	91.0	57	62	1,549	5,496	-3
107	Uzbekistan	85	0.705	72.4	66.7	98.9	99.6 [e]	75	78	1,305	1,983	1
108	Algeria	89	0.688	71.1	68.0	59.6	78.0	69 [h]	72 [h]	2,684	8,794	-2
109	Equatorial Guinea	86	0.691	50.5	47.7	76.0 [l]	92.8 [l]	52	64	16,852 [o]	42,304 [o]	2
110	Kyrgyzstan	..	..	72.2	64.6	..	..	81	80	1,269	1,944	..
111	Indonesia	90	0.685	68.6	64.6	83.4	92.5	64 [h]	66 [h]	2,138	4,161	-1
112	Viet Nam	87	0.689	71.4	66.7	86.9 [m, p]	93.9 [m, p]	61	67	1,888	2,723	3
113	Moldova, Rep. of	91	0.678	72.1	65.3	98.6	99.6 [e]	63	60	1,168	1,788	0
114	Bolivia	92	0.674	65.8	61.6	80.7 [m]	93.1 [m]	82 [h]	89 [h]	1,559	3,463	0
115	Honduras	95	0.662	71.4	66.5	80.2 [m]	79.8 [m]	61 [g, s]	64 [g, s]	1,402	3,792	-2
116	Tajikistan	93	0.668	71.3	66.0	99.3 [e, m]	99.7 [e, m]	67	80	759	1,225	1
117	Mongolia	94	0.664	65.7	61.7	97.5 [m]	98.0 [m]	76	64	1,316	1,955	1
118	Nicaragua	97	0.660	71.8	67.1	76.6 [q]	76.8 [q]	66 [h]	63 [h]	1,520	3,436	-1
119	South Africa	96	0.661	51.9	46.0	85.3	86.7	77	78	6,371	14,202	1
120	Egypt	99	0.634	70.8	66.6	43.6 [m, p]	67.2 [m, p]	72 [k, n]	80 [k, n]	1,963	5,216	-1
121	Guatemala	98	0.635	68.7	62.8	62.5	77.3	52 [h]	59 [h]	2,007	6,092	1
122	Gabon	..	..	57.6	55.7	..	..	70 [k]	74 [k]	4,937	8,351	..
123	São Tomé and Principe	..	..	72.7	66.9	..	..	59	64	..	..	..
124	Solomon Islands	..	..	70.5	67.8	..	..	..	..	1,239	1,786	..
125	Morocco	100	0.604	70.3	66.6	38.3	63.3	52	61	2,153	5,354	0
126	Namibia	101	0.602	46.8	43.8	82.8	83.8	72	70	4,262	8,402	0
127	India	103	0.572	64.4	63.1	46.4 [m]	69.0 [m]	48 [g]	62 [g]	1,442	3,820	-1
128	Botswana	102	0.581	42.3	40.4	81.5	76.1	71	70	5,353	10,550	1
129	Vanuatu	..	..	70.4	67.4	..	..	58	59	..	..	..
130	Cambodia	105	0.557	59.5	55.2	59.3	80.8	53	64	1,622	2,117	-1
131	Ghana	104	0.564	59.3	56.4	65.9	81.9	43	50	1,802	2,419	1
132	Myanmar	..	..	60.1	54.5	81.4	89.2	48 [g]	47 [g]	..	..	..
133	Papua New Guinea	106	0.536	58.5	56.6	57.7 [l]	71.1 [l]	40	42	1,586	2,748	0
134	Bhutan	..	..	64.3	61.8	..	..	..	..	..	..	..
135	Lao People's Dem. Rep.	107	0.528	55.6	53.1	55.5	77.4	53	65	1,358	2,082	0
136	Comoros	108	0.510	62.0	59.2	49.1	63.5	41	50	950	1,699	0
137	Swaziland	109	0.505	36.9	34.4	80.0	82.0	59	62	2,259	7,227	0
138	Bangladesh	110	0.499	61.5	60.7	31.4	50.3	54	53	1,150	2,035	0
139	Sudan	115	0.485	57.0	54.1	49.1	70.8	34 [g]	39 [g]	867	2,752	-4
140	Nepal	116	0.484	59.4	59.9	26.4	61.6	55	67	891	1,776	-4
141	Cameroon	111	0.491	48.1	45.6	59.8 [q]	77.0 [q]	51 [h]	61 [h]	1,235	2,787	2
Low human development												
142	Pakistan	120	0.471	60.7	61.0	28.5 [m, p]	53.4 [m, p]	31 [g]	43 [g]	915	2,789	-6
143	Togo	119	0.477	51.4	48.3	45.4	74.3	55	78	941	2,004	-4
144	Congo	112	0.488	49.9	46.6	77.1	88.9	44 [h]	52 [h]	707	1,273	4
145	Lesotho	117	0.483	39.0	33.3	90.3 [q]	73.7 [q]	66	64	1,357	3,578	0
146	Uganda	113	0.487	46.4	44.9	59.2	78.8	68	73	1,088	1,651	5
147	Zimbabwe	118	0.482	33.5	34.3	86.3	93.8	57 [h]	60 [h]	1,757 [o]	3,059 [o]	1
148	Kenya	114	0.486	46.4	44.0	78.5	90.0	52	54	962	1,067	6
149	Yemen	126	0.436	60.9	58.7	28.5	69.5	37 [g]	66 [g]	387	1,274	-5
150	Madagascar	121	0.462	54.6	52.3	60.6 [l]	74.2 [l]	44	46	534	906	1
151	Nigeria	122	0.458	52.0	51.2	59.4	74.4	41 [k, n]	49 [k, n]	562	1,322	1

HDI rank		Gender-related development index (GDI)		Life expectancy at birth (years) 2002		Adult literacy rate (% ages 15 and above) 2002 [a]		Combined gross enrolment ratio for primary, secondary and tertiary level schools (%) 2001/02 [b]		Estimated earned income (PPP US$) 2002 [c]		HDI rank minus GDI rank [d]
		Rank	Value	Female	Male	Female	Male	Female	Male	Female	Male	
152	Mauritania	124	0.456	53.9	50.7	31.3	51.5	42	46	1,581	2,840	0
153	Haiti	123	0.458	49.9	48.8	50.0	53.8	51 [k, n]	53 [k, n]	1,170	2,089	2
154	Djibouti	..	..	47.0	44.8	55.5 [l]	76.1 [l]	20	28	..	..	..
155	Gambia	125	0.446	55.4	52.5	30.9 [l]	45.0 [l]	41 [h]	49 [h]	1,263	2,127	1
156	Eritrea	127	0.431	54.2	51.1	45.6 [l]	68.2 [l]	28	39	654	1,266	0
157	Senegal	128	0.429	54.9	50.6	29.7	49.0	35 [h]	41 [h]	1,140	2,074	0
158	Timor-Leste	..	..	50.2	48.5	..	..	..	..	..	..	..
159	Rwanda	129	0.423	39.4	38.4	63.4	75.3	50	56	968	1,570	0
160	Guinea	..	..	49.3	48.6	..	..	21 [r]	37 [r]	1,569	2,317	..
161	Benin	130	0.406	53.1	48.5	25.5	54.8	41 [h]	64 [h]	876	1,268	0
162	Tanzania, U. Rep. of	131	0.401	44.4	42.7	69.2	85.2	31 [g]	32 [g]	467	660	0
163	Côte d'Ivoire	132	0.379	41.5	40.9	38.4 [l]	60.3 [l]	34	50	818	2,222	0
164	Zambia	133	0.375	32.5	32.9	73.8	86.3	43	47	571	1,041	0
165	Malawi	134	0.374	38.2	37.5	48.7	75.5	71 [h]	77 [h]	427	626	0
166	Angola	..	..	41.5	38.8	..	..	27 [k]	32 [k]	1,627	2,626	..
167	Chad	135	0.368	45.7	43.6	37.5	54.5	25 [g]	44 [g]	760	1,284	0
168	Congo, Dem. Rep. of the	136	0.355	42.4	40.4	51.8 [l]	74.2 [l]	24 [r, s]	30 [r, s]	467	846	0
169	Central African Republic	138	0.345	41.0	38.7	33.5 [q]	64.7 [q]	24	38	889	1,469	-1
170	Ethiopia	137	0.346	46.4	44.6	33.8	49.2	28	41	516	1,008	1
171	Mozambique	139	0.339	40.0	36.9	31.4	62.3	35	46	840	1,265	0
172	Guinea-Bissau	141	0.329	46.8	43.7	24.7 [l]	55.2 [l]	29 [k]	45 [k]	465	959	-1
173	Burundi	140	0.337	41.3	40.2	43.6	57.7	29	38	561	794	1
174	Mali	142	0.309	49.0	47.9	11.9 [m, p]	26.7 [m, p]	21 [r]	31 [r]	635	1,044	0
175	Burkina Faso	143	0.291	46.3	45.1	8.1 [m, p]	18.5 [m, p]	18 [h]	26 [h]	855	1,215	0
176	Niger	144	0.278	46.3	45.7	9.3	25.1	16	23	575	1,005	0
177	Sierra Leone	..	..	35.6	33.1	..	..	38 [g]	52 [g]	337	815	..

a. Data refer to estimates produced by UNESCO Institute for Statistics in July 2002, unless otherwise specified. Due to differences in methodology and timeliness of underlying data, comparisons across countries and over time should be made with caution. b. Data refer to the 2001/02 school year. Data for some countries may refer to national or UNESCO Institute for Statistics estimates. For details, see http://www.uis.unesco.org/. Because data are from different sources, comparisons across countries should be made with caution. c. Because of the lack of gender-disaggregated income data, female and male earned income are crudely estimated on the basis of data on the ratio of the female non-agricultural wage to the male non-agricultural wage, the female and male shares of the economically active population, the total female and male population and GDP per capita (PPP US$) (see technical note 1). Estimates are based on data for the most recent year available during 1991-2000, unless otherwise specified. d. The HDI ranks used in this column are those recalculated for the 144 countries with a GDI value. A positive figure indicates that the GDI rank is higher than the HDI rank, a negative the opposite. e. For purposes of calculating the GDI, a value of 99.0% was applied. f. For purposes of calculating the GDI, a value of 100% was applied. g. Data refer to the 2000/01 school year. h. Preliminary UNESCO Institute for Statistics estimate, subject to further revision. i. The ratio is an underestimate, as many secondary and tertiary students pursue their studies in nearby countries (see box to table 1). j. For purposes of calculating the GDI, a value of $40,000 (PPP US$) was applied. k. Data refer to the 1999/2000 school year. l. UNESCO Institute for Statistics 2003a. m. Census data. n. Data provided by the UNESCO Institute for Statistics for *Human Development Report 2001* (see UNESCO Institute for Statistics 2001). o. Calculated on the basis of GDP per capita (PPP US$) for 2000. p. Data refer to a year between 1995 and 1999. q. Survey data. r. Data refer to the 1998/99 school year. s. UNESCO Institute for Statistics 2003b.

Source: Column 1: determined on the basis of the GDI values in column 2; *column 2:* calculated on the basis of data in columns 3-10; see technical note 1 for details; *columns 3 and 4:* UN 2003; *columns 5 and 6:* UNESCO Institute for Statistics 2004a, unless otherwise noted; *columns 7 and 8:* UNESCO Institute for Statistics 2004c, unless otherwise noted; *columns 9 and 10:* calculated on the basis of data on GDP per capita (PPP US$) from World Bank 2004f; data on wages from ILO 2004b; data on the economically active population from ILO 2002; and data on population from UN 2003, unless otherwise noted; *column 11:* calculated on the basis of the recalculated HDI ranks and GDI ranks in column 1.

GDI ranks for 144 countries

		23	Hong Kong, China (SAR)	48	Bulgaria	73	Sri Lanka	98	Guatemala	123	Haiti
		24	Portugal	49	Russian Federation	74	Peru	99	Egypt	124	Mauritania
		25	Greece	50	Mexico	75	Paraguay	100	Morocco	125	Gambia
1	Norway	26	Slovenia	51	Belarus	76	Jordan	101	Namibia	126	Yemen
2	Sweden	27	Barbados	52	Malaysia	77	Tunisia	102	Botswana	127	Eritrea
3	Australia	28	Singapore	53	Panama	78	Dominican Republic	103	India	128	Senegal
4	Canada	29	Korea, Rep. of	54	Albania	79	Ecuador	104	Ghana	129	Rwanda
5	Netherlands	30	Cyprus	55	Mauritius	80	Belize	105	Cambodia	130	Benin
6	Iceland	31	Malta	56	Romania	81	Guyana	106	Papua New Guinea	131	Tanzania, U. Rep. of
7	Belgium	32	Czech Republic	57	Ukraine	82	Iran, Islamic Rep. of	107	Lao People's Dem. Rep.	132	Côte d'Ivoire
8	United States	33	Estonia	58	Venezuela	83	Cape Verde	108	Comoros	133	Zambia
9	United Kingdom	34	Poland	59	Colombia	84	El Salvador	109	Swaziland	134	Malawi
10	Finland	35	Hungary	60	Brazil	85	Uzbekistan	110	Bangladesh	135	Chad
11	Switzerland	36	Argentina	61	Thailand	86	Equatorial Guinea	111	Cameroon	136	Congo, Dem. Rep. of the
12	Japan	37	Lithuania	62	Jamaica	87	Viet Nam	112	Congo	137	Ethiopia
13	Denmark	38	Slovakia	63	Kazakhstan	88	Syrian Arab Republic	113	Uganda	138	Central African Republic
14	Ireland	39	Bahrain	64	Lebanon	89	Algeria	114	Kenya	139	Mozambique
15	France	40	Chile	65	Armenia	90	Indonesia	115	Sudan	140	Burundi
16	Luxembourg	41	Uruguay	66	Philippines	91	Moldova, Rep. of	116	Nepal	141	Guinea-Bissau
17	Austria	42	Kuwait	67	Turkmenistan	92	Bolivia	117	Lesotho	142	Mali
18	New Zealand	43	Croatia	68	Oman	93	Tajikistan	118	Zimbabwe	143	Burkina Faso
19	Germany	44	Costa Rica	69	Fiji	94	Mongolia	119	Togo	144	Niger
20	Spain	45	Latvia	70	Turkey	95	Honduras	120	Pakistan		
21	Italy	46	Bahamas	71	China	96	South Africa	121	Madagascar		
22	Israel	47	Trinidad and Tobago	72	Saudi Arabia	97	Nicaragua	122	Nigeria		

25 Gender empowerment measure

HDI rank		Gender empowerment measure (GEM)		MDG Seats in parliament held by women [a] (% of total)	Female legislators, senior officials and managers [b] (% of total)	Female professional and technical workers [b] (% of total)	Ratio of estimated female to male earned income [c]
		Rank	Value				
High human development							
1	Norway	1	0.908	36.4	28	49	0.74
2	Sweden	2	0.854	45.3	31	50	0.83
3	Australia	8	0.806	26.5	35	55	0.71
4	Canada	10	0.787	23.6	34	54	0.63
5	Netherlands	5	0.817	35.1	26	48	0.53
6	Belgium	7	0.808	33.9	30	48	0.50
7	Iceland	6	0.816	30.2	29	55	0.63
8	United States	14	0.769	14.0	46	55	0.62
9	Japan	38	0.531	9.9	10	46	0.46
10	Ireland	16	0.710	14.2	28	52	0.40
11	Switzerland	12	0.771	24.8	28	45	0.50
12	United Kingdom	18	0.698	17.3	31	44	0.60
13	Finland	4	0.820	37.5	28	52	0.70
14	Austria	13	0.770	30.6	29	48	0.36
15	Luxembourg	..	..	16.7	..	..	0.38
16	France	..	..	11.7	..	..	0.59
17	Denmark	3	0.847	38.0	22	51	0.72
18	New Zealand	11	0.772	28.3	38	52	0.69
19	Germany	9	0.804	31.4	34	49	0.52
20	Spain	15	0.716	26.6	31	46	0.44
21	Italy	32	0.583	10.3	21	45	0.45
22	Israel	25	0.614	15.0	26	54	0.53
23	Hong Kong, China (SAR)	..	..	..	26	40	0.56
24	Greece	43	0.523	8.7	26	48	0.43
25	Singapore	20	0.648	16.0	26	43	0.50
26	Portugal	23	0.644	19.1	29	51	0.54
27	Slovenia	31	0.584	12.2	29	55	0.62
28	Korea, Rep. of	68	0.377	5.9	5	34	0.46
29	Barbados	24	0.634	17.6	40	55	0.61
30	Cyprus	49	0.497	10.7	14	46	0.47
31	Malta	53	0.480	9.2	17	40	0.37
32	Czech Republic	30	0.586	15.7	26	52	0.56
33	Brunei Darussalam	..	..	— [d]	..	..	..
34	Argentina	21	0.645	31.3	26	53	0.37
35	Seychelles	..	..	29.4	..	..	..
36	Estonia	28	0.592	18.8	37	68	0.63
37	Poland	27	0.606	20.7	34	60	0.62
38	Hungary	39	0.529	9.8	35	62	0.59
39	Saint Kitts and Nevis	..	..	13.3	..	..	..
40	Bahrain	66	0.395	7.5 [e]	10	19	0.34
41	Lithuania	47	0.508	10.6	44	70	0.67
42	Slovakia	26	0.607	19.3	31	61	0.65
43	Chile	58	0.460	10.1	21	52	0.38
44	Kuwait	..	..	0.0	..	..	0.34
45	Costa Rica	19	0.664	35.1	53	28	0.39
46	Uruguay	46	0.511	11.5	37	52	0.52
47	Qatar	..	..	— [d]	..	..	..
48	Croatia	36	0.560	17.8	26	51	0.56
49	United Arab Emirates	..	..	0.0	8	25	..
50	Latvia	29	0.591	21.0	37	66	0.69

HDI rank		Gender empowerment measure (GEM)		MDG Seats in parliament held by women[a] (% of total)	Female legislators, senior officials and managers[b] (% of total)	Female professional and technical workers[b] (% of total)	Ratio of estimated female to male earned income[c]
		Rank	Value				
51	Bahamas	17	0.699	26.8	31	58	0.65
52	Cuba	..	..	36.0	..	..	..
53	Mexico	34	0.563	21.2	25	40	0.38
54	Trinidad and Tobago	22	0.644	25.4	40	51	0.45
55	Antigua and Barbuda	..	..	8.3	..	..	..
Medium human development							
56	Bulgaria	..	..	26.3	..	..	0.66
57	Russian Federation	55	0.467	8.0	37	64	0.64
58	Libyan Arab Jamahiriya	..	..	..	..	..	..
59	Malaysia	44	0.519	16.3	20	45	0.40
60	Macedonia, TFYR	45	0.517	18.3	19	51	0.55
61	Panama	52	0.486	9.9	38	49	0.50
62	Belarus	..	..	18.4	..	..	0.65
63	Tonga	..	..	0.0	..	..	..
64	Mauritius	..	..	5.7	..	..	0.37
65	Albania	..	..	5.7	..	..	0.56
66	Bosnia and Herzegovina	..	..	12.3	..	..	..
67	Suriname	..	..	17.6	28	51	..
68	Venezuela	61	0.444	9.7	27	61	0.41
69	Romania	56	0.465	9.3	31	56	0.58
70	Ukraine	65	0.411	5.3	38	64	0.53
71	Saint Lucia	..	..	20.7	..	..	..
72	Brazil	..	..	9.1	..	62	0.42
73	Colombia	48	0.498	10.8	38	50	0.53
74	Oman	..	..	–[d]	..	..	0.22
75	Samoa (Western)	..	..	6.1	..	..	..
76	Thailand	57	0.461	9.6	27	55	0.61
77	Saudi Arabia	77	0.207	0.0	1	31	0.21
78	Kazakhstan	..	..	8.6	..	..	0.59
79	Jamaica	..	..	13.6	..	..	0.66
80	Lebanon	..	..	2.3	..	..	0.31
81	Fiji	71	0.335	6.0	51	9	0.36
82	Armenia	..	..	4.6	..	..	0.69
83	Philippines	37	0.542	17.2	58	62	0.59
84	Maldives	..	..	6.0	15	40	..
85	Peru	42	0.524	18.3	27	44	0.27
86	Turkmenistan	..	..	26.0	..	..	0.63
87	St. Vincent & the Grenadines	..	..	22.7	..	..	..
88	Turkey	73	0.290	4.4	7	31	0.60
89	Paraguay	63	0.417	8.8	23	54	0.33
90	Jordan	..	..	7.9	..	..	0.31
91	Azerbaijan	..	..	10.5	..	..	0.57
92	Tunisia	..	..	11.5	..	..	0.36
93	Grenada	..	..	28.6	..	..	..
94	China	..	..	20.2	..	..	0.66
95	Dominica	..	..	18.8	..	..	..
96	Sri Lanka	74	0.276	4.4	4	49	0.57
97	Georgia	67	0.387	7.2 [f]	28	64	0.40
98	Dominican Republic	40	0.527	15.4	31	49	0.36
99	Belize	59	0.455	9.3	31	52	0.24
100	Ecuador	50	0.490	16.0	25	44	0.30

HDI rank		Gender empowerment measure (GEM)		MDG Seats in parliament held by women [a] (% of total)	Female legislators, senior officials and managers [b] (% of total)	Female professional and technical workers [b] (% of total)	Ratio of estimated female to male earned income [c]
		Rank	Value				
101	Iran, Islamic Rep. of	72	0.313	4.1	13	33	0.29
102	Occupied Palestinian Territories	..	..	..	10	33	..
103	El Salvador	60	0.448	10.7	26	46	0.36
104	Guyana	..	..	20.0	..	..	0.39
105	Cape Verde	..	..	11.1	..	..	0.46
106	Syrian Arab Republic	..	..	12.0	..	..	0.28
107	Uzbekistan	..	..	7.2	..	..	0.66
108	Algeria	..	..	..	..	..	0.31
109	Equatorial Guinea	..	..	5.0	..	..	0.40
110	Kyrgyzstan	..	..	6.7	..	..	0.65
111	Indonesia	..	..	8.0	..	..	0.51
112	Viet Nam	..	..	27.3	..	..	0.69
113	Moldova, Rep. of	54	0.469	12.9	40	64	0.65
114	Bolivia	41	0.524	17.8	36	40	0.45
115	Honduras	70	0.355	5.5	22	36	0.37
116	Tajikistan	..	..	12.4	..	..	0.62
117	Mongolia	62	0.429	10.5	30	66	0.67
118	Nicaragua	..	..	20.7	..	..	0.44
119	South Africa	..	..	27.9 [g]	..	..	0.45
120	Egypt	75	0.266	3.6	9	30	0.38
121	Guatemala	..	..	8.2	..	..	0.33
122	Gabon	..	..	11.0	..	..	0.59
123	São Tomé and Principe	..	..	9.1	..	..	..
124	Solomon Islands	..	..	0.0	..	..	0.69
125	Morocco	..	..	..	..	..	0.40
126	Namibia	33	0.572	21.4	30	55	0.51
127	India	..	..	9.3	..	..	0.38
128	Botswana	35	0.562	17.0	35	52	0.51
129	Vanuatu	..	..	1.9	..	..	..
130	Cambodia	69	0.364	10.9	14	33	0.77
131	Ghana	..	..	9.0	..	..	0.75
132	Myanmar	..	..	.. [h]	..	..	..
133	Papua New Guinea	..	..	0.9	..	..	0.58
134	Bhutan	..	..	9.3	..	..	..
135	Lao People's Dem. Rep.	..	..	22.9	..	..	0.65
136	Comoros	..	..	– [i]	..	..	0.56
137	Swaziland	51	0.487	16.8	24	61	0.31
138	Bangladesh	76	0.218	2.0	8	25	0.56
139	Sudan	..	..	9.7	..	..	0.32
140	Nepal	..	..	..	..	..	0.50
141	Cameroon	..	..	8.9	..	..	0.44
Low human development							
142	Pakistan	64	0.416	20.8	9	26	0.33
143	Togo	..	..	7.4	..	..	0.47
144	Congo	..	..	10.6	..	..	0.56
145	Lesotho	..	..	17.0	..	..	0.38
146	Uganda	..	..	24.7	..	..	0.66
147	Zimbabwe	..	..	10.0	..	..	0.57
148	Kenya	..	..	7.1	..	..	0.90
149	Yemen	78	0.123	0.3	4	15	0.30
150	Madagascar	..	..	6.4	..	..	0.59
151	Nigeria	..	..	5.8	..	..	0.43

HDI rank		Gender empowerment measure (GEM)		MDG Seats in parliament held by women [a] (% of total)	Female legislators, senior officials and managers [b] (% of total)	Female professional and technical workers [b] (% of total)	Ratio of estimated female to male earned income [c]
		Rank	Value				
152	Mauritania	..	..	4.4	..	..	0.56
153	Haiti	..	..	9.1	..	..	0.56
154	Djibouti	..	..	10.8	..	..	..
155	Gambia	..	..	13.2	..	..	0.59
156	Eritrea	..	..	22.0	..	..	0.52
157	Senegal	..	..	19.2	..	..	0.55
158	Timor-Leste	..	..	26.1	..	..	..
159	Rwanda	..	..	45.0	..	..	0.62
160	Guinea	..	..	19.3	..	..	0.68
161	Benin	..	..	7.2	..	..	0.69
162	Tanzania, U. Rep. of	..	..	21.4	..	..	0.71
163	Côte d'Ivoire	..	..	8.5	..	..	0.37
164	Zambia	..	..	12.0	..	..	0.55
165	Malawi	..	..	9.3	..	..	0.68
166	Angola	..	..	15.5	..	..	0.62
167	Chad	..	..	5.8	..	..	0.59
168	Congo, Dem. Rep. of the	..	..	7.4	..	..	0.55
169	Central African Republic	..	..	– [i]	..	..	0.60
170	Ethiopia	..	..	7.8	..	..	0.51
171	Mozambique	..	..	30.0	..	..	0.66
172	Guinea-Bissau	..	..	– [i]	..	..	0.49
173	Burundi	..	..	18.5	..	..	0.71
174	Mali	..	..	10.2	..	..	0.61
175	Burkina Faso	..	..	11.7	..	..	0.70
176	Niger	..	..	1.2	..	..	0.57
177	Sierra Leone	..	..	14.5	..	..	0.41

a. Data are as of 1 March 2004. Where there are lower and upper houses, data refer to the weighted average of women's shares of seats in both houses. b. Data refer to the most recent year available during the period 1992-2001. Estimates for countries that have implemented the recent International Standard Classification of Occupations (ISCO-88) are not strictly comparable with those for countries using the previous classification (ISCO-68). c. Calculated on the basis of data in columns 9 and 10 in table 24. Estimates are based on data for the most recent year available during the period 1991-2001. d. Brunei Darussalam, Oman and Qatar have never had a parliament. e. Women were allowed to vote in the referendum of 14-15 February 2001, which approved the National Action Charter. Subsequently, women exercised their full political rights as both voters and candidates in the 2002 national elections. f. Elections were held in November 2003. However, on 25 November 2003, the election results were annuled by the Supreme Court of Georgia. New elections will be held in March 2004. g. The figures on the distribution of seats do not include the 36 upper house special rotation delegates appointed on an ad hoc basis, and the percentages given are therefore calculated on the basis of lower house seats and the 54 permanent seats in the upper house. h. The parliament elected in 1990 has never been convened nor authorized to sit, and many of its members were detained or forced into exile. i. Parliament has been dissolved or suspended for an indefinite period.

Source: Column 1: determined on the basis of GEM values in column 2; *column 2:* calculated on the basis of data in columns 3-6; see technical note 1 for details; *column 3:* calculated on the basis of data on parliamentary seats from IPU 2004b; *columns 4 and 5:* calculated on the basis of occupational data from ILO 2004b; *column 6:* calculated on the basis of data in columns 9 and 10 of table 24.

GEM ranks for 78 countries

1	Norway	19	Costa Rica	40	Dominican Republic	61	Venezuela
2	Sweden	20	Singapore	41	Bolivia	62	Mongolia
3	Denmark	21	Argentina	42	Peru	63	Paraguay
4	Finland	22	Trinidad and Tobago	43	Greece	64	Pakistan
5	Netherlands	23	Portugal	44	Malaysia	65	Ukraine
6	Iceland	24	Barbados	45	Macedonia, TFYR	66	Bahrain
7	Belgium	25	Israel	46	Uruguay	67	Georgia
8	Australia	26	Slovakia	47	Lithuania	68	Korea, Rep. of
9	Germany	27	Poland	48	Colombia	69	Cambodia
10	Canada	28	Estonia	49	Cyprus	70	Honduras
11	New Zealand	29	Latvia	50	Ecuador	71	Fiji
12	Switzerland	30	Czech Republic	51	Swaziland	72	Iran, Islamic Rep. of
13	Austria	31	Slovenia	52	Panama	73	Turkey
14	United States	32	Italy	53	Malta	74	Sri Lanka
15	Spain	33	Namibia	54	Moldova, Rep. of	75	Egypt
16	Ireland	34	Mexico	55	Russian Federation	76	Bangladesh
17	Bahamas	35	Botswana	56	Romania	77	Saudi Arabia
18	United Kingdom	36	Croatia	57	Thailand	78	Yemen
		37	Philippines	58	Chile		
		38	Japan	59	Belize		
		39	Hungary	60	El Salvador		

26 Gender inequality in education

		Adult literacy [a]		Youth literacy [a]		MDG Net primary enrolment [b, c]		MDG Net secondary enrolment [b, c]		MDG Gross tertiary enrolment [c, d]	
		Female rate (% ages 15 and above)	Female rate as % of male rate	Female rate (% ages 15-24)	Female rate as % of male rate	Female ratio (%)	Ratio of female to male [e]	Female ratio (%)	Ratio of female to male [e]	Female ratio (%)	Ratio of female to male [e]
HDI rank		2002	2002	2002	2002	2000/01	2000/01	2000/01	2000/01	2000/01	2000/01
High human development											
1	Norway	..	..	..	..	102 [f]	1.00 [f]	95 [f]	1.01 [f]	85 [f]	1.52 [f]
2	Sweden	..	..	..	..	102	1.00	99	1.01	93	1.54
3	Australia	..	..	..	..	96	1.01	90 [g]	1.03 [g]	72	1.24
4	Canada	..	..	..	..	100 [f, g]	1.00 [f, g]	98 [f, g]	1.00 [f, g]	68 [f]	1.34 [f]
5	Netherlands	..	..	..	..	100 [f]	0.99 [f]	90 [f, g]	1.00 [f, g]	57 [f]	1.07 [f]
6	Belgium	..	..	..	..	101 [f]	1.00 [f]	..	..	63 [f]	1.16 [f]
7	Iceland	..	..	..	..	101 [f]	1.00 [f]	85 [f]	1.05 [f]	61 [f]	1.73 [f]
8	United States	..	..	..	..	93	1.01	85	1.00	94	1.35
9	Japan	..	..	..	..	101	1.00	101 [g, h]	1.01 [g, h]	45	0.86
10	Ireland	..	..	..	..	95 [f]	1.01 [f]	85 [f]	1.07 [f]	53 [f]	1.27 [f]
11	Switzerland	..	..	..	..	99 [f]	0.99 [f]	85 [f]	0.95 [f]	37 [f]	0.78 [f]
12	United Kingdom	..	..	..	..	101 [f]	1.00 [f]	95 [f]	1.02 [f]	64 [f]	1.20 [f]
13	Finland	..	..	..	..	100 [f]	1.00 [f]	95 [f, g]	1.02 [f, g]	94 [f]	1.22 [f]
14	Austria	..	..	..	..	91 [f]	1.01 [f]	88 [f, g]	0.99 [f, g]	61 [f]	1.15 [f]
15	Luxembourg	..	..	..	..	96 [f]	1.00 [f]	83 [f]	1.09 [f]	10 [f, i]	1.14 [f]
16	France	..	..	..	..	100 [f]	1.00 [f]	93 [f, g]	1.02 [f, g]	59 [f]	1.23 [f]
17	Denmark	..	..	..	..	99 [h]	1.00 [h]	91 [h]	1.03 [h]	68 [f, g]	1.35 [f]
18	New Zealand	..	..	..	..	98	0.99	93 [f, g]	1.02 [f, g]	87	1.52
19	Germany	..	..	..	..	84	1.02	88	1.00	48	1.00
20	Spain	..	..	..	..	104	0.99	96	1.04	64	1.19
21	Italy	..	..	..	..	100 [f]	1.00 [f]	85 [g, j]	1.01 [g, j]	57 [f]	1.32 [f]
22	Israel	93.4	96	99.4	100	101	1.00	89	1.01	67	1.38
23	Hong Kong, China (SAR)	..	..	..	..	98 [g]	1.00 [g]	72 [g]	1.02 [g]	26	0.99
24	Greece	..	..	..	..	95 [f]	1.00 [f]	86 [f]	1.03 [f]	64 [f]	1.10 [f]
25	Singapore	88.6 [k]	92 [k]	99.6 [k]	100	..	..	..	..	..	..
26	Portugal	..	..	..	..	..	..	89 [f, g]	1.08 [f, g]	58 [f]	1.37 [f]
27	Slovenia	99.6	100	99.8	100	93 [f]	0.99 [f]	97 [f, g]	1.02 [f, g]	70 [f]	1.35 [f]
28	Korea, Rep. of	..	..	..	..	101	1.00	89	1.00	61	0.60
29	Barbados	99.7	100	99.8	100	103	1.00	86	0.99	52 [f]	2.55 [f]
30	Cyprus	95.1 [k]	96 [k]	99.8 [k]	100	95 [f]	1.01 [f]	89 [f]	1.02 [f]	25 [f]	1.35 [f]
31	Malta	93.4	102	99.8	102	98 [f]	1.01 [f]	80 [f, g]	1.01 [f, g]	28 [f]	1.29 [f]
32	Czech Republic	..	..	..	..	88	1.00	90	1.01	35	1.09
33	Brunei Darussalam	91.4 [k]	95 [k]	99.3 [k]	100	..	..	..	..	17	1.77
34	Argentina	97.0	100	98.9	100	108	1.00	83	1.06	67	1.48
35	Seychelles	92.3 [k]	101 [k]	99.4 [k]	101	106	0.99	101	1.05	..	..
36	Estonia	99.8 [k]	100 [k]	99.8 [k]	100	97 [f]	0.98 [f]	95 [f]	1.06 [f]	74 [f]	1.57 [f]
37	Poland	..	..	..	..	98	1.00	93	1.03	69	1.43
38	Hungary	..	..	..	..	90	0.99	92	1.00	50	1.29
39	Saint Kitts and Nevis	..	..	..	..	107 [f]	1.09 [f]	116 [f]	1.21 [f]	..	..
40	Bahrain	84.2	92	98.9	100	91 [g]	1.01 [g]	86 [g]	1.12 [g]	28 [g, j]	1.86 [j]
41	Lithuania	99.6 [k]	100 [k]	99.7 [k]	100	97 [f]	0.99 [f]	92 [f, g]	1.01 [f, g]	72 [f]	1.53 [f]
42	Slovakia	99.7 [k]	100 [k]	99.7 [k]	100	88	1.02	87	1.01	34	1.13
43	Chile	95.6 [k]	100 [k]	99.2 [k]	100	88 [f]	0.99 [f]	76 [f]	1.03 [f]	36 [f]	0.92 [f]
44	Kuwait	81.0	96	93.9	102	84	0.99	79 [g]	1.05 [g]	32 [g, j]	2.58 [j]
45	Costa Rica	95.9	100	98.7	101	91	1.02	53	1.11	22	1.17
46	Uruguay	98.1	101	99.4	101	90	1.01	76 [g]	1.11 [g]	48	1.82
47	Qatar	82.3 [k, l]	97 [k, l]	95.8 [k, l]	102	94	0.98	80 [g]	1.06 [g]	34	2.69
48	Croatia	97.1 [k]	98 [k]	99.7 [k]	100	88	0.98	87	1.03	39	1.15
49	United Arab Emirates	80.7	107	95.0	108	80	0.97	74	1.05	..	..
50	Latvia	99.7 [k]	100 [k]	99.8 [k]	100	90 [f]	0.99 [f]	89 [f, g]	1.01 [f, g]	80 [f]	1.66 [f]

HDI rank		Adult literacy [a]		Youth literacy [a]		MDG Net primary enrolment [b, c]		MDG Net secondary enrolment [b, c]		MDG Gross tertiary enrolment [c, d]	
		Female rate (% ages 15 and above) 2002	Female rate as % of male rate 2002	Female rate (% ages 15-24) 2002	Female rate as % of male rate 2002	Female ratio (%) 2000/01	Ratio of female to male [e] 2000/01	Female ratio (%) 2000/01	Ratio of female to male [e] 2000/01	Female ratio (%) 2000/01	Ratio of female to male [e] 2000/01
51	Bahamas	..	..	..	..	88 [g]	1.03 [g]	79 [g]	1.01 [g]	..	..
52	Cuba	96.8	100	99.8	100	95	0.99	84	1.01	30	1.25
53	Mexico	88.7 [k]	96 [k]	96.5 [k]	100	102	1.01	61 [g]	1.03 [g]	21	0.95
54	Trinidad and Tobago	97.9	99	99.8	100	94 [g]	1.00 [g]	69 [g]	1.03 [g]	9	1.53
55	Antigua and Barbuda	..	..	..	..	..	..	..	..	..	..
Medium human development											
56	Bulgaria	98.1	99	99.6	100	92 [f]	0.98 [f]	85 [f, g]	0.98 [f, g]	46 [f]	1.35 [f]
57	Russian Federation	99.5	100	99.8	100	..	..	..	..	80	1.33
58	Libyan Arab Jamahiriya	70.7	77	94.0	94	..	..	..	..	61	1.09
59	Malaysia	85.4 [k]	93 [k]	97.3 [k]	100	95	1.00	73	1.10	28 [f]	1.09 [f]
60	Macedonia, TFYR	..	..	..	..	93 [f]	1.00 [f]	81 [f, g]	0.96 [f, g]	28 [f]	1.32 [f]
61	Panama	91.7	99	96.6	99	99	1.00	65 [g]	1.10 [g]	42 [g, h]	1.67 [h]
62	Belarus	99.6	100	99.8	100	93 [g]	0.98 [g]	79 [g]	1.04 [g]	72	1.37
63	Tonga	98.9 [k]	100 [k]	99.1 [k]	100	105	1.00	77 [f, g]	1.13 [f, g]	4 [g]	1.40
64	Mauritius	80.5 [k]	91 [k]	95.4 [k]	102	93	1.00	64	1.08	13	1.29
65	Albania	98.3 [k]	99 [k]	99.5 [k]	100	97 [f]	1.00 [f]	75 [f]	1.03 [f]	19 [f]	1.69 [f]
66	Bosnia and Herzegovina	91.1	93	99.7	100	..	..	..	..	..	..
67	Suriname	..	..	..	..	98 [g]	1.01 [g]	75 [g]	1.43 [g]	15	1.69
68	Venezuela	92.7	99	98.9	101	93	1.01	62 [g]	1.17 [g]	31 [g]	1.37
69	Romania	96.3 [k]	98 [k]	97.8 [k]	100	92 [f]	0.99 [f]	81 [f]	1.02 [f]	30 [f]	1.20 [f]
70	Ukraine	99.5	100	99.9	100	81 [g]	1.00 [g]	91 [g]	1.00 [g]	63	1.17
71	Saint Lucia	..	..	..	..	102 [g]	0.98 [g]	79 [g]	1.29 [g]	24 [g, i]	0.87 [i]
72	Brazil	86.5 [k]	100 [k]	95.7 [k]	103	97	1.02	74	1.08	21	1.29
73	Colombia	92.2	100	97.9	101	86 [g]	0.99 [g]	56 [g]	1.10 [g]	25	1.10
74	Oman	65.4	80	97.3	98	75	1.01	68	1.00	10 [g]	1.67
75	Samoa (Western)	98.4	99	99.5	100	94	0.99	65	1.12	6 [g]	0.90
76	Thailand	90.5 [k]	95 [k]	97.8 [k]	100	85 [g]	0.97 [g]	..	..	38	1.09
77	Saudi Arabia	69.5	83	91.6	96	57	0.92	51 [g]	0.93 [g]	26 [g]	1.49
78	Kazakhstan	99.2	100	99.8	100	89	0.99	83	0.97	43	1.23
79	Jamaica	91.4	109	97.8	107	95	1.00	76	1.04	24	2.24
80	Lebanon	..	..	..	..	89 [g]	0.99 [g]	..	..	48	1.14
81	Fiji	91.4 [k, l]	97 [k, l]	99.4 [k, l]	100	100 [g]	1.00 [g]	79 [g]	1.07 [g]	73 [g]	1.00 [g]
82	Armenia	99.2 [k]	99 [k]	99.9 [k]	100	84	0.99	86	1.04	29	1.17
83	Philippines	92.7 [k]	100 [k]	95.7 [k]	101	94	1.02	62	1.20	35	1.29
84	Maldives	97.2	100	99.2	100	96	1.01	33 [h]	1.13 [h]	..	..
85	Peru	80.3 [m]	88 [m]	95.6 [m]	98	101	1.00	65 [f, g]	0.97 [f, g]	31 [g]	0.98
86	Turkmenistan	98.3 [k, l]	99 [k, l]	99.8 [k, l]	100	..	..	..	..	..	..
87	St. Vincent & the Grenadines	..	..	..	..	92 [g]	0.99 [g]	57	1.21	..	..
88	Turkey	78.5 [k]	83 [k]	93.2 [k]	95	85 [g]	0.93 [g]	..	..	21	0.73
89	Paraguay	90.2 [m]	97 [m]	96.5 [m]	100	92 [g]	1.01 [g]	51 [g]	1.05 [g]	22	1.37
90	Jordan	85.9	90	99.5	100	92	1.01	81	1.03	31	1.02
91	Azerbaijan	..	..	..	..	79	0.98	75 [g]	0.99 [g]	24	1.02
92	Tunisia	63.1	76	90.6	93	97	0.99	69 [g]	1.04 [g]	21 [f, g]	0.97 [f]
93	Grenada	..	..	..	..	80 [f, g]	0.90 [f, g]	..	..	..	..
94	China	86.5 [k]	91 [k]	98.5 [k]	99	93 [f, g]	1.01 [f, g]	..	..	..	..
95	Dominica	..	..	..	..	90 [f, g]	0.98 [f, g]	87 [f]	1.06 [f]	..	..
96	Sri Lanka	89.6	95	96.9	100	105	1.00	..	..	..	..
97	Georgia	..	..	..	..	91	1.00	72 [g, i]	1.03 [g, i]	37	1.02
98	Dominican Republic	84.4	100	92.5	102	95	0.96	47	1.34	..	..
99	Belize	77.1 [k]	101 [k]	84.6 [k]	101	96 [f, g]	1.00 [f, g]	63 [f]	1.07 [f]	..	..
100	Ecuador	89.7 [k]	97 [k]	96.5 [k]	100	102	1.01	50	1.02	..	..

HDI rank	Adult literacy [a] Female rate (% ages 15 and above) 2002	Adult literacy [a] Female rate as % of male rate 2002	Youth literacy [a] Female rate (% ages 15-24) 2002	Youth literacy [a] Female rate as % of male rate 2002	MDG Net primary enrolment [b,c] Female ratio (%) 2000/01	MDG Net primary enrolment [b,c] Ratio of female to male [e] 2000/01	MDG Net secondary enrolment [b,c] Female ratio (%) 2000/01	MDG Net secondary enrolment [b,c] Ratio of female to male [e] 2000/01	MDG Gross tertiary enrolment [c,d] Female ratio (%) 2000/01	MDG Gross tertiary enrolment [c,d] Ratio of female to male [e] 2000/01
101 Iran, Islamic Rep. of	70.4 [l,m]	84 [l,m]	..	..	78 [f,g]	0.98 [f,g]	..	..	20	1.01
102 Occupied Palestinian Territories	..	..	..	..	95	1.01	83 [g]	1.06 [g]	30	0.98
103 El Salvador	77.1	94	88.1	98	89	1.00	47	1.02	18	1.19
104 Guyana	..	..	..	..	97 [h]	0.97 [h]	79 [g,h]	1.10 [g,h]	..	..
105 Cape Verde	68.0	80	86.3	94	100	0.99	54	1.04	3	0.84
106 Syrian Arab Republic	74.2	82	93.0	96	96	0.95	37	0.91	..	..
107 Uzbekistan	98.9	99	99.6	100	..	..	..	..	..	..
108 Algeria	59.6	76	85.6	91	94	0.97	64 [g]	1.06 [g]	..	..
109 Equatorial Guinea	..	..	..	..	78	0.85	19 [g,h]	0.58 [g,h]	2 [h]	0.43 [h]
110 Kyrgyzstan	..	..	..	..	88	0.96	..	..	48	1.14
111 Indonesia	83.4	90	97.6	99	92	0.99	46 [g,h]	0.95 [g,h]	14	0.86
112 Viet Nam	86.9 [k,l]	93 [k,l]	..	..	92 [f,g]	0.94 [f,g]	..	..	9	0.76
113 Moldova, Rep. of	98.6	99	99.8	100	78	0.99	70	1.03	33	1.34
114 Bolivia	80.7 [k]	87 [k]	96.1 [k]	98	94	1.00	67 [f,g]	0.98 [f,g]	22 [g,i]	0.55 [i]
115 Honduras	80.2 [k]	101 [k]	90.9 [k]	105	88 [g]	1.02 [g]	..	..	16 [g]	1.32
116 Tajikistan	99.3 [k]	100 [k]	99.8 [k]	100	102	0.95	72 [g]	0.84 [g]	7	0.33
117 Mongolia	97.5 [k]	99 [k]	98.4 [k]	101	88	1.03	78	1.19	44	1.74
118 Nicaragua	76.6 [m]	100 [m]	88.8 [m]	106	82	1.01	40	1.18	..	..
119 South Africa	85.3	98	91.7	100	90	1.01	65 [f,g]	1.11 [f,g]	16	1.14
120 Egypt	43.6 [k,l]	65 [k,l]	66.9 [k,l]	85	88 [g]	0.96 [g]	79 [g]	0.95 [g]	..	..
121 Guatemala	62.5	81	73.8	86	83	0.95	27 [g]	0.95 [g]	..	..
122 Gabon	..	..	..	..	78 [f,g]	0.99 [f,g]	..	..	5 [i]	0.54 [i]
123 São Tomé and Principe	..	..	..	..	96 [g]	0.94 [g]	..	..	1 [g]	0.56
124 Solomon Islands	..	..	..	..	..	..	..	..	..	..
125 Morocco	38.3	61	61.3	79	85	0.93	28 [g,h]	0.83 [g,h]	9 [g]	0.80
126 Namibia	82.8	99	94.0	104	81	1.06	44	1.36	7	0.84
127 India	..	..	..	..	76 [f]	0.83 [f]	..	..	9 [f]	0.68 [f]
128 Botswana	81.5	107	92.8	109	83	1.04	59 [f,g]	1.15 [f,g]	4	0.82
129 Vanuatu	..	..	..	..	94	1.02	28	1.01	..	..
130 Cambodia	59.3	73	75.9	90	83 [g]	0.93 [g]	15 [g]	0.60 [g]	2	0.40
131 Ghana	65.9	80	90.1	96	59	0.96	30 [g]	0.87 [g]	2	0.39
132 Myanmar	81.4	91	91.1	100	82	1.00	34	0.94	15 [f,g]	1.75 [f]
133 Papua New Guinea	..	..	..	..	73 [g]	0.89 [g]	20 [g]	0.80 [g]	1 [j]	0.54 [i]
134 Bhutan	..	..	..	..	..	..	..	..	..	..
135 Lao People's Dem. Rep.	55.5	72	72.7	85	79	0.92	28	0.81	3	0.57
136 Comoros	49.1	77	52.2	79	50 [g,h]	0.84 [g,h]	..	..	1 [g,h]	0.73 [h]
137 Swaziland	80.0	98	92.1	102	77	1.01	35	1.21	5	1.16
138 Bangladesh	31.4	62	41.1	71	88	1.02	46	1.10	4	0.50
139 Sudan	49.1	69	74.2	88	42 [g,h]	0.83 [g,h]	..	..	6 [i]	0.92 [i]
140 Nepal	26.4	43	46.0	59	66 [f,g]	0.88 [f,g]	..	..	2	0.28
141 Cameroon	59.8 [m]	78 [m]	..	..	..	..	..	..	4 [g]	0.63
Low human development										
142 Pakistan	28.5 [k,l]	53 [k,l]	42.0 [k,l]	64	..	..	17 [g,h]	0.48 [g,h]	1 [h]	0.20 [h]
143 Togo	45.4	61	66.6	75	86	0.84	..	..	1	0.19
144 Congo	77.1	87	97.3	99	..	..	27	1.56	3	1.28
145 Lesotho	90.3 [m]	123 [m]	..	..	88	1.08	13 [f]	0.86 [f]	2 [g]	0.52
146 Uganda	59.2	75	74.0	86	..	..	..	..	3 [g]	0.58
147 Zimbabwe	86.3	92	96.2	97	83	1.01	38	0.91	3 [g]	0.58
148 Kenya	78.5	87	95.1	99	71 [g]	1.02 [g]	24 [g]	0.97 [g]	2 [g]	0.53
149 Yemen	28.5	41	50.9	60	47 [g,h]	0.66 [g,h]	21 [g,h]	0.46 [g,h]	5 [g,h]	0.28 [h]
150 Madagascar	..	..	..	..	69	1.01	12 [g,i]	1.03 [g,i]	2	0.83
151 Nigeria	59.4	80	86.5	95	..	..	..	..	..	..

		Adult literacy [a]		Youth literacy [a]		MDG Net primary enrolment [b, c]		MDG Net secondary enrolment [b, c]		MDG Gross tertiary enrolment [c, d]	
		Female rate (% ages 15 and above)	Female rate as % of male rate	Female rate (% ages 15-24)	Female rate as % of male rate	Female ratio (%)	Ratio of female to male [e]	Female ratio (%)	Ratio of female to male [e]	Female ratio (%)	Ratio of female to male [e]
HDI rank		2002	2002	2002	2002	2000/01	2000/01	2000/01	2000/01	2000/01	2000/01
152	Mauritania	31.3	61	41.8	73	65 [g]	0.96 [g]	13 [g]	0.83 [g]	1	0.27
153	Haiti	50.0	93	66.5	101	..	..	..	..	..	..
154	Djibouti	..	..	..	..	30 [g]	0.77 [g]	13 [g]	0.63 [g]	1	0.80
155	Gambia	..	..	..	..	70 [g]	0.92 [g]	24 [g]	0.75 [g]	..	..
156	Eritrea	..	..	..	..	39	0.86	18 [g]	0.74 [g]	(.)	0.15
157	Senegal	29.7	61	44.5	72	54	0.89	..	..	..	..
158	Timor-Leste	..	..	..	..	..	..	..	..	15	1.58
159	Rwanda	63.4	84	83.6	97	85	1.03	..	..	1 [g]	0.40
160	Guinea	..	..	..	..	54	0.78	7 [g, j]	0.38 [g, j]	..	..
161	Benin	25.5	47	38.5	53	58 [g, h]	0.69 [g, h]	13 [f, g]	0.48 [f, g]	1 [h]	0.24 [h]
162	Tanzania, U. Rep. of	69.2	81	89.4	95	54	1.00	..	..	(.) [f]	0.31 [f]
163	Côte d'Ivoire	..	..	51.5	74	53	0.74	..	..	4 [j]	0.36 [j]
164	Zambia	73.8	85	86.9	95	66 [g]	0.99 [g]	18 [g]	0.85 [g]	2 [f, g]	0.46 [f]
165	Malawi	48.7	64	62.8	77	81 [g]	1.00 [g]	26	0.81	(.) [j]	0.37 [j]
166	Angola	..	..	..	..	28 [g, h]	0.86 [g, h]	..	..	1 [h]	0.63 [h]
167	Chad	37.5	69	64.0	84	47 [g]	0.67 [g]	4 [f, g]	0.31 [f, g]	(.) [h]	0.17 [h]
168	Congo, Dem. Rep. of the	..	..	..	..	34 [i]	0.95 [i]	9 [g, j]	0.58 [g, j]	..	..
169	Central African Republic	33.5 [m]	52 [m]	46.9 [m]	67	..	..	..	..	1 [h]	0.19 [h]
170	Ethiopia	33.8	69	51.8	82	41	0.79	11 [g]	0.61 [g]	1	0.36
171	Mozambique	31.4	50	49.2	64	56	0.88	9	0.69	(.) [g, h]	0.73 [h]
172	Guinea-Bissau	..	..	..	..	38 [h]	0.71 [h]	..	..	(.) [h]	0.18 [h]
173	Burundi	43.6	76	65.1	97	48 [g]	0.82 [g]	7 [g]	0.75 [g]	1	0.42
174	Mali	11.9 [k, l]	44 [k, l]	16.9 [k, l]	52	32 [g, j]	0.72 [g, j]	..	..	..	..
175	Burkina Faso	8.1 [k, l]	44 [k, l]	14.0 [k, l]	55	29 [g]	0.71 [g]	6 [f, g]	0.65 [f, g]	1	0.33
176	Niger	9.3	37	15.1	44	28	0.68	4	0.66	1 [g]	0.34
177	Sierra Leone	..	..	..	..	..	..	..	..	1 [g]	0.40
Developing countries		75.9	88	85.7	95	..	..	..	..	..	..
Least developed countries		43.3	70	57.4	81	..	..	..	..	..	..
Arab States		51.8	70	75.6	87	..	..	..	..	..	..
East Asia and the Pacific		86.2	91	97.6	99	..	..	..	..	..	..
Latin America and the Caribbean		87.7	98	95.3	101	..	..	..	..	..	..
South Asia		40.8	67	45.0	70	..	..	..	..	..	..
Sub-Saharan Africa		55.9	79	72.6	90	..	..	..	..	..	..
Central & Eastern Europe & CIS		99.1	100	99.6	100	..	..	..	..	..	..
OECD		..	..	..	..	..	..	..	..	..	..
High-income OECD		..	..	..	..	..	..	..	..	..	..
High human development		..	..	..	..	..	..	..	..	..	..
Medium human development		..	..	..	..	..	..	..	..	..	..
Low human development		..	..	..	..	..	..	..	..	..	..
High income		..	..	..	..	..	..	..	..	..	..
Middle income		..	..	..	..	..	..	..	..	..	..
Low income		..	..	..	..	..	..	..	..	..	..
World		..	..	..	..	..	..	..	..	..	..

a. Data refer to estimates produced by UNESCO Institute for Statistics in July 2002, unless otherwise specified. Due to differences in methodology and timeliness of underlying data, comparisons across countries and over time should be made with caution. b. The net enrolment ratio is the ratio of enrolled children of the official age for the education level indicated to the total population at that age. Net enrolment ratios exceeding 100% reflect discrepancies between these two data sets. c. Data refer to the 2001/02 school year. Data for some countries may refer to national or UNESCO Institute for Statistics estimates. For details, see http://www.uis.unesco.org/. Because data are from different sources, comparisons across countries should be made with caution. d. Tertiary enrolment is generally calculated as a gross ratio. e. Calculated as the ratio of the female enrolment ratio to the male enrolment ratio. f. Data refer to the 2000/01 school year. g. Preliminary UNESCO Institute for Statistics estimates, subject to further revision. h. Data refer to the 1999/2000 school year. i. The ratio is an under-estimate, as many students pursue their studies in nearby countries. j. Data refer to the 1998/99 school year. k. Census data. l. Data refer to a year between 1995 and 1999. m. Survey data.

Source: Columns 1 and 3: UNESCO Institute for Statistics 2004a; columns 2 and 4: calculated on the basis of data on adult and youth literacy rates from UNESCO Institute for Statistics 2004a; columns 5, 7 and 9: UNESCO Institute for Statistics 2004c; columns 6, 8 and 10: calculated on the basis of data on net enrolment rates from UNESCO Institute for Statistics 2004c.

27 Gender inequality in economic activity

		Female economic activity rate (ages 15 and above)			Female employment by economic activity (%)						Contributing family workers (%)	
					Agriculture		Industry		Services			
		Rate (%)	Index (1990 = 100)	As % of male rate	Total	As % of male rate	Total	As % of male rate	Total	As % of male rate	Women	Men
HDI rank		2002	2002	2002	1995-2002[a]	1995-2002[a]	1995-2002[a]	1995-2002[a]	1995-2002[a]	1995-2002[a]	1995-2002[a]	1995-2002[a]
High human development												
1	Norway	59.9	110	85	2	37	9	27	88	152	63	38
2	Sweden	62.7	102	89	1	32	11	31	88	144	50	50
3	Australia	56.4	108	78	3	56	10	33	87	135	65	35
4	Canada	60.5	105	83	2	40	11	35	87	137	80	20
5	Netherlands	45.8	106	67	2	60	9	29	86	135	80	20
6	Belgium	40.1	106	67	1	52	10	28	82	141	85	15
7	Iceland	66.7	101	83	3	24	10	29	85	157	50	50
8	United States	59.3	107	82	1	42	12	36	87	134	63	37
9	Japan	51.1	104	68	5	113	21	55	73	128	81	19
10	Ireland	37.9	118	53	2	17	14	36	83	167	53	47
11	Switzerland	51.0	104	66	3	67	13	37	84	141	59	41
12	United Kingdom	53.2	106	75	1	35	11	32	88	142	68	32
13	Finland	56.9	98	87	4	50	14	35	82	156	42	58
14	Austria	44.1	103	66	6	113	14	32	80	154	67	33
15	Luxembourg	38.2	104	58	..	..	..	..	..	..	..	..
16	France	49.1	108	77	1	36	13	38	86	136	..	..
17	Denmark	61.8	100	84	2	34	14	38	85	143	..	..
18	New Zealand	58.0	110	80	6	50	12	37	82	146	61	39
19	Germany	47.9	100	70	2	70	18	40	80	153	78	22
20	Spain	38.1	113	57	5	59	15	35	81	160	63	37
21	Italy	38.8	107	59	5	78	20	52	75	136	54	46
22	Israel	49.2	115	69	..	..	..	..	..	..	76	24
23	Hong Kong, China (SAR)	51.1	105	65	(.)	33	10	37	90	123	87	13
24	Greece	38.4	109	59	18	118	12	40	70	127	69	31
25	Singapore	50.0	99	64	(.)	50	18	60	81	119	76	24
26	Portugal	51.6	105	72	14	123	23	51	63	143	70	30
27	Slovenia	54.4	98	81	10	95	29	62	61	143	62	38
28	Korea, Rep. of	54.1	112	71	12	125	19	55	70	122	88	12
29	Barbados	62.3	107	79	4	77	10	35	63	129	..	..
30	Cyprus	49.2	103	62	4	80	13	41	83	142	84	16
31	Malta	26.3	113	38	1	18	21	58	78	129	..	..
32	Czech Republic	61.3	100	83	3	55	28	57	68	155	86	14
33	Brunei Darussalam	50.7	112	63	..	..	..	..	..	..	..	..
34	Argentina	36.7	126	48	(.)	33	12	40	87	127	59	41
35	Seychelles	..	..	..	..	..	..	..	..	..	..	..
36	Estonia	60.4	95	82	4	39	23	55	73	153	50	50
37	Poland	57.1	100	80	19	99	18	46	63	155	58	43
38	Hungary	48.6	102	72	4	41	26	60	71	144	70	30
39	Saint Kitts and Nevis	..	..	..	..	..	..	..	..	..	..	..
40	Bahrain	34.2	120	40	..	..	..	..	..	..	..	..
41	Lithuania	57.5	97	80	12	60	21	61	67	148	59	41
42	Slovakia	62.7	99	84	4	45	26	53	71	161	75	25
43	Chile	38.5	121	50	..	..	..	..	..	..	..	..
44	Kuwait	36.4	96	48	..	..	..	..	..	..	..	..
45	Costa Rica	37.6	113	47	4	19	15	57	80	158	43	57
46	Uruguay	48.6	110	67	2	28	14	43	85	136	74	25
47	Qatar	42.1	127	47	..	..	..	..	..	..	..	..
48	Croatia	48.9	102	73	15	97	21	58	63	133	73	27
49	United Arab Emirates	32.0	110	37	(.)	1	14	38	86	157	..	..
50	Latvia	59.3	94	80	12	63	16	48	72	153	50	50

27 Gender inequality in economic activity

		Female economic activity rate (ages 15 and above)			Female employment by economic activity (%)						Contributing family workers (%)	
					Agriculture		Industry		Services			
		Rate (%)	Index (1990 = 100)	As % of male rate	Total	As % of male rate	Total	As % of male rate	Total	As % of male rate	Women	Men
HDI rank		2002	2002	2002	1995-2002 [a]	1995-2002 [a]	1995-2002 [a]	1995-2002 [a]	1995-2002 [a]	1995-2002 [a]	1995-2002 [a]	1995-2002 [a]
51	Bahamas	67.0	104	84	1	22	5	22	93	134	..	..
52	Cuba	50.8	120	66	..	..	..	..	..	..	..	..
53	Mexico	40.2	118	48	6	26	22	79	72	150	49	51
54	Trinidad and Tobago	44.9	115	60	3	25	13	36	84	160	75	25
55	Antigua and Barbuda	..	..	..	..	..	..	..	..	..	..	..
Medium human development												
56	Bulgaria	56.1	94	86	..	..	..	..	..	..	..	..
57	Russian Federation	59.1	98	82	8	53	23	64	69	140	41	58
58	Libyan Arab Jamahiriya	25.6	125	34	..	..	..	..	..	..	..	..
59	Malaysia	48.9	110	62	14	68	29	85	57	126	..	..
60	Macedonia, TFYR	50.0	104	72	..	..	..	..	..	..	61	39
61	Panama	44.0	114	56	6	19	10	50	85	165	36	64
62	Belarus	59.1	97	82	..	..	..	..	..	..	..	..
63	Tonga	..	..	..	..	..	..	..	..	..	..	..
64	Mauritius	38.4	111	48	13	82	43	110	45	97	..	..
65	Albania	60.0	103	74	..	..	..	..	..	..	..	..
66	Bosnia and Herzegovina	43.1	99	60	..	..	..	..	..	..	..	..
67	Suriname	37.1	124	50	2	21	1	2	97	150	..	..
68	Venezuela	43.9	116	54	2	12	12	42	86	151	..	..
69	Romania	50.5	97	76	45	113	22	72	33	111	71	29
70	Ukraine	55.4	98	80	17	79	22	57	55	168	60	40
71	Saint Lucia	..	..	..	16	59	14	56	71	144	..	..
72	Brazil	43.7	98	52	16	68	10	37	74	150	..	..
73	Colombia	48.9	115	61	7	20	17	90	76	158	58	42
74	Oman	20.0	157	26	..	..	..	..	..	..	..	..
75	Samoa (Western)	..	..	..	..	..	..	..	..	..	..	..
76	Thailand	73.0	97	85	48	95	17	85	35	119	66	34
77	Saudi Arabia	22.0	147	29	..	..	..	..	..	..	..	..
78	Kazakhstan	61.2	101	82	..	..	..	..	..	..	..	..
79	Jamaica	67.3	101	86	10	34	9	34	81	181	66	34
80	Lebanon	30.3	125	39	..	..	..	..	..	..	..	..
81	Fiji	38.7	146	48	..	..	..	..	..	..	..	..
82	Armenia	62.4	99	88	..	..	..	..	..	..	..	..
83	Philippines	49.9	106	61	25	55	12	67	63	172	..	..
84	Maldives	65.4	100	80	5	31	24	149	39	70	57	43
85	Peru	35.3	120	44	6	56	10	42	84	129	66	34
86	Turkmenistan	62.5	105	82	..	..	..	..	..	..	..	..
87	St. Vincent & the Grenadines	..	..	..	..	..	..	..	..	..	..	..
88	Turkey	50.8	116	62	56	232	15	56	29	60	68	32
89	Paraguay	37.3	110	44	20	52	10	50	69	173	..	..
90	Jordan	27.6	163	36	..	..	..	..	..	..	..	..
91	Azerbaijan	55.0	106	76	43	114	7	51	50	103	..	..
92	Tunisia	37.5	114	48	..	..	..	..	..	..	..	..
93	Grenada	..	..	..	10	59	12	38	77	165	..	..
94	China	72.5	98	86	..	..	..	..	..	..	..	..
95	Dominica	..	..	..	14	44	10	42	72	180	..	..
96	Sri Lanka	43.3	108	56	49	129	22	98	27	74	56	44
97	Georgia	55.7	100	78	53	100	6	47	41	118	57	43
98	Dominican Republic	40.8	120	48	2	9	17	64	81	154	23	77
99	Belize	27.5	115	32	6	17	12	62	81	187	32	68
100	Ecuador	33.4	120	40	4	38	16	55	79	132	64	36

		Female economic activity rate (ages 15 and above)			Female employment by economic activity (%)						Contributing family workers (%)	
					Agriculture		Industry		Services			
		Rate (%)	Index (1990 = 100)	As % of male rate	Total	As % of male rate	Total	As % of male rate	Total	As % of male rate	Women	Men
HDI rank		2002	2002	2002	1995-2002[a]	1995-2002[a]	1995-2002[a]	1995-2002[a]	1995-2002[a]	1995-2002[a]	1995-2002[a]	1995-2002[a]
101	Iran, Islamic Rep. of	30.0	139	38	..	..	..	..	..	..	46	54
102	Occupied Palestinian Territories	9.5	151	14	26	281	11	34	62	107	46	54
103	El Salvador	47.1	126	56	4	12	22	90	74	178	39	61
104	Guyana	41.5	116	50	..	..	..	..	..	..	..	..
105	Cape Verde	46.6	109	53	..	..	..	..	..	..	..	..
106	Syrian Arab Republic	29.2	124	38	..	..	..	..	..	..	..	..
107	Uzbekistan	62.8	106	85	..	..	..	..	..	..	..	..
108	Algeria	30.9	162	41	..	..	..	..	..	..	..	..
109	Equatorial Guinea	45.7	101	52	..	..	..	..	..	..	..	..
110	Kyrgyzstan	61.2	104	85	53	103	8	60	38	112	..	..
111	Indonesia	56.0	111	68	..	..	..	..	..	..	..	..
112	Viet Nam	73.5	96	91	..	..	..	..	..	..	..	..
113	Moldova, Rep. of	60.3	98	84	50	97	10	58	40	130	70	30
114	Bolivia	48.4	106	58	3	54	14	36	82	151	63	37
115	Honduras	41.2	122	48	..	..	..	..	..	..	40	60
116	Tajikistan	58.5	112	81	..	..	..	..	..	..	..	..
117	Mongolia	73.8	103	88	..	..	..	..	..	..	70	30
118	Nicaragua	48.1	119	57	..	..	..	..	..	..	..	..
119	South Africa	47.3	102	59	9	72	14	41	75	150	..	..
120	Egypt	35.7	118	45	39	144	7	28	54	112	33	67
121	Guatemala	37.1	132	43	18	36	23	127	56	203	..	..
122	Gabon	63.2	101	77	..	..	..	..	..	..	..	..
123	São Tomé and Principe	..	..	..	..	..	..	..	..	..	..	..
124	Solomon Islands	80.9	97	92	..	..	..	..	..	..	..	..
125	Morocco	41.8	107	53	6	107	40	125	54	86	19	81
126	Namibia	53.7	101	67	29	89	7	39	63	128	..	..
127	India	42.4	105	50	..	..	..	..	..	..	..	..
128	Botswana	62.6	95	77	17	78	14	54	67	133	45	55
129	Vanuatu	..	..	..	..	..	..	..	..	..	..	..
130	Cambodia	80.2	98	97	..	..	..	..	..	..	64	36
131	Ghana	79.9	98	98	..	..	..	..	..	..	..	..
132	Myanmar	65.8	99	75	..	..	..	..	..	..	..	..
133	Papua New Guinea	67.6	100	79	..	..	..	..	..	..	..	..
134	Bhutan	57.1	100	65	..	..	..	..	..	..	..	..
135	Lao People's Dem. Rep.	74.5	101	85	..	..	..	..	..	..	..	..
136	Comoros	62.4	99	73	..	..	..	..	..	..	..	..
137	Swaziland	41.9	107	52	..	..	..	..	..	..	..	..
138	Bangladesh	66.4	101	76	77	144	9	82	12	40	81	19
139	Sudan	35.4	115	41	..	..	..	..	..	..	..	..
140	Nepal	56.8	101	67	..	..	..	..	..	..	..	..
141	Cameroon	49.6	105	59	..	..	..	..	..	..	..	..
Low human development												
142	Pakistan	36.3	127	44	73	164	9	46	18	50	33	67
143	Togo	53.5	101	62	..	..	..	..	..	..	..	..
144	Congo	58.4	100	71	..	..	..	..	..	..	..	..
145	Lesotho	47.6	103	56	..	..	..	..	..	..	..	..
146	Uganda	79.3	98	88	..	..	..	..	..	..	..	..
147	Zimbabwe	65.0	98	78	..	..	..	..	..	..	..	..
148	Kenya	74.7	100	85	16	79	10	41	75	131	..	..
149	Yemen	30.8	109	37	88	204	3	21	9	21	26	74
150	Madagascar	69.0	99	78	..	..	..	..	..	..	..	..
151	Nigeria	47.8	102	56	2	51	11	37	87	131	..	..

	Female economic activity rate (ages 15 and above)			Female employment by economic activity (%)						Contributing family workers (%)	
				Agriculture		Industry		Services			
	Rate (%)	Index (1990 = 100)	As % of male rate	Total	As % of male rate	Total	As % of male rate	Total	As % of male rate	Women	Men
HDI rank	2002	2002	2002	1995-2002[a]	1995-2002[a]	1995-2002[a]	1995-2002[a]	1995-2002[a]	1995-2002[a]	1995-2002[a]	1995-2002[a]
152 Mauritania	63.2	97	74	..	..	..	..	..	..	..	..
153 Haiti	55.7	97	70	37	60	6	41	57	252	..	..
154 Djibouti	..	..	..	..	..	..	..	..	..	..	..
155 Gambia	69.7	101	78	..	..	..	..	..	..	..	..
156 Eritrea	74.6	98	87	..	..	..	..	..	..	..	..
157 Senegal	61.7	101	72	..	..	..	..	..	..	..	..
158 Timor-Leste	73.3	96	86	..	..	..	..	..	..	..	..
159 Rwanda	82.4	98	88	..	..	..	..	..	..	..	..
160 Guinea	77.1	98	89	..	..	..	..	..	..	..	..
161 Benin	73.2	96	90	..	..	..	..	..	..	..	..
162 Tanzania, U. Rep. of	81.5	98	93	..	..	..	..	..	..	..	..
163 Côte d'Ivoire	44.0	102	51	..	..	..	..	..	..	..	..
164 Zambia	64.0	98	74	..	..	..	..	..	..	..	..
165 Malawi	77.7	97	90	..	..	..	..	..	..	..	..
166 Angola	72.6	98	82	..	..	..	..	..	..	..	..
167 Chad	67.3	102	77	..	..	..	..	..	..	..	..
168 Congo, Dem. Rep. of the	60.4	97	72	..	..	..	..	..	..	..	..
169 Central African Republic	67.3	96	78	..	..	..	..	..	..	..	..
170 Ethiopia	57.2	98	67	..	..	..	..	..	..	..	..
171 Mozambique	82.6	99	92	..	..	..	..	..	..	..	..
172 Guinea-Bissau	57.0	100	63	..	..	..	..	..	..	..	..
173 Burundi	81.8	99	89	..	..	..	..	..	..	..	..
174 Mali	69.8	97	79	..	..	..	..	..	..	..	..
175 Burkina Faso	74.7	97	85	..	..	..	..	..	..	..	..
176 Niger	69.3	99	75	..	..	..	..	..	..	..	..
177 Sierra Leone	45.0	106	54	..	..	..	..	..	..	..	..
Developing countries	55.8	101	67	..	..	..	..	..	..	..	..
Least developed countries	64.2	99	74	..	..	..	..	..	..	..	..
Arab States	33.0	118	42	..	..	..	..	..	..	..	..
East Asia and the Pacific	68.8	99	82	..	..	..	..	..	..	..	..
Latin America and the Caribbean	42.5	110	52	..	..	..	..	..	..	..	..
South Asia	43.7	107	52	..	..	..	..	..	..	..	..
Sub-Saharan Africa	62.1	99	73	..	..	..	..	..	..	..	..
Central & Eastern Europe & the CIS	57.4	99	81	..	..	..	..	..	..	..	..
OECD	51.5	106	71	..	..	..	..	..	..	..	..
High-income OECD	52.2	106	74	..	..	..	..	..	..	..	..
High human development	50.9	106	70	..	..	..	..	..	..	..	..
Medium human development	56.7	101	69	..	..	..	..	..	..	..	..
Low human development	56.9	102	66	..	..	..	..	..	..	..	..
High income	52.1	106	73	..	..	..	..	..	..	..	..
Middle income	59.1	100	73	..	..	..	..	..	..	..	..
Low income	51.9	104	62	..	..	..	..	..	..	..	..
World	55.3	102	69	..	..	..	..	..	..	..	..

Note: As a result of limitations in the data, comparisons of labour statistics over time and across countries should be made with caution. For detailed notes on the data, see ILO (2002), ILO (2003) and ILO (2004b). The percentage shares of employment by economic activity may not sum to 100 because of rounding or the omission of activities not classified.

a. Data refer to the most recent year available during the period specified.

Source: Columns 1-3: calculated on the basis of data on the economically active population and total population from ILO 2002; *columns 4-9:* ILO 2003; *columns 10 and 11:* calculated on the basis of data on contributing family workers from ILO 2004b.

28 Gender, work burden and time allocation

| | | Burden of work | | | Time allocation (%) | | | | | |
| | | Total work time (minutes per day) | | Female work time (% of male) | Total work time | | Time spent by women | | Time spent by men | |
	Year	Women	Men		Market activities	Non-market activities	Market activities	Non-market activities	Market activities	Non-market activities
Selected developing countries										
Urban areas										
Colombia	1983	399	356	112	49	51	24	76	77	23
Indonesia	1992	398	366	109	60	40	35	65	86	14
Kenya	1986	590	572	103	46	54	41	59	79	21
Nepal	1978	579	554	105	58	42	25	75	67	33
Venezuela	1983	440	416	106	59	41	30	70	87	13
Average [a]		481	453	107	54	46	31	69	79	21
Rural areas										
Bangladesh	1990	545	496	110	52	48	35	65	70	30
Guatemala	1977	678	579	117	59	41	37	63	84	16
Kenya	1988	676	500	135	56	44	42	58	76	24
Nepal	1978	641	547	117	56	44	46	54	67	33
Highlands	1978	692	586	118	59	41	52	48	66	34
Mountains	1978	649	534	122	56	44	48	52	65	35
Rural hills	1978	583	520	112	52	48	37	63	70	30
Philippines	1975-77	546	452	121	73	27	29	71	84	16
Average [a]		617	515	120	59	41	38	62	76	24
National [b]										
India	2000	457	391	117	61	39	35	65	92	8
Mongolia	2000	545	501	109	61	39	49	51	75	25
South Africa	2000	332	273	122	51	49	35	65	70	30
Average [a]		445	388	116	58	42	40	60	79	21
Selected OECD countries [c]										
Australia	1997	435	418	104	46	54	30	70	62	38
Austria [d]	1992	438	393	111	49	51	31	69	71	29
Canada	1998	420	429	98	53	47	41	59	65	35
Denmark [d]	1987	449	458	98	68	32	58	42	79	21
Finland [d]	1987-88	430	410	105	51	49	39	61	64	36
France	1999	391	363	108	46	54	33	67	60	40
Germany [d]	1991-92	440	441	100	44	56	30	70	61	39
Hungary	1999	432	445	97	51	49	41	59	60	40
Israel [d]	1991-92	375	377	99	51	49	29	71	74	26
Italy [d]	1988-89	470	367	128	45	55	22	78	77	23
Japan	1996	393	363	108	66	34	43	57	93	7
Korea, Rep. of	1999	431	373	116	64	36	45	55	88	12
Latvia	1996	535	481	111	46	54	35	65	58	42
Netherlands	1995	308	315	98	48	52	27	73	69	31
New Zealand	1999	420	417	101	46	54	32	68	60	40
Norway [d]	1990-91	445	412	108	50	50	38	62	64	36
United Kingdom [d]	1985	413	411	100	51	49	37	63	68	32
United States [d]	1985	453	428	106	50	50	37	63	63	37
Average [e]		423	403	105	52	48	37	64	69	31

Note: Data are estimates based on time use surveys available in time for publication. Time use data are also being collected in other countries, including Benin, Chad, Cuba, the Dominican Republic, Ecuador, Guatemala, the Lao People's Democratic Republic, Mali, Mexico, Morocco, Nepal, Nicaragua, Nigeria, Oman, the Philippines, Thailand and Viet Nam. Market activities refer to market-oriented production activities as defined by the 1993 revised UN System of National Accounts; surveys before 1993 are not strictly comparable with those for later years.
a. Refers to the unweighted average for countries or areas shown above. b. Classifications of market and non-market activities are not strictly based on the 1993 revised UN System of National Accounts, so comparisons between countries and areas must be made with caution. c. Includes Israel and Latvia although they are not OECD countries. d. Harvey 1995. e. Refers to the unweighted average for the selected OECD countries above (excluding Israel and Latvia).
Source: Columns 1-10: For urban and rural areas in selected developing countries, Goldshmidt-Clermont and Pagnossin Aligisakis 1995 and Harvey 1995; for national estimates in selected developing countries, UN 2002; for selected OECD countries and Latvia, unless otherwise noted, Harvey 2001.

29 Women's political participation

		Year women received right [a]		Year first woman elected (E) or appointed (A) to parliament	Women in government at ministerial level (% of total) [b]	MDG Seats in parliament held by women (% of total) [c]		
						Lower or single house		Upper house or senate
HDI rank		To vote	To stand for election		2001	1990	2004	2004
High human development								
1	Norway	1907, 1913	1907, 1913	1911 A	42.1	36	36.4	–
2	Sweden	1861, 1921	1907, 1921	1921 E	55.0	38	45.3	–
3	Australia	1902, 1962	1902, 1962	1943 E	19.5	6	25.3	28.9
4	Canada	1917, 1950	1920, 1960	1921 E	24.3	13	20.6	32.4
5	Netherlands	1919	1917	1918 E	31.0	21	36.7	32.0
6	Belgium	1919, 1948	1921, 1948	1921 A	18.5	9	35.3	31.0
7	Iceland	1915, 1920	1915, 1920	1922 E	33.3	21	30.2	–
8	United States	1920, 1960	1788 [d]	1917 E	31.8	7	14.3	13.0
9	Japan	1945, 1947	1945, 1947	1946 E	5.7	1	7.1	15.4
10	Ireland	1918, 1928	1918, 1928	1918 E	18.8	8	13.3	16.7
11	Switzerland	1971	1971	1971 E	28.6	14	25.0	23.9
12	United Kingdom	1918, 1928	1918, 1928	1918 E	33.3	6	17.9	16.7
13	Finland	1906	1906	1907 E	44.4	32	37.5	–
14	Austria	1918	1918	1919 E	31.3	12	33.9	21.0
15	Luxembourg	1919	1919	1919 E	28.6	13	16.7	–
16	France	1944	1944	1945 E	37.9	7	12.2	10.9
17	Denmark	1915	1915	1918 E	45.0	31	38.0	–
18	New Zealand	1893	1919	1933 E	44.0	14	28.3	–
19	Germany	1918	1918	1919 E	35.7	..	32.2	24.6
20	Spain	1931	1931	1931 E	17.6	15	28.3	24.3
21	Italy	1945	1945	1946 E	17.6	13	11.5	8.1
22	Israel	1948	1948	1949 E	6.1	7	15.0	–
23	Hong Kong, China (SAR)	..	..	..	..	..	..	..
24	Greece	1927, 1952	1927, 1952	1952 E	7.1	7	8.7	–
25	Singapore	1947	1947	1963 E	5.7	5	16.0	–
26	Portugal	1931, 1976	1931, 1976	1934 E	9.7	8	19.1	–
27	Slovenia	1945	1945	1992 E [e]	15.0	..	12.2	–
28	Korea, Rep. of	1948	1948	1948 E	6.5	2	5.9	–
29	Barbados	1950	1950	1966 A	14.3	4	13.3	23.8
30	Cyprus	1960	1960	1963 E	..	2	10.7	–
31	Malta	1947	1947	1966 E	5.3	3	9.2	–
32	Czech Republic	1920	1920	1992 E [e]	..	..	17.0	12.3
33	Brunei Darussalam [f]	–	–	–	0.0	– [g]	– [g]	– [g]
34	Argentina	1947	1947	1951 E	7.3	6	30.7	33.3
35	Seychelles	1948	1948	1976 E+A	23.1	16	29.4	–
36	Estonia	1918	1918	1919 E	14.3	..	18.8	–
37	Poland	1918	1918	1919 E	18.7	14	20.2	23.0
38	Hungary	1918	1918	1920 E	35.9	21	9.8	–
39	Saint Kitts and Nevis	1951	1951	1984 E	0.0	7	13.3	–
40	Bahrain	1973 [h]	1973 [h]	–	..	..	0.0 [i]	15.0 [i]
41	Lithuania	1921	1921	1920 A	18.9	..	10.6	–
42	Slovakia	1920	1920	1992 E [e]	19.0	..	19.3	–
43	Chile	1931, 1949	1931, 1949	1951 E	25.6	..	12.5	4.1
44	Kuwait [f]	–	–	–	0.0	..	0.0	–
45	Costa Rica	1949	1949	1953 E	28.6	11	35.1	–
46	Uruguay	1932	1932	1942 E	..	6	12.1	9.7
47	Qatar [f]	–	–	–	0.0	– [g]	– [g]	– [g]
48	Croatia	1945	1945	1992 E [e]	16.2	..	17.8	–
49	United Arab Emirates [f]	–	–	–	..	..	0.0	–
50	Latvia	1918	1918	..	6.7	..	21.0	–

		Year women received right [a]		Year first woman elected (E) or appointed (A) to parliament	Women in government at ministerial level (% of total) [b] 2001	MDG Seats in parliament held by women (% of total) [c]		
		To vote	To stand for election			Lower or single house		Upper house or senate
HDI rank						1990	2004	2004
51	Bahamas	1961, 1964	1961, 1964	1977 A	16.7	4	20.0	43.8
52	Cuba	1934	1934	1940 E	10.7	34	36.0	–
53	Mexico	1947	1953	1952 A	11.1	12	22.6	15.6
54	Trinidad and Tobago	1946	1946	1962 E+A	8.7	17	19.4	32.3
55	Antigua and Barbuda	1951	1951	1984 A	0.0	..	5.3	11.8
Medium human development								
56	Bulgaria	1937	1944	1945 E	18.8	21	26.2	–
57	Russian Federation	1918	1918	1993 E [e]	..	..	9.8	3.4
58	Libyan Arab Jamahiriya	1964	1964	..	12.5	..	..	–
59	Malaysia	1957	1957	1959 E	..	5	10.5	37.0
60	Macedonia, TFYR	1946	1946	1990 E [e]	10.9	..	18.3	–
61	Panama	1941, 1946	1941, 1946	1946 E	20.0	8	9.9	–
62	Belarus	1919	1919	1990 E [e]	25.7	..	10.3	31.1
63	Tonga	..	..	..	..	..	0.0	–
64	Mauritius	1956	1956	1976 E	9.1	7	5.7	–
65	Albania	1920	1920	1945 E	15.0	29	5.7	–
66	Bosnia and Herzegovina	..	..	..	..	..	16.7	0.0
67	Suriname	1948	1948	1975 E	..	8	17.6	–
68	Venezuela	1946	1946	1948 E	0.0	10	9.7	–
69	Romania	1929, 1946	1929, 1946	1946 E	20.0	34	10.7	5.7
70	Ukraine	1919	1919	1990 E [e]	..	..	5.3	–
71	Saint Lucia	1924	1924	1979 A	18.2	..	11.1	36.4
72	Brazil	1934	1934	1933 E	0.0	5	8.6	12.3
73	Colombia	1954	1954	1954 A	47.4	5	12.0	8.8
74	Oman [f]	–	–	–	..	– [g]	– [g]	– [g]
75	Samoa (Western)	1990	1990	1976 A	7.7	..	6.1	–
76	Thailand	1932	1932	1948 A	5.7	3	9.2	10.5
77	Saudi Arabia [f]	–	–	–	..	..	0.0	–
78	Kazakhstan	1924, 1993	1924, 1993	1990 E [e]	17.5	..	10.4	5.1
79	Jamaica	1944	1944	1944 E	12.5	5	11.7	19.0
80	Lebanon	1952	1952	1991 A	0.0	..	2.3	–
81	Fiji	1963	1963	1970A	20.7	..	5.7	6.7
82	Armenia	1921	1921	1990 E [e]	..	36	4.6	–
83	Philippines	1937	1937	1941 E	..	9	17.8	12.5
84	Maldives	1932	1932	1979 E	..	6	6.0	–
85	Peru	1955	1955	1956 E	16.2	6	17.5	–
86	Turkmenistan	1927	1927	1990 E	..	26	26.0	–
87	St. Vincent & the Grenadines	1951	1951	1979 E [e]	0.0	10	22.7	–
88	Turkey	1930	1934	1935 A	0.0	1	4.4	–
89	Paraguay	1961	1961	1963 E	..	6	8.8	8.9
90	Jordan	1974	1974	1989 A	0.0	..	5.5	12.7
91	Azerbaijan	1921	1921	1990 E [e]	2.6	..	10.5	–
92	Tunisia	1957, 1959	1957, 1959	1959 E	10.0	4	11.5	–
93	Grenada	1951	1951	1976 E+A	25.0	..	26.7	30.8
94	China	1949	1949	1954 E	5.1	21	20.2	–
95	Dominica	1951	1951	1980 E	0.0	10	18.8	–
96	Sri Lanka	1931	1931	1947 E	..	5	4.4	–
97	Georgia	1918, 1921	1918, 1921	1992 E [e]	9.7	..	7.2 [j]	– [j]
98	Dominican Republic	1942	1942	1942 E	..	8	17.3	6.3
99	Belize	1954	1954	1984 E+A	11.1	..	3.3	23.1
100	Ecuador	1929, 1967	1929, 1967	1956 E	20.0	5	16.0	–

		Year women received right [a]		Year first woman elected (E) or appointed (A) to parliament	Women in government at ministerial level (% of total) [b]	MDG Seats in parliament held by women (% of total) [c]		
						Lower or single house		Upper house or senate
HDI rank		To vote	To stand for election		2001	1990	2004	2004
101	Iran, Islamic Rep. of	1963	1963	1963 E+A	9.4	2	4.1	– [k]
102	Occupied Palestinian Territories	..	..	..	..	..	..	..
103	El Salvador	1939	1961	1961 E	15.4	12	10.7	–
104	Guyana	1953	1945	1968 E	..	37	20.0	–
105	Cape Verde	1975	1975	1975 E	35.0	12	11.1	–
106	Syrian Arab Republic	1949, 1953	1953	1973 E	11.1	9	12.0	–
107	Uzbekistan	1938	1938	1990 E [e]	4.4	..	7.2	–
108	Algeria	1962	1962	1962 A	0.0	2.	6.2	..
109	Equatorial Guinea	1963	1963	1968 E	..	13	5.0	–
110	Kyrgyzstan	1918	1918	1990 E [e]	..	..	10.0	2.2
111	Indonesia	1945	1945	1950 A	5.9	12	8.0	–
112	Viet Nam	1946	1946	1976 E	..	18	27.3	–
113	Moldova, Rep. of	1978, 1993	1978, 1993	1990 E	..	..	12.9	–
114	Bolivia	1938, 1952	1938, 1952	1966 E	..	9	18.5	14.8
115	Honduras	1955	1955	1957 [l]	33.3	10	5.5	–
116	Tajikistan	1924	1924	1990 E [e]	..	..	12.7	11.8
117	Mongolia	1924	1924	1951 E	10.0	25	10.5	–
118	Nicaragua	1955	1955	1972 E	23.1	15	20.7	–
119	South Africa	1930, 1994	1930, 1994	1933 E	38.1	3	29.8	31.5 [m]
120	Egypt	1956	1956	1957 E	6.1	4	2.4	5.7
121	Guatemala	1946	1946	1956 E	7.1	7	8.2	–
122	Gabon	1956	1956	1961 E	12.1	13	9.2	13.2
123	São Tomé and Principe	1975	1975	1975 E	..	12	9.1	–
124	Solomon Islands	1974	1974	1993 E	..	..	0.0	–
125	Morocco	1963	1963	1993 E	4.9	..	10.8	..
126	Namibia	1989	1989	1989 E	16.3	7	26.4	7.7
127	India	1950	1950	1952 E	10.1	5	8.8	10.3
128	Botswana	1965	1965	1979 E	26.7	5	17.0	–
129	Vanuatu	1975, 1980	1975, 1980	1987 E	..	4	1.9	–
130	Cambodia	1955	1955	1958 E	7.1	..	9.8	13.1
131	Ghana	1954	1954	1960 A [l]	8.6	..	9.0	–
132	Myanmar	1935	1946	1947 E	..	..	.. [n]	.. [n]
133	Papua New Guinea	1964	1963	1977 E	0.0	..	0.9	–
134	Bhutan	1953	1953	1975 E	..	2	9.3	–
135	Lao People's Dem. Rep.	1958	1958	1958 E	10.2	6	22.9	–
136	Comoros	1956	1956	1993 E	..	..	– [o]	– [o]
137	Swaziland	1968	1968	1972 E+A	12.5	4	10.8	30.0
138	Bangladesh	1972	1972	1973 E	9.5	10	2.0	–
139	Sudan	1964	1964	1964 E	5.1	..	9.7	–
140	Nepal	1951	1951	1952 A	14.8	6	5.9	..
141	Cameroon	1946	1946	1960 E	5.8	14	8.9	–
Low human development								
142	Pakistan	1947	1947	1973 E	.. [p]	10	21.6	18.0
143	Togo	1945	1945	1961 E	7.4	5	7.4	–
144	Congo	1963	1963	1963 E	..	14	8.5	15.0
145	Lesotho	1965	1965	1965 A	..	..	11.7	36.4
146	Uganda	1962	1962	1962 A	27.1	12	24.7	
147	Zimbabwe	1957	1978	1980 E+A	36.0	11	10.0	–
148	Kenya	1919, 1963	1919, 1963	1969 E+A	1.4	1	7.1	–
149	Yemen	1967	1967	1990 E [l]	..	4	0.3	–
150	Madagascar	1959	1959	1965 E	12.5	7	3.8	11.1
151	Nigeria	1958	1958	..	22.6	..	6.7	2.8

		Year women received right[a]		Year first woman elected (E) or appointed (A) to parliament	Women in government at ministerial level (% of total)[b] 2001	MDG Seats in parliament held by women (% of total)[c]		
						Lower or single house		Upper house or senate
HDI rank		To vote	To stand for election			1990	2004	2004
152	Mauritania	1961	1961	1975 E	13.6	..	3.7	5.4
153	Haiti	1950	1950	1961 E	18.2	..	3.6	25.9
154	Djibouti	1946	1986	2003 E	5.0	..	10.8	–
155	Gambia	1960	1960	1982 E	30.8	8	13.2	–
156	Eritrea	1955	1955	1994 E	11.8	..	22.0	–
157	Senegal	1945	1945	1963 E	15.6	13	19.2	–
158	Timor-Leste	..	..	..	..	..	26.1 q	–
159	Rwanda	1961	1961	1965 l	13.0	17	48.8	30.0
160	Guinea	1958	1958	1963 E	11.1	..	19.3	–
161	Benin	1956	1956	1979 E	10.5	3	7.2	–
162	Tanzania, U. Rep. of	1959	1959	..	..	..	21.4	–
163	Côte d'Ivoire	1952	1952	1965 E	9.1	6	8.5	–
164	Zambia	1962	1962	1964 E+A	6.2	7	12.0	–
165	Malawi	1961	1961	1964 E	11.8	10	9.3	–
166	Angola	1975	1975	1980 E	14.7	15	15.5	–
167	Chad	1958	1958	1962 E	..	..	5.8	–
168	Congo, Dem. Rep. of the	1967	1970	1970 E	..	5	8.3	–
169	Central African Republic	1986	1986	1987 E	..	4	– o	– o
170	Ethiopia	1955	1955	1957 E	22.2	..	7.7	8.3
171	Mozambique	1975	1975	1977 E	..	16	30.0	–
172	Guinea-Bissau	1977	1977	1972 A	8.3	20	– o	– o
173	Burundi	1961	1961	1982 E	4.5	..	18.4	18.9
174	Mali	1956	1956	1964 E	33.3	..	10.2	–
175	Burkina Faso	1958	1958	1978 E	8.6	..	11.7	–
176	Niger	1948	1948	1989 E	10.0	5	1.2	–
177	Sierra Leone	1961	1961	..	8.1	..	14.5	–

a. Data refer to the year in which right to vote or stand for election on a universal and equal basis was recognized. Where two years are shown, the first refers to the first partial recognition of the right to vote or stand for election. b. Data were provided by states based on their definition of national executive and may therefore include women serving as ministers and vice ministers and those holding other ministerial positions, including parliamentary secretaries. c. Data are as of 1 March 2004. The percentage was calculated using as a reference the number of total seats currently filled in parliament. d. No information is available on the year all women received the right to stand for election. However, the constitution does not mention gender with regard to this right. e. Refers to the year women were elected to the current parliamentary system. f. Women's right to vote and to stand for election has not been recognized. g. Brunei Darussalam, Oman and Qatar have never had a parliament. h. According to the constitution in force (1973), all citizens are equal before the law; however, women were not able to exercise electoral rights in the first legislative elections held in 1973. The first legislature was dissolved by decree of the Emir on 26 August 1975. i. Women were allowed to vote in the referendum of 14-15 February 2001, which approved the National Action Charter. Subsequently, women exercised their full political rights as both voters and candidates in the 2002 national elections. j. Elections were held in November 2003. However, on 25 November 2003, the election results were annuled by the Supreme Court of Georgia. New elections will be held in March 2004. k. As of 1 March 2004, elections were continuing and the number of women in parliament was subsequently unavailable. l. No information or confirmation available. m. The figures on the distribution of seats do not include the 36 special rotating delegates appointed on an ad hoc basis, and the percentages given are therefore calculated on the basis of the 54 permanent seats. n. The parliament elected in 1990 has never been convened nor authorized to sit, and many of its members were detained or forced into exile. o. Parliament has been dissolved or suspended for an indefinite period. p. Pakistan had 7 women in government at ministerial levels in 2000 and 11 in 2004 (UNDP 2004). This is not reflected in the international data series currently available. Updates to this series are expected soon. q. The purpose of elections held on 30 August 2001 was to elect members of the Constituent Assembly of Timor-Leste. This body became the National Parliament on 20 May 2002, the date on which the country became independent, without any new elections.
Source: Columns 1-3: IPU 1995 and IPU 2004a; column 4: IPU 2001; column 5: UN 2004e; columns 6 and 7: IPU 2004b.

30 Status of major international human rights instruments

HDI rank		International Convention on the Prevention and Punishment of the Crime of Genocide 1948	International Convention on the Elimination of All Forms of Racial Discrimination 1965	International Covenant on Civil and Political Rights 1966	International Covenant on Economic, Social and Cultural Rights 1966	Convention on the Elimination of All Forms of Discrimination against Women 1979	Convention against Torture and Other Cruel, Inhuman or Degrading Treatment or Punishment 1984	Convention on the Rights of the Child 1989
High human development								
1	Norway	●	●	●	●	●	●	●
2	Sweden	●	●	●	●	●	●	●
3	Australia	●	●	●	●	●	●	●
4	Canada	●	●	●	●	●	●	●
5	Netherlands	●	●	●	●	●	●	●
6	Belgium	●	●	●	●	●	●	●
7	Iceland	●	●	●	●	●	●	●
8	United States	●	●	●	○	○	●	○
9	Japan		●	●	●	●	●	●
10	Ireland	●	●	●	●	●	●	●
11	Switzerland	●	●	●	●	●	●	●
12	United Kingdom	●	●	●	●	●	●	●
13	Finland	●	●	●	●	●	●	●
14	Austria	●	●	●	●	●	●	●
15	Luxembourg	●	●	●	●	●	●	●
16	France	●	●	●	●	●	●	●
17	Denmark	●	●	●	●	●	●	●
18	New Zealand	●	●	●	●	●	●	●
19	Germany	●	●	●	●	●	●	●
20	Spain	●	●	●	●	●	●	●
21	Italy	●	●	●	●	●	●	●
22	Israel	●	●	●	●	●	●	●
24	Greece	●	●	●	●	●	●	●
25	Singapore	●				●		●
26	Portugal	●	●	●	●	●	●	●
27	Slovenia	●	●	●	●	●	●	●
28	Korea, Rep. of	●	●	●	●	●	●	●
29	Barbados	●	●	●	●	●		●
30	Cyprus	●	●	●	●	●	●	●
31	Malta		●	●	●	●	●	●
32	Czech Republic	●	●	●	●	●	●	●
33	Brunei Darussalam							●
34	Argentina	●	●	●	●	●	●	●
35	Seychelles	●	●	●	●	●	●	●
36	Estonia	●	●	●	●	●	●	●
37	Poland	●	●	●	●	●	●	●
38	Hungary	●	●	●	●	●	●	●
39	Saint Kitts and Nevis					●		●
40	Bahrain	●	●			●	●	●
41	Lithuania	●	●	●	●	●	●	●
42	Slovakia	●	●	●	●	●	●	●
43	Chile	●	●	●	●	●	●	●
44	Kuwait	●	●	●	●	●	●	●
45	Costa Rica	●	●	●	●	●	●	●
46	Uruguay	●	●	●	●	●	●	●
47	Qatar		●				●	●
48	Croatia	●	●	●	●	●	●	●
49	United Arab Emirates		●					●
50	Latvia	●	●	●	●	●	●	●
51	Bahamas	●	●			●		●

HDI rank		International Convention on the Prevention and Punishment of the Crime of Genocide 1948	International Convention on the Elimination of All Forms of Racial Discrimination 1965	International Covenant on Civil and Political Rights 1966	International Covenant on Economic, Social and Cultural Rights 1966	Convention on the Elimination of All Forms of Discrimination against Women 1979	Convention against Torture and Other Cruel, Inhuman or Degrading Treatment or Punishment 1984	Convention on the Rights of the Child 1989
52	Cuba	●	●			●	●	●
53	Mexico	●	●	●	●	●	●	●
54	Trinidad and Tobago	●	●	●	●	●		●
55	Antigua and Barbuda	●	●			●	●	●
Medium human development								
56	Bulgaria	●	●	●	●	●	●	●
57	Russian Federation	●	●	●	●	●	●	●
58	Libyan Arab Jamahiriya	●	●	●	●	●	●	●
59	Malaysia	●				●		●
60	Macedonia, TFYR	●	●	●	●	●	●	●
61	Panama	●	●	●	●	●	●	●
62	Belarus	●	●	●	●	●	●	●
63	Tonga	●	●					●
64	Mauritius		●	●	●	●	●	●
65	Albania	●	●	●	●	●	●	●
66	Bosnia and Herzegovina	●	●	●	●	●	●	●
67	Suriname		●	●	●	●		●
68	Venezuela	●	●	●	●	●	●	●
69	Romania	●	●	●	●	●	●	●
70	Ukraine	●	●	●	●	●	●	●
71	Saint Lucia		●			●		●
72	Brazil	●	●	●	●	●	●	●
73	Colombia	●	●	●	●	●	●	●
74	Oman		●					●
75	Samoa (Western)					●		●
76	Thailand		●	●	●	●		●
77	Saudi Arabia	●	●			●	●	●
78	Kazakhstan	●	●	○	○	●	●	●
79	Jamaica	●	●	●	●	●		●
80	Lebanon	●	●	●	●	●	●	●
81	Fiji	●	●			●		●
82	Armenia	●	●	●	●	●	●	●
83	Philippines	●	●	●	●	●	●	●
84	Maldives		●			●		●
85	Peru	●	●	●	●	●	●	●
86	Turkmenistan		●	●	●	●	●	●
87	St. Vincent & the Grenadines	●	●	●	●	●		●
88	Turkey	●	●	●	●	●	●	●
89	Paraguay	●	●	●	●	●	●	●
90	Jordan	●	●	●	●	●	●	●
91	Azerbaijan	●	●	●	●	●	●	●
92	Tunisia	●	●	●	●	●	●	●
93	Grenada		○	●	●	●		●
94	China	●	●	○	●	●	●	●
95	Dominica			●	●	●		●
96	Sri Lanka	●	●	●	●	●	●	●
97	Georgia	●	●	●	●	●	●	●
98	Dominican Republic	○	●	●	●	●	○	●
99	Belize	●	●	●	○	●	●	●
100	Ecuador	●	●	●	●	●	●	●

30 Status of major international human rights instruments

HDI rank	International Convention on the Prevention and Punishment of the Crime of Genocide 1948	International Convention on the Elimination of All Forms of Racial Discrimination 1965	International Covenant on Civil and Political Rights 1966	International Covenant on Economic, Social and Cultural Rights 1966	Convention on the Elimination of All Forms of Discrimination against Women 1979	Convention against Torture and Other Cruel, Inhuman or Degrading Treatment or Punishment 1984	Convention on the Rights of the Child 1989
101 Iran, Islamic Rep. of	●	●	●	●			●
103 El Salvador	●	●	●	●	●	●	●
104 Guyana		●	●	●	●	●	●
105 Cape Verde		●	●	●	●	●	●
106 Syrian Arab Republic	●	●	●	●	●		●
107 Uzbekistan	●	●	●	●	●	●	●
108 Algeria	●	●	●	●	●	●	●
109 Equatorial Guinea		●	●	●	●	●	●
110 Kyrgyzstan	●	●	●	●	●	●	●
111 Indonesia		●			●	●	●
112 Viet Nam	●	●	●	●	●		●
113 Moldova, Rep. of	●	●	●	●	●	●	●
114 Bolivia	○	●	●	●	●	●	●
115 Honduras	●	●	●	●	●	●	●
116 Tajikistan		●	●	●	●	●	●
117 Mongolia	●	●	●	●	●	●	●
118 Nicaragua	●	●	●	●	●	○	●
119 South Africa	●	●	●	○	●	●	●
120 Egypt	●	●	●	●	●	●	●
121 Guatemala	●	●	●	●	●	●	●
122 Gabon	●	●	●	●	●	●	●
123 São Tomé and Principe		○	○	○	●	○	●
124 Solomon Islands		●		●	●		●
125 Morocco	●	●	●	●	●	●	●
126 Namibia	●	●	●	●	●	●	●
127 India	●	●	●	●	●	○	●
128 Botswana		●	●		●	●	●
129 Vanuatu					●		●
130 Cambodia	●	●	●	●	●	●	●
131 Ghana	●	●	●	●	●	●	●
132 Myanmar	●				●		●
133 Papua New Guinea	●	●			●		●
134 Bhutan		○			●		●
135 Lao People's Dem. Rep.	●	●	○	○	●		●
136 Comoros		○			●	○	●
137 Swaziland		●					●
138 Bangladesh	●	●	●	●	●	●	●
139 Sudan	●	●	●	●		○	●
140 Nepal	●	●	●	●	●	●	●
141 Cameroon		●	●	●	●	●	●
Low human development							
142 Pakistan	●	●			●		●
143 Togo	●	●	●	●	●	●	●
144 Congo		●	●	●	●	●	●
145 Lesotho	●	●	●	●	●	●	●
146 Uganda	●	●	●	●	●	●	●
147 Zimbabwe	●	●	●	●	●		●
148 Kenya		●	●	●	●	●	●
149 Yemen	●	●	●	●	●	●	●
150 Madagascar		●	●	●	●	○	●
151 Nigeria		●	●	●	●	●	●

HDI rank		International Convention on the Prevention and Punishment of the Crime of Genocide 1948	International Convention on the Elimination of All Forms of Racial Discrimination 1965	International Covenant on Civil and Political Rights 1966	International Covenant on Economic, Social and Cultural Rights 1966	Convention on the Elimination of All Forms of Discrimination against Women 1979	Convention against Torture and Other Cruel, Inhuman or Degrading Treatment or Punishment 1984	Convention on the Rights of the Child 1989
152	Mauritania		●			●		●
153	Haiti	●	●	●		●		●
154	Djibouti			●	●	●	●	●
155	Gambia	●	●	●	●	●	○	●
156	Eritrea		●	●	●	●		●
157	Senegal	●	●	●	●	●	●	●
158	Timor-Leste		●	●	●	●	●	●
159	Rwanda	●	●	●	●	●		●
160	Guinea	●	●	●	●	●	●	●
161	Benin		●	●	●	●	●	●
162	Tanzania, U. Rep. of	●	●	●	●	●		●
163	Côte d'Ivoire	●	●	●	●	●	●	●
164	Zambia		●	●	●	●	●	●
165	Malawi		●	●	●	●	●	●
166	Angola			●	●	●		●
167	Chad		●	●	●	●	●	●
168	Congo, Dem. Rep. of the	●	●	●	●	●	●	●
169	Central African Republic		●	●	●	●		●
170	Ethiopia	●	●	●	●	●	●	●
171	Mozambique	●	●	●		●	●	●
172	Guinea-Bissau		○	○	●	●	○	●
173	Burundi	●	●	●	●	●	●	●
174	Mali	●	●	●	●	●	●	●
175	Burkina Faso	●	●	●	●	●	●	●
176	Niger		●	●	●	●	●	●
177	Sierra Leone		●	●	●	●	●	●
Others [a]								
	Afghanistan	●	●	●	●	●	●	●
	Andorra		○	○		●	○	●
	Cook Islands							●
	Holy See		●				●	●
	Iraq	●	●	●	●	●		●
	Kiribati							●
	Korea, Dem. Rep.	●		●	●	●		●
	Liberia	●	●	○	○	●		●
	Liechtenstein	●	●	●	●	●	●	●
	Marshall Islands							●
	Micronesia, Fed. Sts.							●
	Monaco	●	●	●	●		●	●
	Nauru		○	○			○	●
	Niue							●
	Palau							●
	San Marino		●	●	●	●	○	●
	Serbia and Montenegro	●	●	●	●	●	●	●
	Somalia		●	●	●		●	○
	Tuvalu					●		●
Total states parties [b]		135	169	151	148	175	134	192
Signatures not yet followed by ratification		2	7	8	7	1	12	2

● Ratification, accession or succession. ○ Signature not yet followed by ratification.
Note: The table includes states that have signed or ratified at least one of the seven human rights instruments. Information is as of March 2004.
a. These are the countries or areas, in addition to the 177 countries or areas included in the main indicator tables, that have signed or ratified at least one of the seven human rights instruments. b. Refers to ratification, accession or succession.
Source: Columns 1-7: UN 2004f.

31 Status of fundamental labour rights conventions

HDI rank	Freedom of association and collective bargaining		Elimination of forced and compulsory labour		Elimination of discrimination in respect of employment and occupation		Abolition of child labour	
	Convention 87 [a]	Convention 98 [b]	Convention 29 [c]	Convention 105 [d]	Convention 100 [e]	Convention 111 [f]	Convention 138 [g]	Convention 182 [h]
High human development								
1 Norway	●	●	●	●	●	●	●	●
2 Sweden	●	●	●	●	●	●	●	●
3 Australia	●	●	●	●	●	●		●
4 Canada	●			●	●	●		●
5 Netherlands	●	●	●	●	●	●	●	●
6 Belgium	●	●	●	●	●	●	●	●
7 Iceland	●	●	●	●	●	●	●	●
8 United States				●				●
9 Japan	●	●	●		●		●	●
10 Ireland	●	●	●	●	●	●	●	●
11 Switzerland	●	●	●	●	●	●	●	●
12 United Kingdom	●	●	●	●	●	●	●	●
13 Finland	●	●	●	●	●	●	●	●
14 Austria	●	●	●	●	●	●	●	●
15 Luxembourg	●	●	●	●	●	●	●	●
16 France	●	●	●	●	●	●	●	●
17 Denmark	●	●	●	●	●	●	●	●
18 New Zealand		●	●	●	●	●		
19 Germany	●	●	●	●	●	●	●	●
20 Spain	●	●	●	●	●	●	●	●
21 Italy	●	●	●	●	●	●	●	●
22 Israel	●	●	●	●	●	●	●	●
24 Greece	●	●	●	●	●	●	●	●
25 Singapore		●	●	▽	●			●
26 Portugal	●	●	●	●	●	●	●	●
27 Slovenia	●	●	●	●	●	●	●	●
28 Korea, Rep. of					●	●	●	●
29 Barbados	●	●	●	●	●	●	●	●
30 Cyprus	●	●	●	●	●	●	●	●
31 Malta	●	●	●	●	●	●	●	●
32 Czech Republic	●	●	●	●	●	●		●
33 Brunei Darussalam								
34 Argentina	●	●	●	●	●	●	●	●
35 Seychelles	●	●	●	●	●	●	●	●
36 Estonia	●	●	●	●	●	●		●
37 Poland	●	●	●	●	●	●	●	●
38 Hungary	●	●	●	●	●	●	●	●
39 Saint Kitts and Nevis	●	●	●	●	●	●		●
40 Bahrain			●	●		●		●
41 Lithuania	●	●	●	●	●	●	●	●
42 Slovakia	●	●	●	●	●	●	●	●
43 Chile	●	●	●	●	●	●	●	●
44 Kuwait	●		●	●		●	●	●
45 Costa Rica	●	●	●	●	●	●	●	●
46 Uruguay	●	●	●	●	●	●	●	●
47 Qatar			●			●		●
48 Croatia	●	●	●	●	●	●	●	●
49 United Arab Emirates			●	●	●	●	●	●
50 Latvia	●	●		●	●	●		●
51 Bahamas	●	●	●	●	●	●	●	●

31 Status of fundamental labour rights conventions

HDI rank	Freedom of association and collective bargaining		Elimination of forced and compulsory labour		Elimination of discrimination in respect of employment and occupation		Abolition of child labour	
	Convention 87 [a]	Convention 98 [b]	Convention 29 [c]	Convention 105 [d]	Convention 100 [e]	Convention 111 [f]	Convention 138 [g]	Convention 182 [h]
52 Cuba	●	●	●	●	●	●	●	
53 Mexico	●		●	●	●	●		●
54 Trinidad and Tobago	●	●	●	●	●	●		●
55 Antigua and Barbuda	●	●	●	●	●	●	●	●
Medium human development								
56 Bulgaria	●	●	●	●	●	●	●	●
57 Russian Federation	●	●	●	●	●	●	●	●
58 Libyan Arab Jamahiriya	●	●	●	●	●	●	●	●
59 Malaysia		●	●	▽	●		●	●
60 Macedonia, TFYR	●	●	●	●	●	●	●	●
61 Panama	●	●	●	●	●	●	●	●
62 Belarus	●	●	●	●	●	●	●	●
63 Tonga								
64 Mauritius		●	●	●	●	●	●	●
65 Albania	●	●	●	●	●	●	●	●
66 Bosnia and Herzegovina	●	●	●	●	●	●	●	●
67 Suriname	●	●	●	●				
68 Venezuela	●	●	●	●	●	●	●	
69 Romania	●	●	●	●	●	●	●	●
70 Ukraine	●	●	●	●	●	●	●	●
71 Saint Lucia	●	●	●	●	●	●		●
72 Brazil		●	●	●	●	●	●	●
73 Colombia	●	●	●	●	●	●	●	
74 Oman			●					●
75 Samoa (Western)								
76 Thailand			●	●	●			●
77 Saudi Arabia			●	●		●	●	●
78 Kazakhstan	●	●	●	●	●	●	●	
79 Jamaica	●	●	●	●	●	●	●	●
80 Lebanon		●	●	●	●	●	●	●
81 Fiji	●	●	●		●	●		●
82 Armenia		●			●	●		
83 Philippines	●	●		●	●	●		●
84 Maldives								
85 Peru	●	●	●	●	●	●	●	●
86 Turkmenistan	●	●	●	●	●	●		
87 St. Vincent & the Grenadines	●	●	●	●	●	●		●
88 Turkey	●	●	●	●	●	●	●	●
89 Paraguay	●	●	●	●	●	●	●	●
90 Jordan		●	●	●	●	●	●	●
91 Azerbaijan	●	●	●	●	●	●	●	
92 Tunisia	●	●	●	●	●	●	●	●
93 Grenada	●	●	●	●	●	●	●	●
94 China					●		●	●
95 Dominica	●	●	●	●	●	●	●	●
96 Sri Lanka	●	●	●	●	●	●	●	●
97 Georgia	●	●	●	●	●	●	●	●
98 Dominican Republic	●	●	●	●	●	●	●	●
99 Belize	●	●	●	●	●	●	●	●
100 Ecuador	●	●	●	●	●	●	●	●

HDI rank	Freedom of association and collective bargaining		Elimination of forced and compulsory labour		Elimination of discrimination in respect of employment and occupation		Abolition of child labour	
	Convention 87 [a]	Convention 98 [b]	Convention 29 [c]	Convention 105 [d]	Convention 100 [e]	Convention 111 [f]	Convention 138 [g]	Convention 182 [h]
101 Iran, Islamic Rep. of			●	●	●	●		●
103 El Salvador			●	●	●	●	●	●
104 Guyana	●	●	●	●	●	●	●	●
105 Cape Verde	●	●	●	●	●	●		●
106 Syrian Arab Republic	●	●	●	●	●	●	●	●
107 Uzbekistan		●	●	●	●	●		
108 Algeria	●	●	●	●	●	●	●	●
109 Equatorial Guinea	●	●	●	●	●	●	●	
110 Kyrgyzstan	●	●	●	●	●	●	●	
111 Indonesia	●	●	●	●	●	●	●	●
112 Viet Nam					●	●	●	●
113 Moldova, Rep. of	●	●	●	●	●	●	●	●
114 Bolivia	●	●		●	●	●	●	●
115 Honduras	●	●	●	●	●	●	●	●
116 Tajikistan	●	●	●	●	●	●	●	
117 Mongolia	●	●			●	●	●	●
118 Nicaragua	●	●	●	●	●	●	●	●
119 South Africa	●	●	●	●	●	●	●	●
120 Egypt	●	●	●	●	●	●	●	●
121 Guatemala	●	●	●	●	●	●	●	●
122 Gabon	●	●	●	●	●	●		●
123 São Tomé and Principe	●	●						
124 Solomon Islands			●					
125 Morocco		●	●	●	●	●	●	●
126 Namibia	●	●	●	●		●	●	●
127 India			●	●	●	●		
128 Botswana	●	●	●	●	●	●	●	●
129 Vanuatu								
130 Cambodia	●	●	●	●	●	●	●	
131 Ghana	●	●	●	●	●	●		●
132 Myanmar	●		●					
133 Papua New Guinea	●	●	●	●	●	●	●	●
134 Bhutan								
135 Lao People's Dem. Rep.			●					
136 Comoros	●	●	●	●	●			
137 Swaziland	●	●	●	●	●	●	●	●
138 Bangladesh	●	●	●	●	●	●		●
139 Sudan		●	●	●	●	●	●	●
140 Nepal		●	●		●	●	●	●
141 Cameroon	●	●	●	●	●	●	●	●
Low human development								
142 Pakistan	●	●	●	●	●	●		●
143 Togo	●	●	●	●	●	●	●	●
144 Congo	●	●	●	●	●	●	●	●
145 Lesotho	●	●	●	●	●	●	●	●
146 Uganda	●	●	●	●		●	●	●
147 Zimbabwe	●	●	●	●	●	●	●	●
148 Kenya		●	●	●		●	●	●
149 Yemen	●	●	●	●	●	●	●	●
150 Madagascar	●	●	●		●	●	●	●
151 Nigeria	●	●	●	●	●	●	●	●

HDI rank	Freedom of association and collective bargaining		Elimination of forced and compulsory labour		Elimination of discrimination in respect of employment and occupation		Abolition of child labour	
	Convention 87 [a]	Convention 98 [b]	Convention 29 [c]	Convention 105 [d]	Convention 100 [e]	Convention 111 [f]	Convention 138 [g]	Convention 182 [h]
152 Mauritania	●	●	●	●	●	●	●	●
153 Haiti	●	●	●	●	●	●		
154 Djibouti	●	●	●	●	●			
155 Gambia	●	●	●	●	●	●	●	●
156 Eritrea	●	●	●	●	●	●	●	
157 Senegal	●	●	●	●	●	●	●	●
158 Timor-Leste								
159 Rwanda	●	●	●	●	●	●	●	●
160 Guinea	●	●	●	●	●	●	●	●
161 Benin	●	●	●	●	●	●	●	●
162 Tanzania, U. Rep. of	●	●	●	●	●	●	●	●
163 Côte d'Ivoire	●	●	●	●	●	●	●	●
164 Zambia	●	●	●	●	●	●	●	●
165 Malawi	●	●	●	●	●	●	●	●
166 Angola	●	●	●	●	●	●	●	●
167 Chad	●	●	●	●	●	●		●
168 Congo, Dem. Rep. of the	●	●	●	●	●	●	●	●
169 Central African Republic	●	●	●	●	●	●	●	●
170 Ethiopia	●	●	●	●	●	●	●	●
171 Mozambique	●	●	●	●	●	●	●	●
172 Guinea-Bissau		●	●	●	●	●		
173 Burundi	●	●	●	●	●	●	●	●
174 Mali	●	●	●	●	●	●	●	●
175 Burkina Faso	●	●	●	●	●	●	●	●
176 Niger	●	●	●	●	●	●	●	●
177 Sierra Leone	●	●	●	●	●	●		
Others [i]								
Afghanistan				●	●	●		
Iraq		●	●	●			●	●
Kiribati	●	●	●	●				
Liberia	●	●	●	●		●		●
San Marino	●	●	●	●	●	●	●	●
Serbia and Montenegro	●	●	●	●	●	●	●	●
Somalia			●	●		●		
Total ratifications	142	154	163	159	161	159	132	147

● Convention ratified. ▽ Convention denounced.

Note: Table includes UN member states.

a. Freedom of Association and Protection of the Right to Organize Convention (1948). b. Right to Organize and Collective Bargaining Convention (1949). c. Forced Labour Convention (1930). d. Abolition of Forced Labour Convention (1957). e. Equal Remuneration Convention (1951). f. Discrimination (Employment and Occupation) Convention (1958). g. Minimum Age Convention (1973). h. Worst Forms of Child Labour Convention (1999). i. States not included in the human development index that have ratified at least one labour rights convention.

Source: Columns 1-8: ILO 2004a.

		Human development index (HDI)			Human poverty index for developing countries (HPI-1)	Human poverty index for selected high-income OECD countries (HPI-2)	Gender-related development index (GDI)	Gender empowerment measure (GEM)
		1975	1990	2002				
Arab States								
108	Algeria	0.504	0.642	0.704	21.9	..	0.688	..
40	Bahrain	..	**0.808**	**0.843**	..	..	**0.832**	**0.395**
154	Djibouti	..	..	0.454	34.3	..	..	..
120	Egypt	0.438	0.577	0.653	30.9	..	0.634	0.266
90	Jordan	..	0.682	0.750	**7.2**	..	0.734	..
44	Kuwait	**0.761**	..	0.838	..	..	0.827	..
80	Lebanon	..	0.673	0.758	9.5	..	0.755	..
58	Libyan Arab Jamahiriya	..	..	0.794	15.3	..	..	..
125	Morocco	0.429	0.542	0.620	34.5	..	0.604	..
102	Occupied Palestinian Territories	..	..	0.726	..	..	..	..
74	Oman	0.493	0.696	0.770	31.5	..	0.747	..
47	Qatar	..	..	0.833	..	..	..	..
77	Saudi Arabia	0.602	0.707	0.768	15.8	..	0.739	0.207
139	Sudan	0.344	0.427	0.505	31.6	..	0.485	..
106	Syrian Arab Republic	0.534	0.635	0.710	13.7	..	0.689	..
92	Tunisia	0.516	0.656	0.745	19.2	..	0.734	..
49	United Arab Emirates	0.744	0.805	0.824	..	..	..	..
149	Yemen	..	0.392	0.482	40.3	..	0.436	0.123
East Asia and the Pacific								
33	Brunei Darussalam	..	..	0.867	..	..	..	..
130	Cambodia	..	..	0.568	42.6	..	0.557	0.364
94	China	0.523	0.627	0.745	13.2	..	0.741	..
81	Fiji	0.659	0.722	0.758	21.3	..	0.747	0.335
23	Hong Kong, China (SAR)	**0.760**	**0.862**	**0.903**	..	..	**0.898**	..
111	Indonesia	0.467	0.623	0.692	17.8	..	0.685	..
28	Korea, Rep. of	0.705	0.817	0.888	..	..	0.882	0.377
135	Lao People's Dem. Rep.	..	0.449	0.534	40.3	..	0.528	..
59	Malaysia	0.614	0.720	0.793	..	..	0.786	0.519
117	Mongolia	..	0.656	0.668	19.1	..	0.664	0.429
132	Myanmar	..	..	0.551	25.4	..	..	..
133	Papua New Guinea	0.423	0.482	0.542	37.0	..	0.536	..
83	Philippines	0.653	0.719	0.753	15.0	..	0.751	0.542
75	Samoa (Western)	..	..	0.769	..	..	..	..
25	Singapore	0.724	0.821	0.902	**6.3**	..	0.884	**0.648**
124	Solomon Islands	..	..	0.624	..	..	..	..
76	Thailand	0.613	0.707	0.768	13.1	..	0.766	0.461
158	Timor-Leste	..	..	0.436	..	..	..	..
63	Tonga	..	..	0.787	..	..	..	..
129	Vanuatu	..	..	0.570	..	..	..	..
112	Viet Nam	..	0.610	0.691	20.0	..	0.689	..
Latin America and the Caribbean								
55	Antigua and Barbuda	..	..	0.800	..	..	..	..
34	Argentina	0.784	0.810	0.853	..	..	0.841	0.645
51	Bahamas	..	0.825	0.815	..	..	0.813	**0.699**
29	Barbados	**0.804**	**0.851**	**0.888**	2.5	..	**0.884**	0.634
99	Belize	..	0.747	0.737	16.7	..	0.718	0.455
114	Bolivia	0.512	0.603	0.681	14.4	..	0.674	0.524
72	Brazil	0.644	0.714	0.775	11.8	..	0.768	..
43	Chile	0.703	0.784	0.839	4.1	..	0.830	0.460
73	Colombia	0.661	0.727	0.773	8.1	..	0.770	0.498
45	Costa Rica	0.745	0.791	0.834	4.4	..	0.823	0.664

		Human development index (HDI)			Human poverty index for developing countries (HPI-1)	Human poverty index for selected high-income OECD countries (HPI-2)	Gender-related development index (GDI)	Gender empowerment measure (GEM)
		1975	1990	2002				
52	Cuba	..	..	0.809	5.0	..	..	..
95	Dominica	..	..	0.743	..	..	..	..
98	Dominican Republic	0.617	0.678	0.738	13.7	..	0.728	0.527
100	Ecuador	0.630	0.710	0.735	12.0	..	0.721	0.490
103	El Salvador	0.590	0.648	0.720	17.0	..	0.709	0.448
93	Grenada	..	..	0.745	..	..	..	..
121	Guatemala	0.510	0.583	0.649	22.5	..	0.635	..
104	Guyana	0.677	0.697	0.719	12.9	..	0.715	..
153	Haiti	..	0.455	0.463	41.1	..	0.458	..
115	Honduras	0.517	0.624	0.672	16.6	..	0.662	0.355
79	Jamaica	0.687	0.726	0.764	9.2	..	0.762	..
53	Mexico	0.688	0.761	0.802	9.1	..	0.792	0.563
118	Nicaragua	0.565	0.589	0.667	18.3	..	0.660	..
61	Panama	0.708	0.748	0.791	7.7	..	0.785	0.486
89	Paraguay	0.667	0.719	0.751	10.6	..	0.736	0.417
85	Peru	0.642	0.706	0.752	13.2	..	0.736	0.524
39	Saint Kitts and Nevis	..	..	0.844	..	..	..	..
71	Saint Lucia	..	..	0.777	..	..	..	..
87	St. Vincent & the Grenadines	..	..	0.751	..	..	..	..
67	Suriname	..	..	0.780	..	..	..	..
54	Trinidad and Tobago	0.735	0.791	0.801	7.7	..	0.795	0.644
46	Uruguay	0.759	0.803	0.833	3.6	..	0.829	0.511
68	Venezuela	0.716	0.759	0.778	8.5	..	0.770	0.444
South Asia								
138	Bangladesh	0.345	0.417	0.509	42.2	..	0.499	0.218
134	Bhutan	..	..	0.536	..	..	..	..
127	India	0.411	0.514	0.595	31.4	..	0.572	..
101	Iran, Islamic Rep. of	0.565	0.649	0.732	16.4	..	0.713	0.313
84	Maldives	..	..	**0.752**	**11.4**	..	..	..
140	Nepal	0.291	0.418	0.504	41.2	..	0.484	..
142	Pakistan	0.346	0.444	0.497	41.9	..	0.471	**0.416**
96	Sri Lanka	**0.613**	**0.698**	0.740	18.2	..	**0.738**	0.276
Southern Europe								
30	Cyprus	..	**0.835**	**0.883**	..	..	**0.875**	**0.497**
88	Turkey	0.590	0.683	0.751	12.0	..	0.746	0.290
Sub-Saharan Africa								
166	Angola	..	..	0.381	..	..	..	..
161	Benin	0.288	0.356	0.421	45.7	..	0.406	..
128	Botswana	0.503	0.675	0.589	43.5	..	0.581	0.562
175	Burkina Faso	0.239	0.302	0.302	65.5	..	0.291	..
173	Burundi	0.282	0.338	0.339	45.8	..	0.337	..
141	Cameroon	0.415	0.519	0.501	36.9	..	0.491	..
105	Cape Verde	..	0.623	0.717	19.7	..	0.709	..
169	Central African Republic	0.334	0.375	0.361	47.7	..	0.345	..
167	Chad	0.260	0.326	0.379	49.6	..	0.368	..
136	Comoros	..	0.501	0.530	31.4	..	0.510	..
144	Congo	0.451	0.532	0.494	31.9	..	0.488	..
168	Congo, Dem. Rep. of the	0.410	0.414	0.365	42.9	..	0.355	..
163	Côte d'Ivoire	0.382	0.429	0.399	45.0	..	0.379	..
109	Equatorial Guinea	..	0.504	0.703	32.7	..	0.691	..
156	Eritrea	..	..	0.439	41.8	..	0.431	..

		Human development index (HDI)			Human poverty index for developing countries (HPI-1)	Human poverty index for selected high-income OECD countries (HPI-2)	Gender-related development index (GDI)	Gender empowerment measure (GEM)
		1975	1990	2002				
170	Ethiopia	..	0.305	0.359	55.5	..	0.346	..
122	Gabon	..	..	0.648	..	..	..	..
155	Gambia	0.283	..	0.452	45.8	..	0.446	..
131	Ghana	0.439	0.511	0.568	26.0	..	0.564	..
160	Guinea	..	..	0.425	..	..	..	..
172	Guinea-Bissau	0.254	0.311	0.350	48.0	..	0.329	..
148	Kenya	0.445	0.540	0.488	37.5	..	0.486	..
145	Lesotho	0.457	0.544	0.493	47.9	..	0.483	..
150	Madagascar	0.400	0.436	0.469	35.9	..	0.462	..
165	Malawi	0.315	0.368	0.388	46.8	..	0.374	..
174	Mali	0.232	0.288	0.326	58.9	..	0.309	..
152	Mauritania	0.339	0.387	0.465	48.3	..	0.456	..
64	Mauritius	..	0.723	0.785	**11.3**	..	**0.775**	..
171	Mozambique	..	0.310	0.354	49.8	..	0.339	..
126	Namibia	..	..	0.607	37.7	..	0.602	**0.572**
176	Niger	0.237	0.259	0.292	61.4	..	0.278	..
151	Nigeria	0.324	0.430	0.466	35.1	..	0.458	..
159	Rwanda	0.341	0.351	0.431	44.7	..	0.423	..
123	São Tomé and Principe	..	..	0.645	..	..	..	..
157	Senegal	0.315	0.382	0.437	44.1	..	0.429	..
35	Seychelles	..	..	**0.853**	..	..	..	..
177	Sierra Leone	..	..	0.273	..	..	..	..
119	South Africa	**0.655**	**0.729**	0.666	31.7	..	0.661	..
137	Swaziland	0.516	0.611	0.519	..	..	0.505	0.487
162	Tanzania, U. Rep. of	..	0.413	0.407	36.0	..	0.401	..
143	Togo	0.396	0.474	0.495	38.0	..	0.477	..
146	Uganda	..	0.395	0.493	36.4	..	0.487	..
164	Zambia	0.466	0.466	0.389	50.4	..	0.375	..
147	Zimbabwe	0.547	0.617	0.491	52.0	..	0.482	..
Central & Eastern Europe & CIS								
65	Albania	..	0.702	0.781	..	..	0.778	..
82	Armenia	..	0.751	0.754	..	..	0.752	..
91	Azerbaijan	..	..	0.746	..	..	..	..
62	Belarus	..	0.785	0.790	..	..	0.789	..
66	Bosnia and Herzegovina	..	..	0.781	..	..	..	..
56	Bulgaria	..	0.795	0.796	..	..	0.795	..
48	Croatia	..	0.806	0.830	..	..	0.827	0.560
32	Czech Republic	..	..	0.868	..	..	0.865	0.586
36	Estonia	..	0.817	0.853	..	..	0.852	0.592
97	Georgia	..	..	0.739	..	..	..	0.387
38	Hungary	0.777	0.807	0.848	..	..	0.847	0.529
78	Kazakhstan	..	0.767	0.766	..	..	0.761	..
110	Kyrgyzstan	..	..	0.701	..	..	..	..
50	Latvia	..	0.807	0.823	..	..	0.823	0.591
41	Lithuania	..	**0.823**	0.842	..	..	0.841	0.508

		Human development index (HDI)			Human poverty index for developing countries (HPI-1)	Human poverty index for selected high-income OECD countries (HPI-2)	Gender-related development index (GDI)	Gender empowerment measure (GEM)
		1975	1990	2002				
60	Macedonia, TFYR	..	..	0.793	..	..	..	0.517
113	Moldova, Rep. of	..	0.736	0.681	..	..	0.678	0.469
37	Poland	..	0.802	0.850	..	..	0.848	0.606
69	Romania	..	0.771	0.778	..	..	0.775	0.465
57	Russian Federation	..	0.813	0.795	..	..	0.794	0.467
42	Slovakia	..	..	0.842	..	..	0.840	**0.607**
27	Slovenia	..	..	**0.895**	..	..	**0.892**	0.584
116	Tajikistan	..	0.719	0.671	..	..	0.668	..
86	Turkmenistan	..	..	0.752	..	..	0.748	..
70	Ukraine	..	0.798	0.777	..	..	0.773	0.411
107	Uzbekistan	..	..	0.709	..	..	0.705	..
High-income OECD [a]								
3	Australia	0.847	0.892	0.946	..	12.9	0.945	0.806
14	Austria	0.842	0.893	0.934	..	..	0.924	0.770
6	Belgium	0.845	0.897	0.942	..	12.4	0.938	0.808
4	Canada	0.869	**0.928**	0.943	..	12.2	0.941	0.787
17	Denmark	0.872	0.897	0.932	..	9.1	0.931	0.847
13	Finland	0.839	0.899	0.935	..	8.4	0.933	0.820
15	Luxembourg	0.838	0.882	0.933	..	10.5	0.926	..
19	Germany	..	0.887	0.925	..	10.3	0.921	0.804
24	Greece	0.832	0.870	0.902	..	..	0.894	0.523
7	Iceland	0.862	0.913	0.941	..	..	0.938	0.816
10	Ireland	0.810	0.869	0.936	..	15.3	0.929	0.710
22	Israel	0.794	0.857	0.908	..	..	0.906	0.614
21	Italy	0.841	0.887	0.920	..	11.6	0.914	0.583
9	Japan	0.854	0.910	0.938	..	11.1	0.932	0.531
16	France	0.852	0.902	0.932	..	10.8	0.929	..
31	Malta	0.726	0.824	0.875	..	..	0.866	0.480
5	Netherlands	0.865	0.907	0.942	..	8.2	0.938	0.817
18	New Zealand	0.847	0.874	0.926	..	..	0.924	0.772
1	Norway	0.866	0.911	**0.956**	..	7.1	**0.955**	**0.908**
26	Portugal	0.785	0.847	0.897	..	..	0.894	0.644
20	Spain	0.836	0.885	0.922	..	11.0	0.916	0.716
2	Sweden	0.863	0.895	0.946	..	**6.5**	0.946	0.854
11	Switzerland	**0.878**	0.909	0.936	..	..	0.932	0.771
12	United Kingdom	0.845	0.883	0.936	..	14.8	0.934	0.698
8	United States	0.866	0.914	0.939	..	15.8	0.936	0.769

Note: The best value in each index and region is presented in bold.
a. Excludes the Republic of Korea; see East Asia and the Pacific. Includes Israel and Malta, although they are not OECD countries.
Source: Column 1: column 1 of table 2; *column 2:* column 4 of table 2; *column 3:* column 8 of table 1; *column 4:* column 2 of table 3; *column 5:* column 2 of table 4; *column 6:* column 2 of table 24; *column 7:* column 2 of table 25.

33 Basic indicators for other UN member countries

	Human development index components				Total fertility rate (births per woman) 2000-05[c]	MDG Under-five mortality rate (per 1,000 live births) 2002	MDG Net primary enrolment ratio[a] (%) 2001/02[d]	HIV prevalence[b] (% ages 15-49) 2003	MDG Under-nourished people (% of total population) 1999/2001[e]	MDG Population with sustainable access to an improved water source (%) 2000
	Life expectancy at birth (years) 2000-05[c]	Adult literacy rate (% ages 15 and above) 2002	Combined gross enrolment ratio for primary, secondary and tertiary schools (%) 2001/02[d]	GDP per capita (PPP US$) 2002	Total population (thousands) 2002						
Afghanistan	43.1	..	14	..	22,930	6.8	257	..	..	70	13
Andorra	..	..	..	..	69	..	7	..	..	..	100
Iraq	60.7	..	57	..	24,510	4.8	125	91	<0.1 [0.2]	27	85
Kiribati	..	..	..	..	87	..	69	..	..	..	48
Korea, Dem. Rep.	63.1	..	..	..	22,541	2.0	55	..	..	34	100
Liberia	41.4	55.9	61	..	3,239	6.8	235	70	5.9 [2.7-12.4]	42	..
Liechtenstein	..	..	..	..	33	..	11	..	..	..	..
Marshall Islands	..	..	..	..	52	..	66	100	..	..	..
Micronesia, Fed. Sts.	68.6	..	..	..	108	3.8	24	..	..	..	..
Monaco	..	..	..	..	34	..	5	..	..	..	100
Nauru	..	..	55	..	13	..	30	81	..	..	..
Palau	..	..	..	..	20	..	29	97	..	..	79
San Marino	..	..	..	..	27	..	6	..	..	..	..
Serbia and Montenegro	73.2	..	74	..	10,535	1.7	19	75	0.2 [0.1-0.4]	9	98
Somalia	47.9	..	..	..	9,480	7.3	225	..	..	71	..
Tuvalu	..	..	67	..	10	..	52	..	..	..	100

Note: This table presents data for UN member countries not included in the main indicator tables.

a. The net enrolment ratio is the ratio of enrolled children of the official age for the education level indicated to the total population of that age. b. Data refer to point and range estimates based on new estimation models developed by the Joint United Nations Programme on HIV/AIDS (UNAIDS). Range estimates are presented in square brackets. c. Data refer to estimates for the period specified. d. Data refer to the school year 2001/02. Data for some countries may refer to national or UNESCO Institute for Statistics estimates. For details, see http://uis.unesco.org/. e. Data refer to average for the years specified.
Source: Columns 1, 5 and 6: UN 2003; *column 2:* UNESCO Institute for Statistics 2004a; *column 3:* UNESCO Institute for Statistics 2004c; *column 4:* World Bank 2004f; *column 7:* UNICEF 2003b; *column 8:* UNESCO Institute for Statistics 2004c; *column 9:* UNAIDS 2004; *column 10:* FAO 2003; *column 11:* UNICEF 2003b, based on a joint effort by the United Nation Children's Fund and the World Health Organization.

Note on statistics in the Human Development Report

This Report usually presents two types of statistical information: statistics in the human development indicator tables, which provide a global assessment of country achievements in different areas of human development, and statistical evidence on the thematic analysis in the chapters. This year's Report incorporates many of the Millennium Development Goal indicators in the human development indicator tables (see *index to Millennium Development Goal indicators*). Data for these indicators provide a statistical reference for assessing the progress in each country towards the Millennium Development Goals and their targets.

DATA SOURCES

The Human Development Report Office is primarily a user, not a producer, of statistics. It therefore relies on international data agencies with the resources and expertise to collect and compile international data on specific statistical indicators.

HUMAN DEVELOPMENT INDICATOR TABLES

To allow comparisons across countries and over time, the Human Development Report Office, to the extent possible, uses internationally comparable data produced by relevant international data agencies or other specialized institutions in preparing the human development indicator tables (for information on the major agencies providing data used in the Report, see box 1). But many gaps still exist in the data, even in some very basic areas of human development. While advocating for improvements in human development data, as a principle and for practical reasons, the Human Development Report Office does not collect data directly from countries or make estimates to fill these data gaps.

The one exception is the human development index (HDI). The Human Development Report Office strives to include as many UN member countries as possible in the HDI. For a country to be included, data ideally should be available from the relevant international data agencies for all four components of the index (see Statistical feature 2, *Note to table 1: About this year's human development index*). But for a significant number of countries data are missing for one or more of these components. In response to the desire of countries to be included in the HDI, the Human Development Report Office makes every effort in these cases to identify other reasonable estimates, working with international data agencies, the UN Regional Commissions, national statistical offices and UNDP country offices. In a few cases the Human Development Report Office has attempted to make an estimate in consultation with regional and national statistical offices or other experts.

MILLENNIUM DEVELOPMENT GOAL INDICATORS

The United Nations Statistics Division maintains the global Millennium Indicators Database (http://millenniumindicators.un.org), compiled from international data series provided by the responsible international data agencies. The database forms the statistical basis for the UN Secretary-General's annual report to the UN General Assembly on global and regional progress towards the Millennium Development Goals and their targets. It also feeds into other international reports providing data on the Millennium Development Goal indicators across countries, such as this Report and the World Bank's annual *World Development Indicators*.

At the time this Report was being prepared, the United Nations Statistics Division was

BOX 1

Major sources of data used in the *Human Development Report*

By generously sharing data, the following organizations made it possible for the Human Development Report to publish the important human development statistics appearing in the indicator tables.

Carbon Dioxide Information Analysis Center (CDIAC) The CDIAC, a data and analysis centre of the US Department of Energy, focuses on the greenhouse effect and global climate change. It is the source of data on carbon dioxide emissions.

Food and Agriculture Organization (FAO) The FAO collects, analyses and disseminates data and information on food and agriculture. It is the source of data on food insecurity indicators.

International Institute for Strategic Studies (IISS) An independent centre for research, information and debate on the problems of conflict, the IISS maintains an extensive military database. The data on armed forces are from its publication *The Military Balance.*

International Labour Organization (ILO) The ILO maintains an extensive statistical publication programme, with the *Yearbook of Labour Statistics* and the *Key Indicators of the Labour Market* its most comprehensive collection of labour market data. The ILO is the source of data on wages, employment and occupations and information on the ratification status of labour rights conventions.

International Monetary Fund (IMF) The IMF has an extensive programme for developing and compiling statistics on international financial transactions and balance of payments. Much of the financial data provided to the Human Development Report Office by other agencies originates from the IMF.

International Telecommunication Union (ITU) This specialized UN agency maintains an extensive collection of statistics on information and communications. The data on trends in telecommunications come from its *World Telecommunication Indicators* database.

Inter-Parliamentary Union (IPU) This organization provides data on trends in political participation and structures of democracy. The Human Development Report Office relies on the IPU for data relating to elections and information on women's political representation.

Joint United Nations Programme on HIV/AIDS (UNAIDS) This joint UN programme monitors the spread of HIV/AIDS and provides regular updates. The *Report on the Global HIV/AIDS Epidemic,* a joint publication of UNAIDS and the World Health Organization, is the primary source of data on HIV/AIDS.

Luxembourg Income Study (LIS) A cooperative research project with 25 member countries, the LIS focuses on poverty and policy issues. It is the source of income poverty estimates for many OECD countries.

Organisation for Economic Co-operation and Development (OECD) The OECD publishes data on a variety of social and economic trends in its member countries as well as on flows of aid. This year's Report presents data from the OECD on aid, energy, employment and education.

Stockholm International Peace Research Institute (SIPRI) SIPRI conducts research on international peace and security. The *SIPRI Yearbook:* *Armaments, Disarmament and International Security* is the published source of data on military expenditure and arms transfers.

United Nations Children's Fund (UNICEF) UNICEF monitors the wellbeing of children and provides a wide array of data. Its *State of the World's Children* is an important source of data for the Report.

United Nations Conference on Trade and Development (UNCTAD) UNCTAD provides trade and economic statistics through a number of publications, including the *World Investment Report.* It is the original source of data on investment flows that the Human Development Report Office receives from other agencies.

United Nations Educational, Scientific and Cultural Organization (UNESCO) The Institute for Statistics of this specialized UN agency is the source of data relating to education. The Human Development Report Office relies on data in UNESCO's statistical publications as well as data received directly from its Institute for Statistics.

United Nations High Commissioner for Refugees (UNHCR) This UN organization provides data on refugees through its *Statistical Yearbook* or other on-line statistical publications.

United Nations Office on Drugs and Crime (UNODC) This UN organization carries out international comparative research to support the fight against illicit drugs and international crime. It provides data on crime victims from the International Crime Victims Surveys.

United Nations Multilateral Treaties Deposited with the Secretary General (UN Treaty Section) The Human Development Report Office compiles information on the status of major international human rights instruments and environmental treaties based on the database maintained by this UN office.

United Nations Population Division (UNPOP) This specialized UN office produces international data on population trends. The Human Development Report Office relies on *World Population Prospects* and *World Urbanization Prospects,* two of the main publications of UNPOP, and its other publications and databases, for demographic estimates and projections.

United Nations Statistics Division (UNSD) The UNSD provides a wide range of statistical outputs and services. Much of the national accounts data provided to the Human Development Report Office by other agencies originates from the UNSD. This year's Report also presents UNSD data on trade and energy and draws on the global Millennium Indicators Database, maintained by the UNSD, as the source of data for the Millennium Development Goal indicators.

World Bank The World Bank produces and compiles data on economic trends as well as a broad array of other indicators. Its *World Development Indicators* is the primary source for many indicators in the Report.

World Health Organization (WHO) This specialized agency maintains a large array of data series on health issues, the source for the health-related indicators in the Report.

World Intellectual Property Organization (WIPO) As a specialized UN agency, WIPO promotes the protection of intellectual property rights throughout the world through different kinds of cooperative efforts. It is the source of data relating to patents.

updating the Millennium Indicators Database and the World Bank was completing its *World Development Indicators 2004* for publication. By generously sharing data, the World Bank and other international agencies—such as the United Nations Educational, Scientific and Cultural Organization Institute for Statistics (UIS), the United Nations Children's Fund (UNICEF) and the World Health Organization (WHO)—enabled the Report to include not only the existing data in the Millennium Indicators Database but also more recent estimates for some of the Millennium Development Goal indicators, estimates that were later to be incorporated into the database.

DATA FOR THEMATIC ANALYSIS

The statistical evidence used in the thematic analysis in the Report is often drawn from the indicator tables. But a wide range of other sources are also used, including commissioned papers, government documents, national human development reports, reports of non-governmental organizations, journal articles and other scholarly publications. Official statistics usually receive priority. But because of the cutting-edge nature of the issues discussed, relevant official statistics may not exist, so that non-official sources of information must be used. Nevertheless, the Human Development Report Office is committed to relying on data compiled through scholarly and scientific research and to ensuring impartiality in the sources of information and in its use in the analysis.

Where information from sources other than the Report's indicator tables is used in boxes or tables in the text, the source is shown and the full citation is given in the bibliography. In addition, a summary note for each chapter outlines the major sources for the chapter, and endnotes specify the sources of statistical information not drawn from the indicator tables.

THE NEED FOR BETTER HUMAN DEVELOPMENT STATISTICS

While the indicator tables in this year's Report present the best data currently available for measuring human development, many gaps and problems remain.

DATA GAPS

Gaps throughout the indicator tables demonstrate the pressing need for improvements in the availability of relevant, reliable and timely human development statistics. A stark example of data gaps is the large number of countries excluded from the HDI. The intent is to include all UN member countries, along with Hong Kong, China (SAR) and the Occupied Palestinian Territories. But because of a lack of reliable data, 16 UN member countries are excluded from the HDI and therefore from the main indicator tables (what key indicators are available for these countries are presented in table 33). Similarly, the human poverty index covers only 95 developing countries and 17 high-income OECD countries, the gender-related development index 144 countries and the gender empowerment measure 78 countries. For a significant number of countries data for the components of these indices are unreliable and out of date and in some cases need to be estimated (for the definition and methodology of the indices, see *technical note 1*).

DISCREPANCIES BETWEEN NATIONAL AND INTERNATIONAL ESTIMATES

When compiling international data series, international data agencies often need to apply internationally adopted standards and harmonization procedures to improve comparability across countries. Where the international data are based on national statistics, as they usually are, the national data may need to be adjusted. Where data for a country are missing, an international agency may produce an estimate if other relevant information can be used. And because of the difficulties in coordination between national and international data agencies, international data series may not incorporate the most recent national data. All these factors can lead to significant discrepancies between national and international estimates.

This Report has often brought such discrepancies to light. While the Human Development Report Office advocates for improvements in international data, it also recognizes that it can play an active role in such efforts. When discrepancies in data have arisen, it has helped to link national and international data authorities to address those discrepancies. In many cases this has led to better statistics in the Report. The Human Development Report Office is striving to continuously improve data consistency through more systematic efforts.

TOWARDS STRONGER STATISTICAL CAPACITY

A vital part of the solution to the enormous gaps and deficiencies in statistical information is building sustainable statistical capacity in countries, an effort requiring financial and political commitment at both national and international levels. The momentum generated by the Millennium Development Goal process has mobilized the entire international statistical community, and many initiatives are under way, including the Marrakech Action Plan for Statistics (box 2) and the Health Metrics Network launched by the WHO (box 3).

International statistical agencies should continue to play an active part in statistical development by improving, promoting and implementing internationally agreed standards, methods and frameworks for statistical activities. This year's Report highlights the need for conceptual and methodological breakthroughs in the development of cultural indicators (box 4 and box 2.3 in chapter 2). It also calls for greater efforts to improve other basic human development statistics. Recognizing the weakness of the existing literacy statistics, the UNESCO Institute for Statistics is developing new tools for measuring literacy (box 5). And the Millennium Round of the International Comparison Program promises to provide a sounder basis for assessing standards of living across countries (box 6).

METHODOLOGY AND PRESENTATION OF THE INDICATORS

This year's Report presents data for most key indicators with only a two-year lag between the reference date for the indicators and the date

---

BOX 2

The Marrakech Action Plan for Statistics

The emphasis on quantitative targets in the Millennium Development Goals and the growing attention to measuring results have increased the demand for statistics. They have also increased our awareness of the poor state of statistical systems in many parts of the developing world. Good statistics are not a technical issue. As Trevor Manuel has said, "If you can't measure it, you can't manage it". Data and statistics are needed by governments, politicians, and managers. Crucially, they are needed by citizens to hold governments accountable for their actions and results. Improving statistical systems is a development issue, which requires concerted action by the entire global community and not just professional statisticians.

At the Second International Roundtable Conference on Managing for Development Results, representatives of the multilateral development banks, the OECD Development Assistance Committee, and UN programs and agencies proposed an action plan for improving development statistics. The plan has three objectives:
1. To strengthen national capacity to produce, analyze and use reliable statistics.
2. To improve the quality and availability of development statistics for global monitoring.
3. To support countries that are expanding their statistical capacity.

Six broad sets of actions
The Marrakech Action Plan for Statistics (MAPS) builds on existing initiatives and country experience to set out six broad sets of actions needed to improve statistics at both national and international levels.
1. *Mainstream strategic planning of statistical systems and help all low-income countries prepare national statistical development strategies by 2006.* Statistical requirements must be derived from wider development strategies, such as Poverty Reduction Strategy Papers, not treated as a separate issue.
2. *Strengthen preparations for 2010 census.* Censuses are a core source of development statistics and underpin the ability to monitor progress towards the Millennium Development Goals. We must begin now if adequate information is to be in place to assess progress in 2015.
3. *Increase financial support for statistical capacity building.* In many cases countries will need to increase their own financing for statistics, but they will also require external assistance. In the spirit of the Monterrey Conference on Financing for Development, countries that adopt good policies for their

statistical systems should receive needed financial support for statistics.
4. *Set up an international household survey network.* Surveys have become increasingly important for measuring social outcomes, but need better coordination.
5. *Undertake urgent improvements needed for Millennium Development Goal monitoring for 2005.* The world expects a candid and complete report on progress next year.
6. *Increase accountability of the international statistical system.* The international agencies must further improve their own practices.

Costs
The incremental cost of these activities is around US$120 million a year for improving national statistical systems and around US$25 million a year for improving international systems. These are not exhaustive costs. For example, they exclude the costs of the 2010 census. Nor do they include the costs for improvements in other statistical sources such as establishment surveys or administrative reporting. These are first estimates, which will be refined as the proposals are developed and fine tuned. Also note that these costs are for financing from all possible sources, national as well as donors.

Source: World Bank 2004e.

of the Report's release. The main human development indicator tables include 175 UN member countries along with Hong Kong, China (SAR) and the Occupied Palestinian Territories—all those for which the HDI can be calculated. Owing to a lack of comparable data, 16 UN member countries cannot be included in the HDI or, therefore, in the main indicator tables. For these countries basic human development indicators are presented in a separate table (table 33).

COUNTRY CLASSIFICATIONS

Countries are classified in four ways: by human development level, by income, in major world aggregates and by region (see *Classification of countries*). These designations do not necessarily express a judgement about the development stage of a particular country or area. The term *country* as used in the text and tables refers, as appropriate, to territories or areas.

Human development classifications. All countries included in the HDI are classified into three clusters by achievement in human development: high human development (with an HDI of 0.800 or above), medium human development (0.500–0.799) and low human development (less than 0.500).

Income classifications. All countries are grouped by income using World Bank classifications: high income (gross national income per capita of US$9,076 or more in 2002), middle income (US$736–$9,075) and low income (US$735 or less).

Major world classifications. The three global groups are *developing countries, Central and Eastern Europe and the CIS* and *OECD*. These groups are not mutually exclusive. Unless otherwise specified, the classification *world* represents the universe of 193 countries and areas covered—191 UN member countries, plus Hong Kong, China (SAR) and the Occupied Palestinian Territories.

Regional classifications. Developing countries are further classified into the following regions: Arab States, East Asia and the Pacific, Latin America and the Caribbean (including Mexico), South Asia, Southern Europe and Sub-Saharan Africa. These regional classifications are consistent with the Regional Bureaux

---

BOX 3

Health Metrics Network: An emerging global partnership for health information

The Millennium Development Goals have stimulated awareness of the importance of data. They have also highlighted the weakness of existing information systems in many countries. Nowhere is this more apparent than in health. Sound information is essential for achieving the health-related goals, yet rarely available. Everywhere there are too many uncoordinated demands for information, too much useless data and too few solid facts.

The Health Metrics Network, an emerging global partnership funded largely by the Bill and Melinda Gates Foundation, seeks to remedy this situation. It will convene the health and statistical constituencies at global, regional and country levels, including international agencies, bilateral and multilateral donors, foundations and technical experts, to advance the proposition that meeting the health challenges of the 21st century requires building stronger health information systems.

Its aim is to use the growing demand by countries and development partners for good

Source: WHO 2004f.

information to accelerate the building of national level health information systems that serve global, national and subnational needs. Countries themselves will lead this effort, forging consensus among stakeholders around plans for strengthening or reforming health information systems. Implementing the plans will help countries respond to the challenge of monitoring progress towards national and international goals and targets, including the Millennium Development Goals.

The Health Metrics Network will be made up of a board, a small secretariat initially hosted by the World Health Organziation, and technical task forces that will provide the impetus for addressing key health metrics challenges. Board members will include representatives of developing countries, multilateral and bilateral agencies, foundations and technical experts. The network's launch is planned for the first half of 2004, following the first meeting of the board.

BOX 4

The Culture Statistics Programme of the UNESCO Institute for Statistics

Before 2001, the United Nations Educational, Scientific and Cultural Organization (UNESCO) Institute for Statistics (UIS) Culture Statistics Programme collected data based on survey vehicles in six areas: book production, films and cinemas, libraries, museums, print media and broadcasting. In 2002 the UIS began a reevaluation of its Culture Statistics Programme and suspended data collection pending the review. The UIS is currently developing a new programme of work that will better meet the policy needs of member states.

The review began with a three-day international symposium in Montreal in October 2002, jointly sponsored by l'Observatoire de la culture et des communications du Québec, to solicit opinions from researchers around the world on what data the UIS should collect on culture. Suggestions included work in culture participation,

Source: UNESCO Institute for Statistics 2004d.

culture employment and the finance of culture. Those suggestions, along the lines of recent work by the Working Group on Culture Statistics of the European Union, are being investigated for feasibility and relevance to other regions of the world.

Also under consideration is the updating of data on trade flows of cultural goods for recent years in support of the Convention on the Protection of Cultural Goods and Artistic Expression, currently being drafted by UNESCO. In addition, the UIS is participating in UNESCO's cross-cutting project "Initiative B@bel" by sponsoring a report on the status of multilingualism on the Internet. Finally, the new programme of work for culture statistics will likely involve the retooling of one or more of the suspended UIS surveys, probably broadcasting or print media, the two for which external demand for data is greatest.

---

of UNDP. An additional classification is *least developed countries,* as defined by the United Nations (UNCTAD 2001).

Measuring literacy

Literacy is the foundation for social, economic and environmental progress in developing countries. Yet little attention has been paid to measuring literacy, or the underlying factors contributing to the development of reading, writing and numeracy skills in developing countries or obtaining the necessary information to monitor change or to formulate appropriate interventions.

Some developing countries, although a minority, have attempted to follow international guidelines on determining the size of their illiterate population using a census or survey question asking whether an individual is literate. This methodology, referred to as self-declaration, has major limitations. First, it divides the population into two groups—those who are literate and those who are not—and how many are in each group, a vast oversimplification. Second, it underestimates the number of illiterate people because respondents are reluctant to admit their illiteracy. These rates are widely used to indicate the number of illiterate people in countries and regions, but they provide no insight into the literacy levels of these populations, what aspects of reading and writing development require improvement or the relative impact of non-formal education and literacy programmes. Needed instead are measures of each individual's skill level in reading, writing and numeracy, and a means of measuring progress. The United Nations Educational, Scientific and Cultural Organization (UNESCO) Institute for Statistics is developing a sample survey methodology to do this through the Literacy Assessment and Monitoring Programme (see http://www.uis.unesco.org/).

The time has come to replace simple literacy rates with literacy profiles of populations to show the wide range of skills and to monitor changes to these profiles at all levels of literacy. The international community can help by asking the right questions, by formulating associated international goals and by supporting national efforts to obtain more detailed information on literacy.

Source: UNESCO Institute for Statistics 2004e.

AGGREGATES AND GROWTH RATES

Aggregates. Aggregates for the classifications described above are presented at the end of tables where it is analytically meaningful to do so and data are sufficient. Aggregates that are the total for the classification (such as for population) are indicated by a T. As a result of rounding, world totals may not always equal the sum of the totals for subgroups. All other aggregates are weighted averages.

In general, an aggregate is shown for a classification only when data are available for half the countries and represent at least two-thirds of the available weight in that classification. The Human Development Report Office does not fill in missing data for the purpose of aggregation. Therefore, unless otherwise specified, aggregates for each classification represent only the countries for which data are available, refer to the year or period specified and refer only to data from the primary sources listed. Aggregates are not shown where appropriate weighting procedures were unavailable.

Aggregates for indices, for growth rates and for indicators covering more than one point in time are based only on countries for which data exist for all necessary points in time. For the world classification, which refers only to the universe of 193 countries and areas (unless otherwise specified), aggregates are not always shown where no aggregate is available for one or more regions.

Aggregates in this Report will not always conform to those in other publications because of differences in country classifications and methodology. Where indicated, aggregates are calculated by the statistical agency providing the data for the indicator.

Growth rates. Multiyear growth rates are expressed as average annual rates of change. In calculations of rates by the Human Development Report Office only the beginning and end points are used. Year-to-year growth rates are expressed as annual percentage changes.

PRESENTATION

In the human development indicator tables countries and areas are ranked in descending order by their HDI value. To locate a country in these tables, refer to the *key to countries* on the back cover flap, which lists countries alphabetically with their HDI rank.

Sources for all data used in the indicator tables are given in short citations at the end of each table. These correspond to full references in the *statistical references.* When an agency provides data it has collected from another source, both sources are credited in the table notes. But when an agency has built on the work of many other contributors, only the ultimate source is given. The source notes also show the original data components used in any calculations by the Human Development Report Office to ensure that all calculations can be easily replicated.

Indicators for which short, meaningful definitions can be given are included in the *definitions of statistical terms.* All other relevant information appears in the notes at the end of each table.

In the absence of the words *annual, annual rate* or *growth rate,* a hyphen between two years, such as in 1995-2000, indicates that the data were collected during one of the years shown. A slash between two years, such as in 1998/2001, indicates an average for the years

BOX 6

The International Comparison Program

The International Comparison Program is a global statistical initiative begun in the early 1970s. It aims to facilitate cross-country comparisons of economic aggregates by producing internationally comparable price levels, expenditure values and purchasing power parity (PPP) estimates. Through purchasing power parity exchange rates, which are the number of units of a country's money required to buy the same quantity of goods and services as $1 buys in the United States, countries can be compared in real terms, free of price and exchange rate distortions. This is particularly important when studying differences in income, poverty, inequality and expenditure patterns among countries.

Over the past 30 years, the International Comparison Program has grown from a pilot study to a global project. The programme has become an integral part of national statistical work in Organisation for Economic Co-operation and Development (OECD) countries, and much progress has been made in many developing countries. By the time of the last round of international comparisons during 1993 and 1996, 118 countries from all regions of the world were participating in the programme. Yet, the current set of PPP data is still lacking in universal coverage, timeliness and uniformity of quality across regions and countries. Gaps in country coverage of benchmark surveys have been filled with econometric estimates, which are then extrapolated over time. These results are becoming increasingly weak as the distance grows between the reference survey year and the current year.

The importance of purchasing power parities in economic analysis underlines the need for improvement in PPP data. A new International Comparison Program strategic framework has been developed through a global consultative process for improving the methodology and implementation of the exercise and the quality of its outputs. The framework sets out remedial actions for international and regional agencies as well as national partners. The immediate objective is to organize the collection of economic statistics for the new Millennium Round (2003–06), to meet the urgent demand for reliable and timely data to support tracking progress on the Millennium Development Goals. The ultimate objectives are to strengthen national statistical capacity in price and national accounts and make the programme an integral part of national statistical systems, to bring purchasing power parities for the poor into the mainstream of the programme and to promote the use of International Comparison Program data for economic analysis at national, regional and international levels. More than 160 countries (including OECD members) intend to take part in the new round.

Promising research is under way to integrate poverty-specific PPPs within the mainstream of the International Comparison Program work. The results of two pilot studies conducted in Asia and Africa show that poverty-specific PPPs can be generated using data from household expenditure surveys and International Comparison Program sources. The findings of these studies provide a promising approach that can be used for poverty analysis within and across countries.

Source: World Bank 2004d.

---

shown unless otherwise specified. The following symbols are used:

    ..   Data not available.

    (.) Less than half the unit shown.

    <   Less than.

    –   Not applicable.

    T   Total.

Unless otherwise indicated, data for China do not include Hong Kong, China (SAR), Macau, China (SAR) or Taiwan (province of China). In most cases data for Eritrea before 1992 are included in the data for Ethiopia. Data for Indonesia include Timor-Leste through 1999. Data for Jordan refer to the East Bank only. Data for Sudan are often based on information collected from the Northern part of the country. Economic data for Tanzania cover the mainland only. And data for the Republic of Yemen refer to that country from 1990 onward, while data for earlier years refer to aggregated data for the former People's Democratic Republic of Yemen and the former Yemen Arab Republic.

As a result of periodic revisions of data by international agencies, statistics presented in different editions of the Report may not be comparable. For this reason the Human Development Report Office strongly advises against constructing trend analyses based on data from different editions.

HDI values and ranks similarly are not comparable across editions of the Report. For trend analysis based on consistent data and methodology, refer to indicator table 2 (Human development index trends). The HDI values and ranks recalculated for 2001 (the reference year for the HDI in *Human Development Report 2003*) based on data and country coverage comparable to this year's Report are available on the HDRO website [http://hdr.undp.org/].

The data presented in the human development indicator tables are those available to the Human Development Report Office as of 1 April 2004, unless otherwise specified.

CALCULATING THE HUMAN DEVELOPMENT INDICES

The diagrams here offer a clear overview of how the five human development indices
used in the *Human Development Report* are constructed, highlighting both their similarities
and their differences. The text on the following pages provides a detailed explanation.

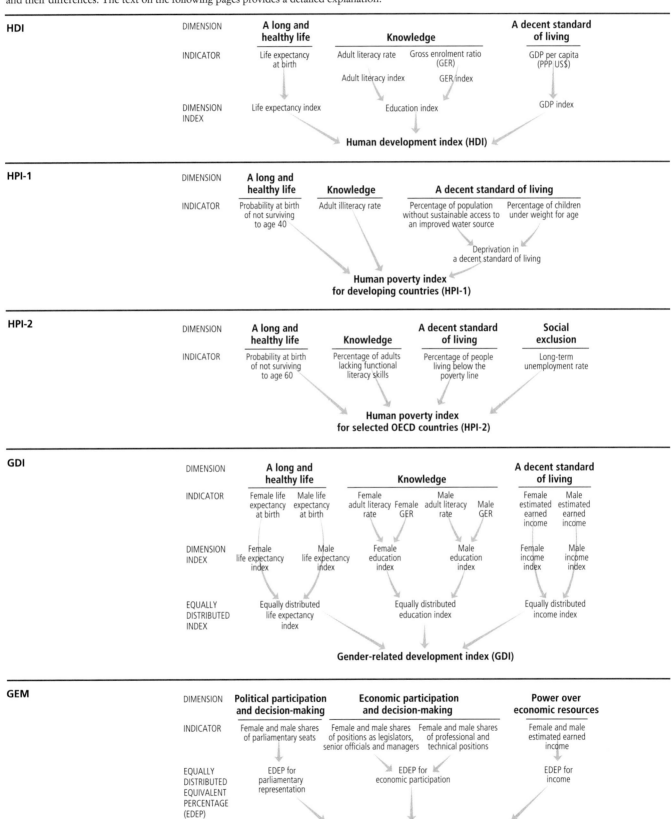

The human development index (HDI)

The HDI is a summary measure of human development. It measures the average achievements in a country in three basic dimensions of human development:

• A long and healthy life, as measured by life expectancy at birth.
• Knowledge, as measured by the adult literacy rate (with two-thirds weight) and the combined primary, secondary and tertiary gross enrolment ratio (with one-third weight).
• A decent standard of living, as measured by GDP per capita (PPP US$).

Before the HDI itself is calculated, an index needs to be created for each of these dimensions. To calculate these dimension indices —the life expectancy, education and GDP indices—minimum and maximum values (goalposts) are chosen for each underlying indicator.

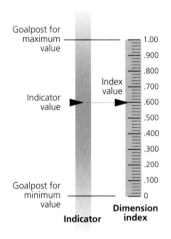

Performance in each dimension is expressed as a value between 0 and 1 by applying the following general formula:

$$\text{Dimension index} = \frac{\text{actual value} - \text{minimum value}}{\text{maximum value} - \text{minimum value}}$$

The HDI is then calculated as a simple average of the dimension indices. The box at right illustrates the calculation of the HDI for a sample country.

Goalposts for calculating the HDI

Indicator	Maximum value	Minimum value
Life expectancy at birth (years)	85	25
Adult literacy rate (%)	100	0
Combined gross enrolment ratio (%)	100	0
GDP per capita (PPP US$)	40,000	100

Calculating the HDI

This illustration of the calculation of the HDI uses data for Costa Rica.

1. Calculating the life expectancy index
The life expectancy index measures the relative achievement of a country in life expectancy at birth. For Costa Rica, with a life expectancy of 78.0 years in 2002, the life expectancy index is 0.884.

$$\text{Life expectancy index} = \frac{78.0 - 25}{85 - 25} = \mathbf{0.884}$$

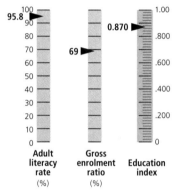

2. Calculating the education index
The education index measures a country's relative achievement in both adult literacy and combined primary, secondary and tertiary gross enrolment. First, an index for adult literacy and one for combined gross enrolment are calculated. Then these two indices are combined to create the education index, with two-thirds weight given to adult literacy and one-third weight to combined gross enrolment. For Costa Rica, with an adult literacy rate of 95.8% in 2002 and a combined gross enrolment ratio of 69% in the school year 2001/02, the education index is 0.870.

$$\text{Adult literacy index} = \frac{95.8 - 0}{100 - 0} = 0.958$$

$$\text{Gross enrolment index} = \frac{69 - 0}{100 - 0} = 0.690$$

Education index = 2/3 (adult literacy index) + 1/3 (gross enrolment index)
= 2/3 (0.958) + 1/3 (0.690) = **0.870**

3. Calculating the GDP index
The GDP index is calculated using adjusted GDP per capita (PPP US$). In the HDI income serves as a surrogate for all the dimensions of human development not reflected in a long and healthy life and in knowledge. Income is adjusted because achieving a respectable level of human development does not require unlimited income. Accordingly, the logarithm of income is used. For Costa Rica, with a GDP per capita of $8,840 (PPP US$) in 2002, the GDP index is 0.748.

$$\text{GDP index} = \frac{\log (8,840) - \log (100)}{\log (40,000) - \log (100)} = \mathbf{0.748}$$

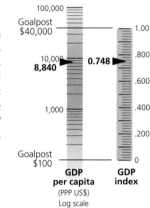

4. Calculating the HDI
Once the dimension indices have been calculated, determining the HDI is straightforward. It is a simple average of the three dimension indices.

HDI = 1/3 (life expectancy index) + 1/3 (education index) + 1/3 (GDP index)
= 1/3 (0.884) + 1/3 (0.870) + 1/3 (0.748) = **0.834**

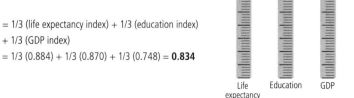

The human poverty index for developing countries (HPI-1)

While the HDI measures average achievement, the HPI-1 measures *deprivations* in the three basic dimensions of human development captured in the HDI:

• A long and healthy life—vulnerability to death at a relatively early age, as measured by the probability at birth of not surviving to age 40.
• Knowledge—exclusion from the world of reading and communications, as measured by the adult illiteracy rate.
• A decent standard of living—lack of access to overall economic provisioning, as measured by the unweighted average of two indicators, the percentage of the population without sustainable access to an improved water source and the percentage of children under weight for age.

Calculating the HPI-1 is more straightforward than calculating the HDI. The indicators used to measure the deprivations are already normalized between 0 and 100 (because they are expressed as percentages), so there is no need to create dimension indices as for the HDI.

Originally, the measure of deprivation in a decent standard of living also included an indicator of access to health services. But because reliable data on access to health services are lacking for recent years, in this year's Report deprivation in a decent standard of living is measured by two rather than three indicators—the percentage of the population without sustainable access to an improved water source and the percentage of children under weight for age.

The human poverty index for selected OECD countries (HPI-2)

The HPI-2 measures deprivations in the same dimensions as the HPI-1 and also captures social exclusion. Thus it reflects deprivations in four dimensions:

• A long and healthy life—vulnerability to death at a relatively early age, as measured by the probability at birth of not surviving to age 60.
• Knowledge—exclusion from the world of reading and communications, as measured by the percentage of adults (aged 16–65) lacking functional literacy skills.
• A decent standard of living—as measured by the percentage of people living below the income poverty line (50% of the median adjusted household disposable income).
• Social exclusion—as measured by the rate of long-term unemployment (12 months or more).

Calculating the HPI-1

1. Measuring deprivation in a decent standard of living

An unweighted average of two indicators is used to measure deprivation in a decent standard of living.

$$\text{Unweighted average} = 1/2 \text{ (population without sustainable access to an improved water source)} + 1/2 \text{ (children under weight for age)}$$

A sample calculation: Cambodia
Population without sustainable access to an improved water source = 70%
Children under weight for age = 45%

$$\text{Unweighted average} = 1/2 \, (70) + 1/2 \, (45) = 57.5\%$$

2. Calculating the HPI-1

The formula for calculating the HPI-1 is as follows:

$$\text{HPI-1} = [1/3 \, (P_1^{\alpha} + P_2^{\alpha} + P_3^{\alpha})]^{1/\alpha}$$

Where:
P_1 = Probability at birth of not surviving to age 40 (times 100)
P_2 = Adult illiteracy rate
P_3 = Unweighted average of population without sustainable access to an improved water source and children under weight for age
$\alpha = 3$

A sample calculation: Cambodia
P_1 = 24.0%
P_2 = 30.6%
P_3 = 57.5%

$$\text{HPI-1} = [1/3 \, (24.0^3 + 30.6^3 + 57.5^3)]^{1/3} = \textbf{42.6}$$

Calculating the HPI-2

The formula for calculating the HPI-2 is as follows:

$$\text{HPI-2} = [1/4 \, (P_1^{\alpha} + P_2^{\alpha} + P_3^{\alpha} + P_4^{\alpha})]^{1/\alpha}$$

Where:
P_1 = Probability at birth of not surviving to age 60 (times 100)
P_2 = Adults lacking functional literacy skills
P_3 = Population below income poverty line (50% of median adjusted household disposable income)
P_4 = Rate of long-term unemployment (lasting 12 months or more)
$\alpha = 3$

A sample calculation: Canada
P_1 = 8.7%
P_2 = 16.6%
P_3 = 12.8%
P_4 = 0.7%

$$\text{HPI-2} = [1/4 \, (8.7^3 + 16.6^3 + 12.8^3 + 0.7^3)]^{1/3} = \textbf{12.2}$$

Why $\alpha = 3$ in calculating the HPI-1 and HPI-2

The value of α has an important impact on the value of the HPI. If $\alpha = 1$, the HPI is the average of its dimensions. As α rises, greater weight is given to the dimension in which there is the most deprivation. Thus as α increases towards infinity, the HPI will tend towards the value of the dimension in which deprivation is greatest (for Cambodia, the example used for calculating the HPI-1, it would be 57.5%, equal to the unweighted average of population without sustainable access to an improved water source and children underweight for age.

In this Report the value 3 is used to give additional but not overwhelming weight to areas of more acute deprivation. For a detailed analysis of the HPI's mathematical formulation, see Sudhir Anand and Amartya Sen's "Concepts of Human Development and Poverty: A Multidimensional Perspective" and the technical note in *Human Development Report 1997* (see the list of selected readings at the end of this technical note).

The gender-related development index (GDI)

While the HDI measures average achievement, the GDI adjusts the average achievement to reflect the *inequalities* between men and women in the following dimensions:

• A long and healthy life, as measured by life expectancy at birth.
• Knowledge, as measured by the adult literacy rate and the combined primary, secondary and tertiary gross enrolment ratio.
• A decent standard of living, as measured by estimated earned income (PPP US$).

The calculation of the GDI involves three steps. First, female and male indices in each dimension are calculated according to this general formula:

$$\text{Dimension index} = \frac{\text{actual value} - \text{minimum value}}{\text{maximum value} - \text{minimum value}}$$

Second, the female and male indices in each dimension are combined in a way that penalizes differences in achievement between men and women. The resulting index, referred to as the equally distributed index, is calculated according to this general formula:

Equally distributed index
$= \{[\text{female population share (female index}^{1-\epsilon})]$
$+ [\text{male population share (male index}^{1-\epsilon})]\}^{1/1-\epsilon}$

ϵ measures the aversion to inequality. In the GDI $\epsilon = 2$. Thus the general equation becomes:

Equally distributed index
$= \{[\text{female population share (female index}^{-1})]$
$+ [\text{male population share (male index}^{-1})]\}^{-1}$

which gives the harmonic mean of the female and male indices.

Third, the GDI is calculated by combining the three equally distributed indices in an unweighted average.

Goalposts for calculating the GDI

Indicator	Maximum value	Minimum value
Female life expectancy at birth (years)	87.5	27.5
Male life expectancy at birth (years)	82.5	22.5
Adult literacy rate (%)	100	0
Combined gross enrolment ratio (%)	100	0
Estimated earned income (PPP US$)	40,000	100

Note: The maximum and minimum values (goalposts) for life expectancy are five years higher for women to take into account their longer life expectancy.

Calculating the GDI

This illustration of the calculation of the GDI uses data for Turkey.

1. Calculating the equally distributed life expectancy index

The first step is to calculate separate indices for female and male achievements in life expectancy, using the general formula for dimension indices.

FEMALE
Life expectancy: 73.1 years

Life expectancy index $= \dfrac{73.1 - 27.5}{87.5 - 27.5} = 0.760$

MALE
Life expectancy: 67.9 years

Life expectancy index $= \dfrac{67.9 - 22.5}{82.5 - 22.5} = 0.757$

Next, the female and male indices are combined to create the equally distributed life expectancy index, using the general formula for equally distributed indices.

FEMALE
Population share: 0.496
Life expectancy index: 0.760

MALE
Population share: 0.504
Life expectancy index: 0.757

Equally distributed life expectancy index $= \{[0.496 \, (0.760^{-1})] + [0.504 \, (0.757^{-1})]\}^{-1} = \mathbf{0.758}$

2. Calculating the equally distributed education index

First, indices for the adult literacy rate and the combined primary, secondary and tertiary gross enrolment ratio are calculated separately for females and males. Calculating these indices is straightforward, since the indicators used are already normalized between 0 and 100.

FEMALE
Adult literacy rate: 78.5%
Adult literacy index: 0.785
Gross enrolment ratio: 61.8%
Gross enrolment index: 0.618

MALE
Adult literacy rate: 94.4%
Adult literacy index: 0.944
Gross enrolment ratio: 73.5%
Gross enrolment index: 0.735

Second, the education index, which gives two-thirds weight to the adult literacy index and one-third weight to the gross enrolment index, is computed separately for females and males.

Education index $= 2/3 \, (\text{adult literacy index}) + 1/3 \, (\text{gross enrolment index})$

Female education index $= 2/3 \, (0.785) + 1/3 \, (0.618) = 0.729$

Male education index $= 2/3 \, (0.944) + 1/3 \, (0.735) = 0.874$

Finally, the female and male education indices are combined to create the equally distributed education index.

FEMALE
Population share: 0.496
Education index: 0.729

MALE
Population share: 0.504
Education index: 0.874

Equally distributed education index $= \{[0.496 \, (0.729^{-1})] + [0.504 \, (0.874^{-1})]\}^{-1} = \mathbf{0.796}$

3. Calculating the equally distributed income index

First, female and male earned income (PPP US$) are estimated (for details on this calculation, see the addendum to this technical note). Then the income index is calculated for each gender. As for the HDI, income is adjusted by taking the logarithm of estimated earned income (PPP US$):

$$\text{Income index} = \frac{\log (\text{actual value}) - \log (\text{minimum value})}{\log (\text{maximum value}) - \log (\text{minimum value})}$$

FEMALE
Estimated earned income (PPP US$): 4,757

MALE
Estimated earned income (PPP US$): 7,873

Income index $= \dfrac{\log (4,757) - \log (100)}{\log (40,000) - \log (100)} = 0.645$

Income index $= \dfrac{\log (7,873) - \log (100)}{\log (40,000) - \log (100)} = 0.729$

Calculating the GDI continues on next page

Calculating the GDI (continued)

Second, the female and male income indices are combined to create the equally distributed income index:

FEMALE
Population share: 0.496
Income index: 0.645

MALE
Population share: 0.504
Income index: 0.729

$$\text{Equally distributed income index} = \{[0.496\,(0.645^{-1})] + [0.504\,(0.729^{-1})]\}^{-1} = \textbf{0.685}$$

4. Calculating the GDI

Calculating the GDI is straightforward. It is simply the unweighted average of the three component indices—the equally distributed life expectancy index, the equally distributed education index and the equally distributed income index.

$$\text{GDI} = 1/3\,(\text{life expectancy index}) + 1/3\,(\text{education index}) + 1/3\,(\text{income index})$$
$$= 1/3\,(0.758) + 1/3\,(0.796) + 1/3\,(0.685) = \textbf{0.746}$$

Why $\in = 2$ in calculating the GDI

The value of $\in$ is the size of the penalty for gender inequality. The larger the value, the more heavily a society is penalized for having inequalities.

If $\in = 0$, gender inequality is not penalized (in this case the GDI would have the same value as the HDI). As $\in$ increases towards infinity, more and more weight is given to the lesser achieving group.

The value 2 is used in calculating the GDI (as well as the GEM). This value places a moderate penalty on gender inequality in achievement.

For a detailed analysis of the GDI's mathematical formulation, see Sudhir Anand and Amartya Sen's "Gender Inequality in Human Development: Theories and Measurement," Kalpana Bardhan and Stephan Klasen's "UNDP's Gender-Related Indices: A Critical Review" and the technical notes in *Human Development Report 1995* and *Human Development Report 1999* (see the list of selected readings at the end of this technical note).

The gender empowerment measure (GEM)

Focusing on women's opportunities rather than their capabilities, the GEM captures gender inequality in three key areas:

• Political participation and decision-making power, as measured by women's and men's percentage shares of parliamentary seats.
• Economic participation and decision-making power, as measured by two indicators—women's and men's percentage shares of positions as legislators, senior officials and managers and women's and men's percentage shares of professional and technical positions.
• Power over economic resources, as measured by women's and men's estimated earned income (PPP US$).

For each of these three dimensions, an equally distributed equivalent percentage (EDEP) is calculated, as a population-weighted average, according to the following general formula:

$$EDEP = \{[\text{female population share (female index}^{1-\epsilon})] + [\text{male population share (male index}^{1-\epsilon})]\}^{1/1-\epsilon}$$

ϵ measures the aversion to inequality. In the GEM (as in the GDI) $\epsilon = 2$, which places a moderate penalty on inequality. The formula is thus:

$$EDEP = \{[\text{female population share (female index}^{-1})] + [\text{male population share (male index}^{-1})]\}^{-1}$$

For political and economic participation and decision-making, the EDEP is then indexed by dividing it by 50. The rationale for this indexation: in an ideal society, with equal empowerment of the sexes, the GEM variables would equal 50%—that is, women's share would equal men's share for each variable.

Where a male or female index value is zero, the EDEP according to the above formula is not defined. However, the limit of EDEP, when the index tends towards zero, is zero. Accordingly, in these cases the value of the EDEP is set to zero.

Finally, the GEM is calculated as a simple average of the three indexed EDEPs.

Calculating the GEM

This illustration of the calculation of the GEM uses data for Greece.

1. Calculating the EDEP for parliamentary representation

The EDEP for parliamentary representation measures the relative empowerment of women in terms of their political participation. The EDEP is calculated using the female and male shares of the population and female and male percentage shares of parliamentary seats according to the general formula.

FEMALE	MALE
Population share: 0.507	Population share: 0.492
Parliamentary share: 8.7%	Parliamentary share: 91.3%

$$\text{EDEP for parliamentary representation} = \{[0.507\,(8.7^{-1})] + [0.492\,(91.3^{-1})]\}^{-1} = 15.70$$

Then this initial EDEP is indexed to an ideal value of 50%.

$$\text{Indexed EDEP for parliamentary representation} = \frac{15.70}{50} = \mathbf{0.314}$$

2. Calculating the EDEP for economic participation

Using the general formula, an EDEP is calculated for women's and men's percentage shares of positions as legislators, senior officials and managers, and another for women's and men's percentage shares of professional and technical positions. The simple average of the two measures gives the EDEP for economic participation.

FEMALE	MALE
Population share: 0.507	Population share: 0.492
Percentage share of positions as legislators, senior officials and managers: 25.6%	Percentage share of positions as legislators, senior officials and managers: 74.4%
Percentage share of professional and technical positions: 47.9%	Percentage share of professional and technical positions: 52.1%

$$\text{EDEP for positions as legislators, senior officials and managers} = \{[0.507\,(25.6^{-1})] + [0.492\,(74.4^{-1})]\}^{-1} = 37.82$$

$$\text{Indexed EDEP for positions as legislators, senior officials and managers} = \frac{37.82}{50} = 0.756$$

$$\text{EDEP for professional and technical positions} = \{[0.507\,(47.9^{-1})] + [0.492\,(52.1^{-1})]\}^{-1} = 49.88$$

$$\text{Indexed EDEP for professional and technical positions} = \frac{49.88}{50} = 0.998$$

The two indexed EDEPs are averaged to create the EDEP for economic participation:

$$\text{EDEP for economic participation} = \frac{0.756 + 0.998}{2} = \mathbf{0.877}$$

3. Calculating the EDEP for income

Earned income (PPP US$) is estimated for women and men separately and then indexed to goalposts as for the HDI and the GDI. For the GEM, however, the income index is based on unadjusted values, not the logarithm of estimated earned income. (For details on the estimation of earned income for men and women, see the addendum to this technical note.)

FEMALE	MALE
Population share: 0.507	Population share: 0.492
Estimated earned income (PPP US$): 10,892	Estimated earned income (PPP US$): 25,601

$$\text{Income index} = \frac{10,892 - 100}{40,000 - 100} = 0.270 \qquad \text{Income index} = \frac{25,601 - 100}{40,000 - 100} = 0.639$$

The female and male indices are then combined to create the equally distributed index:

$$\text{EDEP for income} = \{[0.507\,(0.270^{-1})] + [0.492\,(0.639^{-1})]\}^{-1} = \mathbf{0.377}$$

4. Calculating the GEM

Once the EDEP has been calculated for the three dimensions of the GEM, determining the GEM is straightforward. It is a simple average of the three EDEP indices.

$$GEM = \frac{0.314 + 0.877 + 0.377}{3} = \mathbf{0.523}$$

Female and male earned income

Despite the importance of having gender-disaggregated data on income, direct measures are unavailable. For this Report crude estimates of female and male earned income have therefore been derived.

Income can be seen in two ways: as a resource for consumption and as earnings by individuals. The use measure is difficult to disaggregate between men and women because they share resources within a family unit. By contrast, earnings are separable because different members of a family tend to have separate earned incomes.

The income measure used in the GDI and the GEM indicates a person's capacity to earn income. It is used in the GDI to capture the disparities between men and women in command over resources and in the GEM to capture women's economic independence. (For conceptual and methodological issues relating to this approach, see Sudhir Anand and Amartya Sen's "Gender Inequality in Human Development" and, in *Human Development Report 1995,* chapter 3 and technical notes 1 and 2; see the list of selected readings at the end of this technical note.)

Female and male earned income (PPP US$) are estimated using the following data:

- Ratio of the female non-agricultural wage to the male non-agricultural wage.
- Male and female shares of the economically active population.
- Total female and male population.
- GDP per capita (PPP US$).

Key

W_f / W_m = ratio of female non-agricultural wage to male non-agricultural wage
EA_f = female share of economically active population
EA_m = male share of economically active population
S_f = female share of wage bill
Y = total GDP (PPP US$)
N_f = total female population
N_m = total male population
Y_f = estimated female earned income (PPP US$)
Y_m = estimated male earned income (PPP US$)

Note

Calculations based on data in the technical note may yield results that differ from those in the indicator tables because of rounding.

Estimating female and male earned income

This illustration of the estimation of female and male earned income uses 2002 data for Philippines.

1. Calculating total GDP (PPP US$)
Total GDP (PPP US$) is calculated by multiplying the total population by GDP per capita (PPP US$).

Total population: 79,944 (thousand)
GDP per capita (PPP US$): 4,170
Total GDP (PPP US$) = 4,170 (79,944) = 333,366,480 (thousand)

2. Calculating the female share of the wage bill
Because data on wages in rural areas and in the informal sector are rare, the Report has used non-agricultural wages and assumed that the ratio of female wages to male wages in the non-agricultural sector applies to the rest of the economy. The female share of the wage bill is calculated using the ratio of the female non-agricultural wage to the male non-agricultural wage and the female and male percentage shares of the economically active population. Where data on the wage ratio are not available, a value of 75% is used.

Ratio of female to male non-agricultural wage (W_f/W_m) = 0.94
Female percentage share of economically active population (EA_f) = 38.2%
Male percentage share of economically active population (EA_m) = 61.8%

$$\text{Female share of wage bill } (S_f) = \frac{W_f/W_m (EA_f)}{[W_f/W_m (EA_f)] + EA_m} = \frac{0.94 (38.2)}{[0.94 (61.8)] + 61.8} = \mathbf{0.368}$$

3. Calculating female and male earned income (PPP US$)
An assumption has to be made that the female share of the wage bill is equal to the female share of GDP.

Female share of wage bill (S_f) = 0.368
Total GDP (PPP US$) (Y) = 333,366,480 (thousand)
Female population (N_f) = 39,014 (thousand)

$$\text{Estimated female earned income (PPP US$) } (Y_f) = \frac{S_f(Y)}{N_f} = \frac{0.368 (333,366,480)}{39,014} = \mathbf{3,144}$$

Male population (N_m) = 39,566 (thousand)

$$\text{Estimated male earned income (PPP US$) } (Y_m) = \frac{Y - S_f(Y)}{N_m} = \frac{333,366,480 - [0.368 (333,366,480)]}{39,586} = \mathbf{5,326}$$

Selected readings

Anand, Sudhir, and Amartya Sen. 1994. "Human Development Index: Methodology and Measurement." Occasional Paper 12. United Nations Development Programme, Human Development Report Office, New York. *(HDI)*

———. 1995. "Gender Inequality in Human Development: Theories and Measurement." Occasional Paper 19. United Nations Development Programme, Human Development Report Office, New York. *(GDI, GEM)*

———. 1997. "Concepts of Human Development and Poverty: A Multi-dimensional Perspective." In United Nations Development Programme, *Human Development Report 1997 Papers: Poverty and Human Development.* New York. *(HPI-1, HPI-2)*

Bardhan, Kalpana, and Stephan Klasen. 1999. "UNDP's Gender-Related Indices: A Critical Review." *World Development* 27 (6): 985–1010. *(GDI, GEM)*

United Nations Development Programme. 1995. *Human Development Report 1995.* New York: Oxford University Press. Technical notes 1 and 2 and chapter 3. *(GDI, GEM)*

———. 1997. *Human Development Report 1997.* New York: Oxford University Press. Technical note 1 and chapter 1. *(HPI-1, HPI-2)*

———. 1999. *Human Development Report 1999.* New York: Oxford University Press. Technical note. *(HDI, GDI)*

IDENTIFYING TOP PRIORITY AND HIGH PRIORITY COUNTRIES FOR THE MILLENNIUM DEVELOPMENT GOALS

This year's *Human Development Report* identifies countries that are *top priority* and *high priority* for each Millennium Development Goal for which there are sufficient data, based on human poverty in each goal and trends in the 1990s. Based on the goal-by-goal analysis, the Report then identifies countries that are top priority and high priority overall.

Assessing countries as top priority and high priority for each Goal

For each Millennium Development Goal the assessment of a country is based both on its progress towards the goal—slow or reversing, moderate, fast—and on its level of human poverty in the goal—extreme, medium, low (technical note tables 2.1 and 2.2). Progress is measured against the targets and using the indicators defined for the Millennium Development Goals.

Top priority countries for each goal
A country is designated top priority for a goal if it has both extreme human poverty in that goal and slow or reversing progress towards it (technical note figure 2.1).

High priority countries for each goal
A country is designated high priority for a goal if:
• It has extreme human poverty in that goal and moderate progress towards it.

• Or it has medium human poverty in that goal and slow or reversing progress towards it.

Assessing countries as top priority and high priority across all the Goals

The assessment of whether a country is top priority or high priority for all the goals is based on the number of goals for which the country is top priority or high priority. (This overall assessment includes data for the HIV/AIDS target, though it is not assessed separately).

Top priority countries across all the goals
A country is designated top priority across all the goals if:
• It is top priority for at least three goals.
• Or it is top priority for half or more of the goals for which at least three data points are available for that country.
• Or, where data are available for only two goals, it is top priority for both.

High priority countries across all the goals
A country is designated high priority across all the goals if it does not fall into the top priority category but:
• I is top or high priority for at least three goals.
• Or it is top priority for two goals.
• Or it is top or high priority for half or more of the goals for which at least three data points are available for that country.
• Or, where data are available for only two goals, it is top or high priority for both.

Technical note table 2.1
Defining progress towards the Millennium Development Goals

Rate of progress	Definition
Slow or reversing	Actual progress towards the goal is *less than half* the approximate progress required to meet the target if current trends prevail until 2015.
Moderate	Actual progress towards the goal is *more than half but less than* the approximate progress required to meet the target if current trends prevail until 2015.
Fast	Actual progress towards the goal is *equal to or greater than* the approximate progress required to meet the target if current trends prevail until 2015.

Note: The year in which the target is to be met is 2015 for all except gender equality in education, for which it is 2005.

Technical note table 2.2
Defining the level of human poverty in the Millennium Development Goals

Target	Indicator	Level of human poverty (x = value of indicator)			Source
		Extreme	Medium	Low	
Halve the proportion of people whose income is less than $1 a day	GDP per capita (PPP US$)[a]	$x < 3,500$	$3,500 \leq x < 7,000$	$x \geq 7,000$	World Bank
Halve the proportion of people who suffer from hunger	Undernourished people (%)	$x > 25$	$10 < x \leq 25$	$x \leq 10$	Food and Agriculture Organization
Ensure that children everywhere will be able to complete a full course of primary schooling	Net primary enrolment ratio (%)	$x < 75$	$75 \leq x < 90$	$x \geq 90$	United Nations Educational, Scientific and Cultural Organization (UNESCO)
Achieve gender equality in education	Ratio of girls to boys in primary and secondary education (%)	$x < 80$	$80 \leq x < 90$	$x \geq 90$	UNESCO
Reduce under-five mortality by two-thirds	Under-five mortality rate (per 1,000 live births)	$x > 100$	$30 < x \leq 100$	$x \leq 30$	United Nations Children's Fund (UNICEF)
Halve the proportion of people without sustainable access to safe drinking water	Population with sustainable access to an improved water source (%)	$x < 75$	$75 \leq x < 90$	$x \geq 90$	UNICEF and World Health Organization (WHO)
Halve the proportion of people without access to improved sanitation	Population with sustainable access to improved sanitation (%)	$x < 75$	$75 \leq x < 90$	$x \geq 90$	UNICEF and WHO

a. The average annual GDP per capita growth rate is used as a trend measure.

Technical note figure 2.1
Identifying top priority and high priority countries

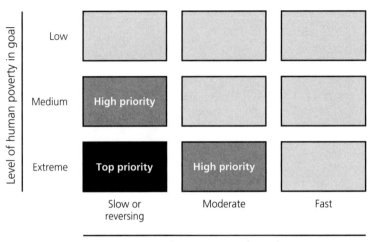

Calculating progress towards each goal

Progress towards each goal is assessed by comparing actual annual progress if current trends were to prevail until 2015 with the annual progress needed to meet the target, under the assumption of linear progress.

Assessing actual progress
The actual annual rate of progress is calculated using the general formula:

$$\text{Actual annual rate of progress} = \frac{(x_{t_1} - x_{t_0})\,/\,x_{t_0}}{t_1 - t_0}$$

where t_0 is 1990 or the year closest to 1990 for which data are available; t_1 is the most recent year for which data are available, generally 2001; and x_{t_0} and x_{t_1} are the values of the indicator for those years. For rates of hunger, poverty and under-five mortality, for which the most desirable value is 0, the formula is applied without modification.

For the net primary enrolment ratio, gender equality in education (ratio of girls to boys) and the proportion of the population with access to safe water and sanitation, for which the most desirable value is 100%, progress is expressed as "shortfall reduction" according to the following formula:

$$\text{Actual annual rate of progress} = \frac{(x_{t_1} - x_{t_0})\,/\,(100 - x_{t_0})}{t_1 - t_0}$$

Assessing required progress
The rate of progress required to meet a target by 2015 (by 2005 for gender equality in education) is dictated by the target: α is $-1/2$ for poverty and hunger, $1/2$ for safe water and sanitation, $-2/3$ for under-five mortality and 1 for primary enrolment and gender equality in education. The annual rate of progress required is then calculated by simply dividing α by the number of years between t_{MDG}, the year by which the target is to be met, and t_0, the year closest to 1990 for which data are available:

$$\text{Required annual rate of progress} = \frac{\alpha}{t_{\text{MDG}} - t_0}$$

Determining priority status: an example

This illustration of determining priority status uses data on the under-five mortality rate for Chad.

Calculating progress
Data for the under-five mortality rate are available for 1990 and 2002:
$t_0 = 1990$
$t_1 = 2002$

The under-five mortality rate is 203 per 1,000 live births for 1990 and 200 for 2002:
$x_{t_0} = 203$
$x_{t_1} = 200$

The required reduction is two-thirds:
$\alpha = -2/3$

Therefore:

$$\text{Actual annual rate of progress} = \frac{(200 - 203) \div 203}{2002 - 1990} = -0.12 \text{ percentage points}$$

$$\text{Required annual rate of progress} = \frac{-2/3}{2015 - 1990} = -2.67 \text{ percentage points}$$

The actual progress towards the goal is less than half the approximate progress required to meet the target.
  Therefore, Chad is making slow or reversing progress towards the goal of reducing under-five mortality.

Determining the level of human poverty
The under-five mortality rate for Chad in 2002 is 200 per 1,000 live births.
  Therefore, Chad has an extreme level of human poverty in under-five mortality (see technical note table 2.2).

Determining the priority status for under-five mortality
Chad has an extreme level of human poverty in under-five mortality and slow or reversing progress.
  Therefore, Chad is categorized as top priority for the goal of reducing under-five mortality.

Determining the priority status across all goals
Of the eight indicators for which Chad has data, it is identified as top priority for two and high priority for another six.
  Therefore, Chad is categorized as a high priority country overall.

Note

To measure progress in income poverty, the GDP per capita growth rate in 1990–2002 is used. It is estimated that average annual growth of 1.4% is required in 1990–2015 to meet the income poverty target. Accordingly, the threshold for slow or reversing progress is annual per capita income growth of less than 0.7%; for moderate progress, 0.7% to 1.4%; and for fast progress, 1.4% or more.
Trend data for the prevalence of HIV/AIDS among adults (age 15 and above) in 1990 and 2000 are also used in the overall assessment of countries as top priority and high priority (UNAIDS and WHO 2003). For determining the level of human poverty in HIV/AIDS, a prevalence rate of more than 3% is considered extreme; 3% or less but greater than 1%, medium; and 1% or less, low. Since the target is to halt and begin to reverse the spread of HIV/AIDS, an increase in the prevalence rate of less than 1 percentage point is considered fast progress; an increase of 1 percentage point or more but less than 3, moderate progress; and an increase of 3 percentage points or more, slow or reversing progress.

Definitions of statistical terms

Armed forces, total Strategic, land, naval, air, command, administrative and support forces. Also included are paramilitary forces such as the gendarmerie, customs service and border guard, if these are trained in military tactics.

Arms transfers, conventional Refers to the voluntary transfer by the supplier (and thus excludes captured weapons and weapons obtained through defectors) of weapons with a military purpose destined for the armed forces, paramilitary forces or intelligence agencies of another country. These include major conventional weapons or systems in six categories: ships, aircraft, missiles, artillery, armoured vehicles and guidance and radar systems (excluded are trucks, services, ammunition, small arms, support items, components and component technology and towed or naval artillery under 100-millimetre calibre).

Births attended by skilled health personnel The percentage of deliveries attended by personnel (including doctors, nurses and midwives) trained to give the necessary care, supervision and advice to women during pregnancy, labour and the postpartum period, to conduct deliveries on their own and to care for newborns.

Birthweight, infants with low The percentage of infants with a birthweight of less than 2,500 grams.

Carbon dioxide emissions Anthropogenic (human-originated) carbon dioxide emissions stemming from the burning of fossil fuels, gas flaring and the production of cement. Emissions are calculated from data on the consumption of solid, liquid and gaseous fuels, gas flaring and the production of cement.

Cellular subscribers (also referred to as cellular mobile subscribers) Subscribers to an automatic public mobile telephone service that provides access to the public switched telephone network using cellular technology. Systems can be analogue or digital.

Children reaching grade 5 The percentage of children starting primary school who eventually attain grade 5 (grade 4 if the duration of primary school is

four years). The estimates are based on the reconstructed cohort method, which uses data on enrolment and repeaters for two consecutive years.

Consumer price index, average annual change in Reflects changes in the cost to the average consumer of acquiring a basket of goods and services that may be fixed or may change at specified intervals.

Condom use at last high-risk sex Men and women who say they used a condom the last time they had sex with a non-marital, non-cohabiting partner, of those who have had sex with such a partner in the last 12 months.

Contraceptive prevalence rate The percentage of married women (including women in union) ages 15–49 who are using, or whose partners are using, any form of contraception, whether modern or traditional.

Contributing family worker Defined according to the 1993 International Classification by Status in Employment (ICSE) as a person who works without pay in an economic enterprise operated by a related person living in the same household.

Crime, people victimized by The percentage of the population who perceive that they have been victimized by certain types of crime in the preceding year, based on responses to the International Crime Victims Survey.

Debt forgiveness, gross bilateral Forgiveness of bilateral debts of developing countries with the support of official funds of donor countries, whether owed to public or private creditors. Offsetting entries for official development assistance (ODA) principal are not subtracted. See *offficial development assistance (ODA), net.*

Debt relief committed under HIPC initiative Forgiveness of loans as a component of official development assistance under the Debt Initiative for Heavily Indebted Poor Countries (HIPCs). The initiative is the first comprehensive approach to reducing the external debt of the world's poorest, most heavily indebted countries, which total 42 in number.

Debt service, total The sum of principal repayments and interest actually paid in foreign currency, goods or services on long-term debt (having a maturity of more than one year), interest paid on short-term debt and repayments to the International Monetary Fund.

Drugs, affordable essential, population with sustainable access to The estimated percentage of the population for whom a minimum of 20 of the most essential drugs—those that satisfy the health care needs of the majority of the population—are continuously and affordably available at public or private health facilities or drug outlets within one hour's travel from home.

Earned income (PPP US$), estimated Roughly derived on the basis of the ratio of the female non-agricultural wage to the male non-agricultural wage, the female and male shares of the economically active population, total female and male population and GDP per capita (PPP US$). For details on this estimation, see *Technical note 1.*

Earned income, ratio of estimated female to male The ratio of estimated female earned income to estimated male earned income. See *earned income (PPP US$), estimated (female and male).*

Economic activity rate, female The share of the female population ages 15 and above who supply, or are available to supply, labour for the production of goods and services.

Education expenditure, public Includes both capital expenditures (spending on construction, renovation, major repairs and purchase of heavy equipment or vehicles) and current expenditures (spending on goods and services that are consumed within the current year and would need to be renewed the following year). It covers such expenditures as staff salaries and benefits, contracted or purchased services, books and teaching materials, welfare services, furniture and equipment, minor repairs, fuel, insurance, rents, telecommunications and travel. See *education levels.*

Education index One of the three indices on which the human development index is built. It is based on the adult literacy rate and the combined gross enrolment ratio for primary, secondary and tertiary schools. For details on how the index is calculated, see *Technical note 1.*

Education levels Categorized as pre-primary, primary, secondary or tertiary in accordance with the International Standard Classification of Education (ISCED). *Pre-primary education* (ISCED level 0) is provided at such schools as kindergartens and nursery and infant schools and is intended for children not old enough to enter school at the primary level. *Primary education* (ISCED level 1) provides the basic elements of education at such establishments as primary and elementary schools. *Secondary education* (ISCED levels 2 and 3) is based on at least four years of previous instruction at the first level and provides general or specialized instruction, or both, at such institutions as middle schools, secondary schools, high schools, teacher training schools at this level and vocational or technical schools. *Tertiary education* (ISCED levels 5–7) refers to education at such institutions as universities, teachers colleges and higher level professional schools—requiring as a minimum condition of admission the successful completion of education at the second level or evidence of the attainment of an equivalent level of knowledge.

Electricity consumption per capita Refers to gross production, in per capita terms, which includes consumption by station auxiliaries and any losses in the transformers that are considered integral parts of the station. Also included is total electric energy produced by pumping installations without deduction of electric energy absorbed by pumping.

Employment by economic activity, female Female employment in industry, agriculture or services as defined according to the International Standard Industrial Classification (ISIC) system (revisions 2 and 3). *Industry* refers to mining and quarrying, manufacturing, construction and public utilities (gas, water and electricity). *Agriculture* refers to activities in agriculture, hunting, forestry and fishing. *Services* refer to wholesale and retail trade; restaurants and hotels; transport, storage and communications; finance, insurance, real estate and business services; and community, social and personal services.

Energy requirements, total Energy consumption plus the traditional fuels which include fuelwood, charcoal, bagasse (sugar cane waste), animal, vegetal and other wastes.

Energy use, GDP per unit of The ratio of GDP (in 1995 PPP US$) to commercial energy use, measured in kilograms of oil equivalent. This ratio provides a measure of energy efficiency by showing comparable and consistent estimates of real GDP across countries relative to physical inputs (units of energy use). See *GDP (gross domestic product)* and *PPP (purchasing power parity).*

Enrolment ratio, gross The number of students enrolled in a level of education, regardless of age, as a percentage of the population of official school age for that level. The gross enrolment ratio can be greater than 100% as a result of grade repetition and entry at ages younger or older than the typical age at that grade level. See *education levels.*

Enrolment ratio, gross, combined for primary, secondary and tertiary schools The number of students enrolled in primary, secondary and tertiary levels of education, regardless of age, as a percentage of the population of official school age for the three levels. See *education levels* and *enrolment ratio, gross.*

Enrolment ratio, net The number of students enrolled in a level of education who are of official school age for that level, as a percentage of the population of official school age for that level. See *education levels.*

Environmental treaties, ratification of After signing a treaty, a country must ratify it, often with the approval of its legislature. Such process implies not only an expression of interest as indicated by the signature, but also the transformation of the treaty's principles and obligations into national law.

Exports, high technology Exports of products with a high intensity of research and development. They include high-technology products such as in aerospace, computers, pharmaceuticals, scientific instruments and electrical machinery.

Exports, manufactured Defined according to the Standard International Trade Classification to include exports of chemicals, basic manufactures, machinery and transport equipment and other miscellaneous manufactured goods.

Exports of goods and services The value of all goods and other market services provided to the rest of the world. Included is the value of merchandise, freight, insurance, transport, travel, royalties, licence fees and other services, such as communication, construction, financial, information, business, personal and government services. Excluded are labour and property income and transfer payments.

Exports, primary Defined according to the Standard International Trade Classification to include exports of food, agricultural raw materials, fuels and ores and metals.

Fertility rate, total The number of children that would be born to each woman if she were to live to the end of her child-bearing years and bear children at each age in accordance with prevailing age-specific fertility rates.

Foreign direct investment, net inflows of Net inflows of investment to acquire a lasting management interest (10% or more of voting stock) in an enterprise operating in an economy other than that of the investor. It is the sum of equity capital, reinvestment of earnings, other long-term capital and short-term capital.

Fuel consumption, traditional Estimated consumption of fuel wood, charcoal, bagasse (sugar cane waste) and animal and vegetable wastes. See *energy requirement, total.*

GDP (gross domestic product) The sum of value added by all resident producers in the economy plus any product taxes (less subsidies) not included in the valuation of output. It is calculated without making deductions for depreciation of fabricated capital assets or for depletion and degradation of natural resources. Value added is the net output of an industry after adding up all outputs and subtracting intermediate inputs.

GDP (US$) GDP converted to US dollars using the average official exchange rate reported by the International Monetary Fund. An alternative conversion factor is applied if the official exchange rate is judged to diverge by an exceptionally large margin from the rate effectively applied to transactions in foreign currencies and traded products. See *GDP (gross domestic product).*

GDP index One of the three indices on which the human development index is built. It is based on GDP per capita (PPP US$). For details on how the index is calculated, see *Technical note 1.*

GDP per capita (PPP US$) See *GDP (gross domestic product)* and *PPP (purchasing power parity).*

GDP per capita (US$) GDP (US$) divided by midyear population. See *GDP (US$).*

GDP per capita annual growth rate Least squares annual growth rate, calculated from constant price GDP per capita in local currency units.

Gender empowerment measure (GEM) A composite index measuring gender inequality in three basic dimensions of empowerment—economic participation and decision-making, political participation and decision-making and power over economic resources. For details on how the index is calculated, see *Technical note 1.*

Gender-related development index (GDI) A composite index measuring average achievement in the three basic dimensions captured in the human development index—a long and healthy life, knowledge and a decent standard of living—adjusted to account for inequalities between men and women. For details on how the index is calculated, see *Technical note 1.*

Gini index Measures the extent to which the distribution of income (or consumption) among individuals or households within a country deviates from a perfectly equal distribution. A Lorenz curve plots the cumulative percentages of total income received against the cumulative number of recipients, starting with the poorest individual or household. The Gini index measures the area between the Lorenz curve and a hypothetical line of absolute equality, expressed as a percentage of the maximum area under the line. A value of 0 represents perfect equality, a value of 100 perfect inequality.

GNI (gross national income) The sum of value added by all resident producers in the economy plus any product taxes (less subsidies) not included in the valuation of output plus net receipts of primary income (compensation of employees and property income) from abroad. Value added is the net output of an industry after adding up all outputs and subtracting intermediate inputs. Data are in current US dollars converted using the *World Bank Atlas* method.

Health expenditure per capita (PPP US$) The sum of public and private expenditure (in PPP US$), divided by the population. Health expenditure includes the provision of health services (preventive and curative), family planning activities, nutrition activities and emergency aid designated for health, but excludes the provision of water and sanitation. See *health expenditure, private; health expenditure, public;* and *PPP (purchasing power parity).*

Health expenditure, private Direct household (out of pocket) spending, private insurance, spending by non-profit institutions serving households and direct service payments by private corporations. Together with public health expenditure, it makes up total health expenditure. See *health expenditure per capita (PPP US$)* and *health expenditure, public.*

Health expenditure, public Current and capital spending from government (central and local) budgets, external borrowings and grants (including donations from international agencies and non-governmental organizations) and social (or compulsory) health insurance funds. Together with private health expenditure, it makes up total health expen-

diture. See *health expenditure per capita (PPP US$)* and *health expenditure, private.*

HIPC completion point The date at which a country included in the Debt Initiative for Heavily Indebted Poor Countries (HIPCs) successfully completes the key structural reforms agreed on at the HIPC decision point, including developing and implementing a poverty reduction strategy. The country then receives the bulk of its debt relief under the HIPC Initiative without further policy conditions.

HIPC decision point The date at which a heavily indebted poor country with an established track record of good performance under adjustment programmes supported by the International Monetary Fund and the World Bank commits, under the Debt Initiative for Heavily Indebted Poor Countries (HIPCs), to undertake additional reforms and to develop and implement a poverty reduction strategy.

HIPC trust fund, bilateral pledges to the A firm obligation undertaken by an official donor to provide specified assistance to the HIPC trust fund. Bilateral commitments are recorded in the full amount of expected transfer, irrespective of the time required for the completion of disbursements.

HIV prevalence The percentage of people ages 15–49 who are infected with HIV.

Human development index (HDI) A composite index measuring average achievement in three basic dimensions of human development—a long and healthy life, knowledge and a decent standard of living. For details on how the index is calculated, see *Technical note 1.*

Human poverty index (HPI-1) for developing countries A composite index measuring deprivations in the three basic dimensions captured in the human development index—a long and healthy life, knowledge and a decent standard of living. For details on how the index is calculated, see *Technical note 1.*

Human poverty index (HPI-2) for selected high-income OECD countries A composite index measuring deprivations in the three basic dimensions captured in the human development index— a long and healthy life, knowledge and a decent standard of living—and also capturing social exclusion. For details on how the index is calculated, see *Technical note 1.*

Illiteracy rate, adult Calculated as 100 minus the

adult literacy rate. See *literacy rate, adult.*

Immunization, one-year-olds fully immunized against measles or tuberculosis One-year-olds injected with an antigen or a serum containing specific antibodies against measles or tuberculosis.

Imports of goods and services The value of all goods and other market services received from the rest of the world. Included is the value of merchandise, freight, insurance, transport, travel, royalties, licence fees and other services, such as communication, construction, financial, information, business, personal and government services. Excluded are labour and property income and transfer payments.

Income poverty line, population below The percentage of the population living below the specified poverty line:

- $1 a day—at 1985 international prices (equivalent to $1.08 at 1993 international prices), adjusted for purchasing power parity.
- $2 a day—at 1985 international prices (equivalent to $2.15 at 1993 international prices), adjusted for purchasing power parity.
- $4 a day—at 1990 international prices, adjusted for purchasing power parity.
- $11 a day (per person for a family of three)—at 1994 international prices, adjusted for purchasing power parity.
- National poverty line—the poverty line deemed appropriate for a country by its authorities. National estimates are based on population-weighted subgroup estimates from household surveys.
- 50% of median income—50% of the median adjusted disposable household income.

See *PPP (purchasing power parity).*

Income or consumption, shares of The shares of income or consumption accruing to subgroups of population indicated by deciles or quintiles, based on national household surveys covering various years. Consumption surveys produce results showing lower levels of inequality between poor and rich than do income surveys, as poor people generally consume a greater share of their income. Because data come from surveys covering different years and using different methodologies, comparisons between countries must be made with caution.

Infant mortality rate The probability of dying between birth and exactly one year of age, expressed per 1,000 live births.

Internally displaced people People who are displaced within their own country and to whom the United Nations High Commissioner for Refugees (UNHCR) extends protection or assistance, or both, generally pursuant to a special request by a competent organ of the United Nations.

Internet users People with access to the worldwide network.

Labour force All those employed (including people above a specified age who, during the reference period, were in paid employment, at work, self-employed or with a job but not at work) and unemployed (including people above a specified age who, during the reference period, were without work, currently available for work and seeking work).

Legislators, senior officials and managers, female Women's share of positions defined according to the International Standard Classification of Occupations (ISCO-88) to include legislators, senior government officials, traditional chiefs and heads of villages, senior officials of special interest organizations, corporate managers, directors and chief executives, production and operations department managers and other department and general managers.

Life expectancy at birth The number of years a newborn infant would live if prevailing patterns of age-specific mortality rates at the time of birth were to stay the same throughout the child's life.

Life expectancy index One of the three indices on which the human development index is built. For details on how the index is calculated, see *Technical note 1.*

Literacy rate, adult The percentage of people ages 15 and above who can, with understanding, both read and write a short, simple statement related to their everyday life.

Literacy rate, youth The percentage of people ages 15–24 who can, with understanding, both read and write a short, simple statement related to their everyday life.

Literacy skills, functional, people lacking The share of the population ages 16–65 scoring at level 1 on the prose literacy scale of the International Adult Literacy Survey. Most tasks at this level require the reader to locate a piece of information in the text that is identical to or synonymous with the information given in the directive.

Malaria cases The total number of malaria cases reported to the World Health Organization by countries in which malaria is endemic. Many countries report only laboratory-confirmed cases, but many in Sub-Saharan Africa report clinically diagnosed cases as well.

Malaria prevention, children under age five The percentage of children under age five sleeping under insecticide-treated bed nets.

Malaria treatment, children under five with fever The percentage of children under five who were ill with fever in the two weeks before the survey and received anti-malarial drugs.

Market activities Defined according to the 1993 revised UN System of National Accounts to include employment in establishments, primary production not in establishments, services for income and other production of goods not in establishments. See *non-market activities* and *work time, total*.

Maternal mortality ratio The annual number of deaths of women from pregnancy-related causes per 100,000 live births.

Maternal mortality ratio, adjusted Maternal mortality ratio adjusted to account for well documented problems of underreporting and misclassification of maternal deaths, as well as estimates for countries with no data. See *maternal mortality ratio*.

Maternal mortality ratio, reported Maternal mortality ratio as reported by national authorities. See *maternal mortality ratio*.

Medium-variant projection Population projections by the United Nations Population Division assuming medium-fertility path, normal mortality and normal international migration. Each assumption implies projected trends in fertility, mortality and net migration levels, depending on the specific demographic characteristics and relevant policies of each country or group of countries. In addition, for the countries highly affected by the HIV/AIDS epidemic, the impact of HIV/AIDS is included in the projection. The UN Population Division also publishes low and high variant projections. For more information, see http://esa.un.org/unpp/assumptions.html.

Military expenditure All expenditures of the defence ministry and other ministries on recruiting and training military personnel as well as on construction and purchase of military supplies and equipment. Military assistance is included in the expenditures of the donor country.

Non-market activities Defined according to the 1993 revised UN System of National Accounts to include household maintenance (cleaning, laundry and meal preparation and cleanup), management and shopping for own household; care for children, the sick, the elderly and the disabled in own household; and community services. See *market activities* and *work time, total*.

Official aid Grants or loans that meet the same standards as for official development assistance (ODA) except that recipient countries do not qualify as recipients of ODA. These countries are identified in part II of the Development Assistance Committee (DAC) list of recipient countries, which includes more advanced countries of Central and Eastern Europe, the countries of the former Soviet Union and certain advanced developing countries and territories.

Official development assistance (ODA), net Disbursements of loans made on concessional terms (net of repayments of principal) and grants by official agencies of the members of the Development Assistance Committee (DAC), by multilateral institutions and by non-DAC countries to promote economic development and welfare in countries and territories in part I of the DAC list of aid recipients. It includes loans with a grant element of at least 25% (calculated at a rate of discount of 10%).

Official development assistance (ODA), per capita of donor country Official development assistance granted by a specific country divided by this country's total population. See *official development assistance, net*.

Official development assistance (ODA) to basic social services ODA directed to basic social services, which include basic education (primary education, early childhood education and basic life skills for youth and adults), basic health (including basic health care, basic health infrastructure, basic nutrition, infectious disease control, health education and health personnel development) and population policies and programmes and reproductive health (population policy and administrative management, reproductive health care, family planning, control of sexually transmitted diseases, including HIV/AIDS, and personnel development for population and reproductive health). Aid to water supply and sanitation is included only if it has a poverty focus.

Official development assistance (ODA) to least developed countries See *official development assistance (ODA), net* and country classifications for least developed countries.

Official development assistance (ODA), untied bilateral ODA for which the associated goods and services may be fully and freely procured in substantially all countries and that is given by one country to another.

Oral rehydration therapy use rate The percentage of all cases of diarrhoea in children under age five in which the child received increased fluids and continued feeding.

Patents granted to residents Refers to documents issued by a government office that describe an invention and create a legal situation in which the patented invention can normally be exploited (made, used, sold, imported) only by or with the authorization of the patentee. The protection of inventions is generally limited to 20 years from the filing date of the application for the grant of a patent.

Physicians Includes graduates of a faculty or school of medicine who are working in any medical field (including teaching, research and practice).

Population growth rate, annual Refers to the average annual exponential growth rate for the period indicated. See *population, total*.

Population, total Refers to the de facto population, which includes all people actually present in a given area at a given time.

Population, urban The midyear population of areas classified as urban according to the criteria used by each country, as reported to the United Nations. See *population, total*.

PPP (purchasing power parity) A rate of exchange that accounts for price differences across countries, allowing international comparisons of real output and incomes. At the PPP US$ rate (as used in this Report), PPP US$1 has the same purchasing power in the domestic economy as $1 has in the United States.

Private flows, other A category combining non-debt-creating portfolio equity investment flows (the sum of country funds, depository receipts and direct purchases of shares by foreign investors), portfolio debt flows (bond issues purchased by foreign investors) and bank and trade-related lending (commercial bank lending and other commercial credits).

Probability at birth of not surviving to a specified age Calculated as 1 minus the probability of surviving to a specified age for a given cohort. See *probability at birth of surviving to a specified age.*

Probability at birth of surviving to a specified age The probability of a newborn infant surviving to a specified age if subject to prevailing patterns of age-specific mortality rates.

Professional and technical workers, female Women's share of positions defined according to the International Standard Classification of Occupations (ISCO-88) to include physical, mathematical and engineering science professionals (and associate professionals), life science and health professionals (and associate professionals), teaching professionals (and associate professionals) and other professionals and associate professionals.

Refugees People who have fled their country because of a well founded fear of persecution for reasons of their race, religion, nationality, political opinion or membership in a particular social group and who cannot or do not want to return. *Country of asylum* is the country in which a refugee has filed a claim of asylum but has not yet received a decision or is otherwise registered as an asylum seeker. *Country of origin* refers to the claimant's nationality or country of citizenship.

Research and development expenditures Current and capital expenditures (including overhead) on creative, systematic activity intended to increase the stock of knowledge. Included are fundamental and applied research and experimental development work leading to new devices, products or processes.

Researchers in R&D People trained to work in any field of science who are engaged in professional research and development (R&D) activity. Most such jobs require the completion of tertiary education.

Royalties and licence fees, receipts of Receipts by residents from non-residents for the authorized use of intangible, non-produced, non-financial assets and proprietary rights (such as patents, trademarks, copyrights, franchises and industrial processes) and for the use, through licensing agreements, of produced originals of prototypes (such as films and manuscripts). Data are based on the balance of payments.

Sanitation facilities, improved, population with sustainable access to The percentage of the population with access to adequate excreta disposal facilities, such as a connection to a sewer or septic tank system, a pour-flush latrine, a simple pit latrine or a ventilated improved pit latrine. An excreta disposal system is considered adequate if it is private or shared (but not public) and if it can effectively prevent human, animal and insect contact with excreta.

Science, math and engineering, tertiary students in The share of tertiary students enrolled in natural sciences; engineering; mathematics and computer sciences; architecture and town planning; transport and communications; trade, craft and industrial programmes; and agriculture, forestry and fisheries. See *education levels.*

Seats in parliament held by women Refers to seats held by women in a lower or single house or an upper house or senate, where relevant.

Smoking, prevalence among adults of The percentage of men and women who smoke cigarettes.

Tariff and non-tariff barriers, average Aggregate measure of trade barriers facing developing countries. It measures monetary barriers (tariffs) as well as quotas and subsidies in manufactures, textiles, agricultural products and fuels, weighted by endogeneity-corrected import volume.

Telephone mainlines Telephone lines connecting a customer's equipment to the public switched telephone network.

Tenure, households with access to secure Households that own or are purchasing their homes, are renting privately or are in social housing or subtenancy.

Terms of trade The ratio of the export price index to the import price index measured relative to a base year. A value of more than 100 means that the price of exports has risen relative to the price of imports.

Tuberculosis cases The total number of tuberculosis cases reported to the World Health Organization. A tuberculosis case is defined as a patient in whom tuberculosis has been bacteriologically confirmed or diagnosed by a clinician.

Tuberculosis cases cured under DOTS The percentage of estimated new infectious tuberculosis cases cured under the directly observed treatment, short course (DOTS) case detection and treatment strategy.

Tuberculosis cases detected under DOTS The percentage of estimated new infectious tuberculosis cases detected (diagnosed in a given period) under the directly observed treatment, short course (DOTS) case detection and treatment strategy.

Under-five mortality rate The probability of dying between birth and exactly five years of age, expressed per 1,000 live births.

Under height for age, children under age five Includes moderate and severe stunting, defined as more than two standard deviations below the median height for age of the reference population.

Under weight for age, children under age five Includes moderate underweight, defined as more than two standard deviations below the median weight for age of the reference population, and severe underweight, defined as more than three standard deviations below the median weight.

Undernourished people People whose food intake is chronically insufficient to meet their minimum energy requirements.

Unemployment Refers to all people above a specified age who are not in paid employment or self-employed, but are available for work and have taken specific steps to seek paid employment or self-employment.

Unemployment, long-term Unemployment lasting 12 months or longer. See *unemployment.*

Unemployment rate The unemployed divided by the labour force (those employed plus the unemployed).

Unemployment rate, youth Refers to unemployment between the ages of 15 or 16 and 24, depending on the national definition. See *unemployment.*

Water source, improved, population without sustainable access to Calculated as 100 minus the percentage of the population with sustainable access to an improved water source. Unimproved sources include vendors, bottled water, tanker trucks and unprotected wells and springs. See *water source, improved, population with sustainable access to.*

Water source, improved, population with sustainable access to The share of the population with reasonable access to any of the following types of water supply for drinking: household connections, public standpipes, boreholes, protected dug wells, protected springs and rainwater collection. *Reasonable* *access* is defined as the availability of at least 20 litres a person per day from a source within 1 kilometre of the user's dwelling.

Women in government at ministerial level Defined according to each state's definition of a national executive and may include women serving as ministers and vice ministers and those holding other ministerial positions, including parliamentary secretaries.

Work time, total Time spent on market and non-market activities as defined according to the 1993 revised UN System of National Accounts. See *market activities* and *non-market activities*.

Statistical references

Aten, Bettina, Alan Heston, and Robert Summers. 2001. Correspondence on data from the Penn World Tables 6.0. Philadelphia. March.

———. 2002. "Penn World Tables 6.1." University of Pennsylvania, Center for International Comparisons, Philadelphia. [http://pwt.econ.upenn.edu/]. Accessed March 2004.

Birzeit University. 2002. *Palestine Human Development Report 2002.* Ramallah, Occupied Palestinian Territories.

CDIAC (Carbon Dioxide Information Analysis Center). 2004. *Trends: A Compendium of Data on Global Change.* [http://cdiac.esd.ornl.gov/trends/trends.htm]. Accessed March 2004.

FAO (Food and Agriculture Organization of the United Nations). 2003. *The State of Food Insecurity in the World 2003.* Rome.

Goldschmidt-Clermont, Luisella, and Elisabetta Pagnossin Aligisakis. 1995. "Measures of Unrecorded Economic Activities in Fourteen Countries." Background paper for *Human Development Report 1995.* United Nations Development Programme, Human Development Report Office, New York.

Harvey, Andrew S. 1995. "Market and Non-Market Productive Activity in Less Developed and Developing Countries: Lessons from Time Use." Background paper for *Human Development Report 1995.* United Nations Development Programme, Human Development Report Office, New York.

———. 2001. "National Time Use Data on Market and Non-Market Work by Both Women and Men." Background paper for *Human Development Report 2001.* United Nations Development Programme, Human Development Report Office, New York.

IISS (International Institute for Strategic Studies). 2003. *The Military Balance 2003-2004.* Oxford: Oxford University Press.

ILO (International Labour Organization). 2002. *Estimates and Projections of the Economically Active Population, 1950-2010,* 4th ed., rev. 2. Database. Geneva.

———. 2003. *Key Indicators of the Labour Market, Third Edition.* [http://kilm.ilo.org/kilm/]. Accessed March 2004.

———. 2004a. *Database on International Labour Standards (ILOLEX)* [http://www.ilo.org/ilolex/english/docs/declworld.htm]. Accessed February 2004.

———. 2004b. *Laboursta Database.* [http://laborsta.ilo.org]. Accessed March 2004.

IMF (International Monetary Fund) and IDA (International Development Association). 2004. "Heavily Indebted Poor Countries (HIPC) Initiative—Status of Implementation." 31 March. Washington, DC.

IMF (International Monetary Fund) and World Bank. 2003. "Status of Bilateral Donor Pledges to the HIPC Trust Fund." [http://www.worldbank.org/hipc/progress-to-date/TrustFundSep03.pdf]. Accessed March 2004.

IPU (Inter-Parliamentary Union). 1995. *Women in Parliaments 1945-1995: A World Statistical Survey.* Geneva.

———. 2001. Correspondence on women in government at the ministerial level. March. Geneva.

———. 2004a. Correspondence on year women received the right to vote and to stand for election and year first woman was elected or appointed to parliament. March. Geneva.

———. 2004b. *Parline Database and World Classification of Women in National Parliaments.* [www.ipu.org]. Accessed March 2004.

ITU (International Telecommunication Union). World Telecommunication Indicators Database, 7th edition. [http://www.itu.int/ITU-D/ict/publications/world/world.html]. March 2004.

LIS (Luxembourg Income Study). 2004. "Relative Poverty Rates for the Total Population, Children and the Elderly." [http://www.lisproject.org/keyfigures/povertytable.htm]. Accessed February 2004.

Milanovic, Branko. 2002. Correspondence on income, inequality and poverty during the transition from planned to market economy. World Bank. March. Washington, D.C.

OECD (Organisation for Economic Co-operation and Development), Development Assistance Committee. 2004a. Correspondence on agricultural support estimates. February 2004. Paris.

———. 2004b. Correspondence on official development assistance disbursed. February. Paris.

———. 2004c. Correspondence on the employment rates. March. Geneva.

———. 2004d. Correspondence on long-term unemployment rates. March. Geneva.

———. 2004e. *DAC Journal: Development Cooperation 2003 Report* (5)1. Paris.

———. 2004f. *DAC Online.* Database. Paris.

OECD (Organisation for Economic Co-operation and Development), and Statistics Canada. 2000. *Literacy in the Information Age: Final Report on the International Adult Literacy Survey.* Paris.

Polity IV. 2002. "Political Regime Characteristics and Transitions, 1800–2000." [http://www.bsos.umd.edu/cidcm/inscr/polity/index.htm]. Accessed April 2002.

Roodman, David. 2004. "The Commitment to Development Index: 2004 Edition." Center for Global Development, Washington, DC.

SIPRI (Stockholm International Peace Research Institute). 2003. *SIPRI Yearbook: Armaments, Disarmaments and International Security.* Oxford: Oxford University Press.

———. 2004a. Correspondence on military expenditure data. March. Stockholm.

———. 2004b. *SIPRI Arms Transfers.* Database. February. Stockholm.

Smeeding, Timothy M. 1997. "Financial Poverty in Developed Countries: The Evidence from the Luxembourg Income Study." In Sheldon H. Danziger and Robert H. Haveman, eds., *Understanding Poverty.* New York: Russell Sage Foundation; and Cambridge, MA: Harvard University Press.

Smeeding, Timothy M., Lee Rainwater, and Gary Burtless. 2000. "United States Poverty in a Cross-National Context." In Sheldon H. Danziger and Robert H. Haveman, eds., *Understanding Poverty.* New York: Russell Sage Foundation; and Cambridge, Mass.: Harvard University Press.

Statec. 2004. Correspondence on gross enrolment ratio for Luxembourg. April. Luxembourg.

UN (United Nations). 2001. *World Population Prospects 1950-2050: The 2000 Revision.* Database. Department of Economic and Social Affairs, Population Division. New York.

———. 2002. Correspondence on time use surveys. Department of Economic and Social Affairs, Statistics Division. February. New York.

———. 2003. *World Population Prospects 1950-2050: The 2002 Revision.* Database. Department of Economic and Social Affairs, Population Division. New York.

———. 2004a. *Comtrade.* Database. Department of Social and Economic Affairs, Statistics Division. New York.

———. 2004b. Correspondence on energy consumption. Department of Economic and Social Affairs, Statistics Division. March. New York.

———. 2004c. Correspondence on traditional fuel use. Department of Economic and Social Affairs, Statistics Division. March. New York.

———. 2004d. Correspondence on 2002 urban population interpolation. Department of Economic and Social Affairs, Population Division. March. New York.

———. 2004e. Millennium Indicators Database. Department of Economic and Social Affairs, Statistics Division. [http://millenniumindicators.un.org]. Accessed March 2004.

———. 2004f. "Multilateral Treaties Deposited with the Secretary-General." [http://untreaty.un.org]. Accessed March 2004.

———. 2004g. United Nations Population Division Database on Contraceptive Use. Department of Economic and Social Affairs, Population Division. March. New York.

———. 2004h. *World Urbanization Prospects: The 2003 Revision.* Department of Economic and Social Affairs, Population Division. New York.

UNAIDS (Joint United Nations Programme on HIV/AIDS). 2004. Correspondence on HIV prevalence rate. May. Geneva.

UNCTAD (United Nations Conference on Trade and Development). 2001. "Third United Nations Conference on the Least Developed Countries." [http://www.unctad.org/conference/]. Accessed April 2002.

UNDP (United Nations Development Programme). 2000. *Human Development Report 2000.* Oxford University Press. New York.

———. 2002a. *Bosnia and Herzegovina Human Development Report 2002.* Sarajevo.

———. 2002b. *East Timor Human Development Report 2002.* Dili.

———. 2004. Correspondence with UNDP Country Office in Pakistan on data on women in government at ministerial level. April. Islamabad.

UNESCO (United Nations Educational, Scientific and Cultural Organization). 1997. International Standard Classification of Education 1997. Available at [http://www.uis.unesco.org/ev_en.php?ID=3813_201&ID2=DO_TOPIC]. Accessed March 2004.

———. 1999. *Statistical Yearbook 1999.* Paris.

———. 2003. *Education for All Global Monitoring Report 2003/4.* Paris.

UNESCO Institute for Statistics (United Nations Educational, Scientific and Cultural Organization). 2001. Correspondence on combined gross enrolment ratio. March. Paris.

———. 2003a. Correspondence on adult and youth literacy rates. March. Montreal.

———. 2003b. Correspondence on combined gross enrolment ratios. March. Montreal.

———. 2003c. Correspondence on education expenditure. February. Montreal.

———. 2004a. Correspondence on adult and youth literacy rates. March. Montreal.

———. 2004b. Correspondence on education expenditure. March. Montreal.

———. 2004c. Correspondence on gross, net enrolment ratios and children reaching grade 5. March. Montreal.

———. 2004d. "Cultural Statistics Programme of the UNESCO Institute for Statistics." Background note prepared for *Human Development Report 2004.* Montreal.

———. 2004e. "Measuring Literacy." Background note prepared for *Human Development Report 2004.* Montreal.

UNHCR (United Nations High Commissioner for Refugees). 2004. Correspondence on internally displaced people, refugees by country of asylum and by country of origin. April. Geneva.

UNICEF (United Nations Children's Fund). 2000. *State of the World's Children 2001.* New York: Oxford University Press.

———. 2003a. Multiple Indicator Cluster Survey (MICS) 2002. Dili.

———. 2003b. *The State of the World's Children 2004.* New York: Oxford University Press.

———. 2004. Correspondence on infant and under-five mortality rates. March. New York.

UNODC (United Nations Office on Drugs and Crime). 2004. Correspondence on data on crime victims. March. Vienna.

WHO (World Health Organization). 2003. *Global Tuberculosis Control: WHO Report 2003.* [http://www.who.int/gtb/publications/globrep/]. Accessed March 2003.

———. 2004a. Correspondence on access to essential drugs. March. Geneva.

———. 2004b. Correspondence on health expenditure. March. Geneva.

———. 2004c. Correspondence on HIV prevalence rate. March. Geneva.

———. 2004d. Correspondence on human resources for health. March. Geneva.

———. 2004e. Correspondence on tuberculosis cases. March. Geneva.

———. 2004f. "Health Metrics Network: An Emerging Global Partnership for Health Information." Background note prepared for *Human Development Report 2004.* Geneva.

WIPO (World Intellectual Property Organization). 2004. *Intellectual Property Statistics.* Publication B. Geneva.

World Bank. 2003a. *Global Economic Prospects and the Developing Countries.* Washington, DC.

———. 2003b. *World Development Indicators 2003.* CD-ROM. Washington, DC.

———. 2004a. Correspondence on data on income distribution. March. Washington, DC.

———. 2004b. Correspondence on GDP per capita annual growth rates. March. Washington, DC.

———. 2004c. "HIPC Initiative: Status of Country Cases Considered Under the Initiative, September 2003." [http://www.worldbank.org/hipc/progress-to-date/status_table_Sep03.pdf]. Accessed March 2004.

———. 2004d. "International Comparison Programme (ICP)." Background note prepared for *Human Development Report 2004.* Washington, DC.

———. 2004e. "The Marrakech Action Plans for Statistics." Background note prepared for *Human Development Report 2004.* Washington, DC.

———. 2004f. *World Development Indicators 2004.* CD-ROM. Washington, DC.

Classification of countries

Countries in the human development aggregates [a]

High human development (HDI 0.800 and above)

Antigua and Barbuda
Argentina
Australia
Austria
Bahamas
Bahrain
Barbados
Belgium
Brunei Darussalam
Canada
Chile
Costa Rica
Croatia
Cuba
Cyprus
Czech Republic
Denmark
Estonia
Finland
France
Germany
Greece
Hong Kong, China (SAR)
Hungary
Iceland
Ireland
Israel
Italy
Japan
Korea, Rep. of
Kuwait
Latvia
Lithuania
Luxembourg
Malta
Mexico
Netherlands
New Zealand
Norway
Poland
Portugal
Qatar
Saint Kitts and Nevis
Seychelles
Singapore
Slovakia
Slovenia
Spain
Sweden
Switzerland
Trinidad and Tobago
United Arab Emirates
United Kingdom
United States
Uruguay

(55 countries or areas)

Medium human development (HDI 0.500–0.799)

Albania
Algeria
Armenia
Azerbaijan
Bangladesh
Belarus
Belize
Bhutan
Bolivia
Bosnia and Herzegovina
Botswana
Brazil
Bulgaria
Cambodia
Cameroon
Cape Verde
China
Colombia
Comoros
Dominica
Dominican Republic
Ecuador
Egypt
El Salvador
Equatorial Guinea
Fiji
Gabon
Georgia
Ghana
Grenada
Guatemala
Guyana
Honduras
India
Indonesia
Iran, Islamic Rep. of
Jamaica
Jordan
Kazakhstan
Kyrgyzstan
Lao People's Dem. Rep.
Lebanon
Libyan Arab Jamahiriya
Macedonia, TFYR
Malaysia
Maldives
Mauritius
Moldova, Rep. of
Mongolia
Morocco
Myanmar
Namibia
Nepal
Nicaragua
Occupied Palestinian Territories
Oman
Panama
Papua New Guinea
Paraguay
Peru
Philippines
Romania
Russian Federation
Saint Lucia
St. Vincent & the Grenadines
Samoa (Western)
São Tomé and Principe
Saudi Arabia
Solomon Islands
South Africa
Sri Lanka
Sudan
Suriname
Swaziland
Syrian Arab Republic
Tajikistan
Thailand
Tonga
Tunisia
Turkey
Turkmenistan
Ukraine
Uzbekistan
Vanuatu
Venezuela
Viet Nam

(86 countries or areas)

Low human development (HDI below 0.500)

Angola
Benin
Burkina Faso
Burundi
Central African Republic
Chad
Congo
Congo, Dem. Rep. of the
Côte d'Ivoire
Djibouti
Eritrea
Ethiopia
Gambia
Guinea
Guinea-Bissau
Haiti
Kenya
Lesotho
Madagascar
Malawi
Mali
Mauritania
Mozambique
Niger
Nigeria
Pakistan
Rwanda
Senegal
Sierra Leone
Tanzania, U. Rep. of
Timor-Leste
Togo
Uganda
Yemen
Zambia
Zimbabwe

(36 countries or areas)

a. Excludes the following UN member countries for which the HDI cannot be computed: Afghanistan, Andorra, Iraq, Kiribati, the Democratic Republic of Korea, Liberia, Liechtenstein, Marshall Islands, the Federated States of Micronesia, Monaco, Nauru, Palau, San Marino, Serbia and Montenegro, Somalia and Tuvalu.

Countries in the income aggregates [a]

High income
(GNI per capita of $9,076 or more in 2002)

Andorra
Antigua and Barbuda
Australia
Austria
Bahamas
Bahrain
Barbados
Belgium
Brunei Darussalam
Canada
Cyprus
Denmark
Finland
France
Germany
Greece
Hong Kong, China (SAR)
Iceland
Ireland
Israel
Italy
Japan
Korea, Rep. of
Kuwait
Luxembourg
Malta
Monaco
Netherlands
New Zealand
Norway
Portugal
Qatar
San Marino
Singapore
Slovenia
Spain
Sweden
Switzerland
United Arab Emirates
United Kingdom
United States
(41 countries or areas)

Middle income
(GNI per capita of $736–9,075 in 2002)

Albania
Algeria
Argentina
Armenia
Belarus
Belize
Bolivia
Bosnia and Herzegovina
Botswana
Brazil
Bulgaria
Cape Verde
Chile
China
Colombia
Costa Rica
Croatia
Cuba
Czech Republic
Djibouti
Dominica
Dominican Republic
Ecuador
Egypt
El Salvador
Estonia
Fiji
Gabon
Grenada
Guatemala
Guyana
Honduras
Hungary
Iran, Islamic Rep. of
Iraq
Jamaica
Jordan
Kazakhstan
Kiribati
Latvia
Lebanon
Libyan Arab Jamahiriya
Lithuania
Macedonia, TFYR
Malaysia
Maldives
Marshall Islands
Mauritius
Mexico
Micronesia, Fed. Sts.

Morocco
Namibia
Northern Mariana Islands
Occupied Palestinian
    Territories
Oman
Palau
Panama
Paraguay
Peru
Philippines
Poland
Romania
Russian Federation
Saint Kitts and Nevis
Saint Lucia
St. Vincent & the
    Grenadines
Samoa (Western)
Saudi Arabia
Serbia and Montenegro
Seychelles
Slovakia
South Africa
Sri Lanka
Suriname
Swaziland
Syrian Arab Republic
Thailand
Tonga
Trinidad and Tobago
Tunisia
Turkey
Turkmenistan
Ukraine
Uruguay
Vanuatu
Venezuela
(86 countries or areas)

Low income
(GNI per capita of $735 or less in 2002)

Afghanistan
Angola
Azerbaijan
Bangladesh
Benin
Bhutan
Burkina Faso
Burundi
Cambodia
Cameroon
Central African Republic
Chad
Comoros
Congo
Congo, Dem. Rep. of the
Côte d'Ivoire
Equatorial Guinea
Eritrea
Ethiopia
Gambia
Georgia
Ghana
Guinea
Guinea-Bissau
Haiti
India
Indonesia
Kenya
Korea, Dem. Rep.
Kyrgyzstan
Lao People's Dem. Rep.
Lesotho
Liberia
Madagascar
Malawi
Mali
Mauritania
Moldova, Rep. of
Mongolia
Mozambique
Myanmar
Nepal
Nicaragua
Niger
Nigeria
Pakistan
Papua New Guinea
Rwanda
São Tomé and Principe
Senegal

Sierra Leone
Solomon Islands
Somalia
Sudan
Tajikistan
Tanzania, U. Rep. of
Timor-Leste
Togo
Uganda
Uzbekistan
Viet Nam
Yemen
Zambia
Zimbabwe
(64 countries or areas)

a. World Bank classification (effective 1 July 2003) based on gross national income (GNI) per capita. Excludes Nauru and Tuvalu because of lack of data.

Developing countries

Afghanistan	Honduras	St. Vincent & the	Djibouti	Croatia	Turkey
Algeria	Hong Kong, China (SAR)	Grenadines	Equatorial Guinea	Czech Republic	United Kingdom
Angola	India	Samoa (Western)	Eritrea	Estonia	United States
Antigua and Barbuda	Indonesia	São Tomé and Principe	Ethiopia	Georgia	*(30 countries or areas)*
Argentina	Iran, Islamic Rep. of	Saudi Arabia	Gambia	Hungary	
Bahamas	Iraq	Senegal	Guinea	Kazakhstan	**High-income**
Bahrain	Jamaica	Seychelles	Guinea-Bissau	Kyrgyzstan	**OECD countries** [a]
Bangladesh	Jordan	Sierra Leone	Haiti	Latvia	Australia
Barbados	Kenya	Singapore	Kiribati	Lithuania	Austria
Belize	Kiribati	Solomon Islands	Lao People's Dem. Rep.	Macedonia, TFYR	Belgium
Benin	Korea, Dem. Rep.	Somalia	Lesotho	Moldova, Rep. of	Canada
Bhutan	Korea, Rep. of	South Africa	Liberia	Poland	Denmark
Bolivia	Kuwait	Sri Lanka	Madagascar	Romania	Finland
Botswana	Lao People's Dem. Rep.	Sudan	Malawi	Russian Federation	France
Brazil	Lebanon	Suriname	Maldives	Serbia and Montenegro	Germany
Brunei Darussalam	Lesotho	Swaziland	Mali	Slovakia	Greece
Burkina Faso	Liberia	Syrian Arab Republic	Mauritania	Slovenia	Iceland
Burundi	Libyan Arab Jamahiriya	Tanzania, U. Rep. of	Mozambique	Tajikistan	Ireland
Cambodia	Madagascar	Thailand	Myanmar	Turkmenistan	Italy
Cameroon	Malawi	Timor-Leste	Nepal	Ukraine	Japan
Cape Verde	Malaysia	Togo	Niger	Uzbekistan	Korea, Rep. of
Central African Republic	Maldives	Tonga	Rwanda	*(27 countries or areas)*	Luxembourg
Chad	Mali	Trinidad and Tobago	Samoa (Western)		Netherlands
Chile	Marshall Islands	Tunisia	São Tomé and Principe		New Zealand
China	Mauritania	Turkey	Senegal	## OECD	Norway
Colombia	Mauritius	Tuvalu	Sierra Leone		Portugal
Comoros	Mexico	Uganda	Solomon Islands	Australia	Spain
Congo	Micronesia, Fed. Sts.	United Arab Emirates	Somalia	Austria	Sweden
Congo, Dem. Rep. of the	Mongolia	Uruguay	Sudan	Belgium	Switzerland
Costa Rica	Morocco	Vanuatu	Tanzania, U. Rep. of	Canada	United Kingdom
Côte d'Ivoire	Mozambique	Venezuela	Togo	Czech Republic	United States
Cuba	Myanmar	Viet Nam	Tuvalu	Denmark	*(24 countries or areas)*
Cyprus	Namibia	Yemen	Uganda	Finland	
Djibouti	Nauru	Zambia	Vanuatu	France	
Dominica	Nepal	Zimbabwe	Yemen	Germany	
Dominican Republic	Nicaragua	*(137 countries or areas)*	Zambia	Greece	
Ecuador	Niger		*(49 countries or areas)*	Hungary	
Egypt	Nigeria	**Least developed**		Iceland	
El Salvador	Occupied Palestinian	**countries**	*Central and*	Ireland	
Equatorial Guinea	Territories	Afghanistan	*Eastern Europe*	Italy	
Eritrea	Oman	Angola	*and the*	Japan	
Ethiopia	Pakistan	Bangladesh	*Commonwealth*	Korea, Rep. of	
Fiji	Palau	Benin	*of Independent*	Luxembourg	
Gabon	Panama	Bhutan	*States (CIS)*	Mexico	
Gambia	Papua New Guinea	Burkina Faso		Netherlands	
Ghana	Paraguay	Burundi	Albania	New Zealand	
Grenada	Peru	Cambodia	Armenia	Norway	
Guatemala	Philippines	Cape Verde	Azerbaijan	Poland	
Guinea	Qatar	Central African Republic	Belarus	Portugal	
Guinea-Bissau	Rwanda	Chad	Bosnia and Herzegovina	Slovakia	
Guyana	Saint Kitts and Nevis	Comoros	Bulgaria	Spain	
Haiti	Saint Lucia	Congo, Dem. Rep. of the		Sweden	
				Switzerland	

a. Excludes the Czech Republic, Hungary, Mexico, Poland, Slovakia and Turkey.

Developing countries in the regional aggregates

Arab States

Algeria
Bahrain
Djibouti
Egypt
Iraq
Jordan
Kuwait
Lebanon
Libyan Arab Jamahiriya
Morocco
Occupied Palestinian Territories
Oman
Qatar
Saudi Arabia
Somalia
Sudan
Syrian Arab Republic
Tunisia
United Arab Emirates
Yemen
(20 countries or areas)

Asia and the Pacific

East Asia and the Pacific
Brunei Darussalam
Cambodia
China
Fiji
Hong Kong, China (SAR)
Indonesia
Kiribati
Korea, Dem. Rep.
Korea, Rep. of
Lao People's Dem. Rep.
Malaysia
Marshall Islands
Micronesia, Fed. Sts.
Mongolia
Myanmar
Nauru
Palau
Papua New Guinea
Philippines
Samoa (Western)
Singapore
Solomon Islands
Thailand
Timor-Leste
Tonga
Tuvalu
Vanuatu
Viet Nam
(28 countries or areas)

South Asia
Afghanistan
Bangladesh
Bhutan
India
Iran, Islamic Rep. of
Maldives
Nepal
Pakistan
Sri Lanka
(9 countries or areas)

Latin America and the Caribbean

Antigua and Barbuda
Argentina
Bahamas
Barbados
Belize
Bolivia
Brazil
Chile
Colombia
Costa Rica
Cuba
Dominica
Dominican Republic
Ecuador
El Salvador
Grenada
Guatemala
Guyana
Haiti
Honduras
Jamaica
Mexico
Nicaragua
Panama
Paraguay
Peru
Saint Kitts and Nevis
Saint Lucia
St. Vincent & the Grenadines
Suriname
Trinidad and Tobago
Uruguay
Venezuela
(33 countries or areas)

Southern Europe

Cyprus
Turkey
(2 countries or areas)

Sub-Saharan Africa

Angola
Benin
Botswana
Burkina Faso
Burundi
Cameroon
Cape Verde
Central African Republic
Chad
Comoros
Congo
Congo, Dem. Rep. of the
Côte d'Ivoire
Equatorial Guinea
Eritrea
Ethiopia
Gabon
Gambia
Ghana
Guinea
Guinea-Bissau
Kenya
Lesotho
Liberia
Madagascar
Malawi
Mali
Mauritania
Mauritius
Mozambique
Namibia
Niger
Nigeria
Rwanda
São Tomé and Principe
Senegal
Seychelles
Sierra Leone
South Africa
Swaziland
Tanzania, U. Rep. of
Togo
Uganda
Zambia
Zimbabwe
(45 countries or areas)